GLOBAL MARITIME GEOPOLITICS

POLICY SERIES: 11

GLOBAL MARITIME GEOPOLITICS

Edited by Hasret Çomak, Burak Şakir Şeker, Mehlika Özlem Ultan

Copyright © 2022 Transnational Press London

First Published in 2022 by TRANSNATIONAL PRESS LONDON in the United Kingdom, 13 Stamford Place, Sale, M33 3BT, UK.

www.tplondon.com

Transnational Press London® and the logo and its affiliated brands are registered trademarks.

Requests for permission to reproduce material from this work should be sent to: sales@tplondon.com

Paperback

ISBN: 978-1-80135-115-7

Digital

ISBN: 978-1-80135-116-4

Cover Design: Nihal Yazgan

Cover Photo by Chris Pagan on Unsplash.com

Transnational Press London Ltd. is a company registered in England and Wales No. 8771684.

GLOBAL MARITIME GEOPOLITICS

Edited by

Hasret Çomak

Burak Şakir Şeker

Mehlika Özlem Ultan

TRANSNATIONAL PRESS LONDON

2022

CONTENTS

i

PREFACE

With its transit facilities and living and non-living resources, the oceans and seas have been at the service of humanity throughout history. The importance of the seas has grown even more in the twenty-first century, and it has begun to play a significant role in the global economy. Sea transport accounts for a significant portion of worldwide trade.

In 1890, American Admiral Alfred Thayer Mahan authored **"The Effect of Sea Power on History 1660-1783,"** which broke new ground in the United States and many other countries. Mahan succinctly said in his philosophy that trade is very important in terms of country-to-country relations, and that the major motivation for large-scale battles between countries is the desire for a say in world trade and domination over the seas. As a result, he proposed the hypothesis that **"control of sea routes is the key to global dominance."**

"...Every marine endeavor of powerful governments must take into account diplomacy and the constraints of national resources," writes Mahan in one of his works. States that fail to do so run the risk of moving forward on shaky basis. An indissoluble power binds foreign policy and strategy together..." (In 1911, Naval Strategy was compared and contrasted with the Principles and Practice of Military Operations on Land.)

The fact that geopolitics specialists attach a priority on naval strength in their theories is unquestionably owing to the sea's importance to governments in terms of politics, economy, security, and defense. Naval power is frequently a requirement of defense policy for coastal states.

The volume of international trade carried out by sea is growing by the day, and it now serves as the primary mode of transportation for goods. All states place a high priority on the safety of marine routes.

The ability of countries to benefit from the international maritime transportation system determines their commercial competitiveness in the twenty-first century. Maritime route security continues to play a critical role in state foreign affairs and will continue to do so in the future.

Maritime transport, in particular, provides a crucial position in the political, economic, military, and energy fields in Europe and the Asia-Pacific area. When countries' "security perceptions" are shaped by rivalry and cooperation, it dramatically alters their "security perceptions."

The Asia-Pacific region has emerged as the world's new power center in the twenty-first century. This circumstance increased the region's geopolitical and geo-economic weight, as well as giving maritime trade a new dimension. This scenario, which has been exacerbated by economic mobility, has begun to have an impact on military and political authority. This introspection has resulted in new developments that could have an impact on geopolitical balances. It is changing ties between world power centers at the same time.

Maritime transportation is now used to a significant extent by global actors to accomplish their economic, political, cultural, and military ambitions and orientations. Oceans, seas, and sea passages have all become major elements of geopolitical competition in this regard.

The proportion of marine-derived foods in general food consumption has begun to rise in our century. Furthermore, as a result of advancements in deep-sea exploration and drilling technology, underwater hydrocarbons have begun to enter the economy at a rapid pace. The introduction of hydrogen as a new energy source, in particular, has increased the importance of coastal areas and increased competition between governments.

Hydrocarbon reserves may now be operated, evaluated, and sold using cutting-edge technology. Many platforms, coastal amenities, and pipelines can be erected in this setting. Energy supply and demand are now being directed by these facilities.

Again, the advancement of contemporary technologies has resulted in several economic advances and developments. With submarine fiber optic cables, communication possibilities have expanded significantly. This system's international trade, banking, and security services have begun to become the lifeblood of economic life.

Maritime trade, maritime transportation routes, energy transmission lines, marine living and non-living resources, strategic infrastructures, and new energy facilities all have a direct impact on the global economy.

As a result of this circumstance, the oceans and seas have become crucial to the countries' economic and security interests. The seas, in fact, have become an essential component of prosperity and security. The seas give authority to those who benefit from them on a worldwide scale, and they generate a zone of influence and interest, thanks to their vast size. While global actors want to preserve sovereignty and access to the high seas, developing maritime powers are adopting asymmetrical methods to limit other countries' access to regional waterways by strengthening their presence on the high seas.

The oceans and seas play a significant role in global trade, raw material transportation, global and regional security measures, and power balances. Mutual confidence between riparian countries can be established and maintained if the parties follow the provisions of the International Treaty and the Convention. In addition, the development and monitoring of policies that promote stability are becoming more important.

In addition, ***the development and monitoring of policies that promote stability*** are becoming more important. Setting and sustaining a positive example of peace and stability on the high seas will considerably contribute to regional and global peace.

"States having a closed or semi-enclosed sea should cooperate with one

another in exercising their rights and meeting their duties emanating from this Convention," according to UNCLOS Article 123. In this situation, riparian governments should prioritize collaboration in accordance with the aforementioned clause.

The Flight Information Region (FIR) Responsibility is to give meteorological information and developments in airspace in general, according to the 1944 Chicago Convention. Only technical services are covered by FIR Liability. No treaty or contract grants the State responsible for the FIR "*sovereignty*" over international airspace over the high seas.

"*Each Search and Rescue zone will be defined by agreement between the parties concerned*," according to Article 2.1.4 of the Hamburg Convention of 1979. Overlapping the Search and Rescue Responsibility Area for marine search and rescue services with the FIR is an undesirable practice. The practice of states overlapping the Search and Rescue Responsibility Region for marine search and rescue services with the FIR area and presenting it as a sovereign area is inappropriate.

Maritime jurisdiction borders of countries with coasts are essential for international law and national interests. The growing relevance of seabed and subsurface energy research has resulted in more disputes and a resurgence of debates over maritime jurisdictional issues. Because they entail strategic plans, countries' aspirations for marine jurisdictions pose political challenges.

The Arctic region, which includes the northernmost parts of these three continents, the Arctic Ocean, and parts of the Atlantic and Pacific oceans, covers an area of approximately 21 million square kilometers and includes the northernmost parts of these three continents, the Arctic Ocean, and parts of the Atlantic and Pacific oceans. Russia, the United States, Canada, Norway, and Denmark are the countries that border the Arctic Ocean (Arctic Five or Arctic countries). Iceland, Sweden, and Finland, on the other hand, are battling for this recognition despite not having direct access to the Arctic Ocean.

The construction of an international management center was necessary by the huge number of actors in the Arctic Ocean and the frequent occurrence of problems in numerous topics. On behalf of the Arctic geography, the Arctic Council, in collaboration with the Arctic Five state-level Arctic governments, and the United Nations, has undertaken this job. The Arctic Council is made up of eight countries (Denmark, Canada, Norway, Russia, USA, Iceland, Sweden and Finland). As observers, 12 countries are represented in the Council (Germany, United Kingdom, Italy, Poland, France, Spain, China, South Korea, India, Singapore, Japan and Switzerland).

The Arctic Council, which was established as an institutional structure for the Arctic Region, coordinates social and political coordination among members, establishes rules governing these countries' relations with one another in the region outside of the military field, coordinates their implementation, and regulates relations with non-regional countries.

Access to Arctic energy resources and control of maritime trade routes have become increasingly important for states as their geopolitical worth has grown. The energy conflict at the poles has taken on new significance, with new changes in trade and security policies.

As the region's glaciers have begun to melt as a result of global warming caused by climate change, new sea lanes have been opened and new energy sources have been discovered, the Arctic region has become a new battleground for major nations. The Arctic has evolved into a new geopolitical battleground.

Increasing the Russian Federation's efficacy in the Arctic Ocean region has resulted in an increase in NATO's sensitivity to the region. It boosted the United States' influence in the Eastern Mediterranean in the framework of the Russian Federation and NATO.

The US is afraid that as China's military organization in the South China Sea improves, it will expand its sphere of influence. Its goal is to keep China under control by bolstering the Southeast Asian Nations Association (ASEAN).

In the medium term, China intends to secure relative peace and economic gains in the Eastern Mediterranean, maintain the power balance, and balance the security of infrastructure and ships. China's military presence in regions critical to the Belt and Road Initiative is becoming more likely.

Countries that compete for energy transportation and commercial routes on major maritime transportation routes are becoming geopolitical players. Many ports and countries have benefited from oil transit routes. Political crises and conflicts may, however, arise over time in numerous countries and regions that receive logistical help. Yemen, Somalia, Sudan, Egypt, Vietnam, Cambodia, Nigeria, Cuba, and South Africa are among the countries along these hazardous and vital routes. Critical maritime competition is taking place in the Suez Canal and the Eastern Mediterranean. Being part of the Belt and Road Initiative may exacerbate difficulties with maritime security, competition, and dangers.

Antarctica is a natural laboratory for climate study, geophysics, biology, space sciences, and other disciplines of science, in addition to its abundant natural resources. Countries that value science and want to advance in it conduct scientific research in Antarctica and establish scientific bases on the continent.

The Antarctic Treaty System's legal order is unique among governance systems around the world, and it grants privileges to the nation states that are affiliated with it. The sovereignty claims of seven countries on the Antarctic continent have been frozen as a result of the United States of America's efforts. The System of Treaties governs activities on the continent.

Mineral exploration and operations are likewise restricted until 2048 on the Antarctic continent. The Antarctic Treaty has 53 countries as signatories. Following the Treaty, scientific activity on the continent are limited to peaceful purposes under different accords and protocols.

Antarctica is the common heritage of humanity. As a result, it is critical for the Treaty's signatories to act in accordance with their knowledge of the Antarctic Continent's common human legacy.

Article 2 of the Madrid Protocol (Environmental Protection Protocol) to the Antarctic Treaty of 1991 protects ecosystems associated to and related to the Antarctic environment. Antarctica is designated as a natural reserve dedicated to peace, serenity, and science, according to the agreement. Mining is prohibited in Antarctica, except for scientific purposes, according to Article 7 of the convention. However, both climate change and future continental shelf challenges are pressuring countries to begin preliminary activities now.

After the Indian Ocean, the Pacific (Great) Ocean, the Atlantic (Atlantic) Ocean, and the Arctic (Arctic Ocean or Arctic Ocean) Ocean, National Geographic Magazine named the "Southern Ocean (Antarctica) Ocean" as the 5th Ocean after the Indian Ocean, the Pacific (Great) Ocean, the Atlantic (Atlantic) Ocean, and the Arctic (Arctic Ocean or Arctic Ocean) Ocean. It declared on June 8, 2021, that a new Ocean with the name "Ocean)" has been established.

In the early 2000s, the International Hydrographic Organization (IHO) declared the Southern Ocean to be the 5th World Ocean. The "Southern Ocean" is the name given to the ocean that joins the southern regions of the Pacific, Atlantic, and Indian oceans. IHO has 68 members from the coastal states. In 2000, 28 members took part in the organization's "Southern Ocean" survey. Outside of Argentina, participants opted to identify Antarctica's waters as a separate ocean. The majority of affirmative voters chose "Southern Ocean," whereas the majority chose "**Antarctic Ocean**." The northern boundary of this new ocean was chosen by 14 countries, with latitudes of 60° South, 50° South, and additional countries with latitudes north of 35° South. As a result, the northern boundary of the Southern Ocean was established to be 60° South latitude.

The development of investments and capacity for the military industry and the marine sector is linked to increasing the naval capabilities of the Naval Forces. Maritime Power; From the standpoint of defense and security, it lends the country's geopolitics an indisputable importance. Construction and modernization of maritime power capabilities, in particular, that will increase economic prosperity, should be discussed further.

In the twenty-first century, restoring order to the seas is critical. Cooperation is critical now to establish this order and to avoid threats from the sea, such as terrorism, all types of smuggling, human smuggling, marine pollution, piracy, and piracy.

"Maritime Power" refers to a power system that encompasses all of the sea's material and spiritual power elements and transfers their whole efficiency to national power. The marine commercial fleet and navy are the backbone of maritime power. Furthermore, Maritime Force encompasses all factors that contribute to this power, whether directly or indirectly.

In the twenty-first century, the "Maritime Industry" includes shipbuilding, yacht design, marine sub-industry, construction and operation of marine platforms, marine biology, marine chemistry, marine geology and geophysics, marine research, entertainment and water sports, marina and operation, surface and diving, tourism, and Maritime Education. All of these elements are vital to the development of a country's maritime power and capability.

The Navy is primarily a defensive force. Furthermore, it is not just a force that guards the coasts, but it is also a force that assures the safety of marine transportation routes. The strengthening of the "Navy's" capabilities will be aided by the development of naval industrial and commercial capacity.

States must develop new concepts, maritime policies, and tactics within the framework of soft power, as well as economic, commercial, and logistics factors, in order to establish marine power. It is critical to promote maritime-related components such as films, serials, literature and art, maritime journalism, and maritime photography as a governmental policy.

Marine and maritime security challenges are becoming more important in today's world. As a result of all these developments, the preparation of a multidimensional and comprehensive work on the oceans and seas at the global level has been brought to the agenda. Our book, GLOBAL MARITIME GEOPOLITICS, has been written to elucidate the above-mentioned concerns and add depth, reality, and richness to the scientific field.

I'd want to offer my heartfelt gratitude and heartfelt congratulations to my valued colleagues and researcher friends who helped and supported me by producing a book chapter.

For his thoughtful, selfless, and dedicated initiatives and advice, we'd like to express our sincere gratitude to Prof. Dr. İbrahim Sirkeci, Chief Publications Editor, who prepared our book for printing and designed the cover. His guidance has been much appreciated. We sincerely hope that the work will be useful for the scientific community.

Editors

Prof. Dr. Hasret Çomak,

Assoc. Prof. Dr. Burak Şakir Şeker

Assoc. Prof. Dr. Mehlika Özlem Ultan

Istanbul, October 2022

PART 1

ANTARCTIC AND ARCTIC CIRCLE GEOPOLITICS

ANTARCTIC AND ARCTIC MARITIME SECURITY INTERACTION WITHIN LIBERALISM, REALISM AND CRITICAL THEORIES

Burak Şakir Şeker[*] and Hasret Çomak[**]

Security Concept Through IR Theories

International security possesses a focal situation within the discipline of international relations. This concept is based upon the nations' sovereignty principle that indicates order and stability in the domestic sphere, and disorder and possible confusion in the international arena. Notwithstanding, the issue of security in the international arena has been the subject of an important theoretical discussion, with various approaches to international security previsions created by liberal, realist and critical theorists. Likewise, various new threats of security have emerged that are especially hazardous, since the end of the Cold War, because these newly emerged threats benefit differently, and more extensively, from the modern world's interconnectedness.

In accordance with the advocates of realism, which has been the predominant viewpoint in international politics since the World War II, international politics is all about power and self-interest. The neo-realist ideology has significant results for security. Kenneth Waltz introduced security as the highest aim of international politics.[1]

According to the realist perspective, states have the essential obligation for guaranteeing security, as articulated in the idea of national security. Thus, the main threats to security take their source from other states. Accordingly, threats of violence and different types of physical coercion are intrinsically connected with the possibilities of interstate warfare. Thusly, national security is generally connected with the prevention of such conflicts through the structure of military ability to prevent potential aggressors. Realists accept that this condition of violence can be restricted by the balance of power. In this manner, realists argued that the balance of power ought to be adopted as a policy utilizing diplomacy or the possibility of a possible war in order to keep any state from reaching a predominant situation in the international system.[2]

According to the liberal ideology, which adopts the basic idea of universal

[*] Assoc. Prof. Burak Şakir Şeker, Ankara Hacı Bayram Veli University, Turkey.
E-mail: buraksakirseker@gmail.com; seker.burak@hbv.edu.tr
[**] Prof. Dr. Hasret Çomak, Istanbul Kent University, Turkey. E-mail: hasret.comak@kent.edu.tr
[1] Waltz, Kenneth N. "Structural Realism after the Cold War." International Security, vol. 25, no. 1, 2000, pp. 5–41.
[2] Grieco, Joseph M. "Anarchy and the Limits of Cooperation: A Realist Critique of the Newest Liberal Institutionalism." International Organization, vol. 42, no. 3, 1988, pp. 485–507.

and eternal peace, the principle of balance or harmony controls in a wide range of social interactions. States, gatherings, and individuals may chase self-interest, yet a natural balance will in general manifest itself. As indicated by liberals; mechanisms to control the ambitions of sovereign nations are needed to demonstrate peace and international order, and these appear as international organizations, or international regimes. On the contrary; liberals upheld the collective security concept, the idea that supported the establishment of the League of Nations and later the United Nations.[3]

Constructivism and feminism are the critical approaches to security concept. Constructivism has obtained more interest since the end of the Cold War and has been the most effective post-positivist method to international theory. According to the constructors, the state identity (beliefs, values) formed by mutual interaction performs a focal part in modifying the perception of security according to the constructivist understanding.[4]

On the other hand, feminists have contended that the traditional thought of international security will in general act self-defeatingly because of the security paradox. This trend generates what is called insecurity of security. Finally, Copenhagen School has sized the concept of security within five main sectors. By explaining the relations and interaction between sectors, it revealed that military threats alone do not create insecurity for the society, and threats in other fields such as political, social, economic, and environmental are also a source of insecurity for society.[5]

The aim of this study is to determine by which treaties the Antarctic continent has been protected within the scope of international maritime security and to analyze the current strategic situation of the continent by placing it in a conceptual framework in the context of international relations theories. For this purpose, first of all, the definition of maritime security will be made, and then the historical development of the Antarctic continent in the field of maritime security will be explained. Finally, the strategies of states and international organizations in the continent will be analyzed in the context of international relations theories.

Maritime Security Concept within Realism, Liberalism and Constructivism

The concept of international security is to be examined in subheadings such as cyber security, border security, cultural security, and maritime security. The concept of maritime security, which is one of these sub-titles, is a concept that is

---

[3] Jervis, Robert. "Realism, Neoliberalism, and Cooperation: Understanding the Debate." International Security, vol. 24, no. 1, 1999, pp. 42–63.

[4] David A. Baldwin, "Constructivism." Power and International Relations: A Conceptual Approach, Princeton University Press, Princeton; Oxford, 2016, pp. 139–154.

[5] Newman, Edward. "Critical Human Security Studies." Review of International Studies, vol. 36, no. 1, 2010, pp. 77–94.

frequently mentioned in the International Relations and Security Studies Literature, but there is no consensus on its definition yet. The global rise of maritime security, a concept that has gained popularity in recent years, especially with the September 11 attacks and the piracy activities that emerged off the coast of Somalia, has brought a scientific interest. Considering that 90 percent of world trade is carried out by sea, the necessity of protecting the flow of goods, services, and money makes maritime security one of the most important problems of the international environment. The need for securitization or making maritime security a matter of security is not only due to the importance of maritime trade. The threat analysis shows that it is predicted that an attack as big or as devastating as the September 11 attacks can only come from the sea.[6]

The concept of "Marine Security", which attracted the attention of the public for the first time due to the spread of maritime terrorism after the September 11 terrorist attacks, was used in terms of geopolitical evaluations (dominance of sea areas, control in territorial waters and sea areas, revealing the picture of the sea) during the Cold War. Since the late 1990s and the beginning of the 2000s, maritime security has been used to describe efforts to prevent illegal activity from or at sea. Today, maritime safety is used in connection with environmental and economic considerations.[7]

The prevailing view in the literature is that there is no universal consensus on the definition of maritime security. According to Chris Rahman, maritime security takes on different meanings by different individuals and organizations depending on organizational interests, political or ideological prejudices, depending on who defines it.[8]

Maritime security is a concept that derives from the systematic nature of the maritime space and addresses traditional and non-traditional security challenges by state and non-state actors, in which multiple and interrelated requirements for joint security are presented. In this respect, maritime security aims to coordinate collaborative security initiatives to ensure and promote national, territorial, and worldwide crucial interests, objectives, and basic beliefs including those connected to maritime security; state sovereignty, political stability, freedom of navigation, economic development, environmental and ocean resources, human and community development.

Modern maritime security defines preventive measures to respond to illegal activities from or at sea since the late 1990s and early 2000s. Maritime security,

---

[6] Mat Salleh, Norhasliza, "Post 9/11 maritime security measures : global maritime security versus facilitation of global maritime trade", 2006, World Maritime University Dissertations. 98.

[7] Basil Germond, The Geopolitical Dimension of Maritime Security, Marine Policy, Volume 54, 2015, 137-142. https://www.sciencedirect.com/science/article/pii/S0308597X14003509#:~:text=The%20 geopolitical%20dimension%20of%20maritime%20security%20accounts%20for%20the%20way,develop ing%20their%20maritime%20security%20strategies. (Retrieved: 01.06.2021)

[8] C. Rahman, "Concepts of Maritime Security: A Strategic Perspective on Alternative Visions for Good Order and Security at Sea, with Policy Implications for New Zealand", New Zealand, Victoria University of Wellington, Centre for Strategic Studies, 2009, No. 07/09, 29-42.

used during the Cold War as a reference to superpower control over maritime areas, today represents destructive activities such as terrorism, piracy, arms, drug and human trafficking, illegal, unreported and unregulated fishing, pollution. The above-mentioned approaches to explain and show the transformation of maritime security according to varying degrees of threat at seas and ports and sometimes intersecting factors, undoubtedly contribute to the definition of maritime security and its basic characteristics. In this context, many risks and threats such as piracy and armed robbery of vessels, terrorism, irregular migration, drug and human trafficking, environmental problems disrupting the ecological order (pollution, illegal-irregular fishing), maritime accidents can be seen in the seas. Therefore, maritime security is turning into an area where states can take appropriate measures and make arrangements at the regional and global level in the face of threats at sea.[9]

Maritime security, which includes being away from these risks and threats; It also points to governance that encompasses many areas of peace and security-based policies regarding the seas, vessels, coasts and ports. Another conclusion that can be drawn from this is that maritime security has an aspect that combines civil and military measures in the international arena in order to ensure the use of seas and ports within the framework of certain rules and to prevent illegal activities in these areas. Therefore, maritime security is turning into an area where states can take appropriate measures and make arrangements at the regional and global level in the face of threats at sea. In this context, maritime security is mostly provided by the UNCLOS[10], which came into force in 1994.[11]

The UNCLOS was signed at the third Law of the Sea Conference on December 10, 1982, to be used in the solution of problems in the international arena related to international maritime security problems. UNCLOS, in terms of its functionality, has led to the functioning of different and new institutions such as the ISA[12], the CLCS[13], and the ITLOS[14]. In addition, the United Nations is one of the leading organizations making efforts to ensure maritime security on a global scale, both with the decisions it has taken and the practices it has created through the IMO. The ICJ[15] carries out judicial activities based on the authority it has received from UNCLOS in the resolution of interstate water problems within the scope of its authority from the UN Charter. However, in order for the court to carry out these activities, first of all, the states party must apply with

---

[9] Crowell, Ben, and Wade Turvold. Hindsight, Insight, Foresight: Thinking About Security in the Indo-Pacific. Report. Edited by Vuving Alexander L. Daniel K. Inouye Asia-Pacific Center for Security Studies, 2020. 209-16.
[10] United Nations Convention on the Law of the Sea
[11] K. Dodds, Fish and Continental Shelves: Maritime Security, Sovereignty, and Stewardship in the Polar Regions. Brown Journal of World Affairs, 2015, 244-246.
[12] International Seabed Authority
[13] Commission on the Limits of the Continental Shelf
[14] International Tribunal for the Law of the Sea
[15] International Court of Justice

entente to the court and recognize the jurisdiction of the court.[16]

Maritime security may be taken into consideration in the framework of a few international relations theories. The realist theory of international relations expresses maritime security as a matter of maritime power. In peacetime, maritime power is related to countries' securing the capacity of conducting transport and exchange by means of the seas. In wartime, maritime power is related to the naval forces' ability to attack different naval forces or different nations' maritime transport vehicles.[17]

On the other side, the Liberalist approach advocates that maritime security is the arranging of the maritime domain. Liberalists underline that international law is the way to change the maritime power of countries towards cooperation to achieve common goals.[18]

In addition, constructivists look at the relations and how the concept of maritime security comes to be through actions, interactions instead of expressing maritime security as a list of threats. Constructivists analyze how various maritime security conceptions are shaped by various political interests and normative approaches.[19]

Realist interpretations of maritime security focus on the new naval power balance and competition based on the rise of China as an economic and naval power and the US shifting its focus to Asia-Pacific. This view shows that the seas will increasingly be the scene of the power struggle of the great powers and will affect the international order in the sea. After the Cold War, within the framework of the establishment of the liberal international order, globalization, and the practices of UNCLOS; the navy has turned to expeditionary mission operations, humanitarian aid, disaster relief, and maritime security missions instead of combat missions. However, after the annexation of Crimea by the Russian Federation and the rise of China, it is possible to see the traces of a return to traditional duties. The fact that competition at sea puts the fight against threats into the background makes cooperation difficult.[20]

Antarctic Maritime Security Process

Historian David Day has said that Antarctica is "a mirror on which centuries

---

[16] IUCN, United Nations Convention on the Law of the Sea. https://www.iucn.org/sites/dev/files/unclos_further_information.pdf (Retrieved: 05.06.2021)

[17] Ross, Robert S. "Nationalism, Geopolitics, and Naval Expansionism: From the Nineteenth Century to the Rise of China." Naval War College Review, vol. 71, no. 4, 2018, pp. 10–44.

[18] Landman, Lennart. The EU Maritime Security Strategy: Promoting or Absorbing European Defence Cooperation? Clingendael Institute, 2015.

[19] Farrell, Theo. "Constructivist Security Studies: Portrait of a Research Program." International Studies Review, vol. 4, no. 1, 2002, pp. 49–72.

[20] Scott, David. "China's Indo-Pacific Strategy: The Problems of Success." The Journal of Territorial and Maritime Studies, vol. 6, no. 2, 2019, pp. 94–113.

of human hopes, fears and desires have been projected".[21] This deserted corner of the world, the coldest and windiest, has not attracted the attention of many people except explorers and whalers for many years after its discovery. However, in recent decades, as a result of technological developments, livable environments have started to be created more easily in this region, it has started to gain importance, especially in terms of scientific studies and research. Even a certain tourist activity is observed here.

When we examined security issues in the continent, In the 1950s, treaties involving international political arrangements in Antarctica became a matter of interest for states. Before an international agreement was reached, the fight for strategic dominance in the Antarctic Peninsula took place in the context of the United States' not recognizing any of its claims to sovereignty over the continent, the Soviet Union's perception of threat from the region within the scope of an alliance to be formed against itself, and the profound changes in international relations during the Cold War happened. The negotiations that carried out by the states parties took place in order not to turn the Antarctic continent into a new battlefield and to stay away from regional tensions.[22]

The tensions experienced in the region, before the international negotiations started, brought along the claims of ownership of the region and the efforts to establish a regime to benefit from the region. Various claims regarding the region were put forward by seven states (England, New Zealand, France, Australia, Norway, Chile, Argentina). The main development in the effort to establish an international order in the region has been within the framework of scientific activities. The first serious attempt began with scientific stations established in the region in 1957-1958 by 12 countries (in addition to the seven above, United States, South Africa, Japan, Soviet Union, Belgium). Then, in 1959, these 12 countries created the Antarctic Treaty, and over the years, new countries with different statuses were added to this number, and the number of signatory countries of the treaty has reached 54 today. Along with the Antarctic Treaty, 3 additional treaties regarding Antarctica constitute the ATS[23]. These are the 1972 CCAS[24], the 1980 CCAMLR[25] and the 1991 Madrid Protocol[26].[27]

However, the ATS is quite inadequate in terms of maritime safety and ship navigational safety. For this reason, the UNCLOS agreement dated 1982 is implemented to ensure the safety of ship transportation in the open seas. The

---

[21] David Day, 'Ice Works: Three Portraits of Antarctica' The Monthly, March 2012, 56. See further David Day, Antarctica: A Biography (Vintage, Sydney, 2013).
[22] Hemmings, A. D., Rothwell, D. R., & Scott, K. N. Antarctic Security in the Twenty-First Century: Legal and Policy Perspectives (1st ed.). Routledge.
[23] Antarctic Treaty System
[24] Convention on the Conservation of Antarctic Bear Fish
[25] Convention on the Conservation of Marine Living Resources
[26] Antarctic Treaty Environmental Protection Protocol
[27] N. Liu, The rise of China and the Antarctic Treaty System? Australian Journal of Maritime & Ocean Affairs, 2019, 11 (2), 120–131.

agreement, which entered into force in November 1994, establishes the applicable rules of international law for the oceans that cover most of the earth's surface. What inextricably links these developments with Antarctica is that the icy continent is surrounded by the Southern Ocean. It is bound by the UNCLOS agreement in the Southern Ocean and the Antarctic agreement does not provide appropriate arrangements for navigation. The states of the Antarctic Treaty continue to apply the basic rules and principles of modern ocean law in their dealings with each other and with foreign ships in the southern polar waters.[28]

The most important problem experienced in the region in recent years has emerged when some Asian-African-Latin American countries started to claim rights over the region within the framework of the concept of "Common Heritage of Humanity", or rather, only some developed countries objected to the establishment of rights in the region. It cannot be said that these views, which are generally expressed within the United Nations, have seriously affected the current situation so far. The results of all these developments can sometimes be the subject of discussion between the scholars.[29]

Liberalism and Antarctic Treaty System

In this section, it will be analyzed the function of the system of interstate agreements in Antarctica, how Antarctica became the most peaceful continent in the world, how international mechanisms have confirmed the basic principles of liberalism, and the effects of the treaties still in force today on Antarctic Maritime security. For this, we must first understand the basic principles of liberalism.

Regarding human nature, which classical realists see as the most determining factor behind state behavior and actions in international society, liberals claim that human nature is mainly inclined towards good and cooperation. According to liberals, one can overcome the problem of insecurity through cooperation and norms that are beneficial to all. People also have the ability to think about the well-being of others, and it is in their own interest to bring this quality forward. As people move in this direction one by one, rules can be set both for the common good and progress towards good, cooperation and the development of mutual common interests as a nation or society and as an international community.[30]

In addition, liberals argue that an authority or regulatory institutions can be established in the international society to eliminate anarchy. War and anarchy are not inevitable situations or consequences. Competition, war or conflict as an international problem can be prevented or completely eliminated not only by

---

[28] C. C. Joyner, The Antarctic Treaty and the law of the sea: fifty years on. Polar Record, 46(1), 2009, 14–17.

[29] M. P. Nevitt, & Percival, R. Polar Opposites: Assessing the State of Enviromental Law in the World's Polar Regions, 2018.

[30] Fawcett, Edmund. "The Primacy of Politics." In Liberalism: The Life of an Idea, Second Edition, 454-66. Princeton; Oxford: Princeton University Press, 2018.

national efforts but also by international collective cooperation and efforts. Liberals argue that states can cooperate with common interests instead of national interests, and instead of power politics to ward off perceived threats from each other. First, they believe that this can be easily achieved through increased cooperation, institutionalization, and the absence of anarchy to be eliminated through norms in the international system.[31]

The Antarctic Treaty System (1959) is an international organization that takes as an example the fundamental principles of liberalism listed above. As long as this treaty, which does not have an expiry date, remained in force, no party could put forward a claim of sovereignty over the region, provided that the situation of those who had previously claimed sovereignty was reserved and in a sense frozen. Thanks to this agreement, Antarctica was no longer the subject of maritime security for a long time. Thus, the region will only be used for peaceful/scientific activities, and cooperation between the parties regarding these issues will be essential.[32]

In this respect, it has been decided to deal with the scientific problems related to the region together with the members of this community, apart from the 12 countries that are party to the treaty and have bases used for scientific activities in the region, within the framework of the ICSU.[33] Observers from the signatory countries of the treaty will be able to make observations and inspections in the whole region whenever and wherever they want. Disputes will be settled by peaceful methods, when necessary, by going to the International Court of Justice.[34]

There is no regulation in the treaty regarding the situation of natural resources and mineral wealth in the region. With this status, the region today (at least for the vast majority of countries) is one of the most prominent examples of what is described as humanity's "Global Commons". Thus, by avoiding the conflict environment, it was shown that human nature is good and that he can give up his own interests for the "good of all" by cooperating when necessary. However, the fact that when the ATS came into force, there has been no military conflict in the region since 1961 proof that it was a successful agreement in terms of maritime security. The three (continuing) treaties signed after the Antarctic Treaty: the 1972 CCAS, the 1980 CCAMLR and the 1991 Madrid Protocol. The transformation of the Antarctic Treaty System was achieved with the adoption of the Madrid Environmental Protection Protocol, and other activities, including mining, were prohibited on the Continent, apart from scientific activities. Parties have waived their mineral exploration and exploitation rights with this Protocol.

---

[31] Harrison, Ewan. "Waltz, Kant and Systemic Approaches to International Relations." Review of International Studies 28, no. 1 (2002): 143-62.
[32] T. Stephens, Antarctic security in the twenty-first century: legal and policy perspectives. The Polar Journal, 2(2), 2012, 464–466.
[33] International Council of Scientific Unions
[34] E. J. Molenaar, The Law of the Sea and the Polar Regions: Interactions between Global and Regional Regimes (Publications on Ocean Development, 2013, Martinus Nijhoff, 432.

The Madrid Protocol constitutes a turning point for the Antarctic Continent to be the common heritage of humanity.[35]

Interaction between Arctic Circle and Antarctic within the Liberalist Approach

Locationally there is no consensus on the boundaries of the Arctic Region. The Arctic Region has somehow been included in the interests of countries, companies and scientists, which are not connected with each other in terms of borders, especially due to the increase in global warming. The importance of the region is its importance in terms of international trade as it can be used as a new commercial route.[36] Another advantage for the states in the region arising from the melting of the glaciers in the Arctic Region is the underground resources in the region. Apart from the fact that the region is rich in reserves such as gold, diamond, zinc, and uranium, it is estimated that there is crude oil equivalent to 6% of the world's oil reserves.[37]

There is an interstate organization called the Arctic Council, where the states in the Arctic Region come together for cooperation and coordination in the region. Russian Federation, Canada, Sweden, Iceland, Norway, United States, Finland and Denmark are the member states of the Artic Council. The formation of the Arctic Council has been instrumental in the regular engagement of states in ecological and social projects in the region. However Arctic Council is beyond from security issues in the region and considering that three of the states in the region are EU countries and four of them are NATO members, it can be said that these actors also have influence in the region. Also considering both NATO member countries and Russia exist in same region, security confrontation between countries could be predictable.[38]

With the melting of the glaciers in the region, the states in the region have made certain claims based on international law. The fact that Russia placed its flag on the bottom of the Arctic Ocean as a symbol for their claim in the region in 2007 is one of the events that increased the tension in the region. Apart from all these, there are various disagreements in the region between the two NATO member states, Canada and the USA, regarding peripheral sovereignty in the region.[39]

---

[35] Freeland, Steven, and Anja Nakarada Pecujlic. "How Do You Like Your Regulation – Hard or Soft? The Antarctic Treaty and The Outer Space Treaty Compared." National Law School of India Review 30, no. 1 2018, 11-36.

[36] Burak Şakir Şeker, Dalaklis Dimitrios, Maritime Energy Security Issues: The Case of the Arctic, Geopolitica, 2016.

[37] Rahbek-Clemmensen, Jon. "When Do Ideas of an Arctic Treaty Become Prominent in Arctic Governance Debates?" Arctic 72, no. 2 (2019): 116-30.

[38] Soare, Simona, Arctic Stress Test: Great power competition and Euro-Atlantic defence in the High North, European Union Institute for Security Studies (EUISS), 2020.

[39] Rowe, Elana Wilson, and Helge Blakkisrud. The Arctic Council and US Domestic Policymaking. Norwegian Institute of International Affairs (NUPI), 2019.

From the point of view of structural or neo-realist theory, it can be said that there is not a bipolar or unipolar system but a multipolar system in the region. However, the conflict of interest between Canada and the USA, which are allied within the same system, in the Arctic Region is an indication that the region is open to a more appropriate interpretation of classical realist theory.[40]

If the collective business consciousness in the region examined, it can be seen that it overlaps with liberal theory. This is because, according to classical liberal theory, harmony between states is possible and this situation can be created through interstate organizations. It is also possible to see the traces of liberal theory, which rejects the thesis that only military events determine international politics with the formation of a non-security organization in the Arctic Region. However, the idea advocated by the liberal view that acting jointly will destroy the regional anarchy situation and that stability and harmony will appear in the region has become unrealistic with the appearance of conflicts despite the existence of the organization in the region. [41]

In addition to the work of the Arctic Council, IMO has taken measures for the safety and design of ships in the Arctic. The IMO Assembly has issued a resolution on the development of guidelines for vessels operating in polar waters that will go beyond the guidelines set out in the Polar Code[42], SOLAS[43] and MARPOL[44] Conventions.[45] IMO's Polar Code, which is entered in to force in January 2017. Code was inspired by a recognition that the polar oceans were likely to become increasingly accessible (especially in the Arctic context) and that there needed to be greater attention given to standards regarding polar vessels, training and navigation, and pollution controls.[46]

Examining the Sovereignty Claims, Maritime Security Issues in Antarctica through Realism

In this section, we will discuss how the system of interstate agreements have been established in Antarctica, the relations and power dynamics that have led to the establishment of this system, the sovereignty claims of the states in the Antarctic region and the connection between these claims and classical realist theory. For this, we first need to understand the basic principles of classical realism.

The most important assumption of classical realism is based on the

---

[40] McArthur, Dan. "Reconsidering Structural Realism." Canadian Journal of Philosophy 33, no. 4 (2003): 517-36.

[41] Williams, Michael C. "Securitization and the Liberalism of Fear." Security Dialogue 42, no. 4/5 2011, 453-63.

[42] International Code for Ships Operating in Polar Waters

[43] International Convention for the Safety of Life at Sea

[44] International Convention for the Prevention of Pollution from Ships

[45] Nevitt & Percival, op.cit., 1688

[46] Dodds, op.cit., 246

importance attributed to the concept of the state. According to the realist view, the state is the most fundamental factor of the international system. The state is the only instrument in the system that has legislative, executive and judicial power. Therefore, in the international community of states, states compete for competing purposes or national interests. Another assumption of realists regarding the behavior of states in international society concerns their emphasis on national interest and power. The interest of power and the state comes first. States take part in power struggles in the international community for at least two reasons. Firstly, because they do not feel safe and secure in an anarchic international society, and secondly, because states act with competitive, selfish and jealous impulses based on human nature.[47]

In this context, it is natural for states and nations to include these assets in the definition of national interest in order to obtain national opportunities, lands and natural resources that they can control. The first element of national interest is security, and the second is to be prepared for threats and attacks from other states and to access the resources and opportunities to ensure this.[48]

A fundamental assumption of realism is that the structure of international society is anarchic. According to this assumption, there is no mechanism in the international community to regulate the relations between the members of the society, to set moral or legal rules, and to enforce the rules in case of non-compliance with these rules. The lack of an authority to establish such a mechanism, to ensure its functionality, and to remove the actors who will engage in attitudes and behaviors that disrupt the rules and order, is the basic feature of the international society and the system. The absence of such a supra-state order, an authority that maintains order, maintains power and dignity in the international community is expressed with the concept of anarchy. According to realists, the structure of the international system is anarchic. Accordingly, in the absence of a regulatory order of norms and an authority to support or enforce the norms with sanctions, states are left alone with threats from outside within the system or society only with their national resources and defense capabilities and capacities. Therefore, the concept of "balance of power" dominates international relations. States shape their policies based on this concept.[49]

Since we have explained the basic principles of classical realism, we can take a look at the sovereignty policies of the states in the Antarctic continent, the conflicts of interest and the international Antarctic Treaties system that emerged as a result of these.

After the Second World War, the 1950s were spent in search of a regime for

---

[47] Williams, Michael C. "Why Ideas Matter in International Relations: Hans Morgenthau, Classical Realism, and the Moral Construction of Power Politics." International Organization 58, no. 4 (2004): 633-65.

[48] Glaser, Charles L. "Realists as Optimists: Cooperation as Self-Help." International Security, vol. 19, no. 3, 1994, pp. 50–90.

[49] Walt, Stephen M. "Alliance Formation and the Balance of World Power." International Security, vol. 9, no. 4, 1985, pp. 3–43.

Antarctica. In 1956, New Zealand's proposal for Antarctica to become a world territory and to be administered under the United Nations was also rejected. In fact, it is stated that during the Cold War years that continued in 1950, the South Pole was the scene of the invisible field war of the superpowers.

The US tried to respond to the USSR's concerns about the future of Antarctica by excluding it. The main reason for this can be suggested as the "Balance of Terror" view that dominated foreign policy at that time. Neither country wanted a nuclear missile threat directed at it from the Antarctic continent.[50] In fact, it is possible to say that the Balance of Power theory, which is one of the basic principles of realism, comes into play here. The two superpowers were balancing each other and due to their national interests, no country, including the riparian countries, did not accept any claim in the region.[51]

During the cold war years, which witnessed the power struggle between the USA and the USSR, it was tried to be careful that the continent was away from militarization. In addition, the fact that the USA and the USSR have a say in determining the status of the land in any part of the world has also been revealed. As a result; The USA could not exclude the USSR and the Antarctic Treaty Conference in 1959 was held under these conditions.[52]

The fact that nation states signed such a treaty and mediated the protection of the continent on behalf of all humanity was also associated with the spirit of the time. The maturation and signing of the Antarctic Treaty in the conditions of the Cold War is more about avoiding the consequences of a global conflict of interest than it is about preserving the Continent for peaceful purposes. With the 1959 Antarctic Treaty, a kind of balance of power was tried to be established, and the two superpowers of the Cold War brought together at a common point.[53]

In fact, the "Antarctic Treaty System", which is seen as a multilateral treaty, was created between two superpowers within the framework of the basic principles of realism. Thus, it has been confirmed that the most important element that can bring balance to the international system is the "bilateral alliance system". It aims to ensure the existence of the members of that system in the absence of a central authority, to ensure order and to limit violence, and to ensure justice in this way, through the balance of powers, international law, diplomacy, war and harmony institutions between the great powers. Based on this understanding, it would be appropriate to say that Antarctica witnessed the conflict of two great powers such as the USA and the USSR, and then they

[50] Wohlstetter, Albert. "The Delicate Balance of Terror." Foreign Affairs, vol. 37, no. 2, 1959, pp. 211–234.
[51] Hoffmann, Stanley. "Weighing the Balance of Power." Foreign Affairs, vol. 50, no. 4, 1972, pp. 618–643.
[52] Hanessian, John. "The Antarctic Treaty 1959." The International and Comparative Law Quarterly, vol. 9, no. 3, 1960, pp. 436–480.
[53] Young, Claire. Eyes on the Prize: Australia, China, and the Antarctic Treaty. Lowy Institute for International Policy, 202.

avoided anarchy by establishing a balance between them through the institutions created by international law.[54]

The 1959 Antarctic Treaty consists of 14 articles and was created for the signatory countries of the treaty. This situation causes the biggest criticisms of the Antarctic Treaty System. The states authorized to carry out activities in Antarctica are the signatory countries of the treaty and they determine the future of the continent. This situation leads to criticism that the states parties hold a disproportionate power in their hands. In fact, this situation was expressed by some countries that are not signatory countries of the treaty as the new colonization efforts of developed countries and it was stated that all economic and environmental activities on the continent should be within the framework of the principle of the common heritage of humanity.[55]

Researchers state that international power policies towards the continent were implemented after the end of the Cold War in the form of taking a position to grab as much resources as possible in the future, and that the rising powers of Antarctica, such as China, India, and South Korea, also used their polar programs to strengthen their international influence and national pride. Emphasizing that the Antarctic Treaty, which is open to the participation of all countries, only gives the right to speak to the countries that carry out scientific programs that are accepted on the continent, the academics are of the opinion that there should be a more democratic management system in the continent. Otherwise, some revisionist countries may use the Antarctic agreement in the name of their national interests and may take initiatives to endanger the maritime security rules in the region.[56]

It is possible to observe that the states claiming rights in the region have developed an ambitious Antarctic policy in recent years. We can comment on this by analyzing China's national strategy. China ratified the Antarctic Treaty in 1983, then it joined the Madrid Protocol in 1998 and become a part of the Atlantic Treaty System. In contrast to all this, China is a developing industrial country. Accordingly, China made 34 expeditions to the continent and established five research stations. The natural resources of the continent attract China, like all countries. In addition to all their increasing activities, the drilling activities of Chinese research centers within the scope of combating climate change are approached with suspicion. There are claims that these studies were carried out to measure the mineral resources of the continent. Besides China, most of the states that are party to the Antarctic Treaty keep their sovereignty claims secret. In other words, the slightest bump in the treaty proves that the

---

[54] Beck, Peter J. "The Antarctic Treaty System after 25 Years." The World Today, vol. 42, no. 11, 1986, pp. 196–199.
[55] Freeland, Steven, and Anja Nakarada Pecujlic. "How Do You Like Your Regulation – Hard or Soft? The Antarctic Treaty and the Outer Space Treaty Compared." National Law School of India Review, vol. 30, no. 1, 2018, pp. 11–36.
[56] Bergin, Anthony, and Tony Press. China in the Antarctic Treaty System. Australian Strategic Policy Institute, 2020, pp. 9–12.

states actually want to return to their realist ambitions. This could indicate that maritime security in and around Antarctica will become a major issue in the future.[57]

Especially after the events of September 11, which took place in the United States and caused a change in the perception of security all over the world, the perspective on maritime security was renewed in the context of terrorism. In this situation, the SUA[58] Convention was enacted, and the safety of sea voyages was protected under this agreement. As it is known, the Antarctic region is located at a point so far away that any national navy cannot intervene under the terrorist threat. Therefore, it is important to ensure the navigational safety of the polar regions within the scope of the updated laws like SUA.[59]

The world, since the perception of security has changed since the September 11 attacks, have focused more on individual attacks, terrorist acts and directing bomb attacks on strategic facilities. In this context, especially the USA gave importance to the security of ports, which are the commercial strategic points of the countries. Within the scope of these developments, updated laws were created to ensure port security. The most important one; the ISPS[60] Code which includes amendments to the 1974 SOLAS Convention. But these security measures were not used much for the Antarctic region. The biggest reason for this is that the region is far from trade routes, it is not located on any of the ship routes and there are no large-scale ports.[61]

Illegal activities in Antarctic waters are generally minor and not cause for concern. The most important of these; The two countries are suing after Japan's whalers are fishing without permission in Australian waters. Apart from such events there are not many problems other than illegal fishing problems in the region.[62]

Conclusion

The view that the state, which dominates the seas in international relations, can have a say in the world, has led the states to spread to the seas and to acquire lands and colonies in overseas countries. In addition, considering that 90 percent of world trade is carried out by sea, the necessity of protecting the flow of goods, services and money has made maritime security one of the most important problems of the international environment today.

---

[57] Liu, op.cit, p. 2-3.
[58] Convention for the Suppression of Unlawful Acts against the Safety of Maritime Navigation
[59] Molenaar, op.cit., p. 382
[60] International Ship and Port Security
[61] Woolner, Derek. "Drowned by Politics: Australia's Challenges in Managing Its Maritime Domain." Security Challenges, vol. 9, no. 3, 2013, pp. 63–91.
[62] Young, Michaela. "Whaling in the Antarctic (Australia v Japan: New Zealand Intervening): Progressive Judgment or Missed Opportunity for the Development of International Environmental Law?" The Comparative and International Law Journal of Southern Africa, vol. 48, no. 1, 2015, pp. 59–88.

World countries have established security organizations and adopted a series of strategies to deal with threats in the area of maritime security. According to the realist approach, maritime security is ensured by maritime power, so the seas are an arena where states compete for power. According to the liberalist approach, maritime security can be ensured through cooperation in the face of any threat. In addition, international organizations to be established in order to ensure cooperation perform a focal point in maintaining peace and order.

The Arctic and Antarctic are the main regions where maritime security problems could be experienced soon. The increasing importance and intensity of global interaction has also encouraged the growth of illegal actors such as piracy, terrorism and criminal organizations; it also connected different maritime regions. Climate change, pollution and overfishing are degrading the marine environment and creating new conflicts and problems for the Arctic and Antarctic. In light of these developments, the European Union has decided to develop a comprehensive maritime security strategy in order to increase its effectiveness in the field of maritime security, taking into account the increasing global nature of maritime problems.

In this context, there is a greater synergy between the Integrated Maritime Policy of the European Union and the Common Security and Defense Policy; explores the possibility of launching regional maritime strategies for areas of increasing strategic importance, such as the Arctic, Indian Ocean, West Africa and Antarctic; It strives to improve its ability to monitor and respond to marine problems by increasing efforts to develop a Common Information Sharing Environment in the marine environment.

With regards to current tensions in the Arctic and Antarctic, the compromise system essentially affects regional stability. Territorial disputes are affected by the character of the countries in question and the nature of the dispute, regardless of whether it emerges from the definition of sea limits, covering regional cases, or questioned sovereignty. The presence of various collaboration initiatives in the Arctic and Antarctic shows that probably some basic interests have effectively been distinguished among the nations in the locale. These initiatives are critical in light of the fact that the increase in exchange flows and social associations won't really result convergence of values and automatic security coalitions. While there is coordination and collaboration between nations in the two sides of the equator to handle maritime security challenges in the region, such initiatives have regularly been seen to happen where the generally financial interests are in question. Regardless of this, there is no uncertainty that there are common security advantages to be gotten from participation towards a more secure Arctic and Antarctic and that will urge key partners to make a move.

GLOBAL GEOPOLITICAL SHIFT: BALANCE OF POWER IN THE ARCTIC

Ferdi Güçyetmez[*]

Introduction

Considering today's conditions, the international arena seems to be anarchic. In order to ensure the anarchic structuring order, there are regional and international organizational structures. There is a new area of this anarchic structuring and balance of power issue: The Arctica. When we examine the relations of the states in the Arctic region or with interest in the region; Since there is no higher authority to decide on the issues in the region, it is observed that the relations of the states in the region are carried out in an anarchic system. In the last seventy years, we have witnessed geopolitical shifts in which post-world wars global conflicts are transmitted regionally. The Arctic region, which is the new focus of global powers, has not yet met any terrorist activity, unlike other conflict areas. The Arctic region, where countries are trying to increase their cooperation, will be the new conflict area for states that want to keep energy in the future. In this study, we will examine America and Russia's policies on the Arctic, which are geo-strategically trying to create a new balance of power and are determined to redesign the bipolar system in this region through the power balance theory.

According to Waltz, the international system is anarchic and decentralized. In this anarchic system, the purpose of the states is to survive as in classical realism. The system's anarchic nature stems from the assumption that states see each other as a rival/enemy. Since states cannot rely on each other in the anarchic system, they must rely on the "tools" they have created to exist.[1] Therefore, the struggle to create power in the new regional system created in the global system begins.

On the other hand, can it be said that there is a power gap in the region? This question is critical for the arctic, the new field of global conflict. As an answer to this question, we can say that Russia already has authority in the region. As we mentioned above, after the glaciers' melting, this power will increase more with new areas opened. At this point, since there is an element of power, it is necessary to balance power. States act similarly in the Arctic. As reflected in the strategy documents, Russia's biggest aim is to preserve its sovereignty in the region, in

---

[*] Ferdi Güçyetmez, Lecturer, Switzerland Neuchatel University, Institute of Humanities, & Kent University, Faculty of Humanities and Social Sciences, Turkey. E-mail: ferdigucyetmez26@gmail.com, Orcid: 0000-0003-1204-2006.
[1] Jensen, Øystein, "Current Legal Developments the Barents Sea", **The International Journal of Marine and Coastal Law.** Vol. 26, No.1, 2011, pp. 151-168.

other words, to maintain its power.

After Russia intervened in Ukraine, the USA, Canada, and the EU's economic and technological embargo disrupted Russian investments in the Arctic. It started the war in the balance of power. After this balance change, China started to support Russia's investments in the Arctic region economically, and all global powers in the regional area determined their ranks. In the balance of power, states that provide balance may have different characteristics. Based on this assumption, a militarily weak but economically strong state is always seen as a potential rival/enemy.[2]

With the balance of power approach, it will be possible to examine countries' policies towards the region and their relations covering the region in three sections. First of all, as the "Arctic Five", actors from Russia, United States of America (USA), Canada, Norway and Denmark (Greenland and Faroe Islands) claiming rights over the region directly bordering the Arctic Ocean are inactive position. Also, the Arctic council member states are seeking rights over the region. When it comes to its resources, it is inevitable for the states bordering on the Arctic to claim rights in the region. Thus, the new balance order started to be established. "Waltz states that the anarchic nature of the international system pushes weak states to balance strong states rather than join the strong."[3] In this balance, all states with the smallest border in the Arctic region will have a significant power effect.

Multipolarity is a structure in which there are more than two dominant powers in the international system. This structural system exists in the Arctic region. The multipolar system is divided into two as balanced multipolarity and unbalanced multipolarity. Balanced multipolarity, dominant states at the level of the international system cannot dominate each other. The powers of the dominant states are close to each other. In this structure, security and power systems can be controlled easily. In the unbalanced multipolar structure, when one of the international system's dominant forces is stronger than the others, it seeks a hegemony. This situation makes war and instability inevitable. When we approach it from this point of view, although the arctic has been under construction for many years, it is impossible to talk about a balanced system yet.[4]

Kenneth Waltz thinks that as the international system's conditions change, his international theories will change day by day, and such situations are normal.[5] In the international system, it is essential which state holds power and how long it will maintain it. Balancing the power will be easier because the power formations in the Arctic region are still new. States with power cannot hold this

---

[2] John. J., Mearsheimer, **The Tragedy of Great Power Politics**, New York, Norton Publishing, 2001, p.143.
[3] Kenneth N., Waltz, "Structural Realism After The Cold War", İnternational Secrurity, 01622889, Vol. 25, No.5, 2000, p.14.
[4] Ibid, Mearsheimer, p.44.
[5] Ibid, Waltz, p.25.

power forever. This power is weakened by states, either by their own mistakes or by other states, or balanced by other states, as has happened many times before. Looking at history, the structuralists came up with various ideas about how the international system was shaped by power distribution.

Although the common working area and the balance of power have just begun to form in the region, the region's riparian countries have started to work for power struggle since the 20th century. In the 1930s, the Arctic region began to attract military attention. The Soviet Union and the USA initiated the first attempts. In this direction, the Soviets rapidly industrialized within their domination areas in the Arctic to neutralize the dangers that could come from the capitalist outside world. Besides industrialization, settlements created in the region. Regional development was aimed with the fields of study. The first population to be settled in the area was Gulag prisoners and took an active part in the work carried out in the area with people of all professions.

On the other hand, Canada and the USA also carried out military work in the region. The Arctic region is the strategic region used against Germany during the Second World War. In this direction, most of the USA and Britain's aid to the Soviets was transported from the Arctic Ocean.

With the Second World War, the Arctic region's geostrategic importance witnessed the USA and the Soviets' power struggle. The USA has built military bases on Greenland and Iceland and established systems in the radar zone[6]. Although the Soviets and the USA actively entered into a power struggle during the Cold War period, Soviet Russia's dominance in the region decreased due to the economic turmoil in the 1980s. These crises, which deepened further, led the Soviet leader Gorbachev to pursue a more peaceful and compromise policy to end the bloc in the region and the international arena.[7] In 1987, Gorbachev declared that the region could become a peace zone with his call for a peaceful solution to the region's problems within the framework of multilateral cooperation.[8] With the end of the cold war, the two states' efficiency level in the Arctic region remained minimal and scientific studies were focused. In the 21st century, the glaciers melting with the effect of global warming and the substantial energy resources that emerged from the research have increased the interest in the region again.

There are several reasons for this increased interest recently. First, Arctic has geostrategic importance that allows us to keep the entire northern hemisphere of the Earth under control. Second, the area is rich in hydrocarbon and biological resources. Namely; Approximately 6% of the world's oil reserves (90 billion barrels) and 24.3% (47 trillion cubic meters) of natural gas resources are located

[6] Surenkov Victor. "Arctic Energy Resources and Global Energy Security", **Journal of Military and Strategic Studies,** Vol. 1, No.22, 2012, p. 12.
[7] Prokhorov Alexander, Great Soviet Encyclopedia Bol'shaya Sovetskaya Entsiklopediya Complete SET (1969-1978), Moskova, Sovetskaya Entsiklopediya, 1970.
[8] Golodnov Antov V., **Mihail Gorbaçov izbranniye Rechi i Statyi,** Moskva: Politizdat, 1988.

in the Arctic Ocean (the US. Geological Survey, 2008 Many scientific studies show that the Arctic region's glaciers will melt significantly and possibly disappear as early as the year 2050. Estimates show that a 12% to 40% reduction in glaciers occurs during the summer periods. In this case, it means that the Arctic Sea passes, which can turn the Arctic Sea into a crucial global trade route, will open for certain periods of the year before 2050. The beginning of global problems is due to the presence of the largest reserves in the Russian Arctic.

Figure 1. Marine ways in the Arctic[9]

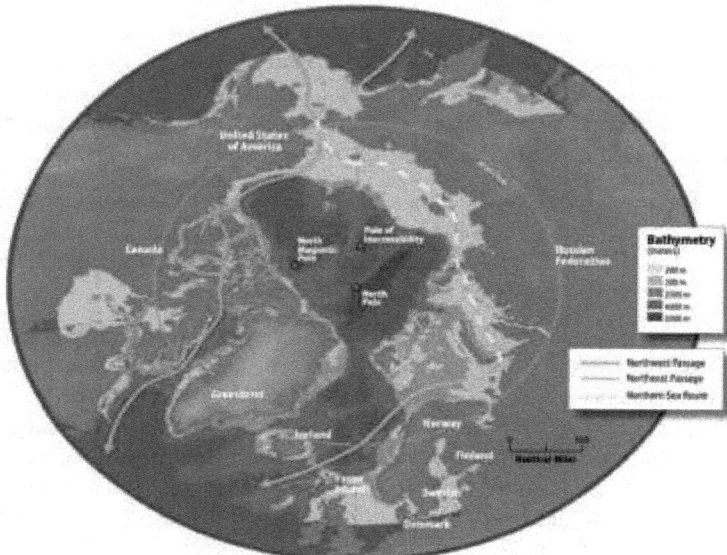

Conflicts of Interest in the Arctic Region

During the Cold War, security concerns were at the centre of the national policies of states. For this reason, the Arctic started to position in the international balance of power in this period. The Arctic does not consist only of the Arctic Ocean. Today, when we look at the Arctic region, we are talking about a multilateral order that includes Europe, Asia and America.

The last of the unshared regions of the world is the Arctic region at the north pole. The Arctic, whose status has not yet been regulated by international law, is today subject to the rules of the 1982 United Nations Convention on the Law of the Sea. The Arctic region, whose status has not been determined by a special contract, is causing tensions due to this uncertainty. The Arctic region is the chessboard of the polar age. There is no single state sovereignty. There are petroleum companies, international organizations, and the Arctic Quintet, coast

---

[9] Marina ways in the arctic, http://www.grida.no/resources/7150, date of access: 04.02.2021.

in the region. The states called the Arctic octet, which are members of the Arctic Council, formed based on international law. The Arctic struggle, covered with glaciers and uncertain legal status, first started in the early 20th century. The regional order provided by the agreements between the Arctic states was tried to be strengthened through bilateral agreements. The region will be the scene of a power struggle both politically and militarily in the future.

The USA's aggressive policies started to spread over time in the Arctic region and other regions. For this reason, the states of the region are now changing their perspective on the USA and looking for a new saviour for themselves. In these saviours, Russia and China stand out as economically steadily progressing. When evaluated in structuralism, this structure of the international system is moving towards a bipolar structure. In this bipolar structure, regional states try to bring other states to become a great power. Accordingly, the USA and Russia's military presence of two superpowers is increasing in the region. Besides, in recent years, both states accuse each other of increasing their military presence in the region. Although the USA took Alaska in 1867 and gained a say in the region, it is not as a deterrent power as Russia.

Although the Arctic region is not the most important Chinese foreign policy issue, its interest in the region has increased in recent years. It has developed diplomatic and economic activities in the region. As a non-regional actor, China is a country that has a significant position in the balance of power. It continues its research activities alongside Russia in order to strengthen its presence and effects in the region. Thus, China has used its role in the balance in favour of Russia. China, like other non-regional actors, plays an active role in science diplomacy in the region. China's Arctic diplomacy strengthens Russia's position vis-a-vis America. China stands by Russia and supports the balance of power. However, it also pays special attention to the development of the Arctic maritime trade. Therefore, it tries to consolidate a legitimate Arctic position to develop bilateral relations with Arctic states. In this way, China takes steps in line with its interests while supporting Russia. Here, it would be more correct to approach China's policy with the Schweller balance of interest theory.

In response to China and Russia's moves[10], the US made new moves in the Eastern Mediterranean to break Russia's energy dominance over Europe and prevent energy transportation from passing through the North Sea. Egypt, Israel, Greece wanted to take the Greek Cypriot Administration and Italy in the Eastern Mediterranean and sent the US navy to the region. In other words, the USA carried its efforts to increase its effectiveness in the Arctic region to the Mediterranean. The aim here is to bring Europe to a level that can meet its energy needs. It is also to minimize the European Union's dependence on China and Russia within the scope of energy. The USA aims to prevent China's trade route

---

[10] Suna Şahin, "Türkiye'nin 1982:01-2015:02 Dönemi Ticaret Bilançosu ve Gayri Safi (Brüt) Değişim Dış Ticaret Hadleri İlişkisi", **Journal of International Trade, Finance and Logistics**, Vol.1, No.1, 2016, pp. 23-36

by moving the conflict zone to the Eastern Mediterranean and puts forward the "Eastern Mediterranean Road" project in response to China's "Silk Road" project. It should also be noted that there is a need for Turkey to increase its influence in the eastern Mediterranean in Russia. It may cause the Dardanelles and Istanbul Strait to lose their importance due to the new trade routes formed with the melting of glaciers in the Arctic region.

Figure 2. International Sea Borders in the Arctic[11]

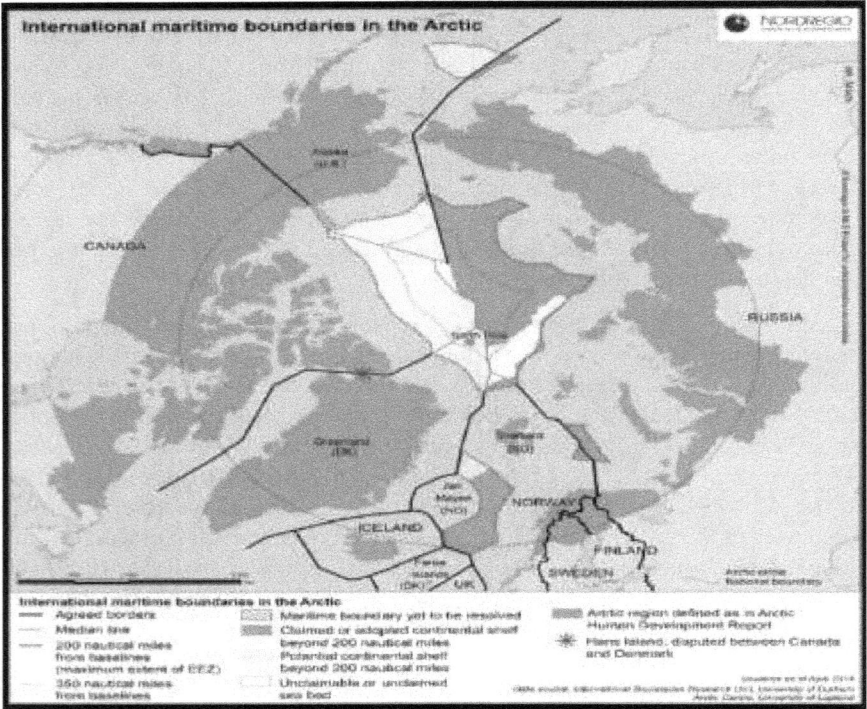

The US is working hard to aggravate its side in the balance of power. One of the reasons for the ongoing geopolitical competition between states in the North Pole is the struggle to access energy resources. The Arctic region has begun to become the source of new international tensions due to this struggle. The conflict area of the USA and Denmark in the region is Greenland. To break Russia's influence in the region, the USA wants to unilaterally take Greenland to increase the land that has a coast to the Arctic. Discourses about taking Greenland from Denmark were met with reactions and objections at the level of state officials. In 2008, a report was prepared for the EU to become an observer member of the Arctic Council. Although there were statements about the conclusion of a treaty

---

[11] Nordregio website, http://www.nordregio.se/en/Maps--Graphs/07-Cooperation-and-eligible-areas/Regional-Cooperation-in-the-North/, date of access: 04.01.2015.

for the Arctic, inspired by the Antarctic Treaty, the regional states opposed and did not accept the agreement.[12] Greenland is a significant issue. This issue will be examined in more detail in the following sections.

As seen in the region, in the 21st century, the energy field has emerged under the glaciers in the region that is called inaccessible. Today, competition for the "Accessible Arctic Region" has become inevitable. This has created the need for a new geostrategic model and geopolitical discourse. The region, which has begun to be known by names such as "New Great Game", "Great Pole Game", "New Cold War" and "Great Arctic Chessboard", will be at the centre of radical changes in the international system in the near future.

Figure 3. Border Claims in the Arctic[13]

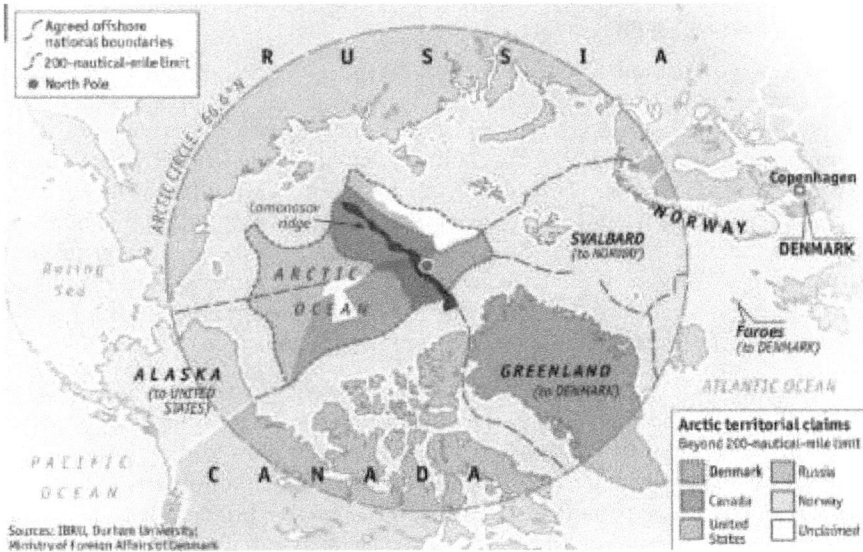

As a result, the balance of power theory is reconstructed in a more specific region than the global meaning. The hegemonic polarizations that we previously saw in many areas such as Africa, the Middle East and Latin America are emerging in a new conflict area. In the balance of power theory, the economic strength of the parties makes it superior. Here, Russia is significant in allies of America as well as the ally China factor. However, the Arctic Council is not trying to make a clear side like China. For example, it is unclear how America will maintain its hegemony in an openly opposed system instead of America in Greenland.

---

[12] The European Parliament, **Resolution of 9 October 2008 on Arctic Governance**. Brussels: The European Parliament, 2009.
[13] Border Claims in the Arctic, https://www.economist.com/international/2014/12/17/frozen-conflict, date of access: 03.13.2021.

On the other hand, it is also essential that Russia's power, which will gain more share from its energy fields by expanding its field after melting glaciers, increases worldwide. It is inherent in the balance of power to stand by the strong countries in the global context. Russia, which started to get stronger after the Cold War and made basic moves in the Mediterranean, especially in the Middle East, seems to be the dominant party in the Arctic region.

Russia's Arctic Strategy

The Arctic region is vital for Russia, unlike other Arctic states. More than half of the Arctic Ocean shores belong to Russia. At the same time, most of the energy resources in this region are located in Russia. The income obtained from Russia's energy resources in the region constitutes 30% of the country's GDP (gross domestic product).

The use of natural resources and trade route under melting glaciers with global warming will emerge as a new conflict area in the region in the following years. From a political point of view, eight countries called the "Arctic Eight" claiming in the Arctic Region. Five countries, including the USA, Russia, Canada, Norway and Denmark (Greenland), have direct borders with the Arctic. Although countries like Sweden, Finland and Iceland do not have direct borders, they are members of the Arctic Council. Although it is an organization structuring to protect the status quo of the region's political, economic and strategic importance, it conducts both military and economic studies on the region, especially within the scope of riparian states' interests.

Russia has a coast to the region and has strategic importance. As a force in the historical perspective, Russia, as a result of its physical location, is a dominant force in matters related to the north pole.[14] Russia is aware of the power it has. According to Heininen; The policies carried out by Russia in the Arctic region are considered as a pragmatic tool used in domestic politics to achieve the stability of the federation and its economy, which was the main goal of the beginning of the century, as well as a response to the new geopolitical situation in the post-Cold War region. Finally, policies towards the region can be seen as a process in which Russia will again become a great power in world politics and a global energy player.[15] The fact that Russia, which owns a large part of the hydrocarbon energy reserves available in the region, is an important player due to these advantages, requires the parties to avoid non-Russian alternatives to solve the problems. Russia's interest in the Northern regions began in 1910 when it sent its navy to the reconnaissance region. In 1926, with a unilateral decision, the Soviet administration drew the new state borders with the Arctic Region. The Soviet Union started to claim the 5842 km² section between the north pole and

---

[14] Gunitskiy, Vsevoled, "On Thin Ice: Water Rights and Resource Disputes In The Arctic Ocean," **Journal of International Affairs,** Vol. 61, No.2, 2008, pp. 261-271.

[15] Lassi Heininen, **Arctic Strategies and Policies: Inventory and Comparative Study,** Published by: The Northern Research Forum & The University of Lapland, 2018, pp. 1-97.

the Bering Strait and the Kola peninsula. In these years, the region does not turn out to be an energy oasis. Considering the Cold War period, it can be described as reflecting the USA-USSR competition in the region. Thus, we can say that Russia's (Soviet) exploration efforts are efforts to dominate new places. For Russia, the Arctic region, where 65% of the ocean coast, is vital. Approximately 80% of the resources in the region are in the region belonging to Russia.

Figure 4. The Border Determined by the USSR in the Arctic[16]

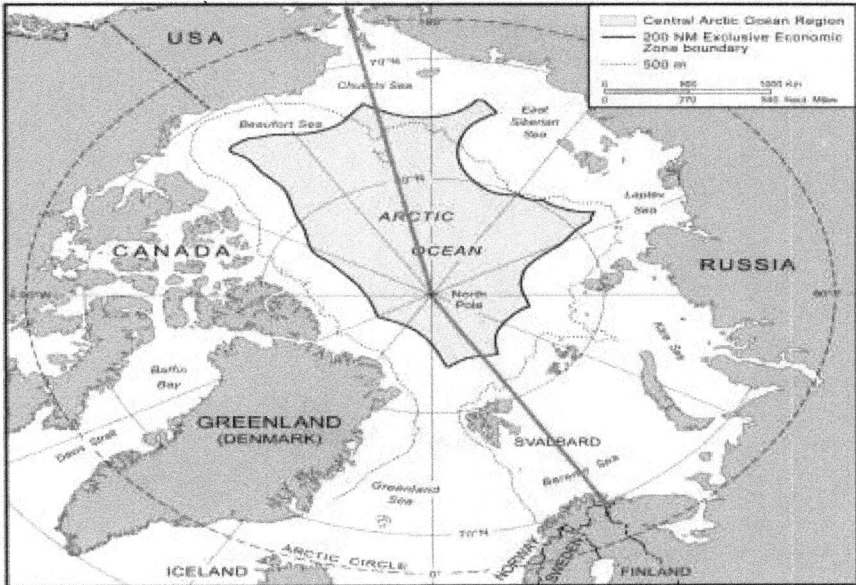

Russia became the first country to apply to the United Nations in 2001 to expand its continental shelf. In his application, he requested the exclusive economic zone to be expanded beyond 200 miles. The international arena condemned this claim, which targets almost half of the Arctic Ocean. Russia's demand includes the Lomonosov and Alpha-Mendelev Mountain ranges of 1,200,000 square kilometres, which extend along the Arctic and contain major oil and gas stocks.[17] If Russia realizes its exclusive economic zone, it will have approximately 48% of the region. While the international community continued to react to Russia's initiatives, in 2007 Russia researched the region to prove that the Lomonosov Ridge is a natural extension of the Siberian lands.[18] During the survey, a titanium-coated Russian flag was erected at a depth of 4200 meters in

[16] Elana Wilson Rowe, **Arctic Governance Power in Cross-Border Cooperation**, Published by Manchester University Press, 2018.
[17] Jarashow M., Runnels, M. B., & Svenson, T., "UNCLOS and the Arctic: The Path of Least Resistance", **Fordham International Law Journal**, Vol. 30, No. 5, 2006, pp. 1585-1652.
[18] Østerud Øyvind, & Hønneland, Geir, "Geopolitics and International Governance in the Arctic." **Arctic Review on Law and Politics**, Vol. 5, No.2, 2014, pp. 156-176.

the region in July 2007.[19]

Outside of the political framework, Russia can maintain a military presence in the Arctic. Russia's military presence in the region poses a threat to the region and EU member states. Russia perceives the country's northern borders as the most vulnerable in terms of security. Therefore, it strives to keep its military units in the region ready for anything at any time. It assumes that it should keep its military presence ready against the USA, Canada, and Denmark, which are members of the North Atlantic Alliance, especially in competition based on underground resources in the future. Accordingly, its main military purpose in the Arctic region is to establish a base.

Figure 5. Arctic North-western Gateway[20]

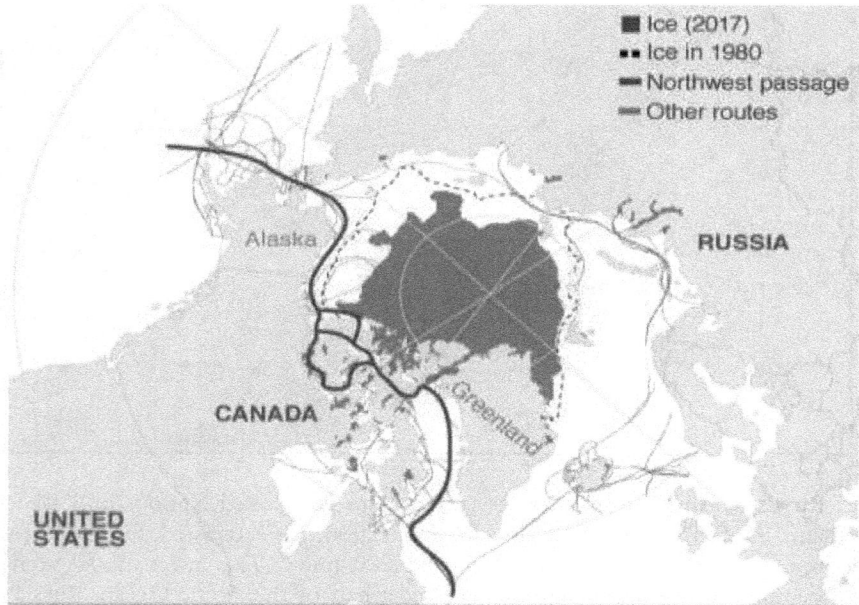

Russia's efforts to dominate the region do not only make efforts to establish a military base. There are also initiatives in the region in the field of energy and to create trade routes. In this direction, there is not just a search for raw materials. Academic Lomonosov, which consists of two reactors, each with a capacity of 35 megawatts, has the capacity to meet the energy needs of a settlement of approximately 100 thousand people. In order to meet the electricity and energy needs of the people living in the region, it actively uses Academic Lomonosov, that is, floating electrical energy in the region. Academic Lomonosov, the first

---

[19] Kefferpütz, Roderick. & Bochkarev, Danila, **Wettlauf um die Arktis: Empfehlungen an die EU**, Brüssel: Heinrich Böll Stifftung, 2009.
[20] Murphy Jessica, (2018), "Is the Arctic set to become a main shipping route?" https://www.bbc.com/news/business-45527531, (date of access: 05.04.2021).

floating nuclear power plant globally, is expected to be the key infrastructure part of the "North Sea Line" project, the shipping route along the North Pole coast of Russia.[21]

In the Russian Arctic region, ten months of the year create a new trade route using giant ice-breaking ships. When using the route, merchant ships must obtain permission from the Russian government's North Sea route administration. Thus, it is seen as Russia has given the dominance of the region. It is considered alarming for US security interests compared to Russia's existing 46 operational 50 icebreakers and 15 new icebreakers planned or under construction, as well as three icebreakers owned by China.[22] In the region, it is necessary to talk about the US initiatives in this region, as in every conflict area, against Russia's attempts to penetrate.

America's Arctic Strategy

The Arctic region is the scene of the states' struggle for new interests. Disputes and conflicts of interest between Russia and the USA continue during the Cold War period and in many regions today. The USA was riparian in the region, that is, the entrance to the Arctic region was provided by taking Alaska in 1987. However, the USA came to the region later than Russia. The Bush administration published the document that forms the basis of the Arctic region of the USA in 2009 under the name of National Security Presidential Directive 66.

According to Turner, natural resources in the Arctic region are also crucial to the US, but natural resources' economic return is not dominant in US politics, unlike Russia. Although Alaska offers some opportunities in terms of natural resources, NSPD-66 acknowledges that "the best-known Arctic oil and gas resources are outside the jurisdiction of the USA"[23]

New Arctic strategy document published by the Ministry of Defence in 2019; It aims to quickly identify threats in the arctic region, respond to these threats quickly and effectively, and shape the security environment to reduce the likelihood of these threats in the future. The document states that, apart from the eight states with sovereign territories in the Arctic region, any other claims regarding the Arctic status will not be recognized[24]

The USA has assumed the role of the World Gendarmerie in many parts of

---

[21] Grätz, James, "The Arctic: Thaw with Conflict Potential." **CSS Analysis in Security Policy**, ETH Zurich, Vol.118, No. 118, 2012, pp.1-4.

[22] Tann Noa. (2018). *New Icebreakers Needed in a Melting Arctic.* 06 03, 2020 tarihinde American Security Project: https://www.americansecurityproject.org/icebreakers-needed-melting-arctic/, (date of access: 02.12.2020).

[23] Turner Jason. A., When the Ice Melts Developing Proactive American Strategy for the Eurasian Arctic. Alabama: Air University Press, 2015, pp. 20-21.

[24] Ministry of Defence, **Department of Defence Arctic Strategy**. Office of the Under Secretary of Defense for Policy, 2019.

the world to achieve its goals of becoming a Hegemonic power.[25] The USA is making many diplomatic and strategic moves to dominate the Arctic Region in the future. The USA reacted strongly to the symbolic flag that Russia has planted in the Lomonosov region. Russia is trying to prevent the USA's struggle to become a hegemon in the region.

Half of the Arctic region resources are under Russia's sovereignty. 1/5 of the Arctic region is under the sovereignty of the USA. These resources make Russia a world giant in Petroleum and Natural Gas imports.[26] Russia has more surface area in the Arctic compared to the USA. This situation is of vital importance for the USA to have a say in the region. Interest in Greenland is increasing concerning this issue. With the news that US President Trump wanted to buy the island covered with glaciers, Greenland suddenly became the international agenda's top. The issue was not taken seriously at first and was considered one of Trump's unusual demands. However, the region is significant.

Thanks to Greenland, Denmark's claims that the Arctic Region are formed.[27] In May 2008, the Danish Parliament adopted Denmark's 2011-2020 Arctic Strategy document. Greenland's total ice volume is 680,000 cubic miles and is about 0.004 per cent of its glaciers each year. (Michael, 2007)

In 2007, Denmark sent a scout to the north pole to gather evidence that the Lomonosov mountains are an extension of Greenland. As a result of new research conducted by Canada in 2008, it was determined that Denmark and Canada have connections with the Arctic ground. The updated information can claim an additional 200,000 km² in the Danish Arctic region[28]

Denmark has a military presence in the region. The 2010-2014 Defence Plan was prepared and announced its military presence in the region to the international public. The biggest reason for Denmark's military presence and exercise attempts in the region is due to the USA's claims on the region. The USA has been maintaining a military presence in the region since World War II. With the increasing strategic importance of Greenland in recent years, US Prime Minister Donald Trump's statements about taking the island make the region's importance for the USA prominent. The region will be the focal point of the EU due to the geological structure and natural resources of the region.

It plays a vital role in the USA's energy field as an inevitable consequence of the oil companies' influence in the USA's politics. It aims to establish dominance in the region by creating cooperation agreements with the region's countries on

---

[25] Kissinger Henry, **American Foreign Policy: Three Essays,** New York, Norton, 1969.

[26] Melnikov, D., Politika Rossii Arktike: Aktualniye pravoviye, ekonomiçeskiyei voyenniye problemi. İTSRON, (2017). http://izron. ru/articles/sovremennye-problemy-obshchestvennykh-nauk-v-mire-sbornik-nauchnykh-trudov-po-itogam-mezhdunarodnoy-/sektsiya-11-politicheskie-problemy-mezhdunarodnykh otnosheniy-globalnogo-i-regionalnogo-razvitiya-sp/politika-rossii-v-arktike-aktualnye -pravovye ekonomicheskie-i-voennye-problemy/ (date of accsess: 04.05.2021).

[27] Kingdom of Denmark, Denmark, Greenland and the Faroe Islands: Kingdom of Denmark Strategy for the Arctic 2011–2020."

[28] Ibid, Kefferpütz & Bochkarev.

the axis of energy companies. For example, in 2011, a strategic cooperation agreement was established between the Russian company Rosneft and the USA Exxon Mobil company for joint work and technology sharing. A year later, although Siberia and the Arctic agreed on joint exploration work, the agreement could not be implemented due to the Ukraine Crisis.[29] The USA will confront us in progress with its expansion policy in both energy and military fields.

Conclusion

Before constructing nation-states, there were indigenous communities in the Arctic, and the peoples' life in this borderless region was generally based on a nomadic lifestyle. From the construction of nation-states to the Second World War, the Arctic borders did not change much. The years when the balance of power started to be established started with the Cold War years when Sweden had a neutral status in the Arctic Region. On the one hand, the Soviets and Finland were compatible with it, on the other hand, NATO formed by Norway, Iceland, Canada, Denmark and the USA. The cooperation that continued with a low profile during the Cold War turned into Arctic regionalism after the Cold War. With the regional activities and the announcement of energy reports one after another, the countries' interest shifted to the region. World politics has now gone far beyond an area where only great powers exist, which could be defined as a power struggle. The Arctic region should also be examined from this perspective.

While we are in a system where global conflicts are not between states, one should not think that countries will clash in the Arctic region. However, the preparations made by the countries as a military force cannot be ignored. Therefore, it is useful to approach this region with caution. While there are many countries that we call the Arctic octet in the region, the events pass between Russia and America may sign that the balance of power will be established between these two. However, whether the European Union will intervene in the region by solving its problems may progress to disrupt all the cycles. As we mentioned above, while America is trying to establish its game establishment in the Arctic over the Mediterranean, Europe can be left alone with Russia with this strategic move. As a result, although the system's regional sides to be established in the balance of power are determined, the rights that will emerge with the melting of the ice will continue to remain confidential as the unknown of the equation in the region. Perhaps the biggest quarterback in the balance of power will be new land fields that will emerge from under melting glaciers.

---

[29] Keskitalo Carina, "International Region-Building: Development of the Arctic as an International Region. **Cooperation and Conflict**, 2007, Vol. 42, No. 187.

BALTIC STATES AND ARCTIC NEGOTIATIONS

Öncel Sençerman[*]

Introduction

Arctic region has become a significant region for the last three decades and thanks to the natural richness of the region and the emergence of a new transportation northern route owing to global warming, even the non-Arctic states have started to have scientific, environmental, economic, logistic and social interests on the region. The interest of the Baltic states has also recently increased despite their traditionally weak links with the Arctic. This study aims to understand how these small Baltic states negotiate their interests regarding Arctic issues. For this reason, this chapter consists of two main parts. The first one deals with the Arctic issue itself and the second part is about the Baltic states' approach towards the Arctic in recent years and their efforts to take part in the Arctic negotiations defending their interests over intergovernmental organizations like the Council of the Baltic Sea States (CBSS), the Arctic Council, the European Union (EU) and the North Atlantic Treaty Organization (NATO).

Arctic as a Region for Cooperation

Arctic is a region that is hard to put into fixed geographical limitations. There are several definitions regarding the Arctic. Moreover, other terms like 'north, far north, high north, circumpolar north, wider-north' are also widely used in the literature.[1] There are several definitions of the Arctic, yet the Arctic Region is commonly described geographically referring to the Arctic Ocean and the lands bordering the Ocean not so different from defining the Mediterranean and the Baltic regions. Apart from this geographical definition, Hough also offers scientific and 'Canadian' definitions for the Arctic. The North Polar circle is mostly accepted as the pinpoint defining the Arctic. These two definitions define two different groups of states as Arctic states. The geographical one defines the littoral states as Arctic, Russia, Canada, Norway, the United States of America (USA), and Denmark (by its land, Greenland) while the scientific one adds three more states on them: Iceland, Finland and Sweden. Not taking the polar circle as the boundary of the Arctic region, Canada considers the 60° northern latitude as the parallel bordering the Arctic region, however this kind of definition for the Arctic region could take the UK inside the region even though this demarcation

---

[*] Öncel Sençerman, PhD, Instructor, Aydın Adnan Menderes University, Aydın, Director of the International Office, Turkey. E-mail: osencerman@adu.edu.tr.
[1] For further details on these definitions please see Klaus Dodds and Mark Nuttall, The Arctic, What Everyone Needs to Know, Oxford University Press, the USA, 2019.

39

is useful for Canada to divide the country into two zones – one has the cities and the other one has the faintly populated areas.[2]

Heininen et. al. mention that the Artic is most commonly defined as "being remote, scattered and having a sparse population" in the strategy documents of several countries and also state that the 60° northern latitude is considered as the border of the Arctic emphasizing that there is not a fixed description of the Arctic.[3] Dodds and Nuttall mention in their book, the Arctic, Everyone Needs to Know, that the Natural Resources Canada (NRC) even goes further showing the Arctic on its map above the 50° northern latitude, which includes much of the Baltic states, Estonia, Latvia and a big portion of Lithuania.[4]

The first inhabitants – Paleo Siberian, Eskimo, the Sami and the Yakut – are believed to come to the Arctic around 5000BC in today's Russian territory and between 4000BC and 2000BC. The Arctic exploration by the Western society started with the expeditions of an English explorer Frobisher, who was looking for the Northwest Passage in the late 16th century. The explorations started with Frobisher, but had a pause about two centuries, resumed in mid-19th century resulting in different claims of territory at different times until the recent history.[5]

The Spitsbergen archipelago in the Arctic region became the scene for whale and seal hunting around the 17th century and at the beginning of the 19th century international cooperation for scientific research replaced the hunting rivalry in the Arctic waters. Nevertheless, the cooperative atmosphere did not take so long since the competition among Norway, Sweden, Russia, Germany and the USA for coal mining began in the 20th century, which resulted in Svalbard (Spitsbergen) Treaty in 1920 confirming the Norwegian sovereignty with some limitations of international regulation, which awarded Norway for its assistance during the World War I and benefited from the situation where the USA did not have any interests in the archipelago while Germany lost the war and the legitimacy of the new Bolshevik regime in Russia was doubtful for the international community.[6]

The Arctic region regained importance during the Second World War and became the scene again for military and scientific competition between the Nazi Germany and the United Kingdom (UK), Norway and Soviet Russia in terms of its geostrategic importance and its usage as radio and weather forecast stations.[7]

Even though, most of the explorers defined the Arctic as *terra-nullius,* land

---

[2] ibid., p. 1-4.

[3] Lassi Heininen, Karen Everett, Barbora Padrtova, Anni Reissell, Arctic Policies and Strategies – Analysis, Synthesis, and Trends, International Institute for Applied Systems Analysis, Laxenburg, Austria, p. 17.

[4] Klaus Dodds and Mark Nuttall, The Arctic, What Everyone Needs to Know, Oxford University Press, the USA, 2019, p. 27-28.

[5] Hough, op. cit., p. 7-9.

[6] ibid, p. 9-10; Adam Grydehoj, "Svalbard: International Relations in an Exceptionally International Territory", The Palgrave Handbook of Arctic Policy and Politics, Ken S. Coates and Carin Holroyd (Ed.), Palgrave Macmillan, 2020.

[7] Hough, op. cit., p. 10-11.

belonging to no one, for some time, the rivalry between the superpowers of the Cold War militarized the region and it became one of the important places useful for the superpowers to show their antagonism through military activities, yet excluding the policies regarding the indigenous people of the Arctic.[8] During the Cold War, the Arctic turned out to be the back garden for the bipolar world for intercontinental ballistic missile trials as it was the closest place both for the USA and the Soviet Russia, therefore the Polar Bear Treaty signed in 1973 was a kind of cooperative agreement setting the benchmarks between the superpowers in the Arctic helping them out to co-exist during the détente years.[9]

Despite being a zone in the far north, as Peter Hough asserts the Arctic region was not the focal point between the two poles during the Cold War, so it could be used as a testing field for further political cooperation between the East and the West.[10] The Arctic almost became the place for Gorbachev to end the Cold War with his famous speeches in Reykjavik and Murmansk respectively in 1986 and 1987.[11] Gorbachev's speeches in the Arctic zone were seemingly ending the Cold War and offering an olive branch to the West and also opening the door for a new era for Arctic negotiations for cooperation on basically environmental security at the beginning. The establishment of Arctic Council started official negotiations over the Arctic among the Arctic states for cooperation and collaboration where the parties take their interests regarding different matters related to Arctic issues on the negotiation desk in a multilateral setting.

The end of Cold War also changed Russia's relations with the Western states pushing it into more cooperation through her integration into the international economic system with her membership to the International Money Fund (IMF), World Bank, World Trade Organization and its close trading partnerships with the European Union (EU) and the North Atlantic Treaty Organization (NATO) members.[12] Following the Murmansk initiative by the Soviet Russia and its gradual integration into the global economic system, Finland came out with the idea of an environmental agreement in late 1980s to be signed in 1991 by the eight Arctic countries, which formed the Arctic Environmental Protection Strategy (AEPS). The action plan of the AEPS was mostly covering scientific cooperation and estimations for environmental effects of industrial enterprises in the Arctic focusing on the work of four different work-groups such as "the Arctic Monitoring and Assessment Program (AMAP), Protection of Arctic Marine Environment (PAME), Emergency Prevention, Preparedness and Response (EPPR) and Conservation of Arctic Flora and Fauna (CAFF)".[13]

---

[8] Teemu Palosaari and Frank Möller, "Security and Marginality, Arctic Europe after the Double Enlargement", Cooperation and Conflict: Journal of the Nordic International Studies Association, Vol. 39, No. 3, 2004, p. 256.
[9] Hough, op. cit., p. 13.
[10] ibid., p. 98.
[11] ibid., p. 13.
[12] Michael Byers, "Crises and International Cooperation: An Arctic Case Study", International Relations, Vol. 31, No. 4, 2017, p. 378.
[13] Hough, op. cit., p. 100.

The meeting of the Parliamentarians of the Arctic Region in Reykjavik in 1993 together with the support of the Arctic Indigenous Peoples' Organization paved the way for the establishment of the Arctic Council by the eight Arctic states (Canada, Denmark, Finland, Iceland, Norway, Sweden, Russia and the USA) in 1996 as a high-level forum for multinational cooperation especially for environmental security.[14] Among these members Russia is the has the biggest portion of the Arctic territory, 50% of the Arctic coastline and 60% of the Arctic land and Russia enjoys this advantage in achieving diplomatic and economic gains owing to its bigger existence in the Arctic compared to other Arctic states and especially the smaller Nordic ones, which were eagerly using the Council for negotiating their interests over the Arctic region as littoral or non-littoral states[15] The Ottawa Declaration is the founding document of the Arctic Council that would absorb the AEPS later on by adding on another work-group dealing with Arctic pollutants.[16]

Upon foundation of the Arctic Council, France, Germany, Netherlands, Poland, Spain and the UK were given permanent observing status in the Council at the very beginning and this status gave these countries to attend the ministerial meetings, make agenda proposals but to vote. The ministerial meeting in Nuuk in 2011 is also an important milestone in the development of the Arctic Council from a high-level forum to an intergovernmental organization that requires establishing stable secretariat and ratification of the Council's agreement called as 'Agreement on Cooperation on Aeronautical and Maritime Search and Rescue in the Arctic', which is legally binding for the members. China, Italy, India, Singapore, Japan, South Korea and Switzerland were then given the same status.[17]

Chater doubts that inclusion of new observing members to the Council could take the focus of the Council from environmental matters to the economic ones and claims that states would like to get the observer status to have economic and environmental gains and the Arctic Council is hence transforming into a more inclusive intergovernmental organization rather than being a closed one mostly dominated by the Western Arctic states with the participation of non-Arctic states, which the Arctic states do not want to have despite their economic and environmental influence in the Council.[18]

Apart from its permanent member states and observing member states the Arctic Council has also different institutions including intergovernmental and non-governmental organizations that have observing status: Nordic Council,

[14] Heininen, op. cit., p. 18; Andrew Chater, "Explaining Non-Arctic States in the Arctic Council", Strategic Analysis, Vol. 40, No.3, 2016, p. 173.
[15] Christian Lemiere and Jeffrey Mazo, Arctic Opening, Insecurity and Opportunity, Routledge, 2014, p. 122.
[16] Hough, op. cit., p. 102; For further details on the foundation of the Arctic Council, its organizational structure, history and functioning, please see Svein Vigeland Rottem, The Arctic Council Between Environmental Protection and Geopolitics, Palgrave Macmillan, 2020.
[17] ibid. p. 102.
[18] Chater, op. cit., p. 173-181.

Nordic Environmental Finance Cooperation, International Union for the Conservation of Nature, International Maritime Organization (IMO), West Nordic Council, World Meteorological Organization, UN Economic Commission for Europe, UN Environment Program, UN Development Program (UNDP), International Federation of Red Cross and Red Crescent Societies, North Atlantic Marine Mammal Commission, International Arctic Science Committee, International Arctic Social Sciences Association, Northern Forum, Advisory Committee on the Protection of the Seas, Arctic Circumpolar Gateway, Circumpolar Conservation Union, International Union for Circumpolar Health, International Working Group for Indigenous Affairs, University of the Arctic, World Wide Fund (WWF).[19] The Arctic Council also has permanent participants representing the four million inhabitants and indigenous people of the Arctic region. These participants are Aleut International Association, Arctic Athabaskan Council, Gwich'in Council International, Inuit Circumpolar Council, Russian Association of Indigenous Peoples of the North and Saami Council.[20]

Ilulissat Declaration was adopted in Ilulissat, Greenland in 2008 by five littoral states of Russian Federation, the United States of America (USA), Canada, Denmark and Norway and put emphasize on the climate change problem in the Arctic Ocean and the usage of its natural resources by underlining the continuation of close cooperation in the Arctic Ocean for scientific research and the conservation of the oceanic environment in the face of increasing maritime activities including tourism, transportation and research in the Ocean.[21] The Ilulissat Declaration is also important since it puts an emphasis on the importance of peaceful negotiation and implementation of international law.[22] The countries signing the Ilulissat Declaration are also called as A5 Club consisting of the five littoral states came out of the Ilulissat Declaration in 2008 underlining the international law and the UNCLOS. Another important summit of the A5 is the meeting in Chelsea, Canada in 2010 created criticism among other three Arctic states, Sweden, Finland and Iceland.[23]

Apart from the Arctic Council, there are also other regional and Arctic related intergovernmental organizations and institutions for cooperation. Barents Euro-Arctic Council is also an intergovernmental organization that cooperates on the issues concerning the Barents region and its members meet at Foreign Minister level under the leadership of the chairing member and the chairmanship rotates every two years among its members, Denmark, Finland, Iceland, Norway, Russia, Sweden and the European Commission.[24] Denmark, Finland, Iceland, Norway, the Russian Federation, Sweden and the Commission of European Communities

---

[19] www.arctic-council.org (Access 13.05.2021).
[20] ibid.
[21] www.arcticportal.org (Access 28.05.2021).
[22] Mikkel Runge Olesen, "Cooperation or Conflict in the Arctic, A Literature Review", DIIS Working Paper, No. 08, 2014.
[23] Hough, op. cit., p. 108.
[24] www.barentscooperation.org (Access 26.05.2021).

together with observing states the United States of America, Canada, France, Germany, Japan, Poland and the United Kingdom came together at a conference in Kirkenes, Norway in January 1993 adopting a declaration – Kirkenes Declaration – on primary cooperation in the Barents Euro-Arctic Region for observing environment and radioactivity in the region, providing security of nuclear plants and rehabilitating the nuclear polluted area. The participating states also showed their interest in economic, scientific, technological cooperation as well as paying attention to the development of infrastructure of the region, the concerns over the indigenous people and possible tourism activities of the region.[25]

The Nordic Council of Ministers, also called as the Nordic Council, was formed in 1971 as the intergovernmental institution for cooperation in the Nordic region and has member states as Denmark, Finland, Iceland, Norway and Sweden aiming a sustainable and integrated region.[26] The Council of the Baltic Sea States is an intergovernmental organization with eleven members states including the small Baltic states, Lithuania, Latvia, Estonia and the European Union. The Council was founded in 1992 to become a forum for cooperation the Baltic Sea Region in the fields of long-term priorities, regional identity, sustainable and prosperous region, safe and secure region.[27]

Northern Dimension (ND) was formed in 1999 with the participation of the European Union, Russian Federation, Norway and Iceland. Later on, this joint policy was restored in 2006 to include Belarus that started to take part in operative cooperation and the USA and Canada as observing states. The ND works for stability, prosperity and continuous progress within the region thanks to operative cooperation in the fields of "environment, nuclear safety, health, energy, transport, logistics, promotion of trade and investment, research, education, and culture" while partnering with other regional bodies as the Council of the Baltic Sea States (CBSS), the Barents Euro-Arctic Council (BAEC), the Arctic Council and the Nordic Council of Ministers.[28]

Regarding the multilateral negotiations held at these organizations mentioned above, Trenin states that "regional institutions, such as the Council of the Baltic Sea States (CBSS); the Barents Euro-Arctic Council (BEAC); and the Arctic Council, need to be turned into platforms for planning and execution of specific projects aimed at promoting and strengthening the culture of multilateral cooperation in the Baltic Sea area and the High North".[29]

The USA initiated a partnership program in 2003 for enhancing partnership with the Nordic and Baltic states – Iceland, Norway, Sweden, Finland, Estonia, Latvia, Lithuania and Denmark – replacing a former program called the

[25] https://www.barentsinfo.fi/beac/docs/459_doc_kirkenesdeclaration.pdf (Access 25.05.2021).
[26] www.norden.org (Access 26.05.2021).
[27] www.cbss.org (Access 26.05.2021).
[28] www.northerndimension.info (Access 26.05.2021).
[29] Dimitri Trenin, "Russian Policies Toward the Nordic-Baltic Region", Atlantic Council, 2011.

Northern Europe Initiative started in 1997 especially aiming the integration of three Baltic states into the European zone of democracy in order to deepen the links for cooperation, helping the region to develop civil society, to build up democratic institutions, to fight against crime and corruption, to establish the rule of law, to offer environmental solutions and economic growth. E-PINE aimed to work for "cooperative security, healthy societies and vibrant economies" cooperating with other multinational organizations like the Arctic Council, the CBSS and the BAEC.[30] The USA, "is a major player in issues dealing with the Arctic, which have relevance to the Nordic-Baltic countries, and can ensure that all differences in the High North are decided peacefully, through negotiation or legal judgment".[31]

Even though the Arctic has started to be seen as a zone of peace with the speech acts of Gorbachev in Murmansk in 1987, the cooperative atmosphere starting in the late 1980s and flourishing especially in 1990s with the foundation of several intergovernmental organizations for cooperation in the Arctic in different fields and the emphasize of the Ilulissat Declaration in 2008 on the rule of law and on enhancing cooperation in the region, this cooperative atmosphere started to get damages especially after the Ukraine crisis in 2014.[32] According to Klimenko, the Ukraine crisis put the Arctic issue around the security issues between the West and Russia and made it an inseparable part of the problem as it was the beginning of the spill-over effect of the crisis over the Arctic.[33]

Even though Russia paid great importance to the Arctic issues under the presidency of Putin and have benefited from the Arctic for her economic boost, after the Ukraine Crisis and sanctions following it, Russia became more aggressive in her policies in the Arctic, for this reason Russia re-activated former Cold War military facilities and resumed military exercise – Vostok in 2018 - and started to seek ways to enhance and increase the ports in the North on the Northern Passage.[34] The crisis undermined the military and economic cooperation and "raised tensions between Russia and other Arctic states to their highest level since the Cold War".[35]

Breitenbauch et. al. think that this crisis was the turning point in the multinational cooperation in the Arctic bringing along the rivalry again in military, security, politics and business as in Cold War era.[36] Unfortunately, for

---

[30] www.2001-2009.state.gov (Access 25.05.2021).

[31] Trenin, op. cit., p. 51.

[32] Heather Exner-Pirot, "Between Militarization and Disarmament: Challenges for Arctic Security in the Twenty-First Century", Climate Change and Arctic Security, Searching for a Paradigm Shift, Lassi Heininen and Heather Exner-Pirot (Ed.) Palgrave Macmillan, 2020, p. 104.

[33] Ekaterina Klimenko, "Russia's Arctic Security Policy, Still Quiet in the High North?", SIPRI Policy Paper, No. 45, February 2016.

[34] Marc Lanteigne, "The Changing Shape of Arctic Security", NATO Review, 2019.

[35] Byers, op. cit., p. 384.

[36] Henrik Breitenbauch, Kristian Soby Kristensen and Jonas Groasmeyer, "Military and Environmental Challenges in the Arctic", New Perspectives On Shared Security: NATO's Next 70 Years, Carnegie Europe, 2019.

the last decade the Arctic has turned into a zone of competition and conflict instead of a zone of peace and cooperation. The Arctic has become an important region for the rivalry among the great powers of the 21st century, China, Russia and the USA owing to the region's rich natural resources and the significance of the northern passage for logistics and transportation.[37] Nevertheless, the Arctic Council is still there for peaceful cooperation among its members through multilateral negotiations.

Baltic States and the Arctic

Baltic states have no traditional links with the Arctic making their hands weak, however, these states have recently started to show interest in the Arctic matters owing to the international tendency over the region for the last two decades.[38] The close relations between the Baltic and Nordic states have influence over the security concerns of Lithuania, Latvia and Estonia regarding Norway's security situation in the Arctic region.[39] The three small Baltic states do not negotiate over Arctic issues in the Arctic Council, so they choose to use the EU and NATO as channels for these matters to negotiate their interests.[40] However, as Berzina mentions the Baltic states are among sub-Arctic European countries and emphasizes that the Baltic states are closer to the center of the Arctic Council in Tromso, Norway than Brussels, so a closer relation is needed between the Arctic and sub-Arctic states.[41] This relationship can be built on negotiating observer state status at the Arctic Council since it is the main organization where Arctic negotiations are held. Below is given a brief discussion on the Baltic states' interests over the Arctic and the actions taken by them to negotiate their interest through different mechanisms, mainly seeking the way for an observer state status in the Arctic Council.

Estonia is more dedicated to take part in the Artic negotiations and for this reason officially states that as the northernmost non-Arctic state Estonia would like to get the observing state status because of her increased interest in the Arctic owing to the latest developments in the region and its polar scientific research experience. The official website of the Foreign Ministry of Estonia sums up four reasons for applying to the Arctic Council: Climate change has its immediate effects on Estonia, Estonia's geographical and cultural closeness to the region, scientific experience and powerful and efficient business solutions for the Arctic supported with environment-care technology. Estonia also claims these reasons

---

[37] Rebecca Pincus, "Three-Way Power Dynamics in the Arctic", Strategic Studies Quarterly, Vol. 14, No.1, 2020.

[38] Lassi Heininen, "The Arctic, Baltic, and North Atlantic Cooperative Regions in Wider Northern Europe: Similarities and Differences", Journal of Baltic Studies, Vol. 48, No. 4, 2017.

[39] Kristian Atland, "Security Perspectives from Norway", Routledge Handbook of Arctic Security, Gunhild Hoogensen Gjorv, Marc Lanteigne and Horatio Sam-Aggrey (Ed.), Routledge, New York, 2020, pp. 165-176.

[40] Kristine Berzine, "Why the Arctic Matters for the Rest of Europe", Perceptions and Strategies of Arcticness in Sub-Arctic Europe, Andris Spruds and Tom Rostoks (Ed.), Latvian Institute of International Affairs, Riga, 2014.

[41] ibid., p.21.

making her a suitable candidate for the observer status: Estonia signed the Svalbard Treaty in 1930 and has been conducting polar research since 1940, Estonia has the advantage of using her expertise in polar research for the Arctic Council and can contribute into genetic studies regarding the inhabitants of the Arctic and enjoys linguistic links with the Northern people and can benefit from its location for swift business related solutions for the Arctic region. Estonia made official application to become an observer state in the Arctic Council after announcing her eagerness publicly in November 2020. However, the Arctic Council gave no decisions regarding the observer status of Estonia in Reykjavik, Iceland on 20 May 2021, which means that Estonia will continue its efforts in the future to become an observer and to be approved during the ministerial meeting of the Council in 2023.[42]

Latvia does not have a formal statement of Arctic interests; however, Latvia has increased her activities in the EU and NATO to contribute into the peace and stability in the Arctic. Besides, Latvia does not have an economic plan for business related investments in the Arctic region, yet there have been discussions within the country regarding an application for an observer status like Estonia but no further action has been taken for this objective.[43] Latvia has only recently started to pay attention to the significance of the Arctic issues and Latvian government made its first official statement regarding the Arctic in late 2019 when the Minister of Foreign Affairs, Edgars Rinkevics emphasized the importance of Arctic for the regional peace and security as Latvia has borders with Arctic states and strategic partnerships with most of the Arctic states. Rinkevics also underlined the role to be taken by the EU especially in the immediate matters as the effects of climate change.[44] According to Janis Eichmanis, Latvia's interests in the Arctic could be gathered under five main issues of concern: climate change, arctic governance, natural resources, shipping and security issues. Again, no different from the reasons behind Estonia and Lithuania's interests in the region, Latvia has been affected by the recent developments in the region in terms of its emergence as a geostrategic and geo-economic area.[45]

As Dolzenkova and Mokhorov mention Latvia takes more active roles in social, healthcare, digital spheres like national minority languages mass media for Arctic matters as a small state.[46] As to Vargulis, "Germany and Poland perceive an increasing availability of Arctic resources as a window of opportunity of diversification, of their energy supplies" and "opposite to Poland and Germany, Latvia has not actively promoted a need for deeper involvement in issues related

---

[42] www.vm.ee/en/arctic (Access 31.05.2021).
[43] Emmet Tuohy, Cooperation and Conflict in the Arctic: A Roadmap for Estonia, International Centre for Defense Studies, 2014.
[44] www.mfa.gov.lv (Access 14.05.2021).
[45] Janis Eichmanis, "Arctic Scenarios: A Latvian Perspective", Latvian Foreign and Security Policy, Andris Spruds and Sintija Broka (Ed.), Latvian Institute of International Affairs, Riga, Latvia, 2020.
[46] E. Dolzhenkova and D. Mokhorov, "Latvia's role in the Arctic. Cooperation Prospects", IOP Conference Series: Earth and Environmental Science, 2020.

to Arctic energy resources".[47] All in all Latvia does not have an official Arctic strategy even though there are some shareholders handling the matters related to the Arctic and trying to increase the public awareness. Besides, as Vargulis states that "several NGOs and scientists have contributed to the discourse of the Arctic in Latvia" and "some of them have prepared a comprehensive assessment on how the processes taking place in the Arctic region affect Latvia".[48]

Lithuania is far away from the region and has no traditional or cultural links with the Arctic except the forcefully deported Lithuanians to the Siberian territory by the Soviet administration. Lithuania pays attention to the region when Russia has military involvements there.[49] The Literature on Lithuania's involvement into Arctic negotiations and Lithuanian interests is also very weak like Lithuania's link to the Arctic. However, Mindaugas Jurkynas has a detailed chapter on dealing with the Lithuanian Arctic policies. His study depends on the official programs of the government and political parties, legal documents, interviews he had with diplomats, officers of ministry of foreign affairs, and high-ranking administrators.[50]

Like other Baltic states, Lithuania also paid great importance in increasing relations and partnerships with the Nordic states, which are also Arctic states especially during the presidency of Dalia Grybauskaite. Since Lithuania have not developed an Arctic policy, it is interested in the EU's increased role within the Arctic Council and again like Latvia and Estonia, Lithuania wants mutual cooperation and stability in the Arctic, for this reason supports EUs soft politics. Lithuania also benefits from regional organizations like the Northern Dimension, the BEAC, the CBSS and E-PINE. However, Lithuania is not a member of the BEAC, but the European Commission is. Hence, Lithuania prefers to have information through the Commission and does not have any interest in taking part in the Council.[51]

Despite not being a Baltic state, Poland as a Baltic Sea Region state, even though has also a Soviet past made scientific investments in the Arctic starting from the 1950s and now trying to maintain its positions and as an observer state in the Arctic Council Poland could negotiate its interests, mainly scientific. Luszczuk et. al. deal with Poland's policy toward the Arctic since her approval of the Svalbard Treaty in 1931 and gaining an observing state status since 1996 and the priorities of this policy such as supporting and promoting Polish scientific

---

[47] Martins Vargulis, "Latvia in the Arctic: A Case Study of Risks and Opportunities for A Small Sub-Arctic Countries", Perceptions and Strategies of Arcticness in Sub-Arctic Europe, Andris Spruds and Tom Rostoks (Ed.), Latvian Institute of International Affairs, Riga, 2014.
[48] Ibid. p. 214.
[49] Mindaugas Jurkynas, "Looking at Northern Lights: A (Non) Existent Arctic in Lithuania", Perceptions and Strategies of Arcticness in Sub-Arctic Europe, Andris Spruds and Tom Rostoks (Ed.), Latvian Institute of International Affairs, Riga, 2014.
[50] For further details on this study please see, Mindaugas Jurkynas, "Looking at Northern Lights: A (Non) Existent Arctic in Lithuania", Perceptions and Strategies of Arcticness in Sub-Arctic Europe, Andris Spruds and Tom Rostoks (Ed.), Latvian Institute of International Affairs, Riga, 2014.
[51] ibid., p. 186.

venture in the Arctic because Polish scientific activities in the region could help her to legitimize its existence in the Arctic Council and boost its image in the international arena.[52] They set four priority goals for Poland's activities in the Arctic and make recommendations on how to achieve them like increasing her activity in the Arctic Council by regular participation into the workshops and promoting cooperation among observers, benefitting from public diplomacy to promote its activities in the Council, getting increased participation into the scientific task forces of the Council, launching 'Go Arctic' initiative together with economic and social shareholders and finally setting up an Arctic agenda among institutional, business, economic, academic and social sectors.[53]

Baltic states are important partners of NATO for its Northeastern flank for its superiority over the Baltic Sea region. Simon states that "if the security of the Baltic States were undermined, Russia's standing in the Arctic would be significantly enhanced" and adds that "in turn, the Alliance's, own geostrategic position in the Baltic Sea could rapidly crumble, like a house of cards, and the Baltic would become again a contested geopolitical space".[54] Emphasizing the importance of the Baltic states for the security of the Arctic, Simon also mentions the interrelation between the Arctic as a sub-theater of NATO's eastern flank and the Baltic Sea.[55] Therefore, as a sub-theater region, the Baltic states can use this interconnectivity between their region and the Arctic to have new interests including security interests as well.

Conclusion

Where is Arctic? Its geographical and scientific description is not so vague and far from states' perceptions. However, its political description changes as to the states' perceptions constructed on their political, economic, historical, environmental, scientific, logistic interests. If China can define itself as a near-Arctic country relying on her ambitions and interest in the Arctic region, why other states in the vicinity and periphery of the Arctic region cannot define their Arcticness depending on their interests over the Arctic and the Arctic states, does not matter littoral or non-littoral?

Baltic states are in the vicinity of the region. As discussed in the literature, the region they are in can be called as sub-theater of the Arctic or basically the sub-Arctic. Therefore, the Baltic states should seek more ways and take necessary measures in the very near future to indulge into the Arctic negotiations at various intergovernmental organizations where Arctic negotiations are held by taking concrete steps to form their own Arctic policies and strategies instead of using

[52] Michal Luszczuk, Piotr Graczyk, Adam Stepien, Malgorzata Smieszek, "Poland's Policy Towards the Arctic: Key Areas and Priority Actions", The Polish Institute of International Affairs, No. 11, 113, May 2015, p.2.
[53] ibid., p. 6.
[54] Luis Simon, "Assessing NATO's Eastern European Flank", The US Army War College Quarterly: Parameters, Vol. 44, No. 3, 2014, p. 72.
[55] ibid., p. 70-71.

actors to negotiate their own interests

UNDERSTANDING THE ANTARCTIC BIODIVERSITY AND TURKISH CONTRIBUTION TO ITS PROTECTION

Bayram Öztürk[1] and Mehmet Gökhan Halıcı[2]

Introduction

Antarctica is called the frozen continent and has been reserved for peace and science since the Antarctic Treaty was signed in 1959 in Washington, D.C. Antarctic research has fundamental societal importance and requirements to have a consultative status cannot be achieved without a substantial scientific and operational presence in Antarctica. The future of this fragile continent depends on international cooperation through the Antarctic Treaty, which Turkey signed in 1995, although it had not performed any scientific study on this continent for more than 20 years.[3] In fact, an expedition appeal and agenda have been established in 1991 in Turkey. Historically, the world map drawn in 1513 by Piri Reis, a great Turkish admiral and the founder of Ottoman Cartography, did not include Antarctica but mapped its adjacent areas, including the Falkland / Malvines Islands.[4] Some Turkish scientists participated in Antarctica expeditions of foreign countries since the 1960's, such as the U.S.A. and Germany, but their main scope was not biodiveristy. Turkey started its own expeditions in 2016 and has been continuing ever since.

Turkish contribution to the biodiversity contains two pillars. The first one is marine biodiversity and the second one is terrestial biodiversity.

Concerning marine biodiversity, there have been studies mainly on marine mammals and planktons. Marine mammals, mainly cetaceans, were studied during the first Turkish–Ukrainian Antarctic Research Expedition conducted on 5–8 April 2016 in the Lemaire Channel, Penola Strait, Flanders Bay, southern Gerlache Strait, and southern Neumayer Channel in the Western Antarctic. Along the Peninsula, 74 humpback whales (*Megaptera novaeangliae*) in 24 sightings and 11 Antarctic minke whales (*Balaenoptera bonaerensis*) in 6 sightings were recorded. The overall encounter rate (number of sightings/survey effort in nautical miles) was 0.333 (0.266 for humpback whale, 0.066 for Antarctic minke

1 Prof. Dr. Bayram Öztürk; Istanbul University, Faculty of Aquatic Scineces and Turkish Marine Research Foundation, Turkey. ORCID ID: 0000-0002-2092-8557, E-mail: ozturkb@istanbul.edu.tr.
2 Prof. Dr. Mehmet Gökhan Halıcı; Erciyes University, Faculty of Science, Biology Department, Turkey. ORCID ID: 0000-0003-4797-1157, E-mail: mghalici@gmail.com.
3 Bayram Öztürk, Bettina A. Fach, Burcu Özsoy Çiçek, Sinan Hüsrevoğlu, Barış Salihoğlu, Halim Aytekin Ergül, Şamil Aktaş, Birol Çotuk, Günay Çifçi, Ayaka Amaha Öztürk, "Towards the Turkish Antarctic science programme", Journal of the Black Sea/Mediterranean Environment, Vol. 20, No. 1, 2014, pp. 92-95.
4 Bayram Öztürk, Turkish Antarctic Research Expedition Antarctica. Infinite beauty and Wilderness for peace and Science, İstanbul, Turkish Marine Research Foundation (TUDAV), 2017, p. 196.

51

whale). According to the sighting distribution, the Lemaire Channel and Penola Strait are important migration and feeding habitats for whales. Five humpback whales were photo-identified individually by natural features on their flukes; one of them had a match in the Antarctic Humpback Whale Catalogue. The matched individual was first recorded on 30 August 2007 at Salinas, Ecuador.[5]

In the expedition in western Antarctic Peninsula, plankton composition was also studied[6] and reported that surface water temperatures ranged between −0.12 °C and −0.97 °C and average chlorophyll-*a* concentrations were 0.65 µg/l. A total of 50 phytoplankton and 24 zooplankton taxa (15 copepods and 9 meroplanktonic species) were identified by this study. Diatom species (78%) predominated phytoplankton and the highest abundance was 820 cells per litre. Zooplankton was prevailed by the dominance of copepods, except contribution of meroplankton at the Neumayer Channel. Highest zooplankton abundance was 101 ind.m^{-3}. The sampling season was the transition period from the productive spring-summer to dormant winter, which explains the low abundances registered, however, on contrary to low cell abundances, diversity was high within the plankton community.

At four coastal stations along the west Antarctic Peninsula (WAP) a total of 37 microplankton species were reported.[7] Diatoms were the dominant group, followed by ciliates. The highest total microplankton cell concentrations were 18370 cells per litre. Although the most common phytoplankton and ciliate species were *Odontella weissflogii* and *Cymatocylis affinis*, respectively, diversity indexes showed that no dominance of a species at any station. Additionally, they observed that the southern part of the WAP is significantly different from its northernmost part in microplankton abundance/composition.

Concerning terrestrial biodiversity, it has aslo been little studied except for lichen species. As it is known comparing with the other continents, Antarctica has the poorest flora and vegetation but also the most unique in the world. As the harshest conditions for living organisms prevail on the continent and the terrestrial biodiversity in Antarctica is predominantly restricted to areas that are permanently ice-free (estimated nearly between 0.2-0.5% of the whole continent)[8] it is understandable that the terrestrial flora and vegetation is so poor.

---

[5] Bayram Öztürk, Mehmet Arda Tonay, Melike İdil Öz, İzzet Noyan Yılmaz, Halim Aytekin Ergül, Ayaka Amaha Öztürk, "Sighting of cetaceans in the western Antarctic Peninsula during the first joint Turkish–Ukrainian Antarctic Research Expedition 2016", **Turkish Journal of Zoology**, Vol. 45, 2017, pp. 955-961.

[6] I. Noyan Yılmaz, Halim Aytekin Ergül, Sinan Mavruk, Seyfettin Taş, Halim Vedat Aker, Melek Yıldız, Bayram Öztürk, "Coastal Plankton Assemblages in the Vicinity of Galindez Island and Neumayer Channel (Western Antarctic Peninsula) during the First Joint Turkish-Ukrainian Antarctic Research Expedition", **Turkish Journal of Fisheries and Aquatic Sciences**, Vol. 18, No. 4, 2018, pp. 577-584.

[7] Ali Muzaffer Feyzioglu, Ersan Başar, Ilknur Kurt Yıldız, Burcu Ozsoy, "Microplankton Composition and Spatial Distribution Along the West Antarctic Peninsula During the Late Summer of 2017", **Turkish Journal of Fisheries and Aquatic Sciences**, Vol. 20, No. 10, 2020, pp. 739-747.

[8] Hannah S. Wauchope, Justine D. Shaw, Aleks Terauds, "A snapshot of biodiversity protection in Antarctica", **Nature Communications**, Vol. 10, 2019, pp. 1-6.

In geological times, Antarctica had been firstly located near the equator. It is estimated that 417 mya (from the beginning of Devonian Period), when Gondwana shifted towards the South Pole, the first terrestrial plants appeared in fairly cold conditions in Antarctica. Starting from Carboniferous-Permian glaciation until the early Cretaceous (142 mya), especially the west part of Antarctica was covered by conifer forests. Finally, with the last glacial period, the majority of Antarctic vegetation is eliminated and the few remaing organisms which are detailed below are forced to survive in one of the harshest conditions in the world.[9]

There are three recognized terrestrial biogeographic zones in Antarctica namely, sub-, maritime and continental Antarctic in which the biodiversity is rather different from each other. The terrestrial biodiversity is highest in subantarctic and Antarctic Peninsula, and these zones also involve the maximum ice-free habitats comparing with the other parts of Antarctica. Besides, the Antarctic Peninsula is one of the three most rapidly warming regions on the planet[10] and it is under the influence of regional and global environmental change.

Today, Antarctica has terrestrial vegetation comprising mostly lower organisms such as microorganisms, algae, lichenized fungi and bryophytes. It is considered as a tundra biome dominated by lichens and bryophytes. Both cryptogams are poikilohydric and the homoiohydric plants are confined to more northern latitudes.[11] Although Antarctica has a large surface area (14,000,000 km^2), almost 1.5 times larger than Europe and 18 times larger than Turkey, there are only two native flowering plants recorded. One of these flowering plants is *Deschampsia antarctica* Desv. (Antarctic hairgrass) classified under the family Poaceae and the other is *Colobanthus quitensis* (Kunth) Bartl. (Antarctic pearlwort) classified under the family Caryophyllaceae. The members of these species occur along the western coast of the Antarctic Peninsula and the distribution range of these species is expanding by the effect of global warming. The Antarctic Peninsula recently experienced relatively fast regional climate changes[12] and it serves as an early warning system in understanding the species and ecosystem responses to climate change.[13]

---

[9] Ivan Parnikoza, Gökhan Halıcı, "Monitoring of Antarctic Vegetation as a Key for Understandibg Global Processes", State Institution National Antarctic Scientific Center (NASC), Kyiv, Ukraine.
[10] Peter Convey, "Antarctic terrestrial biodiversity in a changing World", **Polar Biology**, Vol. 34, 2011, pp. 1629-1641.
[11] Peter Convey, "Antarctic climate change and its influences on terrestrial ecosystems", **Trends in Antarctic Terrestrial and Limnetic Ecosystems**, Bergstrom, D., Convey, P., Huiskes, A.H.L., (Eds.), Springer, Dordrecht, The Netherlands, 2006, pp. 253-272.
[12] John Turner, Nicholas E. Barrand, Thomas J. Bracegirdle, Peter Convey, Dominic A. Hodgson, Martin Jarvis, Adrian Jenkins, Gareth Marshall, Michael P. Meredith, Howard Roscoe, Jon Shanklin, John French, Hugues Goosse, Mauro Guglielmin, Julian Gutt, Stan Jacobs, Marlon C. Kennicutt II, Valerie Masson-Delmotte, Paul Mayewski, Francisco Navarro, Sharon Robinson, Ted Scambos, Mike Sparrow, Colin Summerhayes, Kevin Speer and Alexander Klepikov, "Antarctic climate change and the environment: an update", **Polar Record**, Vol. 50, No. 3, 2014, pp. 237-259.
[13] Claudia Colesie, Burkhard Büdel, Vaughan Hurry, Thomas George Allan Green, "Can Antarctic lichens

Bryophytes including liverworts and mosses form the important part of the terrestrial Antarctic vegetation. About 130 species of these primitive plants have been recorded from Antarctica. They include 100 species of mosses and 25 to 30 species of hepatics, or liverworts. They are typically small leafy plants, either upright or creeping. Because of their poikilohydric lifestyle they can withstand the harsh conditions of Antarctica, especially the drought stress. Compared to lichens, they are most abundant in wet habitats. In other words, bryophytes are successful to colonize the biggest frozen desert of the world, growing much smaller (just 1 mm a year) compared to their relatives in the other parts of the world.

The most dominant life form of Antarctic terrestrial vegetation is lichens, a symbiotic association between fungi (99% Ascomycota) and green algae or cyanobacteria. Unlike the bryophytes, they are also present in continental Antarctica. They are represented by nearly 400 species which can occupy drier sites especially on rock surfaces in Antarctica. In Antarctica, most of the lichens grow on exposed rocks, and the area composed of exposed rocks is very small, just 21,745 km^2, or 0.18% of the continent.[14] The Antarctic Peninsula and Transantarctic Mountains are the areas where most of the exposed rocks are present in Antarctica, and these parts are rich in lichen biodiversity.

It is very important to determine the lichen biodiversity completely and correctly because lichens have been used as biomonitors for multiple purposes. As well as their usage as air pollution indicators around urban and industrial sites, nowadays researchers are interested in lichens because it may have a potential to be used in biomonitoring the climate change especially in alpine and polar regions. In the review paper prepared by Sancho et al. (2019), the value of saxicolous lichens for monitoring environmental changes in Antarctic regions was discussed.[15]

Turkish scientists started to make lichenological studies in Antarctica in 2016, with the first Turkish expedition carried together with National Antarctic Scientific Center of Ukraine. In this first expedition, lichens were collected from Argentine Islands (location of Ukrainian Antarctic Akademik Vernadsky Station) located in the western coast of Antarctic Peninsula. Although many botanical studies were carried in these islands by Ukrainian scientists, the lichens were never studied by molecular methods. Turkish scientists started to evaluate the lichen biodiversity by using modern tools. From the Argentine Islands, they discovered a new species of lichenicolous fungi, and it was named as *Sagediopsis bayozturkii*, to honor Prof. Dr. Bayram Öztürk who was the expedition leader of

---

acclimatize to changes in temperature? ", **Global Change Biology**, Vol. 24, No. 4, 2017, pp. 1123-1166.
[14] Alex Burton-Johnson, Martin Black, Peter T. Fretwell and Joseph Kaluza-Gilbert, "An automated methodology for differentiating rock from snow, clouds and sea in Antarctica from Landsat 8 imagery: A new rock outcrop map and area estimation for the entire Antarctic continent", **The Cryosphere**, No. 10, 2016, pp. 1665-1677.
[15] Leopoldo G. Sancho, Ana Pintado and T.G. Allan Green, "Antarctic studies show lichens to be excellent biomonitors of climate change", **Diversity**, Vol. 11, No. 3, 2019, pp. 42.

the first Turkish expedition to Antarctica.[16]

In 2016/17 austral summer, Prof. Dr. Mehmet Gökhan Halıcı was invited to Mendel Polar Station of Czech Republic in Antarctica on the coast of James Ross Island. It is a large island off the southeast side and near the northeastern extremity of the Antarctic Peninsula, from which it is separated by Prince Gustav Channel. Rising to 1,630 m, it is irregularly shaped and extends 64 km in a north–south direction. James Ross Island (Antarctic Peninsula) is one of the lichen rich islands of Antarctica because of its large deglaciated area, with over 140 species of lichenized fungi reported from the island. Halıcı collected more than 300 specimens of lichens from this island. From these lichen collections, *Toniniopsis bartakii*[17] and *Leptogium pirireisii*[18] were described as new to science and named in honour of Miloš Barták (a Czech botanist who has been carrying botanical studies in James Ross Island more than a decade) and Ottoman admiral Ahmed Muhiddin Piri (ca. 1465–1553), known as Piri Reis who was a cartographer, geographer and navigator.

Besides, some lichen species which were previously not known from Antarctica were reported from for the first time. *Catenarina desolata* Søchting, Søgaard & Elvebakk. was described recently from southernmost Chile, and the presence of this species in Antarctica was discovered by using molecular methods.[19] This species was wrongly present as *Caloplaca* aff. *anchon-phoenicon* in the checklist of James Ross Island. In another paper published by Turkish authors, nrITS gene regions of some specimens were studied and the lichen species *Aspicilia virginea* Hue and *Peltigera ponojensis* Gyeln. were reported from Antarctica for the first time. The data for nrITS of *Candelaria murrayi* Poelt and *Flavoparmelia gerlachei* (Zahlbr.) Hale were provided for the first time. The same authors also informed that *Austroplaca frigida* Søchting & Garrido-Ben., a lichen species previously reported only from continental Antarctica has also distribution in maritime Antarctica[20]. From the collections of James Ross Island, we observed the lichenicolous fungus species *Sphaerellothecium reticulatum* on the lichen *Flavoparmelia gerlachei*. Although this species was identified on other parmelioid lichens, it was never reported on *Flavoparmelia* spp. and it was reported from

---

[16] Mehmet Gökhan Halıcı, Mithat Güllü and Ivan Parnikoza, "*Sagediopsis bayozturkii* sp. nov. on the lichen *Acarospora macrocyclos* from Antarctica with a key to the known species of the genus (Ascomycota, Adelococcaceae)", **The Polar Record**, Vol. 53, No. 3, 2017, p. 271.

[17] Mehmet Gökhan Halıcı, Merve Kahraman, Sonja Kistenich, Einar Timdal, "*Toniniopsis bartakii* - A new species of lichenised fungus from James Ross Island (Antarctic Peninsula)", **Turkish Journal of Botany**, Vol. 45, 2021, pp. 216-223.

[18] Mehmet Gökhan Halıcı, Merve Kahraman, Mayara C. Scur, Marcos J. Kitaura, "*Leptogium pirireisii*, a new species of lichenized Ascomycota (Collemataceae) from James Ross Island in Antarctica", **New Zealand Journal of Botany**, 2021, in press.

[19] Mehmet Gökhan Halıcı, Mithat Güllü and Miloš Barták, "First record of a common endolithic lichenized fungus species Catenarina desolata Schting, Sgaard & Elvebakk. from James Ross Island (Antarctic Peninsula)", Czech Polar Reports, Vol. 7, No. 1, 2017, pp. 11-17.

[20] Mehmet Gökhan Halıcı, Milos Bartak and Mithat Güllü, "Identification of some lichenised fungi from James Ross Island (Antarctic Peninsula) using nrITS markers", New Zealand Journal of Botany, Vol. 56, No. 3, 2018, pp. 276-290.

Antarctica for the first time.[21] Finally, the Turkish researchers discovered *Peltigera castanea* Goward, Goffinet & Miądl., a species in the *P. didactyla* complex from Antarctica and Southern Hemisphere for the first time by using molecular methods[22] and the project aiming to determine the lichen biodiversity of James Ross Island still continues.

In the last Turkish expeditions to Antarctica, the flowering plants were also examined with different methods. For example, the genome size constancy in Antarctic populations of *Colobanthus quitensis* and *Deschampsia antarctica* were studied and it was presented the first genome size analysis focused in several populations from the Antarctic Peninsula and the surrounding islands for both species, with a broad sampling area streching 800 km.[23]

Establishment of Marine Protected Areas is linked to the knowledge of biodiversity. In that sense, both marine and terrestrial biodiversity are crucial for the conservation of Antarctica. The Ross Sea has been called "the last ocean" because it remains relatively pristine and untouched by human activities. More than 1.5 million km² of the Ross Sea around Antarctica will be protected as a Marine Preotected Area, where no fishing nor any commercial activities will be allowed. Significantly, the protections are set to expire in 35 years. Why not protect this beauty and wilderness forever? We believe that more Marine Protected Areas are needed to sustainably support Antactica's ecosystem and biodiversity. Turkey should support all kinds of inititiatives about Antarctica and the protection of Artarctic environment without any condition. This can be another contribution in terms of conservation and sustainability of the frozen continent Antarctica and the Southern Ocean.

---

[21] Mehmet Gökhan Halıcı and Miloš Barták. "Sphaerellothecium reticulatum (Zopf) Etayo, a new lichenicolous fungusfor Antarctica", Czech Polar Reports, Vol. 9, No. 1, 2019, pp. 13-19.

[22] Mehmet Gökhan Halıcı, Osman Muaz Osmanoğlu, Merve Kahraman "A new record of lichenized fungus species for Antarctica: Peltigera castanea Goward, Goffinet & Miadl", Czech Polar Reports, Vol. 10, No. 1, 2020, pp. 50-58.

[23] Joan Pere Pascual-Díaz, Sedat Serçe, Ivana Hradecka, Martin Vanek, Bahar Soğutmaz Özdemir, Nusrat Sultana, Mehtap Vural, Daniel Vitales, Sonia Garcia. "Genome size constancy in Antarctic populations of Colobanthus quitensis and Deschampsia antarctica". Polar Biology, Vol. 43, 2020, pp. 1407-1413.

PART 2

INDIAN AND PACIFIC OCEAN GEOPOLITICS

SECURITIZATION PROCESS OF INDO-PACIFIC AND ASIA-PACIFIC THROUGH IR THEORIES WITHIN MARITIME SECURITY INTERACTION

Burak Şakir Şeker*

Introduction

From ancient times to the present, the Indian and Pacific Oceans have been vital because it is an area that encompasses major trade routes and choke points. Oceans, on the other hand, is vulnerable to a variety of maritime security concerns, including piracy, drug trafficking, significant state conflicts, and terrorist operations. Coastal governments are unable to collectively assure the ocean's security, sometimes due to divergent interests and other times due to issues stemming from internal instability, but they have created regional organizations and are working in this field. Within the context of Indian and Pacific Oceans maritime security, several theoretical explanations of specific aspects can be given.

Before the age of colonialism, people living near the Indian and Pacific Oceans were greatly affected by old world threats such as the slave trade and conquests that came with the links made by the ocean. As the Portuguese and then European countries arrived in the region with stronger naval forces and developed massive colonial empires around the ocean, the balance of power and security challenges shifted dramatically. Over the centuries, the British managed to dominate the region among European nations, and as the leading power, they prioritized maritime security to eliminate threats to the flow of trade. Hegemony of Great Britain in the region, however, came to an end with the start of the decolonization process and the independence of its colonies. Then, as the Cold War continued and the region became more polarized, the Indian and Pacific Oceans' global importance grew, and it came under the influence of various countries.

In the polycentric world, the fact that Asian countries with coasts to the Indian and Pacific Oceans increase their effectiveness every year. Additionally, these countries have important maritime trade networks due to their location and have drawn attention to the maritime security threats of the Indian and Pacific Oceans as well as studies have been conducted to explain and create solutions to them.

The changing structure of international relations creates new topics,

* Assoc. Prof. Burak Şakir Şeker, Ankara Hacı Bayram Veli University, Turkey.
E-mail: buraksakirseker@gmail.com; seker.burak@hbv.edu.tr

challenges, and ideologies for the world to discuss and define. Conflicts, alliances, globalization, industrialization, and other concepts that lie under the structure of international relations emerge different security and safety agendas for the states. According to Buzan's understanding of security, political and military sectors are the main and classic security topics in international relations.[1] Before globalization and industrialization of the world, these two main topics were prioritized by states because they were the essential areas to show their influence and power. However, with globalization, new security agendas started to arise such as cyber, economic, environmental, and maritime security.

This paper has been written with the aim of firstly explaining the buzzword maritime security and then focusing on the Indian and Pacific Oceans, by dividing it into 3 parts, and its maritime security. The main aim of this paper is to examine the state and non-state security threats in the maritime security region in the mentioned Oceans as well as how different states perceive these dangers and the steps they take individually or together to counter them. While doing this, the main objective is to go further into some crucial points to examine various events, actions, or events in a theoretical context. It should be noted that there will always be more than one reality if there are diverse views, hence the subject of this paper is enriched by more than one theory of international relations.

Background of the Maritime Security and its Securitization Process

Maritime security and its importance started to arise in recent years. National security, transnational economic development, the marine environment, and human security, piracy, even climate change and its consequences linked with maritime security concept throughout the years. Therefore, maritime security and safety needed to be assured, defined, and discussed by the states in the international area. As a buzzword in international relations, Maritime Security does not have a specific and accepted definition. Different scholars -such as Rahman, Cordner, Chapsos, Klein, Bueger- define maritime security from different perspectives. According to Bueger, Maritime Security can be explained by linking it with different concepts which can be recent or older, positive, or negative. In his "Maritime Security Matrix", he divided the concepts into 5 sections which include important links and possible threats for Maritime Security.[2] According to Cordner, Maritime Security is a concept that arises from the systematic nature of the maritime space and addresses traditional and non-traditional security challenges posed by state and non-state actors, in which multiple and interconnected requirements for collective security are presented[3].

---

[1] Buzan, Barry. "New Patterns of Global Security in the Twenty-First Century." International Affairs (Royal Institute of International Affairs 1944-) 67, no. 3 (1991): 431-51.
[2] Bueger, C. What is maritime security? Marine Policy, 2015, 159-164.
[3] Cordner, Lee. "Progressing Maritime Security Cooperation in The Indian Ocean." Naval War College Review 64, no. 4 (2011): 68-88.

As mentioned above there is no consensus for the definition of maritime security. Therefore, states and international organizations needed to review this security concept from their perspectives with the securitization framework. They escaped the question of "What is maritime security?" and focused on the questions of "What are the threats in maritime and how these threats can be prevented?". As seen in the definition of Copenhagen School for securitization theory, when subjects securitized by actors in the system, they become the alarming topic of politics and security of the actors and this allows them to take immediate, legitimate, actions on the behalf of their interests[4]. Focusing on the threats that are determined by actors in the favor of their interests rather than the common definition can emerge disorder between actors. Also, looking the maritime security through the securitization theory can cause a lack of proper and long-lasting solutions in the system.[5]

The securitization process of Maritime Security can be divided into two important periods. The first period is connected to the USA's agenda after the September 11 attacks, it is the perception of "Maritime Security" that developed against the terrorist threat. The second period is under the leadership of the UN against the increasing threat of piracy since 2008.

On 11th September 2001, four terrorist attacks were realized by al-Qaeda in the US. This terrorist act triggered the new approach about fighting against terrorism worldwide. President George W. Bush, who used these matters as an excuse for new policies, shifted his approach in support of further involvement in many regions. USA's new policies of military, politics and maritime security had shown and explained to the world. On June 24, 2002, he delivered a speech in support of the creation of "a peaceful and democratic " world order in the Middle East [6]. Creating a peaceful and democratic order was the goal not only in the case of Middle Eastern countries but was more in the liberal understanding of the World by the United States. Its primary foreign policy principle is based on the Democratic Peace Theory which is a branch of liberalism. It claims to be dealing with democracy promotion via intervening territories of non-democracies. However, it is argued that this is not a "democratization" step forward against non-democracies but rather the form of enthrallment of those who do not act following the interests of the US and its allies.[7]

Following days of these events, as mentioned above, new policy approaches on different security subjects started to be discussed by the USA. Maritime Security Strategy was one of them due to its lack of a secure environment which can lead to possible threats like terrorist attacks. Besides the strategy document,

---

[4] McSweeney, Bill. "Identity and Security: Buzan and the Copenhagen School." Review of International Studies 22, no. 1 (1996): 81-93.
[5] Burak Şakir Şeker," International Maritime Security: The 100 Rules", International Security, Beta Publication, Istanbul.
[6] Mohamad, H. (2015). President George W. Bush's Legacy on the Israeli-Palestinian)
[7] Rosato, Sebastian. "The Flawed Logic of Democratic Peace Theory." The American Political Science Review 97, no. 4 (2003): 585-602.

the SOLAS convention (The Safety of Life at Sea), which is an international convention accepted in 1914 that regulates life safety issues in commercial ships, was amended and added new regulations by IMO with the approval and order of the UN in 2002 upon the request of the USA[8].

The United States Maritime Security Strategy document connects the state's national and economic security to the secure usage of the oceans. The strategy emphasizes that the United States' primary interests can only be safeguarded in an environment where maritime security is assured. It also specifically mentions that preventing and ceasing the violations of rogue states, who can be using weapons or preparing an intervention, or the terrorist attacks against the USA and its allies is the primary objective of this strategy. This statement can be seen as proof of the USA's intention to make the "maritime security" concept securitized in order to seek and protect, its and its allies' interests. As Realists emphasize, all states are motivated by national interests, and they seek their survival in the system. As a global power United States seeks its and its allies' interests to protect its position and power in the international area.[9]

The second phase of the securitization process of Maritime Security emerged under the leadership of the United Nations in 2008. Through the UN-sanctioned policing operation against piracy, the UN has gotten increasingly involved in African maritime issues since 2007.

Through four UN Security Council resolutions, the UN has played a significant part in the securitization process by fostering a more conducive operating environment against piracy. These four resolutions are based on cooperation against piracy and other maritime security matters, and they also gave permission to the countries who are fighting against maritime threats to intervene in the territorial waters of Somalia. According to Vreÿ, piracy is presented as an existential threat to the flow of food to the Somali population by the sea in these UN resolutions, while legitimizing a massive deployment of international naval forces to combat the menace.[10]

In the Law of the Sea agreement, UNCLOS[11], the limits of territorial seas and sovereignty of states in waters defined specifically. In this case of Somalia, UNSC took a decision upon Somalia and its territorial seas without its permission. As a weak and injured state, Somalia could not have a word against the decision of the UNSC. This position of Somalia can be examined under the doctrine of acquiescence. When a state remains silent in a position against the acts of other actors in the international area, other actors and international law acknowledge this silence as an acceptance of that state. The securitization process and silent

---

[8] Norris, Andrew J. "The "Other" Law of The Sea", Naval War College Review 64, no. 3 (2011): 78-97.
[9] DHS, National Strategy for Maritime Security, https://www.dhs.gov/national-plan-achieve-maritime-domain-awareness
[10] Vreÿ, F, "Securitizing Piracy", African Security Review, 2011, pp. 54-66.
[11] United Nations Convention on the Law of the Sea

position of Somalia legitimized the decisions of the UN.[12]

Throughout these events, the importance of "Maritime Security" started to be recognized by international areas. With USA's policies to prevent threats in the maritime environment, which also were pointing out this deficiency in maritime security, guided other actors to discuss and find proper solutions for threats in maritime security. Important actors such as the United Nations, European Union, and NATO introduced their maritime security strategies. These actors released their maritime security strategies by explaining and defining the possible threats. There are main threats that accepted generally such as piracy and armed robbery, maritime terrorism, human trafficking, migrant smuggling, illicit trafficking in weapons of mass destruction, drug trafficking, illegal fishing, and unlawful damage to the marine environment[13] .

As seen in the two cases of securitization of Maritime Security, deciding and acting with securitization framework can reveal a situation where actors act in their favor. On the other side, these events created positive outcomes such as recognition of serious threats like illegal human trafficking, terrorist attacks, and piracy in the maritime environment which were causing loss of people and economic damages.

IR Theories and Main Factors Affecting Maritime Security in the Indian and Pacific Oceans

Maritime security, which is becoming a more prevalent notion in the international maritime agenda, can be defined as staying away from natural and human-made threats, as well as threat perception caused by maritime operations extending to ports and the high seas. Therefore, maritime security is turning into an area where international actors can take appropriate measures and develop plans at the regional and global level against maritime threats.

However, in the example of the Indian Ocean, it can be said that there is an environment of turmoil due to reasons such as the fact that some of the states surrounding the region still do not carry out fully independent policies, they approach each other with suspicion, and the efforts of the great powers to be included in the region. While some coastal states with weak and unstable governments cannot contribute to the security of the ocean, while they leave the door open for great powers to the region and enter rivalry with opponents in the region.[14]

We can explain the maritime security of the Indian Ocean under three main

---

[12] UN, United Nations Convention on the Law of the Sea, 1982. https://www.un.org/depts/los/convention_agreements/texts/unclos/unclos_e.pdf (Retrieved: 09.05.2021)
[13] Bateman, Sam, Anthony Bergin, Bob Breen, Satish Chand, Graeme Dobell, Stewart Firth, Andrew Goldsmith, Richard Herr, and Bob Lowry. Australia and the South Pacific: Rising to the Challenge. Report. Australian Strategic Policy Institute, 2008. 55-73.
[14] Brewster, David. Australia's Second Sea: Facing Our Multipolar Future in the Indian Ocean. Report. Australian Strategic Policy Institute, 2019. 17-28.

headings: the security of coastal states, the security of sea lines of communications (SLOCs) and the security of the maritime environment. At this point, it is apparent that the first title, "the security of the coastal states", may be affected by the security of the ocean, but it can also affect the ocean at the same way either. Although the riparian states or others that closely related to the Indian Ocean are rich in underground and surface resources, so that is why 42% of the conflicts in the world are related to these states. There has been a vast list of conflicts and crises, including the Palestinian-Israeli conflict, Iraq, Yemen, Sudan, Iran, Somalia, Myanmar, Sri Lanka, Pakistan and so on so forth.[15]

In Indonesia, insurgents from the Free Aceh Movement[16] routinely attacked ships carrying natural resource products such as oil and aluminum. Although the situation has been taken under control in Somalia, decades of instability have fed a deadly pirate threat. The Iran-Iraq war in the 1980s, the ongoing crisis in Iraq today, and the Yemen issue that has been on the agenda recently. Although the causes of these conflicts vary, many of them are weak or failed states, and they deal with domestic problems such as poverty, underdeveloped institutions, bribery, and corruption.[17]

Figure 1. Connectivity Initiatives of China and India[18]

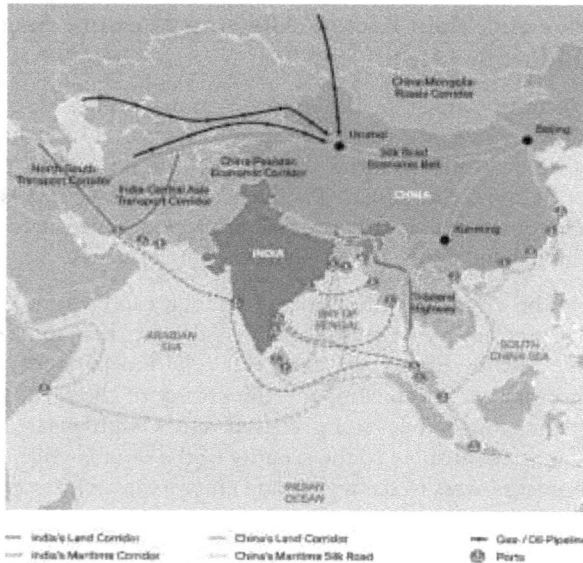

| India's Land Corridor | China's Land Corridor | Gas-/Oil-Pipeline |
| India's Maritime Corridor | China's Maritime Silk Road | Ports |

---

[15] ICC International Maritime Bureau (IMB). Piracy and Armed Robbery Against Ships Report, 2020, 6.
[16] Gerekan Aceh Merdeka-GAM
[17] Suri, G., "India's Maritime Security Concerns and the Indian Ocean Region", Indian Foreign Affairs Journal, 11(3), 2016, 243.
[18] Peter Rimmele, Philipp Huchel, A New Stage in the Rivalry Between the Great Powers?, Konrad-Adenauer-Stiftung. https://www.kas.de/en/web/auslandsinformationen/artikel/detail/-/content/weitere-buehne-im-wettstreit-der-grossmaechte-1 (Retrieved 05.05.2021)

Liberalism, one of the theories of international relations, adds two further criteria to the security of a state at this point: the development of democracy and the security of the individual. In other words, it can be said that liberalism establishes a balanced link between the security of a state and the security of the individuals who compose it.[19] Hence, if we look at such states from the liberal perspective, we can see their insecure or sometimes even threatening position.

Drug zones, called Golden Crescent and Golden Triangle, one of the most dangerous areas in the world, are in the Indian Ocean as well. The Golden Triangle was number one in this sector before Afghanistan became a hub to produce illegal drugs following the civil war. Of course, the Indian Ocean served as an important route for drug smugglers, as security measures could not be as strict as on land and a substandard security environment wasn't already provided. Myanmar, which already has no internal stability, has suffered from these activities.[20]

Figure 2. Golden Crescent and Golden Triangle[21]

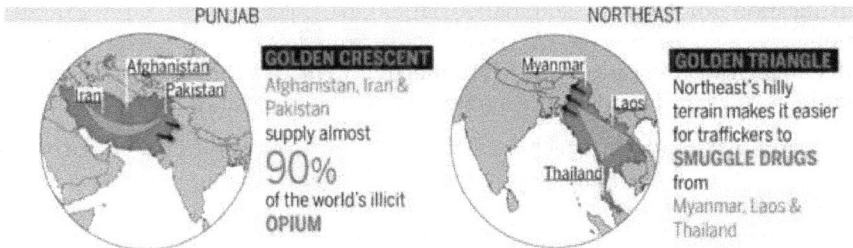

The leading threats perceived by the USA in the Indian Ocean are the ongoing conflicts in the states of the region and the increasing activity of states such as China, Russia, and Iran in the region. The most important aim of the USA is to protect its allies in this region against these undemocratic countries.[22] We can say that these policies are the result of securitizing the target countries.

According to the securitization theory, such national security policies of states are not naturally given but carefully designed by politicians. And political issues are constituted by a 'securitizing actor' as extremely dangerous, menacing, threatening, and alarming problems to be immediately dealt with. So, the security issues are not just "out there" but rather must be reported by the security actors.

---

[19] Owen, John M. "How Liberalism Produces Democratic Peace." International Security 19, no. 2 (1994): 87-125.
[20] Potgieter, T., "Maritime security in the Indian Ocean: strategic setting and features", Institute for Security Studies, (236), 2012, p.2
[21] Hindustan Times, Illicit opium production region in the world. https://www.hindustantimes.com/india-news/india-in-us-list-on-drug-transit/story-k38UkOlpMQ8C9JPDvTPx7K.html (Retrieved: 01.05.2021)
[22] Hughes, Lindsay, The United States and the Indian Ocean Region: The Security Vector, Future Directions International, https://www.futuredirections.org.au/wp-content/uploads/2016/06/The-United-States-and-the-Indian-Ocean-Region-The-Security-Vector.pdf (Retrieved: 22.05.2021)

Calling a non-democracy, a "threat to national and/or international security, for instance, shifts non-democratic states from low priority concern to high priority issue that entails action, such as securing national/international borders.[23]

According to post-structuralist Jacques Derrida, distinctions such as weak and strong actually exist with the definitions constructed by the strong sides of these dualities, and Derrida describes how the definitions of the "other" side will change. Powerful actors that make up security language and discourse, naturally apply a unilateral security definition and practice. In this sense, post-structuralists take a stance against the universally accepted definitions and discourses in traditional security studies. According to them, the fact that the great powers can universally impose their own security concerns and securitized issues on the rest of the system does not mean that these happen this way.[24]

With the growing number of commercial ships passing through the Indian Ocean as part of the Maritime Silk Road Initiative, the United States and its allies see China's enhanced sensitivity to maritime trade routes and port control as a justification for Chinese domination ambitions. Likewise, the USA carefully monitors Iranian territorial waters and its surroundings. In particular, the Gulf of Oman, which connects the Gulf and the Strait of Hormuz to the outside world, is of great importance as a transit route for one fifth of the world's oil.

There was a missile attack by Iran on Saudi Arabian oil facilities between 2019-2021. The United States and Saudi Arabia blamed Iran for this attack, while Tehran denied the allegations. Again, the US and Iranian ships sometimes create a tense atmosphere, especially in the Strait of Hormuz.[25]

Although these are the usual pictures, it should be noted that the identity attributed to each of these actors is not perceived in the same way by others. Albeit each of them tends to legitimize their activities around the Indian Ocean in the context of their identity and culture, a move that one claims to have made to ensure security can be perceived by the other as expansionism. Ultimately, one side's security may create the other's insecurity because each actor has a different perspective. At this point, post-structuralism tries to understand how the concepts produced by "us" are perceived by the "other" through language, culture and ethnography studies that shape its perspective.[26]

Actors can affect each other in different ways, according to constructivists, and this might affect security. They argue that states' approaches to their dealings with one another are based on the situations and interactions of individuals

---

[23] Wæver, Ole. 1995. 'Securitization and desecuritization.' In Ronnie D Lipschutz (ed), On Security. New York: Columbia University Press, pp. 46-86.
[24] Derrida, J. Writing and Difference. London: Routledge, p. 354
[25] Khaled Wassef, Saudi Arabia oil facilities targeted in drone and missile attack by Iran-backed Houthis in Yemen, CBS. https://www.cbsnews.com/news/saudi-arabia-drone-attack-oil-infrastructure-ras-tanura-dhahran-houthis-yemen-iran/ (Retrieved: 29.05.2021)
[26] Young, Robert. "Post-Structuralism: The End of Theory." Oxford Literary Review 5, no. 1/2 (1982): 3-20.

within those states. Constructivists made one more point that is worth mentioning while opening the hostilities between Iran and the USA in the Indian Ocean: the changeability of state identity and interests. Accordingly, the interests and identities of states can change within the social order. Constructivist theory criticizes realist and liberal theories' acceptance of identities and interests as fixed and unchanging.[27]

If we look at the example of Iran, how true is it to claim that there has been no change in Iran's foreign policy identity which known as pro-Western policies and a US gendarme in Persian Gulf during the reign of Mohammad Reza Shah? On the other hand, if someone looks at this example from a different perspective and says that the Shah's policies are not dependent on the situations or social interaction of individuals anyway, and that this disconnection from society has already brought his dynasty's end, then there will be doubt whether the ideas of social constructionists will be sufficiently explanatory for monarchies.[28]

It is possible to see that China and Russia share a neo-realist line on maritime security in the Indian Ocean in parallel with their general security policies. Although Iran, Russia and China held joint security exercises in the Indian Ocean between 2019-2021[29] and built strategic ties in the region, both China and Russia have close relations with Saudi Arabia. It is also clear that Saudi Arabia is perceived as a US military and political base from the perspective of Iran. According to neo-realists, instead of being power-hungry and constantly demanding more, states can use power as a tool for security or to achieve national interests when they feel threatened.[30]

According to neo-realism, when the power used as a tool, can be also organized in cooperation with other states against the problems that will threaten the international system. But of course, this is not a liberal kind of cooperation. In the example of China, Russia, and Iran, we see that these countries can act together in the Indian Ocean because the elements they perceive as threats are similar. This situation can also be explained by the fact that a state must make alliances with other states in order to ensure its own security when confronted with a state that is getting stronger against itself, as stated in the balance of power theories.[31]

Recently, the number of non-state actors and the size of the threats they can pose have been increasing rapidly, contrary to the state-centered attitude of

---

[27] Farrell, Theo. "Constructivist Security Studies: Portrait of a Research Program." International Studies Review 4, no. 1 (2002): 49-72.

[28] Panah, Maryam H. "Social Revolution: The Elusive Emergence of an Agenda in International Relations." Review of International Studies 28, no. 2 (2002): 271-91.

[29] Alex Lantier, Iran, Russia and China launch joint naval exercises in Indian Ocean, WSWS, 2021. https://www.wsws.org/en/articles/2021/02/19/iran-f19.html (Retrieved: 02.05,2021)

[30] Chen, Rong. "A Critical Analysis of the U.S. "Pivot" toward the Asia-Pacific: How Realistic Is Neo-realism?" Connections 12, no. 3 (2013): 39-62.

[31] Jervis, Robert. "A Political Science Perspective on the Balance of Power and the Concert." The American Historical Review 97, no. 3 (1992): 716-24.

realism. Criminal organizations and terrorist groups operating in different parts of the world can work in connection with each other. Indian Ocean coastal states also provide a more flexible environment for these organizations, as mentioned earlier, as they have weak governance structures and contribute little to maritime security, although not on purpose.

It is still possible to find traces of groups affiliated with al-Qaeda in countries such as Afghanistan, Egypt, Indonesia, Iraq and Somalia. These organizations can continue their activities such as sea attacks, arms and drug smuggling by using the ocean besides the land. In 1993 and 2008, there were terrorist attacks in India from the sea. These attacks marked the beginning of significant changes in India's vision for maritime security, and this state gave some incentives and took responsibility for security. For example, it is known that this country has activities in escorting merchant ships belonging to other countries and conducting joint studies with the countries of the region, especially against piracy.[32]

Unfortunately, progress in forming a "strong grouping around the Indian Ocean" in terms of a collective security system or strengthening regional cooperation has been minimal and gradual. This is owing to the Indian Ocean's large geographical size, which creates a divide between its sub-regions, as well as the lack of a unified or convergent narrative or perspective on political and security issues across the region. Despite all the mentioned negative factors, it would be unfair to say that the Indian Ocean states could not develop policies against the threats they perceived, especially piracy, human trafficking and maritime terrorism, and did not at least make any effort for common security. [33]

Economic cooperation has brought people and governments together for mutual economic progress and benefits, which have manifested themselves in a variety of economic groups. Economic security is frequently followed by an extensive understanding of political and security issues.

According to neo-liberalism, the common interests developed by states, relative gains in the international system, cooperation, international law and economic dependency will increase the desire of states to build and protect common security. Liberals explain why common security has not yet reached the extent that it should, as seen in Indian Ocean countries such as: At the systemic level, the most basic elements of common security are understanding of total gain, harmony between security providing parties, clearance of common interests, and destabilizing disputes, conflicts, and wars that are created by states' misunderstanding of each other. International institutionalization and international law will be the solutions to this problem.[34]

---

[32] Potgieter, op.cit., p.11
[33] Suri, Gopal. "India's Maritime Security Concerns and the Indian Ocean Region." Indian Foreign Affairs Journal 11, no. 3 (2016): 238-52.
[34] Lewkowicz, Nicolas. "The Institutionalization of The Postwar International Order." In The United States, the Soviet Union and the Geopolitical Implications of the Origins of the Cold War, 11-30. New

Sub-regional economic commonalities have been effectively transcribed into organizations like the ASEAN[35], ARF[36], APAEC[37], ADC[38], EAC[39], and others. However, the majority of organizations are focused on geography, economy or culture with a limited maritime security charter, 2 pan-IOR[40] organizations namely Indian Ocean Naval Symposium and Indian Ocean Rim Association make notable exceptions, with member states hailing from various parts of the area and belonging to one or more sub-regional economic groups.[41]

Maritime Security Interaction between Indian and Pacific Oceans

The Pacific Ocean and its security have a very significant and strategic role for the coastal states in this region. In this part, there will be an examination of the pacific regions' security by dividing it into three main concepts. These concepts are Indo-Pacific, Asia-Pacific, and America's role in these regions.[42]

Although any debate regarding the region definitions is out of scope of this study, to be able to deliver the differences between Indo-Pacific and Asia-Pacific terms, main points are as like stands shown in Figure 3.

The Strait of Malacca connects the Indo-Pacific region, which runs from the eastern Indian Ocean to the western Pacific Ocean. Maritime geopolitics in the Indo-Pacific region has become a focal point for security, trade, and environmental initiatives. This region has significant importance for powerful nations such as China, India, Australia, Japan, Southeast Asian countries, and even the United States. The Indo-Pacific area is a crossroads for worldwide trade, with millions of barrels of crude oil passing through each year and a major part of worldwide exports coming from the region[43] .

China and United States are the main powers those have been computing in this region. With developments and investments for this region India, Japan, and Australia also have become part of the important actors. China, which controls the security environment in Indo-Pacific, recreates its security strategies due to the rising power and shifting policies of the USA and Japan's cooperation. The USA, which seen as the gendarme of the seas, seeks cooperation to improve its influence. India, which is a new rising power, is also seeking power in order to protect its new position in the system. These competitions and tension between

---

York, NY: Anthem Press, 2018.
[35] Association of Southeast Asian Nations
[36] ASEAN Regional Forum
[37] ASEAN Plan of Action for Energy Cooperation
[38] APAEC Drafting Committee
[39] East Asian Community
[40] Indian Ocean Region
[41] Das, Chinmoyee. "India's Maritime Diplomacy in Southwest Indian Ocean: Evaluating Strategic Partnerships." Journal of Strategic Security 12, no. 2 (2019): 42-59.
[42] Le Thu, Huong. "Southeast Asia and Indo-Pacific Concepts: From Resistance to Reticence to Reaction." Security Challenges 16, no. 3 (2020): 53-57.
[43] Tertia, J., & Perwita, A. A. B, Maritime Security in Indo-Pacific: Issues, Challenges, and Prospects. Jurnal Ilmiah Hubungan Internasional, 2018

states are having, generally, political, and economical outcomes such as shifting policies, using sanctions, signing treaties, and many more.[44]

There are possible threats that all states in this region must combat, such as piracy. Piracy used to be a massive concern in the Malacca Strait, but multilateral treaties have effectively eliminated this threat. Since the beginning of the year of 2005, pirates began equipping the Indian Ocean with useful tools that allows them to operate within 1,500 NM[45] off the Somali coasts.[46]

---

[44] Lang, David. The Not-Quite-Quadrilateral: Australia, Japan and India. Australian Strategic Policy Institute, 2015

[45] Nautical Mile, 1852 metrers.

[46] Jeong, Keunsoo. "Piracy and Crime Embeddedness: State Decay and Social Transformation in Somalia." African Conflict and Peacebuilding Review 9, no. 1 (2019): 72-99.

Figure 3. Main points of Indo-Pacific and the Asia-Pacific[47]

Asia-Pacific	Indo-Pacific
The term 'Asia-Pacific' is associated with the part of Asia that lies in the Pacific Ocean.	The Indo-Pacific is an integrated region that combines the Indian Ocean, the Pacific Ocean, and the landmasses that surround them.
It is a proposed idea and is supported by Asia's Pacific powers as they sought a term to describe their common region.	It is an evolving concept and most analysts see it as an idea that may shift power and influence from the West to the East.
The Asia Pacific has three major constituents-- north-east Asia, south-east Asia and Oceania (South Western Pacific).	Its geographical expanse is undefined, however, it is said to range from the coast of East Africa, across the Indian Ocean, to the Western Pacific, including countries like Japan and Australia.
It is an economic conception rather than a security-related notion. Since the late 1980s, the zone has been experiencing rapid economic growth and is popularly termed as the zone of emerging markets.	It is both a strategic as well as an economic domain comprising important sea-lines of communication. It is associated with maritime security and cooperation.
Asia-Pacific Economic Cooperation forum (APEC) is the only multilateral institution that effectively represents the Asia Pacific.	It has a symbiotic link with the Quadrilateral Security Dialogue (Quad), an informal grouping of like-minded democracies in the region, comprising Australia, Japan, India, and the United States.
India is not a part of the Asia-Pacific region.	India is a part of the Indo-Pacific.

On Indo-Pacific human and drug trafficking are also common cross-border crimes. Illicit markets transport drugs produced in Afghanistan, India, and Indonesia by sea. Oil transfer and offshore drilling, fishing, and cruise shipping are all examples of marine-based economic activities that have the potential to harm the surrounding maritime environment. Large oil spills in the ocean will have an impact on marine ecology and will eventually lead to the extinction of numerous marine species. Illegal fishing, which often involves explosives and

---

[47] Arfa Javaid, What is the Difference Between the Indo-Pacific and the Asia-Pacific? https://www.jagranjosh.com/general-knowledge/indo-pacific-vs-asia-pacific-1612883032-1 (Retrieved 08.05.2021)

cruise ships, threatens coral reefs, which are important habitats for marine life[48]. States affected by threats in this region tend to focus on preventing human trafficking, piracy, and terrorist attacks, which also leads to a lack of solutions to protect the marine environment and its sustainable life.[49]

The Asia-Pacific region is inherently maritime. The sea and issues related to the sea form an important part of international relations in the area, both between the countries of the region themselves and between those countries and the rest of the world. Most Asia-Pacific countries depend on the sea for economical improvements, power, and most importantly access to food and energy. Such dependencies created a need for Maritime Security in the region. To protect these needs, some progress has been made in maritime and naval cooperation in Southeast Asia. Countries have engaged in cooperative marine scientific research, anti-piracy operations, marine environmental protection programs, and bilateral and even multilateral exercises. Different parts of Asia-Pacific are carrying out different significances in international relations. Economically, East Asia is currently one of the most dynamic parts of the world. The expansion of naval forces in the region Asia-Pacific has been particularly rapid in Northeast Asia. Japan is increasingly seeking greater self-reliance in security matters and will rely less on the United States security umbrella in the longer term[50].

Indo-Pacific region also involves the Asia-Pacific region into itself. Therefore, there are similarities at the points of major powers, threats, and security matters. On the other hand, there are different cooperations and forums which were established to promote cooperation on security and economic matters in the Asia-Pacific region such as Asia-Pacific Economic Cooperation, ASEAN Regional Forum, and Security Cooperation in the Asia Pacific.

In the Asia-Pacific region, Pacific Island Countries (PICs) and their security also carry-outs an important weight. Due to their position, PICs grapple with unfamiliar national security threats such as climate change, natural disasters, transnational crime, and border security. In contrast, they don't put any effort into their military power, only three PICs have formulated militaries. PICs have similar strategies on consideration of economic, resource, and environmental security. Most PICs' economies depend on the maritime sector and blue economy. Therefore, the biggest threat to maritime security in PICs is illegal, unregulated, and unreported fishing and piracy. As mentioned above, PICs face problems in managing their natural resources, dealing with transnational crime, protecting their sovereignty especially against major powers such as China[51]. Due to lacking sufficient power and sources, they in a need of cooperation with

---

[48] Tertia & Perwita, op.cit.

[49] Liss, Carolin. "New Actors and the State: Addressing Maritime Security Threats in Southeast Asia." Contemporary Southeast Asia 35, no. 2 (2013): 141-62.

[50] Envall, H. D. P. "The Pacific Islands in Japan's 'Free and Open Indo-Pacific': From 'Slow and Steady' to Strategic Engagement?" Security Challenges 16, no. 1 (2020): 65-77.

[51] Bergin, A., Brewster, D., & Bachhawat, A. Pacific Island Countries. Australian Strategic Policy Institute, 2019, 16-28.

major powers, such as the USA who can be the equal power against China, and between themselves.

As a global power, the USA has a major influence on every security agenda in international relations, and maritime security is one of them. As explained above, after the 11 September attacks, the USA's strategies upon different subject matters were the hot topics for the world to follow. USA's national strategy document for maritime security led other security actors to create their strategies. The United States does not want to lose its influence in maritime security vis-à-vis China, India, or other potential great powers in the maritime environment. Therefore, the United States seeks cooperation with coastal states. The U.S. maritime strategy, A Cooperative Strategy for 21st Century Sea power, places an emphasis on enhancing maritime security cooperation, stating, "Expanded cooperative relationships with other nations will contribute to the security and stability of the maritime domain for the benefit of all. This should be seen primarily as part of the broader U.S. effort to protect the U.S.-led global system - including its maritime and economic elements - rather than as an indication of an intention to pursue cooperative maritime security in the manner postulated by the concept of cooperative security[52] .

The United States' foreign and defense policies in the Indian and Pacific Oceans have evolved over the years. This is at least partly a response to China's advance in the region, as well as a possible perception that the US can no longer leave security in the region to Australia and New Zealand. In a statement to the U.S. Congress, Secretary of State Hillary Clinton warned of the 'unbelievable' competition with China for influence in the Pacific islands[53].

Through the Hawaii-based USINDOPACOM[54] and military bases in Australia, Japan, ROK, Guam, and Diego Garcia agreements with Singapore, Thailand, and the Philippines continue to provide the basis for strategic action in Indo-Pacific for the United States. Especially, engagement with rising power India has also strengthened the United States' presence, particularly in monitoring the Indian Ocean. As tensions rise in Pacific maritime security, the United States remains engaged with multilateral mechanisms such as the ASEAN Defense Minister Meeting Plus, ASEAN Regional Forum, and conducted the largest naval exercise in the world, the Rim of the Pacific, which includes China[55]. As seen in the examples as a gendarme of the seas United States has alliances, military bases, and agreements to protect its position and power in every region of seas which makes the USA one of the most important actors of maritime security around the world.

---

[52] Rahman, C. Concepts of Maritime Security. Centre For Strategic Studies New Zealand, Discussion Papers, 2009, 7(9), 1-66.

[53] Bateman, Sam, and Anthony Bergin. Staying the Course: Australia and Maritime Security in the South Pacific. Report. Australian Strategic Policy Institute, 2011.

[54] United States Indo-Pacific Command

[55] Freier, Nathan, et al.. An Army Transformed: USINDOPACOM Hyper competition and US Army Theater Design. Report. Strategic Studies Institute, US Army War College, 2020. 7-12.

Conclusion

As a buzzword, Maritime Security is one of the security concepts that has been studied and discussed by states in recent years. Major components of international relations such as the United States, United Nations, NATO, European Union have developed their security strategies to protect their maritime environment and interests. As a liberal state, the United States created policies based on cooperation in different regions. This is because the main problems such as terrorism, human trafficking, and illegal markets can only be solved through cooperation. On the other hand, it is clear in the strategies of the United States that the national interests of the United States and its allies have primary importance. Japan, which is an emerging power in the region Indo-Pacific, states that its maritime strategies are based on cooperation with the mentorship of the United States. Japan has a significant position in this region but still does not have enough military power and sources to ensure its security. This situation creates dependence on the US for Japan. The dependence on the great powers is also seen in the case of the countries of Pacific Island and even for Australia. Therefore, it can be said that even the liberal approaches of the states have parts of the realistic view due to the concern of the states for their sovereignty and security.

All states seek cooperation in this area to ensure their survival and protect their national interests. In the securitization process of maritime security, this need for protection interests can also be seen. Declaring and creating strategies for Maritime Security by threats created advantages for actors to decide what is worth protecting according to their interests. These diversified strategies make it even more difficult for actors to find common definitions. The Pacific Ocean is one of the maritime environments where many important components have an influence. Therefore, converging strategies of these components can easily lead to conflicts among these actors. Finding a common definition and creating guidelines for the common good can make it easier for stakeholders to protect their maritime environment.

THE GEOPOLITICS OF INDO PACIFIC REGION

A. İnci Sökmen Alaca[1]

Introduction

The new center of gravity of the world, the Indian Pacific region, is the subject of this article. *"Free and Open Indian Pacific Policy"*, adopted by the USA in 2017, is on the foreign policy agenda. By addressing the geopolitical, geo-economics and geostrategic importance of the region, it will be explained why the USA has implemented this policy. The fact that the competition between China and the US in the global system can result in war is the subject of the article that the dual containment strategy applied to the Soviet Union during the Cold War period and it is a geopolitical area that has gained importance in the context of the alliance relations established with the countries in the region. The importance of the geographical area will be evaluated from the US perspective.

Indian Pacific Region in terms of Geographical Aspect

The Indian Pacific region has gained significance with its American strategic document since 2017 in the field of international policy. This region has become one of the most important geostrategic, geo-economics and world power center regions of the world in terms of the economic, military and political forces of the countries in the Indian Ocean and the Western and Central Pacific Oceans, including the East Asia, South Asia, South East Asia and Oceania regions on a common border. It is the area where the Pacific and Indian oceans merge with trade, infrastructure and diplomacy at the point of the Malacca Strait. In the ancient period, the Indian-Pacific sea region, such as the Mediterranean and the Atlantic Ocean in the 20th century, came to the forefront as the main international sea road in the 21st century. Asia connects Africa, Europe, Oceania and the Americas globally in energy and trade. Geographically, it is also referred to as the Indo-West *Pacific and Indo-Pacific Asia*. There are also those who use *the concept of the Great Indian Ocean* as a single integrated geopolitical domain.[2] Approximately 38 countries, 44% of the world's lands and 65% of the world's population are located in this region.[3]

It covers the western and central areas of the Indian Ocean and the Pacific Ocean. It is subdivided into three subdivisions as Central-East-West Indian

---

[1] Associate Professor, İstanbul Arel University, the Department of International Relations, incisokmen@gmail.com.
[2] Raja Mohan, C. **Samudra Manthan: Sino-Indian Rivalry in the Indo-Pacific,** Washington, DC: Carnegie Endowment for International Peace, 2012.
[3] De, P. "Reshaping Indo-Pacific Cooperation", The Economic Times, 2018, https://economictimes. indiatimes.com/blogs/et-commentary/reshaping-indo-pacific-cooperation/ (Access 22.05.2020)

Pacific. *The Central Indian Pacific* Region has many straits and seas that connect the two oceans. These are the archipelago of Indonesia, the South China Sea, the Philippine Sea, the northern coasts of Australia, the seas surrounding New Guinea, the islands of Micronesia, New Caledonia, the Solomon Islands, Vanuatu, Fiji and the Tonga Islands. Centrally located between the two oceans, this area also boasts a vast marine diversity. Within the *Eastern Indian Pacific*, it originates from the volcanic islands of Marshall, and includes central and south eastern Polynesia, Easter Island, and Hawaii. The *Western Indian Pacific* region covers the western and central parts of the Indian Ocean, which includes the eastern coasts of Africa, the Red Sea, the Gulf of Aden, the Arabian Sea, the Gulf of Bengal and the Andaman Sea, Madagascar, the Seychelles, Comoros, the Mascarene Islands, the Maldives and the Chagos archipelago.

Map 1. Indo Pacific Region[4]

The boundaries of the region are very variable. Most sources include the Indian-Pacific region, Japan to the north, Australia to the south, the Western Pacific islands to the east and India to the west. The eastern coasts of Africa are also located within the borders. Inclusion/removal of China/ Africa within the borders of the region is carried out by politicians who built this new geopolitical area as a competition area of power. Despite this territorial definition that America is not involved in, it is accepted as a part of the region in the USA as a country that carries military and alliance relations to the international policy agenda as a new geopolitical area. The region is of *strategic primary* importance to the American government in terms of its national interest. As a country in the Pacific region, Hawaii, California, Washington, Oregon, and Alaska with five

---

[4] Kumar, A. "Indo-Pacific Security", 2014, http://www.indopacificsecurity.com/2014/05/about.html (Access 22.05.2020).

U.S. states are located on the islands of Guam, American Samoa, Wake Island, and Northern Mariana. It is seen by the American administration as the new center of gravity of the world. It directed the axis of its foreign policy from the Middle East to this region. Chinese authorities refrain from using this definition because it reflects too many American spheres of influence in the Indo-Pacific region.

Importance of the Indian Pacific Region in terms of International Policy

The Indo-Pacific region, which has started to be seen in geopolitical studies since 2011, is not a new conceptualization. In 1920, for the first time, German geopolitical expert Karl Haushofer handled an academic study titled *"Indopazifischen Raum (Indo-Pacific Area)"* and examined the Indian and Chinese civilizations that developed independently of each other as Tibetan borders. Within the conditions of that day, both countries realized more than 50% of the world's gross production and determined that this situation was reached as a result of their activities in sea and ocean areas.[5] Haushofer's evaluations can be argued to have led to the inclusion of India and the Indian Ocean as an element of balance against China in today's American Indian-Pacific strategy. Two very similar countries in terms of population and technological developments, India as a country governed by British colonies and democracy in the past, were chosen as the strategic country to balance America's rival. During the US-India Security dialogue meeting in June 2013, the concept of the *Indo-Pacific Economic Corridor* was adopted. India is connected to East Asia, South Asia, South East Asia via Myanmar. Myanmar is of strategic importance as a gateway. *"Look East"*, which gained importance in India's foreign policy in 1992, was organized as "Act East" in 2014 and it was aimed to be a diplomatic initiative that would increase economic, strategic and cultural relations with Asian Pacific countries at different levels[6]. In September of the same year, China announced its *"One Way One Belt"* project to the world from Kazakhstan Nazarbayev University.

The *geostrategic* importance of the region stems from the fact that it is a buffer zone between the USA and China, that is, between the Atlantic and Pacific regions, which are in great power competition. In addition, by highlighting maritime safety issues, certain transition straits, Bap al-Mandeb and Malacca Straits, have gained strategic importance and regional power conflict areas, especially the South China Sea and East China Sea, have been included.

The three important economies of the world in terms of geo-economics are the USA, China and Japan, and the countries of India, Russia and other

---

[5] Haushofer, E. K., Tambs, A. L. and Brehm, E. J. An English Translation and Analysis of Major General Karl Ernst Haushofer's Geopolitics of the Pacific Ocean: Studies on the Relationship between Geography and History, Lewiston, New York, Edwin Mellen Press, 2002.
[6] Kesavan, V. K. " India's Act East Policy and Regional Cooperation ", Observer Research Foundation, (2020,https://www.orfonline.org/expert-speak/indias-act-east-policy-and-regional-cooperation-61375/ (Access 15.05.2020).

important South Korea and South East Asian Countries (ASEAN), which are among the newly emerging economic forces, are also located in the region. It is known that the ports where the most intense maritime trade takes place and 60% of the global maritime trade takes place in this region.

Geopolitically, the countries with the largest population in the world are the region with the highest number of Muslims and China and India. Three permanent members of the UN Security Council are within the borders of the United States, China and Russia. The fact that the six countries of the world with nuclear power capacity, the USA, Russia, China, India, Pakistan, North Korea, are located within the borders of the region constitutes a *nuclear war risk area* in terms of international and regional security. Sub regional diplomatic formations are available in ASEAN and Quad Security Dialogue (Australia-Japan-India-U.S.). The fact that there are islands under the political rule of France in the Pacific region and that Australia, New Zealand, Papua New Guinea, the Solomon Islands and Tuvalu are members of the British Commonwealth causes both England and France to be included in the region. The free market, led ideologically by the USA, includes pluralism, the liberal world order involving democracy and the economic capitalist, Socialism model encounter based on China's unique communist single party system. At the same time, there are North Korea, Vietnam and Laos communist regimes in the region.[7]

American New Strategy: Transition from the Asia Pacific Strategy to the Indian Pacific Strategy

For the United States, which defines itself as a country belonging to this region, it has been determined as the first important strategy to prevent the emergence of countries/countries that may be rivals/enemies in the region in order to maintain national security and the continuity of its power in the world. Historically, America, which participated in three wars in the Pacific region with World War II, Vietnam War and Korean War, continues to maintain its influence in the region within the framework of a strategic plan based on economy, geostrategy and security/defence.

During the era of former American president Barack Obama, the Asian-Pacific policy developed in the face of the rise of China and the new economic *and political power center of the world was reshaped by the new president Donald Trump, who won the 2017 elections, as "Free* and Open Indo-Pacific-FoIP". This policy, announced at the Asia Economic Cooperation Forum (APEC) 2017 Vietnam meeting, aims to solve problems peacefully, in accordance with international law, free and fair trade based economic development, respecting the sovereign rights of all countries in the region. The term *free* is associated with the continuation of sustainable development, in which all countries can participate regardless of their national power*, and the word free* is associated with the continuation of sustainable

---

[7] Akanksha "Indo-Pacific: The New Geopolitical Construct" Next IAS, 2019, https://blog.nextias.com/indo-pacific-the-new-geo-political-construct (Access 15.05.2020).

development without the obstacle of any state. In both words, it is seen that China's efforts to expand the unilateral sovereignty rights that it wants to make in the region have been opposed. In addition, it was stated that no state alone would be prevented from controlling the Indo-Pacific region.[8] In the 2017 US *National Security Strategy Document*, the region's borders extend from India's west coast to America's west coast, hosting the world's largest population and being the best economically strong area.[9]

Map 2. Asia Pacific and Indo Pacific Regions [10]

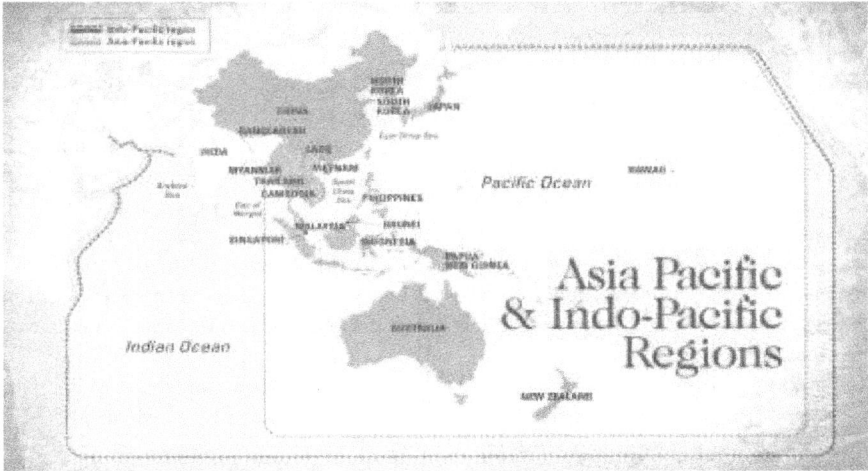

The Free and Open Indo-Pacific Policy is *based* on three issues: economy-regional governance-security. The fact that the region is the most important area for the world economy has also caused economic security to gain importance. The main objective is to maintain international maritime trade uninterruptedly and safely. The presence of pirates off the Malacca Strait and the Gulf of Aden - Somalia is a threat to container trade. Through a region policy based on certain rules and norms, it will be possible to ensure both the continuity of the world economy and the sustainability of the national economies of the countries in the region.

As part of the *"rebalancing"* policy under President Obama, the Asia Pacific region covered the yellow dotted area on the map below. The newly developed

---

[8] FOIP Indo-Pacific Strategy Report, The Department of Defense, (01. 06. 2019), pp. 3-4, https://media.defense.gov/2019/Jul/01/2002152311/-1/-1/1/DEPARTMENT-OF-DEFENSE-INDO-PACIFIC-STRATEGY-REPORT-2019.PDF (Access 20.05.2020).

[9] NSS, National Security Strategy of the United States, The White House Publishing, 2017, p. 46, https://www.whitehouse.gov/wp-content/uploads/2017/12/NSS-Final-12-18-2017-0905-1.pdf (Access 20.05.2020).

[10] Gopalaswamy, B. and Ramachandran, A. " The Shifting Balance of Power in the Indo Pacific", **China & US Focus**, 2017, https://www.chinausfocus.com/peace-security/the-shifting-balance-of-power-in-the-indo-pacific (Access 20.05.2020).

Indian Pacific region shows the red dotted area. This area includes both the Middle East and the eastern coasts of Africa with the addition of the Indian Ocean and India. It has emerged as an important strategic area in terms of including the route of world oil shipment.

The US "Free and Transparent Indo-Pacific Policy " consists of six main issues; 1) Opening of international waters and airspace to everyone without hindrance 2) Elimination of obstacles to international trade and investments 3) Ensuring political liberalization in the region 4) Preventing aggressive behaviour in the region 5) Cooperation with friendly governments 6) II. The continuity of the liberal order established by the USA after World War II.[11]

Within the scope of this policy published on June 1, 2019, in the section related to China, the USA stated that it implemented an external balancing strategy by pursuing both internal balancing and policy of developing alliances and strategic partnerships by trying to increase its own power against China [12]. China is seen as a threat to liberal regional security in the region and as a revisionist country that expands its sovereignty with its military power. In particular, the USA wants the sea and airspace in the region to be safe in its new policy. This policy reveals that China's special privileged rights in the South China Sea, which are not approved by UN Maritime Law, and the declaration of a no-fly zone over the East China Sea in 2013 were not accepted by the USA.[13] In terms of South China Sea problems, the Taiwan Strait and the island of Taiwan have a strategic importance for the American government to reach the region. The Taiwan Strait is also a strategic area in which free passage as international waters should be ensured for American politics and the power diplomacy they apply here is therefore legitimate. The continued flights of the Chinese Air Force on the island and naval exercises in the East China Sea are considered as a demonstration of power for Taiwan by increasing its military presence in the Taiwan Strait and its immediate vicinity, where both Taiwan's independence and the third country involved in this incident are tried to be deterred. [14] The diplomatic alliance relationship he established with Vietnam and the Philippines also brings China and the United States against each other in terms of the South China Sea apart from the Taiwan problem.[15]

In terms of the US, China is seen as an unfair, based on economic intelligence and theft, creating a new addiction relationship by lending, making unfair profits in international trade by decreasing the value of its money, and bringing countries to its environment with coercive practices. This country, which wants to revise

---

[11] Roy, D. Taiwan's Potential Role in the Free and Open Indo-Pacific Strategy: Convergence in the South Pacific, **The National Bureau of Asian Research**, 77, March 2019, pp. 9-10.
[12] FOIP Indo-Pacific Strategy Report, The Department Of Defense, (01. 06. 2019) pp. 7-11, https://media.defense.gov/2019/Jul/01/2002152311/-1/-1/1/DEPARTMENT-OF-DEFENSE-INDO-PACIFIC-STRATEGY-REPORT-2019.PDF (Access 20.05.2020)
[13] FOIP, Ibid, p. 8.
[14] Ibid, p. 31
[15] Carpenter, G. Ted, America's Coming War with China: A Collision Course Over Taiwan, St. Martin's Press, 2006.

the rules-based international order in favour of its own interests, has taken control of the Indo-Pacific region and implicitly referred that China will not be allowed to be the world leader.

In the new global geopolitical environment, the multipolar political structure of the Indo-Pacific region also creates uncertainty and instability due to the power struggle between the United States and China. It is suggested that conflicts may arise in the subjects of land/maritime political domains competition between the two powers, their own space boundaries, expansionism (China annexing Taiwan), encirclement strategy (USA surrounding China with missiles), intervention in their internal affairs (Hong Kong, Tibet and Uighur autonomous regions for China). The establishment of new bilateral and multiple alliance relations with the conflict creates diplomatic solution areas. The United States formed an alliance with Australia, Japan, the Philippines, South Korea and Thailand in the Indian-Pacific region. China, on the other hand, carried out economic cooperation with 51 countries within the scope of the *"One Road One Belt"* project and made serious agreements with France, Germany, Italy and the UK. However, the geographical location of the United States is able to control all three as Pacific, Atlantic and Indian oceans by ensuring that it is more effectively located in the seas than in China. Being a global naval force, which is one of the conditions to be a global hegemony, is in favour of America. We can see the two projects on the map below.

Map 3. One Belt One Road Project Countries and Indo Pacific Region[16]

China considered itself a land power rather than a naval power and determined its dominance in the Eurasian continent as a critical region for world

---

[16] Khadka, D. "Caught Between Indo-Pacific Strategy and BRI", 2020, http://english.lokaantar.com/articles/caught-indo-pacific-strategy-bri/ (Access 25.05.2020).

domination.[17] With the concepts of *"strategic borders"* and *"living space"* developed by the Chinese army since the 1990s, it aims to achieve the national interest goals of China in the lands under the sovereignty of other countries that cross the borders of the state and spread over a wide area. China has implemented a foreign policy and security strategy that combines nationalism and geography and is called *"geopolitical* nationalism. [18] Considering the views of the American historian Alfred Thayer Mahan on being a naval force, the aim of creating a navy with Chinese characteristics was realized. [19] It is among the primary duties of the Chinese army to ensure the safety of energy and commercial goods, especially when transporting by sea. Thus, within the scope of the *"two ocean strategies"* developed, naval activities in the areas of the South China Sea, the Western Pacific and the Indian Ocean have increased their capabilities.[20] The sea bridge road between the lands reaching Indonesia, especially from Thailand via Malaysia and Singapore, is a strategic area in terms of reaching South East Asia. Chinese authorities have adopted the view that a country wishing to control the Pacific and Indian Oceans should keep this region within its political sphere of influence. Chinese leader Xi Jinping's statement that we are *reshaping the geopolitical area* creates the opportunity to penetrate Malaysia, Singapore and Thailand to medium-sized states in the region by controlling this strategic area and connecting both important sea routes and China to Indonesia.[21]

As an energy-dependent country, he determined to make the Indian Ocean effectively safe for the safety of ships coming from the Middle East and Africa within the framework of the *" Pearl Array Strategy"*. Within the scope of this strategy, having the methods of infrastructures of ports whose strategic location is determined, establishing maritime transport companies and becoming dominant in the maritime container are included. The map below shows the ports where China invests in accordance with the Pearl series strategy. These ports are believed to be able to be used as military bases for the Chinese army in the future.[22]

While providing access to the global market, energy transport security and the US/India control power in the Indian ocean are broken. The alternative to the Malacca Strait transit security is the acquisition of the management of the Gwadar port in the southwest of Pakistan in the province of Baluchistan, which is a very important strategic move against the US/India policy.[23]

---

[17] Kaplan, R. D. **The Revenge of Geography,** New York, Random House, 2012, p. 222.

[18] Hughes, C. "Reclassifying Chinese nationalism: The geopolitik turn", **Journal of Contemporary China,** Vol. 20, No. 71, 2011, pp. 602,607.

[19] Diakidis, N. 'An assessment of China's defense strategy in the post-Cold War era: What role for bilateral defense cooperation with Russia?', **Piraeus,** December 2009, pp. 43-46.

[20] Kaplan, op.cit., pp. 53-54.

[21] Fallon, T. 'The new Silk Road: Xi Jinping's grand strategy for Eurasia', **American Foreign Policy Interests,** Vol. 37, No. 3, 2015, p. 140.

[22] Kaplan, op.cit, pp. 50-55.

[23] Khurana, S. G. "China's *String of Pearls* in the Indian Ocean and Its Security Implications", **Journal of Strategic Analysis,** Vol. 32, No. 1, 2008, p. 4.

Map 4. Chinese Pearl Array Strategy and Important Ports[24]

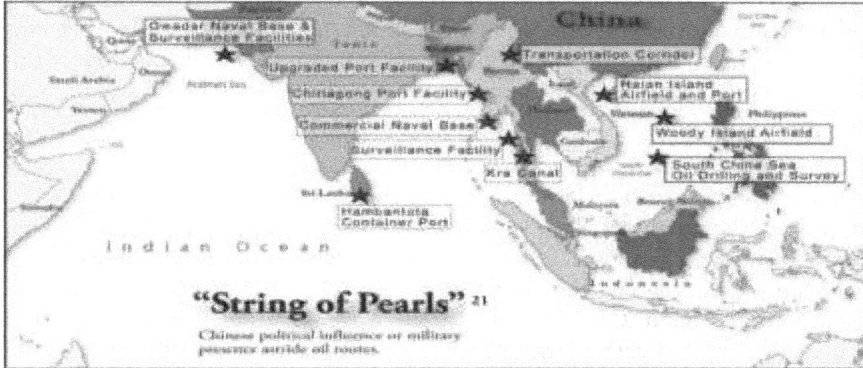

The second country after China in the Indian-Pacific region was shown as Russia, and it was mentioned that it reduced its political isolation after the Ukrainian events by increasing its economic, military and diplomatic relations in the Asian region. During U.S.-China competition and trade/financial wars, it tends to act as an impartial third country. Another country is North Korea. The communist regime, which conducts intercontinental ballistic nuclear missile trials and whose range can reach the US continent, is considered a national threat to the US. Nuclear disarmament and unification with the south is a top priority both for the Korean peninsula, for the region and for the US.

Alliance Relations of the USA in the Indian Pacific Region

In order to achieve America's national goals in the Indo-Pacific region, it has identified a tripartite strategy of being prepared, increasing cooperation with countries, and establishing regional networks. An intensive effort has been made to improve cooperation in the economic, military and defence fields with countries that see China's economic and military strengthening in the region as a competitor/threat against their own interests and that are close to American policies in the region. Japan, India and Australia have been identified as priority countries. In addition, efforts have been made to strengthen their cooperation with South Korea, the Philippines, Thailand, Singapore, Vietnam, Indonesia, Malaysia, Taiwan, New Zealand and Mongolia. The establishment of cooperation with communist Vietnam is a turning point in terms of American foreign policy. Of all these countries, the most critical country is Taiwan, which is on China's primary expansion strategy. This country, which is divided into two as pro-independence and unification within the country, is seen as a hot conflict issue that can bring China and the United States against each other from a military point of view. The United Kingdom, which has island dominance in the Pacific

---

[24] Pejic, I. "China's String of Pearls Project ", Map & Conflict Database, 2016, https://maps.southfront. org/chinas-string-of-pearls-project/ (Access 25.05.2020).

and Indian Ocean region, is thought to be within the regional security network that the United States wants to build in France and Canada. Anti-Chinese alliance relations are not strict blocking as in the cold war, but an opposition or balancing that takes advantage of the opportunities offered by China in economic terms and also cooperates with the United States on security and defence issues.

The most important thing about security is the formation of the Quad-Diamond Alliance, which is formed by Australia-Japan-India-US, as a strategic alliance against China, both to surround it and to prevent it from becoming the only one in Asia. The absence of a unipolar structure under Chinese sovereignty in Asia is a primary priority. They are also seen as a coalition of democracies with naval power in the region, and they also operate within the continuity and spread of liberal world order and values in the region. QUAD is also called *"Three Plus One"* as the US-Japan-Australia and India with a strategic autonomy.[25] India was part of the group of "Non-Aligned" during the Cold War period. In addition to economic cooperation with China-Russia-India and within the BRICS, it is also included in the QUAD in a balanced manner without being a full part of a party. The country concluded strategic cooperation agreements in the economic, defence and political fields with Japan (2000), Russia (2000), USA (2001), China (2005), Australia (2009). In the 1962 war between China and India, due to the support of the USSR, Russia is seen as a more important strategic partner country than the United States.[26] This is considered as a part of multiple alliances in India's foreign policy. It can be argued that the US could not provide the exact unity it wanted against China in the QUAD and that Japan and Australia had intensive economic relations with China and that India was one of the multiple alliances we mentioned.[27]

While the former British colonial India was brought to the forefront as a regional power by the United States, it was also named as the leader of the world economy in 2050 due to low workforce and high technology studies with the second largest world population. India views the Indian ocean as its own geopolitical geographic sphere of influence. The country, which follows a nationalist line in foreign policy, has the idea of uniting with Pakistan, Bhutan, Nepal, Bangladesh, Afghanistan and Burma within the framework of the *"Greater India (Akhand Bharat)"* ideal of far-right nationalist political opinion. In this ideal developed by Arthashastra Chanakya, it was thought that the countries in the region should be under a single administration.[28] Built on Turkish nationalism, this ideal can only allow different religions to coexist with a secular state structure. If Buddhist nationalism prevails in the aforementioned countries,

[25] Doyle, T. and Rumley, D. **The Rise and Return of The Indo-Pacific**, Oxford, Oxford University Press, 2019, p. 54.
[26] Hall, I. "Multi-alignment and Indian Foreign Policy under Narendra Modi", **Round Table,** Vol. 105, No. 3, 2016, pp. 278.
[27] Mohan, ibid.
[28] Parekh, V. "Why "Akhand Bharat" is a pipe dream" , **Huffington Post,** 17 March, 2016, https://www.huffingtonpost.in/varun-parekh/why-akhand-bharat-remains_b_9461132.html (Access 23.05.2020).

unification seems difficult to realize. The same India is included in the concept of economic partnership of Indian-Chinese markets, which is defined as "Chindia" in economic cooperation with China.[29]

The US-Japan alliance relationship has been shown to be the most important factor for peace and development in the Indo-Pacific region. Japan views the North Pacific Ocean, the Sea of Japan and the East China Sea regions as its own sphere of influence. While strengthening its army on the way to re-armament, the policies pursued by China in the East China Sea in the perception of threat to its security, the problem of Russia and the Kuril Islands and the nuclear activities of North Korea on the Korean peninsula, which has geographical proximity to its territories, are considered. In its region, Kuril Islands with Russia, Diaoyu/Senkaku with China and Dokdo/Takeshima island problems with South Korea are still not solved. Japan is of importance in the possible war and defense strategy of the USA in the region due to its geographical proximity in the mainland of China. There are American naval bases and army on the territory of the country. On the island of Okinawa in Japan off the coast of Taiwan, wiretapping systems and American military units carry out the most strategic military missions on the front line. The tripartite defence agreement between the US and South Korea and Japan, the 2007 security agreement with Australia, both strategic cooperation with India in 2000 and unity within the QUAD can be considered as Japan's foreign balancing policies despite China's economic and military rise.

Australia considers the South Pacific region as its own sphere of influence. It attaches importance to its relations in the South Pacific islands and South East Asia. China is Australia's biggest trading partner, but the country is more dependent on the United States in terms of economic and defence/ national security. Joint intelligence sharing is carried out between two countries under the formation of five eyes. In Iraq, Afghanistan and Syria, the country supported US operations. America has more investments in Australia than China on mining, agriculture, and company basis. The SARS-Covid 19 outbreak has increased racist actions against Chinese and Asian individuals in the country. White Anglo-Saxon identity is seen as a threat due to migrations from Asia to its country.[30]

Possibility of War in the Indo-Pacific Region

The Pacific Ocean and Indian Ocean regions are of two distinct strategic importance to the United States. After the war with the Spanish government in the Pacific region in 1898, the United States became a force, including the island of Hawaii. Geographically and geopolitically, it is in a structure that allows American military forces to operate easily. For America, the boundaries of the

---

[29] Ramesh, J. and Talbott, S. **Making sense of Chindia: Reflections on China and India,** India Research Press, 2016.
[30] **Global Times,** "Wolverines represent Washington more than Australia in antagonizing China", 2020, https://www.globaltimes.cn/content/1189993.shtml (Access 22.05.2020).

Pacific region start from Alaska and the Arctic region, extending to Australia. Hawaii, the 50th state of the country, is located in the center of this area. In operations in the Pacific region, the Alaskan and Western coasts, which provide access to the Arctic, are two key regions. What makes the Pacific an important area in terms of national security is the western coasts of the United States and their cities located on these coasts. With the advancement of technology, distances have eliminated their importance, while space capabilities and long-range missile systems have put the preservation of the American mainland at risk.

The Indian Ocean, on the other hand, is the transit route of the energy line from the Middle East and Africa, so a problem here can disrupt all energy needs. China, its biggest rival, is a foreign-dependent country in terms of energy. It is among the priority areas for the continuity of the Middle East and African economy. It can be considered as the most critical region that will determine the result in this period when it competes closely with the USA and China.

American command based in the Indian-Pacific region, USINDOPACOM operates over a wide area. As far as possible in the military defence of the United States, the islands in its own possession close to Asia and India, such as Guam and Diego Garcia, and their bases are trying to stop the arrival towards their own country (such as Japan, Australia). The central point of defence is the island of Hawaii. If the enemy forces cross this line quickly, the eastern coast of America is at risk. For this reason, Hawaii Island was considered on the US defence line as a strategic triangular resistance force field connecting the territory of Guam and Japan and as a manoeuvring area in the equilateral rectangular area connecting the land areas of South Korea, Australia, Singapore and Japan.[31]

The Indian-Pacific region has six nuclear weapons, including China, Russia, India, Pakistan, and North Korea, including the United States. Outside India, in a nuclear missile war within the Chinese-Russian-North Korean alliance, American defences may be insufficient. The missile, which was launched with a one-on-one country during the Cold War, could provide an easier defence. However, the lack of a multi-mechanism system that can neutralize three countries and simultaneously launched missiles may not create the opportunity to realize the second strike capacity of the United States in nuclear missile firing. It may be possible for the United States to be defeated by hitting.

For this reason, it has gained importance that North Korea ceases to be a threat by becoming a nuclear-free country. The country's nuclear capability intercontinental ballistic missile (ICBM-range 5000/5500 km) and submarine ballistic missile (SLBM) trials have led to the implementation of this policy. In 2019, bilateral negotiations between American President Trump and North Korean leader Kim Jong-un on the purification of North Korea from nuclear weapons did not achieve the desired result. Although it is not clear that the North

---

[31] Timberlake, E.; Laird, F. R. and Weitz, R. **Rebuilding American Military Power in The Pacific: A 21st – Century Strategy,** Praeger Security International, 2013.

Korean leader has a health problem and his leadership can be maintained, this issue is of great importance for the US. The goal of uniting the two countries as a single country, which cannot be achieved with the Korean War, may become possible with a new leader after Kim Jong-un. In the South Korean democracy model, it is thought that a threat to the American ally, the new United Korea, the Korean peninsula and US national security will be eliminated by the positive change of the country.

China tries to be prepared for war with a possible America based on asymmetric tactics, which implements the strategy of not giving A2/AD gates as a military system, submarine fleet, satellite warfare exercises in space. China, which is an economic power like Japan but is thought to have no effect on international policy and supported, has assumed the role of the production center of the world economy in accordance with this plan and has followed a foreign policy that determines the principle of peaceful rise and non-interference in internal affairs based on multilateral cooperation as a permanent member of the United Nations Security Council. In fact, the goal is for the US-China to manage the world economy together. Two economically dependent countries have entered a process that has become more tense after the SARS, Covid-19 outbreak and is even thought to be completely completed by the US. In addition to China's spying activities in the field of military and strategic technology, the US Trump government is sceptical of hidden space, artificial intelligence and genetic/bio-technology studies and sees a threat to the national security of the country.

As the leading country of the authoritarian capitalism model, China is also shown to cause the weakening of the liberal political order in the world. Waiting for the outcome of the struggle between globalization and the nation-state/priority-strong US-protective policy lovers within the United States, China is seen as a structural force that will create a revisionist new world order. It is predicted that the British-American interests in many issues will be contradicted, the British-Jewish global capital will take a stand in favour of China and will cause a decrease in its economic and political power for the lonely US. China-India unity comes to the fore for the world economy. The economy of the two rising worlds is thought to place the United States in third place, as Joseph Nye (2015)[32] states in his book The *American Century Is Over?* . It was thought that the US might have problems in its economy, which made China an important force today, before it entered into a hot conflict with China, as its power fell. Decreasing growth rate, high inflation, and rising production costs may shake China economically. The recession of the world economy, the contraction of national economies and the economic collapse of nation states will also have a negative effect on China. It has been considered in counter-policy such as experiencing major natural disasters among the scenarios of experts, being exposed to crises that threaten public health such as SARS and today's SARS Covid-19, failing in armed conflict with any country or internal stability issues related to itself. Hong

---

[32] Nye, J. Is the American Century Over?, Polity Press, 2015.

Kong incidents are an example. An operation that can question its power on global leadership and be exposed to every event in the economic, social and political fields is being implemented against China.

The United States, which still has the strongest army and defence structure in the world, is at risk of losing the islands on which it is located in the Pacific region in sea level rises that will occur with the meltdown of the Arctic region. In addition, the SARS Covid-19 epidemic caused a disease on the USS Theodore Roosevelt aircraft carrier crew, which is located on the open sea and the transmission of which cannot be solved. It has been revealed that its power at sea can be ineffective against a possible virus. Likewise, the epidemic that may spread to the islands may end life in Guam, Mariana, Wake, Midway, Hawaii, Johnston, Howland Baker, Palymra, Jarwis. It can reset obstacles to accessing the American West Coast. In addition, typhoons in the Pacific Ocean, which they experienced in previous wars, can weaken air and sea defence. The American army, which did not experience wars on its own mainland and distributed its military power to the world under various commandments, carries a risk for the national security of the Pacific region within the scope of the new security threats that emerged in 2020.

In the possible war in the Pacific region, Russia is a key country with approximately 6500 nuclear-headed missiles. Like the Soviet Union, which changed the fate of the war in favour of the allies during World War II, the nuclear power capacity will also determine future wars. Using tensions between Cold War-era People's Republic of China leader Mao Zedong and Soviet Union leader Joseph Stalin, the American government visited China in 1972, where President Richard Nixon pioneered the transition to free capitalism in the Chinese economy and initiated a breakthrough in the eastern bloc. China established economically strong ties in the countries within the former Soviet Union, which Russia called the *immediate environment*, and came to an active position in the Eurasian region with Russia's permission. By drawing Russia to their side this time, the Cold War strategy is tried to be applied to a policy aimed at ending China's activities in the Eurasian region. Charles A. Kupcan's (2010)[33] *How Do Enemies Become Friends?* This policy change reminiscent of How Enemies Become Friends seems difficult for Russia. Although the Pentagon waged a limited air and naval war against China in the Pacific region, there is a possibility that this war would turn into a nuclear war and that Russia would be involved. Since submarines are decisive in naval warfare, China aims to improve itself in this field and turn it in favour of superiority.

Today, the Russians experimented in early 2020 and no defence system was established to neutralize the *hypersonic missile systems* in the strategic weapon category faster than the sound entering the military weapon inventory. It is rapidly developing these missiles in China, while in the USA, these missiles are first being tested in the missile firing area in Kauai, one of the Hawaiian Islands,

---

[33] Kupcan, A. C. **How Enemies Become Friends**, Princeton, Princeton University Press, 2010.

and are being prepared to enter them into its inventory. It is planned to develop hypersonic missiles launched from the sea for submarines as well as those launched from the land. In short, military war development competition between the three countries continues rapidly in order to turn the military balance in its favour.

It can be argued that in a possible new Pacific war (such as a low-intensity and conventional hybrid war, information war, cyber war, algorithmic warfare, electromagnetic warfare, space warfare, nuclear war and biological warfare), where more than one war model is used at the same time, it may be difficult for the United States to achieve a definitive victory over China-Russia-North Korea.

Conclusion

With the Free and Open Indo-Pacific Policy, which became the official policy of the USA in 2017, the region has emerged as a new center of gravity in the world's new economic and security issues. The American government, which directed its axis from the Middle East to this region in its foreign policy, aimed to increase its military power and economic cooperation. China, which is in intense competition for the leadership of the world economy in a multipolar international system, North Korea, and Russia, which has become global again, expanded its sphere of influence, reveals the importance of the region for American national interests.

ASEAN AND ITS ROLE IN THE GEOPOLITICS OF THE SOUTH PACIFIC

Ahmet Ateş* and Süleyman Temiz**

Introduction

ASEAN is a key actor in the South Pacific that has the potential to affect geopolitical shifts in the region. Therefore, its role in the geopolitics of the South Pacific should be addressed comprehensively to explain not only the regional politics but also global politics and geopolitical considerations. In that manner, this chapter explores the role of ASEAN in regional politics in two sections. First, this chapter surveys the evolution of ASEAN to explain its main principles over time. Second, it engages two major geopolitical issues in the region, namely Myanmar Crisis and the dispute over the South China Sea, and explores the impact of ASEAN on regional geopolitics.

The Establishment of ASEAN

ASEAN was formed after SEATO,[1] ASA[2], and Maphilindo[3] and has been able to establish relative continuity in its predecessors. It was founded on 8th August 1967 in Bangkok by five countries, Indonesia, Malaysia, Philippines, Singapore, and Thailand, as a multilateral organization of southeast Asian countries. ASEAN gradually expanded with the admission of Brunei Darussalam on 8 January 1984, Vietnam on 28 July 1995, Laos and Myanmar on 23 July 1997, and Cambodia on 30 April 1999.[4] The ASEAN Declaration stated that the aims and objectives of the regional bloc are to accelerate economic growth, social progress, and cultural development in the region through joint efforts in a spirit of equality and partnership to strengthen the foundation of a prosperous and peaceful community.[5] The declaration also stated that the nations of Southeast Asia aim to promote regional peace and stability through respect for justice and the rule of law in relations between countries in the region and adherence to UN principles. ASEAN has adopted certain principles for the effective functioning of the organization, including a consensus-based decision-making mechanism on

---

* Ahmet Ateş, Ph.D. Lecturer, Iğdır University, Faculty of Economics and Administrative Sciences, Department of Political Science and International Relations, Turkey. E-mail: ahmet.ates@igdir.edu.tr.
** Ph.D. Assist. Prof. Süleyman Temiz, Iğdır University, Faculty of Economics and Administrative Sciences, Department of Political Science and International Relations, Turkey.
E-mail: suleyman.temiz@igdir.edu.tr.
[1] Southeast Asia Treaty Organization.
[2] Association of Southeast Asia.
[3] The Greater Malayan Confederation, or Maphilindo (for Malaysia, the Philippines, and Indonesia), was a proposed, non-political confederation of the three Southeast Asian countries in the Malay Archipelago.
[4] https://asean.org/asean/about-asean/history/ (Access 24.05.2021)
[5] https://agreement.asean.org/media/download/20140117154159.pdf (Access 24.05.2021).

the most critical issues, and prioritizes common interests rather than individual interests of member states. It should be noted that the collective stance of the union against communism can be regarded as a great achievement for ASEAN.

The key concepts of ASEAN's enlargement are soft approach and multilateralism. Its slow, quiet but prudent progress in the last five decades led to important achievements for the region, particularly in three issues. First, ASEAN ensured peace and stability in the region. Even though there are controversial border issues between ASEAN members, these issues did not turn into combat between the countries as a result of ASEAN's efforts. Second, it increased regional integration as ten ASEAN members have been integrating their economies and institutions for the last three decades. It is important to note that after the announcement of the ASEAN Charter in 2008, the pace of this integration has dramatically increased. Third, ASEAN is considered as a respected bloc in the international community due to its success at the regional level and its potential to play a role in the issues beyond its borders which can be observed in the ASEAN Plus project (ASEAN +).

There are several internal and external factors affecting the establishment of the ASEAN. However, the most important factor was the emergence of the idea of the need for a regional organization, especially after SEATO, to address the problems in the region. SEATO facilitated external great powers' intervention to the region. Even though it was a political and military pact, its ineffectiveness in preventing member states' actions on their strategic calculations and formulating a common policy caused the states of the region to take a more distant stance against SEATO.[6]

As the Minister of Foreign Affairs of Singapore S. Rajatnam asserts, "ASEAN is considered a capacity to establish practical ways in which it can provide facilities and opportunities not available to each member state on a national basis." [7] Even though it is stated in the ASEAN documents that it can transform a military alliance if the need arises[8], the ASEAN has never become a military pact and has remained a cultural and economic organization.

ASEAN was designed to solve disputes among its members peacefully. However, the political environment of the region tested ASEAN's capacity to promote and sustain peace in the region. For instance, the regime change in Indonesia in the 1960s led to a significant shift in Indonesian policies that posed a challenge to ASEAN's integrity. Likewise, the dispute between the Philippines and Malaysia on the Sabah area and Chinese intervention in former colonial states questioned the ASEAN's power and policies in the region. It should be noted that ASEAN managed to formulate a coherent regional policy particularly

---

[6] Süleyman Temiz, ASEAN ve Güneydoğu Asya Bölgeselciliği Üzerine Etkisi. KAÜİİBFD, Vol 10, No 20, 2019, pp. 1086-1116.
[7] Tarzie Vittachi, "First step to a dream", https://trove.nla.gov.au/newspaper/article/106978000 (Access 05.05.2021).
[8] The Canberra Times, 04.03.1968.

against Chinese intervention in the region.

It was deliberate to reduce the emphasis on political and security issues in ASEAN official documents. The founding leaders of ASEAN intentionally refrained from presenting ASEAN as a new military alliance that may favor or pursue policies of the United States (US) or the United Soviet Socialist Republics (USSR).[9] It is important to note that even though it was not stressed as a regional security organization on purpose, the main aim of the establishment of the ASEAN was increasing the security of the region. In that manner, ASEAN underwent a transformation and became one of the most important international organizations in the world. This transformation started in 1976 after the Bali Summit.

Bali Summit and the Transformation of the ASEAN

The first ASEAN Heads of Government meeting was held on 23-24 February 1976 in Bali.[10] A joint statement was published after this meeting. During the meeting, the activities of ASEAN since its establishment in 1967 were reviewed and current disputes in the region were discussed. It was also announced that ASEAN was ready to cooperate with other regional and global actors to cultivate fruitful relations and to pursue a win-win policy to contribute to the security and prosperity of the region. Thereby, the Treaty of Amity and Cooperation in Southeast Asia and the ASEAN Concord Declaration were signed at this summit.[11]

This first summit was especially crucial and was a milestone in the history of ASEAN because the decisions taken at the summit led to the transformation of the organization. It is important to note that the political environment played a vital role in this summit. On the one hand, the withdrawal of the US from the region, the unification of Vietnam, and the aggression of China were catalysts to the reactivation of the ASEAN in 1976. On the other hand, Malaysia and Thailand pushed their agenda, inclusion of Indochina and Burma to the ASEAN, prior to the summit. While Malaysia aimed to use the expansion of the ASEAN under its neutralization policy, Thailand, under the governance of Kukrit Pramoj, aimed to exploit Communist victories in Indochina.

The Bali Summit marked the beginning of the transformation of ASEAN because efforts for regional integration were intensified after the summit. It should be noted that although economic, social, and cultural cooperation was a clear goal of ASEAN, socio-cultural cooperation has been given an even lower priority in that time, while economic cooperation has also progressed at a slow pace. However, the emergence of a communist Indochina in 1975 brought a

---

[9] Süleyman Temiz, ASEAN Güneydoğu Asya Ülkeleri Birliği Siyasi Yapısı ve Gelişimi, Ankara, Gazi Kitabevi, 2020, p.117.

[10] https://asean.org/?static_post=declaration-of-asean-concord-indonesia-24-february-1976 (Access 24.05.2021).

[11] https://trove.nla.gov.au/newspaper/article/230403588/24788980 (Access 01.05.2021).

common challenge for the member states and cultivated a cooperative environment and a sense of common security. The Bali Summit laid the framework for closer political cooperation and a comprehensive regional integration under the ASEAN, which is the second most successful regional organization after the European Union (EU). [12]

Another milestone in the history of the ASEAN is the 1992 ASEAN Summit. As in the Bali Summit in 1976, leaders of the member states were compelled to cope with significant changes in the regional order. Considering it took nine years for the ASEAN to meet its first summit in 1976, it would be fair to say that ASEAN leaders at the summit in 1992 demonstrated that they came to Singapore with a sense of mission and purpose due to changing political and security environment as then-Malaysian Prime Minister Mahathir stressed the motivation in his speech;

> *"This Meeting is timely because ASEAN needs to consider appropriate responses to the profound changes that have taken place in the world since the last ASEAN Summit in Manila in 1987. The final disposition of the new global political and economic order is uncertain but we must ready ourselves for all the possible mutations of this order. In South East Asia itself changes will take place, and the form of cooperation which will result must be such as to strengthen our region and keep it continuously dynamic."* [13]

Shifts in the global and regional order such as the end of the Cold War and the rapprochement of Vietnam and Laos to member states of the ASEAN have led the organization to reassess the status and membership of these states and the role of the ASEAN in global politics as then-Singapore Foreign Minister Wong Kan Seng asserted in his speech;

> *"In a successful pro-Western third world grouping, ASEAN has been successful because the West has a vital interest… We must work harder to keep ASEAN fit for its purpose. In addition, we must ensure that the union can adapt to the demands of the rapidly changing world."* [14]

This statement essentially summarizes the transformation of the ASEAN after the end of the Cold War and points to the importance of the ASEAN in global politics. As a result of a reduction in security concerns after the end of the Cold War, the primary aim of the ASEAN became financial integration. It is important to emphasize that in addition to bilateral and multilateral agreements signed at the summit, the ASEAN effectively managed the divergent interests and perspectives of the member states which also shows the improving diplomatic capacity of the ASEAN.

ASEAN has expanded over time and incorporated Vietnam, Myanmar, Laos,

---

[12] Barry Desker, "The 1976 Bali Summit: ASEAN Shifts Gears". **50 Years of Asean And Singapore,** Tommy Koh, Sharon Seah, Chang Li Lin (Ed), Singapore, World Scientific, 2017, p. 23.
[13] http://www.mahathir.com/malaysia/speeches/1992/1992-01-27.php (Access 10.05.2021).
[14] **The Straits Times**, (23.03.1990), p.26.

Cambodia. Being a member of the ASEAN brought several geostrategic and practical advantages to these countries. First, ASEAN is a key organization for regional integration and creates a favorable regional environment for nation-building and defense. In the last twenty-five years, Indochina countries have worked with other ASEAN member states to build a war-free and cooperative South Asia. In addition to promoting intra-ASEAN cooperation, it has established strategic partnerships and comprehensive partnership frameworks with neighboring countries, authorities, and other key partners. The rising importance of these countries in ASEAN has helped them to gain international support for the protection of their political and financial interests, including the South China Sea issue.

Second, joining ASEAN helped CMLV[15] countries to receive funding and expertise to foster their development to integrate them into the regional political and financial system. For instance, Vietnam actively participated in financial trade agreements (FTA) via ASEAN such as the Asia-Pacific Economic Cooperation (APEC), the Asia-Europe Meeting (ASEM), the World Trade Organization (WTO), and the Comprehensive and Progressive Agreement for the Trans-Pacific Partnership (CPTPP). Moreover, the EU-Vietnam Free Trade Agreement (EVFTA) allowed it to advance reforms, expand markets, increase exports and attract investment to the country.[16]

Third, the integration of CMVL to ASEAN helped to revise these countries' diplomatic encounters and being a part of multilateral diplomacy. For instance, after joining the ASEAN, Vietnam became temporary members of the United Nations Security Council (UNSC) in 2008-2009 and 2020-2021. Likewise, it hosted the APEC Summit in 2006 and 2017. In other words, Vietnam had the chance to participate in global cooperation to solve global problems such as climate change and COVID19.

Fourth, the inclusion of CMLV to ASEAN helped these countries to improve their diplomatic skills, expertise, and required workforce and to pursue more confident foreign policies. Under the common theme of the ASEAN in 2020, Harmonious and Responsive, these countries actively engaged in diplomatic interactions and played a vital role in ASEAN's policymaking in the last year. [17]

Among CMLV, Myanmar has unique importance due to its geopolitical importance and Rohingya issue. Hence, the role of ASEAN in the politics of Myanmar and ASEAN-Myanmar relations are discussed more in detail below.

ASEAN and Myanmar

It is known that the decision of the Myanmar government to join ASEAN is due to both political and economic reasons. Politically, the Myanmar

---

[15] Cambodia, Myanmar, Laos, Vietnam.
[16] Temiz, ASEAN Güneydoğu Asya Ülkeleri Birliği, Siyasi Yapısı ve Gelişimi, p.138.
[17] https://en.nhandan.com.vn/politics/external-relations/item/8919502 (Access 29.04.2021)

government needed international recognition, especially in the face of international isolation from the US and the EU. Economically, it needs assistance and financial aid for economic development. However, Myanmar officials insisted that the decision to join ASEAN was not a reactive process but rather a proactive process based on changing local and international conditions. As Myanmar Foreign Minister Ohn Gyaw put it, Myanmar wanted to be part of the "common destiny" of ASEAN and increase the welfare of southeast Asian countries. [18]

While ASEAN countries were worried that Myanmar would enter China's sphere of influence and diminish the regional stability, Myanmar has also begun to feel hesitant in the face of China's growing influence in the country. Hence, Myanmar's decision to join ASEAN is also partly due to its desire to be protected against increased Chinese influence in Myanmar. Indeed, in the new geopolitical configuration of post-Cold War international politics, a closer Sino-Myanmar relationship was in the interests of both sides. In the context of China's growing influence, Southeast Asia could be divided again but the region had just come out of a split and could not afford to return. Therefore, Myanmar gained more importance in the geopolitical considerations of the region and ASEAN welcomed the country to the organization. In addition to geopolitical needs, there were individual requests of the member states' leaders to include Myanmar in ASEAN. For instance, then-Malaysian Prime Minister Mahatmir wanted the inclusion of Myanmar to ASEAN to increase the efficiency of the organization as he asserts in one of his speeches in 1996;

> *"Myanmar of today, is quite different from the Myanmar of many years ago. And we claim that it is because of our constructive engagement that Myanmar has changed. So if anybody says that constructive engagement has got no effect on Burma, or Myanmar, then they must be thoroughly blind."* [19]

Indonesian President Suharto also supported Myanmar's involvement in ASEAN to alleviate ASEAN's authoritarian image in the international community. Furthermore, the pressure from Western countries to Myanmar to not joining the ASEAN solidified Malaysian and Indonesian perceptions on this issue and led to the promotion of welcoming Myanmar to ASEAN. In a nutshell, Myanmar's inclusion in ASEAN was a result of the intersection of both Myanmar's and ASEAN's interests.

Joining ASEAN was a major diplomatic success for Myanmar in a time that the Western countries implemented both political and financial pressure tools to Myanmar and ASEAN to prevent its membership in the organization. In that manner, it is possible to argue that Myanmar's inclusion in ASEAN is in spite of the international pressures is a sign of the Asian brotherhood and regional integration. By joining ASEAN, Myanmar was able to resist pressure groups via

---

[18] https://asean.org/?static_post=opening-statement-by-he-u-ohn-gyaw-minister-for-foreign-affairs-of-myanmar (Access 25.04.2021).

[19] https://www.burmalibrary.org/reg.burma/archives/199612/msg00051.html (Access 04.05.2021).

ASEAN forums and held its political stance on several issues. Being a member of ASEAN also led to financial direct investments to countries from the other member states.

When flexible engagement policy[20] on constructive interference was discussed in the ASEAN Foreign Ministers meeting, it was harshly criticized by Indonesia, Vietnam, Myanmar, Laos, and Malaysia. Only the Philippines supported Thailand's proposal. Even though there was not common support for the proposal, the Myanmar government launched a media campaign and declared that any change in ASEAN's long-standing policy of non-intervention in other countries' internal affairs was unacceptable. However, ASEAN's interest in national reconciliation in Myanmar peaked particularly after the massacre in Myanmar on 30th May 2003.[21]

The enhanced interaction of ASEAN has ensured that the Myanmar government cannot remain aloof or indifferent to ASEAN's concerns. At the same time, the Thailand government has introduced the process later known as the "Bangkok Process", a forum for discussing the national reconciliation process in Myanmar regarding the peace, security, and stability of the region. When the Myanmar government realized that the process would draw attention from the international community and receive support from ASEAN, Myanmar found it difficult to make diplomatic maneuvers. Therefore, it prepared a "Myanmar Road Map" at the end of August 2003 as a counter move to refrain ASEAN from intervening in the conflict.[22]

When the ASEAN Summit was held in October 2003, the Myanmar delegation initiated an agenda so that ASEAN would not need to put further pressure on Myanmar. Even at the end of the summit, ASEAN leaders took a conciliatory attitude in their communiqués.[23] This example showed that the Myanmar government cannot remain indifferent to ASEAN's concerns considering the "Myanmar Road Map" would not have been realized without the ASEAN's pressure.

Myanmar's position in the organization was questioned in 2005 again because Myanmar was to take over the ASEAN presidency in 2006. However, this presidential mandate of Myanmar has been challenged by political opposition inside and outside ASEAN. The Myanmar government faced increasing pressure from the western and some ASEAN countries to renounce the ASEAN

---

[20] Maung Aung Myoe, "Regionalism in Myanmar's Foreign Policy", **Asia Research Institute**, Working Paper Series No:73, 2006, p.18, https://ari.nus.edu.sg/wp-content/uploads/2018/10/wps06_073.pdf (Access 29.04.2021).
[21] The Depayin massacre occurred on 30 May 2003 in Tabayin (Depayin), a town in Myanmar's Sagaing Division (now Sagaing Region), when at least 70 people associated with the National League for Democracy were killed by a government-sponsored mob. Khin Nyunt, formerly the country's prime minister, claimed that he personally intervened to save Aung San Suu Kyi's life during the massacre, by mobilising his men to bring her to a safe location at a nearby army cantonment. https://www.irrawaddy.com/news/burma/khin-nyunt-interrogated-over-saving-suu-kyi-claim.html (Accessed 11.05.2021)
[22] Myoe, **ibid**, p.20.
[23] **Ibid,** pp.20-22.

presidency in 2006. The US and the EU have openly declared that they will boycott all ASEAN meetings if Myanmar becomes the term president.[24] Then-US Secretary of State Condolezza Rice explicitly stated that if there is no progress in Myanmar's democratization process, she will not attend the annual ministerial meeting in 2007.[25] Meanwhile, Myanmar received diplomatic support for its term presidency. ASEAN, on the other hand, reiterated organizations' main principle, non-interference in the internal affairs of member states, and let Myanmar come up with a decision.

Even though the Foreign Minister of Myanmar Nyan Win assured that Myanmar would not burden the regional unity in the ASEAN Minister of Foreign Affairs meeting[26], increasing pressure from the ASEAN members, namely Thailand, Malaysia, Cambodia, and the Philippines, forced Myanmar to give up its rotating presidency due to its weak human rights record and the slow pace of progress in the democratic transition led Myanmar to relinquish the ASEAN presidency in 2006.[27] This crisis was a test for Myanmar's commitment to regionalism since Myanmar's decision to take over the ASEAN presidency could split member states and damage the ASEAN's image. The decision of the Myanmar government ended a debate that might have split ASEAN and overshadowed previous ASEAN meetings in Manila and Vientiane. Even though Myanmar's reiteration of its commitment to ASEAN was initially considered a diplomatic success for Myanmar, Myanmar's reluctance for carrying out democratic reforms was considered shameful for other ASEAN members. Malaysian Foreign Minister's speech in the Foreign Ministers meeting held on 9th December 2005 shows the disturbance of other members:

> *"We discussed the Myanmar problem and the need for Myanmar to be more sensitive to the wishes of the international community. We registered our desire to see the political process and the map. Although Myanmar is an internal issue, we believe there should be some concrete actions. In order for all of us to be able to defend Myanmar, Myanmar must show us gestures that respect the roadmap and the position of Aung San Suu Kyi."*[28]

Despite the change in the principle of non-intervention has changed, Myanmar continues its commitment to the ASEAN. ASEAN's constructive engagement, which is later changed to enhanced interaction, fits in Myanmar's policies. Myanmar's Roadmap and Myanmar's decision to leave the ASEAN presidency have shown that Myanmar has given due importance to the ASEAN factor in its decisions particularly because of increasing non-traditional security

---

[24] Magnus Peterson, "Myanmar in EU–ASEAN Relations", **Asia Europe Journal**, Vol. 4, No. 4, 2006, pp.563–581.

[25] https://www.nytimes.com/2005/07/12/world/asia/rice-in-southeast-asia-draws-fire-for-plan-to-avoid-forum.html (Access 10.05.2021).

[26] Myoe, **ibid.**, p.23.

[27] https://asean.org/?static_post=statement-by-the-asean-foreign-ministers-vientiane-25-july-2005-2 (Access 24.04.2021).

[28] https://www.nytimes.com/2005/12/09/world/asia/myanmar-gets-stern-warning-from-asean.html (Access 24.04.2021).

threats both at national and regional levels. However, two key factors will play a crucial role in Myanmar's future in the ASEAN.

First, the degree of foreign involvement in ASEAN affairs will determine Myanmar's future in the organization. If ASEAN cannot pursue its own agenda on the issue and global actors outside of the region start to determine regional affairs, Myanmar will be reluctant to cooperate in regional affairs under ASEAN. Second, ASEAN-China relations will be important regarding Myanmar's future in the organization. Myanmar regularly expresses concern about the deployment of foreign forces in Southeast Asia to balance China.[29]

The ASEAN Way

Several regionalism experts assert that regional integration plays a vital role in resolving disputes.[30] As the most important regional organization in the Southeast Asia region, ASEAN has its own mechanism for resolving the disputes called the "ASEAN Way". It is important to note that ASEAN Way is based on the principles of respecting sovereignty and non-intervention. There are four elements in the ASEAN Way.

First, there is the non-interference principle. Articles 2 (a) and 2 (b) of the ASEAN Charter states that all ASEAN members must respect the independence of each country and not interfere with internal affairs.[31] This principle is also enshrined in Article 2 (4) of the UN Charter.[32] As ASEAN advocates mutual respect, it emphasizes the principle that all internal problems must be resolved by its own government. Second, there is the principle of soft diplomacy. As ASEAN aims to avoid major conflicts between member states that could lead to war, the personal approach becomes a way to resolve disputes. In other words, soft diplomacy is the first and only thing to do in case of a conflict between member states.

Third, there is no use of the power principle. No matter how bad the conflict is, ASEAN member states have stated that they will never use force to resolve the conflict. Unlike the United Nations (UN) which can implement embargoes and military intervention, ASEAN prefers to use informal ways to prevent escalation of the conflict. In the case of human rights violations, ASEAN pledges to assist in humanitarian aid through the ASEAN Humanitarian Aid Coordination Center, rather than engaging in humanitarian intervention or so-called military intervention. Fourth, there is the principle of decision-making through consensus. In ASEAN, each member has the same position as the

---

[29] https://www.state.gov/u-s-relations-with-burma/ (Access 10.05.2021); Myoe, op.cit, pp.29-30.
[30] Jürgen Haacke & Noel M. Morada, Cooperative Security in the Asia-Pacific-The ASEAN Regional Forum, Routledge, Oxon, 2010. Amitav Acharya, Constructing a Security Community in Southeast Asia: ASEAN and the Problem of Regional Order, Routledge, Oxon, 2014. Alice D. Ba, (Re)Negotiating East and Southeast Asia, Stanford University Press, Stanford, 2009.
[31] https://asean.org/wp-content/uploads/images/archive/publications/ASEAN-Charter.pdf (Access 25.04.2021).
[32] https://unctad.org/system/files/official-document/rmt2018_en.pdf (Access 01.05.2021).

decision-makers. Therefore, there is no voting in the process. All issues are discussed with consensus in order to seek the best solution for an issue.

Altogether, these four elements constitute the ASEAN Road, which is different from other regional organizations. Although some experts consider ASEAN to be too lenient in some human rights situations, it should be noted that it successfully maintains peace among ASEAN members. Therefore, disputes in the region have not escalated to war so far.[33]

The ASEAN Regional Forum (ARF)

The ASEAN Regional Forum (ARF) was created in July 1994 to hold formal consultations on peace and security issues and was also designated as a regional multilateral Asia-Pacific forum. Unique among international organizations of its kind, this forum is a structure where minimal institutionalization, unanimous decision making, and "first-class" (official) and "second class" (informal) diplomacy are used. [34] First-line diplomatic meetings consist of interviews with prominent officials to discuss security measures, while second-line meetings take place between delegations of scientists and academics, statesmen, representatives of private think tanks, and other individuals and organizations. Constructive dialogue and consultation mechanisms on political and security issues related to common interests are encouraged in this forum. Furthermore, the ARF makes a significant contribution to the efforts for confidence-building and preventive diplomacy in the Asia-Pacific region. Likewise, the agenda of the ARF includes improving multilateral discussion on regional issues, mutual trust, dialogue, and networking on security issues.[35]

The ASEAN Regional Forum also serves as an important platform for the establishment of a security dialogue in the Indo-Pacific region as it is a platform where members can discuss current security issues and develop joint measures to increase peace and security in the region. The ARF has twenty-seven members: ten ASEAN members[36], the ASEAN dialogue partners[37], together with Bangladesh, the Democratic People's Republic of Korea, Mongolia, Pakistan, Sri Lanka, and East Timor, Papua New Guinea as observers.[38]

The objectives of the ARF were declared in the statement of the first ARF President in 1994 as promoting constructive dialogue and consultation on political and security issues of common interest and concerns and making a

---

[33] Adli Hazmi, **"What is ASEAN Way?"** https://seasia.co/2020/01/21/what-is-asean-way (Access 02.05.2021).

[34] http://aseanregionalforum.asean.org/about-arf/ (Access 26.04.2021).

[35] E. Goh, (2018). "ASEAN-Led Multilateralism and Regional Order: The Great Power", **International Relations and Asia's Southern Tier Bargain Deficit**. G. Rozman, & J. C. Liow (Ed), Singapore, Palgrave Macmillan, 2018, p.49.

[36] Brunei, Cambodia, Indonesia, Laos, Malaysia, Myanmar, Philippines, Singapore, Thailand and Vietnam.

[37] Australia, Canada, China, the European Union, India, Japan, New Zealand, the Republic of Korea, Russia and the USA.

[38] http://aseanregionalforum.asean.org/about-arf/ (Access 26.04.2021).

significant contribution to efforts towards confidence-building and preventive diplomacy in the Asia-Pacific region. At the 27th ASEAN Ministerial Meeting held in 1994, it was stated that the ARF could become an effective advisory Asia-Pacific Forum to encourage open dialogue on political and security cooperation in the region.[39] In that manner, ASEAN emphasized the need to work in harmony with ARF partners to create a more predictable and constructive relationship model in the Asia Pacific. Despite the differences and diversity between the members' perspectives, it was stated that the forum would contribute to security and cooperation in the region.[40]

The survival of the ASEAN Regional Forum (ARF) is a success in itself, given that many policymakers and experts were initially skeptical of its applicability and utility. The regional imbalances of great power, conflicting national interests, and the unfamiliarity of some countries in the region with multilateralism are often cited as obstacles to agreeing and acting on common security issues in the Southeast Asian region. However, while it's important that ARF has a twenty-six-year history, survival does not necessarily mean success.[41]

The ARF members not only have a regional influence but also have the ability to transform regional security because the ARF consists of countries with a total of more than three-quarters of the World GDP and significant military expenditure. To address regional security, the participants identified three stages of the development of the ARF. These are building trust, preventive diplomacy, and peaceful resolution of conflicts.[42]

One of the main aims of the ARF was to interact with North Korea, China, and Russia as responsible members and great powers within the platform. While the three countries did not have the ability to forcefully challenge the status quo, they never internalized the legitimacy of a US-based regional order. On the contrary, as China gained power, it began to develop its relations with other countries in the region, while embracing its regional vision. In that manner, the primary goal was defined as developing a more satisfactory constructive relationship model in the region in the first statement of the ARF's president.[43] An important step with the ARF has been to develop preventive diplomacy mechanisms that will allow designated representatives to actively meditate to relieve tension through their dialogue. However, attempts towards achieving this goal took place in a competitive manner among the participants.[44] Therefore, it took seventeen years for ARF to develop a work plan that includes principles of

[39] Süleyman Temiz, "Asya-Pasifik'te Uluslararası ve Bölgesel Güvenliğe Yönelik Politika Geliştirme Mekanizması: ASEAN Bölgesel Forumu". **Küresel Terör ve Güvenlik Politikaları**, H. Acar (Ed), Ankara, Nobel, 2020, pp.373-374.
[40] http://worldjpn.grips.ac.jp/documents/texts/arf/19940725.O1E.html (Access 19.04.2021).
[41] Amitav Acharya, "ASEAN in 2030", **East Asia Forum**: https://www.eastasiaforum.org/2011/02/15/asean-in-2030/ (Access 29.04.2021).
[42] http://worldjpn.grips.ac.jp/documents/texts/arf/19940725.O1E.html (Access 19.04.2021).
[43] https://2001-2009.state.gov/t/ac/csbm/rd/4377.htm (Access 05.05.2021).
[44] T. Yuzawa, "The Evolution of Preventive Diplomacy in the ASEAN Regional Forum: Problems and Prospects", **Asian Survey**, Vol. 46, No. 5, 2006, pp.785-790.

preventive diplomacy and identifies confidence-building measures that existed or were previously proposed.[45]

The ARF's inability to address current geopolitical realities should not be too surprising. China considers the USA as a non-regional state that intervenes in intra-regional developments with the support of Russia. China claims that it has freedom of movement in Asian waters, while Japan and Australia support the US. The ARF, on the other hand, can be considered as a very favorable showcase for soft competition between the US and China in the region and setting a nuanced agenda in this power struggle. ARF participants acknowledged the need to foster a more common sense of security and establish a more effective regional security framework.[46]

Participants of the twenty-first ARF meeting in 2014 have reached an agreement on identifying the main pillars of cooperation. These are humanitarian assistance and disaster relief, countering terrorism, preventing transnational crime, and disarmament, and maritime security. It is important to note that the importance of non-traditional security threats has been increasing in determining the ARF security agenda. On the one hand, Asia is the continent most affected by natural disasters, and the United Nations predicts that regional countries may lose 160 billion dollars each year by 2030.[47] On the other hand, transnational crime is expected to increase in the region. These shifts in the security environment made the ARF the main security forum in the region. Current geostrategic changes, the increasing need for dialogue, the informal and non-threatening dialogue process of the ASEAN are other factors that boosted the importance of ASEAN in regional and global politics. In other words, Although ASEAN has come under criticism for its growing centrality, ASEAN's position in the driver's seat of the forum remains solid.[48]

The ARF is considered to be a unique organization It also advances to all participants at a comfortable pace. To ensure integrity, ARF is not too fast for those who want to go slow, and not too slow for those who want to go fast. While it looks at what can be done in the long run, it also strives to pursue what is possible. For the further development of the ARF, reaching a common understanding and consensus on the concept, definition, and principles of preventive diplomacy seems extremely strategic for future interactions.[49]

---

[45] R. Emmers & S. T. See, "The ASEAN Regional Forum and Preventive Diplomacy: Built to Fail?" **Asian Security**, Vol. 7, No. 1, 2011, pp. 44–60.

[46] https://www.mofa.go.jp/region/asia-paci/asean/conference/arf/state0306.html (Access 01.05.2021).

[47] D. Guha-Sapir, P. Hoyois, P. Wallemacq & R. Below, "Annual Disaster Statistical Review 2016 The Numbers and Trends" https://reliefweb.int/sites/reliefweb.int/files/resources/adsr_2016.pdf (Access 26.04.2021).

[48] J. Haacke & N. M. Morada, "The ASEAN Regional Forum and cooperative", **Cooperative Security in the Asia-Pacific: The ASEAN Regional Forum,** J. Haacke, & N. M. Morada (Ed), Oxon, UK: Routledge, 2010, p.3-5.

[49] Temiz, Asya-Pasifik'te Uluslararası ve Bölgesel Güvenliğe Yönelik Politika Geliştirme Mekanizması: ASEAN Bölgesel Forumu, p.391.

ASEAN and the South China Sea

The growing influence of ASEAN over the region over time led to regional solidarity against China on the South China Sea issue. China refused to discuss the South China Sea issue with any states or multilateral organization for a long time. On July 22, 1992, under the Philippines presidency, ASEAN called for the Manila Declaration on the South China Sea for the peaceful settlement of judicial problems, the implementation of individual restrictions in the region, and for cooperation on a number of common sea issues.[50] China also rejected the invitation of ASEAN to sign the Manila Declaration. Despite conflict among ASEAN's four members on this issue, ASEAN acted in solidarity and eventually persuaded China to join to discuss issues under the ASEAN-China umbrella.

China began to put signs of sovereignty on the Spratly archipelago in February 1995. In the same year, China settled on the Mischief Reef islands and quickly built military facilities on the islands.[51] By October 1998, China sent four military supply ships and approximately 100 workers to the islands and completed the construction in 1999.[52] The Chinese facilities on the Mischief Reef islands were just over 100 km from the Philippines and constituted a major threat to both the Philippines and regional security. As a result of China's aggressive posture in the region, tensions between China and the Philippines have rapidly risen.

ASEAN stepped in to solve this problem peacefully. In that manner, ASEAN's member states have provided strong support to the Philippines. After ASEAN's involvement on the issue, the Declaration of Action of the Parties in the South China Sea was signed by the foreign ministers of China and ASEAN in 2002. The signatory parties committed to the peaceful settlement of disputes in the region, the freedom of shipping and flight on the South China Sea, and withdrawal of Chinese occupation on the islands.[53] The parties also pledged to cooperate in environmental protection, scientific research, transportation, and communication security, search and rescue and the fight against international crimes in the South China Sea. It should be noted that ASEAN countries have worked together and individually with China on the implementation of the declaration.

The declaration was a crucial milestone in preserving peace and stability in the region because the tension in the South China Sea has begun to calm down after the declaration, with the atmosphere of trust that emerged with both ASEAN's joint action as a unity and China's eventual softening of its policy. However, this maritime zone between China and the territories of

[50] https://asean.org/?static_post=joint-communique-25th-asean-ministerial-meeting-manila-philippines-21-22-july-1992 (Access 03.05.2021).
[51] Temiz, ASEAN Güneydoğu Asya Ülkeleri Birliği Siyasi Yapısı ve Gelişimi, p.134.
[52] https://nationalinterest.org/feature/how-china-slow-conquering-south-china-sea-151811 (Access 24.05.2021).
[53] https://asean.org/?static_post=declaration-on-the-conduct-of-parties-in-the-south-china-sea-2 (Access 01.05.2021).

southeast Asia remained a potential source of contention since the problems within the domain were not fully resolved in the declaration.

The South China Sea is in the heart of southeast Asia. Technically, it has the status of a semi-closed sea, according to the United Nations Convention on the Law of the Sea (UNCLOS), where coastal states are encouraged to "cooperate in exercising their rights and duties."[54] The geographic core of the dispute is the Spratly archipelago, which stretches over 400,000 km^2 of the South China Sea and consists of over a hundred islets, reefs, and rocks.[55] Because each coastal state has been aiming to get sovereignty and jurisdiction over the region, the dominant feature of relations between coastal states has been competition rather than cooperation. Also, the contested regions of the South China Sea are vital because they are part of the strategic waterway of sea routes from East Asia to the Middle East. The US considers the freedom of passage of American naval ships across the South China Sea as a vital security interest. Therefore, it demands a peaceful resolution of disputes.

Regional countries, on the other hand, evaluate the dispute from a more resource-based perspective. For regional countries, the dispute over the region is also a dispute over controlling the oil and natural gas reserves in the area. For instance, the proven reserves in the region are estimated to be 7 billion barrels of oil.[56] Therefore, Brunei, Malaysia, the Philippines, Vietnam, and Indonesia strictly pursue energy-driven policies.

However, there is no reliable data for proven energy reserves since there is not major drilling in the center of the South China Sea. According to the very optimistic and highly speculative Chinese estimates, there are 213 billion barrels of oil in the region, 26 trillion m^3 in the Spratly in Islands, and 56 trillion m^3 in the entire South China Sea. Moreover, a US research indicates that there are 11 billion barrels of oil, 55 trillion m^3 of natural gas reserves in the region.[57] Even though the estimation of the resources differs, the appeal of taking advantage of these potential reserves poses a challenge to regional security.

Nearly half of the Spratly Islands are occupied or garrisoned by China. In addition to China, Malaysia, the Philippines, Vietnam, and Taiwan also claimed rights on the islands. The basis of both China's and Vietnam's claims stems from historical elements. For China, this goes back to the Han Dynasty which ruled twenty-three centuries ago. Per Vietnam, this region is a colonial heritage of the country. The Malaysia and Brunei claims are based on the continental shelf expansion while the Philippines gets involved with claims of proximity and

---

[54] https://www.un.org/Depts/los/convention_agreements/texts/unclos/closindx.htm (Access 01.05. 2021).
[55] Temiz, ASEAN Güneydoğu Asya Ülkeleri Birliği Siyasi Yapısı ve Gelişimi, pp.202-203.
[56] **Ibid**, p. 202.
[57] https://www.eia.gov/international/analysis/regions-of-interest/South_China_Sea (Access 02.05. 2021).

history that dated back to the 1950s.[58]

Part of the reluctance to implement the law to resolve South China Sea disputes is due to the legal weakness of some of the claims, despite adherence to UNCLOS. Large-scale exploration and exploitation of the sea's potential resources will be delayed until sovereignty issues and the resulting jurisdiction conflicts are resolved. The main issue is how to reach a solution. Since 1974, China has shown its willingness to use force to defend its territorial claims. In 1974, China forcibly displaced South Vietnam from Paracel Islands to the north of the Spratly[59] archipelago. Since then, China has expanded its presence and penetrated Vietnam and the Philippines-owned regions. For instance, the Chinese navy sunk two Vietnamese ships near Fiery Cross Reef in 1988.[60] Likewise, the Philippines discovered a Chinese military base in 1995 on Mischief Reef which is in its exclusive economic zone (EEZ).[61] Chinese expansion into the Philippines' EEZ was also a result of the inefficient navy of the Philippines. It was also known that US security obligations to the Philippines did not go beyond the limits of their bilateral security agreement. However, this situation changed in the following years as then-President of the Philippines Arroyo explained in a statement in 2004. The main focal point of the US military education program in the Philippines became training the Philippines army to counter China in the Spratly archipelago.[62]

There are also conflicts between Malaysia and the Philippines and Vietnam and the Philippines on this subject. Especially as China's naval and long-range airpower has grown, increasing conflicts have become a destabilizing factor in the regional international order. Chinese the 1992 People's Republic of China's Seas and Contiguous Territories Act caused a regional backlash in ASEAN. ASEAN's strategy was to maintain the status quo in the South China Sea without alienating China. In parallel to this strategy, ASEAN took over the political agenda with the 1992 "South China Sea Declaration."[63] The declaration emphasized the need to resolve all sovereignty and judicial disputes peacefully and without coercion. Also, it was stated to Beijing that ASEAN would view bilateral issues with a regionalist perspective and that there is a unified ASEAN position on this issue. The Declaration also suggested that functional cooperation activities can be carried out in areas such as pollution, shipping, piracy, and other transnational issues without involving sovereignty and judicial issues. Finally, it called for the application of the principles contained in

---

[58] Donald E. Weatherbee, **International Relations in Southeast Asia: The Struggle for Autonomy,** Lanham-Maryland, Rowman & Littlefield Publishers, 2009, pp.143-144.

[59] It was called as Nansha by China.

[60] https://www.scmp.com/news/asia/article/1192472/spratly-islands-dispute-defines-china-vietnam-relations-25-years-after (Access 25.05.2021).

[61] https://www.globalsecurity.org/military/world/war/spratly-clash.htm (Access 02.05.2021).

[62] https://eresources.nlb.gov.sg/newspapers/digitised/issue/straitstimes20040405-1 (Access 03.04. 2021).

[63] https://asean.org/?static_post=declaration-on-the-conduct-of-parties-in-the-south-china-sea-2 (Access 01.05.2021).

the TAC as a basis for the establishment of an international code of conduct on the South China Sea. The draft of such an agreement has become the main focus of the ASEAN-China dialogue in the South China Sea even though China's expansion continues.[64]

An estimated US $3.37 trillion of global trade, which accounts for a third of global maritime trade[65], crosses the South China Sea every year.[66] Given the eighty percent of China's energy imports and approximately forty percent of China's total trade pass through the South China Sea, it can be fairly argued that the disputes constitute one of many aspects of China's salami strategy.

It is important to note that the disputes are not limited to the Spratly archipelago and Paracal islands. Other parts of the South China Sea including Scarborough Shoal and border issues in the Gulf of Tonkin are also problematic. There are disputes even in the Indonesian Natuna Islands, which many do not consider these islands to be part of the South China Sea. However, the dispute over the Spratly archipelago and Paracal islands drew more attention than other issues, particularly from other global actors outside of the region due to their potential regarding natural resource reserves and their potential to dominate the strategic maritime trade routes.

China has been continuing island construction in the Spratly Islands and Paracel Islands region since 2013.[67] These actions were met with broad international condemnation, and extra-regional powers such as the US, France, and the UK have carried out free movement operations in the region since 2015.[68] An arbitration court established under Annex VII of the UNCLOS ruled against China's maritime claims against the Philippines. Even though the court did not specify possession of the islands or their maritime borders[69], China and Taiwan insisted that the matter should be resolved through bilateral negotiations with other plaintiffs, stating that they do not recognize the court's decision.[70] As a delayed response, France, Germany and the UK released a joint verbal memo recognizing the Permanent Court of Arbitration (PCA) decision and challenged China's claims on 17th September 2020.[71]

However, China finished the construction of the airports on the islands in

---

[64] Weatherbee, **ibid.**, p.144.

[65] https://unctad.org/system/files/official-document/rmt2018_en.pdf (Access 24.04.2021).

[66] https://web.archive.org/web/20190608020005/https:/chinapower.csis.org/much-trade-transits-south-china-sea/ (Access 26.04.2021).

[67] https://amti.csis.org/island-tracker/china/ (Access 24.04.2021).

[68] Eleanor Freund, **"Freedom of Navigation in the South China Sea: A Practical Guide"** https://www. belfercenter. org/publication/freedom-navigation-south-china-sea-practical-guide (Access 24.04.2021).

[69] https://web.archive.org/web/20160712201412/https:/pca-cpa.org/wp-content/uploads/sites/175/2016/07/PH-CN-20160712-Press-Release-No-11-English.pdf (Access 22.04.2021).

[70] https://www.bloomberg.com/news/articles/2016-07-12/china-no-historic-right-to-south-china-sea-resources-court-says (Access 29.04.2021).

[71] https://www.cnnphilippines.com/news/2020/9/18/France-Germany-United-Kingdom-reject-China-South-China-Sea.html (Access 19.04.2021).

2018.[72] Furthermore, Chinese President Xi Jinping declared in July 2019 that China does not recognize and comply with the decision on the status of the disputed islands[73], which is in parallel to one of the primary official Chinese national security documents, the Chinese White Paper entitled "China's National Defense in the New Age."[74]

In response to Chinese actions on the issue, the President of the Philippines, Rodrigo Duterte, in his United Nations speech on September 22, 2020, confirmed The Hague decision, which rejected most of China's claims regarding controversial waters and stated that "the decision is now part of international law, it has reached a point beyond compromise and beyond the reach of passing governments to dilute, shrink or abandon."[75] It would be not wise to expect the resolution of this issue in the near future given the importance of the region for China's geopolitical calculations and its declaration of not complying with any international law on this issue.

Conclusion

ASEAN is a regional organization that brings together different neighbors to address economic, security, and political issues, and has been established between Brunei, Cambodia, Indonesia, Laos, Malaysia, Myanmar, Philippines, Singapore, Thailand, and Vietnam. As a regional group that promotes economic, political, and security cooperation among its ten members, and ASEAN countries have a total population of 650 million and a combined gross domestic product of $2.8 trillion.[76]

The organization plays a central role in Asian economic integration by leading negotiations and signing free trade agreements with other regional economies to form one of the world's largest free trade blocs among Asia-Pacific countries. However, the impact of ASEAN is limited by the lack of strategic vision, differing priorities, and weak leadership among member countries. Even though the organization's biggest challenge is developing a unified approach to balance and contain China, particularly in response to Beijing's claims that overlap with many ASEAN members in the South China Sea and the organizations failed to do that comprehensively so far, it is an undeniable fact that ASEAN contributes to regional stability by developing much-needed norms and providing a neutral environment to tackle common challenges.

Main security issues in the region are maritime disputes such as the South

---

[72] https://csis-website-prod.s3.amazonaws.com/s3fs-public/publication/190724_China_2019_Defense.pdf (Access 02.05.2021).
[73] https://www.navytimes.com/news/your-navy/2019/09/01/beijing-tells-duterte-it-wont-honor-south-china-sea-ruling/ (Access 02.05.2021).
[74] https://csis-website-prod.s3.amazonaws.com/s3fs-public/publication/190724_China_2019_Defense.pdf (Access 02.05.2021).
[75] https://thediplomat.com/2020/09/in-un-speech-duterte-stiffens-philippines-stance-on-the-south-china-sea/ (Access 01.05.2021).
[76] https://www.usasean.org/why-asean/what-is-asean (Access 24.05.2021).

China Sea, human trafficking, drug trafficking, refugee flows, natural disasters, food security, terrorism, and riots. While most issues are addressed outside of ASEAN, including bilateral or external audits, there are several ASEAN-led forums where regional issues are discussed. The ARF is the most important regional initiative regarding addressing the challenges since it represents a broad spectrum, including ASEAN, dialogue partners, the EU, North Korea, and Pakistan, among others. However, its effectiveness is often limited by geopolitical concerns.

Despite all these diplomatic interactions under ASEAN leadership, conflicts over security issues continue to challenge ASEAN's unity. The most robust problem of the organization is still formulating a common response to China's financial and military expansion. The re-emergence of China as the main power in the East Asian region has the potential to transform not only the relations of Southeast Asia with China but also the internal relations of ASEAN itself. It should be noted that not all members have the same level of bilateral relations with China. Therefore, there is a possibility that member states may act based on their national interests and not necessarily based on the ASEAN's interests. In fact, ASEAN members are divided due to their relations with China and the USA. The region needs investment, trade, and infrastructure development, and China tends to seize every opportunity to meet these needs. However, ASEAN members also feel concerned about being economically dependent on China. In addition, some member states also align their policies with the US to prevent Chinese aggression as it is the case in the Vietnam-USA partnership.

Furthermore, ASEAN brings together countries with significantly different economies and political systems. Singapore has the highest GDP per capita among group members at more than $65,000, according to the 2019 World Bank figures, while Myanmar is the lowest at around $1,400.[77] There is a divergence of the member's political systems as well including democracies, authoritarian and hybrid regimes. Demography also differs across the region, with many religious and ethnic groups represented. Given such diversity among its members, ASEAN has to address many issues, including China's allegations in the South China Sea, human rights violations, including ethnic cleansing against the Muslim minority in Myanmar, and political pressure in member states such as Cambodia.

Most of the regional or international organizations are dominated by a single country instead of working based on equality. For instance, it is evident that the US is the dominant actor in the North Atlantic Treaty Organizations (NATO) while China is the dominant actor in the Shanghai Cooperation Organization (SCO). Consequently, other regional actors do not have the required power to set the organization's agenda if their policies contradict the dominant actor which also hurts the sense of membership of other actors. No actors in the ASEAN can fully dominate the agenda of the organization. Therefore, not only do

---

[77] https://data.worldbank.org/indicator/NY.GDP.PCAP.CD?locations=SG (Accessed 24.05.2021).

member states in the ASEAN have a strong sense of inclusion in decision-making processes but also the lack of dominant actors in the ASEAN contributes to its neutral stance for the third parties.

A fundamental paradox with ASEAN also needs to be observed. ASEAN's strength may be its weakness as well. ASEAN has emerged as an indispensable platform for great power participation in the Asia-Pacific region. Because it is too weak to be a threat in the region, all great powers instinctively trust it. Therefore, the ARF is the only platform in which regional governments can engage in sincere dialogue. Indeed, it even offers an opportunity for dialogue with North Korea. Likewise, since it is the only organization in the region that all other actors trust, it fills an extremely serious geopolitical and geostrategic void in the region although it was belittled initially until the 2000s.

REGIONAL CHALLENGES AND INTERNATIONAL RELATIONS: THE COMPLEX REALITIES OF SOUTH PACIFIC GEOPOLITICS

Amba Pande[1]

Introduction

South Pacific also known as *Oceania* is a relatively isolated and remote region and is a home of small island countries apart from two metropolitan powers scattered amidst a vast oceanic area. Yet, the region is not bereft of great power rivalry and both conventional and non-conventional security threats. South Pacific is also a witness to internal turmoils like political upheavals, nuclear tests, resource theft and depletion, environmental challenges, and many other issues. Interestingly, the regional security challenges have been entwined with the intervention of great powers which has given rise to a complex and cluttered geopolitical environment in the South Pacific. This paper seeks to discuss, the geopolitics of the South Pacific region in the context of regional vulnerabilities and international relations that has resulted in a quagmire of political, domestic, economic, ethno-geographic, diplomatic, and environmental issues.

Coined, originally by the Swedish political scientist Rudolf Kjellén, *geopolitics* is an overly used term by scholars and practitioners alike. It generally, denotes international politics related to a geographical region. However, the regional politics arising out of geographic features, natural resources, *oecopolitik,* economic conditions, environmental and security dynamics, race, and religion, too are part of the geopolitical construct. In other words, it is about international relations that arise out of the internal politics of a geographical region. Without dwelling deep on the theoretical aspects of geopolitics (as it is already deliberated at the beginning of the volume), I will simply discuss the South Pacific International relations in the context of the internal power politics of the region. The regional politics and security challenges directly or indirectly guide the foreign policies and the security goals of the Pacific Island Countries (PICs). Since, South Pacific is majorly an oceanic body, the context of Maritime geopolitics will be taken into account to explore the challenges like over/illegal fishing, nuclear testing, seabed mining, global warming, rising sea levels etc.

Remoteness, and Vulnerability: An Introduction to South Pacific Region

The South Pacific region covers a vast area of almost 8,525,989 square

[1] Dr Amba Pande, School of International Studies, Jawaharlal Nehru University, New Delhi, India. Email: ambapande@gmail.com.

kilometres and is home to 14 Island countries and the two metropolitan powers Australia and New Zealand. It is a sparsely populated region with less than 3 percent land area, and fragmented in numerous islands. South Pacific is divided into three geo-cultural or ethno-geographic sub-regions, the first being Melanesia that occupies the island countries of Fiji, New Caledonia, Vanuatu, the Solomon Islands, and Papua New Guinea; The second grouping is Micronesia that occupies the island countries of Nauru, Palau, Federated States of Micronesia (FSM), Kiribati, and the Marshall Islands. The largest group is Polynesia, which occupies the island countries of Tonga, Tuvalu, Samoa, Kiribati, and French Polynesia. Other than these PICs, there is Australia, and New Zealand (together referred to as Australasia) and semi-independent territories of Cook Island and Niue which have a 'free association' status with New Zealand.

South Pacific is an extremely diverse region full of disparities and paradoxes in terms of size, population, ethnicity, topography, ecology, economic resources and level of development. On the one hand Australia and New Zealand are part of OECD countries and on the other Kiribati, Solomon Islands, Samoa, Tuvalu and Vanuatu, are classified as the least developed countries. On the one hand Australia, PNG and Fiji possess large land areas and have a relatively large population base and on the other Tuvalu and Nauru, have exceedingly small land areas with small populations. Niue has a only 1,398 people as its population. Colonialism still exists in the region with the colonisers and the colonised both being part of it. The remotely scattered islands have a troubling combination of small population base (in total 8 million approx.), low economic development, and weak governmental systems on the one hand but on the other, they are in possession of large oceanic areas under their EEZs which have abundant natural resources and Tuna supply, are strategically located at the key sea lines of communication (SLOCs), and have the crucial 14 votes at the UN and other international multilateral fora vast natural resources.[2]

Since the island countries were colonies to the western powers and after independence continued to rely on the former colonial masters for aid and development, Western culture and way of life have made deep inroads in the PICs. Although there is much emphasis on the indigenous cultural heritage and the Pacific way of life, the younger generations are captivated by the pop and fast-food culture. Christianity remains the dominant religion in Oceania with approximately 65.61 percent Australasia, 95 percent Melanesia, 93 percent Micronesia and 96 percent Polynesia being Christians.[3] The church is often involved with domestic and regional politics.

Australia and New Zealand are the most important powers in the region.

---

[2] Amba Pande, "India and the South Pacific: Moving Towards a Closer Partnership", **FPRC JOURNAL Focus: India and Pacific Islands**, No. 1, 201, pp. 18-24.
[3] Pew Research Center's Forum on Religion & Public Life, "The Global Religious Landscape: A Report on the Size and Distribution of the World's Major Religious Groups as of 2010", **Pew Research Center,** 2012.

Former colonial masters, are the largest aid donors (providing approximately half of all aid) and defence partners of the PICs and are responsible for the policing and surveillance of sea lanes. Australia, along with New Zealand, is the founding member of the major regional multilateral organisation. New Zealand has long been Australia's 'principal strategic partner' and the two states have cooperated extensively on a range of security, diplomatic, economic, social, cultural, and political issues. However, geographically, culturally, and ethnically New Zealand is closer to PICs and hosts large Maori and Polynesian populations. It produces a sense of *Tagata Pasifika*, or the 'identity as a Pacific nation'.[4]

For Australia, South Pacific has been the region of geopolitical and geo-strategic importance, and it has as Jim Rolfe describes done, 'heavy lifting' on part of the US. Nevertheless, South Pacific has never been high on Australia's priority. What Australia has been doing is to keep the region under the American or the ANZUS influence. Australia has long viewed itself—and has been viewed by others, as an advocate for Western interests in the South Pacific.[5] The strategic and geo-political goals have often been pursued through economic means by Australia.

The security challenges that the region faces relates to external as well as regional dynamics and concerns with both conventional and non-conventional threats. Vijay Naidu describes two sources of instability and challenge to regional peace,

> External forces constitute one source of threat to regional stability. These include the continuation of colonial rule which has racial implications; super-power rivalry including the nuclear arms-race; and adventurism by various groups seeking material gains in the region. Another source of regional insecurity and threat to national sovereignty derives from internal pressures in the South Pacific Island States. Internal forces include social and economic divisions within island societies; the demands from extremist groups for various policies that support their interests in society; and the emergence of democratic forces which many island states find difficulties in accepting.[6]

The security challenges emanating from the extra-regional powers continue to be the state-centric traditional security concerns while for the PICs, the security threats revolve more around non- conventional threats focused on the needs of people and their societies. The majority of the PICs (except Fiji, PNG, and Tonga) have even rejected the possession of defence and military forces. As Herr, explains, "The Islands have focused on "human" or non-traditional

[4] Jim Rolfe, "The South Pacific: Regional Security and The Role Of External Actors". 2015. https://www.wgtn.ac.nz/strategic-studies/documents/strategic-background-papers/24-the-south-pacific-regional-security-and-the-role-of-external-actors.pdf
[5] A Bergin & R Herr, "Our Near Abroad: Australia and Pacific Islands Regionalism, Strategy", 30 November, **Australian Strategic Policy Institute**, Canberra, 2011.
[6] Vijay Naidu, "The South Pacific: Issues of Regional Security", Sovereignty and Ethnic Freedom. **Peace Research**, 22/23, Vol. 22, No. 4, 1990, pp. 51-56.

security over state or traditional security at the regional level. Consequently, linking the two approaches to security has proved challenging at many levels".[7]

Regional Co-operation in the South Pacific and the Challenges of Sub-regionalism

It is important to discuss regional cooperation as part of South Pacific geopolitics because, in view of the smallness and remoteness, the regional organisations often become a platform for an effective presence and collective voices of the PICs on various issues of regional and international significance. Through regional platforms, the PICs gain weightage while negotiating with external powers, and pursuing international diplomacy. It is also a source to maximise their economic potential and work closely with Australia and New Zealand. By far Pacific Island Forum remains the most important organisation in the region and Australia has been able to influence its agenda and decision-making to a large extent.

Nevertheless, regional co-operation in the South Pacific has remained problematic. Greg Fry writes that "Regional cooperation in the South Pacific has become a highly complex political process"[8]. The initial efforts towards regional co-operation were through South Pacific Commission (1947) which included western colonial powers and excluded the PICs from its membership. As the PICs started gaining independence the necessity for an indigenous organisation resulted in the formation of the South Pacific Forum in 1971 which was rechristened as the Pacific Islands Forum (PIF). SPF has a vast network of sub-groups for economic development SPEC, fisheries management (FFA), Environmental management (SPREP), South Pacific Forum Secretariat and the University of the South Pacific.

In recent, South Pacific regional cooperation has further broadened as PICs have been empowered by a greater choice of non-traditional external partners. the disenchantment with Australia and New Zealand has led the PICs form the Pacific Small Islands Developing States (PSIDS), which was formed under the leadership of Fiji after the 2006 coup leading to economic sanctions by Australia. This Melanesian spearhead group excludes Australia and New Zealand and has added a new challenge to regional geopolitics. The external powers like China, France, and Russia extend their support for PSIDS. To Australia's further displeasure PSIDS has managed to represent as the 'Asia Pacific group' at the UN instead of 'Asia Group' which operated under the auspices of PIF. PSIDS is also the main Pacific body representing South Pacific at various international platforms on environmental issues.[9] Nevertheless, the biggest challenge for the

---

[7] R.A. Herr, 1986. "Regionalism, Strategic Denial and South Pacific Security". **The Journal of Pacific History**, Vol. 21, No. 4, 1986, p 18.

[8] Greg Fry, "The Politics of South Pacific Regional Cooperation". In: R. Thakur (Eds.), London, The South Pacific, Palgrave Macmillan, 1991, p. 169.

[9] Joanne Wallis, "Crowded and complex: The changing geopolitics of the South Pacific". **The Australian Strategic Policy Institute Limited**. 2017, p. 15. www.aspistrategist.org.au

South Pacific regional co-operation is that it is not self-funded. The regional organisations fully depend on extra-regional powers, in addition to Australia and New Zealand for day to day running. Hence, they become a platform for the geopolitical powerplay.

The Regional Security Issues and the Geopolitical Environment in the South Pacific

South Pacific has been known for its atmosphere of relative peace for most of the time. However, the region and the PICs have never been devoid of various kinds of conventional and non-conventional threats. The interstate conflict has been almost absent but the non-conventional security threats and threat perceptions have been present in the region and have dominated the regional geopolitics. As Pande suggests "the regional threat perception means anything that force them (PICs) to compromise with their political and economic sovereignty, and their control over regional development".[10] Even the nuclear threat that the region faced was not so much about being attacked by nuclear weapons but more about the environmental and health hazards because of nuclear testing and dumping.

By the end of the 1980s, the previously dominant picture of the peaceful South Pacific became a thing of the past as several conditions of instability came to the fore. The island of Bougainville faced violent, unrests against PNG due to environmental depletion as a result of excessive copper mining, As the Australian aid was being directed by the PNG to supress the Bougainville unrest, it became a cause of big resentment in the region. For Australia on the other hand, the Indonesian presence in the West Papua was a matter of concern and led it to have its foothold in the PNG.[11] The 1980s also saw the resurgence of the self-determination movement in the New Caledonia from France. These incidents had a huge spillover in the region as the PICs sided with the indigenous populations.

One of the most eminent challenges that the South Pacific has been facing is the environmental threat which is the biggest challenge for regional security. Intriguingly, most of the environmental threats that the region faces are not caused by the PICs but by the countries outside the region. Be it the global warming, dumping of hazardous wastes, nuclear testing, resources depletion or overfishing, all were caused by the extra-regional powers. As the UN report says, "the people of the Pacific islands may be among the smallest contributors to climate change, but they are on the frontline of its impacts".[12] Hence, the

---

[10] Amba Pande, Regional Security in Southeast Asia and the South Pacific: Prospects of Nuclear Free Zone, New Delhi: Authors Press, 2002, p. 105.

[11] Amba Pande, "Australia's Policy Towards South Pacific with Special Reference to PNG and Fiji", in D. Gopal (ed), **Australia in the Emerging World Order**, Delhi: Shipra Publications, 2002

[12] UN, "Informing Action: Pacific Nations Unite on The Environment", UN Environment Program, 2017, Https://Www.Unep.Org/News-And-Stories/Story/Informing-Action-Pacific-Nations-Unite-Environment

environmental issues stirred up the regional geopolitics and galvanised the PICs to come on a common platform and address their challenges through regional cooperation. The nuclear test by France and the US in the 1980s is a good example of anti-nuclear activism of the PICs and a region-wide anti-nuclear movement. Although the PICs depended heavily on the western powers, for aid and economic assistance, they did not hesitate to pull France to the International court of justice against atmospheric testing and signed the Treaty of Rarotonga also known as the South Pacific Nuclear Free Zone treaty in 1985.[13] Another, regional issue that came to head during the 1980s was Tuna Poaching and drift net fishing. The distant water fishing nations (DWFN) were overfishing and juvenile fishing Tuna resources from the EEZs of the PICs. Under the auspices of the Forum Fisheries Agency, the PICs took the issue of drift net fishing and jurisdictional issues of EEZ to the UN. This incident caused great discontent in the US-PIC relations.[14] Although known as the western lake the past PICs did not hesitate to raise anti-western voices and direct the whole anti-nuclear and anti-fisheries movement towards the Western powers. Another significant move was the signing of the Protection of the Natural Resources and Environment of the South Pacific (SPREP) for co-operation on sustainable development. In the past couple of decades, rising sea levels, increasingly extreme weather conditions, and the daily challenges have led to large scale emigration of Pacific islanders. It has resulted in large scale activism in the PICs and they have emerged as the front-runner advocates for urgent action on the environment. The UN has launched a program called INFORM involving the 14 PICs to build capacity in environmental data gathering and sharing around the region.[15]

Another major regional challenge has been the Economic vulnerability of the Island countries. Some of the major features of the PIC economy are small in size with limited natural resources, remoteness from major markets and centre of production, small markets, narrow-based exports, unfavourable balance of trade, heavy dependence on aid and vulnerability to external shocks.[16] The PICs have been subsistence economies with fishing and agriculture as their main source of livelihood. All of these affect economic growth and can lead to a high degree of economic volatility. The declaration of Exclusive Economic Zone (EEZ) in 1982 under the UN Convention on the Law of the Sea, gave a new sense of power and authority to the PICs yet could not generate the desired revenues for them. For much of the region, aid and development assistance are required for state survival, and hence, clearly relates the economy to the regional geopolitics. For the future, tourism holds encouraging prospects, but the lack of

---

[13] Pande, op.cit.

[14] Ramesh Thakur, **The South Pacific: Problems, Issues and Prospects**, UK; Palgrave Macmillan, 1991; Wallis, op.cit.

[15] UN, "Informing Action: Pacific Nations Unite on The Environment", UN Environment Program, 2017, Https://Www.Unep.Org/News-And-Stories/Story/Informing-Action-Pacific-Nations-Unite-Environment.

[16] World Bank, "The World Bank in Pacific Islands", 2020, https://www.worldbank.org/en/country/pacificislands/overview ; James Mak, "Pacific Island Economies. Center for Pacific Islands Studies", https://hawaii.edu/cpis/wp-content/uploads/Pacific_Island_Economies.pdf

infrastructures and internal security is a big impediment in the development of the tourism sector. Migration and remittances are yet another sector that may lead to economic development for the PICs but the COVID crisis poses major challenges for the industry.

As ADB points out, one of the major reasons for the inadequate and stagnated development of most of the island states arises from poor governance. The past few decades saw a decline in the democratic culture, and the state's authority to govern. The 'Melanesian arc of instability' witnessed several coups and political upheavals since the 1980s. Fiji has had five military coups since 1988, Solomon Island had coups and ethnic tensions emerging as a failed state.[17] The collapse of law and order and mutinies of armed forces in PNG also had a major impact on the geopolitics of the region. As a spillover of these incidents, there were interventions and sanctions by Australia and New Zealand in an attempt to restore law and order and stability in the region which in turn gave space to extra-regional powers.

Following the 2006 coup, Australia and New Zealand imposed severe economic sanctions against Fiji. In turn, Fiji adopted a more independent approach under its Look North policy inching towards China, Malaysia, and other countries.[18] As the Fijian Minister, Ratu Inoke Kubuabola pointed out 'Fiji no longer looks to Australia and New Zealand but to the world.' The Fijian coup leader Bainimarama visited Beijing and Russia in 2013, which resulted in the signing of several agreements. Fiji's drift away from Australia and New Zealand was also followed by the PNG, a member of the APEC and Non-aligned movement. Over the past five years, its dependence on Australian aid has been reduced by PNGs own growth. Thus, both PNG and Fiji have expanded their presence on the international stage, taking them further outside the sphere of influence of Australia, New Zealand, and other traditional partners. The weakening of ANZUS further undermined Australia's position.[19] These developments have impacted the regional order and have generated a complex geopolitical situation in the South Pacific. "The Boe Declaration of 2018 is an important call by the PIF countries towards 'a more complex environment with an expanded concept of security and calls for closer coordination in the Pacific region."[20]

In the recent, the threats of terrorism appear imminent in the south Pacific. There are reports of the use of PICs by the al-Qaeda operatives for access to international transit. The presence of Islamic fundamentalism in the nearby

---

[17] Asian Development Bank, ADB, Annual Report 2004, p. 43. Https://Www.Adb.Org/Documents/Adb-Annual-Report-2004.

[18] Amba Pande, "India and Its Diaspora in Fiji", **Diaspora Studies**, Vol. 4, No. 2, 2011, pp. 125-138.

[19] R Ayson, "The "Arc of Instability" and Australia's Strategic Policy", **Australian Journal of International Affairs**, Vol. 61, No. 2, 2007, pp. 215–231.

[20] Boe Declaration on Regional Security, https://www.forumsec.org/2018/09/05/boe-declaration-on-regional-security/

Indonesian and Philippines viewed as future vulnerabilities.[21]

Interests of External Powers in the South Pacific Region

The External actors have been present in the South Pacific region historically as explorers, traders, colonisers, missionaries, and settlers. The US, UK, Germany, and France colonised the region with Australia and New Zealand as their proxies. Even after the PICs gained independence, the former colonial masters continued to hold their authority as economic partners and aid donors. During WW 2, the South Pacific became the hotspot of the Pacific Wars and US bases operated from many island countries such as Fiji. In the aftermath of WW2, the perceived threat of Japan using these island countries as a steppingstone to attack Australia and New Zealand or challenge the western dominance in the region loomed large. Australia, New Zealand, and US collective security treaty ANZUS was signed in 1951. Traditionally, Australia, New Zealand, the US, and France, have worked as close partners, with several new countries increasing their presence in the region, most notably China, Russia, Indonesia, Japan, and India.[22] Yet, the South Pacific region was never under a direct threat from the external powers.

The US has been the most important external power in the region and still has its strong foothold in the Micronesian subregion. Although the US is said to have a benign interest in the region, its nuclear and military bases in Australia and Guam has been dominated by the military focussed security. The US has pursued its interests in the region through Australia under *Burden Sharing* and throughout the cold war era, pursued *strategic denial* towards the spread of communism, as in other parts of Asia.[23] However, US activities related to illegal fishing, nuclear testing, refusal to sign the Treaty of Rarotonga, and support for France created a huge discontent against it throughout the region. The so-called *American Lake/ ANZUS Lake* withered away for some years. Following the demise of the cold war, the US scaled down its presence further only to renew during Hillary Clinton's tenure as Secretary of State. In 2011, 'pivot' to the Asia–Pacific' was announced, by the US, followed by a series of high-level official visits, active multilateral diplomacy, increased strategic military deployments, and increased aid, trade and investment ties through USAID. Secretary of State Clinton attended the Pacific Islands Forum meeting in Rarotonga in 2012 reviving the US presence.[24]

---

[21] Troy E. Mitchell, "Protecting the South Pacific". 2018.
https://thestrategybridge.org/the-bridge/2018/2/27/protecting-the-south-pacific
[22] Jim Rolfe, "The South Pacific: Regional Security and The Role Of External Actors". 2015. https://www.wgtn.ac.nz/strategic-studies/documents/strategic-background-papers/24-the-south-pacific-regional-security-and-the-role-of-external-actors.pdf
[23] R.A. Herr, "Regionalism, Strategic Denial and South Pacific Security". **The Journal of Pacific History**, Vol. 21, No. 4, 1986, pp. 170-182.
[24] Charles Edel, "Small dots, large strategic areas: US interests in the South Pacific" The Lowy Institute, 2018, https://www.lowyinstitute.org/the-interpreter/small-dots-large-strategic-areas-us-interests-south-pacific ; Hong Say, "US Strategic Objectives in the South Pacific Challenged by Sino-American

France is another colonial power in the Pacific which still holds territories like New Caledonia, French Polynesia, and Wallis and Futuna. France had an uncomfortable relationship with the PICs and was considered as the main culprit, because of its nuclear tests till the mid-1990s and its attempt to hold on to New Caledonia. However, by ending its nuclear tests and signing the Matignon Agreements in 1988 and Noumea Accord in 1998, to settle the self-determination in New Caledonia, France sought to bolster its image and deepen its engagement with the PICs. It has invested for the benefit of the indigenous Kanak population and has adopted a more conciliatory approach towards Fiji after the 2006 coup, has provided an active support to the Melanesian Spearhead Group, and has taken a favourable stance for the PICs on climate change. France also plays a key role in facilitating the European Union's presence in the region.[25]

The withdrawal of US interest in the South Pacific in the past few decades gave ample space for China to expand its presence in the region. Beijing has constantly expanded its diplomatic presence and development cooperation, initially driven by its competition with Taiwan and later to increase its strategic weight. It signed protocols 2 and 3 of the treaty of Rarotonga in 1987, has established diplomatic presence with most of the PICs, has pursued its chequebook diplomacy unhindered, has provided significant concessional loan packages and debt relief, has increased trade manifold, and has invested in infrastructure projects heavily in the past few decades. Chinese President Xi Jinping visited Fiji in November 2014 to meet with leaders of those PICs that recognise mutual respect and common development through cooperative initiatives like China – Pacific Islands Countries Economic Development and Cooperation Forum in April 2006, followed by a second forum in November 2013. China provides support to key regional organisations, particularly the Pacific Islands Forum and has a soft power presence through television and Mandarin centres.[26] Several of the PICs are part of China's *One Belt One road initiative* (OBOR) and MOUs have already been signed.

Russia is another, major power that has a growing presence in the South Pacific region. During the cold war, the Soviet overtures in the 1980s with the signing of fishing deals and other incentives had generated moderate responses from the PICs. In recent Russia expressed a renewed interest with aid payments, partly for diplomatic recognition for South Ossetia and Abkhazia, after their independence from Georgia. It succeeded in getting recognition from Nauru and Tuvalu in 2009 and 2011 (but later withdrawn). Russian assertiveness is also due to its desire to emerge as a Pacific Ocean power. It has increased its co-operation

Competition" Xian Strategic Analysis Paper. 2019. https://www.futuredirections.org.au/publication/us-strategic-objectives-in-the-south-pacific-challenged-by-sino-american-competition
[25] Wallis, op.cit.; Frederic Grare, "France, the Other Indo-Pacific Power". 2020. https://carnegieendowment.org/2020/10/21/france-other-indo-pacific-power-pub-83000
[26] Sriparna Pathak, "The Pacific Island Nations: Engagements with India and China". **FPRC Journal**, No. 1, 2018, pp. 33-47; Hong Say, "US Strategic Objectives in the South Pacific Challenged by Sino-American Competition" **Xian Strategic Analysis Paper.** 2019. https://www.futuredirections.org.au/publication/us-strategic-objectives-in-the-south-pacific-challenged-by-sino-american-competition

with Fiji, with a defence agreement, a mutual visa exemption scheme, and agreements on tackling money laundering, public health assistance and university exchanges.[27]

Japan, the initial colonial power, and a World War 2 enemy, increased its favourable presence since the 1970s through aid, trade, fishing, and diplomatic presence. Japan's interest is driven by economic as well as strategic considerations, and free access to sea lines of communication to Australia, New Zealand, and parts of Southeast Asia. It is also driven by the desire of having the support of the PICs in the UN for security council membership. Japan is a dialogue partner of the Pacific Islands Forum, provided medical and technical support and has held triennial Japan–Forum summits, referred to as the PALM (Pacific Islands Leaders Meeting) since 1997.[28]

India has been a relatively new player in the South Pacific, but has a deep strategic interest as part of its emergence as an Asia–Pacific power, manifested in its 'Look East' policy. India traditionally had close ties with PNG and Fiji. Fiji has a large Indian diaspora that was created under the Indenture Labour system during British colonialism. With its increased presence, India announced an annual grant of US$ 100,000, which increased to US$ 125,000 in 2009. Between 2005 and 2012, Indian development assistance was nearly US$ 50 million in the form of Lines of Credit and over US$ 11 million in grants (Balakrishnan 2015). Indian Prime Minister Narendra Modi visited Fiji in November 2014 where he held a summit with the PICs and inaugurated the Forum for India-Pacific Island Cooperation (FIPIC) for cooperation and dialogue on issues of common concern, such as climate change, technical co-operation, human resource development and many other incentives. As Pande says, "FIPIC can provide an important bridge for deepening the economic, political and social engagement in future. India is aiming at a wide range of co-operation based on shared aspirations and interests to build a dynamic relationship with the Pacific Island Countries (PICs) which correspondingly solidifies its position as a geopolitical power in the regional power balance".[29] Maitrayee Shilpa Kishore, in a detailed report for VIF, writes, "the current political climate is best suited for India to increase its engagement with the region, bilaterally and in collaboration with other partners".[30]

The Current Geopolitical Scenario in the South Pacific and the Future Prospects

The above discussion illustrates that the remoteness and smallness have not prevented the PICs and the South Pacific from the involvement of external

---

[27] Wallis, op.cit.

[28] Ibid.

[29] Amba Pande, "India and Pacific Islands Region: Building New Partnerships". **Journal of Alternative Perspectives in the Social Sciences**, Vol. 7, No. 2, 1015, pp. 284-289.

[30] Maitrayee Shilpa Kishore, "Geopolitics of the South Pacific and Opportunities for India", **National Security**, Vivekananda International Foundation Vol. 2, No. 3, 2019, p. 367.

powers in the regional politics giving rise to a complex geopolitical environment. The external powers have competed for the regional influence which opened new opportunities of engagement for the PICs. At the same time, the domestic and regional developments opened space for the external powers for further engagement with the PICs. Of course, Australia's stakes have been the highest given its strategic proximity, but it has represented the interests of the western powers especially the US. Its prime concern has been 'to ensure that no power hostile to Western interests establishes a strategic foothold in the region and on the maritime approaches'.[31] As a result, Australia could never be complacent towards the geopolitical challenges of the region and interestingly, has often pursued its strategic goals through the means of economic assistance.

The geopolitical environment of the South Pacific has been mainly driven by two major factors in the past as well as in the present. First, is the involvement of a multitude of external powers because of their own political and strategic interests. Moreover, there existed a sharp-edged competition between the western and non-western powers for increased influence. It converted the South Pacific into an arena of great power rivalry. During WW2, Japan's advance in the Pacific demonstrated the region's vulnerabilities. In the post-war era security treaties like ANZUS were signed and several economic incentives, aid and efforts of regional co-operation were put into place by Australia led Western powers to keep the PICs under the Western security umbrella. The external vulnerabilities resurfaced again during the Cold War when the former USSR and Libya started their overtures in the South Pacific. USSR established diplomatic relations with Tonga, signed fishing deals with Kiribati (1985) and Vanuatu (1987) and offered other incentives to the PICs. 'Soviets are coming' triggered a sharp reaction among the western bloc leading to critical policy changes. The ANZUS increased its presence in the regional security architecture and much greater financial and technical incentives were offered to the PICs. It also led the US to adopt a more conciliatory approach towards the fishing dispute with the PICs by signing a multilateral fishing agreement. A similar kind of anxiety appeared to have resurfaced again as a reaction to China's expanding involvement in the South Pacific. The threat perception that China's growing regional activism could destabilise the pro-US /Australia power balance was a factor for the Asia-Pacific Pivot', and Clinton's subsequent visit and participation in the PIF meeting. It very well reflects the counterbalancing China approach.

The second factor that drives the South Pacific geopolitics relates to the developments within the region that have created space for external intervention beyond the traditional security partners. The most important development in this regard was five Coups that has took place in Fiji. The economic sanctions imposed by Australia and New Zeeland made Fiji look towards China and some other powers for support and co-operation. Fiji's Look North move gave the much-desired space to China and other external powers, to increase their

---

[31] Defence White Paper. Department of defence, Commonwealth of Australia, Canberra. 2016.

foothold in the region. Moreover, the economic vulnerabilities of the PICs have also led them to increasingly engage with alternative partners whose interests might be inimical to the Western bloc. Some of the PICs appear to be taking advantage of this in order to access aid, concessional loans, military support and international influence. As a counter reaction, significant renovations and regional involvement by the Western bloc with increased incentives, and agreements were witnessed, like Biketawa Declaration and the Regional Assistance Mission to Solomon Islands (RAMSI) for direct intervention, and Enhanced Cooperation Programme by Australia with Papua New Guinea. The continued tussle between the Melanesian Spearhead Group and Australia has facilitated the increased Chinese and Russian presence who have their own strategic and economic goals.

There is hardly any doubt that the South Pacific geopolitical scenario has undergone a paradigm shift in the past few decades. It is no more a Western Lake. China quite deftly turned the power vacuum created by waning Western interests to its advantage and has developed deep bilateral relations with PICs. The geopolitical shift also got reflected when in 2018, the Federated States of Micronesia introduced a resolution to end the compact with the US instead of 2023. Speculations were rife about China stepping in as a guarantor of security. Any such move would make American bases at Guam vulnerable and would have great strategic implications for Australia.[32] Under such circumstances, a situation similar to South China Sea could have been possible. The region is also a hot-spot of other power rivalries with the presence of Taiwan, Indonesia, France, Japan, and India. In this state-centric conventional security concerns of the extra-regional powers, the non-conventional regional challenges too have taken new forms along with environmental, and economic challenges. The threats of sea-lane piracy, drug and human trafficking, smuggling, money laundering, illegal logging and terrorism loom large over the region. Illegal fishing and the management of Tuna resources remains a challenge that might require new platforms of cooperative collaboration.

Nevertheless, Beijing's economic cooperation with PICs suffered a significant loss of goodwill and the initial euphoria of China's cheque-book diplomacy, frittered away over time. The extraction of raw material by large Chinese corporations, closer of local companies, use of Chinese workers by their firms, illegal Chinese immigrants in wholesale and retail trade as well as the service sector, loss of jobs for the locals and above all the Chinese debt trap has presented a major challenge for the PICs and has led to deep resentment. There were anti-Chinese riots and destruction of Chinese business districts in PNG, Tonga and the Solomon Islands in 2006. As Ronald Seib points out, "It is obvious that economic cooperation with the island states has hardly led to the "win-win" situation promised by Beijing. This means that China's acclaimed South-South model of cooperation (the "Beijing Consensus") as an alternative

---

[32] Wallis, op.cit.

to Western development concepts has no empirical basis. As with other economic players, self-interest stands in the foreground".[33]

Against this backdrop, the rise of Quod (India, U.S., Australia, and Japan) can be viewed as a significant development for the South Pacific or in fact for the whole of Indo-Pacific. The coming together of liberal democratic stakeholders of the Indo-Pacific under the Quad umbrella has the ability to provide stability to the South Pacific region. In its initial declaration, the Quad group highlighted its aim as 'promote freedom, liberty and democracy and to make sure liberalism prevails over totalitarianism in the region'. Nevertheless, it clearly has a security agenda to countervail China. Moreover, democracy has been a sensitive issue for several of the PICs and has dragged them into the Chinese lap. The rhetoric of 'Democracy as a foreign concept versus the indigenous culture' has often been used to generate a regional response against the economic sanctions after toppling of democratically elected governments in the past[34]. Hence, taking a pro-democratic stand (at least overtly) while dealing with PICs might not be the correct path. The pro-democratic agenda can be pursued covertly through other diplomatic means.

The Quad can have a more meaningful presence in the South Pacific if it can accommodate the non-conventional security concerns of the PICs and promote cooperation in response to natural disasters, Pandemic situations, human security issues, money laundering, trafficking and terrorism. One of the most gigantic concerns of economic vulnerability and the debt trap is something that can really go a long way in building partnerships with the PICs and countervailing China. In this regard developing a common pool or a regional bank like institution to help the PICs pay back their loans to China and avail development assistance in the future can prove to be a gamechanger. All the Quad members are already providing development assistance to the PICs. A coordinated effort to have a common pool can be a great move ahead. Some other democratic nations like France, and New Zealand can also be regional partners of Quad. It is surely, not going to be a simple task considering Australia's heavy economic dependence on China and lure of OBOR for several of the South Pacific countries.

The Quod outreach towards the PICs should be both as a doner as well as a partner. The PICs can have something like an observer status in Quad for the South Pacific region. Quad@ South Pacific can be the new lynchpin of the regional geopolitical environment. Its clear, consistent and sustained presence can crowd out, the economic and political influence of China and curtail the future penetration by potentially hostile powers. The PICs possess a stronghold over the marine resources holding a vast potential for the blue economy and each one has one vote in the UN and many other international bodies. It makes them

---

[33] Roland Seib, "China in the South Pacific: No New Hegemon on the Horizon", PRIF-Reports No. 90, 2009, https://www.hsfk.de/fileadmin/HSFK/hsfk_downloads/prif90.pdf

[34] Amba Pande, "Coups, Constitutions and the Struggle for Power: Contours of Racial Politics in Fiji, in Manmohini Kaul & Anushree Chakraborty (eds.) **India's Look East to Act East Policy: Tracking the Opportunities and Challenges in the Indo-Pacific**, New Delhi, Pentagon Press, 2016.

diplomatically and economically extremely relevant. The Quad presence with a peaceful geopolitical environment in the South Pacific can open new vistas of cooperation between the external powers and the PICs.

THE WIDER NORTH AND THE NEW GEOPOLITICS OF THE NORTH PACIFIC: CRYOPOLITICS

Ebru Caymaz[1] and Fahri Erenel[2]

Introduction

Asia-Pacific is one of the most important regions in world politics and the 21st century is widely regarded as the Asian century since America's global leadership is being directly challenged for the first time upon the collapse of the Soviet Union. While the states such as the USA, China, Japan and Russia take an active role in the power struggle in this region, India also closely monitors the recent developments, as well as several European countries, which attach importance to Asia-Pacific relations.

This chapter focuses on the northern part of the Pacific since several tensions have been experienced among the different actors due to sea ice loss and the emergence of new economic opportunities accordingly. Therefore, combined with the effects of globalization, the circumpolar North has also turned into an international region underscored by the major interest on a global scale. The main aim of this chapter is to further discuss the concept of the wider north and cryopolitics within the context of the new geopolitics of the North Pacific.

The New Geopolitics of the North Pacific

'The Geographical Pivot of History' was introduced by Mackinder a hundred years ago through which he defended the idea that the control and containment of Euro-Asia were essential for power and therefore it meant control over the world since the heartland of the region was pivotal for the balance on a global scale. Although that view is challenged by stating *"Mackinder's contribution is a good illustration of ... a limited and dubious Western-centric theory of history to claim a neutral and informed intellectual basis for what is, in fact, a very biased or situated view"*,[3] it is noteworthy to mention the influence of this assessment on subsequent studies defining the term 'world order' since Mackinder has taken attention to the discussions of the late Victorian period.[4]

Mackinder's model places Eurasia at the strategic centre that outer crescents are instrumental to containment while Eurasia lays on strategic inner within the

---

[1] Assistant Prof. Dr. Ebru Caymaz, Canakkale Onsekiz Mart University, Turkey.
E-mail: ebru.caymaz@comu.edu.tr, ORCID ID: 0000-0002-9119-7659.
[2] Doç. Dr. Fahri Erenel, İstinye Üniversitesi, Turkey. E-mail: ferenel@istinye.edu.tr,
Orcid: 0000-0003-4681-0861.
[3] C. Flint, **Introduction to Geopolitics**, London, Routledge, 2006.
[4] P. Venier, "The Geographical Pivot of History and Early Twentieth Century Geopolitical Culture", **The Geographical Journal**, Vol. 170, No.4, December, 2004, pp. 330-336.

world. That point of view also places Eurasian Pacific Rim in a more strategic position compared to the North Pacific Rim. Accordingly, a balance of power can be achieved through the European crescent as well as the Atlantic area.[5] In fact, his ideas represent the political culture of Britain in the early 20th century when Russia is used to be perceived as an essential threat. In contrast to previous points of view dictating the dominance of the South, the North Pacific has become increasingly strategic in which several powerful national economies exist within the global economy. Along with the nation states, the North Pacific consist the US, Canada, Japan, Russia, China and North and South Korea as the northern Rimland of the Pacific. In addition to large and fast-growing economies such as China, this region also includes the larger economies of the world such as the US and Japan.

Recent studies focus on China's motivations within the region since its desire to play a larger role has become obvious while Australia's Pacific Step-Up and New Zealand's Pacific Reset initiatives are developed to counter Chinese involvement in the Pacific Islands region. The region has also transformed into a highly competitive region upon the inclusions of the US, New Zealand and Australia as the 'Pacific Pledge' still cannot be defined clearly. Responses of Western powers to China's rise have gained full momentum and increasingly evident across the Indo-Pacific region as well as in Oceania. Indo-Pacific strategy of the Biden administration advocates *"the need for a balance of power; the need for an order that the region's states recognize as legitimate; and the need for an allied and partner coalition to address China's challenges to both".*[6]

Map 1. Oceania Countries[7]

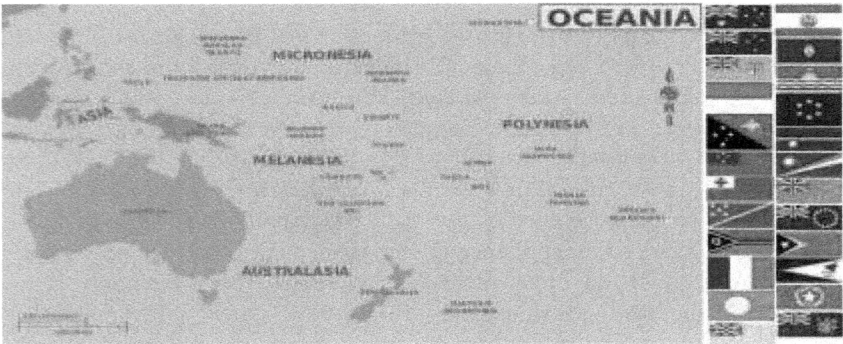

There are strong political and military powers in the region such as the US,

---

[5] H. J. Mackinder, "The Geographical Pivot of History", **The Geographical Journal**, Vol. 170, No.4, December, 1904, pp. 298-321.
[6] K. M. Campbell ve R. Doshi, "How America Can Shore Up Asian Order", **Foreign Affairs**, 12 January, 2021, p.1. www.foreignaffairs.com/articles/united-states/2021-01-12/how-america-can-shore-asian-order (Access 06.06.2021).
[7] https://www.countryaah.com/oceania-countries/ (Access 06.06.2021).

China and Russia. Moreover, there are also a number of growing subregions and cities with flourishing economies, industrial resources such as diamonds as well as areas containing rich energy resources such as the Russian Far East and Alaska. Besides, the circumpolar North is also situated on the northern edge of the North Pacific.[8] Herein, it should be noted that the interest in the Arctic Region is not new, on the contrary, it has been integrated into the international political and economic system for a long time. For instance, with the developments in long-haul flights, Greenland and Iceland became very important refueling points connecting the US and Europe in the Second World War.[9] Similarly, since it was the shortest flight path for newly developed intercontinental missiles and long-range bombers with nuclear warheads between the US and the USSR, the region was militarized for geostrategic reasons and it has played a key role in international security during the Cold War.[10]

Cryopolitics and the Concept of the Wider North

Cryopolitics, as a new field of discussion, can be explained as the competition based on controlling emerging resources and territory engendered by the melting cryosphere. The concept of cryopolitics is derived from the Greek word "kryos" meaning cold. The cryospheric umbrella, outlined by Haverluk,[11] covers wide geography with North and South Polar Regions, Alpine glaciers, ice shelf and strata, icebergs and regions containing permafrost. Therefore, global warming and cryopolitics are closely related concepts; the emergence of cryopolitics requires the recognition that climate change and global warming are scientific facts.

Owing to the great attention recently focused on the data and evidence needed to assert global warming as a scientific fact, speculations about new opportunities for maritime transportation are being voiced more frequently in parallel with the climate change discourse. Unsurprisingly, the scientific tools used to predict new transportation opportunities closely match those used for observations of melting and shrinking sea ice.[12]

The geopolitics of navigation in the Arctic Ocean, which is open to the use of all actors, is based on three fundamental issues: international interests in the mineral resources in the region, changing sea ice patterns due to climate change, and the environmental security of the Arctic Region.[13] Melting sea ice has allowed the seasonal opening of the Northwest Passage on the northern coast of North America and the North Sea Route (NSR) along Russia's northern coast,

---

[8] Lassi Heininen ve H. Nicol, "Canada and the New Geopolitics of the North Pacific Rim", **Position Paper for the 5th NRF Open Assembly,** 2008.

[9] C. Southcott ve L. Heininen (eds), **Globalization and the Circumpolar North,** University of Alaska Press, Fairbanks, 2010.

[10] R. Huebert, "A New Cold War in the Arctic?! The Old One Never Ended!", **Arctic Yearbook,** 2019.

[11] T. W. Haverluk, "The Age of Cryopolitics", **Focus on Geopgraphy,** Vol. 50, No. 3, 2007, pp. 1-6.

[12] M. Bravo ve G. Rees, "Cryo-politics: Environmental Security and the Future of Arctic Navigation", **The Brown Journal of Word Affairs,** Vol. 13, No.1, 2006, pp. 205-215.

[13] Ibid.

allowing ships to navigate without icebreaker guidance. When the increasing demand for resources from the BRIC countries (Brazil, Russia, India and China) is combined with the current high demand for resources from the industrialized states, the Arctic states are making various moves to gain authority over these resources. Russia's flag implementation on the seabed at the Pole can be given as an example of priority in its public policy while Canada offers scientific research to expand its maritime jurisdiction.[14]

Although these competitive moves of the Arctic states manifest great resemblance to the grand geopolitics of the late 19th and early 20th centuries, when states be used to seize land to secure geopolitical power, this approach falls short of describing the current climate-driven geopolitical paradigm that spurred the actions of these states. In this context, the Arctic Region has evolved into a complex and volatile region on its own rather than a buffer zone between superpowers.[15]

Eventually, the "Arctic Ocean" has turned into one of the most serious hegemonic conflict areas of the 21st century. The region has been at the center of the struggle of the great powers owing to its rich seabed and living resources as well as its potential to connect about 75 percent of the world's population due to the melting ice. While the US became a littoral to the Arctic Ocean by purchasing Alaska in 1867, Norway ensured its dominance in the Svalbard Archipelago with the Svalbard Treaty signed in 1920. thanks to this Treaty, the citizens of the signatory states are granted the right to engage in fishing and hunting, maritime and mining activities.[16]

Moreover, Russia accelerated the infrastructure works for the extraction of underground resources in the Arctic and maritime trade routes and Denmark increased its investments in Greenland. Canada, which claims the Northwest Passage, also has disagreements with other littoral states over the exclusive economic zone and the extraction of energy resources. Furthermore, the UK becomes the first non-Arctic state manifesting its major interest in the region by declaring itself as the "nearest neighbour to the Arctic"[17] which has reawakened controversial claims since China has also declared itself as a "near-Arctic state".[18] Besides, the country ranks among the highest gas and oil importers, and its largest partner is Norway. On the other hand, British Petroleum also owns a 19.75% stake in a Russian company, Rosneft, and the two companies have launched

---

[14] Ebru Caymaz, "Arktik Bilim Diplomasisi ve Türkiye", **Novus Orbis: Siyaset Bilimi ve Uluslararası İlişkiler Dergisi,** Cilt: 3, Sayı: 1, 2021.

[15] N. Einarsson; J. N. Larsen; A. Nilsson ve O. R. Young, "Arctic Human Development Report (AHDR)", Iceland: Stefansson Arctic Institute, 2004.

[16] Y. Barbaros Büyüksağnak ve Burcu Özsoy, "Importance and Interest on Arctic and Svalbard Treaty", Polar Conference, Davos, Switzerland, 2018.

[17] Secretary of State for Foreign and Commonwealth Affairs, "The UK and the Arctic", 2015, https://publications.parliament.uk/pa/ld201415/ldselect/ldarctic/118/11809.html (Access 19.04.2021).

[18] The State Council of the People's Rebuplic of China, "China's Arctic Policy", 2018, http://english.www.gov.cn/archive/white_paper/2018/01/26/content_281476026660336.htm (Access 1.07. 2021).

several projects in the Russian Arctic.[19]

Map 2. China's Polar Silk Road[20]

China's Polar Silk Road

Bering Strait

Japan

Alaska, the United States

Canada

China

Arctic Ocean

The Arctic Circle

Northern Sea Route

North Pole
+

The U.S. Military's
Thule Air Force Base

Russia

**Greenland
(Denmark)**

Iceland

Atlantic Ocean **Denmark**

©2019 The Sankei Shimbun /
JAPAN Forward

The non-Arctic states such as China, Japan and South Korea manifested great interest in the region by carrying out large-scale investments. In 2017, China officially declared the list of 'blue economic corridors' which comprise an essential part of China's controversial "Belt and Road" trade and infrastructure initiatives in which the Arctic Ocean was also enlisted among them. In the same year, China and the Nordic Council of Ministers officially agreed to strengthen collaboration between the Nordic region and China on five key areas. On the other hand, the West Nordic Region (Greenland, the Faroe Islands, coastal Norway, and Iceland,) has increasingly been framed as a distinct part of the Nordic region due to its Arctic location, maritime and blue bio-economy focus, albeit these states still have not issued a joint Arctic strategy or approach pertaining to emerging Polar Silk Road.[21]

Turkey also targets to get a larger share from the economic pie with its large number of institutions available in the maritime industry, institutions, and thousands of employees within them. For instance, Yalova-based Tersan Shipyard has received 45 orders from five Arctic states bordering the Arctic

---

[19] BP, "Growing the Business and Advancing the Energy Transition", **BP Annual Report and Form 20-F**, 2018.

[20] The Sankei Shimbun, "China's Polar Silk Road", **Japan Forward**, 2019.

[21] L. Ø. Blaxekær; M. Lanteigne ve M. Shi, "The Polar Silk Road & the West Nordic Region", **The Arctic Yearbook**, 2018; V. Erokhin; G. Tianming ve Z. Xiuhua, "Arctic Blue Economic Corridor: China's Role in the Development of A New Connectivity Paradigm in the North", The Arctic Yearbook, 2018.

Ocean (USA, Russia, Canada, Norway and Greenland /Denmark) since 2010 and delivered the majority of them. Since 2015, there has been a significant increase in the number of orders from the region. While the ship demands are mostly fishing vessels, off-shore support vessels and cruise ships such as ferries,[22] Turkey has manifested its political interest in the High North by applying for the observer membership within the Arctic Council and conducting its first national Arctic Scientific Expedition. Thus, more new and emerging actors are expected to manifest their political will and diplomatic involvement in the region.

On the other hand, due to the views suggesting that the United Nations Convention on the Law of the Sea (UNCLOS), which sometimes acts as a facilitator and sometimes a hindering catalyst for potential conflicts that may occur in the Arctic Region,[23] is insufficient in terms of resolving disputes in the region.[24] Therefore, the concept of cryopolitics has gained even more importance as an essential discussion matter. In parallel to the developments, as reports on Arctic shipping have begun to be evaluated in the context of physical determinism and geopolitical expressions, the basic research questions of cryopolitics can be summarized as below:

1. Will changing sea ice thickness and distribution usher in a new era of Arctic shipping?

2. Do shipping routes with increasing use in the Arctic have the potential to contribute to the security of the G8?

3. What effects will this have on the sovereignty of each littoral state over the northern waters?[25]

There have been several attempts from increasing number of states to mitigate the risks caused by global warming as well as to utilize emerging economic opportunities due to the reduced sea ice cover. The High North has been experiencing a major shift due to climate change, the geopolitics of the Cold War process, globalization and power transitions from the rise of China. This transformation is shaping the future of the region. It also defines the relationship between science diplomacy, geopolitics, law and globalization in the context of climate change, which will bring significant opportunities at the national, regional and global levels. Accordingly, the North has retained its saliency both as a strategic pivot and a wider region with the subsequent and growing interest.

Apart from recent discussions, there has been an obvious gap and an urgent need for an Arctic security forum to address Arctic security or defence issues.

---

[22] T.C. Ulaştırma ve Altyapı Bakanlığı, "Ulaşan Ve Erişen Türkiye-Denizcilik Sektörü", 2019, Https://Www.Uab.Gov.Tr/Uploads/Pages/Bakanlik-Yayinlari/Ulasan-Ve-Erisen-Turkiye-2019.Pdf (Access 01.07.2021).

[23] P. Prows, "Tough Love: The Dramatic Birth And Looming Demise Of UNCLOS Property Law (And What is To Be Done About It)", **Texas International Law Journal**, Vol. 42, 2006.

[24] S. Holmes, "Breaking the Ice: Emerging Legal Issues in Arctic Sovereignty", **Chicago Journal of International Law**, Vol. 9, No.1, 2008, pp. 323-351.

[25] Caymaz, "Arktik Bilim Diplomasisi ve Türkiye".

Upon the growing trend of re-militarization within the region in recent years, the Arctic Council Chairmanship (2021-2023) of Russia could initiate a constructive dialogue among the defence leaders of the Arctic states.

Figure 1. Current Governance Mechanisms in the High North and Their Responsibilities[26]

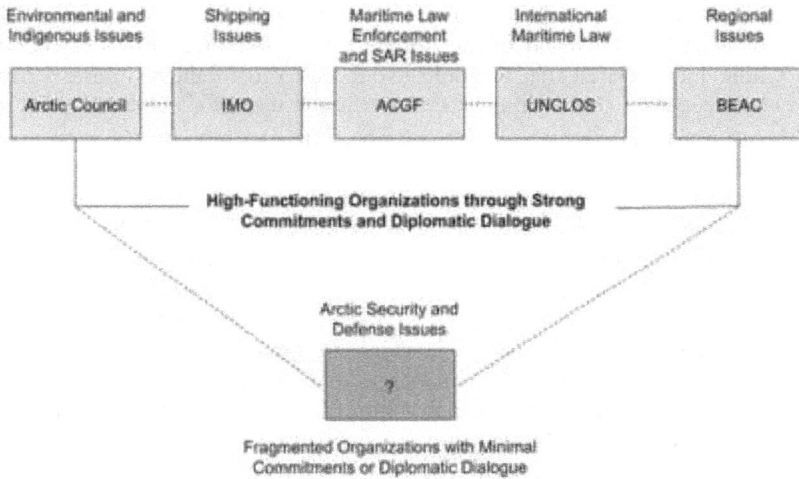

Conclusion

The predictions assert that the recent developments will shift the geopolitical center of gravity of the world from the Middle East to the Arctic Region. The dynamics of the US– China relationship are far more complex compared to the past. Even though some analysts may perceive the US–China competition in the Pacific Islands region as a replay of the Cold War through manifesting sharp reactions to diplomatic and naval activities, a clear understanding of the larger geopolitical developments across Oceania necessitates a broad point of view extending beyond the Cold War narrative.

Mearsheimer, with his 'aggressive reality'[27] approach, argues that states' ambition to gain power is unlimited. In his work titled 'The Tragedy of Great Power Politics', he claims that China would desire to be a hegemonic power in its region and try to drive the US out of the region as it gets stronger. He further discusses that China's low-profile foreign policy or the mutual economic interdependence of the two countries would not prevent the 'hegemonic encounter'. After a decade of implicit agreement between China and Taiwan for

---

[26] T. J. Bouffard, "Arctic Security and Dialogue: Assurance through Defence Diplomacy", 2020, https://moderndiplomacy.eu/2020/07/11/arctic-security-and-dialogue-assurance-through-defence-diplomacy/ (Access 12.05.2021).
[27] J. Mearsheimer, **The Tragedy of Great Power Politics**, W.W. Norton&Company, 2014.

maintaining the status quo of diplomatic ties, Taiwan's internal political dynamics have been changed and became visible in the 2016 national elections. That process has also renewed the competition for official recognition and the competitive dynamic between the US and China has been heavily affected. Currently, US policymakers focus on new opportunities for cooperation along with future economic support for the North Pacific.

On the other hand, in 2015, China designated the Bering Strait, which is the Pacific and Atlantic gateway of the Arctic Ocean, as an area of security concern for China and declared that it would use force to maintain its interests in this strait if necessary. In the same year, five Chinese warships exercised their right of navigation in the Bering Sea for the first time. If China proceeds to use the Bering Strait and other Arctic routes, it can avoid its dependence on the Strait of Malacca and save almost 100 billion dollars a year in transportation costs. China is also developing energy cooperation in the Arctic Ocean with Russia through Gazprom and CNPC companies. Therefore, it is predicted that China would avoid any competition with the US in the Arctic Ocean.[28] Moreover, in the White Paper released by China's State Council Information Office on January 28, 2018, China officially explains its future development goals in the region for the first time – including commercial, resource extraction efforts, scientific, and environmental preservation in which Chinese Arctic interests are aligned with the Belt and Road Initiative.

When the aforementioned developments are evaluated from a critical point of view, it is concluded that a new conceptual framework upon the Pacific Rim, specifically highlighting the North Pacific Rim, is required. In addition to Atlantic connections, recognizing the relationship between the Pacific, the North American continent, the circumpolar North would enhance further dialogue and strengthen the regional linkages among the countries of the North Pacific Rim while the regional powers struggle to utilize the emerging economic opportunities due to climate change in the High North.

---

[28] Cem Gürdeniz, "Kuzey Kutbunda Eriyen Buzların Jeopolitiğe Etkisi", 2021, https://www.denizbulten. com/m-haber-33811.html?islem=anahaber&altislem=anamanset (Access 01.06.2021).

PART 3

MARITIME POLICIES OF GLOBAL AND REGIONAL ACTORS

THE AFRICAN UNION'S MARITIME SECURITY STRATEGY AND ITS IMPACT ON CONTINENTAL PEACE AND STABILITY

Asena Boztaş[1] and Huriye Yıldırım Çınar[2]

Introduction

Africa, the oldest continent in the world, has a lot of problems. The maritime security problem, which has been one of these recently, deeply affects all continental countries. Maritime security, the solution of which must be found by African countries, is the sum of many different sub-elements. In this context, first of all, "Why Maritime Security Strategy is important for Africa?" an answer to this question was tried to be found. The answer to the question was tried to be reached by firstly examining the potentials of the sea and oceans for Africa, then examining threats and vulnerabilities.

They are African countries that will produce their own solution to African maritime security problems. In this context, the African Union, which is the most known organization of Africa, has been put at the basis of the study. In this section, the African Union's continental maritime security has been analyzed with the method of historical analysis.

As a result, it was understood that the African Union could not break away from its Western partners in finding African solutions, and it was observed that these partners were also involved in many meetings on maritime security. Therefore, it is clear that African countries have not yet been given the right to self-determination.

Why Maritime Security Strategy is important for Africa?

Developments regarding the sea and oceans are of vital importance for the African continent to attain peace, prosperity, and stability, which has been subjected to many adversities as a result of colonialist and neocolonialist policies after geographical discoveries. Because 38 of 54 countries in the African continent have seashores. In Africa, it is stated that there are 48,000 coastlines and approximately 13 million square kilometers of sea area. For this reason, the issue of maritime security has been brought to the agenda frequently in recent years, both by African countries and by foreign actors who have interests in Africa.

[1] Assoc. Prof. Dr. Asena Boztaş, Sakarya University of Applied Sciences, Faculty of Applied Sciences, Turkey. E-mail: aboztas@subu.edu.tr Orcid: 0000-0002-3216-3010.
[2] Huriye Yıldırım Çınar, PhD, Kocaeli University, Turkey. E-mail: yildirim.huriye@gmail.com, Orcid: 0000-0003-4681-0861

When considering the issue of maritime security, there are two factors to consider:

1. Protection/sustainability of the gains obtained from the sea, ocean, and seabed

2. Eliminating marine security threats and vulnerabilities

In this context, it can be mentioned that the seas have positive and negative effects on African countries. Factors such as living and non-living resources in the sea, ocean, and seabed, renewable energy that can be obtained from the sea, and trade routes provide some gains for the continent's prosperity and stability. On the other hand, threats from the sea such as pirate and terrorist acts, illegal activities, and environmental problems can cause important security problems for Africa and other foreign actors trying to have interests in the region. It is possible to summarize these two elements and their main sub-components as follows:

Gains and Potentials	Threats and Vulnerabilities

• Fisheries and aquaculture
• Energy
  • renewable energy sources
• Offshore hydrocarbon
  resources
• Seabed mining
• Maritime anc coastal Tourism
• Maritime Transport
• Ports and harbours management
• Shipbuilgind and ship reparing
  industry
	• Piracy
	• Maritime Terorrism
	• Armed Robbery
	• Effects of Inland/Regional
	  İnsecurities (Wars, conflicts,
	  political crises etc.)
	• IUU
	• Smuggling (Arms, goods, people)
	• Environmental Degredations:
	  • Climate change
	  • Pollution
	  • Shipbreaking

Potentials of the Sea and Oceans for Africa

Although the marine areas around Africa have been mostly associated with negative developments such as pirate activities, conflicts, and armed robbery in recent years, they also have a great potential for the peace, prosperity, and stability of the people of the continent. Within the scope of the economic independence of African countries and living in peace and prosperity, the importance of the seas has started to be brought to the agenda more and more at national and international levels. In this context, the concept of "Blue Economy" is frequently mentioned by many international organizations to indicate the importance of seas and oceans for Africa. The concept of "Blue Economy", on which more and more studies are carried out, is defined by the

World Bank as "sustainable use of ocean resources for economic growth, improved livelihoods, and jobs and ocean ecosystem health". Issues such as renewable energy, tourism, fishing, climate change, maritime transport, waste management are evaluated within the framework of Blue Economy. The United Nations Economic Commission for Africa (UNECA) highlighted the great potential of Blue Economy in Africa in its report published in 2016 with the title of "African Blue Economy: A Policy Handbook": "The blue economy as a mechanism to support and sustain rapid and sustainable development in Africa is timely and deserving of appropriate policy attention.[3] Through the blue economy framework, both coastal and land-locked states can harness opportunities, which could yield mutual benefits, including the provision of efficient and coordinated services to each other as well as access to resources.[4]

In this subtitle, the question of "what does/can the African continent gain from the seas and oceans?" will be answered. Fishing is one of the most striking of these areas, with the potential it provides to Africa in terms of both economic gain and food security. Many sources state that the fishing industry provides an income of $ 24 billion to the African continent, corresponding to 1.3% of the total income, and creates employment for more than 12 million Africans. Besides, fishing is tremendously important to the survival of some African peoples who often face food crises. Because fish, which contains half of the animal protein needed by a human, is a cheap and accessible food source for Africans living in coastal areas. It is also known that fish is a vital nutrient for people living in coastal areas in many countries such as Gambia, Sierra Leone, and Ghana.[5]

Another area that has an important potential for the African continent is the maritime transport sector. Approximately 90% of Africa's import and export products pass through the ports around the continent. Also, Africa is home to one of the world's largest shipping registries. The Liberian Registry corresponds to 11 percent of the world's oceangoing fleet.[6] In Africa, where maritime transportation is so important, various sectors such as port management, shipbuilding, and repair are considered sources of income and employment. According to the PMAWCA (Ports Management Association of West and Central Africa), which was established in October 1972 to regulate and develop port management in West and Central Africa, only the shipping line in the west of Africa covers a coastline of 12,000 km. Its ports handle about 300 million tons

---

[3] African Blue Economy: A Policy Handbook, UNECA, 2016.
[4] Cardiff Egede, "A new frotieo for mining? Time for Africa's engagement with deep seabed mining," https://www.ibanet.org/Article/NewDetail.aspx?ArticleUid=afdb69a8-7c83-4184-91b4-2a814556bef7, (Access 11.03.2021).
[5] Asena Özer Boztaş and Huriye Yıldırım Çinar, "Illegal Fishery in Africa and the Recommendations in the context of Turkey-Africa Relations", **Uluslararası Politik Araştırmalar Dergisi**, Vol. 5, No. 2, 2019, pp. 92-109.
[6] Talat Hussain, "Sustainability in Africa's Maritime Industry", 2019, https://www.whitecase.com/publications/insight/sustainability-africas-maritime-industry, (Access 12.03.2021).

of maritime import/export trade for the sub-region excluding crude oil.[7]

Sea and ocean areas around Africa also have great potential in terms of energy. Factors such as offshore hydrocarbon resources, transportation of oil and gas extracted with renewable energy technologies to the world market constitute this potential. Significant amounts of oil and gas resources have been found in the sea areas in recent years in the exploration studies in countries such as Angola, Nigeria, Congo-Brazzaville, Mauritania, South Africa, and Namibia.[8] For example, according to academic studies, it is estimated that Angola has approximately 17.6 billion barrels of oil. It is stated that approximately 95% of these estimated reserves are offshore. Also, Gabon Petronas announced that they found oil in deep waters in recent years. Subsequently, this company signed out a license agreement for 23 blocks in deep water.[9]

On the other hand, the limited and costly supply of fossil fuels offers renewable energy sources as an important alternative in terms of energy supply, after the damage of environmental problems is realized more. With the technological developments in recent years, there have been promising developments regarding energy production from the ocean surface and waves. Recently, various countries in Africa have started to implement projects related to renewable energy resources with the support of international actors. International Renewable Energy Agency (IRENA) reported that "Africa's extensive coastline also suggests long-term ocean energy potential, but this is unlikely to be a significant source by 2030.[10] Although many African countries do not have enough resources to realize this marine renewable energy technology, it is anticipated that many projects will be realized with international cooperation in the coming years. Thus, many developing African countries will be able to obtain much cheaper energy for their growing population and developing industry.[11]

Another promising potential for the African economy is the deep-sea mining industry. According to the report of the European Commission, approximately 10% of global annual mineral production will come from the ocean floor by 2030. In fact, offshore mining is not a new sector for the African continent. Since 1961, offshore mining activities have been found in various parts of Africa with the works of De Beers. For example, today De Beers and the state of Namibia are extracting diamonds from 150 meters with the "Namdeb" project. According to De Beers' statements, in the future, approximately 95% of diamonds will be obtained from reserves off the coast of Namibia. Although it is viewed with

---

[7] PMAWCA's official website, Introduction, https://agpaoc-pmawca.org/introduction/, (Access 12.03.2021).

[8] Zhang, Gongcheng, et al., "Giant discoveries of oil and gas fields in global deepwaters in the past 40 years and the prospect of exploration", **Journal of Natural Gas Geoscience,** Vol. 4, No. 1, 2019, pp. 1-28.

[9] "Oil and Gas Challenges and Opportunities in Africa", **GeoExpro,** Vol. 16, No. 4, 2019, p. 71.

[10] Africa 2030: Roadmap for a Renewable Energy Future, IRENA, 2015, p. 13.

[11] Elana Belleti and Milo McBride, "Against the Tide: Potential for Marine Renewable Energy in Eastern and Southern Africa", **Consilience,** Vol. 23, 2021.

suspicion by environmentalists, many coastal states such as South Africa continue to issue mining licenses to some foreign companies in their maritime areas. For example, in 2012 and 2014, South Africa announced that he would give the licenses to the companies such as Green Flash Trading 251 (Pty) Ltd, Green Flash Trading 257 (Pty) Ltd, and Diamond Fields International., in an area that covers the 150,000 km2 seafloor extending from the mouth of the River Groen on the West Coast to the Mossel Bay.[12]

Maritime and coastal tourism is another topic addressed within the scope of the Blue Economy in terms of the socio-economic development of Africa. Although "Maritime tourism" and "coastal tourism" are often thought of as the same concept, they are actually different. Coastal tourism generally is a beach-based tourism and includes the activities such as swimming, sunbathing, surfing, etc. On the other side maritime tourism covers water-based activities such as cruising, yachting, and sailing.[13] Both types are the key sectors for the African economy providing cash income. Infrastructures such as hotels, resorts, ports and ports built as a result of the investments to be made in this area will provide job opportunities for Africans. Considering only the South African example, it is thought that coastal and maritime tourism in this region will be effective in reducing poverty and unemployment in the country by providing 116,000 jobs by 2026.[14] However, the concern of filling the untouched coastlines with buildings for tourism and causing environmental degradation causes the reaction of both indigenous peoples and environmentalists.

Threats and Vulnerabilities

There is no single answer to the question of "Whose security?" within the concept of African maritime security. As shown in the table above, there are various threats and vulnerabilities coming from the seas and oceans. However, these are not only threats for the states and peoples in Africa, but also for some foreign actors who have interests in the continent. Perhaps that is why, especially in the post-Cold War world, initiatives for African maritime security are on the agenda to secure the interests of these actors. Many international institutions, especially the EU and NATO, aim to ensure the safety of the seas by interacting with the AU.

The concept of security has changed over time. Threats to different levels (international system, state, and individuals) have also changed with this changing character of the concept. For example, after the Second World War, due to the

---

[12] Fidelis Zvomuya, "Africa Eyes Underwater Mineral Treasures, but at what cost?", August 24, 2020. https://www.theoxygenproject.com/post/africa-eyes-underwater-mineral-treasures-but-at-what-cost/, (Access 13.03.2021).
[13] Tonazzini, D., Fosse, J., Morales, E., González, A., Klarwein, S., Moukaddem, K., Louveau, O, Blue Tourism Towards a sustainable coastal and maritime tourism in world marine regions, Ed. Eco-union, Barcelona, 2019.
[14] Cecilia Vos Belgraver, "Growing a sustainable coastal and marine tourism destination", URL: https://www.vukuzenzele.gov.za/growing-sustainable-coastal-and-marine-tourism-destination, (Access 14.03.2021).

ideological, political, and military competition between the USA and the USSR, military issues in the international arena have been in the field of security studies for about 50 years. However, this situation changed after the dissolution of the USSR and the end of the Cold War. The idea that the international system, states, and the survival of individuals can be threatened not only by military issues but also by various sectors, including political, social, economic, and environmental, has been created especially as a result of the studies of the thinkers of the Copenhagen School. The Copenhagen School, which consists of names such as Barry Buzan, Ole Waever, and Jaap de Wilde, expanded the concept of security which focused on military issues during the Cold War with the political, social, economic, and environmental sectors. The issue of the security of the African Seas, as emphasized by the Copenhagen School, includes not only military threats such as piracy and maritime terrorism, but also perceptions of various threats that can be collected under political, social, economic, and environmental topics. It should also be noted that these threats related to African maritime security are often the cause/trigger of each other. For example, global warming and environmental security are a threat to Africans living in fisheries as well as affecting the marine population. Some local fishermen whose livelihoods are under threat sometimes have to commit illegal acts to sustain themselves and their families.

We can summarize the main factors underlying the existence of these threats as follows:

- Political, military, and economic crises in newly independent African states

- Conflict, war, and terrorist acts in the region

- Inadequate cooperation at the regional level

- Postcolonial states' lack of knowledge and vision for maritime security issues

- Conflicts between states over sea areas (For example: between Nigeria and Cameroon over Bakassi Peninsula, and between Kenya and Somalia)

- Negative effects of globalization and neo-patrimonial networks

- The existence of economic and social inequalities and political and economic marginalization on the land

- Initiatives are taken by some foreign actors regardless of local balances

- Global warming and environmental degradation

It is possible to say that piracy is the most frequently mentioned threat to Africa's maritime security in the international area. In history, piracy was one of the methods used by the state and nations to be effective in the seas. However, this situation has changed today. Now, pirates have become a factor that weakens the power and structures of the states. In the early 2000s, East Africa started to be known as the center of piracy activities. At the end of June 2012, while the pirates in the region made a profit of 160 million dollars, this caused a loss of approximately 700 million dollars for the world economy.[15] After a short while, global actors with interests in East Africa and international organizations such as the EU and NATO, in which Western countries are active, took initiatives to combat piracy in Africa. As a result of these initiatives, most of the pirate activities in the east have moved further west and have become active in the Niger Delta and regions with relatively weaker states. Today, especially around Nigeria, pirates earn huge revenues from illegal fishing, smuggling, and illegal obtaining and marketing of hydrocarbon resources.

"Maritime terrorism", which is often put in the same category as piracy, is another important threat to Africa's maritime security. There are important differences between maritime terrorism and piracy. Piracy activities are generally carried out without a political or ideological purpose. However, on the other hand, maritime terrorism involves illegal actions that involve power and armed threats through various methods with a political or political motivation. For example, in the Niger Delta, terrorist organizations such as MEND (Emancipation of Niger Delta) and Boko Haram carry out several actions to achieve their goals in the seas as well as on the land. However, an important point that should be underlined is that sometimes there may be an interaction between pirates and terrorists. For example, there are many sources in the literature indicating that there were deep ties with terrorist organizations such as al-Qaeda and Al Shabaab, the pirates around Somalia after 2005.[16]

Sometimes war, conflict, or political crises on land in Africa can directly affect the situation at sea. For example, conflicts in Yemen threaten maritime security in the Gulf of Aden and the Red Sea. Using the authority gap in the region, illegal criminal organizations can easily carry out their actions here. On the other hand, remote-controlled bomb boots belonging to Houit Rebels pose serious security threats in the region.

Another maritime insecurity element that threatens the African continent and indirectly the international community is smuggling. There are various types of smuggling including people, drugs, goods, and weapons. According to a study conducted in 2007, approximately 60% of the cocaine in the European market reached the region from West Africa that year.[17] In addition to threatening international security, traffickers carrying refugees often cause the loss of their lives by drowning in deep waters. Finally, arms smuggling from the sea is a major

---

[15] Fernandes Capitao Ginga, "Maritime Insecurity In Sub-Saharan Africa And Its Effects In The Economy Of States", **AUSTRAL: Brazilian Journal of Strategy & International Relations**, Vol. 9, No. 18, 2020, p. 7.
[16] C. Singh and A. Bedi, "War on Piracy: The conflation of Somali piracy with terrorism in discourse, tactic, and law", **Security Dialogue,** Vol. 47, No. 5, pp. 440-458.
[17] Ginga, op.cit., p. 197.

threat to the security of both the regional states and the international community. These actions not only deepen the instability in the region but also strengthen terrorist groups and other criminal organizations. For example, after the instability in Yemen, small and medium weapons are illegally delivered from Yemen to criminal organizations in countries such as Somalia, Djibouti, Eritrea, and Ethiopia. The security of the already fragile countries in the region is threatened deeply by arms smugglers.[18]

As mentioned earlier, fishing is an important sector for the economy of many African countries and the food security of the people in the region. However, in recent years, the illegal fishing of foreign industrial fishing companies and other actors has been causing great damage to African states and peoples. This situation, called illegal, unreported and unregulated fishing (IUU), causes various security concerns in African countries. According to the data of FAO, two-thirds of the fish in seas, rivers, and lakes have been hunted excessively and illegally in the last 50 years. Some fish species such as tuna in the oceans have declined by a third. Again, according to the same report, 11-26 million tons of fish are caught each year without reporting.[19] Therefore, it is possible to say that IUU threatens both the livelihood and food resources of Africans who live by fishing on the coasts by significantly reducing fish stocks and species in African seas. According to many sources, only West African countries experience an annual loss of 1.5-2 billion dollars due to illegal fishing. Senegal, which employed a significant number of fishermen in 2012, lost 300 million dollars due to illegal fishing, which corresponds to approximately 2% of its gross national product. Similarly, Guinea was deprived of $ 110 million and Sierra Leone $ 29 million as a result of illegal and illegal fishing.[20] IUU, which causes states to lose a significant income, can cause people employed in the fishing industry to become unemployed and prone to some criminal acts to survive.

The last factor that threatens Africa's maritime security is global warming and environmental degradation. Global warming and pollution affect the water quality (like salinity, acidity degree) of the seas and oceans, causing the living resources here to disappear or migrate to other regions. In addition to the fishing sector, the health of people living in coastal areas is adversely affected by these changes in sea, river, and lake waters. It is possible to summarize the factors that pose these environmental threats that threaten the sea and inland waters in Africa as follows:

- Global warming, water quality, and the destruction of the living spaces of the aquatic creatures.

---

[18] Michael Horton, "Arms from Yemen will Fuel Conflict in the Horn of Africa", **Terrorism Monitor**, Vol. 18. No. 8, https://jamestown.org/program/arms-from-yemen-will-fuel-conflict-in-the-horn-of-africa/, (Access 14.03.2021).

[19] "Illegal, unreported and unregulated fishing", FAO, 2016, p. 2.

[20] lfonso Miren Gutiérrez Daniels et al, "Western Africa's Missing Fish", Por Causa Report, June 2016, p. 11.

- Waste dumping of ships and other marine vessels and toxic wastes

- Emissions from activities in the maritime sector

- Environmental damage caused by ports, seaside hotels, and businesses

- Toxic substances originating from end-of-life-ships, as in the example of 300 ships being left to coast to shore in the Nouadhibou region of Mauritania

As a result, it can be concluded that the threats from the seas and oceans to the African continent and the external actor interested in the continent vary according to time, actor, and place. It can be said that changes in technology and resources directly affect Africa's maritime security problem. A threat/vulnerability that has not yet come to the fore today can have important consequences for both Africans and foreign actors in the medium and long term. For example, today the gravity of issues such as global warming and pollution of the marine environment is not sufficiently understood. However, in the future, these elements are bound to have irreversible consequences for African maritime security. Likewise, an issue that does not pose a danger to any actor can have fatal consequences for other actors. This issue is also suitable for illegal fishing. Foreign actors attempting illegal fishing actions should not interpret this issue as a threat. However, illegal fishing is a major threat to African societies, where fishing is an important source of income and food.

AU and Maritime Security Strategy: Giving Importance

The African Union (AU), which aims to ensure political, social, and economic integration, accelerate development, protect peace and stability, and adopt democracy and good governance principles in all of Africa, in its long-term work in cooperation with the European Union (EU), to the dominance of Africa in the seas, devotes an important place to its rights and security. In fact, until the 2000s, maritime security in Africa was largely not within the scope of its work. In this context, the International Maritime Organization (IMO), which was formed by 37 African countries before the 2000s, was an important formation. So much so that the maritime transport regulations have been in effect in Africa since 1993 thanks to IMO.[21] On the other hand, the issue of African maritime security is an issue that Africans still do not give necessary importance to. In this context, the issue of ensuring security in African seas was first mentioned in the Union at the Cairo Summit in 2000, and then in June 2009, the issue of maritime security was brought back to the agenda of the African Union due to the piracy activities in the Somali coasts. Maritime security, again in terms of combating piracy, formed a part of the Action Plan, which was adopted in August 2009 at the Special Session of the AU Assembly on the Assessment and Resolution of

---

[21] Buerger, Christian, "Communities of Security Practice at Work? The Emerging African Maritime Security Regime", **African Security**, Vol. 6, No. 3-4, pp. 297-316.

the Conflict in Africa in Sirte, Libya.[22]

During this period of international cooperation on African maritime security, IMO invited AU Infrastructure and Energy Department (DIE) to a follow-up meeting to be held in Seychelles on 12-16 October 2009. DIE also participated in a meeting of African maritime transport ministers in Durban. In this meeting held on 12-16 October, "Maritime Safety, Maritime Security and Protection of the Marine Environment in Africa and the related Plan of Action: Maritime Transport, 2009-2012", known as "African Maritime Transport Charter", was accepted[23] The Charter was based on a 1994 document being updated by the AUC between 2007 and 2009.[24]

The breakthrough in African maritime security started with the "AU Experts Workshop on Maritime Security and Safety: Towards Africa's Integrated Maritime Strategy (AIM-Strategy)" held on 6-7 April 2010 the following year, gradually gaining international significance.[25] This workshop came to fruition with the 2050 Aim Strategy in the following years. In this process, the issue of African maritime safety was discussed in the "242nd Meeting of the Peace and Security Council" held on October 4, 2010[26] and in the "The 2010 Africa Maritime Safety and Security Towards Economic Prosperity Conference" on 13-14 October 2010 within AU.[27]

The African maritime security strategic plan, the first steps of which started in 1994, gained momentum again with the arrangement of Task Force to Lead Development and Implementation of 2050 Africa's Integrated Maritime Strategy (2050 Aim-Strategy) on 3 June 2011[28] and was crowned with "Decision on the Report of the Peace and Security Council on its Activities and the State of Peace and Security in Africa" on 25-27 July 2011 prepared 1 month later. In essence, it is obvious that the study, whose EU influence is undeniable, will ultimately contribute to African maritime security. Therefore, Resolution 1851 (2008) was adopted by the Security Council at its 6046th Meeting, on 16 December 2008 the Security Council.[29]Similarly, in 2013 (24-25 June), when the Communiqué of the

---

[22] Ulf Engel, "The African Union, the African Peace and Security Architecture, and Maritime Security" Peace and Security Series. Friedrich-Ebert-Stiftung, 2014, Addis Ababa, pp. 1-32.

[23] "African Maritime Transport Charter", Second African Union Conference Of Ministers Responsible For Maritime Transport 12 – 16 October 2009 Durban, South Africa, https://au.int/sites/default/files/documents/30853-doc-african_mariteme_transport_charter.pdf, (Access 13.02.2021).

[24] Michael L. Baker, "Tozardı an African Maritime Economy"i Empowering the African Union to Revolutionize the African Maritime Sector, **Naval College Review**, Vol. 64, No. 2, 2011, p. 44.

[25] "AU Experts Workshop on Maritime Security and Safety: Towards Africa's Integrated Maritime Strategy (AIM-Strategy)", AU Experts Workshop on Maritime Security and Safety, 6-7 April 2010, Addis Ababa, Ethiopia, https://au.int/ar/node/27460, (Access 16.02.2021).

[26]). "242nd Meeting of the Peace and Security Council", African Union, 4 October 2010, https://au.int/ar/node/27458, (Access 14.02.2021).

[27] "The 2010 Africa Maritime Safety and Security Towards Economic Prosperity Conference", African Union, 13-14 October, Stuttgart, Germany, https://au.int/en/newsevents/20101013, (Access 17.02.2021).

[28] "Task Force to Lead Development and Implementation of 2050 Africa's Integrated Maritime Strategy (2050 Aim-Strategy) Formed, African Union, (Access 02.02.2021).

[29] "Decision On TheThe Report of The Peace and Security Council on Its Activities and The State of

Peace and Security Council of the AU held high-level meetings between the continental states, the 387th meeting in Yaoundé, Cameroon, "Summit of Heads of State and Government on Maritime Safety and Security in the Gulf of Guinea" is very important based on decisions taken on maritime security (African Union, 2013).[30]

AU accepted Turkey as an "observer state" in 2005 and a "strategic partner" in 2008, continues to cooperate with the EU and Western countries to ensure the safety of its seas. Throughout the process, African and European leaders envisioned to act jointly towards shaping the international environment and strengthening collective security understanding, such as supporting reforms in the UN and other important international organizations, establishing the 2050 Africa's Integrated Sea Strategy, as well as finding solutions to the problems encountered.[31]

The African Union strives to ensure its development in cooperation with European countries in the post-colonial period as well as in the historical process. In this context, when the maritime security studies of the African Union are examined, the "2050 Africa's Integrated Maritime Strategy-2050 AIM Strategy", which was developed with the EU in December 2013-January 2014, which was founded in the Cairo Summit, draws attention. The Strategy Document, which was prepared as a result of the cooperation between the EU-AU and prepared to eliminate the threats faced by Africa in inland waters, seas, and oceans, emerged as a result of the work of 2050 Africa's Integrated Naval Strategy Task Force with a delegation of three European vice-admiral (Patrick Hebrard, Anthony Dymock, and Fernando del Pozo). However, the parties agreed that the effective implementation of 2050 Africa's Integrated Marine Strategy and Action Plan would be for the sustainable benefit of the peoples of Africa, and have set up the mission of "Wise Pens International" prepare to maritime analysis, strategies and produce solutions to problems (distrust due to piracy activities, pressure on Africa's inland waters, oceans and seas, traditional maritime activities such as shipping or fishing, aquaculture or offshore renewable energy generation, various types of illegal smuggling, the degradation of the marine environment, the reduction of biodiversity and the aggravated effects of climate change, loss of life, hundreds of billions of dollars of direct total revenue loss).[32]

The fact that the main actors of African maritime security, whose foundations were laid in the late 1990s and early 2000s, are European states rather than African states, can be described as a return of the post-colonial order. Instead,

---

Peace and Security in Africa", African Union, Doc. Assembly/AU/4(XVII)". Assembly/AU/Dec.369(XVII), https://archives.au.int/bitstream/handle/123456789/1273/Assembly%20AU%20Dec%20369%20%28XVII%29%20_E.pdf?sequence=1&isAllowed=y, (Access 17.01.2021).

[30] "Summit of Heads of State and Government on Maritime Safety and Security in the Gulf of Guinea", African Union, Yaoundé, Cameroon, 24-25 June, https://au.int/fr/node/27463, (Access 22.02.2021).

[31] İbrahim Aslan, "Africa-European Union Relations in the 21st Century: Two Unions, One Vision", **Marmara Journal of European Studies**, Vol. 23, No. 1, 2015, p. 116.

[32] İbid, p. 122.

limiting the interventions of European countries to "transfer of experience" would be much more efficient for the continental countries.

Another study created within the African Union, which foresees the maritime security of Africa, is "Africa Agenda 2063", which was accepted in May 2013. What is envisaged in the African Agenda 2063 in the field of maritime security is mostly "Blue Economy or Ocean Economy" and "African Peace and Security Architecture". In this study, which prioritizes economic development, continental eco-policies and performance indicators, from marine biotechnology to accelerating economic growth, are discussed with a regional nature.[33] In the study, which is supported not only by Europe but also by Japan and the whole world, the real predictions are the developments in the 50 years between 2013-2063. The multi-dimensional approach of the 2050 AIM Strategy has also triggered, developed, and supported similar studies such as the Integrated Maritime Strategy of the Intergovernmental Authority of Development (IGAD) in 2015, Djibouti Code of Conduct's 2017 Jeddah Amendment.[34] Described as a foundation for the sustainable development of the maritime industry, the 2050 Aim Strategy was included in the Lomé Charter, a legally binding agreement adopted by the AU in 2016.[35]

As can be seen, although it slowed down for a certain period after 2010, Africa, which attracted the attention of global actors with a rising momentum after 2013, does not fall from the international agenda, especially with the piracy activities in the Gulf of Guinea regarding maritime security. So much so that when we look at Commercial Crimes Services' current Live Piracy and Armed Robbery Report 2021, there was a theft in Angola on February 26, 2021, and two piracy activities in Sao Tome Island on February 8 and 9, 2021.[36] When it comes to maritime security, which is one of the recent priorities of the African Union, Bueger's maritime security matrix comes to mind. In Buerger matrix; draws attention to the importance of the blue economy, coast guard, sea power endurance, climate change, terrorist attacks, pollution, fishing, piracy, smuggling, inter-state disputes, weapons proliferation, accidents in maritime security, which should be examined based on the marine environment, economic development, national security and human security.[37] It is possible to observe the presence of

---

[33] "Agenda 2063: The Africa We Want.", African Union, 2021. https://au.int/en/agenda2063/overview, (Access 07.03.2021).
[34] "Djibouti Code of Conduct: Revised Code of Conduct Concerning the Repression of Piracy, Armed Robbery Against Ships, And Illicit Maritime Activity in The Western Indian Ocean and The Gulf of Aden Area", IMO, 2017, https://www.cdn.imo.org/localresources/en/OurWork/Security/Documents/A2%20Revised%20Code%20Of%20Conduct%20Concerning%20The%20Repression%20Of%20Piracy%20Armed%20Robbery%20Against%20Ships%20Secretariat.pdf, (Access 22.01.2021).
[35] "African Charter on Maritime Security and Safety and Development in Africa (Lomé Charter)", African Union, 15 October 2016, Lome, Togo, https://au.int/sites/default/files/treaties/37286-treaty-african_charter_on_maritime_security.pdf, (Access 14.02.2021).
[36] "Live Piracy and Armed Robbery Report 2021", ICC, 2021, https://www.icc-ccs.org/index.php/piracy-reporting-centre/live-piracy-report, (Access 07.03.2021).
[37] Cristian Buerger, "What is Maritime Security?", **Marine Policy**, 2015, http://bueger.info/wp-content/uploads/2014/12/Bueger-2014-What-is-Maritime-Security-final.pdf, pp. 1-11, (Access 15.02.2021).

the matrix, which is very important in Africa, at the 2016 Summit.

Figure 2.1. Maritime Safety Matrix

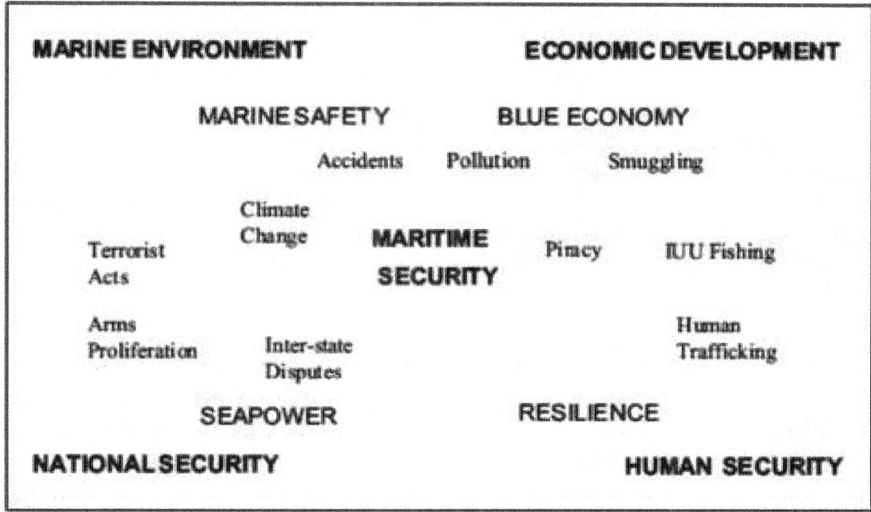

Source: Buerger 2015: 5.

The Maritime Security Declaration was signed at the African Union Maritime Security and Development in Africa Summit held in Togo's capital city Lome in October 2016 Approximately 30 countries have signed the Declaration, which aims to ensure maritime security to effectively combat piracy, illegal fishing, and smuggling in African seas. While the African Court of Human and Peoples' Rights has been responsible for regulating the innovations brought by the declaration, a committee consisting of 15 countries has been appointed to control the implementation of the declaration. The Lome declaration consists of 57 articles divided into 7 sections and has been prepared in accordance with national laws. Also, at the meeting, where the maritime industry envisaged as a part of the African maritime security was not forgotten, "to train, create jobs and wealth in the maritime industry" topics were also discussed.[38]

It could be observed that the Africa maritime security was revived with the Lome Summit, at the "African Day of Seas and Oceans" celebrations in Addis Ababa on 30 May 2018, in the presence of the strengthening Maritime Strategic Task Force, at the 4th Meeting of the Strategic Task Force for the Implementation of the 2050 Africa's Integrated Maritime (AIM) Strategy on 8-10 August 2018, at the AU-ECA High-Level Conference on Africa's Blue Economy on 28 November 2018 and dozens of academic studies in this field.

---

[38] "African Charter on Maritime Security and Safety and Development in Africa (Lomé Charter)", African Union, 15 October 2016, Lome, Togo, https://au.int/sites/default/files/treaties/37286-treaty-african_charter_on_maritime_security.pdf, (Access 14.02.2021).

The African Union, which acts in close relations with the EU on providing peace and security in its seas, also receives the support of the EU in the AU AMISOM operation in Somalia through the APF (African Peace Facility). EU's support to AMISOM for 2014, which was 225 million Euros, is more than 580 million Euros in total. Similarly, after the concerns of piracy and armed robberies in the Horn of Africa and the West Indian Ocean, Operation EU NAVFOR ATALANTA was launched based in Somalia. Maritime Security Center-Horn of Africa/MSCHOA is an important structure in terms of maritime safety, also created as a result of cooperation with the EU. The security of trade lies at the heart of all these EU-supported developments in African maritime security. Therefore, the commercial dimension of the security of African seas, that is, the security of its trade with the Continent, which is an important market for itself, is the main goal of the EU.

Conclusion and Recommendations

Maritime security is one of the issues that started to attract attention with the changing security perceptions in the international arena after the Cold War. The fact that 38 countries have seashores in the African continent consisting of 54 countries makes maritime security important throughout Africa. It is seen that many African states that have gained their political independence, are still economically dependent on the West. and the seas with enormous potential are an integral part of African security when the political and socio-economic crises that do not live in the continent are considered.

The issue of maritime security, which is also about the protection and sustainability of great potentials in various fields such as commercial and economic gains, fisheries, mining and energy, is of great importance not only for Africans but also for external actors who have interests in the African continent. Especially in the rapidly globalizing world after the Cold War, the concern of Western actors to lose their gains from the African seas for various reasons has led to efforts to ensure the maritime security of Africa through bilateral and multilateral initiatives. Other external actors such as the European Union institutionally, the European countries, the USA, and China are closely concerned with the security of African seas. These actors try to take some organizational measures, sometimes through bilateral agreements and operations, and sometimes with the African Union. However, since these measures often center the interests of the relevant actors, there is no permanent solution to Africa's maritime security issue. At this point, the African Union must take concrete and practical steps for the security of the seas and oceans by increasing communication and interaction between continental states.

It is possible to summarize the main issues that should be realized by the continental states, especially the African Union, and external actors regarding the African maritime security strategy as follows:

- Creating national and international security strategies by interpreting the concept of security in a deeper and broader sense and incorporating the security of seas and oceans into the concept.

- Ensuring that African states, external actors related to the continent and international organizations such as the African Union, European Union and NATO have similar perceptions of maritime security to understand the importance of Maritime Security for the security of international peace and stability as well as for Africa

- Establishing suitable platforms for discussing Maritime security issues and creating functional strategies.

- Increasing the sharing of knowledge and experience among actors in order to eliminate threats

- Giving importance to the principle of equal and fair use of the seas by ensuring the benefit of the local people first in profitable activities such as fishing, deep sea mining and energy production

- Strengthening the military and intelligence units of the continental states to combat illegal acts such as UII, piracy, smuggling and armed robbery

- Strengthening the potential of states in order to better observe sea actions and maritime traffic and intervene in emergencies

- Establishing the necessary mechanisms to prevent damage to the environment within the scope of activities such as fishing, maritime transport and deep-sea mining.

- Ensuring the establishment of effective and deterrent legislation for the prosecution and punishment of maritime offenders

These factors, briefly mentioned above, can be effective in obtaining positive results in Africa's maritime security in different fields and degrees. However, in our interview with Mohammed Omar, Senior Advisor to the President of Somalia, within the scope of this study, we concluded that the creation of Joint Regional Group States could be quite functional to ensure the maritime security of the continent. Omar, who has been in the committee formed to resolve the maritime dispute between Kenya and Somalia for many years, underlined that there are different dangers and problems in different regions of Africa, and emphasized that this organization can be more solution oriented. Authorities and scientists from each country in Joint Regional Group States will be able to identify priorities and issues in the areas thay they are responsible for, and offer suggestions for solutions by exchanging opinions, information and experiences. In addition, these entities will be able to contribute to the early detection and intervention of potential threats by undertaking the mission of continuous monitoring in their areas of duty. As a result, it is possible to say that the principle of "African solutions to African problems", which is constantly emphasized, will ensure peace and stability in the continent in the medium and long term. This structure, emphasized by Omar, will prioritize the interests of African states and local peoples over global powers, and will contribute to continental peace and stability regarding African Maritime Security through more effective means of combating.

CONTEMPORARY GEOPOLITICAL ASPECTS OF THE ATLANTIC: ACTORS, ISSUES, AND COOPERATION

Ahmet Ateş[*]

Introduction

Atlantic is one of the most important regions in the world because of at least three reasons. First, several key actors in global politics such as the United States (US), the United Kingdom (UK), and Brazil located in this region. Second, the Atlantic Ocean is crucial for trade flows between North America, South America, Europe, and Africa. Third, this region is vital for global and regional institutions such as the North Atlantic Treaty Organization (NATO) and the Latin American Free Trade Association (LAFTA). In a nutshell, the Atlantic is one of the two epicenters of global politics and international trade.

Due to its importance in global politics, the geopolitics of the Atlantic has always been a key factor not only in political science literature but also in formulating and implementing foreign policies of the countries in the Atlantic in the last fifty years. It is also important to note that the security environment of the region has also dramatically changed in the last fifty years due to incidents in global politics for example the end of the Cold War or 9/11. Even though the security and threat parameters of the region have changed, there is little attention to exploring the region's transformation with a holistic approach. This chapter aims to fill this gap in the literature and provide a holistic approach to analyze and explain contemporary geopolitical aspects of the Atlantic.

To provide an overview of the Atlantic, it is important to focus on key actors and factors that bring into prominence the region. Therefore, this chapter is threefold. First, a brief literature review on geopolitics is provided with a conceptualization of the term in this chapter. Second, key actors both in the North and South Atlantic are presented. Third, key issues of the Atlantic are analyzed.

A Brief Literature Review on Geopolitics and Conceptualization

Even though the concept of geopolitics has been circulating the political arguments for more than a century, the evolution of the concept can be explained under four eras. These eras are 1) Classical Geopolitics, 2) Geopolitics and the Second World War, 3) Back of the Geopolitics in the 1970s, and 4) Current Interpretations of the Geopolitics.

[*] Ph.D. Lecturer, Iğdır University, Faculty of Economics and Administrative Sciences, Department of Political Science and International Relations, Turkey. E-mail: ahmet.ates@igdir.edu.tr.

The introduction of geopolitics into the literature and political discourse started in the nineteenth century. Even though the concept was first studied by German geographer Freidrich Ratzel, the concept was first used by a Swedish professor and politician R. Kjeller in 1899 and defined as the impact of environmental factors on the features of a nation.[1] The concept of geopolitics has been used by several professions since its introduction. Among others, politicians, military professionals, and researchers of geography and political science have used it most.[2] In addition to Kjeller, Alfred Thayer Mahan and Harfold Mackinder played a vital role in building geopolitics as an academic discipline. First, Mahan introduced the concept of sea dominance to explain the importance of the navy to further the US's interests. Even though Mahan explored the importance of geographic location for a country, the academic definition of geopolitics was coined by Mackinder who is also heavily influenced by Mahan's studies.[3]

It would be safe to say that the studies of these four pioneers in the field constitute the classical definition of geopolitics. It is important to explain the two merits of the classical definition of geopolitics. First, the introduction of geopolitics aimed to provide an explanation of global politics other than imperialist explanations.[4] Second, this attempt was also aimed to explain global politics with a focus on sea and land forces and particularly on the security of the Western nations.[5]

After the introduction of the concept in the late 1890s, geopolitics was heavily researched and used by German scholars. Most notably, Carl Hous Houfer's studies on geopolitics paved the way for German political thought before the Second World War and fueled German national socialist discourse before the war.[6] Particularly, the concept of Lebensraum constituted a theoretical background for the German expansion in the 1940s and boosted German ambitions over its neighbors.[7] The use of geopolitics by senior Nazi officials during the Second World War to justify their atrocities diminished the reputation of the concept globally. Hence, both scholars and policymakers refrained from using geopolitics in their studies/explanations between the 1950s and the 1970s. In a nutshell, the concept of geopolitics transformed from an exploration of politics of the Western nations to a theoretical scapegoat of Nazi crimes in the Second World War.

Even though geopolitics became a reprehensible concept after the Second

---

[1] Martin Glasssner, **Political Geography**, Canada, John Wiley and Sons, 1993, p.224 quoted in Mohammed Reza Hafeznia, "A New Definition of Geopolitics." **Geopolitica - Revistă de geografie politică, geopolitică şi geostrategie**, Vol.5, No.22, 2007, pp.21-22.

[2] Mohammed Reza Hafeznia, **ibid**, p.21.

[3] Colin Flint, **Introduction to Geopolitics**, London and New York, Routledge, 2008, p.17.

[4] Colin Flint, **ibid**, p.17.

[5] Colin Flint, **ibid**, p.18.

[6] Sudeepta Adhikari, Political Geography, New Delhi, Rawat Publications, 1997, p.23 quoted in Mohammed Reza Hafeznia, **ibid**, p.23.

[7] Colin Flint, **ibid**, p.20.

World War, it was reintroduced in the 1970s and its usage was expanded by the US political elites in the 1980s to explain the US foreign policy. In the 1970s, geopolitics started to appear in policy analysis and articles.[8] In the 1980s, on the other hand, it became the main factor to explain US foreign policy in the Cold War, particularly after its utilization by Henry Kissinger and Zbigniew Brzezinski.[9] Between the 1980s and early 2000s, geopolitics became one of the most popular concepts in foreign policy and international relations literature, and its scope dramatically expanded to explain other phenomena such as finance and immigration.[10] In other words, once a cursed word to explain inter-state relations due to Nazi atrocities, geopolitics became a popular concept to research not only security relations among countries but also other issues.

After the early 2000s, the focal point of geopolitics dramatically changed. While previous explanations of geopolitics mostly focused on inter-state relations and security, the explanations after the early 2000s interpreted the concept not as the politics of states and borders but as identifying situations in the world.[11] In that manner, the scope of geopolitics research expanded, and non-state actors, domestic issues, and non-material factors such as shared identity were included in the concept.[12] In other words, geopolitics became a handy tool for scholars and policymakers to explain almost everything in global politics.

As briefly explained above, the definition of geopolitics has changed over time in parallel to the changing nature of international relations. Therefore, there are many definitions of the concept. However, all the definitions intertwine with two concepts: geography and politics, as these two concepts constitute geopolitics. However, while some scholars put more emphasis on geography, others pay more attention to politics.

As Anderson or Lee put, in its simplest form, geopolitics is explaining geographical effects' impact on political history[13] or studying international relations from a geographical perspective.[14] In other words, geopolitics refers to the academic consideration of a country's position in the global arena because of its geographical features.[15] Put differently, geopolitics is a way of studying politics

---

[8] Mohammed Reza Hafeznia, **ibid**, p.21.

[9] Oliver M. Lee, "The Geopolitics of America's Strategic Culture." **Comparative Strategy**, Vol.27, No.3, 2008, p. 267.

[10] Jason Dittmer and Klaus Dodds. "Popular geopolitics past and future: Fandom, identities and audiences." **Geopolitics**, Vol.13, No.3, 2008, pp.437-438.

[11] Colin Flint, **ibid**, p.16.

[12] Robbie Shilliam, "The Atlantic as a vector of uneven and combined development." **Cambridge Review of International Affairs**, Vol.22, No.1, 2009, p.73.

[13] Ewan W. Anderson, "Geopolitics: International boundaries as fighting places." **The Journal of Strategic Studies**, Vol.22, No.3, 1999, p.125.

[14] Oliver M. Lee, "The Geopolitics of America's Strategic Culture." **Comparative Strategy**, Vol.27, No.3, 2008, p. 267

[15] Gertjan Dijkink, "GEOPOLITICS DEBATE IV Geopolitics as a Social Movement?." **Geopolitics**, Vol.9, No.2, 2004, p.460.

through geographical traits.

Other scholars, on the other hand, focus more on politics rather than geography. Per Flint, Puntigliano, and Retaillé, geopolitics is inherently about politics. Flint argues that geopolitics is a way of interpreting the world which usually is being used to justify actions within the territorial competition.[16] Puntigliano and Retaillé, on the other hand, assert that geopolitics is one of the approaches to explore imperial and great power policies.[17]

Given the divergent definitions of geopolitics above, the definition of the concept used in this chapter is as follows. Geopolitics is a method to address territorial disputes or cooperation in which key actors, states, international organizations, and non-state organizations, compete or cooperate to further their national or regional interests and improve the security of the region.

Key Actors in the Atlantic

Atlantic is one of the most important regions in the world due to political and geographical reasons. On the one hand, most of the powerful actors in global politics are located in this region. On the other hand, the Atlantic Ocean covers roughly twenty percent of the Earth and 52 countries reside in this region.[18] Due to its magnitude and political differences between the Northern and Southern Atlantic priorities, it would be wise to analyze the region as North and South Atlantic.

North Atlantic

Though there are several countries located in the North Atlantic, it can be argued that four actors vary from others regarding their ability to determine the policies in the region. These key actors are the US, the UK, Canada, and NATO. While the US and Canada are located in the northern part of the North Atlantic, the UK is vital in the southern part of the region. NATO, on the other hand, is a crucial international organization regarding bridging between the northern and southern parts of the North Atlantic and providing the security of the region.

The United States

The US is the main pillar of the North Atlantic alliance and it is the most important actor of the region. Historically, the Atlantic Ocean has been the first of its defensive line and a vital element of the US hegemony, as Mahan argues. Particularly, after the Second World War, politics in the region was shaped by

---

[16] Colin Flint, **ibid**, p.13.

[17] Andrés Rivarola Puntigliano, "21st century geopolitics: Integration and development in the age of 'continental states'." **Territory, Politics, Governance**, Vol.5, No.4, 2017, p.479.; Denis Retaillé, "Geopolitics in history." **Geopolitics**, Vol.5, No.2, 2000, p.37.

[18] US Department of Commerce, National Oceanic and Atmospheric Administration, National Ocean Service, "How big is the Atlantic Ocean?" https://oceanservice.noaa.gov/facts/atlantic.html (Access: 09.05.21)

the US foreign policy agenda.[19] During the Cold War, the main idea behind the US security policy was to deter the United Soviet Socialist Republics and the North Atlantic region was the backbone of this strategy.[20] In other words, North Atlantic was a crucial region for the United States' security during the Cold War. 9/11 also deepened the cooperation between the US and European countries, particularly in countering terrorism.[21]

It should be noted that the importance of the region for the US Grand Strategy relatively reduced after the end of the Cold War. However, revitalization of the Russian military presence after 2008 and Russian expansion after 2011 dramatically increased the importance of the region for the United States. However, it would be not possible to say that this region is as crucial for the US as it was in the Cold War era. Due to the growing economy, rising Chinese military presence, and a shift in the global geopolitics from the Atlantic to the Pacific, it would be safe to argue that the US put more emphasis on the geopolitics of the Pacific.

In a nutshell, the US is still the most important actor in the North Atlantic even though the region's importance for the US is relatively lower than the Pacific. The main geopolitical concern regarding the Atlantic for the US is containing Russian expansionism after 2011 and improving its security via cooperation with European countries.

The United Kingdom

The UK is the most important actor in the southern part of the Atlantic alliance. Unlike the US, the UK is a regional actor rather than a global one. Therefore, the geopolitics of the Atlantic is more crucial to the UK than the US because the security of the Atlantic is strictly aligned with the security of the UK. As Friedman asserts, the British grand strategy requires strong naval force in the Atlantic and durable relations with the European countries.[22] Both in the two world wars, as a leading actor in the region, the UK heavily contributed to the security of Europe. However, the dominance of the UK in setting the European security parameters changed after the Second World War. The US, as a global actor, started to determine the security agenda of the Atlantic in the 1950s and the UK began balancing the US and the USSR. [23] Though it was not a global actor, the UK continued to be the main pillar in the southern part of the Atlantic

[19] John A. Agnew, Is US Security Policy" pivoting" from the Atlantic to Asia-Pacific?: A Critical Geopolitical Perspective. Friedrich-Ebert-Stiftung, Global Policy and Development, 2012, p.4.
[20] John A. Agnew, ibid, p.5.
[21] Jan Ballast, "Merging Pillars, Changing Cultures: NATO and the Future of Intelligence Cooperation Within the Alliance." International Journal of Intelligence and CounterIntelligence, Vol.31, No.4, 2018, p.722.
[22] George Friedman, "The Geopolitics of Britain." **Geopolitical Futures Weekly**. https://geopoliticalfutures.com/the-geopolitics-of-britain/ (Access: 03.05.2021).
[23] George Friedman, **ibid**.

alliance during the Cold War.[24]

Even though it officially left the European Union on 31st June of 2020, the UK is still one of the key actors regarding continental safety of Europe and geopolitics of the Atlantic. Increasing Russian covert activities in the UK such as the Salisbury incident in 2018 prove the importance of the country for the region. However, it should be noted that the majority of British geopolitical concerns after 2010 are not related to the safety of continental Europe but rather are about the Arctic. Therefore, it is possible to argue that the most important issue for the UK in the Atlantic is the Arctic.

Even though the Arctic was one of the important issues in British policymaking, its importance boosted after 2010 due to the impacts of climate change, melting the Arctic.[25] Before 2010, the Arctic was referred to as a logistical corridor which the UK densely used in the Second World War and the Cold War but relatively gave up emphasizing it after the end of the Cold War. [26] After 2010, on the other hand, the impact of climate change provided an opportunity for the UK to connect Wider North through the sea.[27] If melting of the Arctic continues in the same ratio, the Northern Sea Route will be feasible for international trade and the Arctic region may become a commercial hub.[28] Due to this possibility, Russian Federation and China's interest in the region is expanded and they have been intensifying their military presence in the region. Because of these reasons, it would be fair to argue that the Arctic will be the most important issue in the geopolitical considerations of the UK soon.

Canada

Canada is another key actor in the Atlantic not only because of its geographical location but also its role in the region as a vital energy importer considering Canada's proven oil reserves are the third-largest in the world.[29] Therefore, Canada's role in the Atlantic and its policies are strictly related to energy relations. In other words, controlling Western energy resources is the key issue for Canada that impacts its relations with regional actors such as the US and global actors such as China.[30]

It should be noted that the US and Canada are key allies in the region and

---

[24] Benjamin B. Fischer, "Anglo-american intelligence and the soviet war scare: The untold story." **Intelligence and National Security**, Vol.27, No.1, 2012, p.75.
[25] Duncan Depledge, Klaus Dodds, and Caroline Kennedy-Pipe, "The UK's Defence Arctic Strategy: Negotiating the slippery geopolitics of the UK and the Arctic." **The RUSI Journal**, Vol.164, No.1, 2019, pp. 28-29.; James Rogers, "Geopolitics and the 'Wider North' The United Kingdom as a 'Strategic Pivot'." **The RUSI Journal**, Vol. 157, No.6, 2012, p. 42.
[26] Duncan Depledge, Klaus Dodds, and Caroline Kennedy-Pipe, **ibid**, pp.31-33.
[27] James Rogers, **ibid**, p.42.
[28] James Rogers, **ibid**, p.44.
[29] Organization of the Petroleum Exporting Countries (OPEC), "World proven crude oil reserves by country", **2020 OPEC Annual Statistical Bulletin**, p.22
[30] Robert Summerby-Murray, "Trudeau's Liberals 2.0: balancing Canada's regional tensions and international geopolitics in a minority mandate." **The Round Table**, Vol.109, No.1, 2020, p.87.

followed similar energy policies until 2008.[31] After 2008, however, they started to follow different energy policies. While the US reduced its oil imports between 2008 and 2018, Canada did not follow the same path.[32] Moreover, the political divergence between the Trump Administration and the Trudeau Administration, particularly on energy and environmental policies, deepened the dissensus.[33] In addition to the divergence of energy policies, Canada's approach regarding the Atlantic also varied from the US' approach. In parallel to Canada's Global Market Action Plan, which was announced in 2013, Canada improved its relations with the countries in the South Atlantic and initiated several trade agreements in the region.[34] In a nutshell, even though it has been a reliable partner for the US in the region with similar policies, Canada started to pursue its independent foreign and energy policy. In that manner, it would be reasonable to argue that energy security is the most important issue in the Atlantic for Canada.

NATO

NATO was founded in 1949 to secure the Atlantic region and Europe. During the Cold War, NATO conducted several operations on a global scale to deter the USSR and secure the liberal Western order. However, NATO's role in global politics was harshly questioned after the end of the Cold War. After 9/11, on the other hand, NATO's mission was expanded to counterterrorism and transnational criminal networks.[35] It is still one of the most respected international organizations in the world.

While there was a relatively peaceful era between 1993 and 2008, the revitalization of the Russian military started to become the main concern for NATO and the security of the Atlantic. More importantly, increasing Russian military presence in the Arctic became the main challenge for NATO.[36] Therefore, while NATO lost its interest in modernizing the Northern Flank after the end of the Cold War, Russian activities in the region led to an increasing NATO's interest in its elements in the Arctic.[37] In other words, the Arctic became the central defense point of the security of the Atlantic.[38] In parallel to a cognitive change in NATO's strategic planning, a new Joint Force Command (JFC) for North Atlantic and High North operations has been established in

---

[31] Jean-Sébastien Rioux and Jennifer Winter, "Forks in the Road: Energy Policies in Canada and the US since the Shale Revolution." **American Review of Canadian Studies**, Vol.50, No.1, 2020, p.66.
[32] Jean-Sébastien Rioux and Jennifer Winter, **ibid**, pp.67-70.
[33] Richard Nimijean, "Introduction: Is Canada back? Brand Canada in a turbulent world.", **Canadian Foreign Policy Journal**, Vol.24, No.2, 2018, p.130.
[34] Laura Macdonald, "Evaluating Canadian economic diplomacy: Canada's relations with emerging markets in the Americas", **Canadian Foreign Policy Journal**, Vol.22, No.1, 2016, pp.30-31.
[35] Don Thieme, "NATO Renewed: Building the New Transatlantic Strategic Alliance." **The RUSI Journal**, Vol.159., No.3, 2014, p.44.
[36] Duncan Depledge, "NATO and the Arctic: the need for a new approach." **The RUSI Journal**, Vol.165, No.5-6, 2021, p.81.
[37] Duncan Depledge, **ibid**, pp.80-81.
[38] John J. Hamre and Heather A. Conley, "III. The centrality of the North Atlantic to NATO and US strategic interests." Whitehall Papers, Vol.87, No.1, 2016, pp.44.

Norfolk, Virginia, as Depledge puts,[39] and NATO missile capabilities in the North Atlantic was revisited by NATO.[40] As can be seen in the shift in NATO's security agenda and its structural regulations in the last decade, the Arctic is the key concern of NATO regarding the security of the Atlantic.

South Atlantic

Four actors can be categorized as key actors in the South Atlantic. These key actors are Brazil, Argentina, South Africa, and Russia. While Brazil and Argentina are located in the western part of the South Atlantic, South Africa is vital in the southern part of the region. Russia, on the other hand, is a crucial actor due to its relations with regional actors even though it is not located in the region.

Brazil

Brazil is by far the most important actor in the South Atlantic at least for two reasons. On the one hand, Brazil is the most important actor in South America. As several researchers assert, it is a rising power that has the potential to be a global actor.[41] On the other hand, Brazil is the only actor in the region that determines the security and commerce agenda of the region through its bilateral relations with South American and more importantly African countries. In other words, Brazil dominates the geopolitics of the region which is often overlooked by other global actors.

While Brazil was an important actor during the Cold War as well, reformulation of Brazil's grand strategy in the 1990s positioned the country as the key actor in the region.[42] Brazil's contemporary South Atlantic strategy has three aspects: regional security, diplomacy, and economy. An evaluation of Brazilian defense strategy documents reveals that the Brazilian security approach is based on modernizing the military equipment and expanding cooperation on security with African countries. In order to maintain its power in the region, Brazil improved both the quantity and quality of military vehicles and equipment after the Cold War.[43] It is important to note that most of the modernizing occurred in the Brazilian navy due to the shift in the Brazilian strategy: from focusing on regional security to providing the security of the South Atlantic. More importantly, Brazil expanded its security cooperation with several African countries including South Africa and Namibia. While Brazilian-Namibian cooperation on regulating the international maritime space is relatively new,

---

[39] Duncan Depledge, **ibid**, p.82.
[40] John J. Hamre and Heather A. Conley, **ibid**, p.52.
[41] Adriana Erthal Abdenur, Frank Mattheis and Pedro Seabra, "An ocean for the Global South: Brazil and the zone of peace and cooperation in the South Atlantic", **Cambridge Review of International Affairs**, Vol.29, No.3, 2016, p.1116.; Adriana Erthal Abdenur and Danilo Marcondes Neto, "Rising powers and Antarctica: Brazil's changing interests", **The Polar Journal**, Vol.4, No.1, 2014, p.12.
[42] Pedro Seabra, "Defence cooperation between Brazil and Namibia: Enduring ties across the South Atlantic", **South African Journal of International Affairs**, Vol.23, No.1, 2016, p.95.
[43] Adriana Erthal Abdenur and Danilo Marcondes Neto, **ibid**, p.21.

Brazilian-South African cooperation on security began in the early 2000s.[44] Due to the Brazilian-South African partnership on the security of the South Atlantic, not only did both countries expand their influence areas in the region and control the resources in the region but also created a durable security environment that deters other global actors from heavily involved in the region.

In addition to Brazil's expansion in the region on security issues, Brazil also expanded its diplomatic network in the region.[45] Consequently, Brazil restored its relations with South American countries by 2010 and initiated a South-South collaboration with the African countries.[46] Along with Brazil's bilateral relationship with Namibia and South Africa, Brazil also cultivated a better relationship and achieved to sign trade and security agreements of several African countries under the Zone of Peace and Cooperation in the South Atlantic (ZOPACAS).[47] It is also important to note that Brazil is a leading country in shaping decisions on Antarctica since it actively contributed scientific research on Antarctica since 2009.[48]

The last pillar of Brazilian strategy is related to the economy and governing the South Atlantic Ocean. Brazil's main economic agenda, which is also called as blue economy, is becoming a regional economic power through governing the maritime spaces and resources in the South Atlantic. This approach gained more importance particularly after the discovery of reserves of oil and gas on the Brazilian shores in 2007.[49] After this discovery, Brazil's oil reserves increased from fourteen billion barrels to thirty-eight billion barrels.[50] Due to an increase in Brazil's energy resources, South Atlantic became more central in the Brazilian political economy. In that manner, South-South economic cooperation became the main pillar of the Brazilian economic agenda. Particularly, Brazilian-South African economic integration has been playing a key role in the geopolitics of the South Atlantic.[51]

Argentina

Even though Argentina has resources and is located in a significant position in the South Atlantic, its chaotic domestic politics and economic problems prevent Argentina to compete with Brazil and become an important regional actor. Its importance for the region only comes from the Falklands War in 1982 and the status of the islands. Even though the British army defeated Argentina in the war in 1982, the dispute over the islands has not been fully resolved yet.

---

[44] Érico Esteves Duarte and Kai Michael Kenkel, "Contesting perspectives on South Atlantic maritime security governance: Brazil and South Africa", **South African Journal of International Affairs**, Vol.26, No.3, 2019, pp.395-396.
[45] Pedro Seabra, **ibid**, p.97.
[46] Adriana Erthal Abdenur and Danilo Marcondes Neto, **ibid**, p.20.
[47] Adriana Erthal Abdenur, Frank Mattheis and Pedro Seabra, **ibid**, p.1114.
[48] Adriana Erthal Abdenur and Danilo Marcondes Neto, **ibid**, pp.18-19.
[49] Adriana Erthal Abdenur, Frank Mattheis and Pedro Seabra, **ibid**, p.1118.
[50] Érico Esteves Duarte and Kai Michael Kenkel, **ibid**, p.400.
[51] Érico Esteves Duarte and Kai Michael Kenkel, **ibid**, p.403.

Therefore, this dispute makes Argentina one of the important actors regarding the security of the South Atlantic.[52] Furthermore, the location of the Falkland Islands makes these islands a strategic gateway in securing the region which will allow Argentina to be an important actor in the near future.[53] Besides that, it would be hard to argue that Argentina will be an important actor in the region regarding economic or diplomatic issues.

South Africa

South Africa is another key actor in the southern part of the South Atlantic. On the one hand, it is the only stable democracy in the southern part of the region. On the other hand, it is one of the main pillars of South-South cooperation with Brazil. It should be noted that even though Brazil and South Africa have robust cooperation for the last three decades, their approach in regulating the South Atlantic dramatically differs.[54] While Brazil seeks to exploit maritime resources as much as possible through a security perspective, South Africa considers maritime sources in the region as global commons that should be regulated via diplomatic and trade perspectives.[55]

In addition to its collaboration with Brazil, South Africa improved its relations with neighboring countries in the light of the Strategic Plan of the South African Department of Foreign Affairs. Per the document, regional integration is the main goal of South African foreign policy.[56] Moreover, economic integration also played a crucial role in South African policies. For instance, the South African government and private sector were involved in the rebuilding of the Democratic Republic of Congo after the conflict.[57] Apart from regional integration, aiming global integration also drives South African foreign policymaking. On the one hand, South Africa has a unique relationship among African countries with Western countries such as the US and European countries. On the other hand, it also developed a stable relationship with other global actors like China and Russia, particularly under BRICS.[58] In other words, South Africa is the only country in the African continent that has a durable relationship with both global and regional actors. This unique position of South

---

[52] Klaus Dodds and Lara Manóvil, "A common space? The Falklands/Malvinas and the new geopolitics of the South Atlantic", **Geopolitics**, Vol.6, No.2, 2001, p.106.Klaus Dodds, "The Falkland Islands as a 'Strategic Gateway'", **The RUSI Journal**, Vol.157, No.6, 2012, p.21.; Arie M. Kacowicz, "Geopolitics and territorial issues: Relevance for South America", **Geopolitics**, Vol.5, No.1, 2000, p.91.

[53] Klaus Dodds and Lara Manóvil, "A common space? The Falklands/Malvinas and the new geopolitics of the South Atlantic", **Geopolitics**, Vol.6, No.2, 2001, p.106.

[54] Érico Esteves Duarte and Kai Michael Kenkel, **ibid**, p.395.

[55] Érico Esteves Duarte and Kai Michael Kenkel, **ibid**, p.395; Pádraig Carmody, "The Geopolitics and Economics of BRICS' Resource and Market Access in Southern Africa: Aiding Development or Creating Dependency?", **Journal of Southern African Studies**, Vol.43, No.5, 2017, p.865.

[56] Laurie Nathan, "Consistency and inconsistencies in South African foreign policy." **International Affairs**, Vol.81, No.2 2005, p.362.

[57] Elizabeth Sidiropoulos, "South African foreign policy in the post-Mbeki period." **South African Journal of International Affairs**, Vol.15, No.2, 2008, p.110.

[58] Doctor Padraig Carmody, The rise of the BRICS in Africa: The geopolitics of South-South relations. Zed Books Ltd., 2013, p.6.

Africa positions the country as a key actor in setting the security and trade agenda of the South Atlantic.

Russia

Even though Russia is not located in the region, its historical relations and current bilateral agreements with several actors in the South Atlantic make Russia one of the key actors in the region. South American countries, Cuba and Nicaragua in particular, had importance for the USSR during the Cold War due to their geographical proximity to the US and tendencies that aligned with the Soviet ideology. These countries were considered crucial in the Russian global political aspirations and geopolitical calculations. Therefore, the USSR cultivated a stable relationship with several countries in the South Atlantic to conduct intelligence operations in the backyard of the US. As a result of Soviet interest in the region, the US also placed more emphasis on the region to prevent security threats that might come from the region that resulted in a cultural Cold War in the region.[59]

The end of the Cold War resulted in the devastation of the Russian economy and political chaos in the newly founded Russian Federation.[60] Therefore, these factors led to a retrenchment of Russian global ambitions and declining its forces from the South Atlantic after the end of the Cold War. However, after the reformation of the Russian economy in 1995, Russian interest in the region sparked and Russia started to recultivate its relationship with South American countries in 1997.[61] Russian interest in the South Atlantic peaked in 2008 and the region became one of the most important regions in the Russian global geopolitical aspirations.

It would be fair to argue that Russia has been using three instruments in increasing its influence in the region since 2008. These are military aid, financial aid, and Russian mercenaries. While Russia provides military aid and Russian mercenary group Wagner operates in Venezuela, Bolivia, Nicaragua, and Cuba it also provides financial aid to Argentina.[62] In a nutshell, Russia has become a key

---

[59] Víctor Jeifets, "Russia is coming back to Latin America: perspectives and obstacles." Anuario de la Integración Regional de América Latina y el Caribe–América Latina y el Caribe y el nuevo sistema internacional: Miradas desde el Sur coordinado por Andrés Serbin (CRIES, Buenos Aires), Laneydi Martínez (CEHSEU, La Habana) y Haroldo Ramanzi, 2015, p.91.; Patrick Iber, Neither peace nor freedom: the cultural Cold War in Latin America, Boston, MA, Harvard University Press, 2015, p.52.
[60] Andrei Shleifer and Daniel Treisman, "A normal country: Russia after communism." Journal of Economic Perspectives, Vol.19, No.1, 2005, p.154.; Stefan Hedlund and Niclas Sundström, "The Russian economy after systemic change." Europe-Asia Studies, Vol.48, No.6, 1996, p.907.
[61] Stephen Blank and Younkyoo Kim, "Russia and Latin America: The New Frontier for Geopolitics, Arms Sales and Energy", Problems of Post-Communism, Vol.62, No.3, 2015, p. 160.
[62] Stephen Blank and Younkyoo Kim, ibid, pp.160-168.; Ellen Iaones, "There are three countries where Russia's shadowy Wagner Group mercenaries operate", Business Insider, November 19, 2019, https://www.businessinsider.com/russia-wagner-group-mercenaries-where-operate-2018-4, (Access: 14.05.2021).; Brian Katz, Seth G. Jones, Catrina Doxsee and Nicholas Harrington, "The Expansion of Russian Private Military Companies", Center for Strategic & International Studies, 2020, https://russianpmcs.csis.org/, (Access: 14.05.2021).

actor in the South Atlantic through its bilateral relations with countries from the region and financial and military aids.

Key Issues in the Atlantic

Trade

The Atlantic is the most important region in international trade for several reasons. First, North Atlantic is the world's richest region and holds a lion's share in the high-end production of information technologies and financial capital. In other words, the most sophisticated and richest companies such as Apple and Microsoft are located in the region. On the other, the world's financial centers New York and London are located in the region as well. Therefore, not only there are high-density trade flows between the two sides of the North Atlantic but also this region determines the global financial regulations. Second, South Atlantic is a resource-rich region. While countries in South America such as Venezuela and Brazil have substantial oil reserves, countries in Africa are rich in mineral production.[63] Due to these factors, even though it is fair to argue that global production has been shifting to the Pacific in the last two decades, it is fair to argue that the Atlantic is the most important region in the world regarding international trade and finance.

Considering maritime transport is the backbone of the global trade and supply chain[64], maritime trade in the Atlantic Ocean constitutes a significant portion of global trade due to the high volume of international trade through the Atlantic Ocean. Per a report on Statista on global maritime trade routes, twenty-three percent of the maritime transportation in 2020 occurred in the Atlantic region.[65] According to the World Shipping Council report, the US itself is the most importer of containerized cargo.[66] It is important to note that European ports in the region such as Rotterdam, Antwerp, and Hamburg are also voluminous trade centers.

Given the high volume of maritime trade in the Atlantic, the region's importance in energy routes and transportation, and hosting eminent global financial actors, trade is and will be the key factor in the geopolitics of the Atlantic. Even though global mass production has been shifting to the Pacific, it is not expected that the importance of the Atlantic in global finance and trade

---

[63] Mark Aspinwall, "The Atlantic Geopolitical Space: common opportunities and challenges." **Synthesis Report of a conference jointly organised by DG Research and Innovation and BEPA, European Commission**, Belgium, 2011, p.5.
[64] United Nations Conference on Trade and Development, "International maritime trade and port traffic", **Review of Maritime Transport 2019**, 2019, p.4.
[65] Statista, **Maritime trade routes – containerized cargo flows 2020**, https://www.statista.com/statistics/253988/estimated-containerized-cargo-flows-on-major-container-trade-routes/, (Access: 14.05.2021).
[66] World Shipping Council, **Trade Statistics**, https://www.worldshipping.org/about-the-industry/global-trade/trade-statistics, (Access: 14.05.2021).

will diminish soon.

Security

Even though the Atlantic is an enormous geographical location with tens of countries on it, three major security issues in the region have the capacity to influence the geopolitics of the region. These are a) Russian expansion to the Atlantic, b) the growing importance of the Arctic, and c) transnational crime networks and instability.

Russia's global posture strengthened particularly after 2008. Due to the revitalized Russian global politics approach, Russia started to pursue more aggressive policies both in the North and South Atlantic. Hence, it became a major security challenge for NATO and the security of the Atlantic. In response to increasing Russian military presence in the North Atlantic, NATO started to restructure its planning, military deployment plans, and preparations after 2011.[67] The main challenge for the security of the North Atlantic regarding Russian aggression is Russia's use of hybrid warfare. As NATO was founded and operates to counter traditional threats, hybrid threats pose a greater challenge for the security of the North Atlantic.[68]

Since Russian expansion poses a threat to the security of the region, Atlantic countries started to focus more on the security of the Atlantic Ocean. In that manner, the US and British Navy started to cooperate further in the last decade to balance the Russian naval presence in the region.[69] Russian expansion in the Atlantic also poses a grave threat to the sea line of communications (SLOC) between North America and Europe.[70] The security of the SLOC in the Atlantic is particularly crucial because the failure of its security will jeopardize not only military communication between the two continents but also international trade between them.[71]

Russia's growing influence in the South Atlantic also constitutes a threat to the stability of the region. On the one hand, Russian presence in South America constitutes a constant and continuous threat to the US. On the other hand, the increasing role of Russian mercenaries in the conflict in African countries destabilizes the region further.

Given the increasing Russian activities in the Atlantic after 2010, it is fair to argue that Russia is and will be the major security challenge for the Atlantic shortly. It is likely that Russia will pursue more aggressive policies in the next

[67] James Stavridis, "VI. The United States, the North Atlantic and Maritime Hybrid Warfare", **Whitehall Papers**, Vol.87, No.1, 2016, p.93.
[68] James Stavridis, **ibid**, p.97.
[69] Peter Hudson and Peter Roberts, "V. The UK and the North Atlantic: A British Military Perspective", **Whitehall Papers**, Vol.87, No.1, 2016, p. 83.
[70] Steve Wills, "These aren't the SLOC's you're looking for": mirror-imaging battles of the Atlantic won't solve current Atlantic security needs, **Defense & Security Analysis**, Vol.36, No.1, 2020, p.38.
[71] Rolf Tamnes, "I. The Significance of the North Atlantic and the Norwegian Contribution", **Whitehall Papers**, Vol.87, No.1, 2016, p.22.

decade and will employ hybrid warfare tactics in the region to destabilize the region and challenge the liberal Western order. The countries in the region need to assess the Russian threat comprehensively and restructure their response mechanisms to address the Russian threat.

Another major security concern for the region is the growing importance of the Arctic region. On the one hand, as a result of climate change and melting the Arctic, new sealines started to emerge in the Arctic. In other words, securing the SLOC in the Arctic to prevent any disruption between the US and Europe became NATO's priority.[72] On the other hand, Russia and China began involving the politics in the region and started to increase their naval presence in the Arctic that raises grave concern for the security of the Atlantic.[73] Hence, major NATO countries such as the US and the UK started to work on this issue as can be observed in their official security documents.[74] The growing importance of the Arctic for the security of the Atlantic can also be seen in the current NATO activities. As Depledge asserts, not NATO military exercises in the North dramatically expanded in the last decade but also NATO established a joint force command, Joint Force Command for North Atlantic and High North operations, to monitor Russian activities in the Arctic.[75] In a nutshell, as shown above, the Arctic will be one of the major security concerns for the geopolitical calculations of the Atlantic in the next two decades.

The last major security issue in the Atlantic is transnational criminal networks and the instability of the South Atlantic. Even though the North Atlantic is considered a hub for liberal Western democracies, the countries in the South Atlantic have a long history of undemocratic traditions. While several coup d'états occurred in most of the countries in South America such as Chile, Argentina, and Brazil in the 1970s[76], the African part of the region has long been known for civil wars. Further, even the most democratic country of the region, South Africa, has a history of apartheid. Due to historically undemocratic governance in the region, transnational criminal networks are relatively powerful actors in determining local and regional policies. On the one hand, narcotrafficking and corruption play a vital role in the local politics of South America. On the other hand, terror groups and insurgencies frequently take place in Africa. Therefore, ongoing instability constitutes a major security concern not only for the South Atlantic but for global security.

---

[72] John Andreas Olsen, "Introduction: The Quest for Maritime Supremacy", **Whitehall Papers**, Vol.87, No.1, 2016, p.3.

[73] James Rogers, **ibid**, p.42.; Lassi Heininen (2017) "The Arctic, Baltic, and North-Atlantic 'cooperative regions' in 'Wider Northern Europe': similarities and differences", **Journal of Baltic Studies**, Vol.48, No.4, p.441.

[74] Duncan Depledge, Klaus Dodds, and Caroline Kennedy-Pipe, **ibid**, pp.28-29.

[75] Duncan Depledge, **ibid**, p.82.

[76] Franklin Steves, "Regional integration and democratic consolidation in the Southern Cone of Latin America.", **Democratization**, Vol.8, No.3, 2001, p.84.

Cooperation

It is fair to argue that cooperation mostly occurs on a regional scale in the Atlantic. In other words, cooperation occurs within the North or South but not necessarily as North-South cooperation. There are two major cooperation platforms on each side of the Atlantic. For the North Atlantic, cooperation occurs via NATO and North American Free Trade Association (NAFTA), which was renamed as United States-Mexico-Canada Agreement (USMCA). In the South Atlantic, on the other hand, BRICS and Brazil-South African cooperation are the key platforms regarding cooperation.

NATO has been responsible for the security of the North Atlantic for more than seventy years. As mentioned above, it was the key actor in the Cold War to balance the USSR. After the end of the Cold War, however, there was an era that the need for NATO was questioned.[77] Nevertheless, its importance for the security of the Atlantic was realized after 9/11 and NATO's role as a platform for security collaboration was solidified after Russian aggression in the 2010s. Presently, it is still the main institution regarding the security of the Atlantic. NAFTA, on the other hand, is the main institution for financial cooperation in the North Atlantic. NAFTA agreement was signed and entered into force in 1994 to create a free trade area between the US, Mexico, and Canada.[78] NAFTA was replaced with USMCA in 2020.

BRICS is the most important international platform for cooperation in the South Atlantic because two regional powers of the South Atlantic, Brazil and South Africa, are members of the platform. It is particularly important because key actors of the global political and financial system Russia, China, and India are the members of it. It should be noted that there is not a member in this platform from the Western countries. In that manner, it highlights the preference of the South Atlantic: not involving liberal Western democracies into the region and stay with the South-South cooperation.[79] It should also be noted that BRICS allow Russia and China to expand their influence in the region. It is important to emphasize that majority of cooperation in the South Atlantic occurs between Brazil and South Africa. Again, placing more importance on South-South cooperation, these key actors of the region determine the trade agenda of the region.[80] It is fair to argue that ongoing cooperation patterns and institutions will

---

[77] Ruben Zaiotti, "Practising homeland security across the Atlantic: practical learning and policy convergence in Europe and North America", **European Security**, Vol.21, No.3, 2012, pp.330-331.

[78] Gary Clyde Hufbauer and Jeffrey J. Schott. **NAFTA revisited: Achievements and challenges**. Columbia University Press, 2005, p.1.; For the impact of NAFTA on the US Economy, please see. Mary E. Burfisher, Sherman Robinson and Karen Thierfelder. "The impact of NAFTA on the United States." **Journal of Economic perspectives**, Vol.15, No.1, 2001, pp.125-144.

[79] Adriana Erthal Abdenur, Maiara Folly, Kayo Moura, Sergio A.S. Jordão and Pedro Maia, "The BRICS and the South Atlantic: Emerging arena for South–South cooperation", **South African Journal of International Affairs**, Vol.21, No.3, 2014, pp.307.

[80] Lyal White, "South Atlantic relations: from bilateral trade relations to multilateral coalition building", **Cambridge Review of International Affairs**, Vol.17, No.3, 2004, p.523.

be effective platforms in the near future, Therefore, it is not expected a shift in the alliances in the Atlantic.

Conclusion

This chapter provided a holistic snapshot of the contemporary geopolitical aspects of the Atlantic by identifying the key actors, issues, and cooperation platforms. In doing so, it addressed the current geopolitical environment of the region. The Atlantic is an enormous geographical location. Therefore, this chapter analyzed the Atlantic by categorizing it as the North Atlantic and the South Atlantic.

As discussed above, there are four key actors in the North Atlantic, namely the US, the UK, Canada, and NATO. These four actors set the economic and security agenda of the region and constitute the geopolitical pillars of the North Atlantic. The US is the leading actor both in security and financial settings through NATO and global US companies and financial markets. The UK is the eastern pillar of the Atlantic alliance by its military presence in the European continent against mutual threats and the role of London in regulating financial markets. Canada, on the other hand, is a key ally of the US and a regional actor. Finally, NATO is an institution that reflects the embodiment of the Atlantic Alliance which is responsible for securing the region. These four actors altogether form the geopolitics of the region via their strategic preferences and threat perceptions.

Key issues in the North Atlantic are maritime trade security and countering common threats such as Russian aggression in the region and the growing importance of the Arctic. Therefore, a shift in the global production and trade from the Atlantic to the Pacific and increasing Russian aggression both in the Atlantic and the Arctic will be the key security concerns for the North Atlantic in the next decade. In that manner, collaboration platforms in the region NATO and UMSCA will play a major role in the next decade in addressing the regional geopolitical concerns.

There are also four key actors in the South Atlantic, namely Brazil, Argentina, South Africa, and Russia. It is important to keep in mind that Brazil is the most capable actor in the region. While Argentina and South Africa are relatively less capacity to influence the region, Russia's capacity is limited due to its status as an outsider. The South Atlantic is especially important for petroleum and mineral trade, therefore, cooperation patterns in the region are based on resource-rich countries. Brazil-South African cooperation is by far the most successful cooperation in the region. It is worth noting that the region suffers from political instability and transnational criminal networks. These security concerns will not diminish in the immediate future and will constitute a grave security concern not only for the region but also for global security.

THE GEOPOLITICAL SCENARIOS OF THE "QUAD" COUNTRIES, THE UNITED STATES, JAPAN, AUSTRALIA AND INDIA

Duygu Çağla Bayram*

Introduction

The Indo-Pacific, which refers the maritime space stretching from the Indian Ocean to the Western Pacific, surrounding Asia and Eastern Africa, is a relatively new geopolitical concept (re)coined by Indian Captain Dr. Gurpreet Singh Khurana in 2007, attributing to the growing intimacy between India and Japan.[1] Viewed geopolitically, while the geographical location has a determining power over state policies, it is parallelly seen the political interests shape the perception of geography. In this context, all regions are constructs and they are generally defined by states in line with their own purposes. On the basis of such this geopolitical perspective, the Indo-Pacific concept implies the extended Asia-Pacific region across the Indian Ocean in favour of primarily India, the United States and Japan in the face of China's rise.

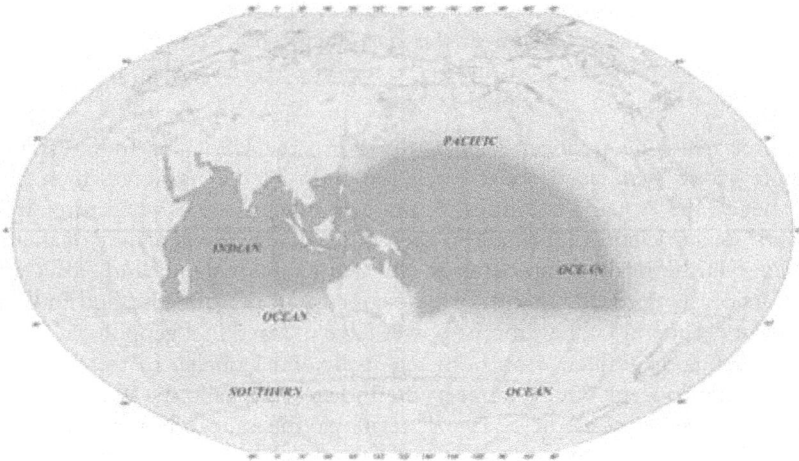

The Indo-Pacific Region (IPR)

The Indo-Pacific is the centre of gravity on earth with the Indian Ocean which is the world's busiest trade corridor, home to four most critical waterways,

* Duygu Çağla Bayram, PhD in International Relations. E-mail: caglabayramm@hotmail.com, ORCID: 0000-0003-0353-1176.
[1] Gurpreet S. Khurana, "Security of Sea Lines: Prospects for India-Japan Cooperation", **Strategic Analysis**, Vol. 31, No. 1, 2007, p. 150.

the Suez Canal, Bab-el Mandeb, the Strait of Hormuz and the Strait of Malacca, carrying roughly half of the world's maritime trade, consisting approximately 20 percent of energy resources, providing nearly 40 percent of the world's offshore oil production, and carrying around three quarters of the oil and gas trade for non-regional states unlike the Pacific and Atlantic Oceans. Furthermore, it is the most dynamic region houses the two most populated countries, China and India, which means over half of the world's population, and three of the largest economies, the United States, China and Japan. Moreover, it is the most militarised region hosting five of the nuclear powers, the United States, China, India, Pakistan and North Korea.

The idea of the Indo-Pacific, which is designed as a super-region where the sub-regions still remain important, prioritises maritime security on the behalf of developing governance arrangement to manage the freedom of movement and trade flows over the "Sea Lines of Communication" (SLOCs). While there have been many criticisms that the Indo-Pacific covers too large area, downplays economic cooperation and prioritises the imperative of managing threats to maritime security,[2] it has widely been embraced by the states whose interests are compatible with the idea. The absence of any mechanism that can solve the problems and insecurity in the region leaves the priority of balancing the stability of the region with its own national interests to the responsibility of each state.[3] With such understanding, rescaling from the Asia- to Indo-Pacific implies a new functional purpose for the regional governance. The Indo-Pacific, hence, is seen not only as a spatial extension of the Asia-Pacific but also as an entirely new conceptualisation of who constitutes the region and what issues are the driving force in the formation of regional orders.[4]

Three major geopolitical changes that form the US-China-India "strategic triangle" have first led to be created the Indo-Pacific narrative, then come together to the "Quad" countries. A strategic triangle exists when three major powers are sufficiently important to each other that a change in any of them or a change in the relationship between any two of them significantly affects the interests of the third. In this context, the concurrent rise of China and India and a relative decline in US hegemonic power have ushered in a geopolitical shift in Asia, exerting an influence on both regionally and globally. In this sense, the Indo-Pacific concept, which connects the Indian Ocean and the Western Pacific as a single strategic construct, is closely related to the issue of how to manage the change in specific to the United States, China and India, which emerged as a

---

[2] See Mark Beeson, Troy Lee-Brown, "The Future of Asian Regionalism: Not What It Used to Be?", **Asia & the Pacific Policy Studies,** Vol. 4, No. 2, 2017; Jeffrey D. Wilson, "Investing in the Economic Architecture of the Indo-Pacific", **Indo-Pacific Insight Series,** Vol. 8, 2017; Jeffrey D. Wilson, "Rescaling to the Indo-Pacific: From Economic to Security-Driven Regionalism in Asia", **East Asia,** Vol. 35, No. 2, 2018; Mark Beeson, "Institutionalizing the Indo-Pacific: the Challenges of Regional Cooperation", **East Asia,** Vol. 35, No. 2, 2018.
[3] Michael Auslin, "The Struggle for Power in the Indo-Pacific", **Turkish Policy Quarterly,** Vol. 10, No. 3, 2011, p. 151.
[4] Wilson, İbid., pp. 181-182.

strategic triangle. As Medcalf points out, the security relations of these countries, which are the big Indo-Pacific three, will shape or shake both regional and global order.[5]

Geopolitically speaking, the crux of this strategic triangle is the systemic rivalry between the United States and China while India and China have often found themselves in a regional rivalry over zone of strategic influence, or "superiority in geographical space". As Østerud summarises, *"geopolitics traditionally indicates the links and causal relationships between political power and geographical space… The geopolitical tradition had some consistent concerns, like the geographical correlates of power in world politics, the identification of international core areas, and the relationships between naval and terrestrial capabilities".[6]* From a geographical point of view, India is an Indian Ocean country, while China is an East Asian and/or a Western Pacific one. In other words, China is an Asia-Pacific country, while India is not. Therefore, India, which is the US "strategic partner", is turning into an Indo-Pacific one in strategic calculations of the United States, American allies and some others. Accordingly, the motivation of the recently spreading Indo-Pacific narrative in strategic language is both geo-economic and geopolitical. The geo-economic dynamic is related to the energy flows and general volume of trade, particularly the protection of SLOCs, in the Indian and Pacific Oceans. As Scott states, *"geopolitics at times involves geoeconomics when it comes to questions of how easily or difficult a state might find it to access resources, especially in the energy field. Sea Lines of Communication are a question of geopolitics, but also of geoeconomics".[7]*

The geopolitical dynamic is related to the rises of China and India. Today, while the United States, Japan and Australia are encountered with a growing "China threat" in the Western Pacific Region (WPR); the United States and India are witnessed to China's expanding strategic footprints in the Indian Ocean Region (IOR). As the leading power in the Pacific since 1945 and the major power in the IOR since the 1980s and also still the single superpower in the world, the United States now needs to control the growing Chinese presence. To this end, the former US government led by Donald Trump has changed the logic of American intervention in the Asian region. Yet, both strategic logics concentrate on the "containment of China". However, the new "Indo-Pacific Strategy" (IPS) seeks to control China through the engagement of some significant actors such as particularly India while the Asia-Pacific aimed to control China by relying on the use of traditional "hub-and-spokes" alliance model.

---

[5] Rory Medcalf, "Pivoting the Map: Australia's Indo-Pacific System", **Centre of Gravity Series,** No. 1, 2012, p. 4.

[6] Øyvind Østerud, "The Uses and Abuses of Geopolitics", **Journal of Peace Research,** Vol. 25, No. 2, 1988, p. 192.

[7] David Scott, "The Great Power 'Great Game' between India and China: The Logic of Geography", **Geopolitics,** Vol. 13, No. 1, 2008, p. 19.

Given the "Quadrilateral Security Dialogue", best known the "Quad", which is a semi-formal strategic forum between the United States, Japan, Australia and India, the Quad countries symbolise the core drivers of the Indo-Pacific narrative. With eye on China's rise, ambitions and military assertiveness across the region, the Quad nations build strategic ties especially focusing on enhancing cooperation for a "free and open Indo-Pacific". Meanwhile, US reaction to the simultaneous rise of China and India has been inversely proportional. While the United States has entered into a strategic competition with China in each field, it has started to attach "particular importance" to India in its strategy to balance and control China's dramatically growing power projection. This means while the rise of China is often cast as a threat, India's rise entails no threat for the United States and the other regional actors. In other words, while "China Threat Theory" has been fed by the mostly West, India has presented as a "natural balancer". The loyal American ally Japan has been focusing its foreign policy attention on the Quad to deepen its relationship principally with India with an eye to "hedging" against "China threat". The other ally Australia, which facing with insecurities derived from China, has also been seeking a developed tie with India, and mainly trying to balance the American and Chinese presences in the Indo-Pacific Region (IPR). On the other hand, India, which traditionally avoids "formal alliances" but also being stuck in the "security dilemma" with China, tries to keep its diplomatic relationships balanced to ensure a peaceful, secure, prosperous and rules-based IPR.

This chapter of the book is divided into four parts, tracing the geopolitical scenarios of the Quad countries towards the Indo-Pacific. The following parts, hence, look at the geopolitical scenarios of the United States, Japan, Australia and India, respectively. To this end, the "US return to Asia" is argued in terms of America's IPS against the rise of China. Then, Japan's moves against "China threat" are addressed as a "hedging strategy" while Australia's attitude is examined in the frame of "niche diplomacy". The last theme to be discussed is "logical nuance" of what one Indian Prime Minister Narendra Modi called a "natural IPR". In discussing them, the chapter ultimately seeks to draw a core picture of the Indo-Pacific geopolitics and concludes by briefly tracing out the implications thereof.

The United States: Balancing China's Rise, Securing American Centrality

Since the 2010s, one can clearly see a shift of US strategic focus from Europe and the Middle East to Asia through its balancing strategies aimed at China. Former US Secretary of State Hillary Clinton's article entitled *"America's Pacific Century"* published in *Foreign Policy* in October 2011 was viewed as the first concrete declaration of the "US return to Asia". Clinton stated in this article, *"the future of politics will be decided in Asia, not Afghanistan or Iraq, and the United States will be right at the centre of the action".[8]* According to Clinton, the time has come for the United States to retake a strategic approach in Asian politics, which has become a key driver of global politics.[9] The Obama administration's Asia policy, originally phrased as the "pivot to Asia" but subsequently renamed as the "rebalance to Asia", has focused on the containment of China and the maintenance of US dominance.

The presidency of Donald Trump did not cause a fundamental change in the Obama administration's Asia policy. Rather, President Trump's "Free and Open Indo-Pacific" (FOIP) is a same strategy but with more strong tone. Indeed, the FOIP is only the conceptual embodiment of the Obama administration's pivot/rebalance to Asia, focusing deeper on the maritime domain. As a response by the United States to China's growing influence in the Pacific and Indian Oceans and with the escalation of US-China rivalry in strategically important areas, President Trump first articulated the vision of the FOIP, calling the "Indo-Pacific dream", during the speech at the Asia-Pacific Economic Cooperation (APEC) Summit in Vietnam in November 2017.[10] Subsequently, the concept of the FOIP was seen in US white papers, the 2017 National Security Strategy and the 2018 National Defense Strategy. These documents stated that long-term strategic competition with China (and Russia) is the principal priority of the United States, as China (as well as Russia) is undermining the international order, and labelled China (together with Russia) as a revisionist power(s), a challenger(s) and a strategic competitor, claiming that China seeks to displace the United States in the IPR through state-led investments and loans and reorder the region in its favour and in the end, wants to shape a world consistent with its authoritarian model.[11]

The Pentagon changed the name of the Pacific Command (USPACOM) to the Indo-Pacific Command (USINDOPACOM) on May 30, 2018, after approximately 4 months the strategy document was released. This means the United States has operationalised the idea of the Indo-Pacific in a more militarised manner. Besides, in June 2019, the US Department of Defense published the Indo-Pacific Strategy Report, which specifies the Indo-Pacific as the "priority theatre" for the Pentagon. This is the most elaborate conceptual document of the United States on the Indo-Pacific to date. The four principles of the FOIP set out in the report are juxtaposed as follows:[12] 1) Respect for sovereignty and independence of all nations; 2) Peaceful resolution of disputes;

---

[8] Hillary Clinton, "America's Pacific Century", **Foreign Policy,** October 11, 2011, https://foreignpolicy.com/2011/10/11/americas-pacific-century/ (Access 21.05.2021).
[9] Ibid.
[10] "Remarks by President Trump at APEC CEO Summit", https://vn.usembassy.gov/20171110-remarks-president-trump-apec-ceo-summit/ (Access 22.05.2021).
[11] See National Security Strategy of the United States of America, The White House, Washington, DC, 2017; Summary of the 2018 National Defense Strategy of the United States of America: Sharpening the American Military's Competitive Edge, The US Department of Defense, Washington, DC, 2018.
[12] Indo-Pacific Strategy Report: Preparedness, Partnerships, and Promoting a Networked Region, The US Department of Defense, Washington, DC, 2019, pp. 3-4.

3) Free, fair, and reciprocal trade based on open investment, transparent agreements, and connectivity; and, 4) Adherence to international rules and norms, including those of freedom of navigation and overflight. It is worth noting that the report strongly restresses China as a revisionist power and identifies US vision of the FOIP *"is a vision which recognises that no one nation can or should dominate the Indo-Pacific".[13]* It should also be pointed out that one can see the specific attention is paid to India in US white papers.

US IPS rests on five main pillars: strengthening alliances across the region; developing deeper security and defence ties or strategic partnerships with non-allies, particularly India; advancing the region's security and economic architecture; active engagement in multilateral structures to promote regional cooperation; and advocating to transparency, the rules-based international order, the peaceful resolution of disputes and adherence to human rights, democracy to single out the ideology of the United States as a reliable partner. One needs to consider the official documents are the tools in which states declare their foreign policy and security perceptions and objectives without explicitly and elaborately reflecting their intentions and strategies to deal with their threat perceptions. Therefore, even if the Indo-Pacific concept may be presented as that has been designed to emphasise the strategic and geopolitical importance of the region, which has a dominant marine character that draws attention to the natural connection of oceans and seas in security, economic and regional issues, one needs to take a careful approach to read beyond its face value.

The Indo-Pacific is inherently a subjective narrative but refers the same tangible region. This means there is a single construct of the region along with many perspectives or intentions or strategies, even if it may sound bizarre. One can clearly view the prefix "Indo-" in the Indo-Pacific concept alludes to the Indian Ocean and what is more, it singles out Indian strategic importance. Moreover, the Indo-Pacific concept US embraced enhances the perception of the strength of India in the "wider" region while dilutes China's. It was not a coincidence that no one could see that China has officially been used the Indo-Pacific concept, and Chinese experts have harshly criticised the concept from the outset, alleging that US usage is aiming to contain China. In March 2018, China's Foreign Minister Wang Yi dismissed it as *"an attention-grabbing idea"* that would *"dissipate like ocean foam."[14]* Likewise, one can witness such criticism in Russia, but probably louder. For example, while addressing the fifth edition of the Raisina Dialogue in New Delhi in January 2020, Russian Foreign Minister Sergey Lavrov remarked that *"Why do you need to call Asia-Pacific as Indo-Pacific? The answer is evident… to contain China. Terminology should be unifying, not divisive"*, adding that *"our Indian friends are smart enough to understand this trap and not to get into it".[15]*

---

[13] Ibid., p. 4.

[14] Lynn Kuok, "Shangri-La Dialogue: Negotiating the Indo-Pacific Security Landscape", **The Straits Times,** June 1, 2018, https://www.straitstimes.com/opinion/negotiating-the-indo-pacific-security-landscape (Access 23.05. 2021).

[15] "Foreign Minister Sergey Lavrov's Remarks and Answers to Questions at a Plenary Session of the

In view of the white papers, it is clear that the American vision toward the IPR essentially concentrates on maintaining its regional dominance against the rise of China rather than improving a comprehensive framework for the region. India occupies a strategic position in the IOR. It can be safely argued that India, hence, carries a lot of weight in the IPS. Therefore, the United States gives high priority to develop deeper relations with India and support it strategically, politically, diplomatically and militarily in its regional prominence, for its own IPS, as India is an essential counterweight to China. Additionally, the United States has been conniving at the resurgence of Japanese militarism, or Japanese steps to boost Japan's "individual" defence capabilities in the IPR. This is the mentality of "offshore balancing" that forming India as "natural balancer" or India and Japan as counter-balancers to China in the IPR, and simultaneously dragging India most likely into a confrontation with China.

Japan: Hedging against the Rise of China

Japan's foreign policy has undergone a tectonic shift with former Prime Minister Shinzo Abe. After the Second World War, which expressed a great defeat for Japan and opened the door to the 7-year (1945-1952) occupation process, Japan had to follow a "pacifist" foreign policy until the era of Prime Minister Abe due to the "Peace Constitution", prepared by the occupation force the United States and took effect in 1947. The pacifist and distinctive nature of the Japanese Peace Constitution stems from the Article 9, which reads as follows: *"Aspiring sincerely to an international peace based on justice and order, the Japanese people forever renounce war as a sovereign right of the nation and the threat or use of force as means of settling international disputes. In order to accomplish the aim of the preceding paragraph, land, sea, and air forces, as well as other war potential, will never be maintained. The right of belligerency of the state will not be recognized".*[16]

Since the early 2000s, with the Abe government(s), Japan has been moving to rebecome a "great power" not only in an economic and a technological manner but also in a "military" manner, which can be exemplified by several steps: First and foremost, in July 2014, the Abe cabinet "officially" reinterpreted Article 9 of the Japanese Constitution, which means moving away from the constitutional limitation that merely allows the use of force in "individual" self-defence. Furthermore, the Abe cabinet ensured the renewal of the "Treaty of Mutual Cooperation and Security" document, signed in 1951 and revised in 1960, which is the basis of today's US-Japan alliance. Moreover, in April 2015, the "US-Japan Defense Guidelines", first codified in 1978 to set the parameters for the military cooperation between the American forces and the Japanese Self-Defense Forces and then reviewed in 1997, was once again updated by the Obama and Abe administrations. Besides, in March 2016, the "Legislation for Peace and

---

Raisina Dialogue", **The Ministry of Foreign Affairs of the Russian Federation,** https://www.mid.ru/en/foreign_policy/ news/-/asset_publisher/cKNonkJE02Bw/content/id/399488 5 (Access 23.05.2021).
[16] The Constitution of Japan, 1947.

Security" came into force, which the Japanese Parliament (Diet) approved in September 2015.

The reinterpretation of Article 9 and the Legislation for Peace and Security permitted for the first time the Self-Defense Forces to exercise force in "collective" self-defence and facilitated the normalisation of Japan's security posture and the Japanese participation in joint military exercises.[17] For example, since 2015, Japan has been participating as a permanent member of MALABAR naval exercise, which is annually being conducted by the United States and India. Additionally, the Japan Maritime Self-Defense Force and the Indian Navy have been holding biennially the joint exercise JIMEX since 2012. Significantly, these changes also paved the way for Japan to develop its "Free and Open Indo-Pacific Strategy" (FOIPS) for the IPR. Admittedly, the conceptualisation of the Indo-Pacific first initiated by Japan, and the FOIPS, mostly espoused by the Trump administration, was initially conceived by the Abe administration.[18] Japan's IPS was first based on Prime Minister Abe's speech to the Indian Parliament on August 22, 2007, entitled *"The Confluence of the Two Seas"*, referring the Indo-Pacific as the "broader Asia", and then the 2012-dated article *"Asia's Democratic Security Diamond"* that envisaged a strategy whereby Japan, the United States, Australia and India *"form a diamond to safeguard the maritime commons stretching from the Indian Ocean region to the western Pacific".[19]* Additionally, the latter has formed the Quad, which makes the Quad is also Prime Minister Abe's initiative, at least ideationally.

Officially, Prime Minister Abe first announced the FOIPS during the keynote speech at the sixth Tokyo International Conference on African Development (TICAD VI) held in Kenya in August 2016, highlighting *"what will give stability and prosperity to the world is none other than the enormous liveliness brought forth through the union of two free and open oceans [the confluence of the Pacific and Indian Oceans] and two continents [and of Asia and Africa]".[20]* Subsequently, in 2017 and the following years, Ministry of Foreign Affairs of Japan (MOFA) released the white papers that promoted the FOIP "strategy/vision" as a new foreign policy "strategy/vision", stressing the "connectivity" between Asia and Africa, and Pacific and Indian Oceans, aiming diplomacy, proactive contribution to peace and stability, rules-based order, freedom of navigation, free trade, economic prosperity, and quality

---

[17] "Cabinet Decision on Development of Seamless Security Legislation to Ensure Japan's Survival and Protect its People", **Ministry of Foreign Affairs (MOFA) of Japan,** July 1, 2014, https://www.mofa.go.jp/fp/nsp/page23e_ 000273.html (Access 28.05.2021); "Japan's Legislation for Peace and Security", April 12, 2016, **MOFA of Japan,** https://www.mofa.go.jp/ fp/nsp/page1we_ 000084.html (Access 28.05.2021).
[18] "Priority Policy for Development Cooperation FY2017", **MOFA of Japan,** 2017, https://www.mofa.go.jp/files/ 000259285.pdf (Access 28.05.2021).
[19] "Confluence of the Two Seas: Speech by H.E. Mr. Shinzo Abe, Prime Minister of Japan at the Parliament of the Republic of India", **MOFA of Japan,** August 22, 2007, https://www.mofa.go.jp/ region/asia-paci/pmv0708/speech -2.html (Access 28.05.2021); Shinzo Abe, "Asia's Democratic Security Diamond", **Project Syndicate,** Dec 27, 2012, https://www.project-syndicate.org/onpoint/a-strategic-alliance-for-japan-and-india-by-shinzo-abe?barrier= accesspaylog (Access 28.05.2021).
[20] "Address by Prime Minister Shinzo Abe at the Opening Session of the Sixth Tokyo International Conference on African Development (TICAD VI)", **MOFA of Japan,** August 27, 2016, https://www.mofa.go.jp/afr/af2/page4e_ 000496.html (Access 28.05.2021).

infrastructure development.[21] It is noteworthy that Japan has described FOIP as a "strategy" up until 2018, but then altered it to a "vision", the word strategy may be viewed as the containment of China by regional actors, especially by the Association of Southeast Asian Nations (ASEAN) states as it has a "zero-sum" connotation.

Due to its economic interdependence with China, expanding domestic economic problems and occasionally shifting strategic priorities that have diminished the American ability to guarantee security of its allies in Asia, US regional allies such as Japan and Australia have turned diversifying their regional partners and seeking the long-term "strategic partnerships" with the other actors notably India. Thus, there appears to be a management dilemma of alliance in US relations with its regional allies and partners. In such a situation, conceptualised by Snyder as the "alliance security dilemma", the allies face two fears, fear of abandonment and fear of entrapment.[22] In this context, given the potential "power transition" due to the rise of China and the relative decline of the United States, Japan seeks to "hedge" against a possible hegemony of a single power, a neighbouring giant China. The power transitions are defined as the periods of strategic change in which the dominant hegemony is questioned by a rising power and the outcomes are highly uncertain.[23] The economic theory argues that uncertainty and volatility in the market drive hedging behaviour, which explained as risk change and where actors invest in different policies to insure against the unexpected failures.[24] Given that the power transitions represent similar uncertainty in the international system, the other states in the system adopt hedging strategies against such future uncertainties. Goh defines hedging as *"a set of strategies aimed at avoiding (or planning for contingencies in) a situation in which states cannot decide upon more straightforward alternatives such as balancing, bandwagoning, or neutrality".[25]* This implies a middle position that scrupulously avoids taking sides with or against a big power or having one straightforward policy stance at the obvious expense of another. Succinctly, one can read here hedging is a strategy in which states attempt to insure/protect themselves against the negative consequences or a possible contingency in an uncertain or fluid environment and taking a soft stance instead certain or possible provocative one. Additionally, this also reflects a kind of soft or indirect balancing.

In view of such theoretical background along with Japan's white papers, "the pursuit of economic prosperity through enhancing connectivities, including through quality infrastructure development in accordance with international

---

[21] "Foreign Policy: Free and Open Indo-Pacific", **MOFA of Japan,** April 1, 2021, https://www.mofa.go.jp/policy/ page25e_000278.html (Access 31.05.2021).
[22] Glenn H. Snyder, **Alliance Politics,** Ithaca, Cornell University Press, 1997, p. 307.
[23] Jacek Kugler, A. F. K. Organski, "The Power Transition: A Retrospective and Prospective Evaluation", **Handbook of War Studies,** Manus I. Midlarsky (Ed.), Abingdon, Routledge, 1989, pp. 171-194.
[24] Joost M. E. Pennings, "What Drives Actual Hedging Behaviour? Developing Risk Management Instruments", **Agribusiness and Commodity Risk: Strategies and Management,** Nigel Scott (Ed.), London, Risk Books, 2003, pp. 63-74.
[25] Evelyn Goh, "Understanding 'Hedging' in Asia-Pacific Security", **PacNet,** No. 43, 2006, p. 1.

standards" seems to form the heart of Japan's vision of ensuring peace, stability and prosperity in the Indo-Pacific region, through establishing a free and open order based on the shared values and principles.[26] In order to improve regional connectivity, Japan has actively been involved in many port development projects in Asia and especially Africa. Given the fact that the Indo-Pacific has a dominant maritime character, it is vital to develop port facilities in coastal areas to provide and increase interconnectivity. In this context, Japan has been supporting port development projects in South and Southeast Asian countries such as India, Sri Lanka, Myanmar, Viet Nam, Cambodia and Indonesia. Similarly, many Japanese companies have a significant presence in Eastern and Southern African countries, particularly in Ethiopia, Uganda, Kenya, Tanzania and Mozambique.

Further, Japan's cooperation with India to contribute to the development of the Chabahar port in Iran was a strategic move that draws attention within the framework of regional connectivity. Besides, since 2017, the "Asia-Africa Growth Corridor" (AAGC) has been the most important and comprehensive collaborative initiative of Japan and India, seeking to develop connectivity and infrastructure in the IPR, promoting cooperation between Asia and Africa. The Corridor, based on development and cooperation projects, quality infrastructure and institutional connectivity, enhancing capacities and skills and people-to-people partnership, signifies a soft or indirect balancing created by the two countries against the influence of China's "Belt and Road Initiative" (BRI). On the other hand, despite the lack of transparency and quality in Chinese projects as well as China's approach to use its own workforce, it is not that easy yet to create a counterbalance or a counterweight to China in terms of the scale of financial investment. Moreover, both India and Japan have a little experience in building infrastructure in other countries unlike China. That said, the Corridor still represents a great potential alternative to China's BRI.

Australia: Looking for a Niche Diplomacy in the IPR

The Indo-Pacific is a very familiar concept for Australia, which possesses the two-ocean characteristic. When tracing back to the 1950s in the foreign policy debates of Australia, the use of the concept has been threefold in the aspect of time and issue: in the 1950s, on the decolonisation of dominions surrounding Australia; in the 1960s, on nuclear proliferation and Commonwealth responsibilities within the region; and in the 1970s, on the description of an Indo-Pacific balance which would ensure Australia's security.[27] Yet, the abovementioned examples represent the limited usage of the concept until it has regained currency since 2000s.

---

[26] "Foreign Policy: Free and Open Indo-Pacific", op.cit.
[27] Melissa Conley Tyler, Samantha Shearman, "Australia Re-Discovering the Indo-Pacific", **Indo-Pacific Region: Political and Strategic Prospects,** Rajiv K. Bhatia, Vijay Sakhuja (Eds.), New Delhi, Vij Books, 2014, p. 42.

In view of Australian white papers, the IPR first called as the "wider Asia-Pacific" in 2009.[28] Subsequently, even if the 2012-dated document replaced this use as the Indo-Pacific,[29] most commonly the 2013-dated one is accepted as the first sample of Australia's official adoption the Indo-Pacific concept, [30] which also makes Australia the first ever state of accepting the concept in a white paper. The latter stated that *"the Indo-Pacific strategic arc, connecting the Indian and Pacific Oceans through Southeast Asia, adjusts Australia's priority strategic focus to the arc extending from India though Southeast Asia to Northeast Asia, including the sea lines of communication on which the region depends".[31]* If one carefully reads the statement, it is evidently seen the Indo-Pacific view for Australia is yet to form in the same way with the other Quad nations, two of whom (apart from the US) embraced it as a region that comprises the whole of the IOR along with the WPR. Instead, the Indo-Pacific approach of Australia explicitly differentiates both regions and distinctly focuses on the eastern part of the IOR confined to India and Southeast Asia in addition to the WPR. Besides, Australia's strategic outlook in the Indo-Pacific context were further concretised in the 2016 Defense White Paper and 2017 Foreign Policy White Paper, the latter of which straightforwardly stated that *"We define the 'Indo-Pacific' as the region ranging from the eastern Indian Ocean to the Pacific Ocean connected by Southeast Asia, including India, North Asia and the United States".[32]* Additionally, this is the reason for which Phillips has a conceptual proposition for Australian style of the Indo-Pacific as "Indo/Pacific" to illustrate that the Indian and Pacific dynamics are handled in different dimensions by virtue of the limited power projection capabilities.[33]

The Australian power scale fairly differentiates the Australian Indo-Pacific stance from the other Quad countries indeed. Australian vision was defined pragmatically in pursuit of taking advantage of the economic opportunities of the IPR, putting a greater emphasis on geoeconomics. In other words, as can be seen in the white papers, the focus is orientated not only in a security manner but also in an economic manner. Australia's maritime-based economy conveyed by the requirements of unfettered access to an open, free and secure trading system to support its economic development, and of minimising the regional instability that would directly affect its interests. Furthermore, Australia's approach is based on the "twin policy" that pragmatically welcomes China's engagement, even if substantially concerned about Chinese assertiveness, while overemphasises the significant role of the United States as a stabilising influence,

---

[28] See Defence White Paper 2009: Defending Australia in the Asia-Pacific Century: Force 2030, Commonwealth of Australia Department of Defence, Canberra, 2009.
[29] See **White Paper 2012: Australia in the Asian Century,** Commonwealth of Australia Department of Prime Minister and Cabinet, Canberra, 2012.
[30] See Defence White Paper 2013: Defending Australia and Its National Interests, Commonwealth of Australia Department of Defence, Canberra, 2013.
[31] Ibid., pp. 2, 7.
[32] 2017 Foreign Policy White Paper: Opportunity Security Strength, Commonwealth of Australia Department of Foreign Affairs and Trade, Canberra, 2017, p. 1.
[33] Andrew Phillips, "From Hollywood to Bollywood? Recasting Australia's Indo/Pacific Strategic Geography", ASPI Strategy Series, 2016.

and therefore placing the US alliance at the centre of its approach, which also makes Australia's Indo-Pacific stance difference compared to the Quad nations in a way how China question would be dealt with.

Admittedly, the main motivation behind the differentiation stems from Australia's "middle power" status and accordingly the pursuit of "niche diplomacy". Australia's diplomats, who casting the nation as a "bridge-builder" between East and West, notably Australian Foreign Minister Gareth Evans, identified the country as a middle power to secure diplomatic autonomy and increase leverage over great powers through coalitions with other "like-minded" countries during the reconstruction period in the early 1990s.[34] There is no conceptual consensus on the definition of middle power, yet the scale of middle power is attributed to states that hold a bridge-like middle position in world politics in respect of great and super powers, a middle position that lacking significant influence in the aspects of material strength on a macro-global sphere and vice versa on micro-regional one, and also substituting this shortage with moral weight or diplomatic capabilities on a micro-specialised one. In addition, the most widely usage of the concept applies four diversifications as geographic (physically or ideologically), material (measurable position as military, economy, population), normative (order-stabiliser with value orientation in diplomatic mean) and behavioural (compromise-positioner, multilateral-solution-seeker in international problems).[35] The traditional characteristics of the middle powers, therefore, can be juxtaposed as follows: the respect of international law and universal values; the contribution to global issues such as peace-keeping, conflict prevention, climate change, official development assistant (ODA); the mediation in the interests of great and small powers; the pursuit of coalition-building with like-minded states; the tendency toward multilateralism; the conduct of niche diplomacy; and the playing the part of agenda-setting and norm-spreading in international development.[36]

The middle powers do not have enough political or military weight in world policy to impose their will, yet still are significantly able to exert their influence over specific issues or decision-making process on the international stage. While

---

[34] Gareth Evans, Bruce Grant, **Australia's Foreign Relations in the World of the 1990s,** Melbourne, Melbourne University Press, 1995, pp. 344-348; also see "Speech to the National Press Club by Senator Gareth Evans", http://www.gevans.org/speeches/old/1991/041191_fm_australiasforeignrelations.pdf (Access 05.06.2021); for a brief-closer reading of the historical evolution of the middle power concept in Australian foreign policy, see Carl Ungerer, "The 'Middle Power' Concept in Australian Foreign Policy", **Australian Journal of Politics and History,** Vol. 53, No. 4, 2007.

[35] See Andrew F. Cooper, Richard A. Higgott, Kim Richard Nossal, **Relocating Middle Powers: Australia and Canada in a Changing World Order,** Vancouver, UBC Press, 1993; for a theoretical (IR) assessment, see James Manicom, Jeffrey Reeves, "Locating Middle Powers in International Relations Theory and Power Transitions", **Middle Powers and the Rise of China,** Bruce Gilley, Andrew O'Neil (Eds.), Washington, DC, Georgetown University Press, 2014, pp. 23-44; for an Australia-focus examination, see Thomas S. Wilkins, "Australia: A Traditional Middle Power Faces the Asian Century", **Middle Powers and the Rise of China,** Bruce Gilley, Andrew O'Neil (Eds.), Washington, DC, Georgetown University Press, 2014, pp. 149-170.

[36] For further conceptual explanation and case study of middle power-niche diplomacy, see Andrew F. Cooper (Ed.), **Niche Diplomacy: Middle Powers after the Cold War,** London, Macmillan Press, 1997.

the middle powers do not ignore the necessity of material strength, they define themselves mostly within the framework of "ideational components" and reflect "ideational beliefs" in the foreign policy roles they adopt. Therefore, the middle powers traditionally possess three characteristics: *"the material capability, the behavioural element and the ideational component."*[37] They, hence, tend to utilise niche diplomacy, also called middle power diplomacy or mission-oriented diplomacy of which Australian Foreign Minister Gareth Evans has been credited with giving the name, which is a strategy that associates with the method of soft power and prevalently labelled as middle power (or sometime small power) foreign policy behaviour. One can define niche diplomacy is to be selective in terms of policy prioritisation or geographical region and accordingly concentrate and specialise the resources in specific areas in order to yield the direct outcome, to have the room to manoeuvre, and for the maximisation of the relevance, impact and benefits.

As a traditional middle power, Australia's response to a rising China or the intensifying competition between the United States and China has been to advance further the Indo-Pacific construct with the hope of redirecting the structural changes through building "like-minded" state coalitions to ensure or guarantee a secure and stable IPR and a rules-based global order, the structural changes in which as recently stressed by Australia, *"strategic competition, primarily between the United States and China, which is playing out across the Indo-Pacific and increasingly in our immediate region, will be the principal driver".*[38] In this sense, the main motivation of Australian Indo-Pacific stance seeks *"to protect an international order in which relations between states are governed by international law and other rules and norms",*[39] an order that China's challenging posture and the increasing strategic competition with US hegemony.

As Gilley and O'Neil point out, *"as influential agents in international politics, middle powers have the potential to reshape and redirect the way in which China's ascent evolves",* further adding, *"more able because of their material power capabilities to take issue with China's preferences, but less able than great powers to balance China's influence unilaterally, middle powers rely on adept diplomatic means, with an emphasis on building coalitions with like-minded powers, to differentiate their policy preferences from great powers".*[40] Hence, Australia places priority on bilateral and multilateral engagement with democracies in the IPR notably Japan, India, Indonesia and South Korea *"to limit the exercise of coercive power and support an open global economy and a rules-based international order",*[41] emphasising, *"since 2016, major powers have become more assertive... including China's active pursuit of greater influence in the Indo-Pacific... Some countries will*

---

[37] Manicom, Reeves, op.cit., p. 33.
[38] **2020 Defence Strategic Update,** Commonwealth of Australia Department of Defence, Canberra, 2020, p. 11.
[39] 2017 Foreign Policy White Paper, op.cit., p. 11.
[40] Bruce Gilley, Andrew O'Neil, "China's Rise through the Prism of Middle Powers", **Middle Powers and the Rise of China,** Bruce Gilley, Andrew O'Neil (Eds.), Washington, DC, Georgetown University Press, 2014, p. 3.
[41] 2017 Foreign Policy White Paper, op.cit., p. 7.

continue to pursue their strategic interests through a combination of coercive activities, including espionage, interference and economic levers. Tensions over territorial claims and the establishment of new military facilities are rising and are involving the use of military or para-military forces more frequently than in the past, including coercive para-military activities in the South China Sea".[42]

Under the shadow of seeking to navigate the escalating risks of the US-China confrontation as a middle power of which has very critical pros and cons in between of these two, Australia might be able to serve as a "norm entrepreneur", as argued by Carr and Baldino, pointing out, Australia's self-identified *"as an agent who can play a critical part in the emergence of certain types of norms as a means of conflict prevention and crisis management in the Indo-Pacific region".*[43] Meanwhile, norm entrepreneurship is a form of practice which comes under the category of niche diplomacy. Hence, Australia's niche diplomacy with like-minded partners toward the IPR might be conducted through norm entrepreneurship. In this sense, Australia seems to rely on its "active" defence diplomacy as a "trust-builder mechanism" in order for conflict prevention and risk management in the IPR, a diplomacy that is voiced in white papers as *"we are trusted to defend, proven to deliver, respectful always",*[44] which seems to become a motto for Australian regional defence activism. Yet 2013 white paper explicitly stated, *"our contribution to regional security is not restricted, to deploying forces in a conflict or crisis. Rather, our efforts are focused on reducing the risk of conflict through building trust and partnerships through regular interaction with other nations",* the efforts that represents *"an active regional defence posture"* that viewed by Australia as *"a vital non-discretionary responsibility"* and an important instrument *"to Australia's security and prosperity".*[45]

On the other hand, Australia's practice of norm entrepreneurship seems to be a great task even if impossible is nothing. Borrowing Björkdahl's framework on norm entrepreneurship, these four steps need to be fulfilled in the establishment of Australia as a norm entrepreneur in the IPR: First, the committed norm by norm entrepreneur is *"framed to make it morally appealing, familiar, and 'good', in order for it to resonate with a global audience... Second, the norm entrepreneur strives to find an organisational home for the emerging norm in order for it to become self-sustaining and institutionalized into the organisational structure of the organisation... Third, the norm entrepreneur then uses norm advocacy, which combines agenda-shaping, norm-negotiation, and coalition-building, to persuade other states to embrace the norm... The final step in the norm entrepreneurial activities is to support the process of institutionalization. This process is characterised by how a norm becomes mainstreamed into an organisation's discourse, procedures, and structures".*[46]

[42] 2020 Defence Strategic Update, op.cit., pp. 11-12.
[43] Andrew Carr, Daniel Baldino, "An Indo-Pacific Norm Entrepreneur? Australia and Defence Diplomacy", **Journal of the Indian Ocean Region,** Vol. 11, No. 1, 2015, p. 30.
[44] See **Defence White Paper 2013,** op.cit., p. 94; also see, **2016 Defence White Paper,** Commonwealth of Australia Department of Defence, Canberra, 2016, p. 154.
[45] Defence White Paper 2013, op.cit., p. 24.
[46] Annika Björkdahl, "Ideas and Norms in Swedish Peace Policy", **Swiss Political Science Review,** Vol.

Given this framework, it is unlikely to imagine that any norm-spreading or "trust-spreading" efforts would successfully be fulfilled. Any kind of the conduct of niche diplomacy is only possible if the international system allows it; in other words, if there is the implicit acquiescence of the international system, and/or if the international society has placed the "niches" on the agenda. If considering the ongoing evolution towards most likely the structural shift, not just regionally, globally as well, it can be safely asserted that the Indo-Pacific cannot be a playground where all sides would peacefully slice the pie. The IPR is an "unpredictable construct-region" mirroring a heavy atmosphere where the precariously growing militarisation is, which has the more likely potential for active interference in some parts like the South China Sea or Taiwan; the ever-increasing misunderstandings and risks of miscalculations are; China is challenging with America's hegemony and seeking to influence the region to suit its own interests; and the potential to execute increasingly coercive strategies in various ways, mostly in the economy is. Hence, the future of the Indo-Pacific construct is full of uncertainties and not suitable to think pollyannaish.

India: Viewing Indo-Pacific as a Natural Region

The Indo-Pacific is not an exciting concept for India. Rather, India is of the opinion that the conceptualisation is a "natural extension" of its own long-running policies which has been, is, and will most likely be exerted from past to present, and to future. Thus, it was not an accident that Prime Minister Narendra Modi unambivalently described the IPR as a "natural region" while delivered the keynote address at Shangri La Dialogue on 1 June 2018, after a relatively long wary silence. First and foremost, the Indo-Pacific construct has been reflecting India's mind even if its name is not or has not been an Indo-Pacific, which is why that needs to be clarified by briefly tracing back to the evolution of India's foreign policy prism. To understand the "logic" behind Prime Minister Modi's assessment, the starting point could be the "Look East Policy" (LEP).

After a long while stuck in South Asia, India decided to turn to the East due to its economic reforms as well as the post-Cold War world allowed. To this end, the LEP, which has been seen a way to get rid of its isolated position from the Asia-Pacific, was launched in the early 1990s. Over a period of about a decade, the LEP has initially focused on the development of India's trade relations with ASEAN countries, which means the first phrase; then expanded its scope of the East beyond Southeast Asia and diversified its trade-based ties to security-oriented, which refers the second phrase; and ultimately after Narendra Modi took office for his first term as prime minister in 2014, it is rebranded as the "Act East Policy" (AEP) to signify a more "proactive" stance. As India's then External Affairs Minister Yashwant Sinha pointed out, *"the first phase of India's 'Look East' policy was ASEAN-centred and focussed primarily on trade and investment linkages. The new phase of this policy is characterised by an expanded definition of 'East', extending from*

19, No. 3, 2013, pp. 325-326.

Australia to East Asia, with ASEAN at its core. The new phase also marks a shift from trade to wider economic and security issues, including joint efforts to protect the sea-lanes and coordinate counter-terrorism activities".[47]

In the context of the LEP, India has first left its "land focus", then built deeper strategic ties with "like-minded" states such as the members of ASEAN, Japan and South Korea to defend its fundamental trade interests in the region, which was the one of the most important security objectives pursued by the country in its LEP. Ironically, even though having a very crucial position, India, let call it the "Indian Ocean giant", has not adequately been realised the importance of the IOR for a long time due to its "northern bias" that arises from Pakistan in the northwest and China in the Himalayas and also its complex and fragile North Eastern Region. In fact, the Indian Ocean is the lifeblood of India. As India's most famous historian K. M. Panikkar commented, *"He who rules on the sea will shortly rule on the land also- declared Khaireddin Barbarosa to Sultan Suleiman the Magnificent. The history of no country illustrates this principle better than that of India. There had been invasions and conquests of India from the land side on many previous occasions. But such invasions and conquests have either led to transient political changes, or to the foundation of new dynasties, which in a very short time became national and Indian. In fact it may truly be said that India never lost her independence till she lost the command of the sea in the first decade of the sixteenth century".[48]* As in a recent addition to Panikkar's comment concerning "maritime logic", Rajiv Sikri, the then Secretary in External Affairs Ministry echoed, *"If India aspires to be a great power, then the only direction in which India's strategic influence can spread is across the seas. In every other direction there are formidable constraints".[49]* Which is why India's LEP, as Indian former Prime Minister Manmohan Singh pointed out, *"was not merely an external economic policy, it was also a strategic shift in India's vision of the world".[50]*

India has been discovering the importance of being a blue sea force and the maritime security for roughly the last three decades, which implies the recovery of its malady of "sea-blindness", the malady that worded by retired Admiral of the Indian Navy Arun Prakash.[51] In parallel to reap the fruits of the maritime awareness along with the LEP, the AEP, which refers an "extension" of the LEP, was declared by former External Affairs Minister Sushma Swaraj in 2014. Thereafter, India's strategic vision for the "Indian Ocean Security and Growth for All in the Region", "SAGAR", which conceptually means "ocean" in Hindi

---

[47] "Speech by External Affairs Minister Shri Yashwant Sinha at Harvard University", **Government of India Ministry of External Affairs (GoI-MEA),** September 29, 2003, https://www.mea.gov.in/Speeches-Statements.ht m?dtl/4744 (Access 07.06.2021).

[48] K. M. Panikkar, India and the Indian Ocean: An Essay on the Influence of Sea Power on Indian History, London, George Allen & Unwin, 1945, p. 7.

[49] Rajiv Sikri, Challenge and Strategy: Rethinking India's Foreign Policy, New Delhi, Sage, 2009, p. 250.

[50] "PM's Keynote Address at Special Leaders Dialogue of ASEAN Business Advisory Council", Government of India Prime Minister's Office National Informatics Centre (GoI-PMO-NIC), December 12, 2005, https://archi vepmo.nic.in/drmanmohansingh/speech-details.php?nodeid=238 (Access 08.06.2021).

[51] See Admiral (Retd.) Arun Prakash, "Rise of the East: The Maritime Dimension", Maritime Affairs: Journal of the National Maritime Foundation of India, Vol. 7, No. 2, 2011, p. 7.

and strategically signifies India's potential role of being the regional "net security provider", was unveiled by Prime Minister Modi in 2015 during his visit to Mauritius. To date, India has relatively regained its strategic strength in the IOR and expanded its strategic outreach across Southeast Asia and the Western Pacific through the AEP and the SAGAR. In this sense, the deeper ties, notably defence-oriented, with Japan and Australia, and most importantly with the United States mark far beyond the tradition of the Indian Foreign Policy.

The main driver of this dramatic shift is undoubtedly the "China factor", a factor that vitally refers geographical proximity, distrust-based relations, conflicted rivalry, disputed borders with many of grey zones, security dilemma in heavily the IOR. On the one hand, the more China pushes India to the US, the more India will close to the US. On the other hand, India will never say "yes" to a "formal alliance" as long as it is not a matter of life and death, as the sole exception. Which is why India has shown a wariness as keeping its long silence against the mostly US-driven, secondary Japan-driven, Indo-Pacific narrative (as well as the Quad narrative) in which the exclusion-oriented approaches converge aiming at China's containment, even if the Indo-Pacific construct was technically first (re)induced by Gurpreet Khurana, that is by an Indian. Rather, India's Indo-Pacific approach is "inclusive" that representing the inclusion of China in which India desires a constructive and stable bilateral relationship to manage its China relations and hedge against the China factor as well as against any possible alliance formation by keeping China engaged in the IPR, maintaining its own strategically advantageous leverage in the IOR and retaining its Non-Alignment Policy tradition.

As Prime Minister Modi stressed, *"the Indo-Pacific is a natural region... Inclusiveness, openness and ASEAN centrality and unity, therefore, lie at the heart of the new Indo-Pacific. India does not see the Indo-Pacific Region as a strategy or as a club of limited members. Nor as a grouping that seeks to dominate. And by no means do we consider it as directed against any country. A geographical definition, as such, cannot be. India's vision for the Indo-Pacific Region is, therefore, a positive one"*, clarifying with seven core elements as: *"One, it stands for a free, open, inclusive region... Two, Southeast Asia [ASEAN] is at its centre... Three, [a common rules-based order] must believe in sovereignty and territorial integrity, as well as equality of all nations, irrespective of size and strength... Four, we should all have equal access as a right under international law to the use of common spaces on sea and in the air that would require freedom of navigation, unimpeded commerce and peaceful settlement of disputes in accordance with international law... Five, ...India stands for open and stable international trade regime. Six, connectivity... must be based on respect for sovereignty and territorial integrity, consultation, good governance, transparency, viability and sustainability... Finally, ...our friendships are not alliances of containment. We choose the side of principles and values, of peace and progress, not one side of a divide or the other... India's own engagement in the Indo-Pacific Region – from the shores of Africa to that of the Americas - will be inclusive".[52]*

---

[52] "Prime Minister's Keynote Address at Shangri La Dialogue", June 01, 2018, **GoI-MEA,** https://www.mea.gov.in/Speeches-Statements.htm?dtl/29943/Prime+Ministers+Keynote+Address+at

Today, in a last word, the AEP along with the SAGAR is the backbone of the strategy orientation in which the IPR has been seen a strategic playground for India. Hence, there is an Indian brand of the "Indo-Pacific Vision" but no an Indian brand of the "Indo-Pacific Strategy" unlike the United States and Japan, which means India has not been specifically (re)developed a strategy regarding the Indo-Pacific construct.

Conclusion

Mental maps guide thoughts about the world and have a real impact on actions. With the Indo-Pacific designation, the mental map of Asia has been redrawing for the last decade. In other words, the Asia-Pacific mentality has been recasting by the Quad countries, by mostly the United States. In this context, the Indo-Pacific concept emphasises the special importance of the Indian Ocean where India naturally has a geographical advantage and which signifies an "India card" for the United States against China. Admittedly, as a geopolitical construct, the Indo-Pacific is literally based on the balancing of the rise of China by promoting and prioritising India's regional power projection in the wider IPR. Hence, the formation of Indo-Pacific is a two-sided coin for India: on one side, it offers India an opportunity of enhancing its regional leverage; on the other side, it carries a risk of confronting China. In the latter sense, India would not fall into the "Thucydides trap" in the IOR, a trap that refers to an inevitable conflict between a rising power and a ruling power in history. Evidently, India's current foreign policy posture that the author of this chapter coins as "Conjunctural Non-Alignment" (CNA) functions as a kind of "risk control strategy" that allows "equal-status and multi-oriented strategic partnerships" including China as well as that guarantees at safeguarding its independence against "alliance formations" and accordingly its own "room to manoeuvre" in world politics.

Given the other Quad countries individually, not only the Quad formation of four but also the FOIPSs of the United States and Japan seem to provoke China. Indeed, the inclusiveness rhetorically raised, whereas the tone of what one the perceived is exclusiveness. In this sense, the institutionalisation or constructive and functional platforms are vital in the IPR. For example, norm entrepreneurship requires a crucial need for a forum or structure for Australia to sell its values or ideas. To give the devil his due, as the old English saying goes, ASEAN has developed a unique method known the "ASEAN Way" that refers the nominal leadership and institutional model of constitutive and shared norms and principles to manage regional security in the Asia-Pacific. On the other hand, it would be unrealistic to think that the ASEAN sample will be adapted to the wider IPR. Hence, to practice its niche diplomacy for a constructive order, Australia can utilise the Quad formation. To conclude, borrowing Khurana's

---

+Shangri+La+Dialogue+June+01 +2018 (Access 09.06.2021).

phrase, *"Indo-Pacific was always about China? Yes, but let's not cross the Red Line".*[53]

---

[53] Gurpreet Khurana, "Indo-Pacific Was Always About China? Yes, But Let's Not Cross the Red Line", **Maritime Perspectives 2017,** Pradeep Chauhan, Gurpreet S Khurana (Eds.), New Delhi, National Maritime Foundation, 2018, pp. 96-99.

RUSSIAN NAVAL DOCTRINE AND RUSSIAN NAVY MODERNIZATION

Ahmet Sapmaz[1]

Introduction

The Russian Federation (RF) is the largest country in the world. It has coastlines on three oceans and thirteen seas. It has one of the most powerful armed forces in the world, especially nuclear weapons. RF is an important country in the world with its permanent member status of the United Nations Security Council, natural resources, defense and space industry, security and foreign policy in line with being a great power. After the collapse of the USSR, RF, which went through a period of collapse in all respects, pursues policies towards being a great power of the multipolar world with the understanding of "strong army, strong economy, strong state" with Vladimir Putin's rise to power.

With the political determination guiding the developing economic and military capabilities, Moscow has been using its military power directly in line with its foreign policy goals since 2008. The Russian Navy, which constitutes an important part of the RF military force, is of great importance to Moscow. First of all, the navy is of great importance in ensuring the safety of the maritime transportation routes of the energy resources that form the basis of the RF economy. On the other hand, the navy has a great contribution to the military security of the RF and its allies. Moreover, nuclear-powered long-range ballistic missile submarines capability of the RF Navy constitute an important part of Moscow's strategic nuclear deterrence and its great power status in the world.

In this study, the naval doctrine of the RF and the modernization of the Russian navy are discussed. First of all, the place and current status of the navy in Russian history, then the Russian naval doctrine and the modernization of the Russian navy will be discussed and the study will be concluded with an evaluation. The main argument of the study is that, with the exception of nuclear-powered ballistic missile submarines and some long-range precision strike missile systems, the RF does not have a significant force multiplier for the navy, and that the navy is not strong enough to support the political and military policies generally outlined in naval strategies and doctrines. However, the RF maintains its status as a major regional power in the current state of the navy.

The Place of the Navy in Russian History and Today

According to Alfred Thayer Mahan, the geography of coastal countries will lead governments to an understanding of maritime policy, which in turn will

---

[1] Dr. Ahmet Sapmaz, E-mail: ahmet_sapmaz@yahoo.com.

affect the foreign, security and economic policy of the country. The naval powers will seek to realize their economic interests through overseas trade. In this context, the aforementioned countries will need a large merchant fleet and a navy to protect this fleet.[2] This was the case for Russia. The geographical, political, economic and cultural isolation Russia faced in the 17th and 18th centuries necessitated the establishment of a regular navy. Tsar Peter I (Peter the Great) realized that Russia could not achieve economic development with intra-continental trade and that overseas trade was necessary for this. Peter I had a large merchant fleet and built St. Petersburg, created the Russian navy to protect the merchant fleet and sea routes.[3] Peter I provided the necessary expertise for the formation of the navy, both from his visits to European countries and through the experts he brought from Europe.[4] The Azov Fleet, which constituted the first permanent naval force of the Navy, was built in 1695-1696 and helped the Russian army occupy the Azov Turkish Fortress. The Council of Boyars approved the regulation submitted by Peter I regarding the navy on October 30, 1696, and this date was accepted as the foundation of the Russian navy.[5] The aim of the Russian navy in the Great Northern War, which lasted between 1700 and 1721, was to carry some elements that have survived to the present day These purposes were to fight the enemy fleet, to keep the transportation lines open, and to present day. These purposes were to fight the enemy fleet, to keep the transportation lines open, and to attempt to attack and infiltrate from the sea.[6]

While Peter I focused on the Baltic region, defeating Sweden, half a century later, Catherine II headed south and tried to reach the warm seas. The Ottoman Navy was sunk in Chesme in 1770 by the Russian Baltic Fleet. Catherine II captured Crimea and founded the port city of Sevastopol. However, the Russians, who landed in the Black Sea, could not advance further south due to the Turkish Straits. In 1860, Vladivostok was established on the Pacific coast. With the commissioning of the Trans-Siberian railway, Vladivostok has become the main port in the Far East. In the 19th century, the Russians fought three times with the Ottoman Empire to reach the warm seas and the Mediterranean. The Baltic Fleet was deployed in the Mediterranean during the Russo-Turkish War of 1806-1812. During the Crimean War (1853-1856), the Russians were defeated by the allied state navies, mostly with steamships. The Russo-Turkish War (1877-1878) was a war in which the predecessors of modern torpedoes were used. The Caspian Flotilla participated in the 1803-1813 and 1826-1827 wars with Persia and gained a firm position in the north of the Caspian Sea. In the Russo-Japanese

---

[2] Alfred Thayer Mahan, **The Influence of Sea Power Upon History: 1660-1773**, New York, Dover Publications, 1987, pp. 25-58.
[3] Klaus A.R. Mommsen, "The Russian Navy", **Routledge Handbook of Naval Strategy and Security**, Joachim Krause, Sebastian Bruns (Eds), New York, Routledge, 2016, p. 305.
[4] David R. Stone, A Military History of Russia: From Ivan the Terrible to the War in Chechnya, London, Praeger Security International, 2006, p. 49.
[5] http://eng.mil.ru/en/structure/forces/navy/history.htm (Access 13.04.2021).
[6] Ibid.

War of 1904-1905, the Russian Pacific Fleet was caught off guard against the powerful Japanese navy. When the Russian Baltic Fleet sought to reinforce the Pacific Fleet, it was defeated by the Japanese Navy.[7] Murmansk was founded on the Kola Peninsula in 1916. Murmansk, an Arctic port, does not freeze even during the winter months. The Russian Navy was not very effective against the German and British navies in World War I, and the German navy and occupation in World War II, and performed limited missions.[8] The fact that the borders of the empire included very wide and distant geographies caused the navy fleets to carry out regional missions in their area of responsibility. In this context, it is based on the Russian fleets to be at a self-sufficient level.[9]

During the USSR period, the Navy continued to support the land forces and carried out the tasks of keeping the sea supply routes open and the defense of the coastal areas. The Navy was in a defensive position in the early years of the Cold War. United States aircraft carrier groups and amphibious task forces were seen as the main threats. The USSR became a military threat to the US from both the Atlantic and the Pacific Oceans, with nuclear submarines second strike capability, ocean cruisers and aircraft carrier in the Northern and Pacific fleets, and relations developed with some of the non-affiliated countries. However, even in this case, the Soviet Navy did not engage into any military conflicts.[10]

Admiral Sergey Gorshkov, Commander of the Soviet Union Navy between 1956 and 1985, greatly improved the navy in surface and submarine ships with the effect of the 1962 Cuban Missile Crisis. The area of responsibility of the Northern Fleet covered the entire North Atlantic, and its powerful submarines and long-range naval bombers reached a level that would cause significant casualties on NATO forces. However, in the Soviet military doctrine, the role of the navy continued to support the ground forces and create favorable conditions for ground operations.[11]

The Navy of the Soviet Union became the most powerful in its history in the mid-1980s. During this period, a force of 100 squadrons and brigades, including four fleets and the Caspian Flotilla, surface ships, submarines and coastal defense units, was reached. With the dissolution of the USSR in 1991, the Navy of the Soviet Union first turned into the Navy of the Commonwealth of Independent States and then the Navy of the Russian Federation. Moscow lost its naval base

---

[7] **The Russian Navy: A Historic Transition**, Office of Naval Intelligence, 2015, pp. 14-15.

[8] Mesut Hakkı Caşın, Rusya'nın Putin Yönetimi Liderliğinde Yeni Deniz Gücü Stratejisi-1, https://m5dergi.com/son-sayi/rusyanin-putin-yonetimi-liderliginde-yeni-deniz-gucu-stratejisi-1/ (Access 18.04.2021)

[9] The presence of naval power in certain maritime geographies in Russian history emerged as a response to the world oceans and international economic and political conjuncture. The Baltic Fleet survived from May 18, 1703, the Caspian Flotilla from November 15, 1722, and the Black Sea Fleet from May 13, 1783. Although the Northern and Pacific Fleets were temporarily established and dissolved, the Pacific Fleet became permanent as of April 21, 1932, and the Northern Fleet as of June 1, 1933. http://eng.mil.ru/en/structure/forces/navy/history.htm (Access 13.04.2021).

[10] Mommsen, op.cit., p. 305.

[11] İbid., p. 306.

rights in the Baltic countries, Black Sea and former Warsaw Pact countries. Only the northern and eastern seacoasts were unchanged.[12] The only naval base located abroad was Tartus naval base in Syria.[13] Moscow signed a division agreement with Ukraine in 1997 for the division of the Black Sea Fleet on the Crimean Peninsula and the lease of the Sevastopol naval base.[14] With this agreement, the RF has officially recognized the sovereignty and territorial integrity of Ukraine. Moscow did not want to lose Crimea, where the Black Sea fleet is located, due to its place in Russian history and the greatest opportunity in the Black Sea to reach the warm seas.[15]

After the dissolution of the USSR, the military power and therefore the navy were also affected by the collapse of the Russian Federation in every field. According to Western analysts, the Russian Navy had a rotting fleet. Due to organizational disruption and insufficient budget, enough attention was not given to the Navy. While the submarine fleet, which constitutes an important element of the USSR Navy, had 400 submarines in 1985, the number of submarines owned by RF decreased to 65 in 2007.[16] While the number of personnel of the USSR Navy was approximately 410,000 in 1990, it was around 171,500 in the RF in 2000.[17] During this period, Russia was trying to maintain one of the world's most advanced navies (with nuclear-capable submarines) with a third world country budget.[18] With Putin's coming to power in 2000, the recovery seen in all areas in the RF was also reflected in the Navy.

The RF Navy is the mainstay of the Russian maritime force. The Russian Navy is an instrument of Russian foreign policy and aims to militarily protect the interests of the RF and its allies in the world oceans. On the other hand, the Russian Navy is used to ensure political- military stability and military security in the seas around the RF.[19] The Navy carries out activities such as strategic

---

[12] Victor Potvorov, "National Interests, National Security, and the Russian Navy", **Naval War College Review**, Vol. 47, No. 4, 1994, p. 62.

[13] The Tartus naval base, which the USSR acquired in Syria in 1971, was used for supply and maintenance purposes in the Mediterranean during the USSR period, as in Ethiopia, Egypt, Vietnam and other places. Manzoor Khan Afridi, Ali Jibran, "Russian Response to Syrian Crisis: A Neorealist Perspective", **Strategic Studies**, Vol. 38, No. 2, p. 62.

[14] Mommsen, op.cit., pp. 306-307. Under the agreement, RF would be able to use more than 100 offshore facilities on the Crimean Peninsula until 2017. Within the framework of the agreement, 82% of the Soviet Black Sea Fleet was given to the RF. Dmitry Gorenburg, "The Future of the Sevastopol Russian Navy Base", **Russian Analytical Digest**, 75/10, p. 11, https://css.ethz.ch/content/dam/ethz/special-interest/gess/cis/center-for-securities-studies/pdfs/RAD-75-11-13.pdf (Access 10.04.2021). RF and Ukraine extended the agreement on the use of bases until 2047 with a new 25-year agreement in 2010. In addition, with the possibility of an additional 5 years extension, the use of the bases could be extended until 2047.

[15] Rasmus Nilsson, "Russian Policy Concerning the Black Sea Fleet and its Being Based in Ukraine, 2008-2010: Three Interpretation, **Europe-Asia Studies**, Vol. 65, No. 6, 2013, pp. 1156-1163.

[16] Alexander V. Krylov, Natan Z. Shuminov, "The Marine Strategy of Russia in the Middle East", **Comparative Politics Russia**, Vol. 12, No. 1, 2021, p. 82.

[17] Marcel De Haas, **Russian Security and Air Power: 1992-2002**, New York, Frank Cass, 2004, p. 29.

[18] R.G. Gıdadhublı, "Kursk Submarine Disaster: Obssolete Technologies, Outdated Governance", **Economic and Political Weekly**, August 26-September 2000, p. 3102.

[19] http://eng.mil.ru/en/structure/forces/navy/history.htm (Access 13.04.2021).

deterrence in peacetime, protection of the interests of the RF and its allies, and short-term ocean presence operations that will support Russian foreign policy[20], such as port visits, participating in exercises, and show of force. Since 2008, the Russian Navy has been navigating the Caribbean Sea, Mediterranean, Atlantic and Pacific Ocean regions with a high level of visibility. For the Navy, the most important element of strategic deterrence is nuclear-powered ballistic missile submarines (SSBN). The protection of the seas and coasts of RF and its allies is provided by a layered defense system. At the forward defense, nuclear powered submarines equipped with anti-ship and anti-submarine missiles, large surface ships and long-range planes will destroy enemy firing platforms that can launch long-range missiles to RF by deploying at a distance of approximately 1000 nm from the Russian mainland.[21] Close-in defense is provided by diesel-powered submarines equipped with anti-ship and anti-submarine missiles, small surface ships, minefields and coastal defense forces.[22] This is a continuation of the "Bastion" concept developed in the 1970s in the period of Admiral Gorshkov. The Bastion concept includes layered defense and buffer zones to ensure security, and prioritizes nuclear-powered ballistic missile submarines for the protection of the Russian mainland and second-strike capability.[23]

The main headquarters of the Russian Navy is located at St. Petersburg. The Russian Navy consists of the Baltic, Black Sea, Northern, Pacific Fleets and the Caspian Flotilla. Naval Aviation includes ship-borne fixed, rotary-wing aircraft and operational tactical aviation troops deployed in Kaliningrad, Crimea and the Kola Peninsula. Coastal Troops includes Naval Infantry[24] and Coastal Missile and Artillery Troops. The Russian Navy has recently upgraded its coastal defense missile systems and deployed them in Kaliningrad, Crimea and Arctic regions.[25]

The Northern Fleet is the most equipped fleet of the Russian Navy. The Northern Fleet, located in Severomorsk, with its 7 nuclear-powered ballistic missile submarines, constitutes an important part of the strategic nuclear weapons of the RF. In addition, Admiral Kuznetsov, RF's only aircraft carrier, and the navys' only nuclear-powered KIROV-class heavy cruiser are also included in the Northern Fleet. The two main missions of the fleet are to provide strategic deterrence with ballistic missile submarines and to protect the maritime

---

[20] V.V. Masorin, "The Navy and Russia's Security", **Military Thought**, Vol. 15, No. 1, 2006, p. 231.

[21] The scarcity of large surface ships in the RF Navy increases the importance of territorial waters defence. Jonathan Evitts, Russian Naval Moderinzation and Strategy, **Naval Postgraduate School**, 2019, p. 68.

[22] The Russian Navy: A Historic Transition, op.cit., p. 10.

[23] Liv Karin Parnemo, "Russian Naval Development-Grand Ambitions and Tactical Pragmatism", **Journal of Slavic Military Studies**, Vol. 32, No. 1, 2019, p. 45.

[24] Marines of the Baltic, Northern and Pacific Fleets participated in the First Chechen Campaign and captured the Chechen Presidential Palace in Grozny on January 19, 1995. In 2008, the marine units of the Black Sea Fleet were deployed to Abkhazia to be used against Georgia. In 2014, the 810th Marine Brigade of the Black Sea Fleet was used to isolate Ukrainian bases in Crimea. In addition, the 810th Marine Brigade of the Black Sea Fleet has been providing the security of the RF's Khmeimim airbase in Syria since 2015. Dmitry Boltenkov, "The Russian Marine Corps", **Moscow Defense Brief**, 2019.

[25] Jonas Kjellen, Nils Dahlqvist, "Russia's Armed Forces in 2019", Russian Military Capability in a Ten Year Perspective-2019, Fredrik Westerlund, Susanne Oxenstierna (eds), **FOI**, 2019, pp. 29-30.

areas extending to the northwest of RF. [26] The great capability of the Russian Northern Fleet, which includes the Arctic region of the RF, is due to the level of threat posed by the West in both Europe and Asia and the great energy potential of the Arctic region.[27]

Although the Pacific Fleet lags behind the Northern Fleet in terms of capability, it is capable of strategically attacking the US mainland and operates from the Pacific to the Horn of Africa with surface ships. Most of the Pacific Fleet's diesel-powered submarines and surface ships with headquarters are located in Vladivostok, and nuclear-powered submarines containing SSBNs are located in Petropavlovsk-Kamchatskiy.[28]

The Black Sea has been the region that has undergone the greatest geopolitical change in the last 30 years among the 5 maritime theaters of the RF. During the Cold War period, it was seen as "Soviet Lake", but the influence of the West has increased since 2000s.[29] The Black Sea Fleet was left to rot with Soviet heritage ships for many years, but after the annexation of Crimea by the RF in 2014, it included surface and submarine units, including modern coastal defense and naval infantry units. Equipped with Kalibr missiles, the fleet allows the RF to increase its effectiveness in the Black Sea and subsequently in the Mediterranean and the Middle East, balances NATO in the region and actively supports the operation in Syria.[30]

The Baltic Fleet is located in the port of Baltiysk in Kaliningrad Oblast. The Baltic Fleet provides security of the sea routes between Kaliningrad and St. Petersburg and balances NATO forces in the region. It is also actively involved in the defense of RF interests in the Eastern Mediterranean and Horn of Africa. The Baltic Fleet is in a position to pose a conventional and nuclear threat to Western Europe with its Kalibr missiles. The Caspian Flotilla enables RF to be the hegemonic power in the Caspian Sea. It is the first naval unit in the Navy to be equipped with Kalibr missiles. With its Caspian Flotilla, Moscow has the opportunity to exert influence over Central Asia, Caucasus, Middle East and Eastern Europe with Kalibr missiles with precision strike capability.[31]

After the RF-Georgia War in 2008, the tension between Moscow and the West increased and Russia, which had recovered under the leadership of Putin in the 2000s, started to use its military power directly in line with its foreign policy goals. In this context, the submarines of the Russian Northern Navy set sail on the Atlantic coast of the USA for the first time in many years. The number of

---

[26] Russia Military Power: Building A Military to Support Great Power Aspirations, Defense Intelligence Agency, 2017, pp. 67-68.

[27] Stephen Blank, "The Arctic and Asia in Russian Naval Strategy", **The Korean Journal of Defense Analysis**, Vol. 29, No. 4, 2017, p. 592.

[28] Russia Military Power: Building A Military to Support Great Power Aspirations, op.cit., pp. 67-68.

[29] Igor Delanoe, "After Crimean Crisis: Towards a Greater Russian Maritime Power in the Black Sea", **South European and Black Sea Studies**, Vol. 14, No. 3, 2013, p. 370.

[30] Russia Military Power: Building A Military to Support Great Power Aspirations, op.cit., pp. 67-68.

[31] İbid., pp. 67-68.

joint exercises conducted by the RF Armed Forces has increased and significant changes have been made in the structure of the armed forces. This was also reflected in the RF Navy. Different naval fleets participated in joint exercises. The exercises that have been carried out since the Vostok-2010 Exercise have started to be carried out in the form of instant inspections. 6 military districts in the RF Armed Forces organization were transformed into 4 joint strategic commands in 2010. Joint strategic commands consist of land, air, naval and air defense forces that can plan and execute large-scale joint operations in their areas of responsibility. In this context, the Northern and Baltic Fleets were included in the Western Joint Strategic Command, the Pacific Fleet in the Eastern Joint Strategic Command, the Black Sea Fleet and the Caspian Flotilla in the Southern Joint Strategic Command.[32]

The fact that navigation between Barents Sea and Bering Strait became possible due to global climate change in the Arctic Region, directed the attention of RF to the region. Moscow has developed policies to protect its interests in the Arctic region and to have strategic natural resources in the region. In this context, the number of missions carried out by the Northern Fleet in the region increased, some of the military facilities remaining from the Soviet period in the region were reactivated, and some military facilities were reconstructed. This process led to the establishment of the Northern Fleet Joint Strategic Command, in addition to the existing joint strategic commands, in order to protect the interests of the RF in the Arctic region in 2014.[33]

In 2013, the Commander of the RF Navy, Admiral Viktor Chirkov, announced that it was planned to have permanent naval power in the Pacific, Indian Ocean and the Mediterranean, in addition to the existing naval bases. Initially, priority was given to the Pacific Ocean as it was the focal point of geostrategic interests and events, but in 2013, the Russian Permanent Mediterranean Fleet was established by giving priority to the Mediterranean. The Russian Permanent Mediterranean Fleet, whose headquarters is located at the Black Sea Fleet in Sevastopol, is supported by the Black Sea, Northern and Baltic Fleets. The Russian Permanent Mediterranean Fleet can supply from the 720th Naval Material-Technical Support Center in the Syrian port of Tartus, and during peacetime from civil ports such as Limassol, Valetta and Ceuta. However, the supply and support of the Russian Navy in trans-Mediterranean missions poses a major problem. Although negotiations were held at permanent bases with various countries such as Libya, Cuba, Montenegro, Nicaragua, Venezuela, Vietnam and Yemen,[34] an agreement was reached only with Sudan in 2020 to establish a naval base.

RF annexed Crimea in 2014. It also supports the pro-Russian separatists in eastern Ukraine. RF was militarily involved in the Syrian civil war to support

---

[32] Mommsen, op.cit., p. 309.
[33] İbid., pp. 309-310.
[34] İbid., p. 308.

Bashar al-Assad, and the operation launched by the Air Force in Syria on September 30, 2015 was carried out under the active support of the Russian Navy. According to the agreement made between the RF and Syria on January 18, 2017, the Tartus naval base in Syria will be used by the Moscow for 49 years and this period will be automatically extended for 25 years if the two parties do not terminate with a written diplomatic notification 12 months before the end of the agreement. With the agreement, RF will be able to have 11 naval platforms at the Tartus base at the same time.[35]

On November 25, 2018, RF opened fire and seized 2 Ukrainian Navy ships and a tugboat by blocking the passage in the Kerch Strait, which connects the Sea of Azov and the Black Sea. 6 Ukrainian soldiers were injured in the incident and 23 Ukrainian soldiers were arrested by the RF. The developments increased the competition between the West and the RF in both the Black Sea and the Mediterranean, and the Russian Navy and especially the Black Sea Fleet gained great importance for RF.

Russian Naval Doctrine

States use their military power to achieve their political goals, and military power is the most dynamic and physical element of national power. Ensuring national security for a state generally involves protecting the country and increasing its welfare. In this framework, states create national security concepts in order to direct their long-term policies, create unity of efforts and synergy. Military doctrines prepared in line with the national security concept are a guide on how to use and develop the armed forces. The great powers issue doctrinal documents for each service of the armed forces within the framework of their military doctrines. In this context, RF is a country that has doctrines to direct the Navy. The aforementioned doctrines are generally influenced by the viewpoint of the RF towards the navy and the regional and global developments.

In fact, in determining the priorities of the Russian Navy, there has traditionally been the question of whether Russia is a major land power or a major naval power. Throughout history, an effective naval force has been seen as a precondition for Russia's great power status and influence in the world, while the Russian Navy remained the second priority behind the country's land forces. An important reason for this is that, unlike other major naval powers, Russia expects most of the threats against it from land. Although RF has the world's largest coastline with 38,800 km and neighbors with 3 oceans and 13 seas, a small portion of these sea areas are suitable for naval operations. The wide coastline and the area suitable for a small number of naval operations lead to the deployment of the RF Navy in different operation areas and to the division of its potential.[36]

[35] Krylov, Shuminov, op.cit., p. 86.
[36] Parnemo, op.cit., pp. 42-43.

The Russian naval strategy and naval structure traditionally evolve under the influence of the dispute between the two main schools for political, military and economic reasons. The first of these is the "old school" of Admiral Alfred Mahan, which is based on establishing a strong, offensive and balanced naval power with the large surface ships. On the other hand, the "young school" believes that land wars are decisive and therefore gives the navy second priority. While this school focuses on active defense for the defense of the coasts, it has adopted an approach that prioritizes small, highly maneuverable submarine and artillery systems.[37]

NATO's interventions in Bosnia and Herzegovina and Kosovo since the 1990s; the eastward expansion of NATO and the EU; missile defense systems that NATO and the USA are trying to develop; USA's withdrawal from the 1972 Anti-Ballistic Missile Agreement (ABM); withdrawal of RF from Treaty on Conventional Armed Forces in Europe (CFE); color revolutions in Moscow's periphery and the Middle East and North Africa; Moscow's recognition of the independence of South Ossetia and Abkhazia by fighting Georgia; the annexation of Crimea and support for the pro-Russian separatist movement in eastern Ukraine; as a result, increasing NATO's military presence in Eastern Europe; the competition in the Arctic region and the Eastern Mediterranean in the axis of the Syrian civil war; US withdrawal from the Intermediate-Range Nuclear Forces Treaty (INF); the economic, military and demographic pressure of China and Japan on Moscow in the east give direction to the said doctrines of the RF.

According to the Navy strategy of the United States in 2020, where the interests of RF conflict most recently, China's growing naval forces and the increasingly aggressive approach of the RF are at an alarming level. Hopes that both China and RF would contribute to global security have been lost, and the two countries have become Washington's main rivals. The US Navy has found itself in competition between major powers for the first time in recent years.[38] The USA especially defines China as a long-term strategic threat.[39] In its current state, the US Navy strategy is more conflict-oriented than peacetime-oriented. The USA, which has more than 300,000 soldiers in 800 military bases deployed in approximately 150 countries around the world, has overseas military bases in Bahrain, Cuba, Greece, Italy, Japan, South Korea, Singapore, Spain, the United Kingdom, Guam and Hawaii. The US Navy operates in the world oceans with 7 naval fleets and 11 aircraft carriers.[40]

---

[37] İbid., p. 44.
[38] Peter Haynes, "What U.S. Navy strategist and Defense Planners Should Think About in the era of Maritime Great Power Competition", **Defense&Security Analysis**, Vol. 36, No. 1, 2020, p. 101.
[39] Advantage at Sea: Prevaling with Integrated All-Domain Naval Power, https://media.defense.gov/2020/Dec/17/2002553481/-1/-1/0/TRISERVICESTRATEGY.PDF/TRISERVICESTRATEGY.PDF (Access 17.03.2021).
[40] Seppo Niemi's, "Naval Forces of Great Powers", Russian International Affairs Counsil, https://russiancouncil.ru/en/blogs/seppo-niemi-en/historical-navalism-navigare-necesse-est/ (Access 15.04.2021).

China, which has grown rapidly in recent years in the military field, including the navy, has two strategies for its naval forces. The first of these is the "close seas defense" that it applies to protect the mainland and its near littoral waters. China is building massive military build-ups on the natural and artificial islands it has built. On the other hand, China has started to follow a "far seas protection" policy in order to protect its global interests. Accelerating the construction of aircraft carriers, guided missile ships and nuclear-powered submarines, China aims to maintain overseas naval power to reflect its great power status. China, which currently has two diesel-powered aircraft carriers, wants to build nuclear-powered aircraft carriers that would allow longer navigation across the oceans. Currently having only, a naval base in Djibouti in the Horn of Africa, China aims to become a naval power capable of winning wars and projecting power globally in the mid-21st century.[41]

Until the early 2000s, RF did not have a naval strategy. RF released the "Fundamentals of the Russian Federation's Naval Policy until the Year 2010" in 2000, and the "Maritime Doctrine of the Russian Federation" and "Strategy for the Development of the Shipbuilding Industry until the Year 2020" in 2001.[42] "The Maritime Doctrine of the Russian Federation" was signed by the President of the RF on July 26,2015. According to the doctrine, which is a comprehensive document, RF has economic, political and military interests in the seas. In the doctrine, RF's maritime interests are specified as Arctic, Antarctica, Indian Ocean and Mediterranean. Most of the political and military threats against RF originate from the west. These regions mostly cover the Black Sea and the Mediterranean. Likewise, the Arctic region is defined as a region where RF has political and economic interests and the risk of future military conflict is high. The concern created by the US' overseas powers has caused Moscow to give importance to the Pacific fleet in the recent period.[43]

A decree entitled "Approval of the Fundamentals of the State Policy of the Russian Federation in the Field of Naval Operations for the period until 2030" was signed by Russian Federation President Vladimir Putin on July 20, 2017. The navy has been defined as a flexible instrument of state policy. This flexibility is provided by long-range precision missiles in the Russian Navy. These missiles allow the Russian Navy to operate in a wide spectrum without having a large number of ocean-capable ships. One of the most important of these tasks is nuclear and conventional strategic deterrence. Another task is the integrated use of the capabilities of the Federal Security Service and the Navy. This has recently become more pronounced with the Sea of Azov.[44]

In the doctrine, it is stated that the RF maintains its status as a major naval

---

[41] Seppo Niemi's, op.cit.
[42] Caşın, op.cit.
[43] Richard Connolly, "Russia's Strategy for the Development of Maritime Activities to 2030", NATO Defense College Russian Studies Series 7/19, https://www.ndc.nato.int/research/research.php?icode= 618 (Access 17.03.2021).
[44] Ibid.

power and the focus of the Navy operation is to provide Moscow with militarily favorable conditions that can fulfill national security priorities in the world oceans. According to the document, intense competition continues between states for access to the natural resources of the oceans. World's leading powers are deploying naval capabilities and military facilities in key areas of the world oceans and around the RF. It is expected that an instable political-military situation will prevail in the world until 2030.[45]

In this context, risks and threats to RF include the efforts of some states, especially the USA, to establish superiority in the world oceans, including the Arctic, the claims of foreign countries to the coastal regions and maritime sovereignty areas of the RF, the increase in the number of states with powerful naval forces, the spread of weapons of mass destruction, new missile technologies, efforts by some states to prevent RF's access to resources in the world oceans, economic, political, legal and military pressure to reduce the effectiveness of RF's maritime activities in the world oceans, trying to weaken its control over the North Sea route, the spreading of activities such as international terrorism, piracy, drug and arms trafficking, the presence of military conflicts in the important regions for the RF and its allies.[46]

In the document, it is emphasized that naval operations in the field of national security are to maintain the legal regime in the Sea of Azov and the Caspian Sea. It is stated that the competition of the armed forces of the countries in the world oceans has increased in the 21st century and that the "Global Strike" concept of the USA directly threatens international security and the military security of the RF. In this context, the Navy is one of the most important means of providing nuclear and non-nuclear strategic deterrence and preventing the USA's "Global Strike" concept. Among the goals of providing strategic deterrence are increasing the effectiveness of the Black Sea Fleet by deploying joint forces in the Crimean Peninsula and the permanent presence of sea power in important regions of the world oceans and maritime transportation areas, including the Mediterranean. It is stated in the document that the RF will not allow the naval forces of other countries to establish superiority over its own navy and will try to maintain the status of the second largest naval force in the world.[47]

In the doctrine, the modernization and development objectives of the Navy are to establish a balanced organization, to keep the operational capability of strategic nuclear units at a high level, and to include conventional systems equipped with new and modern weapons and systems in the inventory. In the medium and long term, modernization priorities are listed as strategic nuclear ballistic missile submarines, conventional naval task forces for non-nuclear strategic deterrence, deployment of naval forces in strategic areas where there is

---

[45] The Fundamentals of the State Policy of the Russian Federation in the Field of Naval Operations for the Period Until 2030, Russia Maritime Studies Institute, 2017, p. 4.
[46] İbid., pp. 4-5.
[47] İbid., pp. 11-12.

a threat to the RF, and increasing the operational capability of the Navy by improving its weapon systems and capabilities in all areas. In addition, until 2025, unmanned autonomous systems, including long-range guided cruise missiles, after 2025, hypersonic missiles and unmanned underwater vehicles will be a priority in procurement.[48]

Various criticisms have been directed at the Russian naval doctrine. One aspect of the criticisms is that the statements in the doctrine aims to make the Navy take a larger share from the State Armament Program 2025, on the other hand, despite the strength of the Russian Navy, the Crimean and the Russian-Japanese wars suffered a great defeat, and it received a large share of the budget required for the ground forces in the the First World War and Second World War. Likewise, although the USSR Navy received a large share of the defense budget in the 1970s and 1980s, it contributed little to the USSR's foreign policy and became the fastest collapsing power after the dissolution of the USSR.[49]

In August 2019, RF Prime Minister Dmitry Medvedev approved the document called "Strategy for the State of Russia's Maritime Activities up to 2030". The strategy document draws attention from two aspects. First, it reveals the weaknesses and obstacles in reaching the targets in the documents published in 2015 and 2017; on the other hand, it determines the measurable criteria that can be used in achieving the goals of the strategy.[50]

In the strategy document in question, the weakness of navigational support in the Arctic region with the Russian merchant fleet and nuclear-powered support ships such as ice breakers is mentioned. On the other hand, attention is drawn to the difficulty in accessing marine mineral and energy resources as a result of the sanctions imposed by the USA and other countries since 2014. The decrease and inadequacy experienced in scientific marine research is another mentioned issue. One of the important issues included in the document is the situation of the Naval Forces Command. First of all, it is stated that there are claims against the maritime sovereign areas of the RF mostly due to the problem with Ukraine in the Sea of Azov. On the other hand, it is stated that the legal regulation regarding the use of warships for special operations in war and peace situations is not sufficient. Thirdly, it is mentioned that the personnel, weapons and equipment of the FSB, that is, the Federal Security Service, do not have sufficient capacity to protect the Russian coasts. In addition, the problems experienced in shipbuilding and navigational safety in the Arctic and the Pacific are among the important shortcomings. In the strategy, large-scale armament and modernization activities are shown as the most important solution to all these problems. However, the limitations in Russian civil and military ship production and the status of the Russian economy are the biggest obstacles to the

---

[48] The Fundamentals of the State Policy of the Russian Federation in the Field of Naval Operations for the Period Until 2030, op.cit., pp. 14-15.
[49] Krylov, Shuminov, op.cit., p. 85.
[50] Connolly, op.cit.

implementation of the strategy. The consecutive publication of three important documents on the Russian maritime and naval forces between 2015 and 2019 shows that the threat perceived by Russia from the seas, especially in the regions close to its coasts, is increasing.[51]

Modernization of RF Navy

With the collapse of the USSR, the maintenance of the surface ships and submarines inherited by the RF was unsustainable due to the economic situation in Moscow. For this reason, a large part of the Russian Navy was left to rot. While a global role was assigned to navy at the official level, in reality the operational core was struggling to survive. During this period, many warships could not be maintained due to lack of spare parts and economic resources.[52] Russian political and military leaders had to make a difficult decision: either try to save everything and save nothing, or focus on units that are operationally cost-effective and gradually write off the others. In this context, the second course of action was preferred[53] and about 2/3 of the inventory left over from the Soviet era was writen off. Some of the Navy personnel quit because of not getting a regular salary, and there were disruptions in training activities. The Russian Navy withdrew from the oceans to the marginal seas. During this period, the only mission expected from the Russian Navy was to keep the nuclear-powered ballistic missile submarines active, which is an important pillar of the nuclear triad.[54]

The Russian Navy, which lost its competitiveness with the West, turned to cooperation with the West in some activities. For example, the Russian Navy participated in the embargo operation against Iraq in the Persian Gulf in 1992 and the US-led "Baltops" multinational exercise in the Baltic Sea in 1993. In 1998, the Pacific Fleet participated in a joint exercise with the Japanese Navy. In 2001, the Black Sea Fleet joined BLACKSEAFOR (The Black Sea Naval Co-Operation Task Group), which was created by the Black Sea coastal countries. With the sank of the Kursk submarine in the exercise carried out by the Northern Fleet on 12 August 2000, there was a worldwide cooperation initiative in the field of submarine rescue technology and procedures.[55]

The main political and military elements driving Russian defense reform were RF's conventional weakness, on the other hand, NATO's conventional superiority, RF's perceived threat from NATO, and the importance given to nuclear power in Russian military doctrines.[56] According to the State

[51] İbid.
[52] While the share of the RF Navy in the defense budget was 23% in 1993, it decreased to 9.8% in 1998. Carolina Vendil Pallin, **Russian Military Reform: A Failed Exercise in Defense Decision Making**, New York, Routledge, 2009, p. 99.
[53] The Russian Navy: A Historic Transition, op.cit., p. 6.
[54] Pallin, op.cit., p. 99.
[55] Mommsen, op.cit., p. 310.
[56] Yuri Krupnov, Defence Reform and the Russian Navy, **NATO Defence College**, p. 4,

Shipbuilding Program published in 2001, it was aimed to modernise the navy significantly by 2020. Aircraft carriers and cruisers with ocean capability were not top priorities in the Russian Navy modernization.[57] The RF Navy was trying to keep the current aircraft carrier, Admiral Kuznetsov, in service to maintain its ocean capability. In the modernization of the Navy, priority has been given to nuclear-powered submarines and small and multi-purpose surface ships in order to perform counter-submarine operations and defense missions in areas close to the coasts and in economic areas. The second priority was for multi-purpose frigates that can operate in high sea.[58] It can be stated that the RF takes care to maintain the nuclear-conventional balance in terms of naval forces, especially for strategic deterrence. The Navy attaches importance to nuclear-powered ballistic missile submarines, but prefers surface and submarine ships with conventional capability to protect the surrounding sea areas.

With the comprehensive military modernization program launched in 2008, Moscow began to spend about half of the defense budget in order for the Navy to reach the level necessary for the Russia to regain its great power status in the world.[59] Putin realizes that RF cannot achieve great power status without a powerful navy. For this reason, Putin attached importance to increasing the operational capabilities of the Russian Navy. In particular, as a result of the political directive of securing and protecting maritime transport routes of natural resources, Russian fleets have started to perform duties outside their areas of responsibility.[60]

Modernization activities in the Russian Armed Forces are directed by the Russian State Armament Programs signed by the President of the RF. The Russian State Armament Program 2018-2027, which is currently in force, was put into effect by a secret decree by RF President Putin on December 14, 2017. A total of four SAPs have been implemented until the current SAP. The 4th SAP was signed and put into effect in 2010 by the President of the Russian Federation, Dmitry Medvedev, in 2010. The aforementioned program aimed to increase modern weapons and equipment from 15% in 2010 to 30% in 2015 and to 70% in 2020.[61] In 2009, Russian political and military leaders officially declared that the Russian navy has overcome the crisis it was in. Russian military shipbuilding has advanced and the Russian Navy is equipped with advanced ship and weapon systems. Especially "Borei", "Akula", "Yasen" in nuclear submarine class, "Steregushchiy", "Buyan-M", "Admiral Gorshkov" in surface ships, and "Admiral Kuznetzov" in aircraft carrier class constitute the most advanced naval

---

https://www.nato.int/docu/other/ru/ndc/pdf/6.pdf (Access 15.03.2021).

[57] RF's larger surface vessels have a service life of more than 30 years. Russian Armed Forces: Capabilities, **Congressional Research Service**, https://crsreports.congress.gov/product/pdf/IF/IF11589 (Access 12.04.2021).

[58] Mommsen, op.cit., pp. 306-307.

[59] Krylov, Shuminov, op.cit., p. 82.

[60] Mommsen, op.cit., p. 308.

[61] Julian Cooper, The Russian State Armament Program 2018-2027, **NATO Defense College**, May 2018, p. 2.

weapons of the Russian defense industry.[62] The Russian Navy continues to develop small platforms that will effectively set the enemy's critical infrastructures under fire at the regional level, but it has difficulties in producing global capability that will achieve its objectives in the doctrinal documents.[63]

Submarines constitute the most striking and effective power of the RF Navy, just like in the USSR period.[64] In this context, Moscow has focused on increasing attack and ballistic missile submarine fleets and other special mission submarines in terms of quality and quantity. While the USA mostly owns nuclear-powered submarines, RF invests in both nuclear-powered and diesel-powered submarines. This is because diesel-powered submarines make less noise, making them more difficult to be detected and promoting survival.[65] The RF Navy is in the process of transitioning from Delta III and IV class ballistic missile submarines to the new Borei-class (Dolgorukiy-class) submarines over the next 15 years.[66] The Borei class nuclear-powered ballistic missile submarine is one of the important strategic deterrents of the Russian Navy. These quieter submarines can shoot targets thousands of kilometers away with their intercontinental ballistic missiles. Construction of the Borei class, the first new type of submarine built by the RF after the Soviet era, started in 1996. Yury Dolgoruky, the first Borei-class submarine, was commissioned to the Russian Navy in January 2013. The problems experienced in the steel used in the construction of the submarine and the long and difficult tests of the Bulava Submarine Launched Ballistic Missile (SLBM) newly developed for the Borei class, extended the duration of the project. Currently, RF Navy has 4 Borei class submarines and 4 Borei class submarines are being built.[67]

Within the framework of SAP-2020, 7 Yasen class nuclear-powered multi-role submarines were planned to enter service by 2020. However, only two of them have entered service (Severodvinsk and Kazan) and the others are planned to enter service by 2027. Yasen-M class submarines will replace the Soviet-era Antey class (NATO: Oscar 2) and Shchuka Class B class (NATO: Akula) submarines. Yasen-M class submarines, which are nuclear cruise missile attack submarines, are equipped with Kalibr and P-800 Onyx cruise missile systems. On the other hand, the modernization of 10 modified Shckuba-B is planned to

---

[62] Krylov, Shuminov, op.cit., p. 83.

[63] Michael B. Petersen, "Strategic Deterrence, Critical Infrastrusture, and the Aspiration-Modernization Gap in The Russian Navy", **Improvisation and Adaptability in the Russian Military**, Jeffrey Mankoff (Ed), Center for Strategic&International Studies, 2020, p. 32.

[64] Different ship types have come to the fore in different periods in the Russian Navy. Surface ships before World War I, naval aviation during the World War II, and nuclear weapons and nuclear-powered submarines after World War II became prominent. By the mid-1930s, the Russian Navy became a multidimensional strategic force consisting of naval aviation, coastal defense units and air defense elements. http://eng.mil.ru/en/structure/forces/navy/history.htm (Access 13.04.2021).

[65] Niemi's, op.cit.

[66] Dmitry Gorenburg, "Russian Naval Shipbuilding: Is It Possible to Fulfill the Kremlin's Grand Expectations?", **Ponars Eurasia**, No. 395, 2015, p. 1, https://www.ponarseurasia.org/wp-content/uploads/attachments/Pepm395_Gorenburg_Oct2015.pdf (Access 05.03.2021).

[67] SSBN Borei Class Nuclear-Powered Submarines, https://www.naval-technology.com/projects/borei-class/ (Access 05.03.2021).

be completed by 2023.[68]

RF currently has 28 Kilo-class diesel powered submarines. 22 of them are old version Kilo-class submarines. 6 of them are improved Kilo-class (Varshavyanka-class) submarines. 6 of the Varshavyanka class submarines with integrated Kalibr missiles were included in the Black Sea Fleet. The other 6 submarines will be included in the Pacific Fleet. 6 Lada-class (NATO: St Petersburg-class) diesel-electric submarines, which are more advanced than the Kilo-class, are planned to be included in the Pacific Fleet by 2024.[69] The fifth generation submarines, which are planned to be produced by the RF, do not seem to be able to enter the inventory before 2030. These include diesel-electric Kalina-class and nuclear-powered Husky-class submarines.[70]

It has been adopted as a principle to modernize large ships as surface ships, and to construct new multi-purpose small ships such as frigates and corvettes. In this framework, two Kirov-class cruisers and Sovremenny-class destroyers will be subject to an extension of service.[71] In order to be more visible and effective in the world oceans, RF plans to acquire a new aircraft carrier, Project 23000E or Shtorm, powered by nuclear energy and equipped with 5th generation aircraft. The new aircraft carrier will cost approximately $5.5 billion and will be 50% larger than the existing Admiral Kuznetsov aircraft carrier and is expected to take at least 10 years to build. The aircraft carrier will embark between 70 and 90 attack, airborne early warning, electronic warfare and reconnaissance aircraft. In addition, there will be approximately 10 general purpose and submarine defense helicopters on the aircraft carrier.[72]

The Russian Navy attaches importance to the production of small coastal defense combatants such as corvettes (Buyan-M, Steregushchiy and Karakurt) and frigates (Admiral Gorshkov). These vessels cost less than guided-missile destroyers and cruisers and can be operated with a lower number of crews. In particular, these small warships can be equipped with new anti-ship cruise missiles and SAMs, causing great losses even to the main surface warships of the enemy. Buyan-M-class corvettes have invisibility technology and a vertical launching system for Kalibr and Onyx anti-ship cruise missiles. These warships, whose main task is to protect the littoral zones of Russian coastal areas, can also navigate in the oceans for a short time. Steregushchiy, which is a large corvette and defined as a frigate by NATO, has the Poliment-Redut SAM system. The

---

[68] Richard Connolly, Mathieu Boulegue, "Russia's New State Armament Programme Implications for the Russian Armed Forces and Military Capabilities to 2027", https://www.chathamhouse.org/sites/default/files/publications/research/2018-05-10-russia-state-armament-programme-connolly-boulegue-final.pdf (Access 21.03.2021).

[69] Niemi's, op.cit.

[70] Mesut Hakkı Caşın, Rusya'nın Putin Yönetimi Liderliğinde Yeni Deniz Gücü Stratejisi-2: Rusların yeni Karadeniz Planı Ne?, https://m5dergi.com/dergi/ruslarin-yeni-karadeniz-plani-ne/ (Access 18.03.2021).

[71] Connolly, Boulegue, op.cit.

[72] Russian Shtorm aircraft carrier to potentially be fitted with S-500 anti-aircraft systems, https://www.navyrecognition.com/index.php/naval-news/naval-news-archive/2020/july/8728-russian-shtorm-aircraft-carrier-to-potentially-be-fitted-with-s-500-anti-aircraft-systems.html (Access 12.03.2021).

Karakurt-class corvette, which has Kalibr and Onyx weapon systems and is the most advanced corvette in Russia, is the version of the Buyan-M class corvettes developed for open seas. The Admiral Gorshkov frigate is the new frigate project of the RF. 6 Admiral Gorshkov-class frigates are expected to enter service by 2027. The first of these was put into service in 2017. Gorshkov-class frigates are equipped with Onyx and Kalibr missiles, and new ones will include Zircon hypersonic missiles.[73] Gremyashchiy-class corvettes will be equipped with new diesel turbines and will have the long-range Kalibr-NK missile system. On the other hand, although 6 Admiral Grigorovich-class frigates should have been put into service by 2020, only 3 of them were put into service due to the end of the defense industry cooperation between RF and Ukraine. RF equips all surface ships and submarines included in the new inventory with Kalibr cruise missiles.

Two Mistral amphibious ships, which Moscow planned to buy from France but could not due to the RF-Ukraine crisis, adversely affected the amphibious assault capability of the RF. Moscow is trying to fill this deficiency with the amphibious ships it has developed. It will acquire amphibious ships in addition to the Zubr-class large hovercrafts used by the Russian Naval Infantry.

According to the data of the RF Ministry of Defense, 2 modern submarines, 7 surface ships and 10 combat boats were included in the Russian Navy in 2020. 74% of the need was met in Bal and Bastion coastal missile systems. The Navy formed a motorized rifle division and a coastal missile brigade. Currently, 16 surface ships are under construction, 19 are in the modernization phase, and the other 6 are in the contract phase.[74]

The US former President, Donald Trump's orientation of his Syria policy from the overthrow of Assad to seeking an alliance with RF against ISIL terrorist organization led to an increase in Moscow's naval presence in the Mediterranean. While the aircraft carrier Admiral Kuznetsov, which was in charge of the Northern Fleet, was deployed in the Mediterranean, the Black Sea Fleet and the Caspian Flotilla played the main role in the developments regarding Syria in the Mediterranean. Considering the presence of the West in the Black Sea as a security threat to itself and limiting this situation only with the Montreux Agreement, Moscow gave priority to the Black Sea fleet in its modernization activities. In this context, considering that countermeasures with surface warships would not be cost-effective despite the increasing effectiveness of the West, priority was given to the development of submarines. Although new types of submarines are planned to be supplied to the Black Sea fleet, modernized versions of Kilo class submarines were delivered to the Black Sea Fleet due to delays. On the other hand, the Buyan-M class corvettes were deployed in the Black Sea Fleet in order to balance the presence of NATO and the EU in the

---

[73] Connolly, Boulegue, op.cit.
[74] Report of the Minister of Defence of the Russian Federation at the Board Session, https://mil.ru/files/files/itogi2020/itogi2020_en/VS_1_en.pdf (Access 15.05.2021).

Black Sea.[75] The priority of RF is the defense of coasts and maritime sovereignty areas until it acquires warships with permanent fleets in the Atlantic and Indian Oceans.[76]

The modernization of the RF Navy was also reflected in the operational field and increased the power projection capability of the RF. While the Russian warships and submarines provided protection and support to the RF's operation in Syria[77], they tested the new opportunities and capabilities of the RF navy and gave a message to the countries in the region, especially the Caucasus and Central Asia, and to their global rivals. For example, on October 7, 2015, the Russian Caspian Flotilla fired 26 cruise missiles at targets in the Syrian cities of Raqqa, Idlib and Aleppo from a distance of 1500 km. Again, the Caspian Flotilla launched 18 more cruise missiles in November 2015. On December 8, 2015, the Rostov-on-Don submarine, which has just joined the Black Sea Fleet, launched Kalibr cruise missiles at two targets in Syria, which was the first attack of the RF from the Mediterranean to Syria from a submerged submarine.[78] RF has reached the level to practice gunboat diplomacy with its abilities. In addition, the Russian navy has increased its maritime deterrence with its Kalibr cruise missiles.[79] RF attaches special importance to long-range air defense, land attack and anti-ship missiles in its modernization activities. It is noteworthy that such weapon systems were prioritized especially in the military deployment to the Black Sea Fleet and the Eastern Mediterranean, and an A2/AD based in Tartus and Hmeymin was tried to be established.

However, RF's armament and modernization activities for the Navy have some limitations. First of all, the sanctions applied to the RF after 2014 and the decrease in oil prices due to the coronavirus pandemic and similar reasons lead to the weakening of the Russian economy, and this affects the budget allocated to the navy. Secondly, the termination of the defense industry cooperation due to the negative political, military and economic developments with other countries, especially with Ukraine, negatively affects the production process in terms of critical equipment that cannot be produced and imported in the RF. Thirdly, it is still not possible to completely eliminate the effects of the decline in the RF's naval defense industry production in the 1990s. Shipyards have long ship production times and low experience in some areas of expertise. RF is trying to close the gap between its demands for the Navy and modernization with nuclear powered submarines and land-attack cruise missiles and hypersonic anti-

---

[75] Johannes Riber Nordby, Matthew Dal Santo, "Russia's Naval Strategy in the Black Sea and The Mediterranean", https://www.lowyinstitute.org/the-interpreter/russias-naval-strategy-black-sea-and-mediterranean (Access 13.05.2021).

[76] Nordby, Santo, op.cit.

[77] Between 2012 and 2018, the RF Black Sea Fleet carried out 318 rotations with the Tartus naval base in Syria and carried 185,500 tons of military cargo. Igor Delanoe, "Russian Naval Forces in the Syrian War", **Foreign Policy Research Institute**, 2020, p. 2, https://www.fpri.org/wp-content/uploads/2020/10/report-chapter-6-delanoe.pdf (Access 13.04.2021).

[78] https://tass.com/defense/843894 (Access 15.03.2021).

[79] Nordby, Santo, op.cit.

ship missiles.[80]

Conclusion

With its global ambitions for Navy, RF has the naval capability to create regional impact. RF Navy is at a level that can threaten the Black Sea, the Eastern Mediterranean, the Middle East, the Caucasus, Central Asia and Europe. The gap between the RF's ambitions for the Navy and its current capabilities is being tried to be eliminated with its two capabilities. The first of these is that the RF can fire 2500 km beyond the position of warships with its long-range precision strike cruise missiles. RF also uses these long-range precision strike cruise missiles on small surface ships. In addition, the nuclear-powered ballistic missile submarines owned by the Russian Navy constitute one of the most important elements of Moscow's strategic deterrence. Navy with superior means and capabilities are a great necessity for the RF, which persistently maintains its claim to be a great power in the multipolar world and actively uses its military power after 2008. The large number of coasts and the fact that the western part of the country does not have a border that is suitable for defense increases the need for a superior navy force to counter the threat from a distance gradually. Furthermore for RF, the Black Sea and the Mediterranean are of great importance in reaching to the south, that is, to the "warm waters". It should not be forgotten that the unipolarity of the USA in the world, which the RF strongly opposed, is mainly based on its naval power. Moscow has accepted the superiority of the USA in the navy, both in its official documents regarding the navy and in terms of the organization, structure and capabilities of the navy. However, the RF is trying not to lag behind China's navy, which is advancing at great speed. Finally, the future status of the RF Navy will be largely shaped by the Russian economy and defense industry, as well as the expectations of the political-military leaders from the navy.

---

[80] Petersen, op.cit., p. 32.

THE STRATEGIC IMPORTANCE OF THE CASPIAN SEA FOR REGIONAL AND GLOBAL ACTORS

Volkan Tatar[*]

Introduction

The Caspian Sea[1], which has been on the agenda for a long time, is a geopolitically important region surrounded by 5 states since the debate about whether it is a sea, lake, or border lake includes different conflicts of opinion about the sharing of important energy resources. The most important factors that increase this geopolitical importance are the energy resources in or around the Caspian Sea and the logistics of this energy. The fact that many developed states, especially the USA, European Union members, and states such as China, are interested in the logistics of energy and energy, increases the importance of the Caspian Sea even more. The Caspian Sea was under the control of the Soviet Union during the interwar period and the cold war period. At that time, most of the coasts were under the control of the Moscow-controlled states, which formed the whole of the Soviet Union, while the other reason was that the only way out for connection with the seas was the Don and Volga rivers and the Soviet territory. In addition, the Treaties made with Iran since the beginning of the 1800s are an important factor in terms of the legal basis of this domination. The defeat of Iran in the wars with the Russian Tsardom and the treaties made afterwards changed the influence in the region in favor of the Russian Tsarist and later the Soviet Union, leaving Iran with only a limited area for fishing activities.

Even in the years when the Cold War ended and the number of states bordering the Caspian increased from two to five, the region relatively preserved this feature. In the post-Soviet period, in addition to Russia's unwillingness to share the region with states other than the riparian states, it is important in this respect that Iran has been in an anti-American policy since the Islamic revolution. Iran's foreign policy, which rejects the Western institutions and systems, has made the southern part of the Caspian relatively autonomous from Western companies and states. After the end of the Cold War period, different conflict and cooperation opportunities emerged, and some changes have occurred in the status quo in the last period. In this study, primarily the geographical features and legal status of the Caspian Sea will be emphasized, its importance in terms of energy, and also the advantages of geopolitics will be explained. Then, in the light

[*] Assoc.Prof. Volkan Tatar, İstanbul Arel University, Faculty of Economics and Administrative Sciences, Head of Department of Political Science and Public Administration, Turkey.
E-mail: volkantatar@arel.edu.tr.
[1] In this study, the expression Caspian Sea is the repetition of the generally accepted name of the region and is used to express a geographical region.

of the historical process and new developments, the legal and actual situation will be discussed in terms of both the countries of the region and some other important actors.

The Caspian Sea in Terms of Geographical, Historical, and Legal Situation

Geographical and Historical Situation

Covering an area of approximately 371,000 km2, the Caspian Sea[2] is approximately 27 meters below the sea surface. Almost 1/3 of the world's inland waters are in the Caspian Sea. It has an average width of 1200 km from north to south and 320 km from east to west, with a maximum depth of 1025 meters.[3] The Caspian Sea[4], which was announced by scientists to be connected to the Oceans through the Azov Sea, the Black Sea and the Mediterranean about eleven million years ago, was reunited with the seas in the 20th century with the channels made between the Don and the Volga after being closed for a long time. The Caspian Sea can be divided into Northern, Central and Southern Caspian based on geomorphological and hydrological features, while the Northern part forms the shallow part with an average depth of 4-6 meters.[5] While the Middle Caspian is a shelf area with an average depth of 100-150 meters, the Southern Caspian consists of depression with a maximum depth of 1200 meters.[6]

From a historical point of view, it is known that in the Caspian Sea, which attracted the attention and interest of the Russians, the Ottoman Empire and Iran in the 1600s, the Russians bought salt, saffron, silk and oil in exchange for fur and leather, and in this way gave importance to their commercial activities.[7] Again, in Baku, which was an important city of the region at that time, mainly Chinese, Russian and Kalmyk merchants are encountered, and it is known to be one of the important trade centers in this respect. While many reasons could be presented for the concentration of trade in the Caspian in those years, perhaps the most important one is that the region attracted traders as a result of the Ottoman Empire's dominance in the Black Sea, at the height of its power, and not allowing piracy activities.[8]

The main entrance of the Russians to the Caspian was in the 18th century, during the reign of Tsar Peter the Great (Deli), although there was competition with Iran and the British on the Caspian in certain periods after this date, the

---

[2] https://earthobservatory.nasa.gov/images/44253/caspian-sea (Access 20.06.2020).
[3] https://www.britannica.com/place/Caspian-Sea (Access 10.05.2021).
[4] Ibid.
[5] Muazzez Harunoğulları, Legal status of the Caspian Sea and sharing of energy resources: Disputes and struggles between the Riparian Countries, **International Journal of Geography and Geography Education,** Vol. 38, p. 204.
[6] Ibid.
[7] https://islamansiklopedisi.org.tr/hazar-denizi (Retrieved 10.05.2021).
[8] Ibid.

Russians gained dominance.[9] Iran remained in a narrow area in the south of the Caspian and carried out its activities here. Especially at the end of the 19th century and the beginning of the 20th century, the increase in the need for oil in Russia, with the effect of the industrial revolution, increased the interest in the Caspian Sea and the interest in the control. In this period, Russian control and dominance over the Caspian was so advanced that from the beginning of the 19th and 20th centuries, until the First World War, only the Russian citizen was authorized to fish. After a long time, however, in 1928, the Soviet-Iranian joint company was established and years later, in 1953, fishing rights in Iranian waters were returned to the Iranian government.[10]

From the interwar period to the break in the Soviet Bloc in 1990, the Soviet Union was again the ruler of the Caspian Sea. Leaving aside Iran's limited dominance in a very small region in the south, the Caspian is a region under Soviet control where natural resources, especially oil, are both supplied and transferred. The break in the international political system in the early 1990s revealed a different ground, especially in the Caspian Sea. Russian domination is under such serious threat for the first time and independent Azerbaijan, Turkmenistan and especially Kazakhstan are states that want their shares.

Legal Status and Treaties of the Caspian

The great change in the international political system in the 1990s brought the end of the bipolar system. For many states, especially in central and eastern Europe and the Caucasus, this change means days of turmoil. The process means unification for Germany and disintegration for some states such as Yugoslavia and Czechoslovakia. Change and transformation have produced new states, new capitals, and also regional conflicts that have sunk into oblivion. The wind of change is a sign that a different period will be experienced not only for the lands but also for the Azov Sea, the Caspian Sea and the Crimean peninsula.

In order to understand the developments in and around the Caspian Sea, the Iran-Russian Tsarist conflict in the early 1800s is important. The attack, which Iran started with great hopes by taking advantage of Russia's struggle with Napoleon, resulted in the defeat of Iran and then the Treaty of Gulistan.[11] The result of the Treaty of Gulistan meant Russian supremacy and only Russian-flagged ships being allowed in the Caspian Sea.[12] Afterwards, the Russian Tsardom, which again entered the struggle with Iran and won, gained the upper hand in both the Caucasus and the Caspian with the Turkmenchay Treaty signed in 1828. The treaty, in addition to ensuring the division of Azerbaijan into two, which has lasted until today, also confirmed the authority of the Russian

---

[9] Ibid.
[10] Bazin, II, 129-130 referral https://islamansiklopedisi.org.tr/hazar-denizi. (Access 13.05.2021).
[11] Murat Aydoğmuşoğlu, 'Abbas Mirza (1789 - 1833) ve Dönemi', **The Journal of International Social Research** 19 Vol. 4 No. 19, 2011, pp. 129-132.
[12] Gulustan Treaty, (https://karabakh.org/treaties/gulustan-treaty/ (Access 20.05.2021).

Tsardom in the Caucasus.[13]

In addition, the article of the Treaty "The merchant ships of both states will be able to sail in the Caspian, but only the warships of Russia can be found" gave the Russians the undisputed superiority in the Caspian.[14] The effects of the Treaty of Turkmenchay on Iran were more than what was thought, the period when it would lose its independence and be seen in the category of weak states, and struggle with economic and political problems have begun.[15]

February 26, 1921, Moscow Friendship Treaty canceled the 1828 Turkmenchay Treaty with a new arrangement and gave Iran rights in the Caspian.[16] Although equality with the USSR was established on navigation, the Treaty signed between the Soviet Union and Iran on October 1, 1927, divided the Caspian between the two states and recorded as the Caspian Soviet-Persian Sea.[17]

Apart from the aforementioned Treaties, there are treaties between the USSR and Iran that define the Caspian Sea as "a piece of water belonging to only two countries", under which the Caspian is closed to foreign interventions.[18]

The confinement of Iran in a small region in the south confirms that the special location of the Sea is the Soviet Sea. During the Cold War period, an important development took place in 1970, and the Caspian, which remained in the Soviet Union, was shared between Azerbaijan, Kazakhstan, Russia and Turkmenistan[19]. The fact that the Iranian border is a clear border with international agreements is important for the axis of the post-1990 debate.

The Caspian Sea in the Light of Developments After 1990

The Caspian Sea and Its Current Importance

After 1990, the Caspian Sea and in this context, the Caspian Sea Basin became the center of the struggle within the scope of the continuous increase in the need for energy. According to Energy information administration data: In the Caspian Sea Basin, 48 billion barrels of oil and 8.27 trillion cubic meters of natural gas reserves are located in the Caspian basins. Almost 75% of oil and 67% of natural gas reserves are found within 160 kilometers of the coast[20]. When the tables are examined, it is clear to see that the oil and natural gas produced in the Caspian

---

[13] 3, 4 and 14th Articles of the Treaty, (Okan Yeşilot, 'Turkmenchay Treaty and Consequences', **A.Ü. Türkiyat Araştırmaları Enstitüsü Dergisi,** No. 36, 2008, p. 190.
[14] Turkmenchay Treaty Article 8 (Ibid).
[15] Ibid., p.194
[16] Selçuk Çolakoğlu, 'Uluslararası Hukukta Hazar'ın Statüsü Sorunu", **Ankara Üniversitesi SBF Dergisi,** Vol. 53, No. 1, 1998, p. 108.
[17] 1935 and 1940 Treaties, (Aidarbek Amirbek, 'Soğuk Savaş Sonrasında Hazar'ın Statüsü ve Sınırlandırılması Sorunu: Kıyıdaş Devletler'in Yaklaşımları Açısından Analizi' **Karadeniz Araştırmaları.**
[18] 1935 and 1940 Treaties, Ibid. p. 27.
[19] Aslıhan P.Turan,"Hazar Havzası'nda Enerji Diplomasisi", Bilge Strateji, Vol. 2, No. 2, 2010, p. 48.
[20] https://www.eia.gov/international/analysis/regions-of-interest/Caspian_Sea (Access 11.06.2021).

basin has shown a significant increase.

The Caspian Sea Basin is very important in terms of oil reserves and natural gas production. When Table 1 is examined, the increase in oil production of Azerbaijan and Kazakhstan between 2000 and 2011 is remarkable. At this point, seeing oil only as an input to the transportation sector would be an understatement of its usage area. Countries with high industrial production have been using oil and natural gas intensively in the production line in the last quarter-century, and they are moving away from coal more and more every day. In this context, as well as the developed European States, the USA, China, and many other states have turned to regions with oil reserves. When Table 2 below is examined, the course of natural gas production in the region can be easily seen. Just like oil, natural gas production has increased in total. When the table is carefully examined, it is seen that Azerbaijan and Kazakhstan stand out more than the others in terms of production.

Table 1. Oil Production from the Caspian Sea Basin Between 2000-2011[21]

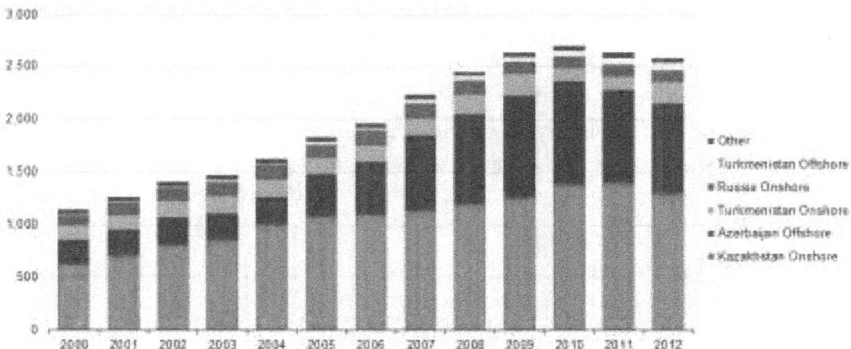

Caspian basins oil production 2000-2012
thousand barrels per day

Sources: U.S. Energy Information Administration, IHS EDIN, Eastern Bloc Energy, Rigzone, Rystad Energy
Note: Oil production includes crude oil and lease condensate production for all fields in Caspian basins.

As can be seen, the Caspian basin has important opportunities for companies as well as regional and global actors, both in terms of reserves and production. The Caspian Sea will inevitably be experienced in a period when the status problem of the Caspian Sea continues, the regional states are turning to alternatives other than Russia and global actors such as China and the USA are trying to infiltrate the region. It is not correct to look at the Caspian Sea Basin only as a reserve. It is also an important area in terms of the logistics of energy. Focusing on some important oil and gas lines such as Atyrau-Samara, Baku-Ceyhan, Baku-Supsa, Baku-Novorossiisk, Caspian Pipeline, Central Asia Oil Pipeline, Baku to Tabriz, Iran Oil Swap Pipeline, Kazakhstan-China Pipeline,

---

[21] Ibid.

Kazakhstan- Turkmenistan-Iran Pipeline, Trans-Caspian (Kazakhstan Twin Pipelines), etc.[22]

Table 2. Natural Gas Production in the Caspian Basin Between 2000-2011[23]

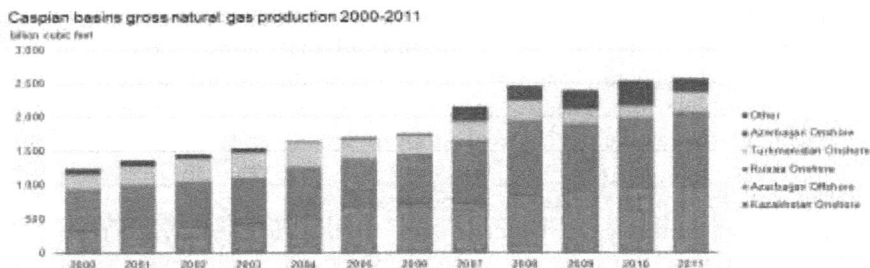

Caspian basins gross natural gas production 2000-2011

Evaluation of the Caspian Sea in the Scope of Global and Regional Actors

When the developments in the Caspian Sea and its surroundings from the 20th century to the present are examined, it would be correct to evaluate them as developments before and after 1990, in line with the developments in the international political system. The October Revolution of 1917, which is of great importance for world history, consolidated the dominance inherited from the Russian Tsardom in the Caspian Sea. For most of the 20th century, the dominance of the Caspian coast continued on the Moscow axis, as in the previous century.

The Cold War after the Second World War and the effectiveness of the Soviet Union in the region means that the dominance in the Caspian is still in the hands of the Soviet Union. Iran, one of the states of the region, has been squeezed into a very small area and with limited activities. In addition, the fact that the Soviet Union was one of the dominant powers in the bipolar system, and Iran's hesitation from this power of the Soviet Union resulted in the use of the Caspian as an inland sea, which is also far from Iranian influence.

The transformation in the international political system brought the bipolar system to an end just a little while before the 21st century. This transformation means the emergence of new states for the Caspian and its surroundings, as well as for the Central and Eastern European states. The Caspian coast is no longer an area surrounded by the Soviet Union and Iran, but a region where 5 states can compete for rich natural gas and oil. The emergence of new states as independent units also means the beginning of a game in which different actors will be active. The new situation In the Caspian, which has a total coastline of 7,010 km, Iran

---

[22] http://parsterminal.com/caspian-sea-region-reserves-and-pipelines-tables/ (Access 11.06.2021).
[23] Ibid.

has 740 km, Azerbaijan 800 km, Turkmenistan 1200 km, Russian Federation 1930 km and Kazakhstan 2,340 km.[24] The issue should be discussed within the scope of regional and global actors as well as the states bordering the Caspian Sea.

States with a Caspian Coast

From the point of view of the states bordering the Caspian Sea, the situation is more complicated. Post-1990 states' thoughts on the Caspian issue can be seen as a reflection of national interest in energy. Until the Treaty in 2018, states' perspectives on the problem are important. Azerbaijan and Kazakhstan, arguing that the Caspian is the Sea, claim that they have 12 miles of territorial waters and 35 miles of exclusive economic zone rights to riparian states, as it should be subject to the 1982 UN Convention on the Law of the Sea.[25] Other areas should be divided by the riparian states. In addition, the effort to divide the Caspian into five national sectors with the midline proposal of Azerbaijan continued for a long time.[26] Kazakhstan is approaching the sharing like Azerbaijan, and with the advantage of having a share of 29.6%, she wanted it to be divided into national sectors and opposed the equal division, which was mostly voiced by Iran.[27]

Russia and Iran, which have limited resources in terms of oil and natural gas on their coasts, have argued that the Caspian is a lake and have taken a stand for equal sharing.[28] The idea of equal sharing is Iran's main argument on the subject, and she is the state that is most reluctant about the middle line. In addition, Iran and Russia are getting closer to the idea of the joint use of the seafloor, which Russia has advocated for a while.[29] On the other hand, Turkmenistan's view is more ambiguous, and in 1994 it made a proposal to form a joint company union to solve the problem, and after a while, it welcomed the 45-mile Russian offer and declared it.[30] After a while, upon the discovery of Azeri-Chirag and Kepez oil fields, he changed his attitude again and started to support the common line principle.[31]

The long-lasting disagreements and negotiations by the Caspian riparian states continued until the Treaty signed in 2018. These discussions were followed by regional and global actors who tried to infiltrate the region in different ways. It can be easily said that riparian states in the Caspian Sea have gained an advantageous position, especially with the 2018 Treaty.[32] Although there is a text in which the Caspian is affirmed as a Sea, Article 3, paragraph 6 of the Treaty

[24] Amirbek, op cit., p. 24.
[25] Turan, op cit., p. 49.
[26] Serkan Uguz, https://tasam.org/tr-TR/Icerik/668/paylasilamayan_bolge_hazar (Access 17.06.2021).
[27] Ibid.
[28] Turan, op cit., p.49.
[29] Uguz, op cit.,
[30] Uguz, Ibid.
[31] Uguz, Ibid.
[32] Treaty determining the Legal Status of the Caspian, http://en.kremlin.ru/supplement/5328 (Access 10.06.2021).

clearly closed the area to the 'armed forces of the states that do not have a coast on the Caspian'.[33] Again, paragraph 7 of the 3rd article of the same Treaty means that the riparian states own the Caspian and closed it to other states, as well as "not allowing the third country forces to use their lands to engage in aggression and other military actions against each other".[34] From the perspective of the treaty as a whole, it would not be wrong to say that Russia's demands were met. Although it is thought that the sharing should be recorded as a loss for Russia (and Iran) when compared to the Russian Tsarist or USSR era, this is not entirely true. Russia and Iran do not want a third country outside the region (eg USA) to be involved in the process.[35] In addition to closing the Caspian to the military presence of other states and powers, the treaty means closing the lands to the third country powers described in the 7th paragraph, and that the powerful state Russia is still the most effective power in the Caspian and her surroundings. In addition, when the 4th, 5th, 6th, 7th articles of the treaty are carefully examined, it divides the Caspian between the riparian states, gives them all kinds of freedom, including the freedom of passage, and leaves little room for other states.[36]

In terms of non-Riparian States and Actors

First of all, it should be noted that the Caspian was an area that many actors wanted to infiltrate before the 'Treaty' in which the states bordering the Caspian Sea determined the status of the Caspian in 2018. For the states that are not littoral to the Caspian, the Caspian Sea has gained the status of a closed lake with the 2018 Treaty. The Caspian Sea and the energy resources of the Sea, especially the USA, the European Union States, China and NATO from international organizations cannot find a place for themselves at this stage. Even in the Black Sea, NATO can make itself felt with limited power, with the advantage of Turkey's geopolitical position. The special situation of the Caspian Sea, the agreement of the regional states on the status, has closed such a chance for states like the USA, Germany, and France, or for NATO, which is alone in terms of effectiveness and power in this field today. However, it should be noted that the USA and the UK control about 27% of the Caspian oil reserves and 40% of the Caspian natural gas through Azerbaijan and Kazakhstan, through their companies, which we can cite as BP, Exxon Mobile, Chevron.[37]

On the other hand, it is also known that the USA pursues a strategy of transferring energy to the EU through allied states such as Turkey and thus reducing the dependence of EU allies on Russia.[38] The Caspian States in cooperation with an ally like Turkey is a very attractive situation for the USA.

---

[33] Ibid.
[34] Ibid.
[35] İsmail Sarı, Hazar Denizi'nin Hukuki Statüsü Konvansiyonu ve Çok Boyutlu Etkileri https://iramcenter.org/hazar-denizinin-hukuki-statusu-konvansiyonu-ve-cok-boyutlu-etkileri/(Access 10.06.2021).
[36] Ibid.
[37] Ibid.
[38] Ibid.

First of all, during the disintegration of the Eastern Bloc, it was tried that the USA followed close policies with Turkey to enter the region and that Russia could change its effective position in this way, but it did not achieve complete success. Russia, especially by taking an anti-US state like Iran with herself, continued her effectiveness both in the south of the Caucasus and in the Caspian basin. But here, Azerbaijan should be considered as a separate case. Azerbaijan's close relationship with the EU and EU states has created a more flexible situation in its foreign policy. The investments of US and EU-based companies are increasing day by day[39], especially in Azerbaijan, which is very important in terms of diversifying Azerbaijan's foreign policy. This relationship should be well followed in terms of the emergence of different situations in the future. The USA aims to exclude Russia as much as possible in energy transportation, wants the transportation to continue through its allies, and bases this on the creation of alternative corridors for the transportation of energy in the Caspian, Central Asia, and the Caucasus.[40]

Conclusion

In many parts of the world, for different reasons, many actors, especially states, enter into conflict, make international agreements and arrangements to strengthen their hands, and form alliances at various levels. These alliances, which sometimes appear as military alliances, are fed by the ideas of states to protect or develop their spheres of influence. These regions, where the struggles of the states continue and sometimes the tension rises enough to result in war, enter the agenda of the states for different reasons and sometimes come to the fore with one or more of their characteristics. As a result of the changing conjuncture and/or developments in the field of technology, a change can be seen in the cause and area of the struggle.

For example, the island of Cyprus has been a priority for British foreign policy for many years and her importance has lasted for many years. The main reason for this can be explained by the fact that she was seen as a base, a fixed port on the way to the colonies, especially to India, which we can call the Imperial Road until the middle of the 20th century. For this reason, the British Empire, taking advantage of the difficult situation of the Ottoman Empire was in, did not leave the island, but tried to make its occupation permanent by annexing the island. It can be easily said that the importance of the island for the UK is her location. However, the developments in technology in the last quarter-century have also changed the perspective of the island of Cyprus, bringing the island's decreasing importance after the Second World War to higher levels again. The fact that the seafloor can be examined more easily with the developing technology and the natural resources can be brought to the surface at relatively cheaper costs have made an island like Cyprus attractive to both the countries in the region and the

---

[39] Uguz, op cit.
[40] Sarı, op cit.

global powers. This small island in the Eastern Mediterranean and her share in natural resources laying under blue waters now has very different importance than it has played in history.

The Caspian Sea should also be analyzed very well in this context. First of all, the fact that it is on an important trade route from the past to the present is a factor that has increased the importance of the Caspian for a long time. For this reason, the civilizations of the region also used the advantages of the passageway, while many cultures were mingling with each other, trade was also very developed in this context. In addition, due to its proximity to the Mediterranean and the Black Sea, it offers convenience in terms of connecting to larger trade routes, while at the same time, the development of agriculture with the advantage of climate and rivers facilitated settlement. The fish richness of the Caspian is also of great importance in this context. After the beginning of the activity of the Russian Tsarist, the Caspian became the center of the conflict, especially between Iran and the Russians, and Iran could not resist much. Russian domination and the industrial revolution that followed mean discussions on 'energy, energy reserves and especially importance on the energy route' for the oil-rich Caspian. Both the interwar period and the cold war and post-war period are very important. The break in the international political system after 1990 marked the beginning of a different period for the Caspian Sea, which the Soviets used as an inland sea. Now, in addition to Russia and Iran, Azerbaijan, Turkmenistan, and Kazakhstan are the states bordering the Caspian Sea. From the 1990s until the agreement signed in 2018, the status of the Caspian was discussed, and both riparian states and regional and global powers followed the issue closely. With the agreement signed in 2018 and determining the status of the Caspian Sea, the states of the region have confirmed that they have a say in the Caspian. Despite this, many states and international actors that do not have a coast to the Caspian, especially the USA, EU states, China and Turkey, are trying to establish activities in the Caspian in different ways. In the spectrum of opportunities and struggles, especially when considering membership in international organizations, the increasing need emerges as a region where more struggle will be experienced in the paradox of decreasing energy resources.

MEDITERRANEAN GEOPOLITICS AND INTERNATIONAL BALANCE

Hüseyin Çelik[*]

Introduction

It is located on a strategic crossroads as a middle sea in Europe, Asia and Africa, on the Mediterranean name. This intersection is expressed by many disciplines with different important definitions. This region is a geographic transition point. It is a sea that facilitates trade economically. It is a set of countries with complete political turmoil, governed by politically different regimes. In terms of religion, it is a sea that has a coast to the regions that are the source of Christianity, Islam and Judaism. This region is racially among the lands that include Latins, Slavs, Arabs, Turks, Jews, Greeks, French and Italians. To the north is Europe, where the European peoples converge at the point of European unity, and to the south, the north African nations consisting of Arabs. With a middle sea that opens to the Atlantic Ocean with the Strait of Gibraltar, opens to the Indian Ocean with the Suez Canal, the less salty Black Sea is reached through the Dardanelles, Marmara Sea and Istanbul Strait through the Aegean Sea. Thus, this sea, which is the middle center of the world connected with huge oceans, creates an interesting situation.

The Mediterranean has always been the scene of tension between countries and has been a sea of war and tensions for thousands of years. Upon the squeezing of Europe by the Ottoman Empire, European countries started new searches and as a result, they made geographical discoveries and Renaissance movements. All these events led to the emergence of the bourgeois class, the enlightenment and the industrial revolution. While Europe was getting stronger, the southern and eastern parts of the Mediterranean began to weaken and become poorer. While Europe is rising in every field, only Turkey and Israel have started to be among the rising countries of capitalism in this region. Especially countries such as North African countries, Syria and Lebanon could not catch up with Europe's enlightenment era and industrial revolution. The Mediterranean, which is located in an area of 4000 kilometers from west to east, witnessed a series of regime changes and tensions, which was called the Arab Spring in the 2000s, after the collapse of the Soviet Union, and the region became quite unstable. Today, this geography continues to be an important geopolitical region and continues to shape the history of the world in terms of international balance. In this section, the Mediterranean region has been geopolitically analyzed, especially in the light of recent developments, efforts to restore the international balance with the discovery of the eastern Mediterranean hydro-

[*] Prof. Hüseyin Çelik, Istanbul Nisantasi University, Turkey. E-mail: hucelik@gmail.com.

korban reserves are evaluated.

Mediteranean

The Mediterranean is located in the center of three continents. These three continents are distinguished from each other only by characteristics such as geographical structure and climate, and it can be seen that they have developed very differently from each other in terms of industrialization, richness of natural resources, culture, religion and race. While Europe consists of countries with high per capita income, the African Continent deals with problems such as thirst, hunger and famine. In the Asian Continent, the Middle East Region emerges as a very rich area in terms of oil and natural gas.

While most of the oil and natural gas needs of industrialized Europe are met by Russia and Norway, the other part is met from the Middle East and African Countries. Natural gas pipelines passing under the Mediterranean and new lines planned to be built, and tankers carrying hundreds of crude oil and petroleum products using the Mediterranean route increase the importance of the Mediterranean with each passing day.

It is one of the main routes in the Mediterranean maritime trade. Container traffic between Asia and Europe uses the Mediterranean by passing through the Suez Canal. All tankers filling at oil terminals in the Black Sea have to pass through the Mediterranean. The crude oil pipelines of the Middle East Region, which feed the sea terminals in the Mediterranean, increase the tanker traffic in the Mediterranean with each passing day.

Human beings have begun to access underground resources on the sea and ocean floor more easily and economically with their increasing technological abilities. Exploration studies in the Mediterranean Basin have yielded results, and rich oil and natural gas resources have begun to be exploited. The issue of sharing resources has become even more important than sharing sea areas in recent years.

Humanity benefits from the seas for two purposes: Firstly, transportation and communication, and the other is to use and operate the natural resources and riches of the sea[1]. With today's technology and the technology that will be available in the future, it will be possible to reach deeper in seas and oceans. Thus, the competition for access to limited resources will become more and more fierce with each passing day. In order to gain competitive advantage, countries have entered into a race to increase their ability and skills to utilize the seas by bearing great costs.

Pipelines, which are widely used in land geography today for the purpose of transporting water, oil and natural gas, have started to be built under the seas with the developing technology. Since 1897[2], when mankind first started to

---

[1] Kuran, Selami; **Uluslararası Deniz Hukuku**, Beta Basım, 5. Baskı, İstanbul, 2016, p. 1.
[2] Song, Guo, B. Chacko, J., Ghalambor, A., **Offshore Pipelines**, Gulf Professional Publishing, Burlington, 2005, p. 1.

extract oil from the seas, underwater pipelines have been on the agenda. Since the beginning of the 1850s, the activities of laying fiber optic cables that can carry all kinds of data, first telegraph, then telephone, and today, on the ocean and sea floor. Today, all continents are linked except Antartica While Europe was getting stronger, the southern and eastern parts of the Mediterranean began to weaken and become poorer. While Europe is rising in every field, only Turkey and Israel have started to be among the rising countries of capitalism in this region.

The Mediterranean is the largest sea in the world. The South China Sea and the Bering Sea are smaller than the Mediterranean Sea. It is five times bigger than the Black Sea. Mediterraneus, which is the Latin equivalent of the word Mediterranean; (medius middle, between and terra place) is a combination of the words of the world and means the middle of the world or between the lands. The area covered by the Mediterranean, which takes Europe to the north, Africa to the south, Asia to the east and connects these three continents, is 2.5 million km².

Within these three continents, there are 23 countries that have a coast to the Mediterranean. Among these, the countries in the Asian continent are Turkey, Syria, Lebanon, Palestine and Israel. Countries in the European continent are Turkey, Bosnia-Herzegovina, Montenegro, Albania, Greece, Spain, France, Monaco, Italy, Slovenia and Croatia, while those in the African continent are Egypt, Libya, Algeria, Tunisia and Morocco. Malta is located in the central Mediterranean, the Turkish Republic of Northern Cyprus and the Greek Cypriot Administration of Southern Cyprus in the eastern Mediterranean. Mediterranean; It is between the Atlantic Ocean in the west, the Black Sea in the north east, the Suez Canal in the south east and the Indian Ocean via the Red Sea[3].

In the early period, trade started in Mesopotamia around 3000 BC and progressed towards the city of Sur (Tyre) of Phoenician in the Eastern Mediterranean. The Eastern Mediterranean Region, which has hosted civilizations throughout history and where the first port cities were established, is a region where maritime trade is concentrated. It extended from there to Rhodes. It then continued to advance towards Greece and Rome. The development of maritime trade has been thanks to the safe corridors provided by the people of the region.

The Suez Canal, which was opened in 1869, further increased the importance of the Mediterranean, removed it from being a regional trade area, and caused the formation of one of the busiest routes of world trade. Before the canal was opened, Asia-Europe routes were possible by touring the Cape of Good Hope. The Asia-Europe route shortens the distance by approximately 1/3 when traveling through Suez. Today, approximately 220,000 commercial ships use the Mediterranean per year. This amount constitutes 1/3 of the world maritime trade

---

[3] https://www.google.com.tr/maps/@34.5306027,32.2263517,8.64z (Erişim 15.05.2018).

fleet[4].

Among the maritime trade fleets, cargo ships with various carrying capacities vary according to the routes they serve. The Suezmax class vessels[5] created in terms of capacity within the tanker fleet are the vessels of the maximum size that can pass in the Suez Canal. Tankers, whose capacities are specified above, loading from sea terminals in the Middle East Region, carry liquid energy resources such as crude oil, LNG, LPG to the ports in the Mediterranean via the Suez Canal or to the coasts of Western Europe and West Africa by crossing the Strait of Gibraltar. Oil exporter Libya transports 70 million tons of crude oil per year and Algeria 83 million tons of crude oil through its terminals in the Mediterranean.[6]

Between Azerbaijan and Supsa and Novorosski Terminal in the Black Sea; Millions of tons of crude oil coming to the oil wells in various regions of Russia and Tuapsa, Novorosski, Kherson and Odessa Terminals via pipelines[7], after loading into tankers at these terminals, they reach the Mediterranean and go to the world markets by passing through this route. 370 million tons of crude oil is transported annually in the Mediterranean. This amount represents more than 20% of the total oil transported in the world. Every day, 250-300 tankers roam the Mediterranean at the same time[8].

The three main routes used in container transportation by sea are Transatlantic (Europe-America), Transpacific (Asia-America) and Far East-Europe lines. Container ships with scheduled voyages between the Far East and Europe with a length of approximately 400 meters use the Mediterranean line, one of the three main lines in the world[9].

The Mediterranean constitutes the longest and undoubtedly the most fundamental area of geopolitical tension at the world level, with 20 countries in the region[10]. This area also creates a contrast in terms of economy, race, culture, Politics and religion. In a sense, this is called north-south relations[11]. It is seen that the USA also participated in these tense relations in the early 20th century. The USA, which wants to have a say in the Middle East, shows its existence by keeping the 6th Fleet of the USA in the Mediterranean with its bases in the countries in this region. Other European states were also very interested in this region and gained colonies in the process of the weakening and collapse of the Ottoman Empire. After the end of the Second World War, these countries declared their independence between 1956 and 1962. But European countries continued to be interested in the former colonial countries.

---

[4] https://en.wikipedia.org/wiki/Mediterranean_Sea (Erişim 20.07.2018).
[5] Martin Stopford, **Maritime Economics**, Oxsford, Routledge, 2009, p. 596.
[6] Stopford, p.: 438.
[7] https://en.wikipedia.org/wiki/List_of_oil_pipelines (25.06.2018).
[8] https://en.wikipedia.org/wiki/Mediterranean_Sea (25.06.2018).
[9] Stopford, p.: 526, 527, 528.
[10] Lacoste, Yves, Büyük Oyunu Anlamak, 2008, NTV yayınlar, p.: 224.
[11] Lacoste, p.: 225.

Natural Resources in The Mediterranean

It is estimated that there are 3.45 trillion m3 natural gas and 1.7 billion barrels of oil in the Levant Basin, the region between Cyprus, Lebanon, Syria and Israel. This forecast indicates that one of the world's largest natural gas deposits is located in the Eastern Mediterranean[12].

Levant gas basin discovered in 2015 and Leviathan gas fields discovered in 2010 in the Levant Basin are the largest gas fields in the Mediterranean. While Zohr remains in Egypt's EEZ, Leviathan and the Tamar gas fields discovered in 2009 are at odds between Israel and Lebanon. He claims that both gas fields expanded into Lebanese waters. The USA declared that it supports Lebanon in this regard[13]. Another rich field in the region, Aphrodite field is an estimated 170 billion m3 potential and is 34 km west of Leviathan[14].

About 1.8 billion barrels of oil in the Nile Delta Basin; It has been announced that it is estimated that there are 6.3 trillion m3 natural gas reserves and that there are 8 billion barrels around the island of Cyprus. In addition, there is a total of 3.5 trillion m3 unproven natural gas reserves, one of which is 1.5 trillion m3 and the other is 2 trillion m3, in the area in the south and southeast of Crete called "Herodotus"[15].

The Bouri oil field is the largest production field in the Mediterranean. It is located 120 km north of Libya. For the first time in 1976 2700 m. The field, which has been discovered at depth, has a proven, extractable 720 million m3 of crude oil, 3.5 trillion cubic meters of natural gas reserves and can produce 6 billion m3 of natural gas per year. Libya, the region called the Pelagian Basin, where the Bouri Field is located; Tunisia is located between Italy and Malta and extends partly to the territorial waters of Italy and Malta. It has 160 million m3 of extractable crude oil and approximately 17 trillion ft3 natural gas reserves[16]. Thus, the Mediterranean maintains its status as a region rich in natural resources. This region has become the economic strategic focal point today.

Mediterranean Jurisdictions

Sharing these areas by various countries is within the scope of their jurisdiction. This subject falls within the field of maritime law.

While the conflicts of maritime law in international law were at the level of 6-7% in the 1960s, this rate reached 40 to 48% in the 1990s. Since 1945, no category of international conflicts has been more than maritime law disputes[17].

---

[12] Ertürk, Muzaffer, "Energy Dispute in the East Mediterranean between Turkey and Greece", **Journal of Current Researches on Social Sciences**, Vol 7, No 2, 2017, p. 16.

[13] https://en.wikipedia.org/wiki/Leviathan_gas_field (24.07.2018)

[14] https://en.wikipedia.org/wiki/Leviathan_gas_field (24.07.2018)

[15] Ertürk, p.: 21.

[16] https://en.wikipedia.org/wiki/Bouri_Field (24.07.2018)

[17] Karaman, I. V., Dispute Resolution in the Law of the Sea. Publications on Ocean Development V. 72,

Out of 427 declared potential sea areas worldwide, only 168 (39%) are officially and the vast majority of them are partially accepted However, this does not mean that the remaining 58% sea area is disputed. Delimitation of marine areas is a complex and costly process. 22% are in disagreement, and most of these are due to islands, overlapping areas, and conflict between land borders and sea areas. It can be said that in the coming days there will be a great deal of disputes. This issue can be summarized with a laconic statement "There is no border problem, only states have problems"[18].

150 coastal states made arrangements on the declaration of territorial waters, 90 on the adjacent region, and 132 on the EEZ in their domestic law. Factors such as geographical location, distances as well as international law and relations, political reasons, diplomacy, economy and engineering play an important role in determining the boundaries of the sea areas[19].

One of the most basic resources to be consulted in this matter is the limitation of territorial waters according to the 15th article of UNCLOS[20];

> "Article 15 Delimitation of the territorial sea between States with opposite or adjacent coasts Where the coasts of two States are opposite or adjacent to each other, neither of the two States is entitled, failing agreement between them to the contrary, to extend its territorial sea beyond the median line every point of which is equidistant from the nearest points on the baselines from which the breadth of the territorial seas of each of the two States is measured. The above provision does not apply, however, where it is necessary by reason of historic title or other special circumstances to delimit the territorial seas of the two States in a way which is at variance therewith. "

The limitation of the EEZ is specified in Article 74 of the UNCLOS and the limitation of the continental shelf in Article 83. (The text is the same for both items.)

> "Article 74-83 Delimitation of the continental shelf between States with opposite or adjacent coasts 1. The delimitation of the continental shelf between States with opposite or adjacent coasts shall be effected by agreement on the basis of international law, as referred to in Article 38 of the Statute of the International Court of Justice, in order to achieve an equitable solution. 2. If no agreement can be reached within a reasonable period of time, the States concerned shall resort to the procedures provided for in Part XV. 3. Pending agreement as provided for in paragraph 1, the States concerned, in a spirit of understanding and cooperation, shall make every effort to enter into provisional

---

Leiden: Brill Nijhoff. 2012.
[18] Prescott, J. R. V. and Clive H. Schofield, p.: 245
[19] Karaman, p.: 170.
[20] Karaman, p.: 183.

arrangements of a practical nature and, during this transitional period, not to jeopardize or hamper the reaching of the final agreement. Such arrangements shall be without prejudice to the final delimitation. 4. Where there is an agreement in force between the States concerned, questions relating to the delimitation of the continental shelf shall be determined in accordance with the provisions of that agreement. "

While the eastern and southern coasts of the Mediterranean are flatter, the northern coasts are indented, protruding, with the main peninsulas of Italy and Greece and many islands, some of which are quite large. There are many disputed regions in the Mediterranean regarding the delimitation of sea areas. Moreover, non-peaceful political relations prevent negotiations between neighboring states[21].

There is no territorial sea announcement for Albania, Bosnia and Herzegovina and Montenegro among the Mediterranean countries. Due to the geographical structure of the Aegean Sea, Turkey and Greece have declared 6 miles of territorial waters. The territorial waters of Cibraltar are 3 miles. The territorial waters of other Mediterranean countries are 12 miles wide[22].

The Mediterranean is divided into two as east and west by 19 ° East longitude. The sea areas of the British bases (Akrotiri and Dhekelia) in Cyprus in the Eastern Mediterranean were limited in 1960. These are the first restricted sea areas in the Mediterranean. This treaty adopted between Cyprus and England includes 4 short borders and their length varies between 6.9 miles and 9.85 miles. These areas do not constitute their territorial waters. Cyprus has not declared a territorial waters region[23]. .

Algeria, Cyprus, Egypt, France, Italy, Malta, Monaco, Morocco, Spain, Syria and Tunisia declared a 24-mile contiguous zone[24]. Algeria (32/52 miles), Libya (62 miles), Malta (25 miles), Spain (designated by coordinates), Tunisia (up to 50 m deep) have declared fishing zones[25].

When evaluated in terms of xclusive Economic Zone (EEZ); There are two EEZ borders in the Eastern Mediterranean, which have been declared UN. These are the Cyprus-Israel and Cyprus-Egypt EEZ borders. The line consisting of 12 points based on equal distances covering 55 miles between Cyprus and Israel was approved in 2011[26]. The Cyprus-Egypt border was determined with 8

---

[21] Karaman, p.: 383.
[22] Costs and benefits arising from the establishment of maritime zones in the Mediterranean Sea Final Report, p.: 46.
[23] Prescott, J. R. V. and Clive H. Schofield, p.:384.
[24] Costs and benefits arising from the establishment of maritime zones in the Mediterranean Sea Final Report, p.: 46
[25] Table of claims to maritime jurisdiction (as at 15 July 2011), http://www.un.org/depts/los/LEGISLATIONANDTREATIES/PDFFILES/table_summary_of_claims.pdf (21.07.2018)
[26] Bulletin No. 75, Division for Ocean Affairs and the Law of the Sea Office of Legal Affairs, Law of the Sea, United Nations New York, 2011, p. 31. http://www.un.org/depts/los/doalos_publications/LOS

points from west to east and was announced in 2003[27]. Turkey objected to this limit. Turkey made an official objection by stating that Turkey has the right from the west of the point on the longitude 320 16'18 "and that the Cyprus Island cannot be considered as a single state, and that the TRNC has the right within the designated area[28].

Except for the lines listed above, all lines in the Eastern Mediterranean are referred to as potential borders, and most of them are considered to be disputed sea areas. The border between Egypt and Israel reaches to the south of Cyprus by making small deviations with equal distances. Its distance from the beach is 115 miles and it ends at 32 ° 54 'N, 32 ° 58' E at 8 points determined starting from the west[29].

The potential border between Israel and Lebanon runs 70 miles towards the sea at equal distances and ends at 33 ° 30 'N, 33 ° 44' E. The potential border with Lebanon and Syria extends 50 miles towards the sea, first to the southwest and then to the northwest. (34 ° 51 'N, 34 ° 59' E) The Cyprus and Lebanon potential border between the specified points has a width of 100 miles[30].

Ten maritime areas were restricted in the Western Mediterranean between 1968 and 1999. Italy has been the most active country in this regard. Between 1968-1992, it signed treaties with Yugoslavia, France, Spain, Tunisia, Greece and Albania. The states that emerged with the dissolution of Yugoslavia comply with the treaties signed between Italy and Yugoslavia in 1969 and 1975. The treaty with France deals with Corsica and the Sardinian Islands. Two other maritime zones were determined between France and Monaco in 1987 and between Croatia and Bosnia-Herzegovina in 1999[31].

The Tunisia-Algeria border was adopted in 2002[32]. The line between Libya and Malta, determined according to the principle of equal distances of 20 miles, was limited in accordance with the provision given by the International Court of Justice in 1986[33]. The Libya-Tunisian border was restricted in accordance with the provision issued by the International Court of Justice in 1988[34].

Bulletins/bulletinpdf/bulletin75e.pdf (20.07.2018)

[27] Bulletin No. 52, Division for Ocean Affairs and the Law of the Sea Office of Legal Affairs, Law of the Sea, United Nations New York, 2011, p. 47, http://www.un.org/depts/los/doalos_publications/LOS Bulletins/bulletinpdf/bulletin52e.pdf (21.07.2018)

[28] Bulletin No. 54, p.: 127.

[29] Prescott, J. R. V. and Clive H. Schofield, a.g.e., p.: 384.

[30] Prescott, p.: 384.

[31] Prescott, p.: 384.

[32] Bulletin No. 52, a.g.e., p.: 44.

[33] Costs and benefits arising from the establishment of maritime zones in the Mediterranean Sea Final Report, s. 69.

[34] Costs and benefits arising from the establishment of maritime zones in the Mediterranean Sea Final Report, s. 69.

Air Space and FIR In The Mediterranean

At the Middle East air navigation meeting held on October 15, 1946, a discussion was held on FIR lines, which did not exist until that day, and a proposal was submitted to the Turkish Government at this meeting. In this proposal, it was envisaged to establish a flight information zone that includes Turkish and Greek airspaces and whose center is Ankara. There is no record of the response given by the Turkish Government. At the Middle East air navigation conference held in Istanbul in 1950, the present Istanbul-Athens FIR lines proposal was concluded and the relevant document was published in November 1950. The southeastern border of the flight information zone line determined in this meeting passes from the east of Hatay province to Hakkari at 37 ° 20 'north latitude and the lands in the south of this line were left to Syria and Iraq for air traffic control. After the cancellation of the Baghdad pact, this line has adapted to Turkey's national borders.

Mediterranean flight areas consist of FIRs connected to Eurocontrol[35] in Brussels and UIR (Upper Flight Information Areas) starting after the vertical limit of FIRs.In the Mediterranean, Madrid UIR, Barcelona UIR, Rome UIR, Brindizi UIR, Malta UIR, Hellas in Greece, Nicosia (Nicosia) in Cyprus were established. These upper flight zones have not yet been established in Istanbul and Ankara.

It is stated that all civil aircraft using these airspaces in the Mediterranean will be used provided that they obtain permission. However, as stated in the Chicago Conference, the states that signed the contract did not open their airspace to the flights of state aircraft, they only made arrangements according to the civil aviation operational needs. Permission for state civilian vehicles depends on internal regulations of other countries and bilateral agreements with neighboring countries. There is only one signed Lausanne agreement on this issue between Greece and Turkey. In this case, it is sufficient to look at the relevant provisions of the agreement. For example, Greece increased the territorial waters around the Aegean islands from 3 (NM) nautical miles according to the Lausanne agreement to 6 NM on 17 September 1930 and started to apply this in 1964. Turkey has determined this to be 10 km (5.4 NM) in the Black Sea, Aegean and Mediterranean. In 1982, in the United Nations Convention on the Law of the Sea, it was envisaged that they could expand their territorial waters up to 12 NM

---

[35] Eurocontrol is the center in Brussels, the capital of Belgium, where all civil traffic in Europe is monitored, where all aviation participants in Europe are coordinated, and a pan-European Air Traffic Management (ATM) system is developed. In this context, the main fields of activity of the organization are the establishment and development of the pan-European ATM network, supporting the preparation and regulation of civil aviation rules across Europe, developing measures to meet these needs by analyzing the future needs of air traffic, Providing training of personnel in air traffic services, Studies on Air Navigation. and conducting experiments, analyzing the results of the work carried out by the member countries, providing the air traffic control service of the central European region and collecting air navigation fees on behalf of the member states. URL: http://www.mfa.gov.tr/eurocontrol.tr.mfa, 22.11.2018.

and Greece claimed that it had the right to increase its territorial waters to 12 NM by citing this issue. According to Turkey's theses, when the territorial waters in the Aegean reach 12 NM, it will not be possible to exit from the Aegean.

Greece has stated that it can widen this distance even more and has brought the 12 NM demands to the agenda today. This situation was accepted in the Greek parliament in 1995, and with Turkey's initiatives, it assured the United Nations and NATO not to expel 12 NM territorial waters in the Aegean Sea. Therefore, in the Aegean Sea, its territorial waters are 6 NM wide and its airspace is 10 NM wide compared to Greece. Turkey accepts both its territorial waters and its airspace as an average of 6 NM. Greece declared its airspace as 10 NM in AIP (Aeronautical Information Publication), an aviation publication in 1975, and Turkey did not accept it. However, every time the warplanes land in the Aegean Sea, Greece reports them as violations and does not allow any state aircraft to cross the border. In the Aegean, the FIR line is accepted as the western side of the 6 NM of Turkish territorial waters as Athens FIR and the east of it is Istanbul FIR.

Turkey has not signed the United Nations Convention on the Law of the Sea. Greece (although it does not represent a right of sovereignty) claims that by assuming control of aircraft over the Aegean Sea via the Athens FIR, and this right is proof that it can increase its territorial waters to 12 NM. Greece sees the Athens FIR line as a line of sovereignty. Although this line, which is a technical issue, does not constitute a right of sovereignty and the sovereign airspace of the countries is only a region on land and territorial waters, Greece occasionally makes this claim up.

Military exercises may be held in international areas, but the place and time of this must be declared. Military exercises may be held in international areas, but the place and time of this must be declared. NOTAM (Notice to Airmen) is a notice declared as a warning to aviators. These NOTAM requests, which have become a problem between Turkey and Greece, and requests for the right to request amendments to the disclosed NOTAM still remain a problem. Greece stated that the 10 NM territorial waters and airspace application applied on the islands are not military (according to the article on disarmament of the islands in the Lausanne Treaty) but for police purposes. Every Aegean departure of Turkish military aircraft is reported as air violations on the Greek side. They claim that when Turkish warplanes land in the Aegean and are under positive radar control with VFR[36] (Visual Flight Rules), they do not have to fill in the flight plan and will not report to the Athens approach control center.

It is observed that some problems are experienced in other regions of the Mediterranean due to airspace and FIR lines. Airspaces were closed for a certain

---

[36] Görerek uçuş veyaVFR uçuş, bir pilotun uçağın irtifa (attitude) kontrolünü ve seyrüseferini uçak dışındaki birtakım görsel referanslara göre gerçekleştirdiği uçuştur. Bu uçuş için uçuş planı doldurulduğunda pilot rotasını yazmak zorunda değildir. DCT olarak ineceği hava alanını yazabilir.

period of time in North African countries (Tunisia, Morocco, Libya, Algeria) due to Arab Spring problems in 2000. In the Eastern Mediterranean, absolute air superiority to Israel continues today. Due to the Syrian war, flights in this region are restricted and the area is closed to air traffic.

Turkey's Existence and Geopolitical Balance or Imbalance

Turkey, which was established as a result of an independence war after the collapse of the Ottoman Empire in the region, demolishes this north and south scheme. Because although Turkey is located in the north like European countries, it has different aspects belonging to the south. Having a specific place in the region, Turkey has prevented the Black Sea located in the north and Russia from reaching the hot seas (ie the Mediterranean) for hundreds of years. Entering NATO in 1952 after the Second World War, Turkey took part in the face of the Soviet Union. After the collapse of this union, the independence of the Turkic republics caused Turkey to be turned away from its geopolitical importance again. In order to prevent Caspian oil from passing through the straits, Turkey signed an agreement with Azerbaijan and started to transfer the oil via pipelines to Ceyhan port located in the Mediterranean in the south of Turkey.

All these problems experienced by Turkey have occurred due to being stuck in the area it belongs to. As a racially separate nation from Arabs in this area, the Turks ruled both Arabs, Kurds and eastern European nations as the Ottoman empire. Kurds, who use a language belonging to an Indo-European class similar to Persian, have spread to many geographies of Turkey and continue to live intertwined with the Turks. The PKK or Kurdish problem that Turkey is experiencing continues today with the support of the West. Western countries, which want to separate nations from each other, advocate uniting in their countries (especially France, England and the USA) when it comes to them. For this reason, Turkey, which continues to deal with the Kurdish problem, continues to consume both humanitarian and economic and military resources. It is remarkable why the region of Syria and Iraq, where the West shows its power, was made unstable. Likewise, the USA and other western states who want to control Iran also want to control the gulf oil. For this purpose, they cooperate with the Arab states in the Persian Gulf.

When we start to examine the Mediterranean strategically starting from the eastern region, the following picture is seen: Syria, Lebanon, Egypt, Turkey and Israel. Here only Turkey and Israel are included in the western blog. However, Israel's expansionist policies are not supported by Turkey. Turkey supports Arabs, namely Muslims, in the Arab-Jewish conflict. The formation of the state of Israel is based on the view that the Jewish nation aims to create a homeland. The Jews who were exiled to various parts of the world by the Roman Empire began to settle in the Palestinian lands within the Ottoman Empire from the 19th century. The idea of the state of Israel, which emerged as a romantic idea, started to form a nation's subjection thanks to the increasing immigration of Jews to this region. The reactions of the Arabs to this formation continued intensely especially after the First World War. Arab uprisings started upon the collapse of the Ottoman Empire. The British, who dominated this region, suppressed these rebellions by stopping Jewish immigration. During the Second World War, Arabs supported Germany, while Jews supported the British. After the Germans' massacre of genocide against the Jews, they started to receive support from the United States of America in establishing a Jewish state. After the Second World War, Israel's independence was declared by the United Nations in 1948. After this date, Israel was attacked by the Arab states around it. After each attack, Israel expanded its territory. It even dominated the Sinai peninsula. Since the British wanted to control the Suez Canal alone, they withdrew from this area. Western countries and the Soviet Union benefited the most from the Arab-Israel War. They have sold huge amounts of weapons to both Israel and the Arab states. Today, Israel, supported by the West, has managed to acquire most of the lands belonging to Palestine and opened these lands to Jewish settlers. With the evacuation of the Gaza strip by Israel in 2005, a small area of Palestine was imprisoned and started to attack this region from time to time. It shows the power of Israel in this way. In 2020, when Israel declared Jerusalem as the capital by taking the United States behind it, riots, protests, attacks and bombardments started and it is seen that these events continue in 2021. With Iran's support for the Hamas organization, Israel further consolidated its position in the west.

As a result of the Arab Spring, the change of the regime in many countries came to the west. The weakening of Lebanon, the weakening of the Arabs and the fact that Turkey was not involved in this event further increased the power of the West. Western oil and gas companies have started to establish drilling zones between Cyprus and Israel and in Southern Cyprus. Turkey's objection to this situation and declaring its own exploration and drilling areas caused Europe to object. Until 2021, Turkey started negotiations with both Libya and Egypt regarding economic regions in the Mediterranean. Since Southern Cyprus is a European Union country, Turkey is no longer dealing with Southern Cyprus and Greece, but the European Union.

Conclusion

The Mediterranean is the world's largest sea located in the middle of three continents. The three surrounding continents are not only distinguished from each other by features such as geographical structure and climate, but also differ from each other in terms of features such as industrialization and richness of natural resources. Therefore, it forms a geography where raw materials and finished products are exchanged. The eastern part of it was the region where sea trade started.

After the Suez Canal was opened, it contains the routes with the world's busiest sea traffic. Some of the oil and natural gas needed by the EU is transported over the Mediterranean, both by tankers and through pipelines. There are hundreds of oil refineries and natural gas liquefaction and gasification facilities along the Mediterranean coasts.

It is estimated that there are very rich oil and natural gas deposits in the region between Cyprus, Lebanon, Syria and Israel. This forecast indicates that one of the world's largest natural gas deposits is located in the Eastern Mediterranean. Mankind with the current technology 2700 m. oil from depths, 12 000 m. It extracts natural gas from the depths. In the following periods, these depths will increase even more and the Mediterranean will be the region where there is a very hard disagreement about the ownership of these resources.

Disputes in the field of maritime law constitute the largest part of international law. These disputes have been increasing every year since 1945. One of the main reasons for this is the opportunity to reach natural resources and riches in deeper waters, as mentioned above. The extraction and operation of resources in the sea floor and the water body above it provides great wealth to the states.

There are many disputed regions in the Mediterranean regarding the delimitation of sea areas. Non-peaceful political relations also make conflict resolution impossible. While the eastern and southern coasts of the Mediterranean are flatter, the northern coasts are indented, protruding, with the main peninsulas of Italy, Greece and Turkey and many islands, some of which are quite large. These types of geographical features cause an increase in conflicts.

Algeria, Cyprus, Egypt, France, Italy, Malta, Monaco, Morocco, Spain, Syria and Tunisia declared a 24-mile contiguous zone. There are fishing zones belonging to Algeria, Libya, Malta, Spain and Tunisia. Other Mediterranean countries do not have any contiguous zone and fishing zone.

There are two EEZs in the Eastern Mediterranean. The lines between Cyprus-Israel and Cyprus-Egypt have been officially recognized. Except for these lines, all lines in the Eastern Mediterranean are referred to as potential borders, and most of them are considered to be disputed sea areas.

The borders of the sea areas in the Adriatic Sea have been determined. The states that emerged with the dissolution of Yugoslavia comply with the treaties signed between Italy and Yugoslavia in 1969 and 1975. This is the only region in the Mediterranean where there is no conflict. Italy has solved most of its problems not only with its neighbors to the east, but also with its neighbors to the west. Between 1968-1992, France signed treaties with Spain, Tunisia, Greece and Albania.

The Tunisia-Algeria border was adopted in 2002. The line between Libya and Malta, determined according to the principle of equal distances of 20 miles, was limited in accordance with the provision given by the International Court of Justice in 1986. The Libya-Tunisian border was restricted in accordance with the provision issued by the International Court of Justice in 1988.

In addition to these problems in the Eastern Mediterranean, problems between Europe and North Africa continue. On the one hand, the balance between a poor southern Mediterranean countries and the rich European Union countries continues to improve for the benefit of Europe. Considering Israel as a western state, the United States of America and the European Union constantly support this country. Russia, which ostensibly supported Arab states (especially Syria) before and after the dissolution of the Soviet Union, continues its ambivalent policy and establishes various bases in Syria. Likewise, the United States of America establishes bases in Greece for the purpose of protecting the Balkan countries against Russia and thus is interested in the Black Sea. The United States, which has good relations with Bulgaria, Romania and Ukraine, indirectly wants to reach the Black Sea. The idea of the Soviet Union to reach the warm seas evolves and the idea of the United States to reach the cold sea, namely the Black Sea continues to mature.

The balance and imbalances in the Mediterranean continue today. Such as the Turkey-Greece dispute in the Aegean Sea, the Turkey, Turkish Republic of Northern Cyprus and the Greek Cypriot Administration of Southern Cyprus dispute, the Israel-Lebanon dispute, the Israel and Palestine dispute, the Spain-Morocco dispute, the Libya-Sirte Gulf dispute. It will be possible to overcome these and the problems that will arise later, by bringing peaceful solutions together with the principle of equity.

EXISTING AND PROSPECTIVE CENTRAL PARADIGMS OF EASTERN MEDITERRANEAN ENERGY GEOPOLITICS IN THE 21ST CENTURY: DO / WILL ALL THE RELATED PARTIES SEEK FOR COLLABORATIONS OR CONFRONTATIONS?

Sina Kısacık[1]

Introduction

The Mediterranean Region which has been continuing to be one of the most critically important regions within the context of world history due to its inclusion of several civilizations, old empires and modern nation-states as well as trade routes, natural reserves is preserving its prominence in today's world. This is because of the discovery of energy reserves in the eastern part of this region since the beginning of 21st century. The finding of especially significant natural gas reserves in Israel, Greek Cypriot Administration and Egypt has been transforming the Eastern Mediterranean region as one of the noteworthy regions that has to be carefully examined in terms of world energy geopolitics.

Since the discovery of natural gas reserves in the Eastern Mediterranean region, there has been an ongoing debate on how to transport them to the world markets. When considered from this perspective, two pipeline and one LNG facility options are discussed. But it has to firstly be underlined that there exist numerous hurdles before the monetization of Eastern Mediterranean natural gas reserves that are namely Cyprus Question, Israel-Palestine, Israel-Lebanon Conflicts, the lack of mutually agreed pact on the Exclusive Economic Zones in the region, the confrontations between Turkey-Greek Cypriot Administration, Turkey-Israel and so on. One can multiply these conflicts. In addition to this, the littoral states, as well as outer-regional states, have been launching their military power capacities into the region in order to defend their declared national interests within the framework of Eastern Mediterranean. So one can state the militarily empowered struggle between the related parties in the Eastern Mediterranean region regarding the discovery, drilling and transportation of primarily natural gas reserves firstly for them and also export these resources to world markets.

By taking into account the aforementioned paradigms, this paper will try to elaborate the current and possible paradigms of Eastern Mediterranean energy security within the 21st century by focusing on the question that "Do / Will All

[1] Asst. Prof. Dr. Sina Kısacık, Cyprus Science University Department of International Relations, Kyrenia (Girne)-Turkish Republic of Northern Cyprus. E-mail: sinakisacik@csu.edu.tr, sina1979@hotmail.com, ORCID NO: 000-0002-3603-6510.

the Related Parties Seek for Collaborations or Confrontations?" In this context, apart from Introduction and Conclusion sections, there will exist three chapters in the development paragraphs. The first chapter will talk over the significant energy findings within the Eastern Mediterranean region. The second chapter will look at the feasible ways of commercializing the Eastern Mediterranean natural gas reserves. The third section will be on the discussion of some noticeable obstacles before the monetization of Eastern Mediterranean natural gas resources. In the Conclusion part, it will be shared some personal evaluations and projections on the researched subject.

Important Energy Discoveries in the Eastern Mediterranean

Energy searches that have been carried out within the Eastern Mediterranean ever since the beginning of 2000s have ended up with the finding of significant oil and natural gas resources. As a result of these findings, the Eastern Mediterranean has transformed into a possibly key energy transference center. Simultaneously, when the Eastern Mediterranean's geographical location as standing a door to the Middle East is considered, the finding of energy resources ensures direct impacts on global geopolitics. Owing to these findings, the high prospective of reserves, and the interests of energy companies within this region, the Eastern Mediterranean has grown into a principal topic of hot clashes within today's world. Instead, Eastern Mediterranean countries have been dealing with political problems, border clashes, and internal disorder. The happening of those struggles in regional, national, and international scopes ought to not perceive as unplanned circumstances. The most noteworthy clashes inside the Eastern Mediterranean remain the disordered political conditions in Egypt, Libya, and Syria due to the outbreak of Arab Revolts (Arab Spring) since 2010, in addition to the long-drawn-out Palestine and Cyprus conflicts.[2]

When we come to the energy aspect within the Eastern Mediterranean, as stated by the "Fact Sheet 2010–3014" , a document of the U.S. Geological Research Institution, 1.7 billion barrels of technically recoverable oil reserves and 3.5 trillion cubic meters (tcm) of technically recoverable natural gas reserves are present within the Levantine East Basin. In line with these findings, as said by "Fact Sheet 2010–3027", a document of the same institution, one can talk about the existence of 1.8 billion barrels of technically recoverable oil resources and 6.3 tcm of technically recoverable natural gas resources have been confirmed inside this area. After these estimates, littoral states located at this region have been escalating their energies to find oil and natural gas inside their offshore areas. Amongst them, particularly in terms of natural gas, the findings of Israel, Greek Cypriot Administration (GCA), and Egypt have stayed the most momentous ones within the framework of Eastern Mediterranean energy geopolitics. When

---

[2] Ozan Örmeci, Sina Kısacık, "Cutting the Gordian Knot: Turkish Foreign Policy Towards Cyprus During AK Party Era (2002–2020)", **Studia I Analizy Nauk O Polityce (Studies and Analyses of Political Science)**, Vol.1, No.1, 2020, p. 36, https://czasopisma.kul.pl/sanp/article/view/9838/8309 (Access 25.04.2021).

we explore Israel's overall natural gas reserves, its most substantial reserves stand situated at Tamar and Leviathan fields in the offshore of this country, calculating as 900 billion cubic meters (bcm) and found by the American Noble Energy. Tel-Aviv has adopted to ship solely 40% of these reserves, and the remaining ones stay assigned for the country's energy demand. In this context, another main natural gas reserves remain placed in Cyprus. In Cyprus, the Aphrodite natural gas field counting 140 bcm has been the case. GCA has been intending to benefit from this quantity of natural gas not only in internal use but also for exporting. Both Israel and Cyprus' natural gas reserves have been found by foreign energy firms at the end of the first decade of the 2000s.[3]

When we come to Israel, a fundamental subject for this country within the context of Eastern Mediterranean in the following years will remain the natural gas discoveries in this region. The initial natural gas found in offshore area from Ashkelon in 1999 and the initial field – Mari B- has been exploited since 2004. The more important fields has been found in 2009 – Tamar in which the production began in 2013- and in 2010 -Leviathan in which the production would begin in 2017- while extra findings possibly will follow. These fields transform Israel not only self-sufficient in terms of energy but also will too enable Israel as an energy exporter as soon as it finds suitable outlet for this gas. While this complicated case forms brand-new incentives for the collaboration among Eastern Mediterranean countries, the reality that maritime boundaries had not been openly determined within the region has too caused a confrontation, most evidently perhaps within the warmongering rhetoric between Turkey and GCA on the one hand, and Israel and also Lebanon on the other. Concerning natural gas offshore from Gaza that was found in 2000, the exploitation has been prevented by Israel primarily since 2006 when Hamas did win parliamentary elections and then held the power within the Gaza Strip.[4]

When the Lebanon case is considered, this country which signed a sea authorization agreement with GCA in 2007 has made important initiatives in terms of commencement of hydrocarbon exploration studies in its own authorization field thanks to the momentum presented by drillings and discoveries. In August 2010, the Lebanese Parliament has adopted the first oil and natural gas law regarding the sea authorization field. By this adopted law, as a result of government's decision, a regulatory commission will be established to review the offers of exploration licences of national oil company. The law determines the searching periods with 10 years and production periods with 30 years in the agreements. Even if the comprehensive seismic researches made in Lebanon have been a promising one, the country's first offshore studies have been delayed five times in that the licensing agreement on the offshore blocks has not been approved by the government due to the political chaos. The drilling of first exploration well that was delayed in 2017 is still awaited. The joint venture

---

[3] Ibid., pp. 36-37.
[4] Daniela Huber, "Israeli Regional Perspectives and The Mediterranean", **Routledge Handbook of Mediterranean Politics**, Richard Gillespie, Frederic Volpi (Ed.), New York, Routledge, 2018, p. 127.

among Total (40%), Eni (40%) and Novatek (20%) has signed a deal for 4. and 9. Blocks in February 2018. It is expected that the exploration drilling presented by this consortium and according to the approved plan will begin very soon. Lebanon which divides its own authorization field into ten blocs increases its drilling activities.[5]

On October 19, 2010, Lebanon has presented the map that defines its sea authorization fields to the United Nations. The Exclusive Economic Zone borders expressed by this declaration encompass the coordinates the demarcation deal signed between Lebanon and GCA. Moreover, it is seen that a part of 9 square kilometers of the EEZs declared by Lebanon and Israel do clash. Following this clash, the EEZ disagreement between the two countries has been unresolved and this situation has increased the tension between the countries. Political instability, war atmosphere and the disagreements within the region negatively affect the process regarding the exploration and drilling activities. Lebanon has sent a note to the United Nations on its opposition to the EEZ agreement between Israel and GCA in 2011. Moreover, Beirut has decided to start exploration activities in 8. , 9. , 10. Blocks determined in 2017. But this initiative has strongly been criticized by Israel and a warning has been sent to Lebanese government. Within this context, Beirut has sent a memorandum to the United Nations including its criticism toward Tel-Aviv's stance as well as its exclusive right to search in its EEZ. Together with this note, Lebanon has once more expressed its opposition regarding the EEZ deal between GCA and Israel.[6]

For Egypt, Italian energy company ENI has discovered an 850 bcm natural gas reserve in the Zohr field in 2015. This stays the biggest gas discovery that has been made up until now. Egypt as an old natural gas and oil producer has the infrastructure that can export the gas by two liquefication terminals and also by the two pipelines which connect the country with Israel and Jordan. It is observed that Mısır being as a net natural gas importer with the increasing consumption, has turned out to be a country that produces more than it consumes thanks to the activation of its Eastern Mediterranean reserves into the production. Following the Zohr discovery, the natural gas located here has been reached into the land just a short period of two and half years. After the starting of production in the Zohr project within the four months, the second production unit has become operational. In the field which the production capacity is increased day by day, nearly daily 22.65 million cubic meters (mcm) of natural gas were acquired in 2018. In August 2019, it has come into the condition of producing more than 76 mcm of natural gas on daily basis in that field. It is envisaged that in the following years, the production capacity within this area is going to be increased into 90 mcm on daily basis. It has been obligated the opening of 254 wells during the production process in terms of the development

---

[5] Yunus Furuncu, "Doğu Akdeniz'de Türkiye Dışındaki Ülkelerin Hidrokarbon Arama ve Sondaj Faaliyetleri", **Doğu Akdeniz ve Türkiye'nin Hakları**, Kemal İnat, Muhittin Ataman, Burhanettin Duran (Ed.), İstanbul, SETA Kitapları, 2020, p. 267.
[6] Ibid., pp. 268-269.

plan of Zohr field. Italian Eni being as the operator of the field has sold its 10 percent shares in the licensing and gas fields to BP, 30 percent of its shares to Rosneft in 2017 (total value 1 billion 125 million dollars) and also 10 percent of its shares to UAE based Mubadala Petroleum in March 2018 (total value of 934 million dollars). Moreover, BP and Rosneft have the options to get more 5 percents. Eni which discovers a huge reserve in the region has set up partnerships before it extracts the reserve found.[7]

Furthermore, it is calculated that the development cost of that field will be more than 7 billion dollars. By the way, the Zohr field is positioned at the 6.5 kilometers far away to the regional border that was unilaterally declared by GCA and just the opposite side of the 11th parcel granted by GCA to French Total Company. It is not completely known that whether or not the reserve in Zohr lies to the waters of Cyprus. The West Nile Delta Field, has met the 20% of Egypt's natural gas consumption by nearly 39 mcm of production in 2019 on a daily basis. The 82.75 percent of this area belongs to BP and the remaining share is possessed by German DEA (Deutsche Erdöl AG). Together with this, within the Nooros field close to the Nile Basin, it is seen that ENI and BP have 50%-50% partnerships. It is too viewed that this field determined to be possessing as 77 billion cubic meters (bcm) of natural gas is one of the important reserves of Egypt and the production in this field has begun in 2015. The discovery of Atoll as another field has been declared by BP in March 2015. The reserve in this field has been calculated as approximately 42 bcm of natural gas and 31 million barrels of condensate. From the field that starts the production in 2018, daily 10 million cubic meters (mcm) of natural gas as well as 10 thousand barrels of condensate are acquired. The gas acquired from this field is directly allocated to the Egypt's natural gas network. It has been planned by Egypt Natural Gas Firm (EGAS) to grant 13 exploration and drilling licences in the natural gas block of Eastern Mediterranean as of the first quarter of 2020. The EGAS which finalizes the studies and seismic researches on this issue has been waiting the final decision of Oil Ministry regarding the timetables. Within the greatest bid round of the Ministry's history, Shell, BP, DEA and Petronas have applied for the hydrocarbon exploration privilege within the context of Mediterranean and Nile Basins. On the one hand when Egypt presents its reserves to the markets following the processing period, on the other hand, it increases the exploration and drilling activities by granting the new licensing fields to the energy firms. Therefore, Egypt plans to become an important natural gas supplier through increasing its natural gas reserves and production thanks to the new discoveries.[8]

When the Syria, Libya and Palestine are examined in terms of exploration and drilling activities with the Eastern Mediterranean, it is observed that they have not been going forward when compared with Egypt, Israel and Lebanon. The continental shelf delimitation agreement between Turkey and Syria in which

---

[7] Furuncu, ibid., pp. 253-254.
[8] Furuncu, ibid, pp. 255-256.

these two states are neighbouring to each other both by land and sea have not been signed. After the signing of the agreement, either the two countries can make exploration and drilling activities in the region or they can develop initiatives related with the determination of EEZ. However, it seems difficult that making such kind of an agreement in Syria experiencing an ongoing war in short term. Moreover, when the making an agreement is the case, it is understood that the Syrian Regime can prefer to talk with GCA[9] because of the existing atmosphere. Actually it has to be taken into account that Russia is going to be the chief determinant actor both in terms of the signing of EEZ agreement as well as the exploration of hydrocarbons in the region here. In this sense, the Russian firms will have priority within the allocation of exploration licences. A cooperation agreement has been signed between Russian Federation's Energy Minister Alexander Novak and Syria's Oil and Mineral Reserves Minister Ali Ghanem within the framework of close commercial relations between the two countries. This cooperation agreement involves the betterment of Syria's oil and natural gas production and also the other developments in the energy infrastructure. The drilling privilege within the coastal part of Syria ranging from Banyas to Tartus has been granted to the Russian firms for 25 years. Damascus has signed an exploration deal with Russian Soyuzneftegaz in December 2013. But there has been recorded no development on the drilling and exploration activities due to the conflicts. Any kind of development in the current atmosphere seems unrealistic.[10][11]

When we come to the Palestine, a littoral country in the Eastern Mediterranean, this country's rights are wanted to be encroached by Israel. The Gaza Marine Field discovered in the offshore Palestine is now unexploited. In 1999, the British Gas has declared its discovery of commercial and recoverable / manageable nearly 40 bcm natural gas reserves in Gaza located at the Palestine's 30 kilometer offshore field and 600 meters depth. Following this, in 2007, the then Israeli Cabinet has declared the acceptance of the offer on the purchasing of natural gas in the Eastern Mediterranean from the state of Palestine by the then Prime Minister Ehud Olmert. It has been stated that the total value of gas is 4 billion U.S. Dollars and it has been decided to give the possible total profit of 2 billion U.S. Dollars to the Palestinians. But the succeeding government has declared the invalidity of this agreement with British Gas.[12]

Libya a critically important country in the Eastern Mediterranean is an important partner for Turkey. On November 27, 2019, "A Memorandum of Understanding on the Delimitation of Sea Authorization Fields" between Turkey

---

[9] The GCA's natural gas reserves and how it impacts on Turkey's Eastern Mediterranean policies will be examined in detail within the third section of this paper.

[10] Furuncu, ibid., pp. 269-270.

[11] Álvaro Escalonilla, "Lebanon silent on Syria-Russia energy deal in eastern Mediterranean waters", https://atalayar.com/en/content/lebanon-silent-syria-russia-energy-deal-eastern-mediterranean-waters (Access 17.05.2021).

[12] Furuncu, ibid., p. 270.

and Libya was signed.[13] By this agreement, the two countries have determined their sea borders in the Eastern Mediterranean. At the same time, by acting from the proportionality principle of international law, both Turkey and Libya have clearly set forth by an international agreement that the Greek approach on granting the continental shelf to the islands is wrong. In the aftermath of this agreement, the possibility for other countries agreeing with the Greeks re-bringing into the agenda of agreements due to such factors as the continental shelf of islands, the coastal lengths and the condition of main land / continent has increased. Because, thanks to this agreement with Turkey, Libya has put forward that it holds rights in more fields within the milieu of the Eastern Mediterranean.[14]

Probable Transportation Ways of Commercializing The Eastern Mediterranean Hydrocarbons

Beforehand anyone can speak the prominence of the Eastern Mediterranean in regional energy security, exclusively for the littoral states together with Europe, the recent energy portraits of Turkey and the EU need correspondingly be distinguished. Turkey stays viewed as the sixth utmost natural gas importer with yearly requirements that overall 50 bcm. Turkey's gas consumption remains anticipated to decline from 2015 to 2030 while its natural gas dependence epitomizes nowadays about ninety-nine percent. Its natural gas consumption stays estimated to reach 60 bcm in 2020 and 70 bcm in 2030. When the European Union (EU) stays noticed in this setting, 53.5% of spent energy by the EU stays traded in. It principally necessitates hydrocarbon imports in an upward tendency. EU's gas import dependence ratio stands at around 67.4%, which are comprised of 39% of natural gas and 33% of oil importations from Moscow. The EU has a lessening share of fossil fuels in the energy set of itself in conjunction with more than 400 bcm gas consumption annually. This is coming into the meaning that the East-Med symbolizes the weightiest adjacent market for natural gas. The EU which already meets 30% percent of its natural gas from Russia remains in quest of different sources and export routes that will lessen its ever-growing reliance on one energy supplier chiefly following the 2006-2009 natural gas disruptions and also the prevailing inner war which has been ongoing since November 2013. In this milieu, also the Caspian natural gas (if reachable Turkmenistan and Iran), the EU searches for accessing energy supplies via the Southern Gas Corridor nevertheless stays similarly following contemporaneously firsthand routes that will bring East-Med natural gas to the EU.[15]

The primary project for transporting East-Med natural gas to Europe

---

[13] This issue will be detailed in the third part of this paper.
[14] Furuncu, ibid., pp. 270-271.
[15] Sina Kısacık, "How Will The Existing and Probable Eastern Mediterranean Energy Security Parameters Affect The Eurasian and Aegean Sea Energy Geopolitics in the 21st Century?", **Ege Jeopolitiği Cilt II**, Hasret Çomak, Burak Şakir Şeker, Dimitrios Ioannidis (Ed.), Ankara, Nobel Akademik Yayıncılık, 2020, pp. 1255-1256.

represents the East-Med Pipeline Project, which stays scheduled to connect Cyprus to Greece through the Island of Crete. Proposed by DEPA and included within the list of Common Interest Projects by the EU, it has been estimated to possess a yearly capacity of nearly 8 bcm. The most notable obstacles of the project stay the technical complications and the high budget. Moreover; Cyprus, Israel, and Lebanon's natural gas resources believably to be found within the forthcoming terms are not anticipated to stay more than 750 bcm capacities. As stated by the Oslo Peace Institute, its over-all cost rests prized at 16 Billion Euros. Even if this project becomes visible, the whole projected revenue represents at 44.7 Billion Euros.[16] This project is totally backed by the White House due to the reason that this pipeline will upturn the affluence and steadiness in the Eastern Mediterranean, then again will likewise make stronger the European energy security and it will assist in the variation of energy resources. For instance US Ambassador Geoffrey Pyatt has stated in the Athens Energy Dialogues 2020 event that *"Washington warmly supports Greece's cooperation with Cyprus and Israel on the EastMed natural gas pipeline that forms part of the US strategy in the region."* He has also underlined that *"the pipeline is a far-reaching project that is fully adjusted to the energy strategy of the US in the Eastern Mediterranean, country's interest in the strategic space of the region. Washington has great confidence in Greece's stabilizing role in the region."[17]* In accordance with these statements, as of December 17, 2020, U.S. Energy Secretary Dan Brouillette has shared Washington's official point of view on the East Med Natural Gas Pipeline in Athens to the journalists as follows:

> *"The United States is backing the construction of a subsea pipeline that would supply Europe with natural gas from the eastern Mediterranean. We are going to continue to work with Israel, Greece and other interested parties to ensure that the infrastructure will be developed. There is still an enormous amount of interest both from private industry and from governments of the region to see that infrastructure developed and to be developed as quickly as we can possibly do it."[18]*

By January 2, 2020, a settlement for constructing a pipeline was contracted by the governments of Greece, Israel, and GCA that may arrange for Europe with 4 % its annual natural gas supplies starting the middle of the decade. The agreement signifies an announcement of political willpower. Yet, it rests at the present time in need of the construction consortium, led by the Public Gas Corporation of Greece (DEPA) and Italy's Edison, to afford the roughly six billion euros ($6.7bn), which remain the predictable budget of the pipeline. East Med will stay positioning only approximately 1,900 kilometers (1,181 miles) from Israeli and Cypriot natural gas fields within the eastern Mediterranean to Italy via Greece. The three participant states of the East-Med Pipeline have been emphasizing that the becoming operational of this pipeline is going to exist a "win-win" situation for all the interrelated parties, and it is not established

---

[16] Kısacık, ibid., p. 1258.

[17] Chryssa Liaggou, "Pyatt voices US support for EastMed", https://www.ekathimerini.com/economy/248780/pyatt-voices-us-support-for-eastmed/(Access 11.05.2021).

[18] https://www.reuters.com/article/greece-usa-energy-int-idUSKBN28R2FV (Access 11.05.2021).

contrary to other countries, first and foremost Turkey.[19] This trilateral settlement taken on among Tel-Aviv (Jerusalem)-Nicosia-Athens regarding the realization of East-Med Pipeline has been tenderly appraised by the EU spokesperson on January 2, 2020, as:

> *"The pipeline should be seen as one option of tapping EastMed gas supplies for the EU alongside shipping it to the EU by tankers in the form of LNG. It's important to explore further the costs and benefits of both main options. In this context, the EastMed pipeline is one option to bring that gas to the continent."[20]*

Here, it had better be defined thoroughly how this trilateral pact is judged by the Republic of Turkey. The Spokesperson of Republic of Turkey Ministry of Foreign Affairs Ambassador Hami Aksoy has assessed this initiative as:

> *"Any project disregarding Turkey, which has the longest coastline in the Eastern Mediterranean, and the Turkish Cypriots, who have equal rights over the natural resources of the island of Cyprus, cannot succeed. Turkey is the most commercially feasible and secure route for the utilization of the natural resources in the Eastern Mediterranean and their transfer to consumer markets in Europe, including Turkey..."[21]*

Prof. Oktay Tanrısever, an expert on energy diplomacy and the International Relations Department chair of the Middle East Technical University, has analyzed this issue as:

> *"The project cannot be realized also because of legal difficulties as the planned pipeline would pass through the Turkish Exclusive Economic Zone. Isolation of Turkey does not benefit anyone, and it is not sustainable in the long run. The parties will eventually consider revising the pipeline project by cooperating with Turkey for the construction of a mutually beneficial pipeline project, with a route from the island of Cyprus passing through Turkey. Turkey has been offering its willingness to cooperate with all the countries concerned..."[22]*

A central difficulty within the perspective of the putting into practice of the project represents in its expensiveness and the necessary volume, for including the costs has not till now actually been realized. For the Greek daily newspaper *To Vima*, it stands projected that the transfer fee of the natural gas is going to stay three times less costly if the pipeline passes on Turkey, instead of the route planned by the EastMed. Consistent with this forecast, Androulla Vassiliou, former Greek Cypriot EU Commissioner for Health and also for Education, Culture, Multilingualism & Youth, has assessed this pipeline as *for a pipeline that will be so expensive that it will be impossible to finance, for natural gas the price of which we do not know if we can justify the expenditure and the quantities of which are still unknown. It*

---

[19] Örmeci, Kısacık, ibid., pp. 42-43.
[20] Ibid., p. 43.
[21] Ibid., p. 43.
[22] Ibid., pp. 43-44.

is all a game of impressions.[23] It should be mentioned that Italy has some doubts on the implementation of East-Med Natural Gas Pipeline. Italy's Foreign Affairs Minister Luigi Di Maio has shared the following statements regarding this issue:

> *"The EastMed pipeline project will fail to be a feasible plan in terms of its cost and construction process. It is obvious that the EastMed pipeline project, proposed by Greece, will not be an option in the medium- and long-term compared to other projects, when its cost and the construction process are taken into consideration. This infrastructure, which can play a positive role in diversifying European resources, must prove that it can attract the necessary capital for its construction and it can be economically sustainable."*[24]

On other hand, as of March 13, 2021, Mikhail L. Myrianthis, energy expert and member of the advisory committee of the Hellenic Foundation for European & Foreign Policy (ELIAMEP) think tank, has evaluated the possible realization of this pipeline project as follows:

> *"The first and main condition for the creation of an interconnection gas pipeline between Greece and Egypt is the proof of its economic viability. The project has similarities with the Turkish-Austrian Nabucco pipeline which was ultimately abandoned. A project of enormous size and importance, analogous to the current EastMed or Nord Stream I & II, its implementation would decisively upgrade Turkey's energy and geopolitical role. Both the EastMed and Nabucco pipelines envisioned the reduction of EU energy dependence on Russian gas. Another common feature is their huge budgets, with the 1,329-kilometer Nabucco in the range of 8-10 billion euros and the 1,250 km EastMed (underwater route only) in the range of 6 billion euros. The estimate of 6 billion euros is clearly underestimated. Costs similar to Nabucco, which had no extra costly underwater links, are more realistic."*[25]

Here in this point, it should be given some important assessments of two famous energy experts concerning the monetization of Eastern Mediterranean natural gas reserves either by pipelines or LNG. The first one is Mehmet Öğütçü, chair of the London Energy Club and a former Turkish diplomat regarding this issue. Some important remarks of Öğütçü are as follows;

> *"Nowadays, there is just so much supply in the market. There are abundant reserves and LNG capacity has also been growing significantly. In the Eastern Mediterranean, Cyprus, Israel and Egypt all have gas fields, with Egypt seen as the superpower of gas in the region. Its offshore Zohr field is the largest in the Mediterranean and twice the size of Israel's nearby Leviathan field."*[26]

[23] Örmeci, Kısacık, ibid., pp. 44-45.
[24] Fahri Aksüt, "Italian FM doubts EastMed pipeline project feasible", https://www.aa.com.tr/en/energy/energy-diplomacy/italian-fm-doubts-eastmed-pipeline-project-feasible/28119 (Access 10.05.2021).
[25] https://www.ekathimerini.com/news/1157014/eastmed-pipeline-viability-under-scrutiny/(Access 10.05.2021).
[26] Jonathan Gorvett, "Mediterranean pipe dream founders on global gas glut", https://asiatimes.com/2021/03/mediterranean-pipe-dream-founders-on-global-gas-glut/(Access 10.05.2021).

Dr Charles Elinas, senior fellow at the Atlantic Council and a regional energy expert, has shared the following analyses on this issue:

"I just don't see how it's ever going to happen. Simply put, there's just too much gas in the world. Israel is now trying to sell its gas to Egypt. Egypt now has a surplus of gas. Shell, ENI, ExxonMobil, Chevron – they are all important for the region's gas and are all cutting spending drastically after recording huge losses in 2020. In these changing times, there's a need to change with them. The problem is, the politicians seem to find this so very difficult to do."[27]

Another conceivable export way characterizes the Liquefied Natural Gas (LNG). The LNG, a more elastic opportunity in comparison with the pipeline, will help rescuing GCA and Israel from being exclusively reliant the European market. Simultaneously, it will likewise offer the natural gas export to the world markets through the elastic pricing way. However then there happen definite difficulties that need be fixed before the implementation of this alternative. Initially, it has broadly been questioned where the assembly place of the LNG terminal will be positioned, which stands foreseen to process the GCA and Israel natural gas resources. In accordance with Tel-Aviv's selection of the situating this facility within its territories with the causes of the security features, this possibility is less probable to turn into reality owing to land problems, environmental dangers, and public reaction. The floating LNG platforms quickly evolving in modern periods has come into the forefront as a replacement to land-grounded LNG terminals. Nonetheless, the floating LNG facility, two times more costly when compared with a standard LNG terminal, anyhow, appears impracticable when the freshly confirmed reserve volumes remain reflected. The most probably facility among the principal LNG options seems to stand the terminal intended to be fabricated in Vasilikos city of GCA. It was anticipated that the project would be finished in 2016 while exports would commence in 2020. So far, in order to make the 10 billion Vasilikos Terminal rewarding, the Aphrodite gas will not stay simply adequate. In addition to the discovery of fresh reserves, which will be taking time, the only alternative remains to pool some capacities of the Leviathan natural gas to the Vasilikos terminal for the liquefaction. Though, Tel-Aviv declines to promise natural gas to the terminal to be set up outside its territories lacking guarantees of a secondary export opportunity for example a pipeline that grasps the regional markets. As stated by the Oslo Peace Institute, its reliable overall cost is estimated at 10.3 Billion Euros and the entire income is anticipated as 41.1 Billion Euros.28

Relating to the commercialization of East-Med's gas, Ankara can suggest the most cautiously reasonable transference route for Leviathan and the Aphrodite gases. In the broader context, Leviathan gas may perhaps be pooled within the European markets by way of the Southern Gas Corridor (SGC). Economically, Leviathan gas may possibly stand supportive to reduce Turkey's growing

[27] Ibid.
[28] Kısacık, ibid., pp. 1260-1261.

dependence on costly Russian natural gas and instable Iranian natural gas. An Israel-Turkey pipeline is able to encourage Ankara as a different alternate gas transit center for Europe as a result of the founding of the hub-centered pricing instrument. It could correspondingly expand the geostrategic worth of Ankara as a principal companion of Brussels's initiatives for variation of its natural gas suppliers. What stands more remarkable, conversely, stays the vagueness within the context of the natural gas volumes. Political and trade-focused difficulties/ obstacles preclude the East-Med natural gas from turning out to be the game-changer within the global natural gas markets. The most dominant fact that ought to stay debated here embodies the distinct appropriate underwater pipeline from Tel-Aviv transitory over GCA's EEZ vetoed by Nicosia while stimulating Turkey till the all-encompassing resolution of the Cyprus Issue. In relation to the calculations of the Oslo Peace Institute, this pipeline is anticipated to cost as much as 4 Billion Euros. When it comes to be operational, the overall revenue stands estimated to exist 56.8 Billion Euros.[29]

When the progresses on this issue were occurring in 2013, Turkey and Israel would make an effort to recover their affiliation. Binyamin Netanyahu, the then prime minister of Israel, offered his position to Recep Tayyip Erdoğan, the then prime minister of Turkey, via a telephone call within the framework of the reconciliation initiatives by then US President Obama on March 22, 2013. This initiative did happen because of the Mavi Marmara Incident and the assertions for compensation requested by the families of those executed by the Israeli soldiers. President Erdoğan positively answered to this compromise and confirmed Ankara's eagerness for reinstating the military cooperation and full diplomatic connections with Israel. Even so, behind closed doors, Turkey and Israel have arranged to upkeep their private firms that have been buttressing for the progression of a potential Israel-Turkey Pipeline. Nevertheless instead, the economic interactions between Turkey and Israel have been harmfully inclined by their clashes concerning the Israeli-Palestinian Conflict. Meanwhile 2017, the relationships between Ankara and Tel-Aviv has worsened attributable to the former's patronage of the Palestinians counter to Washington's pronouncement to shuffle the US Embassy to Jerusalem.[30] Accompanied by the fiasco of the latest round of the UN-led diplomatic talks for the long-lasting resolution of the Cyprus Question, one can mention the improbability of making a Turkey-Israel-Cyprus Island natural gas pipeline.[31]

---

[29] Kısacık, ibid., p. 1262.
[30] Göktürk Tüysüzoğlu, Sina Kısacık, "Türkiye-İsrail İlişkileri", **Soğuk Savaş Sonrası Türkiye'nin Orta Doğu ve Kuzey Afrika Siyaseti,** Pınar Yürür, Göktürk Tüysüzoğlu, Arda Özkan (Ed.), Ankara, Detay Yayıncılık, 2020, pp. 275-280.
[31] Kısacık, ibid., p. 1262.

Some Important Hurdles Before the Monetization of the Eastern Mediterranean Energy Reserves

Energy and International Law Related Obstacles

In 2013, the then Israeli Cabinet has permitted exporting 40% of its gas reserves. Furthermore, the first cabinet decision accepting the gas exports from Tel-Aviv has chiefly concentrated on reserves comparable to 950 bcm. As an alternate, the extra resources encompassed in the Leviathan's basin in June 2014 would bring about roughly 40 bcm growth in terms of the export capacities. This determination stands the supreme overall exports of Israel which stretch the stages of 440-450 bcm by 2040. Ever since the exporting of 20 bcm yearly to its neighbors delivered from the Tamar Field, this seems to propose an extra export volume of 15-18 bcm per annum between 2020 and 2040. In common with the geopolitical problems within the region, the qualms in terms of price and market, the transference of East-Med gas via pipelines remains to be a challenging choice when the European markets stay considered. Exporting Tel-Aviv's natural gas to Europe by a pipeline looks to stand, at least in the interim, a minor plan that stays overwhelmed with very peculiar prompt predictions.[32]

Within this framework, one must describe the possible reserves of GCA plus the causes why the commercialization of these resources remains very demanding at least for the mid and long terms. The initial proper calculations had better perform at the start of the 2000s when GCA permitted Petroleum Geo-Services to discover the country's export prospective. Following this development, Nicosia has endeavoured to allow for 11 blocs in 2007. Instead, simply the three agreements were ratified. Within 2011, the southern offshore region, the alleged Aphrodite fields positioned about 34 kilometers of the Leviathan field of Tel-Aviv, projected to include 140-220 bcm at the 1700 kilometers depth, was found by the Nobel Company. The quantity revealed possibly will be perceived as ample for the meeting of the internal demand of GCA for numerous years and upkeep the progress of this country's natural gas export. The contradictory stands similarly accurate in that this country rests increasingly reliant on the natural gas import largely in terms of petroleum products. Nonetheless, one has to talk over the foremost political complications before the growth of the country's offshore regions. The Turkish Republic of Northern Cyprus (TRNC) and Turkey confront with the GCA's attitude, underwritten by the international community. Lefkoşe and Ankara do advocate that Cyprus cannot stay de jure and de facto described by the GCA. Furthermore, due to the disagreement in the belongingness of the areas, it rests a globally recognized point that the island's offshore natural resources stand possessed by entire Cypriots including Turks and Greeks. Similarly, Ankara rejects the EEZ charges by Greek Cypriots in the western part vis-à-vis the 1, 4, 5, 6 and 7 blocs. For Ankara's official point, that type of maritime declaration can exclusively stay

---

[32] Ibid., p. 1256.

operative in the aftermath of the resolution of the Cyprus Problem.[33]

GCA has put forward numerous initiatives for the announcement of its peculiar EEZs so as to provide advantages more from the Eastern Mediterranean basins within the 2000s. Within this milieu, Nicosia has begun to work regarding the finding of hydrocarbons in its self-stated fields that are reinforced by such regional and exterior players as France, Italy, the U.S., and the EU. In order for this, the GCA has developed many finding movements by the adoption of EEZ contracts with the regional countries in the former years. Though, the search of a self-governing EEZ policy by GCA in the Eastern Mediterranean, the rapprochement proceeding between the troika of GCA-Israel-Greece, and the political backing offered by the EU and France to GCA are reflected as tests to Turkey's security policies and national interests within this region by Ankara.[34]

The GCA, targeting to have an advantage aggressively from the hydrocarbons in the region, has augmented its territorial waters to 12 nautical miles. Within this setting, to begin with, GCA, by manipulation of the standing of "Sovereign Cyprus Republic", has stated its EEZ. Afterwards this, Nicosia has endeavoured to formalize its actions via the opening of those fields to international energy firms. Yet, it ought to be remembered that it is rigid to describe the EEZs of territorial waters in awkward regions for instance Cyprus. In order for getting maximum advantage from the East-Med, GCA has signed EEZ contracts with Egypt in 2003, Lebanon in 2007 and Israel in 2010 on the basis of the "Median Line Principle". Owing to these settlements, a contested condition with Turkey's territorial waters and the continental shelf has been formed by GCA. Within the framework of this condition, GCA has been in licensing activities headed for the finding of hydrocarbons. For this, American Noble Energy in the 12th parcel, Italian ENI in the 2nd, 3rd, and 9th parcels, and French TOTAL in the 10th and 11th parcels have been authorized by GCA.[35] Conversely, these permissions have strictly been condemned by Ankara. In a reaction to this, Turkey and TRNC have made an EEZ deal in September 2011. It need be highlighted within this situation that, excepting other Mediterranean states, Turkey remains not one of the party states of the 1982 UN Convention on the Law of Seas. Turkey and TRNC have been calling attention to that lacking the presence of a multilaterally settled EEZ treaty between the littoral states within the Eastern Mediterranean, other than the resolution of the Cyprus Dispute, the one-sided initiatives of GCA within the milieu of demarcation of EEZ and authorizing the international energy firms regarding the finding of hydrocarbons stand unlawful and also unsafe.[36]

The discovery of 129 bcm-natural gas by American Noble Energy in Aprohodite Field has attracted the interests of all energy firms into the GCA's

---

[33] Kısacık, ibid., pp. 1256-1257.
[34] Örmeci, Kısacık, ibid., p. 38.
[35] For a detailed analysis on this issue please see, Emete Gözügüzelli, "Güney Kıbrıs Rum Yönetimi'nin Doğu Akdeniz'de Deniz Yetki Alanlarını Belirleme Stratejisi ve Hukuki Rejimi", **Akdeniz Jeopolitiği Cilt I**, Hasret Çomak, Burak Şakir Şeker (Ed.), Ankara, Nobel Akademik Yayıncılık, 2019, pp. 250-266.
[36] Örmeci, Kısacık, ibid., pp. 38-40.

EEZ. Later on the declaration of Italian Eni on the discovery of 169-226 bcm natural gas reserves in Calypso Field within 2018 has strengthened the outlook that the region will be rich in terms of reserve. On the other hand, due to Turkish Cypriots' also having rights in these fields, it has been granted an exploration license to TPAO. Thus, it is understood that 90 percent of TPAO's exploration license fields and the fields declared by GCA do clash. The first gas discovery in declared areas of GCA has been made in Aprohodite Field. The Aprohodite Field takes place within a region that stays 30 kilometers northwest of Leviathan Field and the sea depth is 1700 meters. The field has come into the forefront after A-1 Drilling Well that reaches into the depth of 5600 meters from the sea field and continues 116 days as well as started on September 20, 2011. In November 2015, the British Gas has declared that it has bought 35 percent of Aprohodite reserves from Noble Energy. As of today, in the Aprohodite field, Delek Drilling has 30 percent, Noble: 35% and British Gas: 35 % shares. The production period for the reserve found in Aprohodite is not yet certain. But for the latest plan, in the first phase, it will reached into nearly 5000 meters depth from 1700 meters sea depth in which the proven reserve exist and later on five production wells having high stream speed will be formed. It is planned the provision of yearly 8 bcm of natural gas production from the Aprohodite Field wherein the daily production capacity is expected to be 22 million mcm at maximum within the framework of first production phase. This volume accounts for nearly the 15 percent of Turkey's natural gas consumption per annum.[37]

It is also seen that the GCA makes plans for the transfer of the natural gas to be produced, The GCA has signed cooperation letter of intentions with the Egyptian government regarding the transportation of natural gas from Aprohodite to both the Egyptian market and to the liquefication facility owned by Shell in Idku, Egypt. However, it is understood that within the context of this region wherein TRNC also has rights, in case of the unilateral extraction of the reserve by GCA, the confrontations will be much more when compared with today. In February 2018, the Italian Eni has explained the discovery of Calypso-1 situated at 2000 kilometers depth with the total volume of 169-225 billion cubic meters. As a significant discovery, the Calypso is situated at the sixth parcel. Within the 10th parcel staying out of the contested fields, Exxon-Mobil and Qatar Petroleum have continued their exploration studies and as a result of these researches, they have declared the existence of 142-227 bcm of natural gas in Glaucus-1 Field at the end of February 2018 according to their first results. Moreover, it has been stated that the drilling will be continued in order for the fully determining the reserve volume in this field.[38]

By the announcement issued on January 6, 2015, the Turkish Cypriot part has underscored that Barbaros Vessel will not pause its researches. Simultaneously, it has requested Nicosia to resume the peace discussions with the aim of

---

[37] Furuncu, ibid., pp. 264-265.
[38] Ibid., pp. 265-266.

achieving a comprehensive and practicable resolution advantageous for all parties and which would bring about the re-integration of the island. Egypt as a noteworthy gas producer (850 bcm reserves) has approved to import gas owing to the growing internal consumption. Furthermore, it has been discussed that the unused LNG facilities for the liquefaction of gas ought to be benefited for the transportation from Greek Cyprus and the export of Cyprus gas to the world markets via Cairo.[39]

Here it has to briefly be discussed the international law aspect of this issue. The signing of demarcation agreements by Greece and GCA by accepting and taking the Grete, Kaşot, Çoban, Rodos, Meis Line as the basis and also with the median lines among them or with other littoral states as well as declaring EEZs so as to limit Turkey with a very few continental shelf and EEZ is the violation of international law norms regarding the equity. This also lacks from legal reasoning. The islands when looked from the median line drawn between the Greek main land and Anatolian coasts, do situate at the opposite side. Therefore, they cannot form a coast on the delimitation and except from the territorial waters, they cannot have the continental shelf. This fact is openly stated in the International Court of Arbitration's decision on the confrontation between United Kingdom and France on Channel Continental Shelf. Within this context, it is impossible to form a new coast through the abandoning of related coastal string to the delimitation zone of Turkey for Greece via the unification of Grete, Kaşot, Çoban, Rodos, and Meis Islands with a line. On the other hand, it can be come into the forefront that in any kind of a delimitation practice, a list of equity principles in which among them, the suitable ones can be chosen from the related judicial and arbitration decisions. The principle that is mostly prioritized by the decisions is the "superiority of the geography". It is understood from the geography concept, the main land geography within the area in which it stands the subject of delimitation between the two countries. The most important geographical factor is the length of main land coasts. This principle has been defined by the International Court of Justice in the decision of North Sea Cases as " it is out of question to the reshaping of the geography", in the case of United Kingdom-France as "the geographical conditions determine the suitability of equal distance or any kind of delimitation methods and also within the case of Libya-Malta as "the coasts of the parties form the starting line" and lastly in the decision of Tunisia-Libya Case as " the land / continent is sovereign over the sea."[40]

The superiority of the geography principle has too been prioritized within the jurisdictions on the cases in which the EEZ and continental shelf are delimited in one case. While the international courts are starting to the delimitation

---

[39] Kısacık, ibid., p. 1264.
[40] Cihat Yaycı, "Türkiye ve KKTC'nin Doğu Akdeniz'de Münhasır Ekonomik Bölgeleri", **Ege Jeopolitiği Cilt I**, Hasret Çomak, Burak Şakir Şeker, Dimitrios Ioannidis (Ed.), Ankara, Nobel Akademik Yayıncılık, 2020, pp. 917-918.

practice, they firstly determine a delimitation line that reflects the geographical features of mainland countries between the two mainland countries. If the coastal lengths are approximate and coastal shapes are identical, the coastal line is the equidistant line. When there are important differences on the coastal lengths and coastal shapes, there emerge necessary factors which should include a border apart from the equidistance. In the second phase of delimitation, it is evaluated by the courts that whether this determined border is accounted as equitable or not when other related geographical factors are taken into the account. Amongst the other factors, the islands come into the forefront and in this stage, it is assessed what should be the effect that will be granted to the islands. Primarily, how much effect will be given to the islands between the main lands is determined by such factors as geographical stability and population, location and greatness. Even if the islands have continental shelves, this situation does not mean that the islands are not at the same status with the mainland states. In some circumstances, the islands can either limitedly affect or never affect the delimitation line based on their features. The role of the delimitation of the islands close to the coasts of another country is much more subjected to the limitation. Because the distortion effect of such positioned islands are more over the delimitation line necessitated by the mainlands in terms of the delimitation between two mainlands and therefore in most times, it is granted very limited effect to such located islands or they are completely ignored. If these islands are socially weak and small as volume / size, it is very hard for them to have effects. When the equidistant line between two mainlands that are not close to the coasts of another state is considered, it is seen the underestimation of the islands close to another country unless they possess an important social life in a similar way.[41]

In order to reach an equitable solution, it has to be taken into account all other related factors in addition to the geographical factors. For this reason, in the following stage of delimitation, the related factors apart from the geography are assessed by the international courts. According to the court decisions, the natural resources within the areas to be delimited come into agenda as a primary one among the related factors. A delimitation line that unjustly allocates the natural resources will not be accepted as a border suitable for equity. Here it is also taken into account the factors such as formerly defined areas for oil exploration fields by the parties or the borders to be determined with the third states. It has been developed some principles regarding the impacts of related factors to each other in judicial and arbitration decisions. The first principle is proportionality. According to this, it is necessary to include closeness between the proportion between the coastal lengths of two states as well as the proportion granted to these states in terms of continental shelves and/or EEZs as a result of the delimitation. The proportionality serves for the final control principle that tests the justness of the concluded delimitation. In line with this principle, any other factor will not be evaluated as a method that provides the justness in the delimitation if it has an effect that will importantly change the reflection of the

---

[41] Yaycı, ibid., pp. 918-919.

proportion between the littoral lengths into the delimitation. The non-encroachment is another similar principle. Especially together with the acceptance of the distance factor in the determination of width of continental shelf, it has been acknowledged that the delimitation line has to leave every country the adjacent fields to the coasts or in other words the necessity of provision of the non-encroachment before the islands. That is to say, it has been emphasized that a delimitation method that will result in the granting of a sea field close to a country to another country is against the justness. Therefore, such critically significant factors as the islands located at the opposite sides, lengths of land coasts, the important differences in the coastal shapes, the limited or non-impacting of islands over the delimitation line, the just sharing of natural resources, the previously determination of oil discovery authorization fields, the proportionality principle as well as non-encroachment principle in terms of the delimitation abandon the legal reasonings of Greece's EEZ allegations within the Eastern Mediterranean. But in case of the realization of such unlawful case in terms of international law, the EEZ of Turkey is limited with Bay of Antalya and will be 41.000 square kilometers. Therefore, as an estimate, Turkey will have lost a 104.000 square kilometer-sea authorization field at a minimum level.[42]

In line with the growing of finding and drilling undertakings within the Eastern Mediterranean region, one can straightforwardly perceive military activities within the region. When ENI's Saipem 12000 drilling vessel would move for drilling in the third parcel which is located at the southeastern part of the island and also under the operatorship of ENI, Turkey has declared that it would make military exercise in the region. On February 10, 2018, the drilling ship belonged to ENI has been stopped by Turkish warships. Owing to the understanding of continuing of Turkish military exercise for a long time, the Italian ENI's Saipem 12000 ship has obliged to leave the field.[43] Even if France does not have a coast to the Eastern Mediterranean, it is observed that this country has a presence in the region with its exploration and drilling ships as well as with military activities. The GCA which continues its exploration and drilling activities tries to be influential within the Eastern Mediterranean region by acting together with the regional countries and also excluding Turkey and TRNC. Up until now, by the three licensing bids, it has licensed 90 percent of EEZs that are unlawfully declared to the energy firms.[44]

Another outstanding problem that need be emphasized remains the steady and complete support of Washington and Brussels' to the coalition of Tel-Aviv-Nicosia-Athens-Cairo. In this logic, this alliance has been constantly condemning Ankara's contemporary initiatives within the framework of the Eastern Mediterranean. The EU Foreign Affairs Ministers' decision of June 15, 2019, can be noticed as an additional sample of these kinds of disapprovals. Within this

---

[42] Yaycı, ibid., pp. 919-920.

[43] https://www.maritime-executive.com/article/eni-s-drillship-blocked-by-turkish-armed-forces (Access 18.05.2021).

[44] Furuncu, ibid., pp. 266-267.

decision, it was acknowledged:

> *17. The European Council expresses serious concerns over Turkey's current illegal drilling activities in the Eastern Mediterranean and deplores that Turkey has not yet responded to the EU's repeated calls to cease such activities. The European Council underlines the serious immediate negative impact that such illegal actions have across the range of EU-Turkey relations. The European Council calls on Turkey to show restraint respect the sovereign rights of Cyprus and refrain from any such actions. The European Council endorses the invitation to the Commission and the EEAS to submit options for appropriate measures without delay, including targeted measures. The EU will continue to closely monitor developments and stands ready to respond appropriately and in full solidarity with Cyprus."[45]*

Additionally, the U.S. Deputy Assistant Secretary for European and Eurasian Affairs, Matthew Palmer has highlighted the following noteworthy details:

> *"I don't want to get into hypotheticals, but what I can tell you is that we've made clear to Turkey that we consider the actions that it has undertaken in terms of its announced intentions to begin drilling as provocative and we've encouraged Turkey to stop those actions."[46]*

It remains similarly correspondingly imperative to scrutinize the response of some regional states to Turkey's current drilling activities so as to better comprehend the existing and likely developments concerning this issue. For instance, GCA's Ministry of Foreign Affairs has handed out the next declaration when Ankara has commenced its drilling activities:

> *"Turkey's provocative action is a serious violation of the sovereign rights of the Republic of Cyprus under international and E.U. law. At the same time, it reveals Turkey's real intentions with regard to the Cyprus issue, but also explains why Ankara rejected the proposal for an informal Crans Montana-like meeting to discuss the Cyprus issue. The Republic of Cyprus, aware of the intentions of Turkey, has taken and is taking all appropriate steps to deal with the situation as a Member State of the European Union and the United Nations, and as a State playing an active role in the Eastern Mediterranean region."[47]*

Another announcement with reference to this issue has been shared by the Ministry of Foreign Affairs of Greece which is as: *"We urge Turkey to immediately stop its illegal activities, to respect the inalienable rights of the sovereign Republic of Cyprus that it exercises for the benefit of the whole Cypriot people and to refrain from further actions that undermine stability in the region, as well as resuming talks on a just and viable solution to the Cyprus problem."[48]*

Egypt has remained one of those countries that have been condemning

---

[45] Kısacık, ibid., pp. 1264-1265.
[46] Kısacık, ibid., p. 1265.
[47] Ibid., p. 1266.
[48] Ibid., p. 1266.

Turkey's existing hydrocarbon exploration in the East-Med. As said by the Egyptian Ministry of Foreign Affairs, *"This provocative action by Turkey constitutes a blatant violation of the sovereign rights of the Republic of Cyprus in accordance with the International Law and the Law of the European Union.* In accordance with this, Israel has been another country condemning Turkey's undertakings in the East-Med. The Israeli Ambassador to Cyprus, Sammy Revel has underlined that *"Israel is following with serious concern recent steps taken by Turkey in Cyprus EEZ, off its western coast. Israel reiterated its full support and solidarity with Cyprus in exercising its sovereign rights in its EEZ and expresses its opposition to any attempt to violate these rights."* Paris has similarly requested Ankara to abstain from provocative actions and repeated its support of the independence of the Republic of Cyprus. According to the spokesperson of the U.K. High Commission in Cyprus, *"they are following developments with concern. They are in close touch with the governments of Cyprus and Turkey. They wish to see the situation deescalated.* Alternatively, The Russian Foreign Ministry has declared that: *"We firmly believe that any economic activity must comply with the rules of international law. We call for no action to be taken which could cause tension and create additional obstacles to the settlement of the Cyprus issue."*[49] The July 15, 2019 sanctioning decision of Brussels concerning Ankara due to the latter's recent undertakings in the East-Med has been criticized by Moscow. On July 17, 2019, the Russian Foreign Ministry spokeswoman Maria Zakharova has voiced her country's formal posture vis-à-vis this topic as:

> *"Sanction is not 'a tool of diplomacy' and it cannot be a basis of the international politics. We have an extremely negative attitude towards any sanctions that are not authorized by the [UN] Security Council. As a reciprocal measure, we are forced to say that it is a part of the modern reality. But we cannot accept such a unilateral, illegal, aggressive pressure and policy that aims at promoting one's own interests..."*[50]

In accordance with these declarations, Recep Tayyip Erdoğan, the President of the Republic of Turkey, has stressed Ankara's strength of mind regarding the newest changes in the framework of Eastern Mediterranean on July 24, 2019, the celebration of 96th anniversary of the Lausanne Peace Treaty, a breakthrough treaty recognizing the modern Turkish state as: *"Turkey's recent steps in the eastern Mediterranean and northern Syria - including drilling for natural resources and counter-terrorism operations - clearly demonstrate its determination to protect the rights of both the Republic of Turkey and Turkish Cyprus. No threat of sanctions, either covert or overt, can deter Turkey from her just cause."*[51]

As one of the most significant developments regarding this subject has remained the gathering of representatives from the energy ministries of Israel, Italy, Greece, Egypt, the Greek Cypriot Administration of Southern Cyprus (GCASC) and the Palestinian Authority, a representative of the Jordanian Energy Minister under second ministerial meeting of the Eastern Mediterranean GAS

[49] Kısacık, ibid., p. 1266.
[50] Örmeci, Kısacık, ibid., pp. 53-54.
[51] Kısacık, ibid., p. 1270.

Forum (EMGF) on July 24, 2019. In addition, U.S. Energy Minister Rick Perry, EU Commission Energy Director Dominique Ristori and delegates from France and the World Bank have been amongst the partakers of this meeting. At the finale of this meeting, it's been detailed that *"The group looks to raise EMGF at international level to assure the rights in natural resources. The next meeting will be held in 2020 in Cairo. The main objective of the forum, which will include Egypt, GCASC, Greece, Israel, Italy, Jordan and Palestine, is the establishment of a regional gas market that will serve the interests of the member countries".*[52] The Cairo-based EastMed Gas Forum's Charter was taken on by several Mediterranean members on September 22, 2020. Here some analyses will be shared regarding this subject. Stefan Wolfrum, a researcher at the Germany Institute for International and Security Affairs (SWP has remarked that;

> *"The EMGF [EastMed Gas Forum] is the first example to bring Israel together with Arab countries, with the involvement of European member states. The bilateral structures we know are giving way to more complex geopolitical structures. the forum creates the framework for the Palestinian Authority to sit at the same table with Israel."*[53]

Charles Ellinas, a senior fellow at the Atlantic Council, has analyzed that;

> *"Outside the region, the markets for gas from the east Mediterranean are theoretically in Europe and Asia. Competition in Asia is very intense, also because of the continued use of coal in power generation. For instance, Egypt tried to sell cheap gas to Asia, "but buyers were not interested.. Europe can't be a market for EastMed gas either. The European Union plans to decarbonize its economy by 2050, "which means that its gas consumption by 2030 must go down by 20-25%. That means EastMed gas could only be used regionally. But regional markets are not massive, prices will have to be low and margins will be low. This gas, targeting regional markets, will not make anybody rich. The EMGF could still open the way for the Saudis to buy gas from the region."*

Seth Frantzman, executive director at the Middle East Center for Reporting and Analysis, has assessed the EMGF as follows;

> *"If you tie together these countries, adding Jordan and the Palestinian Authority, it creates a form of arch, from which you can create better political alliances. The question is whether some adversaries might want to oppose it. Turkey's leadership wants to create crisis every few months to deflect the attention from internal difficulties. If it shifted toward a more collaborative standing, it would be invited to join the forum."*[54]

Mehmet Öğütçü, chairman of the London Energy Club, has evaluated this subject as:

---

[52] Kısacık, ibid., p. 1270.
[53] Sergio Matalucci, "EastMed Gas Forum fuels energy diplomacy in troubled region", https://www.dw.com/en/eastmed-gas-forum-fuels-energy-diplomacy-in-troubled-region/a-55206641 (Access 10.05.2021).
[54] https://www.dw.com/en/eastmed-gas-forum-fuels-energy-diplomacy-in-troubled-region/a-55206641

"Without a stable environment conducive to the new investment it is unlikely that financiers and operators will pour investment dollars into new infrastructure projects in the region. Like it or not, Turkey is game maker or spoiler in the region. Turkey must be invited at the earliest possibility; otherwise positions within the forum will be entrenched and will be difficult to bring Turkey in due to concessionary demands from Cyprus and Greece, in particular in return for opening the door to Turkey. Ankara could be weakening the forum on purpose creating alternative structures that may deepen hostilities and make the EastMed energy development a distant prospect."[55]

The last assessment on this issue has come from Luca Franza, head of energy at Istituto Affari Internazionali. Franza's noteworthy statements with regard to this subject are the following:

"Italy clearly wants to be part of a platform for dialogue and producer-consumer coordination in an otherwise difficult context for energy resource exploitation. Italy aims at a mediating role, not least because it has good relations with all the other players involved. Rome and Ankara have compatible interests in Libya, and beyond: in August 2020, the two countries conducted joint military drills in the Mediterranean. The same month, Italy conducted drills with Cyprus, Greece and France. Germany could be another mediator but its reach is somehow limited as the largest European economy has no direct stakes in EastMed. the US, despite its reduced presence, maintains a catalyst role in the project. We should not forget that with the Eastern Mediterranean Security and Energy Partnership Act of 2019, the US facilitated the Israel-Greece-Cyprus alliance in the EastMed. The aim to counter Russia is very explicitly mentioned in the act, through which the US took the very significant step of lifting its arm embargo on Cyprus. It is no coincidence that the EastMed Gas Forum was launched a couple of weeks later [on January 16, 2020]"[56]

In accordance with these incidents, a judgmentally vital initiative has been developed by Turkey and Libya on November 27, 2019. On this date, the Turkish government and the Libyan government legitimately accepted by the United Nations-led by Fayez al-Sarraj- have taken on a Memorandum of Understanding (MoU) concerning the definition of EEZs between them. The settlement stands entitled as "Restriction of Marine Jurisdictions", awaited for the extension of security and military partnership between Turkey and Libya. Turkish Foreign Ministry spokesman Hami Aksoy has assessed this initiative as follows:

"The agreement was following the court decisions that create the international juris-prudence and international law, including the relevant articles of the United Nations Convention on the Law of the Sea. Turkey has the longest continental coastline in the Eastern Mediterranean. The islands, which lie on the opposite side of the median line between two mainlands, cannot create maritime jurisdiction areas beyond their territorial waters and that the length and direction of the coasts should be taken into

---

[55] Ibid.
[56] Ibid.

account in delineating maritime jurisdiction areas...[57]

On January 29, 2019, this agreement has been intensely condemned by the Foreign Ministers of Italy and GCA as "unacceptable", and as a defilement of international laws pay no attention to the independence privileges of other countries. Italian Foreign Minister Luigi Di Maio and his Cypriot counterpart Nikos Christodoulides have too emphasized in a mutual declaration subsequently meetings in Rome that *the deal cannot have any legal impact on other countries*. Turkish Foreign Ministry spokesman Hami Aksoy in contrast, on January 30, 2020, has condemned Rome's unfortunate elucidations concerning the maritime agreement between Turkey and Libya. Aksoy has likewise highlighted that Turkey has been requesting from all EU members to alter their conducts, ignoring as well as underestimating the privileges of Turkish Cypriots. Additionally, Aksoy has underscored that, as co-surviving communities, Turkish Cypriots possess identical privileges with Greek Cypriots relating to oil and natural gas resources nearby the island. In this way, Hami Aksoy has similarly reminded the permitting of search and drilling authorizations to Turkish Petroleum Corporation (TPAO) by TRNC in 2011. In accordance with these permits, the present exploration and drilling activities of the TPAO object to defend the privileges of Turkish Cypriots, not Turkey. Aksoy has similarly emphasized that the TPAO's initiatives will not be concluded up until these privileges remain guaranteed through joint cessation of all "off-shore" undertakings, or when cooperation will be accomplished between the TRNC and the GCA. Also, Aksoy has revealed that Ankara rejects denunciation counter to its MoU with Tripoli, recollecting the point that EU countries, containing Italy, have stayed mute on the comparable agreement between the GCA and Egypt in 2003. Finally, it has been highlighted by Aksoy that Turkey is determined to carry on preservation of the privileges of Turkey along with Turkish Cypriots in the Eastern Mediterranean.[58]

When we come to the possible transportation of Eastern Mediterranean gas reserves primarily to the European markets, one can also easily deliberate some important problems regarding the probable gas suppliers. In the case of Algeria, the country's natural gas output had reached its maximum level at 88 bcm per annum in 2005 prior to the decrease to the estimation of 85 bcm within 2015. The expected flow of brand-new south-west gas projects has anticipated augmenting the output to 100 bcm per annum as of 2020. On the other hand, the same thing will occur with the internal usage. For the Observatoire Méditerranéen De L'Energie's (OME) conservative scenario, Algerian gas exportation stays envisioned to be slightly more in 2030 when compared with the situation in 2010-over 50 bcm and also just 35 bcm as of 2040).Within the context of OME's proactive scenario study, Algeria's exportation capacity possibly be doubling as of 2030 to over 70 bcm and stand more than 60 bcm as

---

[57] Örmeci, Kısacık, ibid., pp. 40-41.
[58] Örmeci, Kısacık, ibid., pp. 41-42.

of 2040. However, there have similarly existed criticisms on the absence of adaptation of European foreign policies toward Algeria, primarily the design of an attractive model to incorporate Algerian gas within the European energy market. The Algerians do view an absence of clarity within the framework of designing future European energy markets specifically the natural gas's position within the European energy mix, the effect of decarbonization goals or the absence of intra-EU natural gas interconnections between Mediterranean Europe and the remaining parts of the continent. Furthermore, the current Euro-Mediterranean framework stands incapable of addressing Algerian choices or to incentivize energy reform within the country. In this context, Algeria stays uninterested in deepening its free trade area with the EU – even if the latter intends for the renegotiation- in that in contrast to what might occur within Morocco, Egypt, Tunisia, it does not grant any preferential tariff access for its exportations that stand nearly mostly oil and natural gas. European energy policy accompanied by brand-new global realities may importantly impact on Algerian policies, decreasing or augmenting the incentives for internal energy reform.[59]

Libya may stand another important alternative for forthcoming oil and natural gas supplies however the existing security framework hinders the country to benefit from its current output and exportation capacity not to discuss for attracting the foreign investment. When we talk about other Mediterranean natural gas reserves exclusively the brand-new offshore eastern Mediterranean findings stand years ahead of commencing the production. Such factors as low natural gas prices, the uncertainty over the evolution of global LNG markets, absence of infrastructures and geopolitical volatility might further postpone important quantities to be presented within the market. The Cairo case shows the uncertainties related to the global LNG market developments, geopolitics and also energy policy reform. In the aftermath of turning out to be a net natural gas buyer over the past years, it remains anticipated that within the early times of next ten years, Cairo will begin to be a gas exporter again. According to the OME's conservative scenario study, its export potential will stay some 17 bcm as of 2030, however as of 2040, Egypt will turn out to be a marginal gas exporter, on the other hand, according to the proactive scenario study, Cairo's export capacity may reach above 30 bcm as of 2030 and decrease to nearly 25 bcm by 2040.[60]

Here in that case, Israel and GCA can too transform themselves from energy importers to exporters thanks to advancing their offshore natural gas fields. When we come to the Israel, 60 percent of the electricity acquired is originated from the natural gas generated from the Tamar field. The advancement of the Leviathan field has not begun yet because of regulatory problems, which have resulted in the advancement hardly competitive with inexpensive LNG

---

[59] Gonzalo Escribano, "The Political Economy of Energy in the Mediterranean", **Routledge Handbook of Mediterranean Politics**, Richard Gillespie, Frederic Volpi (Ed.), New York, Routledge, 2018, pp. 239-240.
[60] Escribano, ibid., p. 240.

importations. The firms that control both fields have made numerous deals for the natural gas exportations to Egypt, Jordan and Palestine however geopolitical confrontations, absence of regional exportation infrastructure, low natural gas prices as well as unclear regulatory contexts bring important challenges into the agenda. According to the outlook of OME's, it is projected that Tel-Aviv's natural gas exportation capacity to reach its highest level within the second half of the 2020s at nearly 20 bcm per annum, however to decrease sharply to unimportant stages as of 2040. When GCA is considered, this country may add another 5 bcm per annum between 2025 and 2040 for the exportation capacity of the region if the Aphrodite field were to be advanced. But, in order to realize this, the differences / confrontations with Turkey ought to be resolved. Some analysts think that a more balanced geopolitical order does come into the forefront in the Eastern Mediterranean and envisage a Turkish-Israeli rapprochement that will result in a breakthrough in terms of benefiting from its natural gas reserves. However, the geopolitical complexities do assist to a depressed natural gas market condition in decreasing firms' willingnesses to make investments towards the offshore natural gas reserves of the region.[61]

When considered from the LNG option on the transportation of Eastern Mediterranean natural gas, it should be discussed that the European market is one of the most important markets that is coming into the agenda. The countries within the Europe continent are dependent on the natural gas that they are highly consuming. Due to this structure, Europe facing with several challenges in the energy supply security attaches sui generis importance to the LNG transfer in constantly and uninterruptedly accession places to the energy reserves and also to lessen the associated risk situations the Eastern Mediterranean geography which is very strategically positioned between the east and the west in terms of market opportunities does not suffice in within the context of LNG facilities. Regarding the transfer of the resources to be acquired from the region in the form of LNG, the facilities in the Egypt come into the forefront. Here, the LNG facilities having the total capacity of 19 bcm in Idku and Damietta regions exist. Those facilities are 90 kilometers far away from Egypt's Zohr and GCA's Aprohodite fields and also nearly 7 kilometers away from Israel's Leviathan Basin. Thus, it will be benefited from already existing unused facilities via the pipelines to be constructed from the joint fields to Egypt's LNG terminals. Additionally, Israel plans to construct floating LNG storage and floating storage regasification units (FSRU) in the field that belong to it. Within this context, the Israeli Delek and its American partner Noble Energy firms have agreed on the pre-feasibility studies of those floating LNG terminal with Golar LNG and Exmar companies. With these facilities, it is envisioned to transfer into the energy markets by LNG tankers after the processing of nearly 2,5-5 million tons (approximately 3,5-7 bcm) of natural gas per annum.[62]

---

[61] Escribano, ibid., p. 240.
[62] Sina Kısacık, Gamze Helvacıköylü, "Doğu Akdeniz'deki Enerji Temelli Askeri Güvenlik Gelişmelerinin Türkiye'nin Doğu Akdenizli Komşuları ve Küresel Güçlerle Olan İlişkilerine Yansımaları", **UPA**

In line with these issues, one of the countries that possess an important superiority with regard to the geographical location, energy infrastructure in terms of LNG remains Turkey. In Turkey, there exist four facilities – two of them are LNG and two of them floating storage regasification facilities which can be enlisted as follows:

Marmara Ereğli LNG Plant: being operational since 1994, it includes the capacities of 17 million cubic meters (mcm) of gasification daily and 225 hundred thousand cubic meters storage in total,

Egegaz-Aliağa Plant: being operative since 2001, it encompasses the capacities of 40 mcm gasification on a daily basis and 280 hundred thousand storage in total,

Etki Liman Floating Storage Regasification Plant: Under the ownership of Etki Liman İşletmeleri Doğalgaz İthalat and İhracat A.Ş., it has become operational in 2016 as Turkey's first FSRU terminal. In terms of storage, this terminal has the capacity of 170 hundred thousand cubic meters on a daily basis and it is able to supply 28 mcm to national gas network and lastly,

Hatay-Dörtyol Floating Storage Regasification Facility: being formally operational in 2018, this terminal supports Turkey's energy infrastructure thanks to its 263 hundred thousand storage and daily 20 mcm gasification capacities.[63]

In addition to these facilities, with the third FSRU to be constructed by BOTAŞ and stationed at offshore Saros, Turkey will have an important strategic superiority regarding this issue within its region. Turkey makes LNG imports from 11 different countries by the abovementioned facilities. Thanks to this feature, Turkey comes after Spain and France in Europe region within the context of LNG imports. In addition to this, when the last ten years are examined, it is observed that there has been twofold increase in the LNG imports of Turkey. Therefore, when the progress concerning this issue is taken into the account, we can easily see the strategic superiority of Turkey on the transportation of Eastern Mediterranean natural gas in the form of LNG. In case of the fully becoming operational of these plants, Turkey will technically be able to re-gasify 30 bcm of LNG per annum. Within this context, Turkey is an important global player in terms of LNG. Together with this, Turkey which targets to increase its underground natural gas stock capacity to the levels of 10 bcm is making progresses to transform into purchase / buy-sale center rather than a transit route within the framework of global energy markets.[64]

On the other hand, within this framework, it has to be set forth that on

---

Strategic Affairs, Vol. 1, No.1, 2020, pp. 105-106, https://dergipark.org.tr/tr/download/article-file/1646181 (Access 10.05.2021).
[63] Kısacık, Helvacıköylü, ibid., p. 107.
[64] Kısacık, Helvacıköylü, ibid., pp. 107-108.

January 28, 2021, Catharina Sikow Magny; Director DG Energy European Commission (EC) has underlined the natural gas prospects for the EU from today to 2050s. Charles Elinas has mentioned that according to Magny, Europe is likewise refraining from gas and also new gas pipelines. For Sikow, the EU will need zero natural gas. Magny believes that together with the EU's commitment toward net zero emissions as of 2050, due to this factor, there will stand zero unrestricted gas spent in Europe. Furthermore, because of EU's increase the emissions lessening objective from 40% to 55% as of 2030, the consumption of gas in Europe will remain declining with the aim of meeting the 2030 and 2050 climate targets. Magny considers that continuing natural gas projects are anticipated to stand finalized as of 2022 and therefore there will not be any more required. Also in line with this, due to the increasing difficulty exporting gas to international markets, there exist other alternatives to benefit from the natural gas up until now within the East Med encompassing the power generation to support alternating renewables and petrochemicals, as it is done by Egypt. The freshly established East Med Gas Forum (EMGF) ought to focus on these issues.[65]

Here it should be mentioned that on December 31, 2019, the huge Leviathan field has begun the production.[66] Following this, Israel has speedily begun exporting some portion of its new gas resource to Egypt through the reversal of the pipeline within the Sinai which had previously transferred Egyptian gas to Israel. Just because Egypt represents self-sufficient in terms of gas at the moment, the Israeli natural gas will assist in the activation of Egypt's mothballed liquefaction facilities and enable Egypt again to turn out to be a LNG exporter.[67] In line with this development, the then Egyptian Energy Minister Tarek el-Molla has stated that "Europe stands our customer. We possess the ready-made solution. We hold the infrastructure." After this, Israel Energy Minister Yuval Steinitz has underlined that "We have discovered much more than we can consume" which is applicable not only for Israel. Then as it has mentioned above, Greece, Israel and GCA have made a deal for constructing an 1180-mile undersea pipeline that will be able to transfer Eastern Mediterranean natural gas to Greece and later on to Italy. In that point, as discussed above in detail that Turkey has quickly expressed its objections to the project by claiming that this pipeline will be crossing its waters. Then Ankara has sent its warships in order to escort the drilling ships into the waters that GCA alleges as its own EEZ.[68]

According to Daniel Yergin, a world-famous expert on international energy issues, has underscored the Israel Energy Minister Steinitz's statement on the

---

[65] Charles Ellinas, "Gas developments in the East Med", https://energypress.eu/tag/iea/ (Access 11.05.2021).

[66] https://www.voanews.com/middle-east/israels-leviathan-field-begins-pumping-gas (Access 11.05.2021).

[67] https://www.timesofisrael.com/in-milestone-israel-starts-exporting-natural-gas-to-egypt/ (Access 11.05.2021).

[68] Daniel Yergin, **The New Map: Energy, Climate, and the Clash of Nations**, Great Britain, Allen Lane- An Imprint of Penguin Books, 2020, p. 257.

findings in the Eastern Mediterranean has come for us a complete surprise. Yergin believes that this should not be regarded as a surprise anymore. Yergin underlines that in today's conditions, those waters stand barely considered of as a lifeless sea when examined within the context of resources. Yergin is of the opinion that the Eastern Mediterranean remains a brand-new and lively component within the global energy industry and in terms of geopolitics as well as stays altering the map for both of them. Yergin highlights that the Eastern Mediterranean geography possibly will stay potential natural gas supplier not only for Europe but also for the world markets via liquefied natural gas. However, for Yergin, it should be kept in mind that the regional politics occur in such a way that it will similarly carry on to stand as a sea of confrontation.[69]

On the other hand, as of March 9, 2021, Israel Energy Minister Yuval Steinitz has stated that his country has had negotiations about the exportation of natural gas to Turkey but this has not put forward any concrete results. Steinitz has also mentioned that Turkey might stand as the part of the Eastern Mediterranean Gas Forum in the forthcoming years. Tel Aviv stays prepared to collaborate with Turkey concerning natural gas within the Eastern Mediterranean. When the East-Med Pipeline is considered, according to the experts on this issue, it will not be probable for filling the pipeline with the existing proven natural gas resources located at the Israel's Eastern Mediterranean offshore and also even if Egypt is included in the project, the feasibility of the project sets on prospective fresh findings of reserves in the region. Moreover, the GCA and Israel have settled for starting talks regarding the commercial use of contested natural gas resources overlapping their maritime border within the Eastern Mediterranean. Within this context, a deal has been made by Nicosia and Tel-Aviv following a nine-year dispute on the basis that the border of Israel's Yishai natural gas field overlaps with the border of the Aphrodite gas field situated at the parcels one-sidedly proclaimed by the GCA. This deal has been declared by Natasa Pilides, energy minister of the GCA, and Israel Energy Minister Yuval Steinitz. Pilides has underlined that *"an important step was taken to resolve the nine-year deadlock regarding resources in the open seas. We have agreed on a framework to solve the problem during Steinitz's visit. The guidelines will be conveyed to the companies involved in the project. The framework will be set out in a joint letter which is being prepared. We are both very satisfied we are now at this point after nine years of discussion."[70]*

As of April 22, 2021, Turkey has invited Israeli Energy Minister Yuval Steinitz to join an international diplomacy conference held in Antalya in June 2021. The request, the first since relations between the countries have collapsed following the killing of 60 Palestinians in Gaza by the Israeli forces in 2018.[71] In case of the approval decision of Steinitz to take part in the event, it might stand the first such high-level visit to Turkey by an Israeli official within recent terms. The

---

[69] Ibid., pp. 257-258.
[70] Jeyhun Aliyev, "Israel says ready to cooperate with Turkey on E.Med gas", https://www.aa.com.tr/en/middle-east/israel-says-ready-to-cooperate-with-turkey-on-emed-gas/2170312 (Access 05.05.2021).
[71] Tüysüzoğlu, Kısacık, ibid., pp. 281-287.

Turkish official, talking namelessly, has stated Middle East Eye that Steinitz may well be present some conferences in the conference as a speaker, encompassing such subjects as energy, specifically gas, and regional issues. Here within this framework, it has to be pointed out that Turkey and Israel have been carrying out negotiations to overhaul their lowered relationships ever since last year via intelligence services. Israel, openly and via the media, has required Ankara fire some Hamas leaders from Turkey, who Israel considers as terrorists. Turkey has recommended in the negotiations to interchange ambassadors and return relationships in ordinary diplomatic canals, nonetheless reiterated Israeli elections and the nonexistence of a steady government there has until now blocked any improvement. Within that, the decision of Ankara for the invitation of Steinitz should not be a surprising one when considered from Steinitz remarks at the beginning of March 2021. In line with these developments, Turkish Foreign Minister Mevlüt Çavuşoğlu has previously addressed that Turkey is prepared for the reexamination of its affiliations with Israel if its leaders alter their policies headed for the Palestine.[72] However, this offer has formally been withdrawn by Turkey as of May 11, 2021 due to the increasing attacks toward the Palestinians by Israel.[73]

On March 13, 2021, Turkish Foreign Minister Mevlut Çavuşoğlu has stressed that subsequently years of unsettled links; "Turkey and Egypt[74]" have started again diplomatic-level dialogues. In accordance with this statement, Çavuşoğlu has further shared the details of this issue as follows;

> *"We have contacts at both the level of intelligence and foreign ministries with Egypt. Diplomatic-level contacts have started. Neither side put forth preconditions, since ties were derailed back in 2013; they cannot be mended quickly or easily. A lack of trust is also normal in such situations and may exist for both parties. For this reason, negotiations take place and continue under a certain strategy, a roadmap. There used to be occasional talks with Egyptian Foreign Minister Sameh Shoukry when they met at international meetings, including when they met in New York two years ago."*[75]

In line with this initiative, as of April 15, 2021, Foreign Minister Mevlut Çavuşoğlu has mentioned that "Turkey will send a diplomatic delegation to Egypt early next month or talks intended for repairing relationships tense for

---

[72] Ragip Soylu, "Turkey invites Israeli energy minister to Antalya forum in rare outreach", https://www.middleeasteye.net/news/turkey-israel-high-level-visit-invitation-energy-minister-yuval-steinitz (Access 05.05.2021).

[73] https://www.ekovitrin.com/politika/turkiye-israil-enerji-bakani-na-gonderdigi-daveti-geri-cekti-h250975.html, https://www.dailysabah.com/politics/diplomacy/turkey-cancels-israeli-ministers-invite-over-recent-aggression, https://www.middleeasteye.net/news/turkey-withdraws-invitation-israeli-minister-attacks-palestinians, https://www.middleeastmonitor.com/20210512-turkey-cancels-invite-issued-to-israel-minister-following-attacks-on-al-aqsa/ (Access 19.05.2021).

[74] For the relations between Turkey and Egypt from 1990 to 2020 please see, Arda Özkan, "Türkiye-Mısır İlişkileri", **Soğuk Savaş Sonrası Türkiye'nin Orta Doğu ve Kuzey Afrika Siyaseti,** Pınar Yürür, Göktürk Tüysüzoğlu, Arda Özkan (Ed.), Ankara, Detay Yayıncılık, 2020, pp. 793-850.

[75] https://www.middleeastmonitor.com/20210313-turkey-egypt-restart-diplomatic-talks/ (Access 05.05.2021).

years due Islamist politics and regional conflicts." Within this context, Turkish Foreign Affairs Minister Çavuşoğlu has added that "Egypt has summoned a delegation from Turkey. The delegation will visit Egypt at the beginning of May. The talks will be made at the level of deputy foreign ministers."[76] The possible rapproachment between Ankara and Cairo has been evaluated by Turkey's Presidential Spokesperson Ibrahim Kalın on April 26, 2021 as follows;

> *"Given the realities on the ground I think it's in the interests of both countries and the region to normalize relations with Egypt. Rapprochement with Egypt will certainly help the security situation in Libya because we fully understand that Egypt has a long border with Libya and that may sometimes pose a security threat for Egypt. Turkey would discuss security in Libya, where a United Nations-backed transitional government took over last month, with Egypt and other countries. We have an agreement that is still holding there with the Libyan government."[77]*

It should be underlined here that freshly, conversely, symbols of a potential settlement have emanated from both countries, predominantly owing to the changing aspects within the Eastern Mediterranean and the Turkey-Greece crisis regarding the energy reserves in the region. In a sign to Cairo last month, Turkey has demanded from Egyptian opposition television channels working within its territory to temper criticism of el-Sisi. Egypt has greeted the initiative nevertheless has been openly careful on Turkish appeals for healthier connections between the two countries which have correspondingly sponsored conflicting parties within the framework of existing confrontation in Libya.[78] On May 5, 2021, in the early times, Egypt has verified that political talks with Turkey will occur in Cairo on May 5-6. The discussions will be made under the leadership by Deputy Foreign Affairs Minister and Ambassador Sedat Önal and his Egyptian counterpart Hamdi Sanad Loza, the Foreign Ministry. It has been underlined that *"the exploratory talks will focus on necessary steps that may lead to normalization of relations between the two countries at the bilateral and regional context."*[79][80]

---

[76] Selcan Hacaoglu, "Turkey, Egypt Plan Talks on Restoring Ties in Early May", https://www.bloomberg.com/news/articles/2021-04-15/turkey-egypt-plan-talks-on-restoring-ties-in-early-may (Access 05.05.2021).

[77] https://www.dailysabah.com/politics/diplomacy/turkish-egyptian-talks-may-bring-peace-to-libya-kalin (Access 05.05.2021).

[78] Ibid.

[79] Iyad Nabulsi, "Egypt confirms talks with Turkish delegation to be held May 5-6", https://www.aa.com.tr/en/middle-east/egypt-confirms-talks-with-turkish-delegation-to-be-held-may-5-6/2229726 (Access 05.05.2021), https://www.reuters.com/world/middle-east/egypt-turkey-hold-two-days-talks-normalisation- push-2021-05-04/ (Access 05.05.2021).

[80] On May 4, 2021, the official statement on this issue by the Republic of Turkey Ministry of Foreign Affairs of Turkey is as follows: *"Political consultations between Turkey and Egypt, co-chaired by H.E Ambassador Mr. Sedat Önal, Deputy Minister of Foreign Affairs of Turkey and H.E Ambassador Mr. Hamdi Sanad Loza, Deputy Minister of Foreign Affairs of Egypt will be held on 5-6th May 2021 in Cairo. These exploratory discussions will focus on necessary steps that may lead towards the normalization of relations between the two countries bilaterally and in the regional context."* https://www.mfa.gov.tr/no_-174_-turkiye-ile-misir-arasinda-gerceklestirilecek-siyasi-istisareler-hk.en.mfa (Access 05.05.2021).

Escalation of the Conflict Through Militarization Initiatives

Within this context, it stands correspondingly assumed that countries evaluate their naval power sets in accordance with their initiatives in the Eastern Mediterranean. When the NATO undertakings stay also take part in this picture, 71 warships from 19 countries stay profoundly positioned in the region presently. When the continuous increase in the numbers accompanied by the deployment is considered, as detailed by Alfred Mahan, the states energetically exercise their naval powers to achieve their hegemonic objectives. It should to be thought about in this routine that, according to the National Defence Ministry of Republic of Turkey on June 23, 2019, Turkish Fatih and Yavuz deep-sea drilling vessels and Barbaros Hayrettin Paşa Seismic Vessel that have been working at the Eastern Mediterranean are safeguarded by the Turkish Naval Forces. As put forward by the Ministry, the Naval Forces ensure the complete defense of Turkey's drilling ships all over the sea and also underneath the water underlining that the defensive drones, planes, helicopters, corvettes, frigates, and submarines remain organized intended for the taking part when it stays prerequisite.[81] As a significant constituent of Turkey's initiatives protecting both its and TRNC's privileges resulting from the international law for Cyprus, Ankara has adopted to establish a drone base in Northern Cyprus.[82] Within this framework, Bayraktar TB2 armed unmanned aerial vehicles from Naval Air Command in Dalaman, Aegean Turkey, did land in TRNC at 10 a.m. (0700GMT) after granting a green light by Turkish Cypriot government on December 16, 2019.[83]

Professor Nurşin Ateşoğlu Güney, a member of Turkey's Presidential Security and Foreign Policy Council, states that Turkey's initiative should be viewed noteworthy for the vessels' security inside the waters adjacent northern Cyprus. Furthermore, it stays respectively underscored by Güney that, thus far, Turkey was executing operations, exactly surveillance or information placed out of Dalaman. Güney mentions that this initiative of Ankara will empower the alertness of these actions along with making certain security. As stated by Güney, this maintains the safety accompanied by information gathering and inspection undertakings of the Turkish Navy, which is backing up in the drilling actions wherein this initiative ought to be perceived as a weighty message for the GCA. In contrast, Professor Güney has highlighted that as a result of this initiative of Ankara, the U.S. Senate may perhaps perform to cancel the 1987 arms embargo on Southern Cyprus. She has similarly put emphasis on within this circumstance that *if this embargo is lifted, it would encourage Southern Cyprus to arm itself and exacerbate instability in the region as well as hurt peace talks referring to the decades-long, on-and-off peace*

---

[81] Erdoğan Çağatay Zontur, "Turkish Navy protecting Oruc Reis in East Mediterranean", https://www.aa.com.tr/en/europe/turkish-navy-protecting-oruc-reis-in-east-mediterranean/1937752 (Access 11.05.2021).

[82] Michael Jansen, "Turkish military drone begins patrols off Cyprus", https://www.irishtimes.com/news/world/europe/turkish-military-drone-begins-patrols-off-cyprus-1.4119585 (Access 11.05.2021).

[83] Örmeci, Kısacık, ibid., pp. 47-48.

talks between the two sides of the island".[84]

Compared to these initiatives of Turkey, Greece and GCA have not been irresolute to pursue security opportunities contrary to Turkey. One of these initiatives stands the backing of the EU via military power. For example, the EU has agreed to advance its security collaboration with the PESCO (Permanent Structured Organization) initiative in 2017. This initiative includes 25 EU member states, plus Greece and GCA (PESCO). As a component of this organization, the transfer of French and German naval forces to the region has been considered, as well as monetary aid thought through for GCA. The organization has been viewed within the Greek Cypriot media as "The Protection Shield Agreement for Cyprus".[85]

GCA has wished to empower its stance counter to Turkey similarly through increasing collaboration in terms of its mutual relationships with other states. One of them has stayed the ratification of a military assistance pact between the Defence Ministers of Greek Cypriot administration and France on May 15, 2019. In line with this pact, France has held the privilege to benefit from Evangelos Florakis Naval Base situated in the Mari region of South Cyprus. Furthermore, it has been affirmed that this naval base will remain updated so as to ensure continuously positioning of French Navy within the region. Among the clause of this pact, the required funding will be delivered by Paris. In conjunction with the deal, unrestricted deployment of French Charles de Gaulle aircraft carrier stands intended for. Consistent with another clause within the deal, the French Navy particularly promises over the safeguarding of the ships discovering hydrocarbons belonging to TOTAL nearby Cyprus.[86] Similarly, according to this deal, France and GCA will stay working together counter to the undertakings of the Turkish Navy within the region. Within the framework of this arrangement, it is identified that France will too look at the settings within the military bases positioned at the Greek part of the island, will contribute to the modernization of weaponry systems of Greek National Guard Army, and will upturn the amounts of mutual exercises. On the other hand, this pact does come into the meaning of the open abuse of Security and Guarantee Agreements that founded the Cyprus Republic in 1960. Additionally, France has sponsored the GCA's membership into the PESCO plus its partaking in 8 programs within the milieu of this initiative. The upgrading of Mari Naval Base under the EU support has been intended to be finished in 2021.[87]

---

[84] Örmeci, Kısacık, ibid., pp. 48-49.

[85] Sina Kısacık, Fahri Erenel, "Doğu Akdeniz Güvenlik Algılamaları Bağlamında, Kalıcı Yapılandırılmış İşbirliği Savunma Anlaşması (The Permanent Structured Cooperation- PESCO) ve Enerji Güvenliği Meselelerinin Avrupa Birliği-Türkiye İlişkilerine Olası Yansımalarını Anlamak", **Türkiye Siyaset Bilimi Dergisi**, Cilt 2 Sayı 1, 2019, pp. 64-67, https://dergipark.org.tr/en/download/article-file/856440 (Access 15.05.2021).

[86] Xavier Vavasseur, "Defense Cooperation Agreement Between Cyprus And France Comes Into Force", https://www.navalnews.com/naval-news/2020/08/defense-cooperation-agreement-between-cyprus-and-france-comes-into-force/ (Access 11.05.2021).

[87] Örmeci, Kısacık, ibid., pp. 49-50.

On January 29, 2020, Greece's Prime Minister, Kyriakos Mitsotakis, has welcomed the French decision to transport war frigates to the Eastern Mediterranean as a standoff with Turkey concerning regional energy resources develops. With severities between Athens and Ankara prompting ascending international fear, Mitsotakis has named the vessels as "guarantors of peace" and underlined that *the only way to end differences in the Eastern Mediterranean is through international justice. Greece and France are pursuing a new framework of strategic defence.* Mitsotakis stood there in the French capital on a visit anticipated to collecting EU sponsorship at a time when hostile relations with Turkey have masked all other problems on the agenda of his nearly seven-month-old government.[88] French President Emmanuel Macron, instead, has guaranteed that France will increase its strategic connection with Greece[89], accusing Turkey of not only deteriorating regional severities but also failing to commit on its assured strategy within battle-damaged Libya.[90] Two French Rafale jets have flown over South Cyprus on February 2, 2020, to display French existence on the island.[91] This issue has been evaluated by the Ministry of Foreign Affairs of Turkey as follows:

> *"The agreement in question is against the 1960 Treaties and the equilibrium established by these treaties. There is also a risk of disrupting the efforts to ensure stability and security in the eastern Mediterranean. The Greek Cypriot administration, which does not represent the entire island nor Turkish Cypriots, is not competent and authorized to make such an agreement. It is unacceptable for France to take steps to further increase the tension in the current period, to organize joint exercises with the Greek Cypriot Administration in this context and to deploy military aircraft here contrary to the 1960 Treaties, albeit temporarily. Turkey supports the reaction and statements made by the authorities of Turkish Cyprus on the defense deal between Greek Cyprus and France. We invite France, permanent member of the U.N. Security Council, to act more responsibly on Cyprus-related issues that are on the U.N. agenda."*[92]

Along with these developments, Greece has similarly augmented its military operational exercises with the GCA in terms of land, and Athens has organized land and air exercises with Tel-Aviv. Besides this, the formation of an army shielding the seas in the name of protecting the pseudo EEZs between Israel and the GCA has been settled in 2012 and has been established to guarantee this by

---

[88] Nicholas Paphitis, Suzan Fraser, "Greece welcomes French navy presence in Meditteranean", https://apnews.com/article/turkey-cyprus-athens-mediterranean-sea-france-5c92284d081e82e9db4f2361b0d37194 (Access 12.05.2021), Bobby Ghosh, "Macron's Muscle-Flexing Will Make Mediterranean Tensions Worse", https://www.bloomberg.com/opinion/articles/2020-08-14/macron-s-muscle-flexing-will-make-turkey-greece-conflict-worse (Access 12.05.2021).

[89] https://www.france24.com/en/20200913-greece-arms-up-with-new-fighter-jets-frigates-amid-heightened-turkey-tensions (Access 12.05.2021), https://primeminister.gr/en/2021/01/25/25723 (Access 12.05.2021).

[90] Örmeci, Kısacık, ibid., p. 50.

[91] https://www.duvarenglish.com/diplomacy/2020/08/12/french-jets-land-in-greek-cyprus-as-part-of-defense-agreement (Access 11.05.2021).

[92] https://www.hurriyetdailynews.com/turkey-slams-french-greek-cyprus-defense-deal-157424 (Access 11.05.2021).

submarines and torpedoes. In accordance with this, Egypt has likewise preferred to extend military collaboration with GCA. Within this perspective, Cairo has augmented the multinational military exercises namely Medusa 6 and Arab Shield-1 in the sea fields plus has instigated to build 3 naval bases to defend its supposed EEZs, which have been incompatible with Turkey. Contrariwise, the U.S. has likewise commenced a rapprochement process with Nicosia in recent years. For example, consistent with "H.R.1865 – Further Consolidated Appropriations Act, 2020" law presented by Republican representative Bill Pascrell, U.S. arms embargo concerning GCA (Cyprus Republic) – which has been in force ever since 1987 – has newly abandoned by Washington (U.S. Congress). TRNC Foreign Ministry and Deputy Prime Ministry have harshly criticized this decision, while Turkey has correspondingly assessed the decision and judged U.S. policy as a determination to impede solution in the Island of Cyprus and collaboration chances within the Eastern Mediterranean by underscoring the prevention of the transfer of F-35 aircraft to Turkey.[93]

On the other hand, as of March 18, 2021, EU leaders in December had suggested asset restrictions and travel embargoes on Turkey's "unauthorized drilling undertakings" for natural gas in unclear waters in the eastern Mediterranean, even though they did not identify persons. Moreover, the EU had similarly decided to deliberate harder economic sanctions at a summit on March 25-26, afterward a tough year in which Turkish President Tayyip Erdogan articulated openly his expectation that demonstrations in France would knock down President Emmanuel Macron. Nevertheless a more positive attitude from Erdogan this year, German Chancellor Angela Merkel's backing for a more peacemaking attitude and the first direct discussions between old adversaries Turkey and Greece within five years have completely facilitated to transform the temper. The new administration of U.S. President Joe Biden has correspondingly advised Brussels not to enforce sanctions at a time when Turkey, a NATO ally and EU candidate country, seems more eager for cooperation. According to an EU diplomat, "Work has stopped on additional blacklistings of Turkish individuals, and we are not talking of economic sanctions anymore." For another EU diplomat, "the work at no time actually launched" and also a third EU diplomat has underscored "the diplomatic trajectory is being prioritised".[94] In accordance with these developments, by March 25, 2021, EU leaders would make a debate through video conference regarding the circumstances in the Eastern Mediterranean and concerning the EU's relationships with Turkey, proposing to develop collaboration with Ankara, however similarly impended to execute sanctions if Turkey resumes search over undecided hydrocarbons within the eastern Mediterranean. The important points of the European Union Council Meeting are as follows:

---

[93] Örmeci, Kısacık, ibid., pp. 50-51.
[94] Robin Emmott, John Chalmers, Tuvan Gumrukcu, "Exclusive: EU halts sanctions on Turkey oil executives as ties improve", https://www.reuters.com/article/us-turkey-eu-exclusive-idUSKBN2BA1KP (Access 11.05.2021).

"We recall the European Union's strategic interest in a stable and secure environment in the Eastern Mediterranean and in the development of a cooperative and mutually beneficial relationship with Turkey. We welcome the recent de-escalation in the Eastern Mediterranean through the discontinuation of illegal drilling activities, the resumption of bilateral talks between Greece and Turkey and the forthcoming talks on the Cyprus problem under the auspices of the United Nations. Turkey has shown a more constructive attitude. However, we also know this process of de-escalation remains fragile."[95]

These conclusions of EU Council Meeting issued on March 25, 2021 have been evaluated by Turkey as follows:

"It is in contravention of international law to "adjudicate" that the drilling activities of Turkey and the TRNC are "illegal" by the EU which, in the name of solidarity, overlooks or fails to restrain the maximalist stance and unilateral provocative actions of the Greek-Greek Cypriot duo. The EU has neither authority nor jurisdiction on this matter. Statements regarding Cyprus on the other hand, intended to defend Greek Cypriots' interests, are detached from reality and do not contribute to a possible reconciliation. Non-reference yet again to the Turkish Cypriots and their legitimate rights and interests in the conclusion, attests to the continuation of EU's partial and prejudiced stance regarding Cyprus."[96]

Conclusion

With the discovery of energy reserves in the Eastern Mediterranean region at the beginning of 21st century has transformed this region as one of the most noteworthy regions in terms of regional and global energy security parameters. In line with this, especially the finding of huge natural gas reserves in the offshore regions of Israel, Egypt and GCA as well as in other parts of the Eastern Mediterranean such as Lebanon and so on, the inner and outer regional countries have been directing their concentrations over the drilling and transportation of these resources into the international markets. Therefore, all related parties independent from being inner regional or outer regional countries, have been putting forward several comprehensive strategies to be influential on the benefiting from the natural gas bonanza within the Eastern Mediterranean region.

In accordance with these developments, Israel-GCA-Egypt troika has been focusing on the commercialization of their natural gas reserves via pipelines or LNG. But one has to be kept in mind that the monetization of natural gas resources in the Eastern Mediterranean region faces with some problems. One can enlist some of them as the protracted Cyprus Question, Israel-Palestine,

---

[95] Kostis Geropoulos, "EU offers Turkey deeper ties but threatens sanctions over East Med drilling", https://www.neweurope.eu/article/eu-offers-turkey-deeper-ties-but-threatens-sanctions-over-east-med-drilling/ (Access 11.05.2021).

[96] https://www.mfa.gov.tr/no_-120_-ab-devlet-ve-hukumet-baskanlari-mart-zirvesi-sonuclari-hk.en.mfa (Access 18.05.2021).

Israel-Lebanon Confrontations, the impacts of Arab Revolts within the Middle East region and so on. In this sense, it should also be remembered that due to the lack of mutually agreed compromise among the regional countries on the delimitation of EEZ within the region, each state declares their EEZs, signs agreements and also invites international energy companies to pursue discoveries and drillings within their self-declared areas. This initiative ends up with the border confrontations between the littoral states as in the cases of Turkey-GCA-TRNC and also Israel-Lebanon, Israel-Palestine in terms of international law.

When we come to the commercialization of Eastern Mediterranean natural gas reserves, two pipeline and one LNG plant projects have been put forward by the associated parties. However, when these three options are thoroughly examined, it is clearly seen and supported by many international energy experts and some countries that firstly the construction of a pipeline between Turkey and Israel and later on the transportation of Eastern Mediterranean gas to international markets will stand as the most economical, rational and profitable one. Such offers to monetize Eastern Mediterranean gas as East-Med Pipeline as well as in LNG form are considered by many energy experts as uneconomical, hard to construct, lack of sufficient volumes and so on. However, some states like Israel, GCA have been working on the realization of East-Med Natural Gas Pipeline in which this is strongly supported by Washington and Brussels. Nonetheless, when considered from the Tel-Aviv's point of view, there have been continuing discussions to implement a pipeline option with Turkey. On the other hand, I do believe that the recent massive attacks towards the Palestinians in Al-Aqsa Mosque in Jerusalem and also in Gaza by Israel within May 2021, together with Turkey's right and harsh criticisms toward Israel[97], this option will highly likely to be postponed into some indefinite time within the forthcoming terms.

When the militarization of the Eastern Mediterranean energy geopolitics, the inner as well as outer regional countries that have been attaching sui generis prominence towards the energy reserves in the region, have been increasing their efforts on this issue via comprehensively benefiting from their military powers in order to protect their national interests. Although it is generally considered as a rational choice to benefit from the military capacities for the preservation of national interests, especially the intervention of such outer regional countries as France and USA to support Israel-Egypt-GCA-Greece Quartet diplomatically and militarily as well as to prevent as well as criticize Turkey's legitimate initiatives derived from international law in the Eastern Mediterranean do force Ankara to use its hard and soft power capabilities so as to protect not only its interests but also the rights of TRNC in a right manner grounded on international law.

Consequently, when the current and possible energy security paradigms within the Eastern Mediterranean in the 21st century is examined by taking into

---

[97] For a detailed analysis on this issue please see, Deniz Tansi, "Mescid-i Aksa'da Çağların Yangını", http://politikaakademisi.org/2021/05/11/mescid-i-aksada-caglarin-yangini/ (Access 19.05.2021).

consideration the abovementioned assumptions, it can clearly be inferred that the existing as well as prospective energy security paradigms in terms of Eastern Mediterranean in the contemporary era will definitely be determined by inner / outer regional countries' all-inclusive strategies either work for collaborations or confrontations with the intention of benefiting from natural gas richnesses positioned at this region in the near and longer terms

TURKEY'S INTEGRATION OF ITS MIDDLE EAST - EASTERN MEDITERRANEAN (ME-EM/MEM) AND CYPRUS (MEM-C) STRATEGIES IN ITS FOREIGN POLICY

Soyalp Tamçelik*

Introduction

Turkey, which is a medium-sized power in world politics, has been confronted with many regional and global problems over the past 40 years. Faced with numerous chaotic issues in its foreign affairs, Turkey's main policy, strategic plannings, areas of action or political attitudes have inevitably been disrupted. This has created difficulties for Turkey in structuring its global and regional policies and has revealed the need to reconsider its foreign policy.

Turkey's structural and traditional values in the foreign policy, which can be called as *The Paradigm of Turkish Foreign Policy* (TFP), is far from meeting the requirements of the currently changing regional and global political developments. Facing these difficulties Turkish governments either find *temporary (paliatif)* solutions to the problems or fail to develop a *fundamental* approach. The *fear of indeterminity* that a change of TFP might cause, leads Turkey to a timid and overcautious approach in diversifying its foreign policy. This approach in TFP has long been pursued or been effective in its international relations. At present, Turkish policymakers need more than ever to produce new policies, develop new strategies, and even restructure or revise their major policies. It can be said that the new strategic approach that Turkey should develop for its foreign policy stem from external, in other words, global and regional forces and pressures rather than the country's internal dynamics.

From this point of view, this study is based on the thesis that while addressing Turkey's policies towards the *Middle East (ME)* and the *Eastern Mediterranean (EM)*, the operational policies of both regions should not be considered separately, one should not fall behind the other, or one should not be prioritized while the other is neglected. Accordingly, it is considered that policies implemented on the contrary will not constitute a sustainable model for the TFP. In this study, it is suggested that Turkey should re-plan its policies towards the two problem areas and in this regard, create policies that anticipate change. This argument is considered to be the *basic assumption*. Accordingly, the foreign policy paradigm suggested in Turkey's practices regarding both regions is based on being *integrative* rather than regionally separating, assuring regional rather than

---

* Professor. Dr. Soyalp Tamçelik, Ankara Hacı Bayram Veli University, Faculty of Economics and Administrative Sciences, International Relations Department, E-mail: soyalp@hotmail.com, ORCID ID: 0000-0002-2092-8557.

local transitivity in the execution of national interests; and in terms of realization of political goals, being *deep* rather than superficial and developing an *intellectual education* and *diplomacy tradition* related to this.

Some of the problems Turkey experienced in adapting to the changing international system after the Cold War era were strongly reflected in its foreign policy. Continuing its efforts to adapt to the global system, TFP and its leaders have resorted to various means to protect Turkey's interests and meet its needs. Since 1991, while assessing the changing global conditions, TFP decision-makers have considered the worldview based on *regional security* and *stability* as the only immutable element of Turkey's foreign policy. Therefore, Turkey; since it evaluates all national and international issues from regional stability to energy policy, from climate policies to global health, from liberal economy to global terrorism, in Cold War terms or with this worldview, could not break the habit of defining or interpreting its foreign policy with securityist approaches, perceptions or imaginations. This stance on foreign policy has become a traditional pattern of behavior as it became more radical and has gradually turned into an extremely conservative trend. This situation has led Turkey to evaluate many events and crises in its foreign policy from a *desecuritizing* perspective.

Although Turkey has made some current changes in its foreign policy conceptions after the Cold War, it has considered and evaluated the political stance towards each region as separate, non-integrated or independent. As a result, Turkey's policies towards the *ME* and *EM* are disconnected or separated from one another.

Evidently that the radical changes in the *ME* after the Cold War and the recent conflicts of interest in the *EM* have caused serious problems in Turkey's foreign policy. It is clear that the common value of these two problem areas is *to establish superiority in energy policy* and *to expand the field of domination*. Therefore, in this study, the propositions put forward for the *ME* and the *EM* will be tried to be structured within the framework of energy policy and on an integrated conceptual map.

In the scientific literature, it is known that Turkey has prepared many reports regarding the *ME* or the *EM*. However, in no report or study have Turkey's policies towards the *ME* and the *EM* been evaluated from an *integrative* perspective. In this study, this geography, which is considered as two independent fields, is examined as a whole and therefore a strategic meaning has been assigned to it by conceptualizing the policy towards it as the *ME-EM Diplomacy*. Thus, it is aimed to balance Turkey's political, strategic and national security interests towards the region with an *integrated* perspective, to draw a political framework and finally to avoid wasting time and effort.

There is no doubt that the political framework we are trying to outline with this study is assertive and stimulating. In fact, another aspect that makes this study important is the emergence of energy, immigration and economic dynamics in the *EM*, the determination of maritime jurisdiction areas and numerous related conflicts, and the risk of terrorism, irregular migration and the fragmentation of states in the *ME*.

In order to consider the two areas as a whole, it will be essential to evaluate the old and new considerations for the region and to make political inferences. Therefore, it is necessary to make historical and political evaluations about the region. In this study, instead of dealing with daily events in both regions, a method suitable for process analysis was chosen to determine where the phenomena evolved to or in which direction the transformation took place. In order not to complicate the study, the subject has been systematized with a diachronic perspective and analytical evaluations. However, as this was done, Turkey's interests and political considerations in the region were examined and evaluated together.

In this study, the main objective of the new doctrine proposed for the TFP is to evaluate the political considerations about the *ME* and the *EM* within the framework of *energy politics*, to understand these two independent areas as a whole or as a monolithic field (*ME-EM*) and to develop a new foreign policy towards this region. Without a doubt, this doctrine, which can also be called "*ME-EM Diplomacy*" in the TFP, or the foreign policy proposed to be implemented on this basis, is a new approach.

The main idea of this study arose from the need to revise Turkey's strategy towards the *EM*. For, Turkey's regional policies have reached a difficult point, due to the alliance structures in which it finds itself or the EU's *spirit of solidarity*. The policies pursued by some actors in the international system toward the affected regions after 2015 have caused order-changing or destabilizing events in the *ME* and the *EM*. This situation has undermined TFP's priorities, restricted its activities, hindered its interests and enabled regional actors to adopt an aggressive and confrontational approach against Turkey.

It is evident that Turkey needs a *comprehensive, integrated* and *holistic* strategy in order to increase the stability in the *ME* and the *EM* and to transform the regional balance in its own favour. Regarding the *ME*, a holistic strategy for Turkey is based on the peaceful resolution of the conflict in Syria, the purification of the region from terrorist organizations such as the PKK/YPG, and the prevention of the process of state construction of terrorist structures while in the *EM*, it is based on the stabilization of the region and the protection of the legal rights and interests of Turkey/TRNC. The intensity of conflicts of interest, anti-democratic practices, deterioration of the demographic structure etc. destabilize the region and challenge Turkey's approaches and decision-making mechanisms towards this region.

Due to these difficulties, it is desired to draw attention to the thesis that Turkey's policies towards the *ME* and the *EM* should not only be interdependent, but should also be *combined* with a *unified* and *integrated* approach. Based on this thesis, it's argued that while regional actors or global powers have not yet determined their *grand strategies* regarding the region, Turkey should redefine its *ME* and *EM* strategy, turn it into an encompassing, inclusive and integrative *high policy document*, conduct doctrinal work on this subject and that Ankara should maintain its presence in the region and expand its sphere of influence.

In this context, the study consists of three parts. In the first chapter, the place and the importance of the *EM* in international politics and global system will be discussed and evaluated in terms of regional and global actors. In addition, the specific gravity of the actors emerging and playing an active role in the region and the policies they want to shape according to their own interests will be examined. In this chapter, the Russian Federation (RF), Iran and Turkey will be specifically evaluated and the future of the region which transforms the *EM*, undermines the state structures, causes irregular migration, accelerates social transformation and provokes arguments on security and sovereignty as a result of energy discoveries will be discussed. In the second chapter, the catalysts for transformation and change in the region will be highlighted. In the third and final chapter, strategic objectives and instruments that can be used will be discussed.

It is considered that this study, which is intended to be seen as a modest contribution to Turkey's regional policies, will enable an Ankara-centered foreign policy evaluation, guide Turkey in its process of establishing relations with the international system, in its strategic depth and tactical efforts and provide an opportunity to analyze systematic data and to implement accessible policies. In this respect, it is proposed that Turkey may realize its interests in the region, play a role in shaping the region, help increase its security and economic prosperity, and as a result, it can gain the ability to build and implement the *ME-EM Doctrine* and the diplomacy related to it.

High Goals Strategy Towards the ME-EM in Turkish Foreign Policy

The list of goals proposed for the *ME-EM* in the TFP, consists of systematized standards of judgments and patterns. However, these patterns are not composed of static normative rules. Hence, it would be appropriate to state that it consists of a series of values that can change, be shaped or revised in time and space. In this study, the framework of the *ME-EM* or the *MEM* Diplomacy conducted in Turkey's foreign policy can be better explained and the issues dealt with and the basic approaches will be better grounded through the utilization of the Normative Theory, which has been used in the analysis of various international issues since the end of the Cold War and is known as one of the most important International Relations Theories. Based on the "normative theory", the set of values desired to be constructed for the TFP or the set of goals related to it was constructed on the "founding theory" of Mervyn Frost, who contributed to the associated theory.[1] It is argued that the two regional and problematic areas in international relations, such as the *ME* and the *EM*, can

---

[1] Mervyn Frost, "The Role of Normative Theory in IR", **Millennium**, Vol. 23, No.1, 1994, pp. 109-118.

help define, interpret, and produce permanent solutions to "hard cases",[2] as Frost stated. One of the main objectives has been to assess the Constitutive Theory[3] understanding based on "established norms" in the International Relations discipline with regard to Turkey's *ME-EM* and *MEM* Diplomacy, solve major normative issues and create a "background theory". It will be essential to base Turkey's and TRNC's social rights and historical interests on the *ME-EM* and *MEM* Diplomacy by making a change in the Constitutive Theory[4] which aims to solve the normative dilemma[5] between *individual rights* and *sovereignty*, and thus prioritizing the subject of being a community instead of individual rights.

Turkey's Strategic Objectives Regarding the Resolution of the Syrian Issue and the Stabilization of the Region

It is clear that Turkey's interests and security will be severely damaged if the decade-long conflict in Syria is not resolved in the near future. The irregular migration flows from Syria mainly affect Turkey, Jordan and Lebanon, and then Europe, undermining and threatening the social order.

This is mainly due to the fact that Salafi jihadist groups have used the geography of Syria as a base to coordinate attacks in Europe and beyond. Other international actors who use these factors as an excuse, are taking advantage of this situation to intervene on the ground and basing their positions on the principle of legitimacy. Based on this, the RF used the conflict in Syria as a tool to increase its power and influence in the *EM*, while Iran considered Syria as a proactive policy element. On the other hand, Turkey has started a diplomatic process to end the conflict in Syria, unlike the RF and Iran; however, it could not manage this process as it wanted. The risk of division in Syria due to its internal problems has increased the *insecurity* by threatening Turkey's interests or destabilizing the region. Accordingly, the biggest challenge for Turkey is that the humanitarian drama in Syria is great and the persecution against humanity will continue for many years.

As can be seen, none of the options that the Ankara administration faces in Syria are particularly desirable. First of all, the conditions of the uprising period that began in Syria in 2011 are very different from those of today. However, the Ankara administration's inaction or moderate behavior in foreign policy has reduced Turkey's influence in the region or has caused it to become controversial. In addition to Turkey, the involvement of the RF and Iran in particular has completely changed the balance. The military intervention of the

---

[2] Mervyn Frost, **Ethics in International Relations**, Cambridge: Cambridge University Press, 1996, p. 98.
[3] See Mark Hoffman, "Normative International Theory: Approaches and Issues", **Contemporary International Relations: A Guide to Theory**, GROOM, A.J.R./Light, Margot (eds.), London, 1994, pp. 27-44.
[4] Peter Sutch, "Global Civil Society and International Ethics: Mervyn Frost's Restatement of Constitutive Theory", **Review of International Studies**, Vol. 26, No.3, 2000, pp. 485-489.
[5] Zerrin Ayşe Bakan, "Normative Theory in IR: Frost's Constitutive Approach", **Ankara Üniversitesi SBF Dergisi**, Cilt. 63, No.1, Ocak-Mart 2008, pp. 3-16.

RF in September 2015 to protect the Assad regime has profoundly changed the conflict on the ground and shifted all balances in the region. This attitude of Iran and the RF has naturally limited the military and political options of Turkey, the United States and other allies, and restricted their activities on the field.

Ankara's *Euphrates Shield Operation* in northern Aleppo in August 2016 and *Operation Olive Branch* in Afrin in January 2018, weakened the dominance of terrorist groups in Syria such as the Democratic Union Party (Partiya Yekitiya Demokrat/PYD), People's Protection Units (Yekineyen terrorists such as Parastina Gel/YPG) and the Syrian Democratic Forces (SDF), which are known to have connections to Turkey's separatist terrorist organization PKK, and reduced expectations for an independent Kurdish state in the region.[6] While this has re-shifted the balance on the ground, it has also complicated U.S. foreign policy preferences and options in the region.[7] Meanwhile, Iran's growing military presence in Syria was considered as a challenge to Turkey's interests in the region, or to the U.S. and its allies. However, by not repeating previous mistakes, Turkey has not excluded or ignored Iran as an actor in its regional policies, or has not engaged directly in a conflict with it.[8] The Ankara administration has foreseen Iran's acting capacity in the new period and has preferred to locate itself and its power according to the methodology of systemic behavior in foreign policy.

Turkey, for its part, feels that the RF and Iran's interventions in the region are undermining the political will to resolve the dispute, while the U.S. and its allies believe that this situation endangers their interests in the region. In particular, the U.S. and its allies perceive that while shaping their policies for the region, their foreign policy scope is progressively narrowing and their options are significantly limited. For example, although the U.S. has deployed about 2,000 troops to fight the Islamic State of Iraq and Damascus (DAESH) and attempted to provide humanitarian assistance to forced migrants, it is known that one of its main objectives is to help and protect the PYD/YPG elements, which are terrorist organizations. The U.S. administration, which has supplied tens of thousands of truckloads of ammunition and weapons, has provided $7,4 billion[9] in aid to those elements in the region since 2011, yet has faced a high foreign policy cost as a result of the serious problems it has had with Turkey.

Though the U.S. as a global and hegemonic power supported the UN-led *Geneva Process* to find a solution in Syria, this process has fallen behind and been overshadowed by the Turkey-RF-Iran led *Astana Process*. The U.S. administration,

---

[6] Deniz Yıldırım, "Zeytin Dalı'nın Beş Kritik Sonucu", Aydınlık.com.tr, 24.1.2018, https://www.aydinlik.com.tr/zeytin-dali-nin-bes-kritik-sonucu-deniz-yildirim-kose-yazilari-ocak-2018, (Access 01.02.2020).

[7] Necati Tarakçı, "Afrin Harekâtı'nın Güncel ve Potansiyel Stratejik Sonuçları", TASAM, 22.02.2018, https://tasam.org/tr-TR/Icerik/50198/afrin_harekatinin_guncel_ve_potansiyel_stratejik_sonuclari, (Access 01.02.2020).

[8] Anoushiravan Ehteshami, "Middle East Middle Powers: Regional Role, International Impact", **Uluslararası İlişkiler**, Vol. 11, No.42, 2014, pp. 36-39.

[9] "U.S. Humanitarian Assistance in Response to the Syrian Crisis", U.S. Department of State, 21 September 2017, https://www.state.gov/r/pa/prs/ps/2017/09/274360.htm, (Access 01.02.2020).

which remained only an observer in the Astana Process, was unable to carry out the desired foreign policy action and could not achieve the desired outcome in the Russian-led *Sochi* talks. The U.S. administration, seeing Turkey as the cause of this situation, has held the Ankara administration responsible.

However, in terms of Ankara's administration, the *Astana* negotiations represent a number of important processes such as the reduction of tensions, the implementation of a ceasefire, the provision of humanitarian aid, the establishment of military bases in the region and the inclusion of local elements in the process.[10] However, the regime's attacks in the rural areas of Idlib and Damascus in early 2018 completely shifted the balances.

At a time when the U.S. expanded its military operations to fight DAESH in Syria in 2017, it focused on political and power discussions with its ally Turkey and its global rival RF. Subsequently, the U.S. focused on ceasefire zones in the region and to that end, engaged in a political and military power struggle with Turkey, the RF and Iran. However, none of this means that Turkey has no political options.

After a decade of violence in the region, the Assad regime was revealed to have *"won"*[11] the civil war with the help of the RF and Iran, although it had only partially reunited the country. However, the fact that Bashar Assad's legitimacy is problematic or that the consent of the Syrian population is unclear, was far from confirming this view. It is clear that the Damascus administration must maintain control over the political, social and economic spheres within Syria's borders in order to restore stability and put an end to the violence. Turkey, which asserts that anything that guarantees Syria's territorial integrity will also guarantee regional integrity and stability,[12] argues that any result that undermines Syria's territorial integrity will lead to further conflicts, destabilize Syria's neighbors and will not be limited to Syria.

The actors who want to shape the post-conflict environment in Syria, particularly Turkey, the U.S. and other actors, are in a constant political struggle and tension. For example, the U.S., which wants to play an active role in this process, has intensified its diplomatic efforts and tried to encourage the Kurds of the region and their terrorist regime to assume limited autonomy in northern Syria.[13] This has disturbed many actors in the region, including Turkey, and led them to undertake efforts to neutralize U.S. foreign policy actions. For, the

---

[10] "Astana Toplantısında Sonuç Uzlaşması", Haber Türk, 15.05.2018, https://www.haberturk.com/astana-toplantisinda-sonuc-uzlasmasi-1966764, (Access 01.02.2020).

[11] Mehmet Barlas, "Esad Savaşı Kazandı Ancak Barışı Kazanamadı", Sabah, 04.09.2018, https://www.sabah.com.tr/yazarlar/barlas/2018/09/04/esad-savasi-kazandi-ama-barisi-kazanamadi, (Access 01.02.2020).

[12] Ceyda Karan, "Suriye'nin Parçalanması, Türkiye'nin Parçalanması Demektir", Sputnik Türkiye, 11.10.2016, https://tr.sputniknews.com/ceyda_karan_eksen/201610111025247776-turkiye-suriye-politikasi-ismail-hakki-pekin/, (Access 01.02.2020).

[13] "YPG: Yerel Bir Örgütten, NATO Ülkelerinin Desteklediği Bir Güce Nasıl Dönüştü?", BBC News Türkçe, 29.10.2019, https://www.bbc.com/turkce/haberler-dunya-50180068, (Access 01.02.2020).

optional foreign policy action proposed by the U.S. jeopardizes the social and territorial integrity of the other states or peoples in the region.[14] In this regard, the U.S. administration both worries and threatens many countries by its foreign policy in Syria.

According to the U.S., the parameters outlined by former Foreign Secretary Rex Tillerson on Jan. 17, 2018, should be considered a starting point for Syria. Accordingly, the U.S. administration proposed not to provide direct aid to the Syrian regime, to negotiate a post-conflict political agreement, to keep the affected regions under the current regime until the implementation of a political solution and to provide assistance for the reconstruction of these regions after that.[15] Consequently, the government control in Syria will be ensured and, thereby, the intervention or effectiveness of foreign powers in Syria, such as Turkey, the RF and Iran, will be gradually reduced. On this basis, the U.S. has led the current regime in Syria, which has violated human rights, to restore its control over the country and has partially attempted to legitimize it. This proposal of the U.S. shows that it does not hesitate to ignore regional balances, the moral situation and human rights. According to the Syrian Human Rights Group, until mid-2017, Assad's forces killed 192,793 civilians, including 21,631 children.[16] It is also alleged that the regime used banned chemical weapons against civilians.[17] As long as Assad remains in power, the Syrians that revolted in 2011, the main driving force, have almost no chance of escaping the brutal regime's authoritarian rule. Moreover, once the Assad regime has taken control, it is out of the question for opposition groups that had turned to violence to remain or to disappear. From this point of view, it does not seem possible to reach a solution in the near or distant future in Syria, and the conflict is expected to continue.

Certainly, Turkey and other foreign actors are not in a position to resolve Syria's internal problems and decide who will rule Syria. Therefore, Turkey must clearly determine its objectives such as accelerating the future settlement process for Syria, balancing its regional interests and ensuring its security. While determining its foreign policy actions in Syria and the ME, Turkey also is confronted with a mission to prevent U.S. influence in the region, the Russian or Iranian dominance on the ground and other actors' (PKK/PYD/YPG/SDF and

---

[14] Amur Gadjiev, "ABD'nin Çok Ata Oynama Yaklaşımı, Türkiye'yi Oyalayıp Suriye'yi Parçalamaya Yönelik", Sputnik Türkiye, 23.07.2019, https://tr.sputniknews.com/columnists/201907231039742898-abdnin-cok-ata-oynama-yaklasimi-turkiyeyi-oyalayip-suriyeyi-parcalamaya-yonelik/, (Access 01.02.2020).
[15] Rex W. Tillerson, "Remarks on the Way Forward for the United States Regarding Syria", U.S. Department of State, 17.01.2018, https://www.state.gov/secretary/remarks/2018/01/277493.htm, (Access 01.02.2020).
[16] "Civilian Deaths", Syrian Network for Human Rights, 01.09.2017, http://sn4hr.org/, (Access 01.02.2020); **Restoring Eastern Mediterranean as a U.S. Strategic Anchor**, A Report of the CSIS Europe Program and CSIS Middle East Program, Authors: Jon B. Alterman, Heather A. Conley, Haim Malka, Donatienne Ruy, Center for Strategic and International Studies (CSIS), New York, 2018, p. 32.
[17] Dan Kaszeta, "Suriye İç Savaşı: Sinir Gazı Dehşeti Geri Döndü", BBC News Türkçe, 05.04.2017, https://www.bbc.com/turkce/haberler-dunya-39502236, (Access 01.02.2020).

Assad regime) forces. This mission leads to having a say on the situation in the region, the progress of the negotiation process and the future of Syria. However, this is not an easy problem to solve as Turkey expects. Although conflicts seem to have decreased in some parts of the country, the conditions for a political solution are quite challenging. Firstly, it is necessary to reach an agreement on some serious issues such as the reconstruction of Syria, the withdrawal of foreign fighters, the return of refugees and the rehabilitation of internally displaced persons.

In addition to its military actions in the region, Turkey wants to play an active diplomatic role, realize its regional interests, prevent the destructive activities of the U.S. and its allies, ensure regional credibility and restore stability. With *"Operation Peace Spring"* launched on October 9, 2019, Turkey seems to have neutralized the U.S.' and other actors' strategy to establish the Kurdish corridor/state. Turkey, while preventing the planned "terror corridor" from being built on its southern borders, is trying to make this outcome permanent by cooperating closely with the RF and Iran.[18] To this end, Turkey is directly engaged in the fight against terrorist groups and DAESH on the ground, continuing its diplomatic and military power struggle with non-regional actors in Syria, trying to balance local forces apart from Kurdish separatist groups on the ground, and it is trying to implement its own plan through the *Astana* and *Sochi* processes in addition to the UN-led *Geneva Process*. This indicates that the Ankara administration is openly reacting to and distrusting the Syrian policy of the U.S and its allies, and the Kurdish separatist elements. Although the Geneva process is proceeding slowly, DAESH's dominance in the region has decreased significantly. However, in Idlib and many parts of the country, Salafi-Jihadist groups and their affiliates continue to challenge regional and global actors and the international system. Therefore, it would be advisable for the Ankara administration to pursue the following four main objectives as foreign policy actions in order to suppress these and similar separatist terrorist groups and to ensure a permanent success. Accordingly:

Analysis of Turkey's Perception of Security Threats towards the *ME* and Possible Hypotheses

Turkey's security analyses for the *ME* are based on a hypothetical 4-step case. Accordingly, when Turkey's foreign policy behavioral analysis is evaluated, these four elements are expected to appear:

- Turkey's Prevention of the Expansion and Use of Force of Iran itself or Iranian-Backed Armed Elements in the *EM* via Syria

Turkey needs to take a pre-emptive position against Iranian military attempts in Syria by preventing Tehran's capability to use force. Iran's efforts to make

[18] **Gülsen Solaker,** "Barış Pınarı Harekâtı: Tamam mı, Devam mı?", Deutsche Welle Türkçe, 29.11.2019, https://www.dw.com/tr/bar%C4%B1%C5%9F-p%C4%B1nar%C4%B1-harekat%C4%B1-tamam-m%C4%B1-devam-m%C4%B1/a-51457261, (Access 01.02.2020).

Syria and the Syrian regime dependent on itself disturb Turkey and other regional powers and pose a serious threat by destabilizing the *ME*. More specifically, the U.S. and Israel want to prevent Iran from establishing permanent military bases in Syria, setting up weapons production facilities, establishing a *land bridge* that will open to the Mediterranean, and are pushing hard for the withdrawal of Iranian soldiers and Iranian-backed foreign fighters.[19] Given the Tehran administration's strategic partnership with the Assad regime, it is expected that Iran will maintain its military and intelligence units in Syria in the near future. Since Iran's approach towards the PYD/YPG and its behavior in line with the Shiite policy in the region will disturb Turkey, it is considered that Turkey should aim to limit or minimize the Iranian presence in Syria as much as possible. In order to quell Iran's foreign policy actions in Syria and the region, the Ankara administration will first have to gradually reduce Iran's prospective operational presence in Syria or keep it to a permanent minimum. Therefore, developing an effective *ME* policy for Turkey and preventing the Iranian policy of establishing a land bridge to the *EM* is a behavior consistent with the *ME* and the *EM* policies that must be integrated.

- Turkey's Defining All Salafi-Jihadist Groups in the *ME* and the PYD/YPG/SDF Elements as Terrorists

It is a fact that Turkey's intense struggle on the ground and the joint efforts of the U.S. and its allies played a critical role in DAESH's defeat in Syria. By the end of December 2017, DAESH had lost nearly 98% of its area in Iraq and Syria.[20] However, Salafi-Jihadist groups affect or threaten Turkey and Western powers in various ways. The first location of Salafi-Jihadist groups is in northwestern Syria, particularly in Idlib and Hama, where the Al Qaeda affiliated Heyet-i Tahrir al-Sham (HTS) and other Salafist militant groups operate.[21] As Al Qaeda and other Salafi-Jihadist groups find a safe environment in Syria, they threaten Turkey and other regional/global actors, harm their interests, and cause further instability as a party to the internal conflict in Syria.

Reasons such as DAESH terrorist groups in the region of Der ez-Zor (Deir ez-Zor) located in northeastern Syria and on the Euphrates River apply irregular warfare techniques in the region, oppose the PYD/YPG groups, which are among other terrorist elements in northern Syria, commit destructive terrorist activities beyond the southern border of Turkey and in Western Europe have led them to be considered as threats.

Turkey's security bureaucracy and decision makers view and consider DAESH as a divisive and destructive element of terrorism at least as much as the

---

[19] "Suriye'nin Güneyindeki Amerikan Üssünün Dolaylı Hedefi: İran", Amerika'nın Sesi, 26.07.2018, https://www.amerikaninsesi.com/a/suriye-nin-g%C3%BCneyindeki-amerikan-%C3%BCss%C3%BCn%C3%BCn-dolayl%C4%B1-hedefi-iran/4500601.html, (Access 29.01.2020).
[20] "Update on the D-ISIS Campaign", U.S. Department of State, 21 December 2017, https://www.state.gov/r/pa/prs/ps/2017/12/276746.htm, (Access 29.01.2020).
[21] Lina Sinjab, "İdlibliler Türkiye'nin HTŞ'nin Gücünü Kırmasını Umuyor", BBC News Türkçe, 28.02.2019, https://www.bbc.com/turkce/haberler-dunya-47404409, (Access 02.02.2020).

PYD/YPG elements. According to the opinion of the Ankara administration, in the fight against DAESH it is stated that there is no country more effective than Turkey; that time, manpower, money and especially human resources are used for this and that a high price is paid for this purpose. Another assessment of the Ankara administration is that it considers DAESH as a terrorist group such as elements of the PYD/YPG,[22] that no distinction should be made between them, that the use of another terrorist group while fighting Salafi-Jihadist groups justifies terrorism and it must be avoided, and the terrorist elements of the PYD/YPG in northern Syria should not be considered as *"freedom fighters"*.[23] However, most NATO allies and regional actors do not agree with this assessment of Turkey and legitimize those elements by engaging with them. This shows that many actors in the region do not support Turkey in its fight apart from DAESH, neutralize the intervention against the PYD/YPG elements and leave Turkey alone in its policies towards Syria. However, when Turkey's activities towards Syria in particular and towards the region and terrorist elements in general are systematically assessed, they are found to be consistent and synchronized with each other. Turkey advocates for the territorial integrity of Syria, the change of the Assad administration that caused instability in the region, a total reconciliation, the restoration of democratic order, the defining of all illegitimate elements in the region as terrorists, as well as ensuring that the PYD/YPG are not considered separate from the elements of DAESH and believes that this situation is essential to ensure regional and global stability.

- Turkey's Prevention of the Creation of a "Regional Kurdish Administration" In Syria or an "Autonomous Kurdish Administration" within the United Syrian Borders

The U.S., France, Israel, the United Arab Emirates, Saudi Arabia and many other regional and global actors support a limited autonomous administration for the Kurds in northern Syria. As in Iraq, there is a desire to start a negotiation process with the central government in Damascus and to establish autonomy by making the necessary constitutional changes to ensure the autonomy of the Kurds in Syria. However, to achieve this, it is argued that this should not imply risks for other actors defending Syria's territorial integrity, that competing interests should be balanced and that diplomatic skills should be maximized. Ankara is seriously concerned about this situation, is alerting NATO allies and other actors about the difficulties that the current situation will create, and is using diplomatic channels to address these concerns. However, when the Ankara administration failed to achieve a result from these, it launched the *"Olive Branch Operation"* in Afrin on January 28, 2018 against YPG terrorist elements. *Operation Olive Branch* was the operation launched by the Turkish armed forces and the Syrian National Army (SNA) groups in the Afrin district of Aleppo province in Syria and in the city of Tel-Rifat of Azez district and has brought Turkey to a

---

[22] **Türkiye'nin DEAŞ ile Mücadelesi**, T.C. İçişleri Bakanlığı, Ankara, 2017, p. 16.
[23] "In Pictures: PKK Fighters Prepare for Battle with IS", BBC News, 20.08.2015, https://www.bbc.com/news/world-middle-east-33991464, (Access 29.01.2020).

position that altered the balance[24] in the region.

With this operation of Turkey, the U.S. administration stood with its *conjunctural allies*, in an environment dominated by the YPG and SDF consisting of many ethnic groups, but it had difficulties in supporting them. The U.S. did not approve of this operation and stated as its grounds for objection that SDF elements supported by coalition forces fighting DAESH were harmed and that Turkey was not supportive of the fight against DAESH. According to the U.S. and its allies, the most effective force fighting DAESH is the SDF, the PYD/YPG and a number of other groups.[25] According to this view, the Kurdish administration is in a relatively stable position in the areas controlled by SDF elements in northeastern Syria, and it is stated that the SDF has a number of important economic assets from holding some of the largest oil and gas fields in the country.[26]

In fact, one of the reasons for the U.S. to support the terrorist elements of the SDF and the PYD/YPG is to present them as an important source of influence against Turkey, the RF, Iran and the Assad regime in the negotiations for Syria. Supporting the creation of a Kurdish corridor in northern Syria and the establishment of a partial autonomy in the region, the U.S. is trying to eliminate Iran's efforts to establish a *land-bridge* through its forces in Syria, Iraq and Lebanon.[27] Moreover, the U.S. administration prefers to call them *"freedom fighters"* rather than *"terrorists"* as expressed by Turkey, as it considers the aforementioned Kurdish groups to be the most powerful elements fighting terrorist elements such as DAESH.[28] U.S. administration's willingness to keep the terrorist elements of the PYD/YPG on its side is due to the fact that they can prevent the emergence of DAESH and other groups from arising in the future, and that it considers these groups as potential troops it can deploy to this end.

The U.S. administration believes that even a limited *autonomy* in northern Syria, where the Kurdish population has a majority, will offer a series of strategic advantages and will facilitate regional balances. It is believed that if a large number of Syrian Kurds from other parts of Syria gather in the northern regions of the country and if autonomy is given to this region, relative stability will be

---

[24] Murat Yeşiltaş, "Zeytin Dalı Harekâtı: Kazananlar ve Kaybedenler", SETA, 20.03.2018, https://www.setav.org/zeytin-dali-harekati-kazananlar-ve-kaybedenler/, (Access 02.02.2020).

[25] "SDG Lideri Mazlum Kobani: SDG, Suriye'nin Milli Gücüdür Yasal Boyut Kazanmak İstiyoruz", Şarkul Avsat, 17.12.2019, https://aawsat.com/turkish/home/article/2039586/sdg-lideri-mazlum-kobani-sdg-suriyenin-milli-g%C3%BCc%C3%BCd%C3%BCr-yasal-boyut-kazanmak, (Access 02.02.2020).

[26] "Suriye'nin Ne Kadar Petrolü Var? Kim Kontrol Ediyor?", Euronews, 07.11.2018, https://tr.euronews.com/2019/11/07/suriye-ne-kadar-petrolu-var-kim-kontrol-ediyor-trump-bagdadi-oldu-petrol-sahalari-guvenlik, (Access 02.02.2020).

[27] David Adesnik and Behnam Ben Taleblu, **Burning Bridge The Iranian Land Corridor to the Mediterranean, Center on Military and Political Power**, Foundation for Defense of Democracies Washington, DC, FDD Press, 2019, p. 7, 13.

[28] "In Pictures: PKK Fighters Prepare for Battle with IS", BBC News, 20.08.2015, https://www.bbc.com/news/world-middle-east-33991464, (Access 29.01.2020).

achieved and the refugees will not flee to other countries.[29] Apart from that, if the local Kurdish elements gain autonomy in northern Syria, the U.S. administration will not deal with the central administration in Damascus or the Esat dictatorship. In addition, it will allow the U.S. administration to organize or design the local and regional Kurdish administration as it desires. With this method, the U.S. administration is trying to legitimize the existence of Kurdish regional elements, which it considers and evaluates as *core allies* in the region and in the diplomatic field., Trying to reconstruct Syria, the U.S. administration aims to avoid being perceived as an unreliable actor who left the Kurds halfway or did not stand behind them, as happened in Iraq, at least it does not want to jeopardize its credibility. However, none of these views are considered to be satisfactory by the Ankara administration. Therefore, Ankara's administration proposes to go directly to the field with the U.S. and other allies, not to use intermediary elements and to fight against all kinds of terrorist organizations.[30] When this view of the Ankara was not accepted by the U.S. and its allies, Turkish decision-makers predicted that the establishment of the *'Regional Kurdish Administration'*, could prepare the ground for a *'Kurdish State'* in the future through a reasonable, moderate and rationalized political consideration process and by making radical decisions to prevent this, they felt the need to reconsider Turkey's foreign policy behavior.

- Turkey's Prevention of Conflict between Israel and Iran in Syrian Territories and Deepening Its Strategy towards the Region

Israel, which has long fought the Iranian-backed Hezbollah, sees Iran's presence in Syria as a serious threat. Therefore, Israel is prepared to use any means to eliminate Iran's military and technological activity in Syria. In fact, the Israeli administration has made it clear that it can use military power against the Iranian regime, Hezbollah forces, Assad's authoritarian rule and other targets in Syria. The Israel Defense Forces (IDF) are currently positioned to counter Iran-Hezbollah forces in an area near Israel's Syrian border.[31] Israel fears that Iran will establish permanent military bases in Syria, build production facilities capable of delivering sensitive munitions to Hezbollah, or support elements of proxy wars similar to Hezbollah in the region.[32]

---

[29] Joost Jongerden, "Governing Kurdistan: Self-Administration in the Kurdistan Regional Government in Iraq and the Democratic Federation of Northern Syria", **Ethnopolitics,** Vol. 18, No.1, 2019, pp. 61-75, DOI: 10.1080/17449057.2018.1525166, ISSN: 1744-9057 (Print) 1744-9065 (Online) Journal homepage: https://www.tandfonline.com/loi/reno20, p. 69-73.

[30] "No: 297, 11 Ekim 2019, Uluslararası Toplumda Barış Pınarı Harekâtı'nı Hedef Alan Bazı Yorumlar Hk.", T.C. Dışişleri Bakanlığı, 11.10.2019, http://www.mfa.gov.tr/no_297_-baris-pinari-harekati-ni-hedef-alan-yorumlar-hk.tr.mfa, (Access 02.02.2020).

[31] Udi Dekel and Zvi Magen, "Israel's Red Lines on Iran's Foothold in Syria", **INSS Insight 993**, Institute for National Security Studies, 22.11.2017, http://www.inss.org.il/publication/israels-red-lines-irans-foothold-syria/, (Access 02.02.2020).

[32] Daniel C. Kurtzer, "Israel and Hezbollah: Deterrence and the Threat of Miscalculation", Council on Foreign Relations, 11.09.2017, https://www.cfr.org/report/israel-and-hezbollah-deterrence-and-threat-miscalculation, (Access 02.02.2020).

In the security analyses prepared by the Israeli army, the possibility of a high-intensity conflict with Iran or Hezbollah in the region or in the Syrian territory was discussed.[33] However, it seems unlikely that a high-intensity conflict will occur, as military actions by both sides in the region will harm the interests of Turkey and other global/regional players. There is no doubt that the engagement of Iran and Israel in any intense conflict in Syria will undermine the security and stability of the region. Therefore, it is expected that both actors will display a low-intensity conflict profile in the Syrian field and continue their struggle in such terms. Moreover, the strengthening of the Assad regime in Syria and its regaining of control of many parts of the country will trigger greater reactions to Israel's military operations in Syria. A direct war with Iran or Hezbollah is seen as a choice Israel would not want to make, as it would be far more damaging than the 2006 intervention.[34] Otherwise, the negative effects of the intervention on the Israeli economy will be significant.

Israel has not been neutral in the Syrian conflict, but has refrained from joining any side. Since 2011, the Israeli administration has conducted more than 100 military operations to strengthen its deterrence power in Syria and to balance its own interests.[35] As reported in the national press, on December 2, 2017, the Israeli administration staged an air operation on a facility 50 km east of the Israeli-occupied Golan Heights, suspected that it was an Iranian military base and caused the death of 12 Iranian citizens.[36] In April 2018, Israel announced that it had destroyed an Iranian aviation facility after an armed drone entered its airspace. On February 10, 2018, after an Iranian plane infiltrated Israeli airspace and a Syrian SA-5 air defense missile shot down an Israeli F-16, Israeli airstrikes accelerated and many elements that are believed to belong to the Islamic Revolutionary Guard Corps (IRGC) and half of the Syrian regime's air defense system has been destroyed.[37]

Israeli Prime Minister Netanyahu has met with then President Trump and Putin on several occasions to limit the activities of Iran and Hezbollah in Syria. Although Israel, which has significantly lost its air defense capability with the S-

---

[33] Ben Caspit, "Israel, Iran Duel on Syrian Soil", Al-Monitor, 04.12.2017, https://al-monitor.com/pulse/originals/2017/12/israel-iran-russia-syria-us-nuclear-agreement-attacks-idf.html, (Access 02.02.2020).

[34] Lamia Estatie, "2006 İsrail-Lübnan Savaşından Bugüne: Beş Başlıkta Hizbullah'ın Dönüşümü", BBC News Türkçe, 12.07.2016, https://www.bbc.com/turkce/haberler-dunya-36772501, (Access 02.02.2020).

[35] Amos Harel, "'We Prevented Israel from Going to War': Outgoing Air Force Chief on Iran, Gaza and the Conflicts Ahead", Haaretz, 07.12.2017, https://www.haaretz.com/israel-news/1.808556, (Access 02.02.2020).

[36] "Arab Media: 12 Iranians Killed in 'Israeli Strike' in Syria", Times of Israel, 02.12.2017, https://www.timesofisrael.com/arab-media-12-iranians-killed-in-israeli-strike-in-syria/, (Access 02.02.2020); Bassem Mroue, "Syrian State Media: Israeli Missiles Strike Near Damascus", Washington Post, 02.12.2017, https://www.washingtonpost.com/world/middle_east/syrian-state-media-israeli-missiles-strike-near-damascus/2017/12/02/e17c15c0-d73d-11e7-9ad9-ca0619edfa05_story.html, (Access 02.02.2020).

[37] Amos Harel, "Downing of Israeli F-16 Cost Syria Half of Its Air Defences, Claims the IDF", Haaretz, 18.02. 2018, https://www.haaretz.com/middle-east-news/israel-took-out-half-of-syria-s-air-defenses-military-beliefs-1.5808981, (Access 02.02.2020).

400 missile systems deployed by the RF for the Syrian regime, has received President Trump's support on this, its relations with RF are proceeding at a cautious pace. For example, the Tel Aviv administration is aware that its relationship with the RF is tested each time as its planes have to get permission from the RF every time they enter Syrian airspace.

Israel initially requested and insisted on that in any ceasefire agreement in the southwestern region of Syria, the Iranian forces and Iranian-backed Hezbollah elements should remain within 60 to 80 kilometers of the Israeli-Syrian border, as determined for the Golan Heights. According to reports in the Israeli press, the RF administration refused this request of the Tel Aviv administration. RF stated that it could keep Iranian forces and its allies only 5 kilometers from the border.[38]

In fact, the Israeli administration can clearly see that the threat it receives from the region and from Syria is high, that there are many indications that support this and that the tension with Turkey is at the core of this situation. The refusal of the Ankara administration to respond to Tel Aviv's wishes and needs, its strong interest in the Palestinian issue, its establishment of relations with Hezbollah and Al-Fatah groups, its emergence as a disruptive factor in the *ME* that Israel is trying to establish, and its more radical decisions on the *EM*, has caused the Israeli administration to lose its former reliable partner and the balancing actor in the *ME* and the Arab world, and led to a number of new problems.

Therefore, the Ankara administration used the Iranian factor and other actors as triggers and tried to balance its interests in order to control Israel's interests in the region in general and in Syria particularly. While the Israeli administration has more intense problems than Turkey in the *ME*, Ankara's problems with maritime jurisdiction areas in the *EM* are deeper than those of Tel Aviv. This situation may prevent two conflicting forces from balancing each other in *ME* and the *EM* and even provoke a conflict. Therefore, it is expected that the conflict between the parties cannot continue for long.

Turkey's Instruments and Approaches towards its Strategic Goals in Syria

While evaluating the Syrian issue, the Ankara administration is giving priority to its national objectives, strategic expectations and military operations as well as diplomatic initiatives to preserve regional stability. Since American, Russian, British and French military units are currently deployed in Syria, Turkey had to use its military presence and operational power to achieve its strategic objectives. All of Turkey's political and military actions in Syria are intended to rebuild the country, guarantee post-conflict security, protect local/regional interests and

---

[38] Amos Harel, "Israel Demanded 60km Buffer but Russia Let Iranian Forces in Syria Approach the Border", Haaretz, 15.09.2017, https://www.haaretz.com/middle-east-news/syria/1.812328, (Access 02.02.2020).

establish a political order based on the new balances. To achieve this goal, Ankara's administration is trying to use Turkey's significant and sustainable diplomatic initiatives together with its historical and social memory, supported by military and economic instruments.

Accordingly, it is evaluated that the Ankara administration has 4 objectives aimed at finding a solution under acceptable conditions regarding the Syrian issue, and while doing so, Turkey engages in mutually reinforcing and sometimes overlapping actions, develops instruments and approaches as indicated below:

- TFP's Creating a Political Solution for the Syrian Crisis and Building Post-Conflict Security in Syria

Turkey is in direct or indirect communication with all regional and global actors regarding the Syrian issue. However, the actors Turkey has difficulty dealing with are usually Western countries or NATO allies. On the other hand, it appears that the Ankara administration has been successful in creating solutions regardless of the fact that it has not been able to agree on many issues with the RF and Iran, yet. The main reason for Turkey's conflict with its European partners is centered on political, diplomatic, strategic and military issues.

The U.S. continues to participate in the UN-led Geneva negotiations and is trying to lead the process according to its own interests. Although the Ankara administration did not prevent this process, it paid more attention to and contributed more to the Astana process than the other. RF, on the other hand, aims to end the conflict in Syria by proceeding with the Sochi process and pursues its political initiatives in this regard. However, it would not be correct to consider these processes as separate, disconnected or as alternatives to each other. In particular, the attacks on Idlib in late 2017 and on Eastern Ghouta in early 2018 showed that Russia, Iran, and the Syrian regime could violate the agreement reached in Astana.[39]

Another reason for the impasse is that the U.S.-led committee for amending the Syrian constitution failed and that the Syrian regime rejected the constitution. Thereupon, French President Macron proposed the formation of a large "Contact Group on Syria" extending to Turkey, Jordan, Saudi Arabia and Iran.[40] Although the U.S. reappointed the Syrian special envoy to advance Macron's proposal, it was unable to achieve the desired result.

The United Kingdom, France and Germany have shown their support for the military mission by taking the lead in anti-DAESH operations in Syria. Their air forces have coordinated airstrikes against DAESH. In addition, in 2015, the German parliament approved sending 1,200 German troops from Northern Iraq

[39] Veysel Kurt, "İdlib Saldırıları Astana'yı Anlamsızlaştırır Mı?", SETA, 12.01.2018, https://www.setav.org/idlib-saldirilari-astanayi-anlamsizlastirir-mi/, (Access 02.02.2020).
[40] "France's Macron Says New Syria Contact Group to Meet at UN Next Month", Reuters, 29.08.2017, https://af.reuters.com/article/commoditiesNews/idAFP6N1KX00E, (Access 02.02.2020).

to Syria to support military operations in Syria, and within a short period those troops were deployed in the region.[41] Britain and France sent special troops to train opposition forces in Syria, and both countries attacked regime forces on April 13, 2018, accusing the Syrian government of having used chemical weapons in Eastern Ghouta.[42] Likewise, the EU, by providing significant support, wanted to be involved in the issue and tried to strengthen its position as an effective means of influence between the Syrian regime and Russia.

As evidenced, there are many actors involved in the Syrian issue. The radical changes in the region have also drawn in actors from distant geographies. Hence, for Turkey it is not possible to stay out of its issue, neither in theory nor in practice. It should be considered natural for Turkey to provide a reliable solution to the Syrian crisis, to restore post-conflict order in Syria or to build a new one. However, it is not possible for Turkey to be the sole driving force in this crisis, to reshape Syria and the region, and to influence other actors. In this respect, it is assessed that Turkey's foreign policy can be more effective on *what not to do* rather than *what to do* in Syria and the *ME*. While it is certain that Turkey cannot disrupt or direct the order in the region alone, it will be more effective if it shows what cannot happen by using its hard power or activating its military operating capability. Turkey's most important operation in this regard was the *Operation Peace Spring*.

With this move, Turkey is viewed to have prevented the formation of a Kurdish administration with limited autonomy in a united Syria or the creation of a Kurdish state in the future.[43] With its military operation, Turkey has shown that this situation, which it has difficulty in discouraging the RF and other stakeholders from undertaking, *cannot happen* or that it will not allow it to happen. The U.S. administration, on the other hand, supported the transformation of the Syrian Kurds into a body that would meet their own needs, and wanted to turn it into a structure which would not be a threat to the existential values of both the Assad regime and Turkey. For that reason, the U.S. administration chose to define the Syrian Kurds as *"freedom fighters"* or *"those who protect democracy"* by demonstrating their struggle against DAESH and aimed to show the world public their well-deserved autonomy.[44] Yet, in doing so, the U.S. administration has ignored the organic link of the PYD/YPG elements with the PKK terrorist organization. Therefore, the Turkish and Syrian regimes do not accept granting autonomy to the political union formed by the PYD/YPG on behalf of the

---

[41] "Germany Involved in Deadly Syria Airstrike", Deutsche Welle, 29.03.2017, http://www.dw.com/en/reports-germany-involved-in-deadly-syria-airstrike/a-38200203, (Access 02.02.2020).

[42] "Promising Money, EU Tries to Woo Assad into Syria Peace Talks", Reuters, 16.02.2018, https://www.reuters.com/article/us-mideast-crisis-syria-eu/promising-money-eu-tries-to-woo-assad-into-syria-peace-talks-idUSKCN1G01MY, (Access 02.02.2020).

[43] "Dışişleri Bakanı Sayın Mevlüt Çavuşoğlu'nun TBMM Genel Kurulunda Barış Pınarı Harekâtı Hakkında Yaptığı Konuşma, 16 Ekim 2019, Ankara", T.C. Dışişleri Bakanlığı, 16.10.2019, http://www.mfa.gov.tr/sayin-bakanimizin-tbmm-de-yaptigi-konusma-2019.tr.mfa, (Access 02.02.2020).

[44] Fehim Taştekin, "Suriye'de Kürtlerin Özerklik Projesi Neden 'Sırat Köprüsünde' Görülüyor?", BBC News Türkçe, 31.07.2019, https://www.bbc.com/turkce/haberler-dunya-49165120, (Access 02.02.2020.

"Syrian Kurds", even at a minimum level.[45]

While the U.S. considers the establishment of an autonomous Kurdish administration in northern Syria to be in its own interest, it argues that this will be the most appropriate tool for regional stability and will bring a new balance to the *ME*. This process has resulted in a deep difference of opinion and a conflicting environment between the Assad regime and American and Turkish foreign policy-makers. PYD/YPG terrorist elements, which progressively took control of Syria's borders, have gradually begun to expand their territory, to create an international public opinion, to establish legitimacy and to become a political interlocutor in the region.[46] To some extent, the terrorist elements of the PYD/YPG have gone beyond to be an instrument and have emerged as a founding element. With the ceasefire agreement signed in Der ez-Zor, this view was further reinforced.[47] Consequently, it can be said that there is a desire to create an environment of security and legitimacy for the SDF elements and to create a basis for dialogue in the negotiations on Syria. However, this process was interrupted by Turkey's Afrin operation.

- Turkey's Expanding Its Influence and Maintaining its Military Existence in Syria

Turkish military troops are located in the Syrian regions of Afrin, Jalabrus, Al-Bab and, since the last operation, in the areas between Tal Abyad and Rasul Ayn. The largest military units of the Turkish Armed Forces (TAF) are known to be in the area between Tal Abyad and Rasul Ayn. Although the number of Turkish troops based here remains unknown, their operational strength and capability is quite high. With the deployment of the TAF units, the terrorist elements in the area where the SNA units are located have been dispersed and the region has purified. These troops in the region are not expected to clash with the Syrian regime's army. The deployment of the TAF in the region and its continued existence have bought Turkey some time, both at the negotiating table in the diplomatic process and in finding a solution to the problem. The continuing deployment of TAF and SNA forces in the region is reducing the dominance and political authority of the YPG/ PYD terrorists and shows that the fight against the remnants of DAESH is proceeding.

As Turkey discusses Syria's new post-conflict order, it aims to eliminate terrorist elements such as the YPG/PYD or the SDF or to destroy separatist elements. SDF, which is the current umbrella organization led by the YPG and

---

[45] Suzan Fraser and Josh Lederman, "US Cutting Off Its Supply of Arms to Kurds Fighting in Syria", Associated Press, 25.11.2017, https://www.apnews.com/945405f808f04d3a898c0b826bbabcc1, (Access 02.02.2020).

[46] Suzan Fraser and Josh Lederman, "US Cutting Off Its Supply of Arms to Kurds Fighting in Syria", Associated Press, 25.11.2017, https://www.apnews.com/945405f808f04d3a898c0b826bbabcc1, (Access 02.02.2020).

[47] Donna Abu-Nasr, "Final Islamic State Defeat Brings Syria's War to a Crossroad", Bloomberg, 09.11.2017, https://www.bloomberg.com/news/articles/2017-11-09/final-islamic-state-defeat-brings-syria-s-war-to-key-crossroads, (Access 02.02.2020).

backed by the coalition, is the most influential organization in northern Syria and is addressed or supported by the U.S. and many other actors. Accordingly, the SDF is seen as an important tool that should be kept on America's side and which can later be used as a pioneer for regional policies. However, U.S. military assistance to SDF elements has been disturbing to Turkey and has led Turkey, which sees the YPG as a PKK-affiliated "terrorist organization", to position itself on the opposite side. Former Secretary of Defense James Mattis explained that the reason for the Pentagon to provide military assets to the SDF and YPG was to avoid casualties of American troops on the ground.[48] However, the Ankara administration believes that there is more to the U.S. strategic mindset. Accordingly, the U.S. administration is trying to form its police force in the region from the SDF and the YPG units and to gain land in northern Syria which it will transform into an autonomous administration. Although the sensitivity of the Turkish national security bureaucracy and policymakers on this issue is known, the U.S. administration continues to arm the YPG and shows no evidence of a policy change. Although Turkey has openly and officially reacted, the U.S. support for the SDF is considered as an indicator that it is unlikely for the U.S. to abandon such a strategic instrument in Syria, at least unless it is replaced.

In addition, the U.S. has supported SDF elements in northern Syria in collaboration with its European allies to jeopardize the achievements of Turkey, the RF and the Assad regime and has sent its troops to reduce Iran's regional influence and to cut the area in the Middle Euphrates Valley, also known as Der ez-Zor Province, where Iran is trying to build a *land bridge* towards Lebanon.[49] Currently, the U.S. maintains its physical presence in the Middle Euphrates River Valley, albeit limited, to prevent Iranian regional gains or military strategies. In doing so, the U.S. controls the oil fields on the ground, enabling their sale and providing arms and logistical support to SDF and YPG/PYD units with these oil revenues.[50]

Since February 2018, U.S.-backed SDF elements have been located on the eastern bank of the Euphrates River, while pro-regime forces, including pro-Iranian forces, have encircled the west bank. U.S.-led coalition forces have attempted to prevent the expansion of both the Assad regime and pro-Iranian forces in the eastern Euphrates by supporting SDF elements.[51] The efforts of the

---

[48] Tuvan Gumrukcu and Angus McDowell, "Turkey Says U.S. Has Promised to Stop Arming YPG, Warns Washington on Manbij", Reuters, 28.01.2018, https://www.reuters.com/article/us-mideast-crisis-syria-turkey/turkey-says-u-s-has-promised-to-stop-arming-ypg-warns-washington-on-manbij-idUSKBN1FG0P4?il=0, (Access 02.02.2020).

[49] Donna Abu-Nasr, "Final Islamic State Defeat Brings Syria's War to a Crossroad", Bloomberg, 09.11.2017, https://www.bloomberg.com/news/articles/2017-11-09/final-islamic-state-defeat-brings-syria-s-war-to-key-crossroads, (Access 02.02.2020).

[50] Tom Perry, Ellen Francis and Laila Bassam, "Assad Sets Sights on Kurdish Areas, Risking New Syria Conflict", Reuters, 31.10.2017, https://www.reuters.com/article/us-mideast-crisis-syria-kurds-analysis/assad-sets-sights-on-kurdish-areas-risking-new-syria-conflict-idUSKBN1D02CN, (Access 02.02.2020).

[51] Karen DeYoung and Liz Sly, "U.S. Moves toward Open-Ended Presence in Syria after Islamic State Is

coalition forces have been successful and SDF forces in the region have excessively expanded. The provision of sufficient military, intelligence, and logistical support from the U.S. administration has enabled SDF elements to expand.

These developments in the region have deeply affected Turkey and thus the perception of a threat from the region has been intensely felt. These developments have led to Turkey's desire to increase its influence in the region, to take military and political measures and to maintain its military presence in Syria. The reason that the Ankara administration, which is trying to prevent the PYD/YPG terrorist elements in the region from operating in Turkey or resorting to terrorist acts, is facing solitude is due to the fact that its main objectives are not consistent with the U.S. and its allies. For, the U.S. and its allies do not feel or see themselves under an intense threat as does Turkey. In addition to the perception of the imminent threat it feels, Turkey shows a great reaction due to the fear of "separation" arising from its historical memory or the anxiety arising from the possibility of the establishment of *"Kurdistan"*. This situation, explained by *"geophobia"*[52], seriously disturbs the Ankara administration and drives it into political and strategic conflict with all the actors responsible for it. The conflict in the region is forcing Turkey into a further tense position and leading to an evaluation of its military options as well as its political and diplomatic ones.

- Turkey's Bringing the Disagreements in the Region to the Agenda of the International Community and Internationalizing the Issues of Conflict

When the terrorism of DAESH in the region and the actions of the terrorist elements of the PYD/YPG are evaluated together with the oppressive attitude of the Assad regime in Syria, the scope of the struggle becomes larger and more challenging. In addition, the involvement of other regional and non-regional actors, who have some influence in the region, further complicates the issue. Another difficulty with the region is that the states and non-state actors involved in the issue do not trust each other or consider each other in an inimical way. The most obvious example of this is Turkey's serious lack of trust in many actors in the region, and this reflects negatively on the TFP and further fuels the *distrust*.

Another example is that U.S. officials talk about the unreliability of the RF and the ongoing conflict between the U.S. and the RF. When describing this dilemma, General Joseph Votel, the central commander of the U.S. Army, stated that the Russians play the role of *"both incendiary and firefighter"*, which is why they

---

Routed", Washington Post, 22.11.2017, https://www.washingtonpost.com/world/national-security/us-moves-toward-open-ended-presence-in-syria-after-islamic-state-is-routed/2017/11/22/1cd36c92-ce13-11e7-a1a3-0d1e45a6de3d_story.html?utm_term=.7484899d662c, (Access 02.02.2020).

[52] Soyalp Tamçelik, "Analysis of Greek Policy Activities and Political Action in the Eastern Mediterranean from the Aspect of Geo-Phobia", **Cyprus: Alternative Solution Models**, Hüseyin GÖKÇEKUŞ and Hüseyin IŞIKSAL, (Eds.) Peter Lang (SCOPUS index), Internationaler Verlag der Wissenschaften, Berlin, 2021, pp. 147-174; Soyalp Tamçelik, "İsrail Örneğinden Hareketle Uluslararası Güvenlik Değerlendirmelerinde Yeni Bir Kavram: Jeofobi Geo-Phobia)", **Güvenlik: Kargaşa ve Belirsizlik Çağından Nereye?**, Mehmet Akif Okur, (Ed.) İstanbul, KOCAV Yayınları, 2018, pp. 119-150.

are constantly tensing the atmosphere and trying to change the conditions in their favor.[53] Though, Turkey makes similar evaluations on the U.S. However, Turkey tends to strengthen its cooperation with the RF to minimize the cost of these evaluations. It is not an easy task for Turkey to strengthen its cooperation with the RF under the current conditions, because Turkey knows that the RF, like other players in the region, is a serious rival. Nonetheless, it is known that Turkey wants to reduce the effectiveness of the U.S. and its allies in the region by using the RF, is trying to invalidate traditional religious and social alliances, and ultimately to re-establish Ankara's existence and influence there. Therefore, Turkey wants to consider the Moscow administration as a great boost. In this context, Ankara tends to increase its diplomatic diversity by engaging in military and political cooperation with Moscow. Turkish policymakers believe that the primary cause of the many problems and political impasses in the region is the U.S. and its allies. Turkish Foreign Minister Mevlüt Çavuşoğlu, while pointing out the things the U.S. has done, stated that the biggest threat felt in the region is the U.S.-backed armed opposition groups and the large amount of weapons and ammunition supplied to them.[54] Therefore, Turkish policymakers and the national security bureaucracy usually hold the U.S. responsible in this process. According to the Ankara administration, U.S. foreign policy behavior, intentions and rhetoric are unreliable and insincere. Although the U.S. has announced that it will withdraw its troops from the region, it is clear that it is permanent and will maintain its military presence in Syria. As such, the Ankara administration keeps this behavior on the agenda at every opportunity and ensures that it is constantly debated in international arena. Turkey claims that the U.S. administration has formed a partnership with separatist terrorist organizations, developed strategies with them, and considers the existence of these organizations as "legitimate". Turkey is trying to broaden the scope of its foreign policy by attempting to *internationalize* the issue.

One of the reasons for Turkey to pursue this policy is the coexistence of two global players such as the U.S. and the RF on the ground, the presence of various terrorist groups in the region and the proxy wars being conducted. The presence of regular and irregular forces operating in the region and their increasing effect on the ground is a serious risk for Turkey. The Ankara administration therefore tends to reduce this risk, to define the problem with a value policy and to *internationalize* political facts and concepts with the actors it cooperates with. This is expected to lead Turkey to find allies in the international system and to overcome its solitude. For this purpose, Turkey tried to sign a memorandum of

[53] Robert Burns, "US General: Russia is Both Arsonist and Fireman in Syria", ABC News, 27.02.2018, http:// abcnews.go.com/Politics/wireStory/us-general-russia-arsonist-fireman-syria-53390106, (Access 02.02.2020).
[54] "Dışişleri Bakanı Sayın Mevlüt Çavuşoğlu'nun Afrika Birliği Komisyon Başkan Yardımcısı Thomas Kwesi Quartey ve Ruanda Dışişleri Bakanlığı'nda Devlet Bakanı Olivier Nduhungirehe ile Ortak Basın Toplantısı, 12 Şubat 2018, İstanbul", T.C. Dışişleri Bakanlığı, 12.02.2018, http://www.mfa.gov.tr/disisle ri-bakani-sayin-mevlut-cavusoglu_nun-afrika-birligi-bsk-yrd-ve-ruanda-devlet-bakaniyla-ortak-basin-toplantisi.tr.mfa, (Access 02.02.2020).

understanding on certain issues by developing diplomatic and military dialogue with the U.S. and the RF several times.

This type of communication between the parties has resulted in the formation of a physically incompatible line between the SDF and the regime-backed forces. This line runs along the Euphrates and reaches the Iraqi border. The presence of YPG/PYD terrorist elements on the north of this line near the Turkish border poses a threat to Turkey's southern borders as well and turns the surrounding area into a conflict zone.

It is clear that such lines established in Syria have failed, commercial and political lines have been violated and there is an environment of conflict. For example, in September 2017, this line had again been violated when forces belonging to the Syrian regime, supported by the Russian air force, followed DAESH militants to the eastern part of the Euphrates River. More than 300 Russian citizens were injured or killed as a result of the U.S. and coalition forces attacks on pro-regime forces in February 2018, in response to the Russian airstrikes on SDF elements close to U.S. Special Forces based in the region.[55]

These events show that the opposing actors in the region can clash and that this can undermine the security of Syria or the neighbouring areas. However, it is obvious that Turkey will have to take precautionary measures of its own despite the controversial actions of the YPG/PYD terrorist elements and the Assad regime. Policy-makers in Ankara have been monitoring the terrorist organizations in Syria since the very beginning and have been warning the U.S.and its allies not to allow or support these formations.[56] However, the U.S. and its Western allies have continued to assist terrorist elements in the region and have even defined them as *"freedom fighters"*. This has encouraged terrorist organizations in the region and has left Syria and Turkey with the impression of being captured in a terrorist grip both within and beyond the border. Feeling this pressure and threat as the internal conflict continues in Syria, Turkey has cleared terrorist structures by conducting military operations in the western parts of the Euphrates River. However, the threat from the east of the region persists and the negative effects of the political and diplomatic consequences of a possible operation on the international community have not disappeared. Turkey will have to explain the reasons for the operation east of the Euphrates to the international community and the public.

As a member of the Syrian Contact Group, Turkey, while conducting its foreign policy, aims to send back the displaced Syrian population, not to increase the number of those who had to migrate, to end the violence, to ensure economic

[55] Thomas Gibbons-Neff, "In Wake of Airstrike, U.S. Military Moves to Establish Closer Communication with Russian Forces in Syria", Washington Post, 17.09.2017, https://www.washingtonpost.com/news/checkpoint/wp/2017/09/17/following-airstrike-u-s-military-moves-to-establish-closer-communication-with-russian-forces-in-syria/?utm_term=.05f8b8b9c465, (Access 02.02.2020).
[56] "No: 302, 14 Ekim 2019, AB Dış İlişkiler Konseyi'nin Kabul Ettiği Kararlar Hk.", T.C. Dışişleri Bakanlığı, 14.10.2019, http://www.mfa.gov.tr/no_302_-ab-dis-iliskiler-konseyi-nin-kabul-ettigi-kararlar-hk.tr.mfa, (Access 02.02.2020).

prosperity and to prepare the ground for a political agreement. However, the massive bombardment of Eastern Ghouta by the RF and the regime's aircrafts killed more than 500 people in just one week in mid-February 2018, and thousands fled to the Turkish border.[57]

The intention of the U.S. to declare a ceasefire in the areas where the Kurdish majority is located in northern Syria and its meeting with the Russian officials for this purpose was made in order to avoid the exhaustion of the "local Kurdish forces" against the Assad regime. Thereupon, the parties agreed on a ceasefire in the northern town of Hasaka in August 2016.[58] The *non-conflict situation* between the parties continued despite some individual attacks. Understanding that the *non-conflict situation* in northern Syria could not be achieved without reconciliation with Turkey, the U.S. made an effort to convince the Ankara administration on this issue.

While the U.S. has been successful in maintaining the ceasefire in southwestern Syria through its cooperation with the RF and Jordan, it has not achieved the desired result with the Turkish authorities in northern Syria. The Ankara administration is very uncomfortable with the fact that the U.S.-backed forces are becoming more effective in the region. The concern of the Ankara administration is that this situation will lead to a decrease of dominance in and the destabilization of the region. This situation, combined with Turkish-American coordination, is a serious problem of insecurity and instability for military units deployed in the region. Therefore, the reconciliation of the U.S. with Turkey in the region is a requirement for the regional mechanisms established to function and achieve their interests. The U.S. prefers to use this issue as an element of pressure in small, closed, bilateral meetings to reach an agreement with Turkey, and Turkish officials prefer to pressure the U.S. in front of the international community to some extent by publicizing the issue internationally.

Turkey wants to maintain its foreign policy for Syria and the surrounding region in a transparent, open, sincere and fair manner. Turkey's foreign policy in this sense is generally based on a *values diplomacy*. In fact, the reason for this foreign policy behavior of Turkey is that it encounters difficulties in balancing the demands or maximalist interests of global and regional actors, which causes chaos in the region. While pursuing this policy for a certain period of time, Turkey, unable to balance the actors, shifted from the diplomacy of values, started using hard power as a diplomatic means under the effect of the classical realist theory, and tried to balance its interests with the interests and demands of

---

[57] "The Besieged Eastern Ghouta has been Witnessing Since Today Morning Targeting by 107 Airstrikes, Barrel Bombes, Shells and Missiles Killing 6 Civilian Martyrs and Injuring 26 Others before, During and After The Truce", Syrian Observatory for Human Rights, 27.02.2018, http://www.syriahr.com/en/?p=85800, (Access 02.02.2020).

[58] Ralph Ellis, "Syrian Military, Kurdish Fighters Reach Ceasefire in Hasaka", CNN, 23.08.2016, http://www.cnn.com/2016/08/23/middleeast/ceasefire-syria-kurds-hasaka/index.html, (Access 02.02.2020).

other actors. However, Turkey's desire in Syria policy is to ensure that the foreign policy behaviors of the U.S. and its European allies proceed within a transparent and reassuring mechanism. Therefore, Turkey wishes to increase the pressure of the international community on the other actors by internationalizing all the relevant issues and thus urge them to compromise.

There is another objective of the Ankara administration that stems from the same concern with its Western allies. Accordingly, Turkey intends to prevent the deployment of Iranian and pro-Iranian allied forces or any other permanent forces in the region. As a result, Ankara and its Western allies do not want Iran and its affiliates to set up bases, build weapons production facilities and acquire the power to control the region in the Syrian geography. In addition, Western powers, Israeli and Syrian governments are seeking to prevent the redeployment of Iranian-backed forces and Hezbollah elements along the Syrian-Israeli border. The Ankara administration, on the other hand, aims to prevent the PYD/YPG terrorist elements in northern Syria from being supported by Iran rather than this structuring in southwestern Syria. Therefore, in order to eliminate the dilemma of goals in the region, Turkey is trying to establish a serious mechanism that will include the forces of the U.S., the RF and Turkey, and to achieve a unity of purpose while respecting the international borders, independent state structure and sovereign power of Syria.

- Turkey's Prevention of the Establishment of a "Kurdish Autonomous Administration" in Syria and Getting the Support of the Western Powers

For the United States and its Western allies, the establishment of an "autonomous Kurdish administration" in northern Syria and its promotion is considered to be one of their main objectives. On the other hand, the RF has focused more on reconciling the regional Kurdish population with the Syrian regime by contacting the Kurds in Syria directly. The RF proposed a new constitution between May 2016 and January 2017 to end the hostilities in Syria. In the constitutional draft, the RF brought up the issue that a limited *decentralized* form of administration could be introduced to the Kurds in northern Syria.[59]

Immediately after this proposal, the Moscow administration provided air support to the Kurds, allowing them to fight against DAESH forces in the Raqqa and Der ez-Zor regions in late 2017.[60] Yet, while it is known that the RF supports the Kurds in Syria, it is difficult to claim that it shares the same feelings and thoughts about all Kurdish communities. First of all, it is unclear whether the RF wants more *self-rule* for all Kurds in Syria, or whether it is pursuing a policy

---

[59] Samer Abboud, "Russia's Draft Constitution: End of Syria's Baath Era?", Al Jazeera, 29.05.2016, http://www.aljazeera.com/news/2016/05/russia-draft-constitution-syria-baath-era-160529064231915.html, (Access 03.02.2020); Maxim A. Suchov, "Russia Offers Outline for Syrian Constitution", Al-Monitor, 27.01.2017, https://www.al-monitor.com/pulse/originals/2017/01/russia-meeting-syria-opposition-moscow-constitution.html, (Access 03.02.2020).

[60] Ellen Francis, "Syrian Kurdish YPG Says Seized Eastern Region from Islamic State", Reuters, 03.12.2017, https://www.reuters.com/article/us-mideast-crisis-syria-ypg/syrian-kurdish-ypg-says-seized-eastern-region-from-islamic-state-idUSKBN1DX0GB, (Access 03.02.2020).

designed to use the Kurds as a means against Turkey and the Assad regime. However, it is clear that one of the main objectives of the RF is getting Turkey out of the NATO bloc.

Essentially, Russia is one of the countries that has been playing the *"Kurdish card"* in the *ME* for a century.[61] However, recently RF has not preferred to deepen relations with regional powers (Kurds) and increase tension by disturbing Turkey and Iran. But the U.S. is keen for a Kurdish population that respects Syria's international borders and state structure to establish an autonomous Kurdish administration in northern Syria and shares a common stance on this with some European and Arab allies.[62] In terms of the U.S., it is possible to say that this policy, which will be supported by the European allies and some Arab states, will put serious pressure on Turkey and this "Kurdish card" will play an important role in foreign policy.

Turkey's foreign policy attitude and stance on this issue is quite clear. Turkey is against any form of Kurdish political structure in northern Syria or in any region parallel to the southern borders of Anatolia.[63] In this regard, Turkey has tried to support its political stance with power elements by conducting military operations in the northern region of Syria. Moreover, with the Olive Branch Operation in northern Syria, the Ankara administration has even shown that Turkish and coalition-backed forces deployed in the region could clash. After that, Turkey drew attention to the fact that its military operations in the region could extend to Manbij, which the U.S. forces has been reinforced with SDF elements. In August 2017, the U.S. and Turkish officials averted the risk of an attack on U.S. forces when Turkish-backed Free Syrian Army (FSA) forces began targeting SDF elements in Manbij.[64] However, the U.S. administration changed its stance on this issue and initiated a process of convincing Turkey that the ceasefire in the region should continue and that the Kurdish autonomous administration in northern Syria would not pose a threat to Ankara's administration.[65]

As the U.S. realized the difficulty of getting Turkey to agree, it launched a

---

[61] **Beklan Kulaksızoğlu**, "Ortadoğu'da Kürt Kartı Rusya'ya Geçti", Deutsche Welle Türkçe, 23.10.2019, https://www.dw.com/tr/ortado%C4%9Fuda-k%C3%BCrt-kart%C4%B1-rusyaya-ge%C3%A7ti/a-50955203, (Access 03.02.2020).

[62] Süheyla Demir ve Derya Yaşar, "Büyük Kürdistan Hayal Ama Irak ve Suriye'de Kürt Devletleri Kurulabilir", Sputnik Türkiye, 18.06.2015, https://tr.sputniknews.com/columnists/20150618101607283 1/, (Access 03.02.2020).

[63] "Dışişleri Bakanı Sayın Mevlüt Çavuşoğlu'nun A Haber'de Yayınlanan "Özel Röportaj" Programına Verdiği Mülakat, 29 Aralık 2016, Ankara", T.C. Dışişleri Bakanlığı, 29.12.2016, http://www.mfa.gov.tr/ disisleri-bakani-sayin-mevlut-cavusoglu_nun-a-haber-_ozel-roportaj_-programina-verdigi-mulakat_-29-aralik-2016_-ankara.tr.mfa, (Access 03.02.2020).

[64] "Department of Defense Press Briefing by General Townsend via Teleconference from Baghdad, Iraq", U.S. Department of Defense, 31.08.2017, https://www.defense.gov/News/Transcripts/Transcript-View/Article/1297228/department-of-defense-press-briefing-by-general-townsend-via-teleconference-fro/, (Access 03.02.2020).

[65] Yurdagül Şimşek, Hikmet Durgun ve Elif Örnek, "ABD, Türkiye'ye Rağmen Suriye'de Bir Kürt Yönetimi Oluşturur Mu", Sputnik Türkiye, 24.03.2017, https://tr.sputniknews.com/columnists/201703 241027789459-abd-turkiye-suriye-kurt-bolgesi/, (Access 03.02.2020).

number of initiatives. As such, the U.S. has promised to promote transparency and confidence-building measures to address Turkey's national security, border security, and counterterrorism concerns, and to minimize conflicts between Turkey and *"armed Kurdish elements"*.[66] The second step was for the U.S. to support the northern regions of Syria with regard to trade and reconstruction, as it has done with the Kurdish regional administration in Iraq, and thus encourage Turkey to play a constructive economic role in northern Syria. The third step for the U.S. was to focus on efforts to persuade the Ankara administration to withdraw Turkish troops from Syria. In addition to all those efforts mentioned above, the U.S. administration's endeavors can be expressed as strengthening the Turkish border with Syria, preventing the influx of refugees from Syria, and also preventing the infiltration of Salafi-Jihadist groups at the Turkish border.[67]

It is believed that the U.S. is trying to create pressure through political and regional arrangements in Syria to convince Turkey. In this regard, it is clear that the U.S. will be willing to use the terrorist elements of the PYD/YPG along with its allies in southeastern Europe. The U.S. and its European allies stated that they could develop an acceptable autonomy agreement and an accompanying mediating agency by reconciling the Kurds in Syria, the regime in Syria and Turkey by limiting the political and regional objectives of the PYD. In fact, the U.S. and European officials are trying to create a triple combination by supporting the terrorist elements of the PYD/YPG, establishing a dialogue between regional powers or enhancing the capabilities of Kurdish elements in northern Syria. This is a highly important task for the U.S. because it cares for and wants to promote the PYD, which it considers a separate unit from the PKK that is a terrorist organization. The U.S. security bureaucracy and policymakers want to present the PYD to the international public by emphasizing that the PYD, unlike other Kurdish formations, includes non-Kurdish populations, regulates local governance in its regions, adopts a democratic and secular life and works in coordination with Western allies.[68] But, regional Kurdish elements such as the PYD have created significant disruption to the Arab and Turkmen population in the areas they have conquered, and subsequently have caused non-Kurdish elements to migrate from the areas where they used to live.

Turkey, on the other hand, has stated that the Kurdish structuring in the region was by no means a benign development, it has turned the region completely insecure and that these areas would eventually turn into a corridor for terrorism, and further explained that this causes serious security problems for itself. One of the factors that supports this concern of Turkey is what the Israeli government has done in Syria.

It is a known fact that Israel has been seeking to shape the Kurdish structure

---

[66] Restoring Eastern Mediterranean as a U.S. Strategic Anchor, op.cit., p. 35.
[67] "ABD Başkan Yardımcısı Pence Türkiye'de: Ziyaretten Neler Bekleniyor?", BBC News Türkçe, 17.10.2019, https://www.bbc.com/turkce/haberler-dunya-50077578, (Access 03.02.2020).
[68] For further information see... Denise Natali, **The Kurdish Quasi-State: Development and Dependency in Post-Gulf War Iraq**, Syracuse University Press, New York, 2010, p. 107-122.

in northern Syria, first as an autonomous region and then as a state.[69] Israel, which wants to ensure the creation of a second non-Arab state in the region, envisages that if it accomplishes this, it will transform the conflict scheme in the region into an Arab-Kurdish-Turkish-Iranian one, and thus it can live in security by eliminating its own security, territorial integrity and survival problems. The Israeli administration, which has turned the social conflict scenario into a political discussion, is determined never to let Iran and its supporters have a presence in Syria or expand their sphere of influence. As reported in the press, Israeli officials have been trying to figure out the extent of the Iranian presence in Syria during consultation meetings with U.S. policymakers.[70] Therefore, it is considered that Turkey should establish a reverse proportional relationship in the conduct of foreign policy in order to balance Israel's policy. Therefore, it should be kept in mind that Turkey can disrupt the Israeli administration and follow a policy of deterrence against Israel by carrying out the actions that Israel has been carrying out in northern Syria, in an area close to the Israeli border in southwestern Syria, with the groups that it supports. However, it should not be forgotten that many problems can be solved if Turkey establishes direct relations with Israel or, conversely, if Israel establishes direct relations with Turkey.

Turkey's Identification of its Foreign Policy Towards the ME-EM and Setting its Strategic Objectives

Turkey is going through a period where it has serious difficulties in implementing its foreign policy towards the *ME* and the *EM* and has to make difficult decisions. Certainly, there are a number of reasons why the Ankara administration is experiencing difficulties in its policies towards the two regions. Though external factors dominate the list of reasons, internal factors such as decision-making mechanisms, cultural accumulation, social memory and the adequacy of the bureaucratic system are also known to be critical in this regard. However, in order to limit the subject of discussion, only the external factors will be examined.

It is to be noted that for the Ankara administration, the risk of confronting terrorist elements and regime forces is gradually increasing due to military operations, especially in the *ME*, the relations among regional and global actors are strained due to the conflict of interests, and that Turkey is increasingly isolated as a result of the political instruments it uses. In fact, Turkey's problems with the *ME* are not entirely the result of Ankara's actions. These problems, which arose in the region, outside Turkey's control, but affected Turkey, led to the emergence of a *syndrome of insecurity*.

In this regard, relations between Turkey and the U.S. can be counted among

---

[69] Yıldız Yazıcıoğlu, "İsrail'in Kürt Bağımsızlığından Beklentisi Ne?", Amerika'nın Sesi, 28.09.2017, https://www.amerikaninsesi.com/a/israilin-kurt-bagimsizligindan-beklentisi-ne/4048326.html, (Access 03.02.2020).
[70] Ece Göksedef, "Savaş Sonrası Suriye İçin Güç Mücadelesinde Dengeler Değişiyor Mu?", BBC News Türkçe, 01.03.2019, https://www.bbc.com/turkce/haberler-turkiye-47422505, (Access 03.02.2020).

the most affected relationships. It is not acceptable for the two NATO allies to be unable to reach an agreement on the future of Syria, to define terrorist elements, to develop a common political stance and to reconcile national interests. Therefore, the Syrian issue is seen as a problem that will affect the direction and intensity of Turkish-American relations. The U.S. administration asserts that Turkey has facilitated the fight against the Assad regime rather than preventing DAESH, has even preferred to fight the Syrian Kurds rather than fighting DAESH, and that it has close relations with the RF and Iran rather than with NATO members.[71] In addition, the U.S. officials claim that the government in Ankara manipulates Turkish public opinion and openly supports anti-Americanism.[72] Therefore, under the current circumstances, it is not really easy for the conflicting foreign policy interests of Turkey and the U.S. to free themselves from such internal opposition and for the parties to reach an agreement in a near future. The U.S. administration associates anti-Americanism in Turkey with the degrading perception of trust in America and NATO and with *Eurasians* who intend to cooperate with Russia and Iran as strategic partners.[73] However, the situation is different in the Turkish public opinion from that indicated by the U.S. Behind this anti-Americanism there are many other reasons such as the belief of Turkish President Recep Tayyip Erdogan and his government that the U.S. is among those who conceived or supported the heinous coup attempt of July 15, 2016, that the U.S. wants to control the *ME* and tries to establish an autonomous Kurdish administration in the region, supports terrorist elements, helps to establish a gas forum against Turkey's interests in the *EM*, acts against Turkey in the determination of the maritime jurisdiction areas.

This policy of the U.S. towards Turkey's vital interests or existential issues has been perceived negatively and even as a hostile attitude by the Ankara administration and the Turkish public. Turkey's reaction was not well received by the U.S. as it was not consistent with the usual pattern of Turkish-American relations, and soon after, relations between the two allies began to deteriorate.

Due to the actions of both sides, anti-Americanism in Turkey has increased, while in the U.S., Turkey's *credibility* and *loyalty* have begun to be questioned.[74] This has led to Turkey's identification as the *other* within the alliance structure by some NATO allies.[75] Reasons such as the temporary closure of Incirlik Air Base

[71] "Erdoğan: Koalisyon DEAŞ, YPG ve PYD'ye Destek Veriyor", BBC News Türkçe, 27.12.2016, https://www.bbc.com/turkce/haberler-turkiye-38444990 (Access 03.02.2020).
[72] "Türkiye'de ABD Karşıtlığı ve Hayat Pahalılığı Kaygısı Zirve Yaptı", Amerika'nın Sesi Türkiye, 01.02.2019, https://www.amerikaninsesi.com/a/turkiye-de-abd-karsiligi-ve-hayat-pahaliligi-kaygisi-zirve-yapti/4769156.html, (Access 03.02.2020).
[73] Gonul Tol and Omer Taspinar, "Erdogan's Turn to the Kemalists", Foreign Affairs, 27.10.2016, https://www.foreignaffairs.com/articles/turkey/2016-10-27/erdogans-turn-kemalists, (Access 03.02.2020).
[74] "Avusturyalı General: Türkiye, Rusya'yla İşbirliği Yaparak NATO'ya Olan Güveni Bozuyor", Sputnik Türkiye, 30.07.2019, https://tr.sputniknews.com/analiz/201907301039796282-avusturyali-general-turkiye-rusya-isbirligi-yaparak-nato-olan-guveni-bozuyor/, (Access 03.02.2020).
[75] Yıldız Yazıcıoğlu, "İdlib Mutabakatıyla Barış Yolu Açıldı mı?", Amerika'nın Sesi Türkiye, 19.09.2018,

in July 2016, the accusation of U.S. officials for having supported the coup, the refusal of allowing German MPs to visit German soldiers in Turkey in 2017, the acquisition of the S-400 missile defense system, incompatible with the NATO system, triggered an objection against Turkey in NATO.

These events, which took place shortly after 2016, and the political behavior of the parties vis-à-vis each other caused a decrease in mutual trust and harmed the spirit of alliance. However, the problem that severely eroded Turkey-U.S. relations was the fact that the U.S. donated tens of thousands of truckloads of weapons to terrorist organizations in northern Syria, openly supported terrorist elements in the region and launched an initiative to create an autonomous Kurdish administration. The fact that Turkey showed the capacity to act independently in January 2018 to neutralize Kurdish terrorist elements, asked the U.S. not to provide weapons to terrorist elements and to withdraw its special forces from areas where they are deployed has further strained relations. As senior U.S. officials declared that they would take into account Turkey's security concerns, there was no change in U.S. security policy, and the U.S. even showed some resistance in dealing with issues related to the SDF and the YPG/PYD.

Along with the political conflicts Turkey has been experiencing in the *ME*, a series of conflicts of interest are being experienced as well in the *EM*. The issue of maritime jurisdictions zones, which is seen as a projection of developments in the *ME*, has been emerging in the *EM* and affecting the politics pursued in this region. It is being observed that the *ME* countries have acted against Turkey in determining their maritime jurisdiction and have used Greece and the Greek Administration of Southern Cyprus (GASC) as proxies, and both actors have brought this to the EU acquis agenda for their own interests.

Turkey has not only ensured its own border security with the launch of Operation Olive Branch in western Syria, but has also prevented terrorist elements in the region from reaching the Mediterranean shores and turning this area into a terrorist corridor. As a result, Turkey's Syrian policy has evolved into a new and increasingly complex policy, which has been inconsistent with the policy of the U.S. and its European allies. In this context, Turkey is neither an enemy nor an ally of the U.S. and its European allies. Given that the same is true for Turkey, there is no doubt that the severe crisis of confidence experienced by both sides will have consequences for the security of Europe and the *EM*, as well as for NATO. In particular, this will affect U.S. military operations against DAESH, its military bases in the region, the security of maritime trade, the irregular migration problem, the security of Europe, and Washington's global hegemony. It is clear that Turkey's attitude towards NATO, especially the U.S., will have an effect on preventing irregular migration, determining energy transit routes, establishing a security umbrella for the *ME*, assessing energy deposits in the *EM*, limiting areas of maritime jurisdiction, and ensuring regional stability.

---

https://www.amerikaninsesi.com/a/idlib-mutabakati-ile-baris-yolu-acildi-mi/4578314.html, (Access 03. 02.2020).

Above all, it is believed that Turkey's attitude can lead to the questioning of the NATO itself and its existence.

This attitude of Turkey, which joined NATO in 1952, would lead to the perception of Turkey as a *less reliable* or *unfaithful* ally. It is not possible for the Turkey-U.S. relations, which are conducted with this mentality of conflict, to benefit either these two states or the NATO. Unlike the Cold War era, the U.S. needs to seek new ways to stabilize and develop its relationship with Turkey. Turkey, on the other hand, needs to shed its image as an actor in the international system that opposes the U.S. and takes revenge on it. However, it is certain that the current relations of the parties will not return to the state which the Ankara administration obeyed unconditionally, as it did during the Cold War.

Currently, Turkey is not an *indispensable strategic partner* for the U.S.[76] However, while it is not desirable for relations to be in this state, it is a fact that Turkish-U.S. relations are strategically significant. In particular, the U.S. administration will need to know in advance and be able to manage the position and actions of the Ankara administration so as not to undermine Turkey's interests. Turkey, on the other hand, will have to shift slowly and gradually from being a reliable ally to a confrontational and competitive one in its relations with the U.S.

The fact that the U.S. adopts a *conceptual approach* in its policy towards the *EM*, as it does in its policy towards the *ME*, which is the adjacent geopolitical area of the *EM*, causes Turkey to feel besieged and to experience a *security syndrome*. For the Ankara administration, this new situation reveals the need to redefine and reinterpret Turkey-U.S. relations along with the need for new regional political strategies.

The U.S.-induced *security syndrome* experienced by the Ankara administration in the *ME*, which can also be assessed as a result of *geophobia*[77], leads Turkey to see the policies of Western allies towards the *EM* as hypocritical, insincere, marginalizing or supportive of their adversaries. This attitude of Western allies towards Turkey is in contradiction with Ankara administration's image of *"New Turkey"*, the image of the great state and the vision of a powerful leader.

In fact, there are many legitimate reasons for Turkey's distrust of the U.S. or its Western allies. The U.S. disturbs Turkey in many issues such as its refusal to extradite the so-called leader of the FETO terrorist organization, which Turkey considers a threat, its serious support for the PYD/YPG terrorist organization in Syria and its willingness to establish a Kurdish autonomous administration, its filing the Zarrab case on the pretext of breaking the sanctions against Iran and targeting President Erdogan, his cabinet and his family, its excluding Turkey

[76] Elif Sudagezer ve Hüseyin Hayatsever, "ABD ile Türkiye'nin Stratejik Ortak Olmadığı Şimdilerde Daha Net Anlaşılıyor", Sputnik Türkiye, 14.08.2018, https://tr.sputniknews.com/columnists/201808141034749341-abd-turkiye-kriz-ortaklik-nato-yaptirim/, (Access 03.02.2020).
[77] On Geophobia see... Soyalp Tamçelik, "Yunanistan Dış Politikasında Doğu Akdeniz Politiği ve Jeofobi (Geo-Phobia) Açısından Davranışsal Analizi", **Türk Dünyası Parlamenterler Birliği Türk Dünyasından Parlamenter Bakış Dergisi**, Cilt. 2, No. 5, 2019, pp. 91-114.

from the *EM* gas forum and depriving Turkey of maritime jurisdiction areas. There is no doubt that Turkey's disturbance is not about regular and simple issues. Almost all these issues correspond to one of Turkey's existential problems. This is why we believe that Turkey should adopt a monolithic approach in its policies towards the *ME* and the *EM*, transforming it into a *ME-EM* policy and developing its strategic interests accordingly. In addition, it was observed that Turkey-EU relations have been seriously strained due to the refusal of European governments to allow the Turkish authorities to campaign in European countries, prior to the referendum on the local constitutional amendment in April 2017, their avoidance of diplomatic courtesy and their insulting behavior.

Turkey's increasingly critical stance and harsh remarks towards its European allies have prompted them to act in a *spirit of solidarity*. It has been observed that harsh behavior on both sides at the political level is not consistent with the relationship of alliance and can be defined as a hostile attitude.[78] However, given its economic relationship with the EU, Turkey has gradually softened its rhetoric and realized the importance of its influence on European security. EU member states, aware of Turkey's role in preventing irregular migration from Syria and Salafi-Jihadist terrorist movements, have tended to ease their relations with Turkey. However, the EU continues to seriously disrupt Ankara's administration due to the limitation of maritime jurisdictions in the *EM*, its unconditional solidarity with the "Republic of Cyprus", the distribution of energy resources, its ignoring of Turkey in the region and the violation of international law.

From this point of view, it is imperative that Turkey's policies towards the *ME* and the *EM* are not seen as separate from each other, but rather as complementary or integrative of each other. Turkey has to pursue a two-pronged strategy that seeks to reinvest in the Turkey-Euro-Atlantic relationship while developing alternative partnerships with other regional actors to realize similar strategic interests. In order to make this complex situation understandable and systematized, it is argued that Turkey's main policy and strategy for sustainable development can be achieved by focusing on the four main objectives explained below and on their strategic planning.

Turkey's Re-determination of Its Foreign Policy towards the EM in Terms of Conceptual, Phenomenal and Actor Dynamics

As can be assumed, Turkey's recent policy decisions regarding the *EM* are the result of a radical and sharp transformation. Although some Western allies claim that Turkey has adopted this attitude in order to break its relations with the West,[79] long-time European countries and U.S. officials know that the intention

---

[78] "Türkiye Artık Müttefikimiz Değil", Time Türk, 21.11.2015, https://www.timeturk.com/turkiye-artik-muttefikimiz-degil/haber-97315, (Access 04.02.2020).
[79] "Financial Times: Erdoğan'ın Türkiyesi Batı'dan Kopuyor", T24, 19.01.2015, https://t24.com.tr/haber/financial-times-erdoganin-turkiyesi-batidan-kopuyor, 284256, (Access 04.02.2020).

was not to break off relations. Therefore, it is certain that there is no separation of Turkey and the West, because, within the dynamics of foreign policy, the West needs Turkey and Turkey needs the West. It has been observed that the West has been drawing attention to the fact that the relationship with Turkey is more of a dependency than a need, leaving Turkey vulnerable, especially with the economic crisis being manipulated by the U.S. With this incident, the distrust of the Ankara administration towards the West and in particular towards the American administration was once again confirmed.

This treatment from its western allies has led to a diversification in Turkey's foreign policy, which the western allies have viewed as a withdrawal from the Euro-Atlantic alliance and have claimed that this withdrawal will leave Turkey vulnerable to Russian policies and pressures. However, Turkey has shown that it can enter into a series of relations of common interest with the RF as well as with the Euro-Atlantic bloc.

Although it is known that Turkey and the RF have been in competition for a long time, there is little understanding of the cooperation and development of new relations between these two actors on the part of the Western powers. The U.S. and its European allies are only beginning to understand that Turkey has radically changed its stance against the West, that the likelihood of realizing the strategic interests they have negotiated with Turkey is reduced or that the strategic gap has between Turkey and the West has expanded beyond closure.

Ankara, on the other hand, is busy constructing and planning its new foreign policy framework and is making great efforts in this regard. It is obvious that while shaping its foreign policy, Turkey will have to assess the global and regional dynamics within its own capacity, not only in terms of being in the West or in the East, and for this purpose, it will have to develop concepts, facts and alternatives of the actors with which it will cooperate. Therefore, it becomes clear that Ankara should prioritize the *diversification of axis* rather than the *shift of axis* in foreign policy.

One of the most striking examples of this was the signing of the Agreement on Delimitation of the Maritime Jurisdiction Areas with the Libyan Government of National Accord on November 27, 2019 in an effort to restore balance in the *EM*. This is the most serious example of how Turkey tried to eliminate the imbalance in the region by creating and cooperating with alternative actors. However, in order for Turkey to maintain its foreign policy behavior in this direction, it will have to reach an agreement first with Israel and Egypt and then with the legitimate administration in Syria which will show that it has behaved with factual integrity in its foreign policy. In this context, Turkey will transform its new concept of security and foreign policy, which it defines as being conceptual and factual, from "attitude" to "behavior" and will emphasize that it is permanent in its actions.

Turkey's Minimization of the Conflict Environment in the *EM*

Turkey is expected to solve the problems arising from the conflict areas in the *EM* through a comprehensive and holistic dialogue rather than through narrow patterns, and to follow a foreign policy based on rights and justice together with the regional actors, with the exception of the GASC. Therefore, Turkey's policies towards the *EM* should be conducted in a broad and consensual approach. Emphasizing that the current policies followed by regional actors may lead to military conflicts and that confidence-building measures will have to be put in place, it is clear that Turkey should minimize the conflict areas in the *EM* and actively lead this process. Considering that the sea mass of the *EM* surrounds the continental mass of the *ME*, it will not be misleading to claim that the problem in this area relates to the domination of the Middle Eastern actors over the sea. Reasons such as the significant economic value of the energy reserves discovered in the region, their attractiveness to Western markets and the possibility of creating an alternative route to those of the RF have raised the question of determining the maritime jurisdiction area in the *EM*, whereas Turkey has been left alone in this process and has been treated as a country creating a conflict atmosphere. Therefore, Turkey can be expected to show that it can direct the threat emanating from the *EM* through diplomatic relations with regional actors, that it can regulate its areas of maritime jurisdiction under the principle of equity, and that hard power can be used when necessary to protect Turkey's and the TRNC's rights.

In order for Turkey to generate constructive ideas for the future of the *EM*, two issues are thought to be addressed. The first is for Turkey to enter into a similar agreement as it did with Libya with the other three countries in the region, and the second is the possibility of the existence of significant energy resources in the areas of maritime jurisdiction that it has declared, in which case Turkey can become a key player. Both scenarios, shifting the regional balance of power, will strengthen Turkey's position, reduce the regional threat and the risk of conflict, and lead to stability.

Turkey's Adherence to Its Fundamental Rights and Interests and the Protection of Its Raison d'être while Establishing Relations with Actors Related to the *EM*

Turkey will have the opportunity to realize its vital interests by not separating its political attitude towards the *EM* region from the *ME* and presenting the two as a whole. Clearly, to prevent its vulnerability in the *EM*, Turkey must first identify or reconstruct its complementary strategic objectives. If Turkey fails to do so, its strategic advantages in the region may be limited or eliminated precisely. In this case, while planning alternative actions towards the *EM*, Turkey should ensure that the southern coasts of Anatolia are always kept open, that a third party doesn't enter the maritime zone between the TRNC and Turkey, that the maritime jurisdiction areas are not limited by any faits accomplis, that there is no declaration of an exclusive economic zone for the land parts in the sea of the

Greek islands, and that the rights of the TRNC and the Turkish Cypriots are protected.

Turkey must maintain its position by making it clear to the parties concerned at all times that it is committed to these issues and considers them to be its raison d'être. For this, it is clear that Ankara will expand its *ME-EM* Diplomacy to the *ME-EM-C (MEM-C)* Diplomacy. Therefore, it would be appropriate to define this particular policy, which will include the island of Cyprus, located between the *ME* and the *EM*, as *MEM-C* Diplomacy. However, it is not an easy task for the Ankara administration to pursue this new foreign policy or to create a new environment. Given that the internal dynamics of the three problem areas are different from each other, that they include complex issues, that the variables are diverse and that the disagreements have their roots in the ancient past, it may seem like a very difficult task for the Ankara administration to develop a common foreign policy approach toward those three areas.

While Turkey is trying to resolve the deep differences of opinion in the *ME* and produce its own security doctrine, as well as conduct inter-communal negotiations on the future of Cyprus; the Greek Cypriot administration's attempt to link the stalemate on the Cyprus issue to the maritime jurisdictional area in the *EM*, bringing the Cyprus issue to the *EM* and the fact that neighbouring countries are also involved in this issue, has inevitably brought the issue to another dimension. As such, it was seen that Turkey has been drawn into an interconnected set of problems that includes the *ME* on the one hand and the *EM* on the other. Therefore, Turkey needs to consider these two issues as a whole and assess them in a holistic perspective.

Since it would not be possible for Turkey to achieve this with the U.S. and its Western allies, whom it has always trusted, developed a transparent alliance with and harmonized its relations of interest, it is considered that it will have to develop a new political doctrine, policy or strategic position regarding the region, and this can be accomplished through the *MEM-C* Diplomacy.

Turkey being located within the three related problematic areas (*ME-EM-C*), regardless of whether the circumstances are favorable or not, it cannot leave its raison d'être in this region to the will or refusal of other actors, and it is therefore essential to consider these regions as a *whole* and to apply the tactic of mutual concessions in a broader area when necessary. It is clear, therefore, that Turkey will have to develop its long-term political and strategic plans. Accordingly, Turkey will have to make assessments by examining first the overall situation in the *EM*, then the characteristics of regional locations, and finally the power of individual actors, and structure its strategic plans on that basis.

Turkey's Use of Soft Power Elements for the *ME-EM* or *MEM-C* Diplomacy and Its Receiving Support from the International Public

Turkey considers negative developments either in the *ME-EM* or *MEM-C* Diplomacy or in the integrated region as an attack on its own values. In fact,

Turkey's assessment of these actions as attacks on its economic, political, legal, diplomatic and heritage values is seen as the product of a comprehensive approach. According to Ankara, given Turkey's size, security and regional economic value, it is considered that any kind of instability in the Anatolian geography will also occur in Europe, the Balkans, the Middle East, North Africa and the Caucasus. In this assessment, the Ankara government shows that any potential negativity in the *ME-EM* or the *MEM-C* Diplomacy will not only be Turkey's loss, but also the loss of all the actors who contribute to it. It will be an important move for Turkey to reach out to the public opinions of the countries in the region or the world powers, to make an effort in this regard, to give a positive message and to insistently repeat its own justification. Despite the attack on Turkey's fundamental rights and interests, Ankara must declare that it balances justice, international law, diplomacy and interests, refrains from doing otherwise, but will use all means possible to protect its rights. In this regard, certainly international meetings, international publications, television programs or briefings will be necessary, as well as the use of other elements of soft power.[80]

Diplomatic Instruments that Turkey can Use in the ME-EM And Their Characteristics

The instruments that Turkey can use in its foreign policy are related to the internal dynamics and characteristics of the regional geography it will address. As long as the objective-means relation in foreign policy is proportional, the chances of success will increase. However, for the instrument used to be successful, the objective must be achievable, applicable, or its functional characteristic must be predictable. In accordance, some of the instruments that the TFP can use in implementing in the *ME-EM* and *MEM-C* Diplomacy are assessed to be the following.

- Turkey's Development of Objectives for the ME-EM Diplomacy and Its Identification of the Related Instruments

The biggest challenge Turkey will face while realizing its interests regarding the *ME-EM* Diplomacy will be the unilateral practices of the U.S. towards the region and the inability to overcome the strategic differences between the two countries' policies. The strategic gaps between the two countries regarding the region are widening due to the fact that the security bureaucracy, foreign and defense ministries, intelligence services, etc. do not trust each other, are overly focused on achieving their own interests and lack coordination. In the near future, it seems difficult for policymakers and the security bureaucracy in both countries to assess and reconcile the different interests and strategic objectives of the parties involved.

In order to manage the growing divergence of political interests or deep

---

[80] For further information see... Benno Signitzer and Timothy Coombs, "Public Relations and Public Diplomacy: Conceptual Convergences", **Public Relations Review**, Vol. 18, No.1, 1992, pp. 137-147.

differences of opinion with the United States and its Western allies, Turkey must first determine a set of objectives that will include ten steps, link them together, operate within a certain logic, and develop the instruments or approaches that can be used as outlined below.

- Turkey's Developing Its Relations with Regional Actors Related to the EM

It would be appropriate for Turkey to contact all national actors in the *EM*, with the exception of the GASC on the grounds that it is not a national actor; and to establish diplomatic relations and initiate a high-level dialogue, regardless of their political differences. Clearly, Turkey needs to establish a formal mechanism to discuss political differences and mutual concerns by holding a series of meetings with other actors in the *EM* region. Secondly, it appears to be a necessity for Turkey to establish a dialogue group under the leadership of an *International Coordination and Strategy Commission*, which will include the Ministries of Foreign Affairs, Defense, Economy and Security and the international law bureaucracy of the other regional countries involved, and to produce coherent and reliable policies towards the *EM*. Through this method, it will be determined how Turkey and the relevant actors can cooperate or to what extent they can agree on the differences between them or why they cannot reach an agreement, and this will facilitate the parties determining their political attitudes. Thus, Turkey will ensure the initiation of a dialogue regarding the delimitation of maritime jurisdiction areas in the *EM*, including the implementation of international law, the determination of maritime jurisdiction areas, the implementation of the principle of equity and the understanding of regional dominance, the prevention of the creation of blocs, the restoration of the regional balance of forces, and by addressing all bilateral issues, related or not, it will allow for the determination of a *set of policy objectives* for the actors involved.

One of the goals will be the *set of political objectives* to evolve towards a broader dialogue into an international congress, and to achieve regional reconciliation and cooperation by involving the key actors of the region. Although it is envisaged that this will not be easy, Turkey undoubtedly needs to achieve this in order to develop a comprehensive *strategic dialogue* towards the *EM* or to re-organize the basis of the partnership. Understanding that otherwise Turkey will not be able to achieve any results from this dialogue, it will have to resort to unilateral actions like other actors in the region and realize its own rights and interests by attempting *de facto* practices. In both cases, Turkey will have to argue that it does not pursue a policy of confrontation by ignoring the absolute interests of the relevant actor(s) in the region. In this environment, Turkey, unable to build alliances in the *EM*, will find itself in a situation where its rights and interests and those of regional actors cannot be protected or crises cannot be managed.

It would be beneficial to establish a formal *working group* that will be formed around Turkey-Libya, Turkey-Israel, Turkey-Egypt and Turkey-Syria in order to develop a broader *strategic dialogue* towards the *EM*. Turkey will have to position itself as fair and equitable as well as transparent in the resolution of related issues in the *EM*, but will have to demonstrate its determination and intransigence regarding its fundamental rights and interests. Based on the success of the above-mentioned countries' working groups, it would be appropriate to turn to the Turkey-Greece working group and initiate the studies to determine the boundary of the Turkish-Greek maritime jurisdiction areas in the northwest of the *EM*. However, since the concerned working group in the northwest is unlikely to succeed or solve the problems, it is obvious that Turkey will obtain legal, political and diplomatic results having the advantage of reconciliation in the east, south and northwest of the *EM*, excluding Greece. Thus, while Turkey will be spared from isolation during the process, Greece and the GASC will be isolated. It is expected that in this process, the administration in Athens will use the terrorist elements that will disrupt the EU or Turkey as a means or will attempt to balance the actions of the administration of Ankara, with that of Haftar, as it did in Libya.

The biggest challenge regarding the delimitation of maritime jurisdictions in the *EM* is undoubtedly to find a solution that is acceptable to both Ankara and Athens. From the viewpoint of Ankara, the delimitation of the Greek and Turkish maritime jurisdiction areas in northwestern *EM* depends on the recognition that it should not pose an existential threat to Turkey's sovereignty and national security strategy.

For Turkey, reasons such as the growing threat originating from the *EM*, Turkey's non-inclusion in the gas forum and its exclusion from the sharing of maritime jurisdiction areas have caused serious disruptions in its *EM* policy. The bilateral or trilateral relations between Israel-GASC, Egypt-GASC, Israel-Greece have almost turned into a policy of encirclement of South Anatolia and the TRNC. Moreover, EU support for this policy and the U.S. patronage have caused political turmoil rather than transformation in the region. Having received regional and global support, the GASC aimed to turn this strength into an advantage in the Cyprus issue, to use it against the Turkish theses and to take revenge for the 1974 peace operation. Although the Ankara administration has a strong hand in the Cyprus issue, it is very uncomfortable with its own impasse in the energy equation in the region. The rise of the GASC as a regional player, attempting to consolidate its gains, and following a restrictive policy towards Turkey, which is a regional power despite the fact that its interlocutor is the TRNC or the Turkish Cypriots, has paved the way for the Ankara administration to take radical decisions and undertake actions that completely change the game. Thus, Turkey, as in the *ME*, has gone beyond moderate diplomacy in the *EM* and has acquired the identity of being a *game changer* or *playmaker*. With the agreements limiting the areas of maritime jurisdiction signed between 2003 and 2013 with the support of Greece and the EU, the GASC attempted to link the areas of maritime jurisdiction of Cyprus to the Greek islands and present this process as a requirement of the Acquis Communautaire. Turkey signed a Memorandum of Understanding with the legal government of Libya on November 27, 2019, in order to demonstrate the ineffectiveness of the efforts of

Greece and the GASC administration to assume jurisdiction in the *EM* and invalidate the EU acquis in this regard. With this approach, Turkey responded to the policy of the GASC-Greece, which intended to expand on the east-west axis in the *EM*, with a policy of expansion on the north-south axis and succeeded in turning the political action of Athens-South Nicosia into a failure.

Turkey has improved its relations in the *EM*, first with Libya and then with Algeria. However, the Ankara administration will also have to normalize and improve its relations with Israel and Egypt in the near future. With this method, Turkey will have reduced the scope of action of the GASC and Greece by establishing a wide network of relations regarding the *EM*, prevented the expansion of the EU's sphere of influence and hindered the U.S. from establishing unilateral policies in the region. Hence, it is expected that the maritime jurisdiction agreement between Turkey and the Government of National Accord of Libya will contribute to the resolution of conflicts in the region and to the reform of energy policies.

Clearly, Turkey's efforts towards the *EM* will have benefits in improving its relations with all regional powers, with the exception of the GASC, and increasing the potential opportunities, and its political results may be satisfactory. For, this approach may turn into a great benefit that will revise the dynamics and parameters of Turkish power in the region.

Turkey's Building Closer Relationships with the Key EU States

Partnership relations with the EU are important for Turkey and undoubtedly Turkey is an important partner for the EU. While the EU supports the rule of law, freedom of expression, the demands of democracy and a welfare society, it evidently needs Turkey's help and support in its fight against terrorism and irregular migration. Under the current circumstances, establishing a more coherent and integrated approach between Turkey and the EU will link the administrations in Ankara and Brussels as well as the major European capitals and help them to work in coordination for mutual interests.

While the most important issues that will push the EU and Turkey into a fruitful cooperation may be refugees, irregular migration, terrorism, trade and humanitarian aid, it would be worthwhile to continue discussions on the status issues such as accession or visa liberalization by emphasizing the benefits of the customs union, and to draw attention to the importance of Turkey's integration into the European production chain.

While Turkey has supported the EU in preventing irregular migration routes in the *EM* or in developing an emergency plan, the EU has tried to support transit countries such as Greece, the Western Balkans, Southeast Europe and Turkey with financial, humanitarian and security assistance to prevent irregular migration flows. However, the EU's unconditional support for the GASC and Greece in a *spirit of solidarity* while determining the zones of maritime jurisdiction in the *EM* and adopting an adverse attitude towards Turkey has reduced the opportunities for regional cooperation between Turkey and the EU and has led to the emergence of an atmosphere of conflict. In fact, the reason for the EU's attitude is that the exclusive economic zones, which the GASC and Greece have tried to determine unilaterally and with a fait accompli, are seen as new spheres of influence. Consequently, the EU extends its presence toward Asia Minor and supports the political position that can be in favor of this.

EU's attitude can be understood by its support for the preparation of the Seville map and its presentation it to the international community, its disregard for the rights of the TRNC and the Turkish Cypriots under the founding agreements of 1960, and its failure to take Turkey's power in the region seriously despite the fact that Turkey has the longest coastline in the Mediterranean. In fact, the support provided by the EU in terms of the *spirit of solidarity* is due to the fact that the policies of the GASC and Greece towards the *EM* are in line with the main policy of the Union or coincide with the national interests of the main member states of the Union. To some extent, the main member countries of the Union have preferred to do this in the *spirit of the Union*, as it would be difficult to intervene in the *EM* independently or to have a presence there. From this perspective, it is considered that the activities of the GASC and Greece might be instrumentalized for other leading countries.

Therefore, Turkey is obliged to express the Turkish point of view and defend its rights by meeting separately with the other EU member states, mainly Germany, France, Italy and Greece, and then constantly using the diplomatic channel within the Union. In order to be effective on the ground, the Turkish Foreign Ministry, which supports any kind of discourse with action, must remain coherent and consistent. For this reason, it is considered that it would be appropriate for the drilling vessels Fatih and Yavuz, the seismic research vessels Barbaros Hayrettin Paşa and Piri Reis to be present in the area and for the navy warships to appear there in order to ensure the safety of these vessels. Meanwhile, Turkey's cooperation with international foreign companies in oil and gas exploration and drilling or seismic exploration activities in the region in order to increase its sanctioning and deterrent power in this area would further enhance the strength and value of Turkey's activities in the *EM*. For, Turkey's pursuit of natural gas exploration activities on its own is not sustainable in terms of costs and funding, and it also comes at a diplomatic cost.

Making efforts to establish permanent contact and common work environments with the leading EU countries will transform these efforts into cooperation over time and thus increase the likelihood of acceptance the plausibility of Turkish theses. In order not to encounter a de facto situation in the meantime, it would be advantageous for the Ankara administration to support its arguments on the basis of international law. The agreement that Turkey has signed with the legal government in Tripoli is therefore important and appropriate.

Turkey's Establishment of New Base Areas in the EM or Demonstrating Its Military Presence

It is an important issue for Turkey to support cooperation and trade with regional actors in order to strengthen its economic structure. There is no doubt that this cooperation will not only improve Turkey's regional relations and its sanctioning power at the governmental level, but will also deepen it.

In fact, Turkey's policies towards the *EM* draw attention as policies with strategic depth while being powered by historical and legal developments. However, Turkey has been isolated because of its recent policies and its relations with many actors have deteriorated. The Ankara administration, whose relations with Israel deteriorated with the Mavi Marmara raid in 2010, with Syria due to the internal unrest in 2011, and with Egypt after Sissi came to power in 2013, has gradually toughened its regional policies toward the *EM*, as well.

The rivalry and hostility of Greece and the GASC towards Turkey arising from the Cyprus question has taken on a new dimension over time, leading to the problem of maritime jurisdictional zones in the *EM*. This new situation, put forward by the GASC and supported by the EU member states with the *Union's spirit of solidarity*, is seen as a confirmation of the solitude of Ankara and the Turkish thesis. Moreover, it is understood that the *EM*, which a global and hegemonic power such as the United States sees as an area where its foreign policy interests are challenged, has become a value which contributes to the solitude of the Ankara administration.

The changing balances and the formation of a new value system in the *EM* have led to troubling experiences in Turkey's relations with regional actors, in a new conflict environment. In particular, the GASC's signing agreements with Egypt in 2003, with Lebanon in 2007 and with Israel in 2010 that determine the areas of maritime jurisdiction, beginning to parcel out areas around the island of Cyprus, granting licenses for these areas and opening them up to the international community have created serious concerns. After these developments, first Greece-GASC-Israel, then Egypt and Italy started demarcating blocks in the *EM* based on bilateral agreements, and this was followed by the establishment of a gas forum in the *EM* which excluded Turkey and the TRNC. This demonstrates that Turkey and the TRNC have no place in the new order to be established in the *EM*, and that they are even isolated or marginalized through distinctive behavior.

The conflict between Turkey and Greece regarding the islands, islets and rocks whose sovereignty are disputed in the Sea of Islands, has taken a new dimension with the problem of maritime jurisdiction areas, which inevitably led to the establishment of a causal connection between the Sea of Islands and the *EM*. It is no coincidence that Greece considers the structures derived from its geographical formation as extensions of mainland Greece, claims that the areas of maritime jurisdiction start from the external border of these regions[81] and wishes to bring the areas of maritime jurisdiction of the GASC and that of Greece to one border. With this method, the TRNC's rights will be completely eliminated, while Turkey's rights will be severely limited.

The desire of some EU member countries to have a military location on the island of Cyprus has led them to request bases from GASC. This demand seriously conflicts with the importance and position of Cyprus in terms of Turkey's immediate environment policy. Therefore, the fact that Cyprus is in the hands of opposition forces, the construction of a settlement base on the island, the provision of military facilities and resources, or the presence of any force other than the legal guarantor states are reprehensible as this will cause a great threat and insecurity to the Turkish mainland.[82] It is clear that the resulting threat will force Turkey to take action and operate under the principle of reciprocity. As a result, it was found that Turkey can bring issues such as the establishment of a small base of drones and sombat drones in the north of the island, the construction of a naval base in the east of the TRNC, the increase in military capacity and power, the establishment of the Defense and Security Cooperation Office in accordance with the military cooperation agreement signed with the Libyan Government of National Accord and thereafter, the subsequent delivery of land, sea and air vehicles and associated weapons, as well as the allocation of training bases to the agenda.

If Turkey succeeds in perpetuating this situation, it will acquire strategic superiority and extend its dominance in the region. With the recent developments, Turkey will have the opportunity to dominate the eastern and western regions of the *EM* more easily. It is therefore natural for Turkey to want to restructure the regional equation. There is no doubt that even Turkey's willingness to maintain its naval elements on the Algerian coast will strengthen its position in the west of the *EM* and that this will affect the entire eastern region.

Turkey's foreign policy today has gone beyond a policy of reaction to actions and has turned into an *active* foreign policy. Ankara administration's change in foreign policy towards the *EM* has also been reflected in Turkey's relations with regional actors. However, such changes can lead to serious fragility in the region. To resolve this problem, Turkey will have to launch a high-level diplomatic campaign and restore its national and regional interests within the framework of the principle of fairness in its relations. Currently, Turkey cannot dominate the region either because its participation in regional alliances, forums, and other

---

[81] Deniz Bölükbaşı, **Turkey and Greece, The Aegean Disputes**, London, Cavendish Publishing, 2004, pp. 41-49; Sertaç Hami Başeren, **Doğu Akdeniz Deniz Yetki Alanları Uyuşmazlığı**, Ankara, İlke Basın Yayım, 2011, pp. 78-86.
[82] Soyalp Tamçelik and Burcu Ayhan, **Geopolitical Theories and Cyprus – The Importance of Cyprus Island in Geopolitical Theories**, Saarbrücken, Germany, Lambert Academic Publishing, 2013, pp. 56-81; Soyalp Tamçelik, **Kıbrıs'ta Güvenlik Stratejileri ve Kriz Yönetimi**, Ankara, Ortadoğu Teknik Üniversitesi (ODTÜ) Yayınları, 2009, pp. 201-220.

institutions and organizations is either incomplete or insufficient or because it refuses to be involved in them. The crises that have emerged in this process are damaging or undermining the interests of both Turkey and the regional actors.

Despite all the tensions in the region, Turkey continues to be a constant force and actor in directing the *EM*. Turkey's emphasis on military alliances along with political and economic cooperation with regional actors in order to make this power operational will further strengthen Turkey and may hinder the actions of GASC and other actors who support it.

It is therefore considered that Turkey will have to increase the number of bases in the *EM*, expand them or establish a new base area in Mersin in accordance with the implementation of a joint land, air and sea group command. In the future, should Turkey normalize its relations with Israel and Egypt, it would be able to ensure that two bases equivalent to its own will be established by the Israeli and Egyptian governments, thus establishing a tripartite structure for security and stability in the region.

Aside from these, Turkey needs to establish and develop a strategically oriented defense dialogue with all regional actors with the exception of the GASC, in order to overcome the insecurity syndrome existing in the *EM* since 2007. Furthermore, it would be beneficial for Turkey to invest in the economies and financial structures of the countries in the region by establishing partnerships with regional powers and foreign investors, and by enriching the political and military balance with an economic one.

Turkey's Establishment of a Military Base in the TRNC and Strengthening its Presence

The island of Cyprus in general, and the TRNC and the GASC in particular, are constantly experiencing security problems due to the developments in the *ME*, the Levant and North Africa. In this regard, the island of Cyprus is geographically open to all kinds of external attacks. The recent irregular migratory flows threaten the peoples of the island and force them to be on alert. The constant state of *security and vigilance* of the people of the Island leads to a security dilemma in their social and political identities. The GASC, on one hand, wants the support or patronage of the EU, NATO, the U.S., France and sometimes the RF, while on the other hand, the TRNC rejects all of the above and prefers only the effective and de facto guarantee of Turkey. Due to the particular position of the island, the insecurity from both sides grows from each other, as well as from the guarantor states and the international actors, institutions or organizations they wish to be protected by. However, due to the lack of trust between the two communities on the island, the need to be under the protection of one or more actors is becoming more prevalent than ever. In this regard, while Turkey is the only reliable ally of the TRNC, it constitutes the greatest threat and an unequal challenger to the GASC.

Another powerful element on the island is Great Britain. Britain has a significant opportunity and strategic advantage in the region due to its bases in Dhekelia and Akrotiri since the independence of Cyprus.[83] These two bases, located approximately 350 miles from Raqqa and 650 miles from Baghdad, provide support for air and naval operations of British and allied forces, and enables the British aircraft, operating against Daech, to take off from Akrotiri.[84]

Cyprus, which is closely linked to Euro-Atlantic society and values in general, was divided in two following the developments of 1974. To this date, the negotiations and incentives of the international community to reunite the peoples living on the island have not lead to any results. However, the biggest problem expressed by the Western allies regarding Cyprus is that the island has been divided since 1974, that the TRNC has been established in the North and that Turkish soldiers are on the island.[85]

But neither the Western allies nor the GASC and Greece state that Turkey interfered on July 20, 1974, as a consequence of the overthrow of Makarios by the clandestine organization EOKA-B and the annexation of the Republic of Cyprus to Greece. Thereafter, the new balance of power on the island was in favor of the Turkish Cypriots and Turkey. The GASC, which wanted to shift the balance of power in its own favour, tried to be deterrent by purchasing the S-300 missile system in 1997.[86] However, this attempt by the GASC was hindered by intense objections from Turkey and the pressure from Britain and NATO.

Due to the new developments in the international system, the US and EU countries, who do not consider this situation of Cyprus as sustainable for their national interests, want to redefine the international and regional status of the island and build a *Cyprus without Turkey* and a *federal system without the TRNC*. If the actors concerned achieve this goal within the new world order, they will have reunited Cyprus and integrated it into the Euro-Atlantic community and its system. In 2014, elements of the GASC naval forces increased their visibility and presence in the international system for the first time by participating in search and rescue operations with the U.S., Israeli and Greek navies.[87]

In this context, it is seen that Turkey is faced with an essential challenge of ensuring the security of the Anatolian geography rather than supporting the TRNC in Cyprus and the security in the region. Turkey must protect and monitor the national security and interests equation on the island of Cyprus in general and in the TRNC in particular. To this end, Turkey must protect its rights under

---

[83] Soyalp Tamçelik, "Kıbrıs'taki İngiliz Üslerinin Stratejik Önemi", **Uluslararası İnsan Bilimleri Dergisi,** Cilt. 8, No. 1, 2011, pp. 1510-1539.
[84] "RAF Akrotiri", Royal Air Force, https://www.raf.mod.uk/rafakrotiri/stationinformation/index.cfm, (Access 06.02.2020).
[85] "Cyprus: The Turkish Invasion", EURYDICE, 28.12.2019, https://eacea.ec.europa.eu/national-policies/eurydice/content/historical-development-15_en, (Access 06.02.2020).
[86] Soyalp Tamçelik, "Rum-Yunan İttifakında Ortak Savunma Doktrini ve Özellikleri", **Stratejik Araştırmalar Dergisi**, Cilt. 6, No. 12, 2008, pp. 13-39.
[87] "Kıbrıs'ta Arama Kurtarma Tatbikatı Yapıldı", Deniz Haber, 25.05.2014, https://www.denizhaber.com/guncel/kibrista-arama-kurtarma-tatbikati-yapildi-h35803.html, (Access 06.02.2020).

the founding agreements that established the Republic of Cyprus in 1960 and maximize its relations with the TRNC. Above all, the TRNC, with its military and law enforcement forces, is not equipped to ensure its internal and external security directly and independently in terms of the content of equipment. Hence, Turkey must support the TRNC's internal security,[88] but assure its external security. Cyprus, for its part, aims to ensure its external security by working with the U.S. and by becoming partners with NATO and the EU's Permanent Structured Cooperation (PESCO).[89]

Currently, confronted with a new problematic area, Turkey and the TRNC are receiving the greatest threat of all times from the *EM* or the maritime jurisdiction areas around Cyprus. Hence, Turkey refers to the threat emanating from the GASC for the sharing of maritime jurisdictions or to benefit from energy resources because it is an issue related to the existential concerns of Turkish Cypriots. While intensifying its foreign policy efforts towards the *ME* and the *EM*, it has become imperative for Turkey to articulate its policy towards Cyprus to this area and to conduct its foreign policy in these three regions with integrity. It would not be wrong to call this type of diplomacy *ME-EM-C* Diplomacy (also called *MEM-C*) since Cyprus, with its energy and security dimension, needs to be articulated within the main vector line of *ME-EM* Diplomacy.

With this method, policymakers in Turkey and the TRNC will have the opportunity to examine and evaluate the parameters of both Cyprus and the *ME* in their foreign policy practices related to *EM*. Despite many issues such as the fact that the criteria for the *ME*, the *EM* and Cyprus are different from each other in terms of foreign policy theory and practices, that they have different counterparts, and that different sources fuel their dynamics and achievements, their existence in the same political geography makes it necessary to consider this problematic areas as a whole. Although these problem areas were strictly separated from each other during the Cold War period, due to certain changes in the post-Cold War period and the ruptures that have taken place today, it was necessary to evaluate the three problem areas in terms of energy, security and maritime jurisdiction, in other words, as a three-leg coaster. Therefore, although the internal dynamics of these problems are different from each other, a new *set of concepts* was created based on the three parameters related to the state of the *energy, security,* and *maritime jurisdiction areas*, and by naming it the *ME-EM-C (MEM-C)* Diplomacy, a new universe of meanings was produced.

Although offshore energy is expected to improve the economic position and structure of Cyprus in particular, it will undoubtedly create a great opportunity.

---

[88] KKTC Anayasası'nın geçici 10. maddesinde, KKTC iç güvenliğinin Kıbrıs'taki Güvenlik Kuvvetleri Komutanlığına bağlı olduğu belirtilmektedir. For further information see... **KKTC Anayasası**, Devlet Matbaası, Lefkoşa, 2011.

[89] Yvonni-Stefania Efstathiou, "PeSCo - The Cyprus Perspective", The Armament Industry European Research Group (Ares Group), 2019, pp. 1-11, https://www.iris-france.org/wp-content/uploads/2019/02/Ares-35.pdf, (Access 06.02.2020).

In order for Turkey to support Cyprus' energy development and its establishing closer ties with European energy markets, it should register the TRNC's rights and interests in these areas, have a say in the parcelling out of energy deposits and in the issuing of exploration and drilling licenses, should be taken into account in the determination of maritime jurisdiction areas and that the GASC should not create a fait accompli with unilateral agreements.[90]

This approach, which Turkey has determined on behalf of itself and the TRNC, will strengthen the orientation of Cyprus, which is an island country, towards Turkey and will contribute to balancing its influence and dominance over the Euro-Atlantic axis to some extent. Meanwhile, it would not be correct for Turkey to support efforts to reunite the island and the two communities in an enhanced *ME-EM-C* Diplomacy for Cyprus. In an environment where collapsing states and regimes have emerged in the *ME*, fears of fragmentation or rights claims are spreading to the *EM*, and efforts to reunite an island like Cyprus, long divided and with separate authorities, under the roof of the EU, leads to discussions about the extent to which Turkey's claims, rights and interests will be beneficial. It is clear that Turkey will need to conduct short- and long-term benefit-cost analyses and undertake joint action with the TRNC. Taken from this perspective, the reunification of Cyprus is viewed as more disadvantageous for many reasons, in terms of the *ME-EM-C* Diplomacy requirements in the *ME-EM* region. Turkey must show that it can take countermeasures without abandoning its arguments for disarmament and demilitarization of the island, but taking into account attempts by other actors to establish bases for military or civilian elements given the island's location.[91] That is why the issue of Turkey's UAV and SİHA deployment on the island is based on the UAV and SİHA purchased by the GASC from Israel. Indeed, it must be taken into account that Turkey, which has shown that it will retaliate against any action that disrupts the balance of power and arms on the island, may establish a base, build a military facility within the borders of the TRNC, or may send arms or military reinforcements there on the grounds that any base that is established in the GASC will disrupt the balance of power on the island and in the region. It is a fact that Turkey has strengthened its *doctrine of retaliation and deterrence* through its recent foreign policy. However, it should be taken into account that this action may also have many disadvantages, such as provoking the rearmament and militarization as well as the establishment of base areas on the island and its surroundings.

[90] "No: 203, 13 Temmuz 2019, KKTC'nin Hidrokarbon Kaynaklarına İlişkin Yeni İşbirliği Önerisi Hk." T.C. Dışişleri Bakanlığı, 13.07.2020, http://www.mfa.gov.tr/no_203_-kktc-nin-hidrokarbon-kaynaklarina-iliskin-yeni-isbirligi-onerisi-hk.tr.mfa, (Access 06.02.2020).
[91] Soyalp Tamçelik, "Kıbrıslı Rumların Bölge Barışını Tehdit Eden Silahlanma Çabaları", **Turkish Studies International Periodical for the Languages, Literature and History of Turkish or Turkic**, Cilt. 6, No. 3, 2011, pp. 391-424.

Turkey's Increasing Its Cooperation Potential with Greece

Turkey and Greece occupy an important place in Europe and in the Atlantic region and they are actors linked to each other with a certain mission. Based on the new balances developing in the world, these two actors are sometimes in conflict and sometimes in cooperation. The advantages for Turkey and Greece to be partners in regional problems or global crises or to act jointly in a spirit of alliance are numerous. Yet, it is very difficult to expect the two countries to have a common objective and foreign policy behavior for many reasons such as the long historic legacy of the Turkish-Greek problems, the strong sense of revenge, and the pursuit of zero-sum policies. In particular, the fact that Greece bases its political interests on the *"nothingness"* of neighboring Turkey, and the GASC on the *"absence"* of Turkey inevitably leads to a conflict between their and Turkey's interests. Therefore, it would be more advantageous for the administrations in Ankara and Athens to develop mutual cooperation on a *minimalist* rather than *maximalist* basis. It is clear that especially if the energy resources of the region are to serve as a catalyst for cooperation between the two actors, it will be necessary to make it feasible with joint investments and cooperation doctrines, and adopt the principle of mutual benefit by proposing alternative routes. The establishment of a joint dialogue group between Turkey and Greece and its functionality will create significant value. It is expected that the proposed joint dialogue group will be able to negotiate on issues such as energy infrastructure and production in the *EM* and even in the Sea of Islands, prioritization of maritime security, and guaranteeing the fundamental rights and interests of the parties and thus reach a consensus on common ground. However, it is clear that the desired outcome cannot be achieved if the parties involved in this dialogue group act with a maximalist point of view.

Greece, the GASC and Israel have been holding annual trilateral dialogue meetings since 2014, in part to form an alliance against Turkey, with the participation of Egypt or Italy at times.[92] With the transformation of this group into a potential power in the form of the *"Eastern Mediterranean Triad (EM-3)/Quartet (EM-4)/Quintet (EM-5)"*, Turkey's rights and interests in the *EM*, the existence and rights of the TRNC are being ignored, and a new equation that completely excludes Turkey and the TRNC is being established. It would be more appropriate to formulate this system as *EM5+1*, as it is known that the U.S. often supports it. It seems very difficult for Turkey to cooperate with Greece in this system. Although Greece would have to change or revise its main policy towards the *EM* to achieve this, it is not expected to happen in the near future. Besides, it is not possible for Turkey to accept the GASC as an interlocutor since it does not recognize it. It is not realistic for Turkey to contact and cooperate with the GASC on the island, on the assumption that the interlocutor of the GASC is the TRNC. Therefore, it appears that the only option for Turkey is to contact the Greek government on this issue. However, there is no doubt that if

---

[92] Restoring Eastern Mediterranean as a U.S. Strategic Anchor, op.cit., p. 57.

the Ankara administration normalizes its relations with regional actors and synchronizes its foreign policy, this will limit the scope of action of the GASC and force Greece to cooperate. The use of external pressure instruments and rational suggestions will strengthen Ankara's position and by signing agreements with other regional states, similar to the agreement signed with Libya, Ankara will be able to fully suppress the above-mentioned actor.

Turkey's Developing and Transforming Its Relationship with Israel into a Strategic Partnership to Ensure Maritime Security

It would be wise for Turkey to include Israel's maritime resources and capabilities in the maritime activities in the *EM*. Because Israel, having national shipping companies and a long maritime history, is considered as an important player of strategic depth in the *EM*. On the other hand, Israel's naval capabilities are weaker than those of other regional actors. Israel tends to reorganize its naval forces in the *EM*, transforming its coastguard-type maritime vessels into more strategic and operational forces. This change will undoubtedly give Israel an advantage over time and strengthen its position in maritime security in the *EM*. However, the GASC, Lebanon and Israel are currently not in a position to pursue long-term military operations or to bear the potential risks of such operations in their maritime areas. For example, during the Israel-Hezbollah war in 2006, Israeli naval elements were attacked by Hezbollah militants. This attack revealed Israel's vulnerability to future attacks from maritime jurisdictions. Israel is expected to increase its maritime security capabilities including search and rescue and disaster relief capabilities.

With regard to energy cooperation, Israel's relations with Egypt are at the expected level, but that level is likely to increase in the coming period. The U.S. administration also supports and encourages Egypt and Israel to cooperate more closely in the field of energy. However, the interruption of gas supplies from Egypt in 2012 inevitably caused a dispute and led Israel to demand compensation.[93] Although the parties' demands were met with U.S. assistance, the issue of facilitating Israeli access to Egyptian LNG facilities arose. In this regard, Israel aims to establish a pipeline between the natural gas fields in the Leviathan region and the Egyptian liquefaction facilities, and Egypt aims to obtain additional economic benefits. This pipeline, which Israel wants to build for export purposes, will clearly be much less expensive and risky than any pipeline to Turkey or Cyprus. It is anticipated that this line, which will extend Israeli-Egyptian relations beyond security, will also encourage other actors in the region to cooperate.

The fact that the authorized operators of Israel's Tamar and Leviathan fields signed a $15 billion agreement to supply natural gas to an Egyptian company on

---

[93] Ora Cohen, "Egypt Signals That Giant Gas Deal Will Hinge on Israeli Concessions", Haaretz, 26.02.2018, https:// (Access www.haaretz.com/israel-news/egypt-signals-that-giant-gas-deal-will-hinge-on-israeli-concessions-1.5848582, (Access 06.02.2020).

February 19, 2018, shows that the Tel Aviv administration has prioritized this route over the others.[94]

Israel, which wants to conduct a broader cooperation in the *EM*, is making plans in accordance with the theory of unified containers and in this sense, by connecting the West Bank to Israel through a gas pipeline, it wants to integrate the administrative and energy infrastructure of Jordan and Palestine into its own.[95]

Reconciliation among Palestinians, in other words, coordination of the Palestinian administration based in the West Bank with the administration in Gaza and normalization of economic activities will create a great opportunity. Turkey's support for the reconstruction of Gaza will also benefit its own interests. The same applies to Israel, as it is considered that the Kurdish settlement in Syria and northern Iraq will have significant benefits for the Tel Aviv administration. In both cases, it is expected that the actors involved will be able to reach a compromise, even if their national interests and expectations are contradictory.

However, Israel's agreements, joint exercises or alliances with the GASC and Greece inevitably disturb Ankara's administration and result in controversy over the areas of maritime jurisdiction and the subject of sovereignty in the *EM*.[96] As such, the two countries would be able to normalize their relations, first by reaching an agreement on energy policy and the delimitation of maritime jurisdiction areas in the *EM*, and then by reconciling their interests in the *ME*. In fact, it is evident that reconciliation will be much better and less costly than conflict for both parties. For this reason, it is considered that the best route to use for the marketing of natural gas in the *EM* will be the route that crosses Cyprus and reaches first Turkey and then the European markets. This will also be the cheapest and most reliable route.[97] Based on this assessment, the main point that both administrations should pay attention to is to focus not on "*must haves*" but on *possible values* when it comes to foreign policy implementation.

The deepening of Turkey-Israel relations after the normalization and its transformation into a strategic partnership over time will bring many benefits to both sides, as both sides will be freed from their maximalist demands, will not threaten each other's raison d'être and can act in a spirit of solidarity against the

---

[94] Rory Jones and Jared Malsin, "Noble Energy, Israel's Delek to Supply Gas to Egypt in $15 Billion Deal", All Street Journal, 19.02.2018, https://www.wsj.com/articles/noble-energy-israels-delek-to-supply-gas-to-egypt-in-15-billion-deal-1519070941, (Access 06.02.2020).
[95] "Ortadoğu'da Sular Duruldu", Enerji Günlüğü, 11.11.2013, https://www.enerjigunlugu.net/ortadogu da-sular-duruldu-6029h.htm (Access 06.02.2020).
[96] Soyalp Tamçelik ve Emre Kurt, "İsrail'in ve GKRY'nin İzlediği Hidrokarbon Politikası ve Türkiye'ye Muhtemel Etkileri", **Artvin Çoruh Üniversitesi Uluslararası Sosyal Bilimler Kongresi (15-17 Ekim 2014) Bildiriler Kitabı**, Ankara, Nobel Akademik Yayıncılık, 2015, pp. 673-699.
[97] Özer Balkaş, "Doğu Akdeniz'de Doğal Gaz Keşifleri, Pazarlama Senaryoları, Enerji Güvenliği ve Jeopolitika", TMMOB Jeoloji Mühendisleri Odası, 01.03.2019, https://www.jmo.org.tr/resimler/ekler/9a30643920bb533_ek.pdf, (Access 06.02.2020).

complications that may arise in international politics

Emergence of the "Blue Homeland" Concept and Its Development in the Regional Seas as Turkey Expands Its Multilateral Naval Exercises

The naval elements of the TAF and the Turkish Navy will have to consider the Black Sea, the *EM* and the Sea of Islands as a whole and in a purely monolithic manner in order to maintain their presence in the seas surrounding the territorial borders of Turkey, and evaluate these maritime spaces as integrated units. For this purpose, it is believed that Turkey should be able to evaluate the three sea areas under the concept of *"Integrated Maritime Policy"*. With this method, the three sea areas will be synchronized with each other. This synchronization will make it possible to evaluate Turkish maritime policy with terrestrial geopolitics and to optimize Turkey's presence in the region's seas. In this case, Turkey will acquire a new understanding, perception and culture as a "land mass + water mass" country, instead of being a purely land-based country. For the first time, Turkey has defined a monolithic sea concept with regard to the water mass surrounding it and named it the *"Blue Homeland"*.[98] Then, for the first time in the history of the Republic, the Naval Forces Command conducted an exercise with 103 ships in three seas surrounding the country and called it *"Exercise Blue Homeland 2019"*.[99] In fact, this is nothing more than a new analytical foreign policy for Turkey.

Turkey's new maritime strategy means to use the Black Sea and its ports repeatedly, to use the Sea of Islands and its ports carefully, and to use the Mediterranean Sea and its ports deliberately and to integrate them into the new action plans as a part of a whole or to articulate integrated maritime areas. It seems essential to ensure the boundaries of the maritime jurisdictional areas in the region and their legitimacy under international law so that Turkey and the TAF can actively and effectively use them. Furthermore, in order for Turkey to protect its maritime rights and interests and maintain the *non-conflict status* between regional powers, all parties involved will have to ensure *fairness* and *compliance with international law*.

In order for Turkey to diversify its military deployment options in the *EM*, it is essential to expand its presence at sea, if possible, to acquire new deployment areas in North Africa, and to expand its commercial and transportation fleet. Should Turkey accomplish this, it will provide a great opportunity and capability area to its naval elements. In fact, it is argued that Turkey, having this opportunity, will get a wider strategic access in the *EM* and can provide greater

---

[98] Cihat Yaycı, **Doğu Akdeniz'in Paylaşım Mücadelesi ve Türkiye**, Ankara, Kırmızı Kedi Yayınevi, 2020, p. 56-62.
[99] Durmuş Genç, "Mavi Vatan'daki Dev Tatbikat Göz Kamaştırdı", Anadolu Ajansı, 07.03.2019, https://www.aa.com.tr/tr/turkiye/mavi-vatandaki-dev-tatbikat-goz-kamastirdi/1411433, (Access 06.02. 2020).

security, in part through Libya and the TRNC. However, in order to achieve more benefits and stability in the region, it will be able to establish joint maritime positions, as well as new areas or ports, with other players in the region, and thus mutually ensure and even balance the sharing of assets and power combination in the *EM*.

It is anticipated that this step, which is intended to secure the stability and peace of the *EM*, will contribute significantly to the concept of security, if implemented on a larger scale, not only in the EM, but in the entire Mediterranean. However, this may prove disadvantageous as not all countries bordering the *EM* are governed by democratic regimes, countries in the region prioritize maximizing their own interests, they fail to agree on issues such as terrorism and irregular migration, and disagree on common values. Considering that in the not very distant future, security needs will increase in the *EM*, expenditures on armaments are estimated to increase, the number of naval elements will outnumber those of today, and the risk of conflict will increase significantly. Therefore, for its own maritime security, it is imperative that Turkey integrates its strategy and structure in a monolithic manner to avoid any waste of resources.

Turkey's Exclusion of the *EM* from NATO's New Mission

Recent developments have led to the inclusion of the *ME* and the *EM* in Turkey's security concept. The unilateral decisions of the GASC to limit and authorize areas of maritime jurisdiction in Cyprus have led to the inclusion of Cyprus in the problematic area of the *ME-EM*. Therefore, a new problem area has been added to the *MEM-C* Diplomacy, which is included in Turkey's new security concept. Since this new problem area has entered NATO's security concept or sphere of influence, it is very likely for NATO to intervene here. In fact, while analyzing the situation in the *ME* and the related *EM* in early 2005, NATO stated that the *ME* had a close and profound effect on the security of European and Atlantic societies, and then drew attention to the importance of new developments in the *EM*.[100] Since *insecurity* in both regions threatens the *security* of the wider region and the global system, it is possible that NATO will undergo a radical transformation to focus and intervene in both regions. When the actions of NATO's global coalition forces against DAESH in Mosul and Raqqa are evaluated, the meaning is obvious. The emergence of a conflict in the *EM* or the spread of proxy wars from the *ME* to the *EM* will lead to an increase in counterterrorism operations in Turkey's southern waters and the involvement of non-regional actors in the region. It is envisaged that the NATO Military Committee, when assessing the operational constraints and vulnerabilities related to the presence of Russian air power and naval forces in the *EM*, will not want to deal with issues related to the maritime jurisdiction of the island of Cyprus or

---

[100] Gunther Altenburg, "An Opportunity We Cannot Miss", Middle East Round Table, 17.02.2005, http://www.bitterlemons-international.org/previous.php?opt=1&id=72#298, (Access 06.02.2020).

will prefer not to do so because of the high risk of conflict. Given the military presence, deployment, and accumulation of the RF in the *EM*, it is understood that the presence of Russian forces in the region will be permanent and may impede NATO's presence, area of operation, and access to energy resources.

Given that there is a geographic division of power and responsibilities between NATO's military and political missions, that common threats are regionally determined, and that they will be jointly addressed, it can be seen that the subject matter of the threat in the *EM* originates from regional structures and poses a serious threat to NATO's southeast flank. Therefore, as NATO seeks to create a new balance between the emerging *threats* and the *security issues* in the *EM*, it may attempt to increase its military build up in the region, identify military deployment areas and patrol with its navy. This may lead to the narrowing of the areas of sovereignty or influence of regional states, including Turkey, and the formation of a new threat perception. To some extent, NATO's entry into the *EM* will signify the entry of other global actors into the region as well, and this may fundamentally change the power pyramid and hierarchy in the region. The realization of this possibility could force Turkey to reconsider its foreign policy actions and preferences, and thus the Ankara administration must ensure that NATO or coalition forces do not enter the region.

Turkey's Establishment of a Security Dialogue for the EM

It would be beneficial for Turkey to take small steps using the technique of high-level diplomacy in order to establish a *security dialogue* with the *EM* and the riparian countries. At the next stage, it will be essential to start *dialogue-seeking* conferences, deepen this process with defense, foreign affairs, intelligence and security officials, and to bring it to a point where leaders can make the final decision through summit diplomacy. In this process, all riparian states and leaders will be addressed first, with the exception of the GASC, and the public opinion will be determined as the target audience. In the second stage, the European countries, the U.S. and the RF will be approached. Turkey's main gains from this process will be to define the concept of regional security in the *EM*, reach consensus on key discussions, draft a framework for an agreement, balance regional interests and generate new ideas on security trends. To this end, Turkey will need to identify two separate working groups and two separate security dialogue strategies regarding conflict areas in the *EM*. As a result, the Ankara administration must on the one hand communicate directly with all the relevant actors in the *EM*, and on the other hand, by establishing first indirect and then direct contacts with actors such as the European states, the U.S. and the RF, it should focus on private and bilateral meetings and expand its political space using diplomatic means. While Turkey's main objective should be to engage with the governments of the region and reach an agreement with them on the principle of fairness, it is expected to resort to all kinds of political actions and behaviours in order to break or weaken the GASC-Greece-EU bloc. In this process, Turkey should intensify its efforts to share maritime jurisdiction areas in the *EM*, use the revenues from energy resources for the development of regional peace, transmit the discovered natural gas to international markets, determine alternative routes and choose the cheapest, simplest and most cost-effective of them.

The foreign affairs, energy, and security bureaucracy should focus on showing what the *EM*, the *ME* and global actors will gain from this process, noting the importance of addressing issues with a comprehensive approach and establishing an equation in which all parties can benefit. Turkey's security dialogue regarding the *EM* will have to balance and satisfy the interests, priorities and objectives of the actors in the region. Therefore, as Turkey initiates the security dialogue for the *EM*, it should convince all parties within the framework of rational thinking, political gain and national interest, and should make them feel that otherwise, with the use of coercive diplomacy, the gains will be less and the costs will be higher.

Conclusion

While Turkey was once powerful and influential in the *EM* and its region, it is intended to be reduced to a country whose power is being tested, whose influence is being diminished, and whose ability to sanction is being reduced. In the new world order that emerged after the Cold War period, certain regional actors and world powers resorted to actions that limited Turkey's effectiveness in the *EM*, challenged its power and even disrupted its influence.

From this, it is understood that Turkey is caught between the values of the Cold War and the values of the post-Cold War world orders. The conflict between old and new values in the TFP is nothing more than a conflict of foreign policy paradigms. It has become clear that the old set of values in Turkey's foreign policy is not compatible with the new one, and is even diametrically opposed to it. Turkey has faced a threat from its immediate environment due to the fact that it had failed to realize or had difficulties in realizing its regional interests with its former set of values. While discussing Turkey's inadequacy in the face of regional and global competition, the activities of global and regional actors in *ME* and *EM* have gradually increased and they have made progress towards building a new value system. In this process, the old values of the TFP began to be consumed as it could not produce a counter-value or display a balancing political position. The change in the *ME* since the end of the Cold War and the ten-year war in Syria had a great impact on this exhaustion of the TFP. Although they seem to be separate from each other, the change experienced in both regions accelerated the transformation of the region as a whole. While the climate of conflict in Syria has provided strength and dominance to Salafi jihadist groups, the most significant aspect for them has been that it has facilitated the formation of a security zone. This has triggered the refugee crisis and started to erode the power, sovereignty, social peace and territorial integrity of the nation-states in the region.

The same situation was experienced in the *EM*, although the actors and interests were different. Although developments in the *EM* were triggered primarily by the GASC and Greece, they were supported by the EU and the U.S., and gained momentum through the efforts of regional actors. However, TRNC and Turkey were excluded from this process. This situation, which was considered the first phase, gained new value when it moved to the second phase, due to the fact that the actors with a coastline in the Mediterranean were from the Middle East and had now also started claiming the mass water in the *EM*, in addition to their ongoing struggle for dominance in the *ME*. The main catalyst for this phenomenon, which is expressed as the limitation of areas of maritime jurisdiction in international law, is the same as that of the actors mentioned in the first phase and has developed in the context of *energy policy*. It is believed that assessing the *ME* and the *EM* as a whole would be more appropriate in Turkey's regional foreign policy practices, rather than assessing them as separate, disconnected or independent from each other. It would be appropriate to call such a foreign policy practice *ME-EM* Diplomacy.

The emergence of terrorist structures such as DAESH, in addition to the radical changes and economic crises in the region, have inevitably brought the issue of security to the forefront. The proxy wars in the *ME*, the inhumane activities of DAESH, the reduction of the peoples of the region to the status of refugees, and the efforts of regional actors to maximize their own interests have led to an increased attention to the region by some regional countries such as Turkey, Iran, Egypt, and Israel, as well as some world powers such as the U.S., the RF, and some of the EU member countries. On the other hand, the developments in the *EM* have enabled the interested parties to construct a broader *foreign policy* and *defense strategy*. Thus, each actor in the region has shown that it can use a range of economic, diplomatic, and military means or take unconventional and legal initiatives in the region to more effectively implement its main strategic objectives or increase its influence. For this reason, it was found that many states in the region cooperate with groups relevant to proxy wars, value terrorist groups such as DAESH, PYD/YPG/SDG/PKK and take unconventional initiatives. However, there are two main elements of the use of terrorist elements in the region. One is that actors seeking to achieve their own interests are unwilling to enter the field directly and prefer not to enter with their own forces. Otherwise, there would be problems in terms of the cost and legality of the actor entering the field with its own power elements. The second is the use of terrorist elements to create a zone of legitimacy, as it will call into question the adequacy and validity of interventions on the ground. Therefore, it is possible to conclude that proxy wars will be maintained and that terrorist elements will continue to be used for a certain period of time due to the reluctance of the relevant global and regional actors to enter the field directly.

Contrary to the *ME*, on the other hand, in the *EM*, rather than proxy wars, there is an environment where regional states are directly involved, trying to extend their dominance over the seas, joining their forces against Turkey, transforming economic and energy cooperation into a military-political alliance and seeking the support of the international community in this regard. Developments in the *EM* and the *ME* have shown that Turkey is seen as either an external actor, an ineffective member, or a partner to be excluded completely.

In this case, Turkey finds itself in the position of a state that behaves atypically, is marginalized, feeds on contradictory doctrines, uses its military power, is aggressive in its policies, or engages in largely reactive foreign policy practices whenever it opposes the foreign policy practices of the relevant actors and engages in the discourse, actions and attitudes that relate to them. Turkey's current foreign policy position leads it to be perceived as a hesitant, insecure, inconsistent, undemocratic, lawless and violent state and to be seen as a partner that creates suspicion in its alliances and gaps in its relations, by both regional and global powers. In their assessments of Turkey's foreign policy, these actors argue that the practices of the Ankara administration pose a threat to regional cohesion and scenarios, and are fundamentally disruptive to the global political order. The reaction of regional actors to Turkey's reactive stance has been to turn to alternative regional structures, formations and alliances instead of seeking a diplomatic solution and vision. The reactions of global actors against Turkey are to support alliances, actions and forums without Turkey or to create environments where Turkey has no specific gravity.

After 40 years of fighting separatist terrorism and 25 years of internal unrest linked to the *ME*, Turkey has acquired the skills and experience to resolve regional conflicts and formulate policies against them. However, Turkey's several failures regarding the *ME* stem from its inability to understand the change in the region after the end of the Cold War and its inability to foresee where the current situation might lead. It can be said that Turkey has a similar lack of vision towards the *EM*. Consequently, the question of what *is* or *should be* the solution to these two main problematic areas remains a serious matter for Turkey's policymakers.

The first problem is how to *eliminate* the instability in the *ME*, and the second one is how to *establish* the disrupted balance in the *EM*. Turkey's interest in the *ME* is primarily to prevent further destabilization of Syria and the surrounding region. For Turkey, this is a phenomenon that must be pursued despite the lawlessness of the Assad regime and the territorial integrity of Syria. Regarding the *EM*, Turkey's priority is to establish closer cooperation with EU countries, to discourage the U.S. from marginalizing Turkey and to protect the interests of Turkey and the TRNC in this region. Since Turkey's objective is to achieve its own national interests and protect its fundamental rights, one of its fundamental needs has been to develop an integrated strategy for the *ME* and the *EM*. In this regard, Turkey has to develop the *ME-EM* policy that was expressed before. If this doctrine includes the Cyprus phenomenon as well, it would be appropriate to call it *ME-EM-C* Diplomacy *(MEM-C)*. This doctrine, which will allow Turkey to expand its power projection and gain dominance in terms of energy policy, will help increase the capacity and avoid the waste of time/work in an integrated political spectrum.

There is no doubt that the gap between the objectives and interests of the Ankara administration in the two regions will narrow if the integration of the *ME* and the *EM* policies and their harmony with Turkey's interests are ensured. However, the Ankara administration will have to re-evaluate its relations with regional actors and initiate the normalization process, because Turkey is an important actor, partner and catalyst for both the *ME* and the *EM*. Moreover, it is one of the three guarantor countries of the island of Cyprus in the *EM*. Therefore, there is no harm in adding the *C* (Cyprus) partnership to the *ME* and the *EM* partnership, since it appears that otherwise it would be impossible for Turkey to pursue its regional policies and ensure its integrity. Turkey must make every effort to ensure the continuity of its integrated regional policies and to maintain its partnership. Therefore, the strategic advantage that *MEM-C* will bring to Turkey will be to produce alternatives to Turkey's regional political practices and interests, and to develop relevant tools and opportunities. Knowing the existence of regional actors with clear objectives or negative agendas against Turkey, it is clear that the Ankara administration will have to compete with them simultaneously and in a coordinated manner, and will have to balance and manage their interests.

Turkey needs to calculate and evaluate how it will deal with these three interconnected problem areas at the regional level (*ME-EM-C/MEM-C*), the future of the region and what Ankara's role will be in the near future. Firstly, Turkey does not have a simple formula or hierarchy of preferences regarding *ME-EM-C* or *MEM-C*. On the other hand, Turkey needs to protect its sphere of influence and effectiveness against its allies and regional rivals, strengthen its position and determine a strategic plan based on achievable goals, and even a main policy. When this is the case, Turkey's main objective should be to evaluate the above-mentioned regions as an integrated whole, to build an integrated political algorithm for this and to set up its determination on it.

Since it will be difficult to predict in advance how the *ME-EM* region has changed or what the direction of change will be, it is of great importance for Turkey to be the guide, determinant or at least the influencer of this change and development in terms of protecting Turkish interests and rights. First of all, Turkey is one of the most important and significant players in the region, and its diplomatic presence cannot be ignored. Recently, Turkey has disrupted the plans of global and regional powers with a series of operation plans developed in the *ME*. As for the *EM*, on the other hand, the dispatch of seismic and drilling vessels in the area, using naval forces as a deterrent, the signing of the Memorandum of Understanding with the legal government of Tripoli of Libya to determine the areas of maritime jurisdiction have confirmed the tactical behavior of Ankara's method, showed that it could also use military elements when necessary, and above all, it has demonstrated its political will and determination. This attitude of Turkey has clearly demonstrated its presence in both regions, and the need to use common sense and coordinate regional interests within the framework of the principle of fairness in order to establish a lasting peace. In this regard, the Ankara administration had to resist the challenge by using diplomatic, economic and military power and demonstrate its determination. Conflicts in the region or the perceived threat posed by the crises have forced Turkey to pay more attention to regional developments, reconsider its strategies and re-arrange its priorities. In fact, while the emerging regional crises have produced a perception of threat to Turkey, they have also brought along new opportunities. It is a known fact that countries that manage crises and threats well often turn them into opportunities. Turkey's indifference to this situation or its assessment with Cold War paradigms will not only cause it to miss regional opportunities, but will also result in a geometric increase in existing threats or the inability to prevent or direct those threats. For, the changes in the region or the political construction processes are too important to be delayed. The cumulative changes experienced in the region have long surpassed the preferences of regional actors and have completely eliminated the possibility of waiting.

The biggest challenge for Turkey in the coming period will be to determine whether it will make a vital strategic choice of combining the *ME* and the *EM* and whether it will add the *C* to it. Turkey must accept that the protection of its strategic interests and rights derived from international law and the historical past is an absolute necessity rather than a choice. Therefore, if the Ankara administration fails to make the aforementioned change, it will confront an environment in which it will have to make many decisions with strategic consequences in the near future. A Turkey that does not have an integrated and broader vision in its regional policies will not be able to execute, manage or protect its regional interests. Turkey's small tactical actions or pursuing its policies with a narrow vision will further reduce its power in the *ME* and the *EM* regions and make its influence more and more insignificant. If Ankara's administration proceeds as before, not only will it harm Turkey's interests in the region and create an environment in which it will feel threatened, but will also strengthen Turkey's regional rivals. In this regard, Turkey's new strategic mindset is not based on what exists under the current conditions, but on anticipating what the future of the region will be and protecting its fundamental rights and interests. The proposed *ME-EM* and *MEM-C* Diplomacy would be comprehensive and relevant in this regard, and capable of addressing Turkey's needs collectively and cumulatively.

THE INFLUENCE OF SEA POWER AND TURKEY'S STRUGGLE IN THE BLUE HOMELAND

Doğan Şafak Polat*

Introduction

A nation's military force is extended to the sea through naval power. It consists of many elements such as warships and weapons, auxiliary vehicles and trained troops, merchant ships, naval bases; and a nation's naval power is measured by its capacity to use the seas against its enemies and adversaries. The potential for naval power is determined by elements such as population, government character, economic soundness, the quantity and quality of harbors and coastline, and the number and location of a country's bases and colonies relative to desirable maritime trade. The primary purpose of naval power has always been to protect allied ships from hostile attacks, as well as to destroy or intercept enemy military and commercial cargo. One of the belligerent states can dominate the seas only if that state has de facto control over surface transport in some parts of the seas and prevents enemy communications while maintaining its own maritime communications. Naval power can be used to exert military and economic pressure on an enemy by restricting or blocking the import of goods needed for war. Naval power might also prevent an enemy from getting finances through commodity exports to neutrals, as well as neutrals trading with the enemy. Blockade is the term for the use of sea power in this manner, which is normally done in accordance with international law. Land targets have also been bombarded from the sea by naval troops. This function of naval power developed greatly in importance in the first half of the twentieth century. The introduction of the aircraft carrier, as well as the missile-firing nuclear submarine, introduced a new dimension to this bombardment potential. In general nuclear warfare, the nuclear submarine was the single most important tool of naval power in the 1960s and 1970s; functionally, it was not much different from strategic air power and land-based missiles.

Based on his studies into maritime history, Alfred Thayer Mahan, a US Navy strategist, proposed modern naval strategy and sea force theory. His 1890 book *The Influence of Sea Power on History, 1660-1783* is a classic explication of the importance of sea power as the foundation of national power and grandeur. This book explores the role of sea power in the seventeenth and eighteenth centuries, as well as the different conditions required to sustain and acquire it, with a focus on possessing the largest and most powerful fleet. His theory rapidly drew the

* Assoc. Prof. Dr., Istanbul, Turkey, E-mail: dpolat@hotmail.com, ORCID ID https://orcid.org/0000-0003-0786-1789.

attention of the world and became a significant concept.

The rhetoric of Turkey's "Mavi vatan" or "blue homeland" is more than just political branding. Cihat Yaycı, the navy's previous chief of staff, is widely credited with inventing it. However, after Yayc's departure, observers have developed a new respect for the concept's creator and major promoter, retired Turkish Rear Adm. Cem Gürdeniz. The term is most commonly used to refer to Turkey's maritime claims in the eastern Mediterranean. The presence of substantial natural gas resources off the coast of Cyprus is key to these interests. The majority of these reserves are located within what Turkey considers to be its exclusive economic zone. However, such a stance contradicts allegations made by Greece and the Greek Cypriot side. Both governments have claimed that Turkey violates important provisions of the UN Convention on the Law of the Sea, which Turkey has never ratified.

There are two parts to this article. The first section contains information on naval strategy and naval power. The seminal contributions of Mahan and Corbett are highlighted in particular. The second section discusses Turkey's new naval strategy, "blue homeland" as well as its consequences.

Naval Power and Naval Strategy

The ability to achieve and keep control of the sea is known as naval power. It refers to a country's military authority being extended to the seas. The term is collective, referring to the whole of all devices used to achieve and exercise control over the water.[1] It comprises of such diverse aspects as fighting vessels and armaments, auxiliary craft, commercial shipping, bases, and trained troops, and is measured in terms of a nation's potential to exploit the seas in defiance of rivals and competitors.[2] Even when operating from a land base, aircraft employed to control seaborne transportation serve as instruments of naval power; aircraft flying from carriers reflect the extension of naval power even when hitting targets deep interior. The functions of naval power in World War II were the same as they were in the 16th century, when warships particularly designed for battle first appeared, with the exception of a significant rise in bombardment of coastal or interior targets from the sea. The number and quality of harbors and coastline, as well as the number and position of a nation's colonies and bases in relation to desired sea commerce, all influence seanaval power power capabilities. The primary goal of naval power has always been to protect allied shipping from hostile attack while also destroying or impeding enemy commercial and military cargo. When one of the belligerents has virtual control of surface shipping in areas of the seas, he is said to have command of the seas, with the capacity to defend his own maritime communications while denying

---

[1] Ernest J. King, "The Role of Sea Power in the International Security", **Proceedings of the Academy of Political Science**, Vol. 21, No. 3, World Organization: Economic, Political and Social, May, 1945, pp. 79-86.
[2] Britannica, **Sea Power**, https://www.britannica.com/topic/sea-power (Access 13.04.2021).

enemy communications. Sea power can also be used to put military and economic pressure on an adversary by restricting the import of goods required for warfighting. It might also hinder him from getting finances through commodity exports to neutrals, as well as neutrals trading with the enemy. Blockade is the term for the use of naval power in this manner, which is normally done in accordance with international law.

Naval strategy is the naval equivalent of military strategy on land, and it involves the preparation and waging of war at sea. The tactics of military operations conducted on, beneath, or above the sea are referred to as naval warfare. The overall strategy for winning victory at sea, as well as the related idea of maritime strategy, is referred to as naval strategy. It comprises campaign planning and execution, the movement and positioning of naval forces that allows a commander to fight at a location that is convenient to them, and enemy deception. Naval tactics is concerned with the execution of combat plans and the maneuvering of ships or fleets. Tactics, as warfare actions, are designed and carried out in the actual and figurative heart of war's violence. Tactical science is a systematic description of these actions, whereas tactical art is the ability to perform them in conflict. Willpower and courage must constantly complement tactical art and science in order to gain success, and often determine the result of combat. These characteristics are not tactics, but they are linked to tactics in the same way that a good decision is linked to the resolution with which it is carried out.[3] Naval strategy is defined as the pursuit of naval power, or the ability to use the seas for military or commercial objectives while preventing an adversary from doing so. "The first and most obvious light in which the sea shows itself from the political and social point of view is that of a gigantic highway," says Captain Alfred Thayer Mahan, a naval history lecturer and president of the United States Naval War College. The importance of technological improvement on tactics was arguably exaggerated by the American naval strategist Mahan. Mahan provided a groundbreaking analysis of the relevance of naval force in the creation of the British Empire in 1890.[4] He finished a companion work, *The Influence of Naval power on the French Revolution and Empire, 1793–1812*, two years later. He concentrated on the use of ships in large-scale wars and the strategies required to carry them out. "From time to time, the framework of tactics has to be completely broken down due to new fighting systems," he wrote, "but the foundations of strategy so far endure, as though set upon a rock." Mahan recognized the value of naval history in identifying strategic constants, or principles of strategy that have stayed constant despite technological progress.[5] Mahan begins the book by looking at the reasons that led to a mastery of the seas, particularly how Great Britain came to be so close to its near dominance. Mahan maintained that British control of the seas, along with a matching

---

[3] Wayne P. Hughes, "**Naval warfare**", https://www.britannica.com/topic/naval-warfare#ref511280 (Access 13.04.2021).
[4] Alfred Thayer Mahan, **The Influence of Sea Power upon History, 1600–1783**, London, Sampson, Low, Marston, 1890, p. 25.
[5] Hughes, op.cit.

reduction in the naval strength of its major European opponents, cleared the way for the United Kingdom's rise to the top of the world's military, political, and economic powers. He listed characteristics such as location, population, and administration, as well as broadening the definition of naval power to include a strong navy and commercial fleet. Mahan also pushed the idea that a strong naval blockade would defeat any army.[6] The Mahanian notion of naval power was fundamentally predicated on the belief that the best defense is a good offense. The victor's "command of the sea" which opens and secures the victor's unfettered use of the ocean, gives security by denying the opponent's use of the sea.[7] In summary, Mahan's doctrine argued that the United States should be a world power; control of the seas is required for world power status; and a powerful Navy is the best method to retain such control.[8]

These principles, according to Mahan and some top American politicians, may be applied to U.S. foreign policy, notably in the effort to grow U.S. markets abroad. At the turn of the century, Mahan's writings and lectures influenced Theodore Roosevelt, Henry Cabot Lodge, and other world leaders, including German Emperor Wilhelm II, in creating global policy based on maritime power.[9] The 1890s in the United States were marked by social and economic upheaval, culminating in the commencement of an economic crisis between 1893 and 1894. Mahan's writings were published before much of the chaos associated with the 1890s, but his ideas struck a chord with many major intellectuals and politicians concerned about the period's political and economic issues, as well as the continent's dwindling lack of economic opportunity. Mahan suggested that the United States' economy will soon be unable to absorb the huge amounts of industrial and commercial commodities produced domestically, and that the country should look for new markets abroad. The most important thing to Mahan was assuring that the US government could guarantee access to these new international markets. Securing such access would necessitate three things: a merchant navy capable of transporting American goods to new markets across the "great highway" of the high seas; an American battleship navy capable of deterring or destroying rival fleets; and a network of naval bases capable of supplying fuel and supplies to the enlarged navy, as well as maintaining open lines of communication between the US and its new markets. Mahan believed that effective control of thesea required and guaranteed the necessary communications in the broad sense, which allowed a nation to project its power and influence into the farthest reaches of the globe, right into the teeth of those forces that might threaten that nation's security or prosperity. The Marshall Plan

---

[6] Philip A. Crowl, "Alfred Thayer Mahan", **Makers of Modern Strategy from Machiavelli to the Nuclear Age**, Princeton University Press, 1989, pp. 444–478.

[7] B. Mitchell Simpson III (ed.), **The Development of Naval Thought: Essays by Herbert Rosinski**, Newport, RI, 1977, p. 24.

[8] Kaminer Manship, USN Admiral, "Mahan's Concepts of Sea Power", **Naval War College Review**, Vol. 16, No. 5, 1964, pp. 15-30.

[9] Britannica, "**The Influence of Sea Power upon History, 1660–1783 work by Mahan**", https://www.britannica.com/topic/The-Influence-of-Sea-Power-upon-History-1660-1783 (Access 13.04.2021).

is credited with launching a tremendous political, economic, and psychological transformation of free Europe. However, European recognition of the United States and Allied supremacy of the North Atlantic's marine regions and logistic supply lines made its effects -both material and moral- possible. This nation and its friends in the free world have been able to knit together and sustain a concert of strength around the periphery of the continental communist states thanks to the application of naval power in its broadest definition. With the exception of political suffering, the projection of communist authority and influence has been restrained within a narrowly defined continental ring by this chain. This approach has been defined by one author as an updating of Mahan's concepts, which he refers to as "peripheral strategy."[10]

Mahan identified six key factors that directly influence a nation's ability to achieve naval power, laying the groundwork for a naval strategy: geopolitical position, physical conformation, including natural production and climate; extent of territory; population; culture; and, finally, the nature of its government and inherent institutions.[11] In his books, Mahan cites the United Kingdom as the preeminent practitioner of maritime strategy, and he emphasizes the need of a strong navy in international politics. "Control of the sea through maritime commerce and naval supremacy signifies international dominance...and is the most important among the purely material components in a nation's strength and prosperity.[12] Because globalization and trade are so important to any maritime nation, his proposals for a considerably more global and diplomatic use of the navy may be applied right away to current geopolitical situations when even small-scale fleet war is extremely unlikely. The situation in the Asia-Pacific, in particular, backs up his assertion that the navy's role, conduct, and training must be tempered by political realities. He also believes that the navy and its use, whether on a vast scale or merely by its presence, cannot produce long-term stability and success on their own, but must be integrated into a larger political, economic, or military strategy.[13]

Mahan's concept of naval power, on the other hand, is now considered as overly limited in terms of its application to the United Kingdom and difficult to apply to an universal philosophy or maritime strategy. The term "sea power" is traditionally attributed to a country that has a nautical focus and strategic vision and relies heavily on marine trade and commerce for its economic well-being. These elements, he and others claimed, necessitated a maritime policy to attain sea control in order to safeguard the country's national security and global interests, particularly trade and commerce. His greatest success is not his concentration on naval diplomacy, about which he wrote relatively little, but his

---

[10] Manship, op.cit., p. 29.

[11] Ibid., pp. 28–29.

[12] Ibid., p. 5.

[13] U.S. Department of State, **"Mahan's The Influence of Sea Power upon History: Securing International Markets in the 1890s"**, https://history.state.gov/milestones/1866-1898/mahan (Access 13.04.2021).

effect on subsequent naval strategists, particularly how the navy functions as an additional arm of the government. This is also connected to Sir Julian Stafford Corbett, a British naval historian and geostrategist who studied the role of warships in foreign affairs in the early twentieth century. Naval warfare, according to Corbett, is a facet of a country's larger policies. Carl von Clausewitz, a Prussian military thinker, was a major influence on his work in this regard. Corbett, like Clausewitz, believed in the primacy of politics in war and the importance of formulating an effective strategy to safeguard national interests. Corbett, on the other hand, was interested in the diplomatic alliance systems and coalitions created before and during a war, as well as the economic and financial sides of war, as well as the technological and material aspects of war, which Clausewitz was uninterested in. John Knox Laughton, possibly the first naval historian, was another key influence, and Corbett has been referred to as his "protégé."[14] Corbett's writings influenced the Royal Navy's reforms at the time. *Some Principles on Maritime Strategy*, which is now considered a classic among naval warfare scholars, highlighted that strategy must be consciously linked to a government's foreign policy and that war is a political act. Corbett's main goal was to formalize the ideas and concepts of naval warfare in order to fill a gap in British naval doctrine. Corbett's naval warfare methods concentrated on the art of naval warfare and defined the distinctions between land and naval combat. He centered his initial efforts on the application of manoeuvre doctrine. Today's naval manoeuvre warfare is built on Corbett's ideas of sea control, enemy focus, and manoeuvre for tactical advantage. In contrast to Mahan, Corbett placed a larger emphasis on confined maritime wars, in which the navy's political shaping function is obvious. He claimed, contrary to Mahan, that because maritime warfare is about sea control, an enemy fleet blockaded in its home ports is equally as effective as one destroyed in a decisive battle. Most importantly, Corbett thought that navies enabled governments to analyze the costs and advantages of any mission both before and during their engagement. When opposed to conventional, messy land operations, maritime operations were more manageable in the sense that they were less prone to disastrous escalation; they were also typically more cost effective.[15] Naval strategy, according to Corbett, should be viewed as a component of a larger war rather than a separate entity. Naval strategy, according to Corbett, should be viewed as a component of a larger war rather than a separate entity. Corbett has grown much more prominent in strategic circles as a result of the shifting global environment since the Cold War ended. Economic globalization, political unpredictability, and the predominance of little conflicts and local warfare between regional governments lend far more credence to his conception of maritime strategy and power than Mahan's vision of huge fleet engagements and rivalry which was more readily relevant to the Soviet Union's and the United States' big fleets. According to

---

[14] Stanley J. Adamiak, "The Foundations of Naval History: John Knox Laughton, the Royal Navy and the Historical Profession", Review of book by Professor Andrew Lambert, **Journal of Military History**, Vol. 64, No. 4, 2000, pp. 1169-1170.
[15] Geoffrey Till, **Seapower, A Guide for the Twenty-First Century**, London, Frank Cass, 2004, p. 47.

Corbett's tenets, using marine forces to increase strategic flexibility; appreciating the limits of naval diplomacy, notably, complete sea control; and the ability to project military power around the world is not always useful, and command of the sea, on the other hand, is a means to an end, not an end in itself.[16] "Since men live on land and not at sea, great issues between nations at war have always been decided -except in the rarest of cases- either by what your army can do against your enemy's territory and national life, or by the fear of what the fleet makes possible for your army to do," Corbett explained.[17]

Mahan and Corbett both shaped maritime strategists in subsequent generations, and their influence on maritime strategy continues to this day. Mahan's lectures and books established naval power and maritime strategy as critical tools of state power, and they continue to impact current thinking in the US Navy as well as other navies across the world, particularly in China. The importance of maritime diplomacy and the function of warships in larger political and strategic endgames exemplifies Corbett's relevance today. While replicating theories put out by 19th century military thinker Clausewitz on land warfare, he realized that the Navy's function as an element of a political arm was revolutionary to maritime strategy at the time. Over the next 50 years, until the end of World War II, these two strategists were the principal shapers of global naval strategy.[18] Large naval deployments and the importance of naval engagements can be observed in both World Wars, as highlighted in the Pacific theater during World War II, as massive fleets engaged each other to gain sea control and eventually global dominance. Their theories were continually developed and built upon until the formation of modern naval strategy during the Cold Conflict to reflect modern geopolitical realities such as globalization and the use of naval diplomacy as an alternative to war. Because of the nature of future war, the strategic direction of the major world and regional powers, and the advantages of naval might for a variety of objectives, the sea is likely to be at least as significant as it has been in the past. Armed conflict will continue to play a major role in international affairs, with naval war accounting for the majority of it. There will continue to be a mix of on-the-sea and off-the-sea operations. The former will involve maritime security and counter-terrorism activities, as well as shipping protection and assertion of navigational rights or contested waters. Strikes on shore targets, as well as amphibious raids and Special Forces operations, will be carried out on a scale ranging from short, quick interventions—which are expected to be prominent and carried out by a broader range of states—to lengthy campaigns.[19]

---

[16] Geoffrey Till, "Sir Julian Corbett: Ten Maritime Commandments", **The Changing Face of Maritime Power**, Andrew Dorman, Mike Lawrence Smith and Mathew R. H. Uttley, (Eds.), London, Macmillan Press, 1999.

[17] J. S. Corbett, **England in the Seven Years War**, Vol. 1, London, Longmans Green, 1907, p. 67.

[18] Michael A. Schelcher, **The Asia-Pacific Rebalance: Impact on Naval Strategy**, Unpublished M.S Thesis, Naval Postgraduate School, Monterey, California, March 2014.

[19] Tim Benbow, "The Future of Naval Conflict and Lessons From History", **Routledge Handbook of Naval Strategy and Security**, Routledge, 21 Dec 2015, https://www.routledgehandbooks.com/doi/10.

It's possible that the people in charge of naval operations will alter much more. The old naval powers, especially the United States, the United Kingdom, France, and probably Russia, will remain significant, but developing powers such as China and India, both within and outside their own regions, as well as a slew of smaller navies, will gradually join them. The spectrum of fully capable, restricted global, and local navies will become increasingly stretched as technology advances. Developing technology has long been and will continue to be a major driver of change in naval conflict. Some new technologies pose a threat to warships and navies, while others aid and augment them, and the majority of them do both. As a result of the continuous cycle of technological advancement, some governments will fall behind and the roles and capabilities to which others aspire will be reduced; however, these laggards will be replaced by emerging world and regional powers eager to use the sea. The strategic environment, as well as the risks and opportunities posed by new technology, form the basis for future naval combat questions. What regional powers will emerge as significant participants, and what maritime roles will they pursue? Turkey, as a prominent actor in the area, is in a geopolitically precarious position. Turkey needs a robust, determined, and ready naval force to ensure its survival on solid foundations, to fulfill its national interests with zeal at all times, and to avoid any flaws in the surrounding waters of the maritime sphere of security.

The following section of this article discusses Turkey's primary vision of having a strong naval force based on national strength that can defend Turkey's interests and rights in international waters.

Turkey's New Naval Strategy, "Blue Homeland", And Its Effects

The objective of the Turkish Naval Forces is to contribute to homeland security and to preserve the Republic of Turkey's sovereign rights and privileges at sea. In October 2015, the Turkish Naval Forces Command published the Turkish version of a new strategy document on its official website.[20] "*The Turkish Naval Forces Strategy is prepared in light of National Military Strategy, which encompasses the marine sector, and which is driven from the National Security Policy,*" according to the document, which was released for the first time. It is critical not only for Turkey's national interests, but also for creating knowledge about its national naval policy, that this detailed book reaches a wider audience. The Turkish Navy has signed a very important study in order to provide a greater knowledge of our national naval strategy, in keeping with its traditional spirit of planning, forecast, and innovation, by issuing such a document. "Turkey is exposed to the negative impacts of numerous on-going crises in the north of the Black Sea and in various hot spots throughout Turkey's southern borders," said then Commander of the Turkish Naval Forces Admiral Bülent Bostanolu during his address at the

---

4324/9781315732572.ch3 (Access 27 May 2021).
[20] MSI, "**Turkish Naval Forces Strategy**", 17 October 2016, https://www.savunmahaber.com/en/article-turkish-naval-forces-strategy/ (Access 29 May 2021).

Pakistan Navy War College on February 17, 2016.[21] According to Admiral Bülent Bostanolu, Commander of the Turkish Naval Forces, "Turkish Naval Forces Strategy" is being developed in order to meet these challenges, ensure doctrinal unity among Turkish Navy personnel, and provide information on the future prospects of our forces to a variety of audiences, ranging from decision-makers setting Turkey's international course and conducting defense planning activities to relevant academic circles." However, objectives based on the protection of the Republic of Turkey's sovereignty rights and maritime interests include maintaining a high level of readiness at all times to respond immediately to situations involving violations of rights arising from international treaties and international laws, as well as disputes over the delimitation of maritime jurisdiction areas, as well as the prohibition of illegal search/drilling operations in Turkey's maritime jurisdiction. Further crises are likely to arise as a result of historical disagreements in the Aegean and rising tensions in the Eastern Mediterranean. Turkey's security situation may continue to be impacted by current and upcoming crises. In the next 5-10 years, this fact will be a major element in the Turkish Navy's operations and force posture. The task in the Black Sea will be to re-establish stability and mutual trust among littoral states, which were both impeded by the onset of the Ukrainian crisis. The Turkish Navy will continue to promote regional ownership and maritime systems like Operation Black Sea Harmony. At the same time, NATO's assurance measures, which are tailored to the changing security environment and threat perception, will continue to be actively supported. The Turkish Navy will maintain friendly and allied connections in the Aegean, as well as confidence-building initiatives. Simultaneously, we will maintain our deterrent posture to deter attempts to alter the status quo and limit the usage of the high seas. Due to ongoing disagreements over marine jurisdictional delimitation, the Turkish Navy will concentrate its efforts in the Eastern Mediterranean. The ongoing crises with Russia have exacerbated an already delicate situation in the Eastern Mediterranean. The Turkish Navy, on the other hand, will continue to be a responsible player in the region. Nonetheless, in our marine jurisdiction regions, we will continue to actively protect Turkey's marine rights and interests. Beyond Turkey's borders, the Turkish Navy's principal missions will be to promote regional and global peace and stability. Turkish Naval Forces will continue to secure Sea Lines Of Communications (SLOCS), which are regularly utilized by Turkish commerce ships, support Turkish foreign policy as needed, and contribute to the Alliance Maritime Strategy through national, alliance, and coalition structures." Turkey's foreign policy goal is built on stability, cooperation, and continental scale endeavors, as stated in the Turkish Naval Forces Strategy. These aims have created the Turkish Naval Forces as a vital foreign policy instrument with access to all regions, including neighboring waters and seas, in line with Turkey's areas of interest, and activities thanks to its mobility capabilities. Turkey's new forceful

---

[21] Defence Turkey, **"Turkish Naval Forces' New Strategy Document & Future Plans"**, https://www.defenceturkey.com/files/issues/5aa6720d2ed70.pdf (Access 16.04.2021).

naval policy governs its seas from the Black Sea to the Aegean and Mediterranean, and the term "Blue Homeland" represents more than a political branding exercise. To a considerable extent, it represents a significant shift in philosophy within Turkish political and military circles, with the goal of increasing Turkish presence and asserting firm control over its maritime rights. Turkey's "blue homeland" theory, which is a shorthand word for Turkey's maritime claims in the eastern Mediterranean, is often credited to Cihat Yaycı, the navy's previous chief of staff, and later to former Turkish Rear Adm. Cem Gürdeniz, the concept's inventor and major advocate. Gürdeniz was given the pleasure of leading the Turkish navy's policy-planning division between 2009 and 2011, in addition to serving on various vessels and a tour at NATO headquarters. Throughout his career, he worked closely with the US for long periods of time (including two years in residence at the Naval Postgraduate School).[22] "Defending the country's territorial waters, its "blue homeland," is just as vital to him as protecting Turkish soil, he said. As a result, Gürdeniz has urged the Turkish government to adopt a tough stance against Greece and its Aegean and Mediterranean counterclaims. According to him, the waters bordering Greece's islands deny Athens the right to exploit the region's natural gas reserves. Greece relies on the United States and Europe to act on its behalf in the lack of military strength. "Greece may dwell inside the dream world of its past and generate countless fantasies," Gürdeniz claims. However, these things should not be imposed on Turkey's sovereignty and interests in the Aegean, Mediterranean, and Black Seas. They should be aware of their surroundings."[23] There is substantial evidence that Gürdeniz's ideas had a considerable influence.[24] The now-common use of the word "mavi vatan" or "blue motherland" is the most visible proof of his influence. The Turkish navy conducted large-scale drills in March 2019, 2020 and 2021 under the operating designation "Blue Homeland."[25] Along with its NATO duties, Turkey will "continue unabated in its blue homeland operations."

Despite the fact that Turkey was not a party to the United Nations Convention on the Law of the Sea (UNCLOS) when it was established in 1982,

---

[22] Ryan Gingeras, **"Blue Homeland: The Heated Politics Behind Turkey's New Maritime Strategy"**, 2 June 2020 https://warontherocks.com/2020/06/blue-homeland-the-heated-politics-behind-turkeys-new-maritime-strategy/ (Access 16.04.2021).

[23] Ibid.

[24] Evangelos Areteosthe, "Mavi Vatan and Forward Defense", Analysis, Diplomatic Academy, University of Nicosia, https://www.unic.ac.cy/da/wp-content/uploads/sites/11/2020/07/Mavi-Vatan-and-Forward-Defence-Evangelos-Areteos.pdf (Access 16.04.2021). As former Turkish Rear Admiral Cem Gürdeniz, the author of the said doctrine, explained in a recent interview with the Greek daily *To Vima*, "the (Mavi Vatan) doctrine has essentially two pillars. The first is intended to indicate Turkish areas of maritime jurisdiction under national sovereignty, such as territorial waters, the continental shelf, the EEZ. The second was intended to create a maritime worldview for Turkey". See To Vima, Τζεμ Γκουρντενίζ: «Η Γαλάζια Πατρίδα είναι η θαλάσσια κοσμοθεωρία της Τουρκίας» https://www.tovima.gr/2020/06/09/politics/tzem-gkournteniz-i-galazia-patrida-einai-i-thalassiakosmotheoria-tis-tourkias/; published 9 June 2020, (Access 16.04.2021).

[25] Turkish Naval Forces, Excercices, https://www.dzkk.tsk.tr/en-US (Access 17.04.2021).

it defined its maritime jurisdiction using the convention's standards. Today, based on UNCLOS principles and judgements of the Court of Arbitration and the International Court of Justice (ICJ) Turkey's maritime jurisdiction areas are governed by the following principles, as stated by Admiral Cihat Yaycı:

"(1) Equity (States with opposite coasts share the seas fairly.)

(2) Superiority of Geography (Based on the mainland as the delimitation means that the islands that are on the opposite side of the bisector line have sea authority as much as their territorial waters.)

(3) Proportionality (In the delimitation, it means that the maritime jurisdiction states will have is proportional to their coastal lengths.)

(4) The State of 'Not closing' (means that the islands close to the coasts of another state should not prevent this coast from sailing.)" [26]

In those nautical charts, Turkey has opposing coasts with the Turkish Republic of Northern Cyprus (TRNC), Libya, Egypt, Israel, Palestine, and Lebanon, as well as a side maritime boundary with Syria. The gnomonic and geodetic maps utilized in these computations have already been employed in other countries' marine delimitation. As a result, Turkey is not a country located on the world's east-west axis. It's a country with a first-degree incline, and scientists have proven that this creates an 18-degree viewpoint.[27] Admiral Cihat Yaycı drew a map of the Blue Homeland based on these concepts, which covers 462 thousand square kilometers. The Blue Homeland Struggle refers to Turkey's fight to legally claim exclusive rights to all living and non-living resources in this area. The obedience of Turkey's neighbors, as well as NATO, the United States, and Russia, is closely observed by this philosophy, which defends Turkey's

---

[26] Cihat Yaycı, **Doğu Akdeniz'in Paylaşım Mücadelesi ve Türkiye**, İstanbul, Kırmızı Kedi Yayınları, 2020, p. 160.
[27] Cihat Yaycı, **Sorular ve Cevaplar ile MEB Kavramı**, İstanbul, Deniz Kuvvetleri Komutanlığı Yayınevi, 2019.

interests. The strengthening of the doctrinal approach to Turkey's "blue homeland" could lead to increased tensions in the Eastern Mediterranean. The presence of substantial natural gas resources off the coast of of the island of Cyprus is key to these interests. It's a message to the Eastern Mediterranean Gas Forum (EMGF), a recent coalition comprised of Egypt, Israel, the Greek Cypriot administration, Greece, Italy, Jordan, and the Palestinian Authority that has compounded the issue over energy development in the Eastern Mediterranean Sea.[28] It will not be surprising if tensions in the Eastern Mediterranean escalate to the point where they constitute the most severe contemporary threat to Turkey's essential national security interests. The majority of these natural gas resources are located within what Turkey considers to be its exclusive economic zone. However, such a viewpoint contradicts claims made by Greece and the Greek Cypriots. Both governments have claimed that Turkey disregards the sovereignty of Greeks and Greek Cypriots, as well as important provisions of the United Nations Convention on the Law of the Sea, which Turkey has never ratified. The bloc of Greek Cypriots, Greece, Israel, and Egypt's irresponsible behavior in the Eastern Mediterranean is a key source of concern that has heightened tensions in the region for years. Many issues have developed as a result of Greece's mind-blowing concept. Because their legal standing differs, these issues must be divided into two categories: Aegean and Eastern Mediterranean.

The subject of islands, islets, and rocks is the most pressing problem in the Aegean. The main problem with the property is the territorial seas. Greece enlarged its territorial waters to 6 miles in 1936 after violating the Lausanne balance, reducing the open sea space in the region to less than 50%. Only one open river leads down to the Mediterranean, according to the 6-mil-regime. Other countries will not be affected by this regime, but Turkey will be affected by the extent of the continental shelf offshore areas shared. As a result, Turkey should begin legal preparations for the reintroduction of the point 3-mile-regime and initiate a formal call. Because all of the problems in the Aegean are interconnected, it would be helpful for Turkey to discuss them all at once. Greece has obstructed access to the International Court of Justice, stating that they have no issues with Turkey in the Aegean other than the continental shelf. As a result, when the time comes, Turkey's government must begin applications for the approximately 152 island group in the Aegean. However, the Aegean concerns, which were locked by the Bern Agreement in 1976, allow Turkey to emphasize the importance of rights and interests in the eastern Mediterranean. While the 152 Aegean island group's entire marine authority area is 15 thousand square kilometers, Turkey's sea territory attempted to be seized by Greece in the eastern Mediterranean is 150 thousand square kilometers.

The situation in the Eastern Mediterranean is far more serious than in the

---

[28] SETA, "**Turkey's Geopolitical Landscape in 2020**", https://setav.org/en/assets/uploads/2020/01/R151En.pdf (Access 13.04.2021).

Aegean. According to a map of maritime jurisdiction developed by the University of Seville in 2003, Turkey's territory in the eastern Mediterranean was determined to be 41 thousand square kilometers, and GCASC announced its EZZ based on the map. From the sea, Greece and Southern Cyprus appear to be neighbors on the map. Turkey's sailing to the open seas was prevented, and Greece's islands facing the Eastern Mediterranean were given full impact.[29] Greece's Eastern Mediterranean shore is 167 kilometers long. Turkey, on the other hand, has an 1870-kilometer coastline. As a result, according to the concept of equity, Turkey must obtain 13 times greater maritime jurisdiction than Greece.[30] Worse, Meis Island, which lies two miles off Turkey's coast, has been granted maritime authority over 40 thousand square kilometers. Meis, Karaada, and Fener Island, on the other hand, are more of a rock than an island. Islands that cannot develop their own economy and do not have a settled population are not allowed to have maritime borders, according to the South China Sea Arbitration Case. The status before to alteration is what matters in marine law. In other words, Greece's settlement policy toward the islands will have no effect on the islands' maritime sovereignty.[31] Furthermore, ownership of Karaada and Fener Islands has never been transferred to Greece; the islands remain under Turkish control. In conclusion, it is clear that Greece has no say in the Eastern Mediterranean from any standpoint. Greece's exclusive economic zones (EEZ) accords with Italy and Egypt did not fully apply to the islands, thus Athens has given up its claims.

Turkey's shifting attitude toward Libya demonstrates the country's resolve to execute the Blue Homeland ideology. While the Turkish Navy was conducting massive drills in Turkey's sovereign territories, Turkey and Libya's Tripoli government (Government of National Accord-GNA) signed a memorandum of understanding (MOU) on the "delimitation of maritime jurisdiction regions in the Mediterranean" on November 27, 2019.[32] As a result, Turkey's western Mediterranean boundary was delineated.[33] The MOU, which established a mutually expanded maritime border between the two countries, has been hailed as a victory for Turkey's blue homeland by politicians across the political spectrum. It was an important step in solidifying Turkey's military and political

---

[29] Yaycı, İbid., pp. 43-53.
[30] Ahmet Alemdar, **Cihat Yaycı'nın Doğu Akdeniz'deki son durum hakkında görüş ve değerlendirmeleri**, Cihat Yaycı ile Reportaj, 09.08.2020, https://www.defenceturk.net/cihat-yaycinin-dogu-akdenizdeki-son-durum-hakkinda-gorus-ve-degerlendirmeleri.(Accessed on: 27 May 2021).
[31] Uğur Bayıllıoğlu, "BMDHS'nin 121. Maddesi'nin Doğu Akdeniz'de etkisi: Meis, Karaada ve Fener Adası'nın statüsüne ilişkin bir değerlendirme", **Ankara Hacı Bayram Veli Üniversitesi Hukuk Fakültesi Dergisi**, Vol. 23, No. 2, 2019, pp. 185-223.
[32] "Memorandum of Understanding Between the Government of the Republic of Turkey and the Government of National Accord-State of Libya on Delimination of the Maritime Jurisdiction Areas in the Mediterranean", UN, 11.122019, https://www.un.org/Depts/los/LEGISLATIONAND TREATIES/PDFFILES/TREATIES/Turkey_11122019_%28HC%29_MoU_Libya-Delimitation-areas-Mediterranean.pdf (Access 27 May 2021)
[33] Elif Sudagezer, **'BM'nin Türkiye-Libya deniz anlaşmasını tescili ne anlama geliyor"**, Cihat Yaycı ile Reportaj, Sputnik Türkiye, 02.10.2020, https://tr.sputniknews.com/columnists/20201002104295690 5-cihat-yayci-anlatti-bmnin-turkiye-libya-deniz-anlasmasini-tescili-ne-anlama-geliyor/ (Access 13.04. 2021).

stance in this conflict. This MOU has the potential to be a game-changer, reshaping the region's current balance. If no settlement is achieved between the rivals, Turkey's military involvement in the Libyan crisis will be a significant geopolitical and strategic upheaval in Turkey's geopolitical landscape in 2020. A national energy fleet was constructed, consisting of three drilling and seismic research vessels. The Blue Homeland map has been included to the search and rescue responsibility area.[34] A shift in public opinion of the federation's demands had begun to emerge, paving the way for a two-state solution in Cyprus. The national defense industry was built to fulfill the geopolitical demands of the twenty-first century. Navy diplomacy has been initiated in response to actions that jeopardize the Mediterranean's peace.

Turkey's current commitment to its "blue homeland" policies appears to be conditional on two important elements. To begin with, Turkey's maritime posture, as dreamed up by Gürdeniz, Yayc, and others, has piqued the interest of a large segment of the Turkish political elite. Calls for a tenacious defense of Turkey's vast "mavi vatan" echo the aggressive, independent attitude of the country's current foreign policy. There is now little reason for Turkey to change from its current path. The second, and most crucial, element is that the Turkish government has capitalized on the blue homeland's greater relevance and endorses this broader strategic orientation. Turkey's efforts in the Blue Homeland, on the other hand, are viewed by Greece and other Mediterranean countries as aggressive Turkish behavior. The United States has grown closer to Greece as a result of its disapproval of Turkey's actions in the Aegean and Mediterranean, and the US Congress has even eased the decades-long arms embargo on Cyprus. Regardless, there is no condition in Turkey's official stance that would jeopardize its relations with NATO, particularly with the United States. On the other hand, the Turkish navy's official strategy document, published in 2015, makes no mention of the "blue homeland" and states unequivocally that the Turkish navy will defend to the end its international law-enforced rights to an equitable distribution of economic wealth in the Eastern Mediterranean.

As a result, as the Republic of Turkey approaches its 100th anniversary, it is confronted with global, multi-dimensional, and multi-layered security challenges at the regional level. Turkey, which is in a geopolitically precarious situation, needs a strong, determined, and ready naval force to ensure its survival and to fulfill its national interests with zeal at all times, as well as to avoid any flaws in the surrounding waters of the maritime domain of security. Turkish Naval Forces Command is aware of these sensitivity issues and is prepared to perform a variety of tasks in the complex security environment of the twenty-first century in order to preserve its country and national interests on the high seas. In this light, the existence of the Turkish Navy is critical for the Republic of Turkey's security and

---

[34] Vatan, "Bakan duyurdu! Mavi Vatan'da harita genişletildi" http://www.gazetevatan.com/bakan-duyurdu-mavi-vatan-da-harita-genisletildi--1348583-ekonomi/ (Access 13.04.2021).

prosperity. Given the foregoing, it appears likely that Turkey will pursue its goal of having a "stronger" naval force to preserve its interests in the Blue Homeland. A stronger Turkish naval force will help the country to meet its operational needs both now and in the future. As a result, in order to avoid making additional enemies in the region, Turkey should make it clear to its Mediterranean littoral states and NATO allies what the "blue homeland" concept entails.

Conclusion

The Blue Homeland doctrine of Turkey is a geopolitical reality of the twenty-first century, expressed by Mustafa Kemal Atatürk, the founder of the Republic of Turkey, as a necessity for survival for a democratic, secular republic whose borders are determined by the international maritime law. According to Atatürk, a Turkey that cannot navigate the seas, is condemned to fail. The wounds had to be healed fast with the establishment of the Republic, and a "strong Turkish Navy" had to be built. Within the scope of international law, the doctrine expresses Turkey's lawful maritime rights. In terms of both applying international law and the potential of regional countries benefiting equitably from all resources, efforts to defend these rights make a significant contribution to global and regional peace. Contrary to claims made by critics of the Blue Homeland doctrine, it appears that complete implementation of the doctrine will benefit not only Turkey, but also all countries in the region. Furthermore, considering how the Blue Homeland doctrine expects the formation of cooperation mechanisms with riparian governments in the Eastern Mediterranean, this doctrine is far from advocating a "expansionist" approach. This doctrine's adoption will significantly contribute to the growth of international trade and the more efficient use of energy resources. When it comes to countries whose attitudes are still influenced by "maritime piracy," it's important to remember that Turkey has a superior naval fleet to preserve its rights as well as modern military-industrial infrastructure. Turkey's more assertive naval policy will play a critical role in the future years, not just as a means of defense and deterrence, but also as a means of projecting influence abroad. Turkey, being conscious of the importance of the seas, has defined its maritime borders in accordance with all international law principles. It is on the way to become a regional energy player with its fleet of national seismic and drilling vessels. The Turkish merchant navy transports commodities all over the world.

As a result, the Blue Homeland doctrine is widely regarded as the most significant intellectual framework for safeguarding Turkey's national security and regional interests. This doctrine also helps friendly and brotherly states beyond the Blue Homeland's borders and contributes to global peace. Considering that Turkey's struggle for survival is symbolized by the Blue Homeland, it is obvious that Turkey will never give up even a drop of Blue Homeland water.

THE GEOPOLITICAL REALITY OF THE ISLAND SEA

Hüseyin Çelik[*]

Introduction

The Aegean Sea, which connects Europe, located on the eastern side of the Mediterranean and Anatolia, called Asia Minor, or the Sea of Islands, where over 3000 islands of various sizes are located, constitute an important geopolitical area. The sea of Island is largely dominated by Greece. Except for Bozcaada and Gökçeada, the majority of the islands at the entrance of the Dardanelles Strait are dominated by Greece. This situation strategically creates a situation in favor of Greece and against Turkey. Because it is seen that the provision of disarmament of the eastern Aegean islands in the Treaty of Lausanne is not valid today and it has been repeatedly violated by Greece. Greece opposes the claim that it is arming the Aegean islands, claiming that it only has detective practices and coast guard ships on the islands. There are many disputes between Turkey and Greece, the two states that have a coast on the Aegean Sea. These are: Territorial Waters and the Continental Shelf, the disarmed status of the Eastern Aegean Islands, the legal status of the geographical formations, the Flight Information Region (FIR) and Search and Rescue (SAR) activities. It repeatedly emphasizes that it is a part of the European Union.

In this section, it is claimed that Greece still continues today. As a result of these claims that neutralized the Lausanne agreement, a new geopolitical reality has emerged in the Aegean Sea. In line with this realism, Aegean problems have the potential to cause new tensions. Therefore, it is necessary to focus on these geopolitical realities and the way in which these problems evolve.

Aegean or Islands Sea: Geographical Situation

The Aegean Sea is located on the eastern side of the Mediterranean. The Dardanelles Strait is a passageway to the Black Sea via the Sea of Marmara and the Bosphorus. Due to the tectonic structure under the Aegean Sea, there are many islands, so the Turks named this sea as the sea of islands.

There are over three thousand large and small islands and islets and many peninsulas in the Sea of Islands. Thus, there are many coves, gulfs, straits and peninsulas in the sea. It is estimated that the Aegean Sea was formed by the collapse of a large land called Aegeis or Egeid into the sea due to the eruption of tectonic and volcanic volcanoes.

The depth of the Soros Gulf, located in the north of the Aegean Sea, reaches

---

[*] Prof. Hüseyin Çelik, Istanbul Nisantasi University, Turkey. E-mail: hucelik@gmail.com.

up to 1000 meters. The Mediterranean climate is experienced on the islands and on the coasts on both sides. The Aegean Sea is compressed by the African plate from the south and the Anatolian plate from the east. The Aegean Sea is a region where volcanic activities continue today and produces earthquakes of seven to eight magnitudes.

The North Anatolian Fault line system reaches the Aegean Sea under the Marmara Sea in the north of the Aegean Sea, and the central parts of the Aegean Sea are filled with fault lines parallel to the grabens in the west. To the south, there are active fault lines in the form of arcs that reach the Greek shores and the villages of Rhodes and Turkey. The Santorini volcano in this region has erupted in many places. It was last seen that it became active in 1950. It can be estimated that the eruptions of the Nysiros volcano between 1422 and 1885 formed the Datça Peninsula. They came from the volcanic centers in Nysiros and Yelli islands located in the west of the Datça peninsula to the peninsula with violent explosions and were generally accumulated in hollow basins[1]. Earthquakes are always caused by tectonic and volcanic causes. There are 12 volcano islands to the north of the Crete peninsula, Milas, Santorini and three volcanic islands under the Gökova gulf[2]. Apart from these, volcanic movements in the Sea of Islands are always ready for new island production. It is considered that new island formations may cause new problems between Turkey and Greece.

The thesis that the islands in the Aegean Sea are extensions of Turkey is claimed by Turkey. Considering the geological evolution of the Aegean Sea, it is seen that the region is under the influence of the continental tectonic stress of Arabia and Eurasia. The Aegean region and the Aegean sea located in the west of Anatolia have been formed in this interaction. The basin, which is injured in the northernmost part of the Aegean Sea, extends to the Hagion-Oros region of Greece, which is the continuation of the North Anatolian Fault Line and then starts in the Soros Gulf[3].

The second large bowl to the south is called the Skiros Bowl. This bowl is a natural continuation of Edremit Bay. It is located in the Icarian Basin and in the north of the islands of Patmos and Samos[4]. This region shows the proximity between the Aegean region and the Aegean Sea. Gokova graben is 150 km long. It is seen that the continuation of the fault zone is off the island of Kos[5] . It is noteworthy that the geology of the Aegean Islands is similar to that of Western Anatolia. Metamorphic rocks are common in some of these islands, while

---

[1] Ercan, Tuncay, et.al.. (1984) "Datça Yarımadasındaki Kuvaterner Yaşlı Volkanik Kayaçların Petrolojisi ve Kökensel Yorumu" MTA Derg.,97-98, **s.: 47**, https://dergipark.org.tr/tr/download/article-file/583491.

[2] Ercan et.al. p..: 49.

[3][3] Yılmaz, Y., et.al., (1998) "Ege Denizi ve Ege Bölgesi'nin Jeolojisi ve Evrimi", *Türkiye Denizlerinin ve Yakın Çevresinin Jeolojisi.*(Editor N. Görür), İstanbul, p.: 216.

[4] Yılmaz, et.al., p.: 217.

[5] Yılmaz, et.al., p.: 232.

volcanic and/or neogene aged sedimentary rocks are common in others. Neogene rocks are also seen in the northeastern points close to Western Anatolia[6]

As a result of the compression of the Anatolian plate by the Arabian and Eurasian plates and moving to the west, changes have occurred in the Aegean Sea and Western Anatolia. As a result, the entire region from the Gökova graben to the Edremit graben was affected and caused the region to be shaped[7].

After the beginning of the northern and southern stretching, it started to intrude from the Mediterranean into the Aegean. This sea occupied a very large area in the northern Aegean. Due to the sea intrusion, the western part of the Aegean region, the Dodecanese (dodecanese islands) is located on the natural extension of the Western Anatolian land[8]. This information supports Turkey's claim that the eastern islands in the Aegean Sea are part of Turkey's continental shelf. What needs to be done; Due to the geostrategic structure of the Aegean Sea, it is the fair distribution of jurisdictions by the two states. Turkey's thesis is the Aegean Sea, the distribution of the islands, the fact that it is a semi-enclosed sea, and that these islands create a special position because they are almost adjacent to the Anatolian land. Turkey's claim is that international general principles will not be applied in this region[9].

Aegean or Islands Sea Problems

The Aegean Sea is an area of tension between Turkey and Greece that sometimes brings the two countries to the brink of hot conflict. It is seen that Greece, by interpreting the United Nations Convention on the Law of the Sea (UNCLOS), which was negotiated in 1973 and signed in 1982, as it wishes, took action to turn the balances in the Aegean Sea completely in its favor this time[10].

The abundance of the islands in the Aegean Sea and the lack of borders have brought the two countries to the brink of war many times[11]. The Aegean Problem has geographical reasons as well as political reasons. Many of these islands are within sight of the Anatolian coast, and many of them are as close as swimming distance[12].

Among the problems experienced between Turkey and Greece are the Continental Shelf, the Territorial Waters, the demilitarized status of the Eastern

---

[6] Yılmaz, et.al., p.: 232-233.
[7] Yılmaz, et.al., p.: 211.
[8] Yılmaz, et.al., p.: 323-324.
[9] Aksu, F., (2005) Ege Sorunlarının Geleceği ve Türkiye: AB Üyelik Sürecinde Türkiye'nin Seçenekleri" *Stratejik Araştırmalar Dergisi*, vol.3, no.5, p.: 265.
[10] Çelikol, A. O, S. Karaduman (2017) "Türkiye Yunanistan İlişkileri ve Denizden Kaynaklanan Uluslararası Sorunlar" *Bilge Strateji, Cilt 9*, Bahar 2017, p.: 16.
[11] K Kıyanç, S. (2020) "ABD Merkezi İstihbarat Teşkilatı (CIA) Arşiv Belgelerine Göre Ege Sorunu" Dokuz Eylül Üniversitesi Sosyal Bilimler Enstitüsü Dergisi, 22,1,2020, p.: 11, url: Http://Dx.Doi.Org/10.16953/Deusosbil.518841ıyanç., p.: 12.
[12] Kıyanç., p.: 12.

Aegean Islands, the legal status of islands, islets and reefs, Flight Information Area (FIR) and Search and Rescue (SAR) activities.

The continental shelf is the natural extension of the coastal state under the sea. Geographically, the seabed generally does not reach great depths after the shore. An average of 130 m from the coast. gradually deepens. Depths from a slope of 1:1000 are less than 20 m. Shelf widths can vary from a few kilometers to 400 kilometers. The average distance is 78 km. After this depth, it takes the form of a sharp slope. The area between the coast and the continental slope is considered to be the continental shelf[13].

Turkey stated that since the Aegean issue is a political issue, not a legal one, it should be resolved in an agreement rather than an international court. He argued that the islands with natural extensions belonging to Anatolia do not have a separate continental shelf. In addition, Turkey stated that the two countries from the Aegean Sea have equal rights based on the balance between Turkey and Greece after the Lausanne Peace Treaty[14].

Greece argues that the islands should be treated as a whole with the mainland, without leaving the continental country, and that the islands have a continental shelf in accordance with the 1958 Geneva Convention. Another thesis of Greece is that the continental shelf delimitation between Turkey and the islands should be made according to the principle of "equal distance". Accordingly, the Turkish-Greek border should also be the border of the continental shelf[15].

The continental shelf issue, which was not a problem between Turkey and Greece until 1974, became a problem with the determination of oil resources that year[16]. Greece acts on the thesis that the islands are a continental shelf, while Turkey, on the other hand, gives weight to the 'natural extension' thesis based on the view that the Aegean continental shelf is the continuation of the Anatolian continent in the sea, and wants the Aegean continental shelf to be shared with the middle line to be drawn between the continents of the two countries.[17]

At the NATO Heads of State and Government summit held in Brussels on May 31, 1975, the Prime Ministers of the two countries[18], Demirel and Karamanlis, came together. In the statement published as a result of the meeting, despite harsh criticism, "The two Prime Ministers had the opportunity to review

[13] Prescott, J. R. V. and Clive H. Schofield. The Maritime Political Boundaries of the World. vol. 2nd ed, Brill, 2005. EBSCOhost.
[14] Fırat, M. (2009). 1960-1980: Göreli özerklik-3, Yunanistan'la ilişkiler. B. Oran (Ed.), *Türk dış politikası kurtuluş savaşından bugüne olgular, belgeler, yorumlar 1919-1980* p.: 758, İstanbul: İletişim.
[15] Kocakaplan, G "Ege Denizi Sorununa Dair Yunanistan ve Türkiye'nin Tezleri ve Bunların Uluslararası Antlaşmalar/Sözleşmeler Düzleminde İncelenmesi", *TUIC Akademi*, p.: 5., URL: https://www.academia.edu/45005607/EGE_DEN%C4%B0Z%C4%B0_SORUNUNA_DA%C4%B0 R_YUNAN%C4%B0STAN_VE_T%C3%9CRK%C4%B0YE_N%C4%B0N_TEZLER%C4%B0_VE _BUNLARIN_ULUSLARARASI_ANTLA%C5%9EMALAR_S%C3%96ZLE%C5%9EMELER_D% C3%9CZLEM%C4%B0NDE_%C4%B0NCELENMES%C4%B0
[16] Kıyanç., p.: 17.
[17] Çelikkol, Karabel, p.18.
[18] Milliyet Newspaper, 01.06.1975: 1).

the problems between their countries. It has been decided that these problems will be resolved through peaceful negotiations and the Aegean continental shelf by the International Court of Justice." Karamanlis had Süleyman Demirel accept the International Court of Justice's move[19].

Territorial waters refer to the maritime area of the coastal state extending to a certain width in accordance with international law surrounding the landlocked state of the coastal state. The territorial waters are the sea areas that constitute the sea country of the coastal state and are subject to the sovereignty of the state[20]. The coastal state has absolute property rights over all living and non-living natural resources under, in, at the bottom and on the surface of the sea[21]. This sovereignty also includes the airspace over the territorial waters.[22]

In the Lausanne Peace Treaty, the territorial seas of Turkey and Greece were determined as 3 miles. In 1936, Greece announced that it had unilaterally increased its territorial waters to 6 miles by presidential decree, taking advantage of the relations between the two countries. Turkey did not object to this situation and accepted the territorial waters as 6 miles by enacting the Law No. It was also stated in the same law that the principle of reciprocity would apply[23].

The UNCLOS, signed in 1982, was ratified by the Greek parliament on 1 June 1995. However, Greece gave assurances to the United Nations (UN) and NATO that they would not extend its territorial seas to 12 miles unless necessary. In response, the Grand National Assembly of Turkey, on 8 June 1995, included military force to the government in order to provide freedom of action in possible developments regarding this stance of Greece. He gave full authority to take the necessary measures, including the war, and thus declared that he would consider this situation as a reason for war (casus belli)[24].

Greece stated that Turkey armed the islands in front of the Dardanelles. While the Dodecanese and Meis Island were left to Greece by the 1947 Paris Treaty, it was decided to disarm the islands; Greece argued that Turkey could not claim rights by stating that it did not accede to the treaty. Within the scope of these claims, he armed the islands[25].

Turkey established the Aegean Army in 1975 in the face of Greece's arming of the Aegean Islands and the USA's appearance in favor of Greece in the Cyprus Issue. The Aegean Army is not in the presence of Turkey's NATO[26]. Greece also objects to this situation.

Military exercises can be held at international sites, but the place and time of

---

[19] Fırat, p.: 756.
[20] Selami Kuran; Uluslararası Deniz Hukuku, Beta Basım, 5. Baskı, İstanbul, 2016, s. 73.
[21] Kuran, p.: 74.
[22] UNCLOS, Article 2/c
[23] Kıyanç, p.: 16.
[24] Kıyanç, p.: 16.
[25] Kıyanç, p.: 21.
[26] Kıyanç, p.: 22.

this must be reported. NOTAM (Notice to Airmen) is an announcement announced as a warning to airmen. These NOTAM requests, which have become a problem between Turkey and Greece, and the requests for the right to request changes on the announced NOTAMs still continue to be a problem. Greece stated that the 10 NM territorial waters and airspace implementation on the islands is not for military purposes (according to the article on the disarmament of the islands in the Lausanne Treaty) but for police purposes. Every Aegean departure of Turkish military aircraft is reported as an air violation on the Greek side. They argue that when Turkish warlords land in the Aegean and are under positive radar control with VFR[27] (Visual Flight Rules), they do not have to fill out the flight plan and will not report to the Athens approach control centre[28].

On June 2, 1974, Greece made an application to the International Civil Aviation Organization (ICAO) and announced to the international public that its airspace was 10 miles. Against this move, Turkey adopted NOTAM 714 on August 4, 1974. Thus, for the safety of Cyprus, information will be given about each flight towards Turkey. In the face of this situation, Greece reacted strongly and declared NOTAM 1157 on 13 September 1974 and closed the Aegean Sea to civil flights. Turkey, which applied to ICAO on April 15, 1975, stated that this situation was unacceptable and declared the area beyond 6 miles dangerous. In the message he sent to Greece on 5 May 1975, he stated that he accepted the airspace as 6 miles[29]. Then, on February 22, 1980, Turkey canceled NOTAM 714, and a day later, Greece canceled NOTAM 1157. Thus, civil air traffic was opened in the Aegean Sea[30]. With the coming to power of Papandreou in 1981, the problems started again. It was aimed to prevent Turkey's Aegean exercises by passing the route of the Greek G-18 air corridor over the island of Lemnos. In 1985, a new route for the G-18 was determined by ICAO. The desire of Greece to apply its airspace as ten nautical miles has led to various problems[31]. Since Greece dominates the civil airspace in the Aegean Sea, it wants to use it as a military airspace. Turkey does not accept the request for permission before approaching Athens by filling the flight plan. Thus, tensions arise and are experienced from time to time in the Aegean.

The issue of arming the Eastern Aegean Islands seems to have been resolved in the Lausanne agreement. The fact that a full maritime border between Turkey and Greece has not been determined in the agreement creates a problem today. Despite the provisions of the Lausanne Treaty, the invasion of the islets by

---

[27] Visual flight, or VFR flight, is flight in which a pilot performs altitude control and navigation of the aircraft relative to some visual reference outside the aircraft. When the flight plan is filled in for this flight, the pilot does not have to write down his route. He can write the airport he will land as a DCT(Direct).
[28] Arı, T . (2014). Ege Sorunu ve Türk-Yunan İlişkileri : Son Gelişmeler Işığında Kara Suları ve Hava Sahası Sorunları. Ankara Üniversitesi SBF Dergisi, 50 (01), .URL: http://dergipark.gov.tr/ausbf/issue/31 12/43114, 22.11.2018, p.: 64.
[29] Kıyanç, p.: 23.
[30] Arı, P.: 62.
[31] Arı, p.: 62.

Greece brought the two countries to the brink of war in 1996[32]. The 12 islands in Lausanne, which are still in the hands of Italy, were transferred to Greece in 1947. Thus, the fact that almost all of the three thousand islands in the Aegean Sea belong to Greece has created a significant problem for Turkey. It is considered that the occupation of these islets one by one by Greece and subsequent arming is a very clear indication of Athens' desire to disrupt the Turkish-Greek balance in the Aegean. Eastern Aegean islands and 12 islands; It was disarmed by the Lausanne Peace Treaty, the Lausanne Straits Convention and the Paris Agreement. It is seen that these islands were left to Greece under these conditions. Despite this, Greece armed the islands especially in the 70's and Turkey started to see this as a threat against itself. A significant number of unidentified islands, islets and reefs still pose a problem today[33]. It is noteworthy that the islands and islets close to Turkey in the Aegean Sea are economically dependent on Turkey due to its proximity to Turkey.

There are historical, geographical and legal differences between the concepts of continental shelf and EEZ. (Exclusive Economic Zone). While the definition of continental shelf was first made in the 1958 Geneva Continental Shelf Convention, it is available in the EEZ 1982 Convention. While the continental shelf is related to the exploration and exploitation of inanimate and natural resources, the EEZ emerged with the idea of fishing in the 1970s. While the continental shelf has a geographical and geological nature, the EEZ has a legal character. In terms of the rights granted to the coastal state, the EEZ has broader rights than the continental shelf. While only fixed-species living organisms are included in the continental shelf, all living or non-living resources are covered in the EEZ[34]. The EEZ shall not extend beyond 200 nautical miles from the baselines from which the territorial seas are measured[35].

Turkey is a party to the "Hamburg Sea Search and Rescue International Convention" of 1979 and the "Chicago International Civil Aviation Treaty" of 1944. According to the provisions of these contracts, it has agreed to abide by the practices determined on SAR (Search And Rescue). Greece has put a reserve in these two contracts, especially due to the disputes in the Aegean Sea[36].

Based on these articles of the agreement, Turkey has expressed its readiness for negotiations on the determination of SAR responsibility areas in the Aegean Sea in all national and international environments. Greece, on the other hand, takes a different approach and bases the SAR Region in the Aegean Sea on the Flight Information Region (FIR), which is another service area such as Search

[32] Kocakaplan, p.: 10.
[33] Çelikkol, Karabel, P.: 18-19.
[34] Kuran, p. 260, 261, 262.
[35] UNCLOS, Article 57.
[36] Olgaç T., A. C. Cemal Töz (2017) "Türk Arama ve Kurtarma Organizasyonu: Uluslararası İş Birliği Faaliyetleri ve Yaşanan Anlaşmazlıklar", *Gemi ve Deniz Teknolojisi Dergisi Sayı: 217, Haziran 2020* ISSN: 1300-1973, e-ISSN: 2651-530X, URL: http://www.gmoshipmar.org/ - 44 - Gemi ve Deniz Teknoloji, p.: 50.

and Rescue. The Flight Information Region (FIR) is the airspace with designated boundaries, within which only flight information and warning services are provided[37].

According to the rules of international law, the airspace over the area outside the territorial waters is international airspace. Although the width of the territorial waters of Greece in the Aegean Sea is 6 miles, based on a decree issued in 1931, it claims that the width of its national airspace is 10 miles. Turkey does not accept this claim of Greece, which has no other example in the world[38].

Turkey published the "Turkish Search and Rescue Regulation" on 11 December 1988, based on the 1st article of the 1979 Hamburg Convention, which is titled general obligations. The coordinates of the sea areas to be provided with SAR service have been declared[39]

In March 1989, Greece determined and published its own SAR areas in the Aegean Sea, designating all sea areas to cover the Athens FIR Line as its SAR area. These areas it determined are intertwined with the Turkish SAR Region. The problem here is that Greece sees the concept of SAR region as a maritime jurisdiction[40].

According to the Hamburg Convention, if search and rescue areas cannot be determined by agreement between the relevant parties, it is foreseen that the parties will make efforts to coordinate these activities until they reach an agreement. However, such a coordination between Greece and Turkey has not been established so far.

Exclusive economic zone is the name given to the region with a maximum length of 200 nautical miles from the line from which the territorial waters are measured and which grants the coastal state rights over the surface and submarine resources[41]. Articles 55 and 75 of the 1982 United Nations Convention on the Law of the Sea relate to the Exclusive Economic Zone. For example, article 56 gives important powers to the country that has a coast in terms of exploration, operation, conservation and management of living and non-living natural resources in the region described above, and benefiting from water, current and wind[42]. Article 72, on the other hand, includes measures such as embarking on the ship in these regions, inspection of the ship, and filing a lawsuit for the seizure of the ship[43]. It is striking that the State, which has a coast in the Exclusive Economic Zone, has authorized the activities such as fishing, as well as natural resources such as oil, natural gas and mines under the sea. An

---

[37] Olgaç T., A. C. Cemal Töz, p.: 50.

[38] Olgaç T., A. C. Cemal Töz, p.: 50.

[39] Olgaç T., A. C. Cemal Töz, p.: 51

[40] Olgaç T., A. C. Cemal Töz, p.: 51.

[41] Tamçelik S., E.Kurt (1993) " Türkiye'nin Ekonomik Bölge Algısı ve Yakın Tehdit Alanı: Kıbrıs", International Security Congress, 8-9 Oct 2013, Proceeding Book,Vol:3,2014:Kocaeli University, p.: 884.

[42] Tamçelik S., E.Kurt, p.: 884.

[43] Tamçelik S., E.Kurt, p.: 884.

important element draws attention in Article 74: States with adjacent or opposite coasts, such as the Aegean Sea, must make the delimitation of the exclusive economic zone by agreement within the framework of equity[44].

Conclusion

The strategic and geopolitical area of the Aegean Sea, which only has coasts between Turkey and Greece, causes problems between the two countries. Of course, the source of these problems stems not only from natural but also from human causes. Geographical reasons originate from this area where there are over three thousand islands and this is called the Sea of Islands. The human reason is that they could not reach a common consensus due to Turkish-Greek, Muslim-Christian and cultural differences.

Due to the geopolitics of the Aegean Sea, there are problems between Turkey and Greece regarding territorial waters. Greece wants to continuously increase its territorial waters to 12 nautical miles and Turkey refuses this because the Aegean Sea will be almost completely under Greek domination. Greece claims rights on the continental shelf on the grounds that the islands belong to them. Especially the eastern islands are an extension of Anatolia and this geological reality is clearly seen. Greece acts in violation of the Lausanne agreement by arming the Eastern Aegean islands.

Another problem between Turkey and Greece is the exclusive economic zone. Turkey is compressed to the east with its western Anatolian coasts. Greece claims that due to the islands, the resources on and under the Aegean Sea belong to it. It also does not agree to an agreement with Turkey on this issue.

It is still unclear how and by which country the search and rescue activities in the Aegean Sea will be carried out. Greece did not make an agreement with Turkey on this issue, and did not reluctant to form an agreement.

The desire of Greece to continuously extend 12 seas to its territorial waters in the Aegean Sea shows that it cannot reach an agreement with Turkey on the exclusive economic zone. Currently, six nautical miles of territorial waters are not enough for Greece, and it wants the resources of the entire Aegean sea above and below this sea. Thus, the Aegean Sea and Greece will be a united state. Because of this thought, it definitely does not want to come to an agreement with Turkey. It uses various opportunities to show that Greece is the sole ruler of the Aegean Sea, even in search and rescue services. It has been seen that he has made applications about dominating this sea in various maritime accidents that took place in the Aegean Sea.

---

[44] Tamçelik S., E.Kurt, p.: 885.

PART 4

MARITIME COMMERCE, ECONOMICS AND MARINE ENVIRONMENT

A SHORT HISTORY OF MARITIME TRADE

Haldun Aydıngün*

"The ships were always the most complicated piece of engineering of their own time throughout the history"

Introduction

The history of ships goes so far back in time that, we don't have any written text to prove, no folks tales to hint and no surviving remains of the first ships, but just bones, human bones; Australian archaeologist Michael Morwood found a number of humanoid bones in the island of Flores, part of the Indonesian Archipelago. Radiometric measurements gave a date of 840,000 BC.[1]

We know that humans and its predecessors went out of Africa more than once and the date obtained by Morwood was not an anomaly by itself, but there was a problem to be solved; Flores was always an island out of the big land masses. In the last 2,5 million years world had many episodes of glaciations during which huge quantities of water from the oceans were trapped in land, making sea levels drop down ca. 120 meters worldwide. As a result, many of the islands we know today were part of the continents, like British islands being part of Europe. The theory was that; our ancestors were simply walking from these land bridges and reached all parts of the world. But in order to reach Flores they had to cross two straits; one being 15 km and the other 9 km long and both being much deeper than 120 m.

These humanoids lived in Flores until about 15,000 BC before being extinct. It was proposed that they made the crossing unintentionally by a tsunami or by some other natural phenomena. Against this arguments Morwood claimed that to be able to survive for such a long time the original group had to contain at least two dozen individuals, to be able to have enough genetic diversity. Consequently, it is said that the original arrivers somehow built some kind of vessels and made the crossing intentionally. The crafts they created can be named as the first known open sea boats.

A similar but a much later historic discovery came from the island of Crete in Aegean Sea. Archaeologists discovered human settlements going back to 130,000 years ago. Crete also was always an island during the time when humans

---

* Archaeology Lecturer

[1] M. J. Morwood and W. L. Junkers, "Conclusions: Implications of the Liang Bua Excavations for Hominine Evolution and Biogeography", **Journal of Human Evolution**, Vol. 57, 2009, pp. 640-648; Josephine Flood, "**The Original Australians – Story of the Aboriginal People**", Sydney, Allen & Unwin, 2006, p. 171; Alan H. Simmons ve Katelyn Di Benedetto, "**Stone Age Sailors – Paleolithic Seafaring in the Mediterranean**", California, Left Coast Press Inc., 2014, p. 27.

were roaming the earth. These settlers had to make two consecutive voyages each at least 45 km long.[2]

Sometime around 50,000 to 60,000 years ago a more advance kind of seafaring were realized by the ancestors of Australian aborigines; They reached Australia. The difference of their voyage from the two previous ones mentioned above was the fact that from the point they set sail they were not able to see the land mass of Australia. They were sailing towards an empty horizon. One has to admit that they had to have much advance navigation skills and vessels capable to cross a sea of at least 70 km.[3]

Material Evidences of the Voyages

Till now the existence of humans in unlikely places were the sole evidence of the most ancient seafaring. 13 to 10 thousand years ago we reach a time we can see some useful materials carried by sea and probably traded.

Island of Melos in Aegean Sea is well known for its famous obsidian quarries. People certainly visited the island, quarried obsidian and carried to many sites in Peloponnese and many islands in western Aegean. There are evidences that the voyages to Melos were repeated regularly, thus purporting an advance seamanship.[4]

These obsidians are the first known items carried long distances from their sources to be used. We don't know if the people carrying them were trading or not but we can say that these people who were handling these obsidians solved one of the most important problem of the maritime trade; namely the logistics.

The Oldest Boat yet found

The ancient mariners were using natural materials to build their boats. These materials were decaying fast and disappeared completely from the archaeological records. So it was a good surprise to find a simple dugout canoe in a peat bog. The acidic environment of the bog were not allowing the bacteria to live and decompose natural materials. The oldest of the many dugouts recovered by archaeologists came from Pesse in Holand. It was almost intact and was showing some traits of early naval engineering; the prove was sharpened to reduce the drag when sailing. The C14 dating gave about an age of around 10,000 years. The replicas of the boat were built and showed that it actually floats and it is possible

---

[2] Katerina Kopaka and Christos Matzanas, "Palaeolithic Industries from the Island of Gavdos, near Neighbour to Crete in Greece", **Antiquity Project Gallery**, Vol. 83, 2009, p. 321. http://antiquity.ac.uk/projgall/kopaka321/index.html (Access 27.05.2018).

[3] Huw S. Groucutt et al., "Rethinking the Dispersal of Homo Sapiens out of Africa", **Evolutionary Anthropology**, Vol. 24, 2015, pp. 149-164; Richard A. Gould, **Archaeology and the Social History of Ships**, Cambridge, 2011, Cambridge University Press.

[4] Agathe Reingruber, "Early Neolithic Settlement Patterns and Exchange Networks in the Aegean", **Documenta Praehistorica XXXVIII**, 2011, pp. 291-305.

to make short trips in calm water of lakes and rivers.[5]

We know that prehistoric environment had more pristine forests having much older and bigger trees. Thus, it was easy to find long and large tree trunks to dig much bigger canoes.

Learning from the Drawings (Petroglyphs)

Early in 7th millennium BC (roughly 9000 years ago), a picture of a ship drawn on a pebble was recovered from an excavation by the Nile river in Sudan. The boat depicted shows a more sophisticated design than a simple dugout canoe; it seems to have a rudder, which should be quite unexpected for such an early date.[6]

There are other pictures (petroglyphs) of boats drawn on rocks in Sudan, not far from the previously mentioned excavation site. But their dating is contentious; there are some seeing them for 4. Millennium BC and some others proposing a much earlier date. In any case, the boats show a wide spectrum of different designs and sizes with sails or rowers.

During the same millennium more petroglyphs were recovered from Aegean island of Andros; in the settlement walls of Strofilas archaeologist Christina Televantou found a series of ship's depictions. It is understood that these ships are long boats with many rowers which can tackle the winds and currents of the Aegean Sea. For the communities living in such isolated islands the existence of the sea going vessel were vital. We can assume a lively trade between islands and the mainland.[7]

In the excavations he is carrying out in the eastern part of Crete, archeologist Yiannis Papadatos found the evidence of the materials coming from distant islands and the mainland Greece. He proposes that the people of that settlement were making direct voyages to obtain much needed resources and trade with other communities in 4th millennium BC.[8]

Learning from the Models

The beautiful ceramics produced by the Ubaid culture of Mesopotamia (6500-3800 BC) was in much demand by the people around Persian Gulf and some of the potteries were discovered in Arabian sites as far as 800 km from their source. Such journeys were the norm of 6th millennium BC in that part of the world. Robert Carter discovered a model of a ship and bitumen pieces, used

[5] Simmons and di Benedetto, op.cit, p.79

[6] Donatella Usai and Sandro Salvatori, "The Oldest Representation of a Nile Boat", **Antiquity Journal,** Vol. 314, 2007, http://www.antiquity.ac.uk/projgall/usai/ (Access: 28.02.2017).

[7] Christina Televantou, "Strofilas: A Neolithic Settlement on Andros", **Horizon-A Colloquium on the Prehistory of the Cyclades,** Neil Brodie, Jenny Doole, Giorgos Gavalas, (Eds.) Colin Renfrew, McDonald Institute for Archaeological Research, Cambridge, 2008, pp. 43-53.

[8] Yiannis Papadatos, Peter Tomkins, "The Emergence of Trade and the Integration of Crete into the Wider Aegean in the Late 4th Millennium: New Evidence and Implications", **AJA,** Vol. 117, No. 3, 2014, pp. 329-343.

to make reed boats water tight in an excavation in Kuwait. We know that during the 5th millennium, trade from India also started and the maritime trade network became widespread.[9] Besides many other prestige items, Lapis Lazuli, a semi-precious stone quarried in Afghanistan, were being shipped as far as Egypt in 4th millennium BC. These stones were transported from their quarries to their final destinations following Oxus river, Indus river and Arabian sea.[10]

In 3rd Millennium BC a number of ship models were found from the cemeteries of Ur in Mesopotamia. Also, from the Cycladic islands further metallic models came. In general, these models depict long but very narrow vessels easy to row against mild currents and winds. But this design brings a problem for trade; there is precious few spaces for cargo in the hull.

An Actual Colossal Ship

Ancient Egyptians are known to give splendid treasures and luxurious daily use items to their deceased pharaohs in their passage to other world, but nobody was expecting to find 43 meters long, full size, perfectly preserved ship from the 3rd Millennium BC dedicated to one of them. The ship was discovered right next to the pyramid of Keops in a dismantled state, containing detailed instructions for reassembly.[11] Experts say, after 4600 years it can still be seaworthy. It also shows us the surprising technological levels reached by that time in ship building. It is known that at that time Egypt was making trading voyages to Levant and to the land of Punt, a southern country reached via Red Sea, being probably Yemen or Somalia.[12]

Around the same epoch, during mid 3rd millennium BC, the trade activities show a sudden increase in Eastern Mediterranean region. Archaeologists finds objects from considerable distances. It is possible to assume that sailors of that time had mastered the use of sails. Because even with a primitive sail it is possible to propel a vessel in open sea and carry heavy loads of 20-25 tons for long distances with a small number of crew.

Rivers or Open Seas

When studying the history of the ships and trade one needs to know the different possibilities and difficulties of the rivers versus open sea.

The fact that there were no big waves in rivers provided two very important advantages in the design of the river going crafts;

---

[9] Robert Carter, "Boat Remains and Maritime Trade in the Persian Gulf During the Sixth and Fifth Millennia BC", **Antiquity**, Vol. 80, No. 307, 2006, pp. 52-63.
[10] A. H. Dani and V. M. Masson (Eds), "History of Civilizations of Central Asia-The dawn of civilization: earliest times to 700 B.C. Volume I", UNESCO Publishing, Paris, 1992, p. 212.
[11] https://en.wikipedia.org/wiki/Khufu_ship (Access 27.01.2017).
[12] William J. Bernstein, **A Splendid Exchange - How Trade Shaped the World**, Atlantic New York, Monthly Press, 2008, p. 59.

1. The boats' high shipboards which is paramount for open sea vessels was not needed,

2. Open sea vessels need to be structurally much stronger than river boats. Because, in case of storms the vessels can be suspended either from its middle of the hull on top of a big wave or on two waves, one from the bow and the other from the stern, in both cases the vessel can be broken from its mid-section.

The advantages of rivers compared to open sea became to such an high mark by the mid 2nd Millennium BC, that while the open sea merchant ship can only carry 20 – 25 tons of cargo, Egyptians were able to transfer a single piece of obelisk weighing 413 tons from the quarries of Aswan till the temple of Amon in Karnak from the river of Nile.[13]

Historically, major rivers played a very important role in inland transport. Until the advent of railroads in the first half of the 19th century and the intercities in the first half of 20th centuries, the rivers like Danube, Volga, Euphrates, Elbe, Vistula and myriads of others were like highways crisscrossing the continents.

There was another very important advantage of the rivers compared to seas; when navigating in rivers it was not possible to lose the way. On the contrary, the technology of pinpointing the exact position of the vessel in open sea can only be reached at the end of 18th century AD[14]. That's why most of the time the ships had to follow the coastal routes in antiquity, which were dangerous both because of the rocky outcrops these coasts may contains and pirates who were active all along the history.

2nd Millennium BC

By the 2nd millennium BC the ships' designs were diversified according to different needs of sailors and merchants. A fresco found on the wall of a house buried under the ejecta of the volcano in the Aegean island of Santorini is probably the most studied of its kind for the entire period of Bronze Age. It depicts a procession of ships in which different designs with or without sails can be seen.[15]

Gelidonya and Uluburun Ship Wrecks

During the second half of the 20th century AD, two shipwrecks changed all our understanding of the trade relations on the eastern Mediterranean. These two ships from the southern coast of Turkey thought us about the trade goods which don't leave archaeological record. It was always known that organic materials like

---

[13] https://en.wikipedia.org/wiki/Lateran Obelisk (Access 25.06.2021).
[14] Heather, Mervyn Hobden, **"John Harrison and the Problem of Longitude"**, London, 2013, p. 27.
[15] Annette Højen Sorensen, et al., "Miniatures of Meaning – Interdisciplinary Approaches to the Miniature Frescoes from the West House at Akrotiri on Thera", **Tagungen des Landesmuseums für Vorgeschichte Halle**, Band 9, 2013, pp. 149-162.

food stuff or textile can hardly survive and they leave precious few records of their existence. But the cargo of these two ships, Uluburun[16] from 13th century BC and Gelidonya[17] from 12th century BC, provided us with tons of copper and tin, raw glass ingots and turpentine. If these goods were able to reach their destination they will be changed to metal tools, arms, glass cups and different daily use items, losing the information about the source of the raw materials. We understood that 3300 years ago there was an important trade between far away distances such as southern Scandinavia, Central Europe, Soudan, Egypt, Levant, Mesopotamia, India and Central Asia. These ships informed the scientific community that the ancient traded goods were rarely prestige items of high value but mostly raw materials as it is today. And the bulk of this trade were carried by vessels.

Especially the tin metal, were brought to Anatolia first from Central Asia via the route of Caspian Sea and Black Sea during the period of 2400-2200 BC, then the transportation from the same source shifted to Indus Valley and it reached Anatolia via Arabian Sea, the Gulf and Mesopotamia during the period of 1970-1700 BC. After 1600 BC the tin was brought from Cornwall of UK, passing through Central European river systems such as Danube.[18]

In order to realize such a complicated trade system, it was necessary to have a very sophisticated political atmosphere, standardized weights and measures, so that merchants from faraway lands can communicate and can realize commercial orders, and strong trade laws applicable to these transactions.

1st Millennium BC

At the end of the 2nd millennium BC the civilized societies of the Eastern Mediterranean all collapsed with the exception of the Egypt. In the following millennium a completely new political landscape emerged. Phoenicians from today's Lebanon and Israel were the leading figures in long distance trading. They were able to navigate in open sea and during nights following the stars. They were also able to go beyond Gibraltar and circumnavigate the Africa. Sub Saharan Africa was utterly rich at that time and there are accounts of ships making this voyage in every three years bringing back gold, precious stones, rare wood etc.[19]

During the same period, starting from 8th century BC, The Greeks started to colonize, first Aegean coasts of Western Anatolia, later Marmara Sea, Western

---

[16] George Bass, "A Bronze Age Shipwreck at Uluburun (Kaş)-1984 Campaign", **American Journal of Archaeology**, No. 90, 1896, pp. 269-296.
[17] , George Bass, Peter Throckmotron, "Excavating a Bronze Age Shipwreck", **Archaelology**, Vol. 44, No. 2, 1961, pp. 78-88.
[18] Haldun Aydıngün, "Orta Tunç Çağı'nda Ege Karadeniz Arasındaki Ticarette Bathonea: Bir Aktarma Limanı Modeli", Unpublished PhD Thesis, Çanakkale Üniversitesi, 2019, p. 246.
[19] Robert R. Stieglitz, "Long-Distance Seafaring in the Ancient Near East", **The Biblical Archaeologist**, Vol. 47, No. 3, 1984, pp. 134-142.

Mediterranean and the Black Sea coasts.

Like other Greek city states, Athens was short of grain and it has to import 100,000 metric tons yearly. The largest part had to be brought from the Crimea.[20] By the mid of the 1st millennium BC, Greek merchant ships were able to carry up to 250 tons of cargo. While the propulsion system was based on one or two square sails, rowing was not an option. These ships were able to carry such heavy loads in Aegean and Mediterranean seas using both the known currents and winds. But transportation of grain from Crimea necessitated the negotiation of both Dardanelles and Bosporus, which was very difficult and dangerous most of the time and downright impossible for these merchant ships. To solve this problem, Athens created a huge organization and strategic transportation of grain was helped by Athenian navy, both for its protection against foes and pirates and against straits' currents by towing them with navy's triremes.

The best military ships of that era; the triremes were long and narrow vessels.[21] They had 170 rovers and were easily able to beat both the northeast wind and the currents of Bosporus, which was more difficult than Dardanelles. During the passages of these two straits, military ships were towing the grain ships in both directions.

Roman Era

In Mediterranean, during the period of mid 1st century BC to the mid of 1st century AD we know that there is a huge shipping activity reaching its climax in the turn of the millennium. The best evidence comes from the dating of the shipwrecks as the table-01 shows. Also, it is obvious from the same chart that the shipping volume of the Classical period cannot be reached till the end of the Middle Ages.

Roman Era cargo ships becomes huge and there are texts purporting the existence of wheat ships which can carry 1000 tons of grains. Unfortunately, we didn't have any solid evidence of them. But we have a number of other ships, identified by their wrecks, although with lesser capacities, still considerable for their period.

One of them is Albenga Shipwreck. It is dated to 100-90BC and sunken in north Italian coast. The major part of its cargo consists of 11,500 to 13,000 Dressel 1B amphorae, it is said to carry walnuts and grains too. The total cargo is calculated to be between 500 to 600 tons.

The other important wreck is Madrague de Giens, the total cargo was calculated to be around 400 tons and was carrying 6000-7000 Italian wine amphorae. It is interesting to note that both ships belong to the first century

---

[20] Lionell Casson, **The Ancient Mariners**, 4th edition, New York, The McMillan Company, 1967, p. 168.
[21] Nicolle E. Hirschfeld, "Appendix G: Trireme warfare in Thucydides", **The Landmark Thucydides: A comprehensive guide to the Peloponnesian War**, R. B. Strassler, (Ed.), New York, NY Free Press, 1996, pp. 608-613.

BC.[22]

The antique writers mention a ship named Syracusia commissioned by King Hieron. She is mentioned as the largest ship of the antiquity, probably a Titanic for her time, containing a library, gymnasium, bath, a small temple, a promenade lined with flowers and she could accommodate hundreds of passengers. Unfortunately, we don't have any exact information about her size, estimations vary between 2000 tons to 4000 tons.[23]

The epitome of the Roman naval engineering, at least the one we were able to find archaeological records were the two Nemi ships. The bigger ship had a length of 73 m. and a width of 24 m, the other one had a length of 70 m and a width of 20 m. They were two floating palaces constructed by Roman emperor Caligula in the 1st century AD at Lake Nemi near Rome. These two ships were the solid evidence that Roman were able to construct very heavy vessels. They were unearthed from the bottom of Nemi Lake in the first half of the 20th century, exhibited in a specially constructed museum and were completely burned down in 1944 during the WWII.[24]

After the 5th century AD Europe was entering its Dark Ages and the size of the biggest Roman ships could not be matched on the 13 centuries which would follow.[25]

The Pirates

The Aegean Sea with its intricate coasts and islands were always a paradise for pirates. The oldest records of pirate activities are dated to 14th century BC and comes from Egyptians. During a period of increasing commercial activities and shipments of goods pirates were becoming a serious threat. In the first century BC Roman admiral Pompey (*Gnaeus Pompeius Magnus*) fought and wiped out almost all the pirates out of Mediterranean, opening the Pax Romana in the sea transport as well.[26] As a result, the relative security of Mediterranean and the single currency provided by Rome (with the exception of Egypt), provided a very positive environment for the increase of long-distance trade within the Roman borders.

The Harbors

When the sea going crafts were small and can be easily beached, the harbors were no more than the small estuaries in the entrance of the rivers. With the increasing size of the vessels, proper infrastructures and port facilities started to

[22] Johan Opdebeeck, "Shipwrecks and Amphorae: Their Relationship with Trading Routes and the Roman Economy in the Mediterranean", Unpublished Thesis, University of Southampton, 2005, p. 10.
[23] Nicolle E. Hirschfeld, op.cit, p.84
[24] Nemi ships - Wikipedia (Access 23.06.2021).
[25] James Beresford, **"The Ancient Sailing Season",** Leiden-Boston, Brill, 2013, p. 108.
[26] https://en.wikipedia.org/wiki/Pompey (Access 25.06.2021).

be needed. In order to be able to coop with the huge maritime trade Romans built a number of very impressive harbors around Mediterranean. We can name a few of these as Carthage, Alexandria, Sebastos at Caesarea, Ostia and Leptis Magna. These harbors were permitting deep draft heavy merchant ships to berth and to upload and unload their cargos easily. They were paramount to cope with the ever-increasing volume of the sea trade during Roman era.

In order to be able to construct these huge jetties into the sea, Roman engineers invented a concrete which can solidify inside the sea water.[27]

Middle Ages

From the point of view of the ongoing maritime trade in the Mediterranean, the Middle Ages, which followed the classical period, were truly a dark era. Only about 1000 years later, with the discovery of new maritime technologies, such as magnetic compass, and new continents, maritime trade started to match again its once glorious days of Roman era.

Table 1. The numbers of shipwrecks per century in Mediterranean[28]

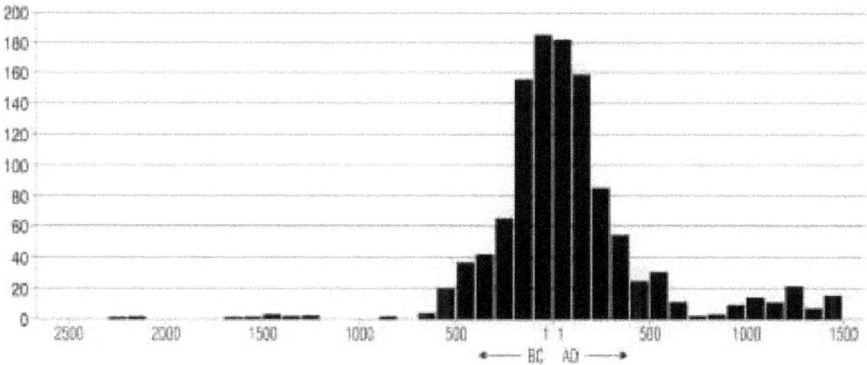

[27] Benjamin Herring and Stephani Miller, "The Secrets of Roman Concrete", **Constructor**, September 2002, pp.13-16
[28] Andrew Wilson, "Developments in Mediterranean Shipping and Maritime Trade from the Hellenistic Period to AD 1000", **Maritime Archaeology and Ancient Trade in the Mediterranean**, Damian Robinson and Andrew Wilson, (Eds.), Oxford Centre for Maritime Archaeology, Oxford, 2011, pp. 33-59.

AUTOMATION AND CYBERSECURITY IN MARITIME COMMERCE

Alaettin Sevim[1]

Introduction

A ship's various intelligent subsystems ensure smooth operation: from tank and ballast water management to propulsion control, alarm, and monitoring systems. All of them work using industrial automation technology. As network communication increases in the maritime industry, the exchange of sensitive data also increases. Electronic systems such as navigation, monitoring, and collision warning systems require connections with off-ship, thus creating potential targets for cybercrime. With the increasing digitalization and network connections on ships, the risk of data misuse and cybercrime is also increasing. Anyone considering the possibilities of Maritime 4.0 also needs to consider the growing requirements for cybersecurity and, more importantly, find suitable solutions to implement it.

At many points, networking these subsystems offers advantages - for example, ship operators can work with greater resource or energy efficiency. Sensitive data exchange also increases wherever systems are connected over a network. As such, this is not enough. compared to applications on land, ships have additional electronic systems such as navigation, tracking and collision warning systems. They serve the security of the ship; However, in addition to increasing the level of network connectivity on board, they also pose an additional threat, as they also establish external connections. Internet-based network technologies or mobile services are increasingly used for these connections. These communication paths provide access points for manipulation - especially at points between ship and land.

Access to or reading data belonging to others is relatively minor compared to the effects caused by hackers who introduce malware into usage systems, alter data, and deflect coordinates and routes. These actions can also endanger cybersecurity, operational safety and ultimately the safety of the crew. This is precisely why suggestions on cyber security are increasing with digitization and network connectivity. Many national and international maritime organizations have published regulations on cyber security in maritime. In general, these regulations define processes, model approaches or technical measures for cyber security implementation; these mostly comply with regulations for automation technology.

Hacking attempts in the maritime environment have been reported to have

[1] Alaettin Sevim, PhD Student, Piri Reis University, Turkey. E-mail: asevim@pirireis.edu.tr.

increased by 400 percent since February 2020.[2] The primary reason for the increase, which is seen as more malware, ransomware, and phishing emails, is the measures taken due to the Covid-19 pandemic. Global travel restrictions, social distancing measures and the recession are limiting companies' ability to defend themselves. As service technicians struggle to navigate to ships and offshore platforms for maintenance and repair purposes, system operators are increasingly performing system maintenance and repairs themselves, with remote service calls requiring them to bypass security protocols and creating an opening for a cyberattack. More vessel and offshore platform operators perform diagnostics by connecting their systems to coastal networks and upload software updates and routes themselves. This similarly disrupts the isolation of systems and makes them more vulnerable to cyber risks. The introduction of remote work and remote, autonomous technologies seems to be faster in the future regardless of the impacts of the Covid 19 pandemic. This will see what cybersecurity risks shipping companies face if they fail to implement adequate safeguards. The aim of this study is to reveal the risks as well as the advantages and conveniences that digital transformation brings to the maritime industry. In the study, the increasing automation in the sector and the cyber risks against it were identified and the cyberattacks recently exposed were examined. Within the scope of the study, the cyber risks faced by the maritime sector were comprehensively discussed.

Automation

Automating the operation and management of a system is to enable the system to operate automatically according to the references previously given. It can be defined as *"the technique, method, or system of operating or controlling a process by highly automatic means, as by electronic devices, reducing human intervention to a minimum"*.[3] The Encyclopedia Britannica on the other hand defines automation as *"application of machines to tasks once performed by human beings or, increasingly, to tasks that would otherwise be impossible. Although the term mechanization is often used to refer to the simple replacement of human labor by machines, automation generally implies the integration of machines into a self-governing system"*.[4] Considering that the common point of the definitions is to reduce human intervention, it is understood that the basic approach of automation is to minimize human intervention and to ensure rapidity and efficiency in operations and to minimize the losses that may result from human errors. Some institutions or private organizations, facilities and factories have generally integrated their systems and operation method on an automatic control system. As a result of this integration, they benefit from increasing production quality and productivity and the benefits of systematic work. Usually, touchscreen industrial computers are used in ship automation

[2] The Maritime Executive, Report: Maritime Cyberattacks Up by 400 Percent, Published Jun 4, 2020, https://www.maritime-executive.com/article/report-maritime-cyberattacks-up-by-400-percent (Access 14.04.2021)
[3] "Automation - Definitions from Dictionary.com". dictionary.reference.com. http://dictionary.reference.com/browse/Automation.(Access 14.04.2021)
[4] https://www.britannica.com/technology/automation (Access 14.04.2021)

systems. Thanks to the software installed on these computers, the user can control the system here and access all the data and reports about the system with an interface. The reasons for choosing the automation system.

- Workforce economy,

- Control stability,

- Zero error or near zero error.

- The fact that everything is flexible and controllable in the automation system is in the interest of operators because this situation shows the operation of the system on the computer screen, the location of the fault, if any, data, and warnings about the system, etc. It provides easy access and control to much information. Time, quality, cost, speed, and profit are returned to the operators and managers. However, automation systems also have disadvantages.

- The biggest disadvantage of these systems is that the initial setup is very costly. However, the cost also pays for itself in most automation systems in a certain term.

- Another disadvantage is that because of excessive reliance on these automated systems, the operators' situational awareness may decrease or lose.[5]

- In addition, the fact that they cause a decrease in the workforce can cause social problems if this damage not being balanced in some way.

Cybersafety and Cybersecurity

Today, the use of technology is developing in all sectors, and automation and digitalization are rapidly spreading. Industry, as well as all commerce, has used various systems, programs, and equipment all this time. As mentioned above, these factors have economic and operational benefits. However, the fact that the effective operation of all these systems needs to be networking with each other and with external systems also reveals cyber risks. Various information and data are exposed on different internet platforms and networks. Risks such as unauthorized access to these systems, unauthorized acquisition, use or modification of data bring the concepts of cybersafety and cybersecurity to the agenda. The Cybersafety and Cybersecurity concepts can be defined as follows:

"Cybersafety: Guidelines and standards for computerized, automated, and autonomous systems that seek to shape those systems to be designed, built, operated,

---

[5] Emin Deniz Özkan, Oğuz Atik, "Gemi Köprüüstü Otomasyon Sistemlerinin Kaptan ve Kılavuz Kaptanların Durumsal Farkındalık Seviyesiyle İlişkisi", Dokuz Eylül Üniversitesi, Denizcilik Fakültesi Dergisi Cilt:8 Sayı:2 Yıl:2016, Sayfa:293-320, ISSN:1309-4296 E-ISSN:2458-9942

and maintained so as to allow only predictable, repeatable behaviors, especially in those areas of operation or maintenance that can affect human, system, enterprise or environmental safety. CyberSafety is required for the deterministic behaviors found in engineered functional assurance, and it includes software integrity management to manage technical risk in software intensive systems." and "Cybersecurity: The activity or process, ability or capability, or state whereby information and communications systems and the information contained therein are protected from and/or defended against damage, unauthorized use or modification, or exploitation."[6]

The maritime industry is increasingly using information technologies (IT), operation technologies (OT) and cyber-physical systems (CPS) due to advances in technology. These systems provide force multipliers to assist the captain and crew in operating the ship effectively and efficiently with engine and ship controls, monitoring and warning. Navigation, propulsion, ship maneuvering, system management, cargo management, and security sensors and alarms - all support management and decision-making, provide functions and assist people while working. The IT, OT and CPS systems are expected to work in a way that is compatible and supportive of each other if they are to support the crew's processes and procedures.

The number of ship and platform automated systems is increasing, and these systems are more interconnected than ever before. There are several reasons for this: crew, company officials, platform or facility managers and original equipment manufacturers (OEMs) request more functions at station locations, backup capability among systems, more capability for remote access, more frequent and faster data flow and feedback from sensors, frequent reporting and more and new data types and functions. Shipping companies using remote solutions get remote diagnosis for their ships, enabling them to optimize their ships and remarket the recorded data. They can also get support from engineers on land for repairs, do not have to keep high-cost technicians on board, and reduce labor costs by using less and less qualified crew. To fulfill these requirements, many control systems are combined via industry standard communications and networking, interfaced with internet-connected networks, and operated in multiple modes. The efficiency of the systems depends to more intercommunication, but the risk of infiltration increases. The result is that special purpose control systems are often connected to general purpose systems and exposed to cyber risks that can have adverse operational consequences. IMO defines the maritime cyber risk as *"a measure of the extent to which a technology asset could be threatened by potential circumstance or event, which may result in shipping-related operational, safety or security failures as a consequence of information or systems being corrupted, lost or Maritime compromised."*[7]

---

[6] American Bureau of Shipping, GUIDANCE NOTES ON THE APPLICATION OF CYBERSECURITY PRINCIPLES TO MARINE AND OFFSHORE OPERATIONS ABS CyberSafetyTM, VOLUME 1, SEPTEMBER 2016
[7] https://www.imo.org/en/OurWork/Security/Pages/Cyber-security.aspx (Access 15.4.2021)

In this environment where linkage opportunities are increasing, protective isolation concepts are approaching their limits. Opportunities offered by network communication, which increase the frequency of external access and provide a much deeper penetration into the ship's automation systems than before, limit the isolation and its effectiveness. The increase in additional communication relationships produced by Industry 4.0 or Marine 4.0 provides increased potential for cyberattacks in maritime environment.

Types of Cyberattacks

Cyberattacks affecting ships and shipping companies can be broadly classified into two categories.

- Untargeted attacks where a company's or ship's systems and data are not specifically targeted but could be one of many potential targets. Most intentional cyberattacks are untargeted attacks without targeting a specific person or organization. The main goal is to influence as many devices or users as possible rather than a particular person or organization. These attacks are made by taking advantage of the Internet's openness to everyone. No distinction is made between those who have been attacked, in short, the identity of the victim is insignificant.

- Targeted attacks where the systems and data of company or ship are the intended target. Cyber criminals attack or infiltrate a critical infrastructure system for malicious use, targeting a specific person or organization. Advanced cyberattacks can now nest within a network for days before being discovered, and until then thousands of private and confidential data can be collected, stolen, or exchanged.

Some of the cyberattack types in these groups can be listed as follows.

Malware: Malware designed to gain access to or damage a computer without the owner knowing. There are various types of malwares such as Trojans, ransomware, spyware, viruses, and worms.

Spyware: A malware used by cybercriminals to spy on the target and obtain sensitive information.

Ransomware - A type of malware designed to block access to a system until the ransom is paid.

Watering Hole: The attacker observes or predicts which websites are used frequently and infects one or more of them with malware. Ultimately, some members of the targeted group will become infected.

Scanning: The attackers scan devices in the system and collect network information of those devices to find security vulnerabilities before launching sophisticated attacks. Scanning techniques commonly used to gather computer network information include IP address scan, port scan, and version scan.

Phishing: Sending emails to large numbers of targets, redirecting them to the similar copy of the site they frequently use or a fake site, or asking for certain sensitive or confidential information. There is also a targeted attack type called Spear-Phishing. In this attack, cybercriminals email a malicious attachment to the target or a link that downloads malware. Unlike phishing emails of the same format that are sent to a large number of people, Spear-Phishing often includes disguised emails that appear legitimate as they seem to be sent by a person or organization known to the recipient.

Typo squatting: It is a form of cybersquatting and possibly brand theft based on errors such as typing errors (typos) made by internet users when entering a website address into a web browser. If a user accidentally enters an incorrect website address, it may be redirected to any website, including an alternative website owned by the cyber squatter.

Distributed Denial of Service: Sending a large amount of data requests to the target, causing the target to interrupt its operation or even crash completely.

Spoofing: Cybercriminals act like a resource known to the user or recipient of a message and try to obtain sensitive information. Common types include email spoofing, IP spoofing, and website spoofing.

Man-in-the-middle attack (MITM): An attacker breaks into communication between two parties to spy on victims, steal personal information or credentials, or perhaps somehow alter the conversation. Nowadays, it is rarely seen as all communications become end-to-end encrypted.

Password (Password Hunting) attack: It aims to guess or crack a user's password. There are many different techniques. The main ones are the Brute-Force attack, Dictionary attack, Rainbow Table attack, Credential Stuffing, Password Spraying and Keylogger attack. Phishing techniques can also be used.

Brute-Force Attack: It is a method of guessing passwords by trying all possibilities with software running systematically. Uses the trial-and-error approach. With the use of strong passwords, finding the password takes a long time and becomes difficult.

Dictionary Attack: Determining the decryption key or password by trying thousands or millions of possibilities, such as words in a dictionary or passwords often obtained in the past.

Rainbow Table Attack: It is possible to save a time by preparing a list of dictionary words in advance and storing them in a database using hashes as keywords. This requires a significant amount of preparation time but allows the actual attack to be carried out faster once the tables are prepared.

Credential Stuffing Attack: Stolen account credentials, which typically include lists of usernames, email addresses, and passwords often obtained because of breaches, are used to gain unauthorized access to user accounts through large-scale automatic login requests to a web application.

Password Spraying Attack: Multiple user accounts are tested using many common passwords. Trying a single password on several user accounts before trying different passwords on the same account allows hackers to bypass the usual account lockout protocols and keep trying more passwords.

Keylogger Attack: Keyloggers are software that records keystrokes made by a user. It records the user's keystrokes typed on a website or application and transfers them to third parties.

Business Email Compromise (BEC): Usually target people with financial transaction authority. The goal is to deceive them and make them to transfer money to the attacker's account.

SQL Injection: Hackers write SQL (Structured Query Language) commands to fields such as login boxes, search boxes, or sign-up boxes. The goal is to use complex code to access a system. If the attack is successful, it may be possible to reproduce, change and delete data. The motivations behind the attack are often financial. Hackers can sell sensitive data or transfer it to groups who want to disrupt target business to gain advantage.

Drive-by Attack: The unsuspecting victim visits a website that is directly controlled or compromised by the attacker, and then their device is infected with malware.

Zero-day Exploit: Exploiting a vulnerability discovered in certain commonly used software applications and operating systems and targeting the users of that specific software.

Social Engineering: A non-technical method used by potential cyber attackers generally through social media to manipulate the stakeholders using the system, leading them to violate security procedures.

Subverting the Supply Chain: Attacking a company or ship by creating confusion in equipment, software, or support services delivered to the company or the ship.

The cyberattack types are not limited to the examples above. The techniques and tools used in attacks are evolving and it is possible to encounter a new type of cyberattack every day. The rates of cyberattacks in the maritime in 2016 and 2018 are given in Figure 1.

Figure 1. Types of Cyberattacks in Maritime (Percentages). Source: Derived by author using the results of previously conducted surveys [8] [9]

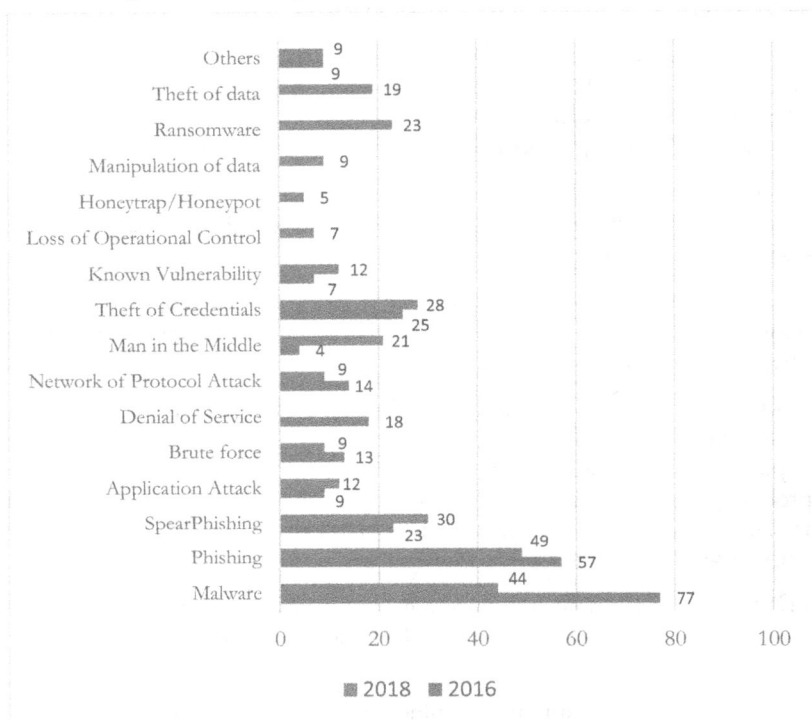

Cyberattack Incidents

Some of the cyberattacks reported in the maritime sector are discussed according to their types in the following section.

GPS (Global Positioning System) Jamming/Spoofing Attacks

- In April 2016, South Korea forced many ships to return to port as they had problems with their navigation systems due to GPS jamming, claiming North Korea was behind the glitch. South Korean officials said the campaign lasted for about a week beginning on March 31 and originated from five different points on the North Korean border. It affected the signal reception of more than 1,000 aircraft and 700 ships. North Korea denied the allegations. The

---

[8] Fairplay and BIMCO Maritime Cyber Security Survey 2018, https://bi-cd02.bimco.org › cyber-security › 2018 (Access 16.04.2021)
[9] Cybersecurity survey 2016, https://cybersail.org/wp-content/uploads/2017/02/IHS-BIMCO-Survey-Findings.pdf (Access 16.04.2021)

jamming was an attempt to block and stop the reception of GPS signals. AIS (Automatic Identification System), ECDIS (Electronic Chart Display and Information System) and VDR (Voyage Data Recorder) systems receiving data from GPS on board were also affected. In the same period, it was stated that many South Korean fishing boats returned to their ports due to GPS jamming, which caused problems in finding the positions of their nets in the sea. South Korea decided to secure the technology needed to build an alternative land-based radio system called eLoran, which it hopes would provide reliable alternative location and timing signals for navigation.[10]

- The UK and Ireland General Lighthouse Authorities conducted a series of trials to examine the effect of GPS jamming on shipping. In one trial, a jammer was operated from a lighthouse and targeted ships. GPS receivers on ships at a distance of about 30 km from the coast were strongly affected in the trial. It has been stated that GPS receivers are affected differently. While some GPS receivers could not receive any signals, some GPS receivers started to give incorrect ship positions (spoofing). Ships that were at sea appeared to be on land. In a second attempt, a jammer was installed on a ship, causing multiple systems to malfunction, including navigation systems, emergency systems, clocks, and AIS. There were ships in the wrong position and ships that suddenly started moving very slowly without anyone noticing.[11]

- On June 22, 2017, the captain of a ship off the in the Russian Black Sea port of Novorossiysk, found that his GPS was showing the wrong location. Its location was 32 kilometers inland in the vicinity of Gelendzhik Airport. After checking that the navigation equipment was working properly, the captain contacted other nearby ships and asked them to check their position as well. AIS traces also docked other ships in the vicinity of the same airport. At least 20 ships were affected. It has been claimed that Russia is testing a new system for GPS spoofing, although it has not been confirmed yet.[12]

- In June 2013, UT Austin university students and researchers

[10] The Maritime Executive, "South Korea Revives GPS Backup After Cyber Attack", 2 May 2016 https://www.maritime-executive.com/article/south-korea-revives-gps-backup-after-cyber-attack (Access 17.04.2021)
[11] Luke Graham, "Shipping industry vulnerable to cyber attacks and GPS jamming", 1 Feb 2017,: https://www.cnbc.com/2017/02/01/shipping-industry-vulnerable-to-cyber-attacks-and-gps-jamming.html (Access 17.04.2021)
[12] David Hambling," Ships fooled in GPS spoofing attack suggest Russian cyberweapon" https://www.newscientist.com/article/2143499-ships-fooled-in-gps-spoofing-attack-suggest-russian-cyberweapon/ (Access 18.04.2021)

managed to deflect the yacht White Rose (formerly White Rose of Drachs) off course with a spoofing attack while it was about 60 km off the coast in southern Italy. Acting as an attacker, the UT student transmitted a counterfeit signal to the yacht's GPS antenna, increasing the strength until it became stronger than the true GPS signal. Control of the yacht's navigation system was seized. Takeover was stealthy. No alarms were triggered, and the bridge crew was not suspicious. When control of the ship's navigation system was taken, the attacker changed the ship's course 3 degrees. The chartplotter on the bridge showed that the ship was drifting. Fig.2 To compensate, the crew diverted the yacht. In reality, they were turning the ship off its intended course because their GPS was showing the wrong, offset position. [13]

Figure 2. Demonstration of GPS Spoofing attack

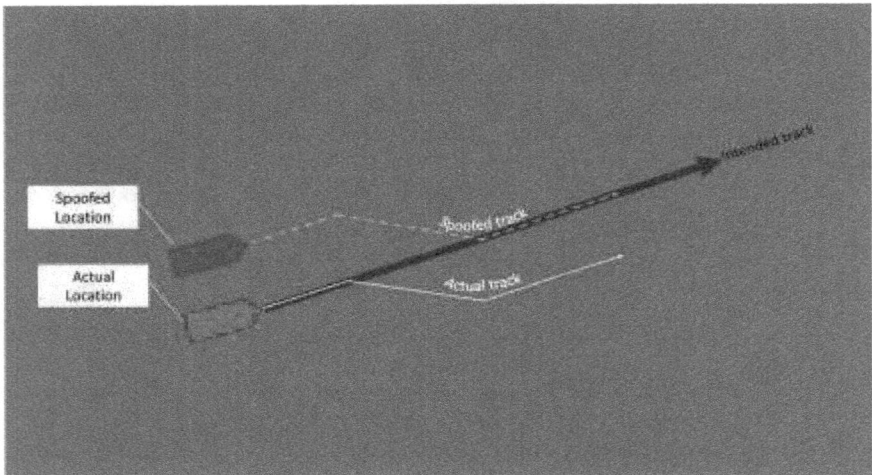

Ransomware Attacks

Port of Kennewick is on the Columbia River 290 km southeast of Seattle. On November 2020, this regional port in western US has become one of the latest maritime victims of a cyberattack, disrupting the services at a key transportation hub. Cyber criminals circumvented Port of Kennewick's IT security and placed an extremely sophisticated encryption lock on the port's server. They then demanded US$200,000 in ransom to restore access to the port's servers and files. Port of Kennewick reported this ransom threat to the Federal Bureau of Investigation (FBI) and Washington State Office of Cyber Security. According to these agencies, this variant of ransomware virus has no known decoder.

---

[13] The Maritime Executive, "Hacker Demonstrates Attack on Superyacht IT Systems", 17 May 2017, https://www.maritime-executive.com/article/hacker-demonstrates-attack-on-superyacht-it-systems (Access 17.04.2021)

Following direction from the FBI and technology professionals, Port of Kennewick did not pay ransom. The port started to rebuild the port's digital files from offline backups after being struck by ransomware. However, this was a significant process takes time to restore port data in a manner which ensures additional redundancies, security, and protection.[14]

On September 28, 2020, French container shipping and logistics company CMA CGM reported that it had suffered a cyberattack on its peripheral servers. The attack was carried out on the company's units based in China, using the Ragnar Locker ransomware. Ragnar Locker scouts and leaks sensitive information to be returned in exchange for ransom payment. The company suspended the container booking system to protect its customers. The suspension interrupted operations since employees lost access to internal emails and apps necessary to perform routine operations, with limited options left for customers contact by phone.[15]

The Port of Barcelona fell victim to the cyberattack on September 20, 2020. It was reported that the attack did not affect the movement of ships entering and leaving the port and only affected ground operations such as loading or unloading, but the port denied any serious disruption. In a tweet two days after the initial attack, Port officials said only internal IT systems were affected, but offered no further details.[16]

The Port of San Diego was the victim of a serious cybersecurity incident in September 2018, same week with the attack on the Port of Barcelona, that disrupted the port's IT systems. Using the SamSam ransomware, the attackers sought bitcoin as ransom. The amount of ransom demanded from the port has not been disclosed. In addition to the Port of San Diego, SamSam virus attacks have involved municipalities, a major university, government agencies, and private sector organizations. The US Department of Justice said that hackers used the virus to get a $6 million ransom from American and Canadian organizations seeking to get their stolen data back. The attack kept cyber security teams busy for a 34-month period that seemed ended with the attack to the Port of San Diego, the last target. It caused $30 million in damages and losses in addition to the ransoms paid before ended. A year-and-a-half FBI investigation led to a grand jury indictment naming the alleged perpetrators, purveyors of the SamSam ransomware virus, as state-sponsored hackers operating inside the

---

[14] Martyn Wingrove, "Cyber attack shuts down US port servers", 23 November 2020, https://www.rivieramm.com/news-content-hub/news-content-hub/cyber-attack-shuts-down-us-port-servers-61955 (Access 18.04.2021)

[15] Everstream analytics, "Ransomware Attack on French Carrier CMA CGM Disrupts Shipping Operations", https://www.everstream.ai/risk-center/special-reports/cyber-attack-on-cma-cgm/ (Access 20.04.2021)

[16] Catalin Cimpanu, "Port of San Diego suffers cyber-attack, second port in a week after Barcelona", 27 September 2018, https://www.zdnet.com/article/port-of-san-diego-suffers-cyber-attack-second-port-in-a-week-after-barcelona/ (Access 18.04.2021)

Islamic Republic of Iran.[17]

A ransomware attack took place in the US Long Beach Port in July 2018. The attack was diverted to the terminal operated by the China Ocean Shipping Company (Cosco) in the port. Port authorities explained that the attack did not affect other parts and operations of the port, probably because the Cosco Shipping terminal has a separate operating system. On Cosco's website, it was reported that there was a network failure only in the US region, all connections with other regions were closed for further investigation as a security measure, all Cosco ships were operating normally, and their main business operation systems were stable.[18]

Danish logistics company Maersk announced that it lost $200-300 million after the cyberattack in June 2017 that disrupted critical systems. Using the NotPetya ransomware, the attack left Maersk unable to process shipping orders and gain revenue from some container lines for weeks. Three of the holding's nine business units were affected by the attack.[19] Despite the fact that NotPetya infected computers showed a message demanding $300 in Bitcoin, the virus caused a lot of destruction for the ransomware. For this reason, it was considered to be a virus for disruption as well as a ransom. According to Maersk officials, 49,000 laptops and all end-user devices, including printing capacity, were destroyed. 1200 applications were inaccessible and around 1,000 were destroyed. The data in the backups was preserved, but the applications could not be restored from them, as they would be re-infected immediately. About 3,500 of the 6,200 servers were destroyed and could not be reinstalled. The cyberattack also affected communications. All fixed line phones were rendered inoperable due to network damage, and all contacts were deleted from mobiles-seriously hindering any coordinated response.[20]

Spear Phishing Attacks

On May 9, 2020, there was a cyberattack on shipping traffic at Iran's bustling Shahid Rajaee port terminal. Shahid Rajaee port facility is the newest of two major shipping terminals in Iran's coastal city of Bandar Abbas on the Strait of Hormuz. The computers that regulate the flow of ships, trucks, and containers crashed, creating massive accumulations on the sealines and roadways leading to the facility. Satellite photos showed traffic jams on the highways leading to

---

[17] Thom Senzee,"What happened in ransomware attack on Port of San Diego-Iran-backed hackers demanded Bitcoin", 10 April 2019, https://www.sandiegoreader.com/news/2019/apr/10/city-lights-happened-ransomware-port-san-diego/ (Access 18.04.2021)
[18] Michael Juliano, "Cosco's Long Beach terminal hit by cyber-attack", 25 July 2018, https://www.tradewindsnews.com/safety/coscos-long-beach-terminal-hit-by-cyber-attack/2-1-386327 (Access: 18.4.2021)
[19] Nate Lord, "The cost of a malware infection? For MAERSK, $300 million.", https://digitalguardian.com/blog/cost-malware-infection-maersk-300-million (Access 14.05.2021)
[20] Rae Ritchie, "Maersk: Springing back from a catastrophic cyber-attack", https://www.i-cio.com/management/insight/item/maersk-springing-back-from-a-catastrophic-cyber-attack (Access 15.05.2021)

Shahid Rajaee port, and dozens of loaded container ships waiting in the anchorages just off the coast. Iranian officials announced that the cyberattack failed to penetrate the Ports and Maritime Organization (PMO) systems and only infiltrated several private operating systems. It was claimed that Israel was behind the attack, to retaliate the previous attack attempts on two Israeli facilities distributing water to rural areas.[21] Iran announced in October 2020 that one of the targets of new cyberattacks against two Iranian government agencies is the electronic infrastructure of the country's ports. It has been reported that deterrent measures have been taken to ensure that the agencies' missions are not interrupted. No information was given about the source of the attacks.[22]

A large-scale targeted attack took place at one of Antwerp's port terminals in Belgium over the course of nearly two years, between 2011 and 2013. A drug cartel took control of containers movement and retrieved the data needed to collect it before legitimate owner.[23] Drug traffickers have hired hackers to breach IT systems that control the movement and location of containers. A Dutch-based drug cartel hid cocaine and heroin among legal cargoes, including lumber and bananas transported in containers from South America. The cartel used Belgium-based hackers to infiltrate the computer networks of at least two companies operating in the port of Antwerp. The breach allowed hackers to access secure data by providing the location and security details of the containers. This meant that the smugglers could send truck drivers to steal the cargo before the legal owner arrived.[24] The hacking operation took place in several stages. A criminal group that began by emailing malware to port staff in June 2011 gained remote access to the data and then used it to identify and redirect to containers with drugs on board. After the software was discovered and neutralized, the attackers broke into offices in the port and deployed keyloggers hidden in everyday objects to intercept data from the systems, including keyboard inputs from staff and screenshots from workstations. The incident was discovered after a large number of containers disappeared from the port without any clear explanation.[25]

Danish officials announced that along with several official offices, the Danish Maritime Authority (Søfartsstyrelsen) was subjected to cyberattacks in April

[21] Joby Warrick, Ellen Nakashima, "Officials: Israel linked to a disruptive cyberattack on Iranian port facility", 19 May 2020, https://www.washingtonpost.com/national-security/officials-israel-linked-to-a-disruptive-cyberattack-on-iranian-port-facility/2020/05/18/9d1da866-9942-11ea-89fd-28fb313d1886_story.html (Access 16.05.2021)
[22] Reuters, "Iran says one of two cyber attack targets was country's ports - news agency", 16 October 2020, https://www.reuters.com/article/iran-cyber-attacks-int-idUSKBN271135 (Access 16.05.2021)
[23] European Union Agency for Cybersecurity (ENISA), Port Cybersecurity, Good practices for cybersecurity in the maritime sector, November 2019, page 32, ISBN 978-92-9204-314-8, DOI 10.2824/328515
[24] Tom Bateman, "Police warning after drug traffickers' cyber-attack", 16 October 2013, https://www.bbc.com/news/world-europe-24539417 (Access 12.05.2021)
[25] Seatrade Maritime News, "Antwerp incident highlights maritime IT security risk", 21 October 2013, https://www.seatrade-maritime.com/europe/antwerp-incident-highlights-maritime-it-security-risk (Access 12.05.2021)

2012. The statement was made in 2014 after an American IT expert warned the Danish authorities after seeing files belonging to the Maritime Authority on a US server known to be controlled by hackers. The investigation made after the warning giveaway that the system was infiltrated by opening the infected PDF file attached to the email sent to a Maritime Authority employee. Once the file opened, the hackers were able to infiltrate the employee's computer and then the Maritime Authority network. Danish officials announced that the attack was state-sponsored and very sophisticated, targeting sensitive information on Danish maritime companies and their merchant fleet. It is thought that China is behind the attack, but the Chinese Embassy in Copenhagen has stated that they have no information about the attack.[26]

In 2012, cyber attackers working for a criminal organization managed to break into the Australian Customs and Border Protection Service's cargo system. The aim of the attackers was to detect containers that police and customs officials suspected and to see if they would abandon the containers carrying the contraband.[27]

The Iranian Shipping Line (IRISL) was hacked in August 2011. Company officials explained that the attack was heavy and showed that the attackers were supported by powerful sources.[28] Company systems crashed, and container tracking data was lost. The company suffered huge losses due to lost containers and incorrectly delivered cargo.[29]

Malware Attacks

The Mediterranean Shipping Company (MSC) was exposed to a malware attack that began on April 10, 2020. The company shut down some of its digital gadgets and website for a malware attack. The outage was affecting the company's digital booking tool, myMSC, and the company's agents around the world had to use more traditional operating methods to keep the uninterrupted cargo flow. The Geneva-based container shipping company said the attack had a limited impact on its operations and cargo operations continued as normal.[30]

In 2013, while drilling in the Gulf of Mexico, employee of a US-based oil company accidentally installed malware on the main computer system of the Mobile Drilling Unit (MODU). An employee unintentionally installed the malware via a flash drive that held corrupt files. Corrupted files downloaded from

---

[26] The Local, "State-sponsored hackers spied on Denmark", 22 September 2014, https://www.thelocal.dk/20140922/denmark-was-hacked-by-state-sponsored-spies/(Acsess 14.05.2021)

[27] Threatspan News, " Top 11 maritime security compromises of all time", 29.12.2017, https://threatspan.com/2017/12/29/top-11-maritime-security-compromises-of-all-time/ (Access 15.05.2021)

[28] Yeganeh Torbati, Jonathan Soul, "Iran's top cargo shipping line says sanctions damage mounting", 22 October 2012, https://www.reuters.com/article/us-iran-sanctions-shipping-idUSBRE89L10X20121022 (Access 12.05.2021)

[29] Threatspan News, op.cit

[30] Jasmina Ovcina, "MSC confirms malware attack", 16 April 2020, https://www.offshore-energy.biz/msc-confirms-malware-attack/ (Access 15.05.2021)

the Internet passed into the rig's computer systems when the devices were plugged in. The thrusters and navigational equipment in MODU were immobilized, causing MODU to move away from the drilling site and ultimately causing it to be shut down.[31]

Two similar cases offshore drilling platforms involved have been reported. In the first incident, the oil rig off the African coast tilted one side by hackers, resulting in a seven-day loss of production. In the second case, during the transport of the platform from South Korea to Brazil, the malware infiltrated the platform's propulsion system, and the transfer was delayed by 19 days.[32]

Findings

Some general conclusions can be drawn from the examination of the cyberattacks incidents:

It is clear that digitalization will take more place in the future of maritime sector due to the advantages and conveniences it brings. However, this situation attracts the attention of cyber attackers targeting the IT systems of the sector. Cyberattacks continue at an increasing rate in the maritime sector. These attacks are commonly seen as ransomware, USB malware and worms, GPS jamming and spoofing. Attacks have become more sophisticated, more difficult to take countermeasures, and, once inside the system, spreading rapidly and causing more damage. For example, while the earlier attacks on the navigation systems of the ships were mostly jamming attacks aimed at preventing the systems from receiving GPS signals, it is seen that the attacks in the new period are mostly spoofing attacks aimed at seizing and misleading the navigation systems of the ships.

Although the cyberattacks on the systems of the ships intensify, it is not the ships but the shore facilities and the systems of the maritime companies that are usually attacked in the big events. The most damaging incidents of malware gangs are attacks targeting shore-based systems in offices, business offices and data centers. In attacks, the systems that manage personnel, receive e-mail, operate ships, and especially container booking applications are targeted. In this context, the maritime sector offers an interesting example. The four biggest shipping companies in the shipping – MAERSK, COSCO, MSC and CMA CGM – have all been hit by cyberattacks. There is no other sector where all the biggest of the sector have been cyberattacked. Even if the attacks took place at different times and types, it can be concluded that the maritime sector is a preferred target for cybercriminals, even for different reasons.

In the press and in some academic studies, there are claims that some

---

[31] Christopher R.Hayes, Maritime Cybersecurity:The Future of National Security, Master Thesis, Monterey, California, Naval Postgraduate School, June 2016, p. 17.
[32] İbid., p.17.

cyberattacks in the maritime sector are state sponsored.[33] Although no state has so far accepted these claims, the nature of the attacks, the fact that they are intended to do nothing but harm, and that they require sophisticated and expensive equipment and technologies, strengthens this possibility. These attacks had purposes such as information theft, defense research, testing of developed defense or attack systems, or sabotage. China, Iran, Israel, North Korea, and Russia were allegedly behind some of the cyberattacks. If these claims are true, a new dimension introduced to the problem. The resources of individuals and private companies will often be insufficient against the resources that states can allocate for cybersecurity. For this reason, they may need to find resources other than their own for the establishment of cybersecurity, and they may often need the support of another state.

It is seen that cyberattacks are mostly realized by infiltrating the systems through ways such as opening infected e-mail attachments, downloading infected files from the internet, clicking on infected advertisements and links, and unauthorized and uncontrolled USB loadings. This is an important indicator of the lack of awareness for cybersecurity among the personnel and operators of the maritime sector. The lack of cybersecurity awareness is exploited by cybercriminals and seen as the most important weakness that enables them to infiltrate systems. It is well clear that increasing the awareness for cybersecurity among the personnel is one of the most important steps of cyber defense.

The vast majority of cyberattacks cause financial losses. Information theft, the sale of information to third parties, or the return of information for ransom are the main motivating factors behind most attacks. However, some cyberattacks have the potential to cause significant loss of life and environmental disasters, such as MODUs being shifted from drilling sites or being tilted by disturbing their balance or the ships navigation control taken over.

Conclusion

The aim of this study was to make a comprehensive review of the Cybersecurity risks that arise in the maritime world as digitalization and automation becomes more and more involved in ship and maritime company operations. The growing number of cyberattacks in the maritime domain has proven that the risk turned out to be real. The magnitude of the risk and threat can be better seen considering the study only dealt with known events and many of the events were not reported. Ships, platforms, and companies' relationships with the cyber world, which have become indispensable, make them potential targets for threats lurking in this world. These threats can cause operational, financial, and environmental damage and may even endanger the safety of personnel. Within the scope of this study, some cyber risks that threaten the maritime sector have been defined and the recent cyberattacks and their effects

[33] Aybars Oruç, Claims of State-Sponsored Cyberattack in the Maritime Industry, Conference Proceedings of INEC, 9 October 2020, DOI: 10.24868/issn.2515-818X.2020.021

in the maritime sector have been examined. Lack or inadequacy of access protocols, misconfigured, obsolete and unpatched systems, and lack of security policies were seen as shortcomings in defense against cybercriminals in the maritime sector. The study also showed that the lack of cybersecurity awareness among industry workers at sea and on the land can be exploited by cybercriminals. Because of this lack of awareness, it was seen that cybercriminals who infiltrated the systems gained the freedom to obtain, steal and change confidential and private data, severe the systems or prevent them from proper work.

As conclusion, digital transformation is completely changing operations in the maritime sector. The innovations and conveniences brought by this change attract the attention of the sector and make it indispensable. The digital age has irreversibly changed our world. However, in addition to these conveniences and advantages, threats that we did not know beforehand and therefore were not prepared for, entered our lives. We must learn to identify these risks and threats in a short time and to live with them. The maritime industry should also recognize the challenges and develop measures to take advantage of the digital transformation. In the future, cyber threats and attacks will become more common and cyber security will become a necessity. It is inevitable that the stakeholders, who see this necessity and take their steps and precautions beforehand will become more advantageous in the sector.

GEOSTRATEGIC AND GEOPOLITICAL CONSIDERATIONS REGARDING MARITIME ECONOMICS

Murat Koray[*]

Introduction

The most crucial strategic mode of transport for world trade is the sea. Shortly, it will be inevitable to think of space as an endless ocean. The concept will change sea power theories and also controlling methods of main seaborne trade routes. Establishing area dominance in any part of the world geography will only keep sea control as in the past. The imbalance between the countries' military capacity and their foreign trade volume changes the maritime strategies to be implemented. A long time has passed since Mahan's famous "influence of sea power" strategy. Therefore, it will no longer be possible to maintain classical naval doctrines. As innovative marine technologies industrialized, the capacity of maritime trade will be increased simultaneously. However, these conversions brought up new hybrid alliances and changed the dominant actors of sea control. The articulation of the space economy to the maritime trade will bring all aspects of geopolitical factors and changed the main shipping lanes. The term geopolitics has been defined in three different meanings in The Dictionary of Turkish Language Association (Turkish: Türk Dil Kurumu, TDK)[1];

- *The influence of geography, economy, population, etc., on a state's policy,*

- *The relationship between the policy implemented in a region in a state and the geography of that place,*

- *Political doctrine to justify the aggressive expansion of a state in terms of economic and political geography.*

Also, geopolitics is described by Yves Lacoste[2] as; *"Geopolitics describes everything about the competition for influence and power over the land and the people living in those lands between all political forces struggles to gain control and domination over all kinds of land, big or small."* Based on these definitions, strategic nodes in terms of maritime trade, global logistics, and naval forces and the geopolitical impact of Sea Lines of Communications (SLOCs) will be examined, and their reflections on the maritime economy will have been revealed. Main oceanic routes for maritime transportation are such as South Atlantic Oceanic Route, North Atlantic Oceanic Route, Routes of Mediterranean Sea, Cape of Good Hope route, North Pacific Oceanic Route, South Pacific Oceanic Route, Routes of Indian Ocean. The main

* Asst.Prof.Dr. Murat Koray, Piri Reis University, Lecturer, Turkey. E-mail: nmkoray@pirireis.edu.tr.
[1] https://sozluk.gov.tr/ (Access 14.03.2021).
[2] Yves Lacoste, Büyük Oyunu Anlamak, NTV Yayınları, 2008, Syf.8

routes connecting the maritime transport lanes to the ports pass through the primary and secondary chokepoints as necessary by geography. These chokepoints play essential roles in formulating marine strategies and calculating geopolitical impacts. The national strategies developed by the states to achieve their national interests depend on the strategic power elements. When the mentioned elements are multiplied by specific coefficients, the value obtained is multiplied by the strategic mindset, and thus, power comparison between states can be obtained. Political, economic, military, social, cultural, technological, legal, historical, geographical, environmental, and other factors are considered in the situational awareness and estimation analysis before determining the national strategies. Many kings, sultans, or commanders have developed sovereignty strategies and expressed valuable words regarding the acquisition of power in history. However, Sir Walter Raleigh stated[3] in the following gnomic motto that in 1829 it would be possible to command the world only with the ability to control the world trade.

"For whosoever commands the sea commands the trade; whosoever commands the trade of the world commands the riches of the world, and consequently the world itself,"

This motto has a lot of meaning in it. The implications that make reflections are as follows:

- 90% of the goods subject to trade are transported by sea,

- Maritime trade can only be made safely depending on the freedom of the high seas,

- Reliability can be built with naval capacity,

- The advantages and disadvantages of geography change while technology variates,

- Sea control and sea denial can only be achieved with a strong navy,

- All of these mentioned above depends on a robust economy.

Therefore, firstly, the relationship between maritime economy and geopolitics will be tried to be explained. Then the effect of maritime law and geopolitics on the maritime economy will be evaluated.

Relations Between Maritime Economy and Geopolitics

Regardless of the form of governments and their organizational structures, there are two commitments that the sovereign powers offer to the Peoples ruled. These are peace and prosperity. World history has witnessed struggles for domination. The main reason for these struggles was to provide the necessary

---

[3] Genevieve Wanucha, "For whosoever commands the sea commands the trade", MIT Department of Mechanical Engineering, 2014 http://meche.mit.edu/news-media/%E2%80%9C-whosoever-commands-sea-commands-trade (accessed 02.05.2021)

resources for the establishment of prosperity. The existence of scarce resources has driven the sovereign powers to develop strategies and, achieve their goals using these strategies in appropriate geopolitical environments. The dissolution of the bipolar balance of powers, forming a multipolar world order first, and then the emergence of complex alliances by transforming into a microlateralism[4] structure have changed all the conventional geopolitical approaches in the classical sense. Hybrid alliances create such a situation that two states in a diplomatic and military geopolitical struggle can engage in a high-volume commercial relationship. In fact, a State subject to an embargo resulting from international sanctions can continue its commercial relations thanks to hybrid alliances. Although geopolitics and gunboat diplomacy is the approach of the previous century, it is getting ready to take the stage again but with a renewed version in the micro-lateral world. The critical question to be asked is why the geopolitical approach is wanted to be revitalized. One of the possible answers to this question is the acceleration of the collapse of the imperials after the second half of the 18th century, the emergence of nationalist movements, the disintegration of empires, and building states and nations in their place, and emerging economic crises.

The continuation of geopolitical fluctuations due to the outbreak of the Great Economic Depressions and World Wars in the early 20th century and the emergence of new world order is the end of the cold war after the bipolar challenge of the world and emerge multi-polar world order. Global, continental, regional or national strategies are directly or indirectly linked to each other. Sometimes they move in parallel, and sometimes they intersect. Grey areas between intersection points form geopolitical conflict zones. However, your intervention in one of these grey areas triggers the other grey areas and affects their entire surrounding areas and adjacent regions. At the same time, unstable grey areas are also conflicted zones, so the risk factors are very high. Besides, there are intensive commercial activities in these zones. Since there are armed conflicts in these areas, they turn into an actual test station where new war technologies are tested. In addition, the old ammunition in stock has an opportunity to be consumed, and the weapon industry finds a trading scope. Since there will be no law and justice in the areas where weapons are fired, illicit activities will increase naturally. These unfair economic climates accelerate transactions and act as a catalyst that increases the turnover of money by reversing the world's economic conditions, preventing stagflation and even negative inflation. Unless the current economic system changes, even if permanent peace is achieved globally, armed regional conflicts will continue, as sustainable economic prosperity cannot be provided for each country or individual. Unfortunately, technology or other options cannot keep the economy alive and fair distribution cannot be achieved. The existence of state

---

[4] Jared Cohen and Richard Fontaine, "The Case for Microlateralism: With U.S. Support, Small States Can Ably Lead Global Efforts", Foreign Affairs, 2021, pg.1 https://www.foreignaffairs.com/articles/world/2021-04-29/case-microlateralism (Accessed, 29.04.2021)

organizations will eventually become controversial since a world in which wars are an interim remedy for the economy will not provide peace and prosperity. The blockchain system provides a good example of this contradictory situation. The concept design of the blockchain system describes a world where each individual is like a state and existing states' organizations lose their functions. A new world order in which all mediators between individuals are eliminated. However, the tools of geopolitics are a strong military capacity and a solid state structure. However, the well-being of individuals depends on a strong economy, and today's order does not provide total welfare.

Nobody has endured a world where the strong reach prosperity and the weak are enslaved. The COVID-19 process has triggered the individualization revolution and caused a great awakening in individuals. Suppose states fail to form effective hybrid alliances. In that case, they will enter the process of disintegration within a century. So, the world will find stability in a point of equilibrium consisting of a combination of non-governmental actors. Therefore, individuals will also exist in an NGO where they can express themselves, not under the auspices of the state. Regardless of the world's political structure today and in the future, basic needs will continue, technology will advance, production, consumption, and trade will continue for individuals. According to the data of January 31, 2019, it is articulated that the total of banknotes, coins, savings, and checks is 37 trillion USD per year in the world. If treasury bills and gilts are taken into account in addition to the liquidities mentioned, it is estimated that a total of 90.4 trillion USD per year is in circulation[5]. The value of merchant ship-owning economies[6] as of January 1, 2020, is approximately 952,213 million USD. More than 80 per cent of world merchandise trade by volume[7] is carried by sea. Maritime shipping activities related to the vessel crew changes, capacity deployed, port operations, warehousing capacity, hinterland connections, and internal logistics are affected by economic crises such as petroleum, financial, technological leaps, global or regional wars. Although the geography did not change, London, Rotterdam, and New York, the busiest ports of transatlantic trade, lost their place to Asian ports due to the change in capital intensive power centers after the crises. Therefore, the colonial approach and gunboat diplomacy have changed dimensions, and the center of gravity has been transferred to the regions where there is cheap production cost. According to the data obtained from UNCTAD's Maritime Transport Report 2020, the apparent superiority of Asian ports in cargo handling is shown in Figure 1.

The maritime trade capacity is showing an increasing trend, as shown in Figure-2. The Asia-based developing maritime trade, transatlantic, transpacific,

---

[5] RankRed (2021), "How Much Money Is There In The World? " 2021 Edition,
https://www.rankred.com/how-much-money-is-there-in-the-
world/#:~:text=There%20is%20approximately%20US%20%2437,and%20cryptocurrencies%20exceeds
%20%241.2%20quadrillion. (Accessed, January 1, 2021
[6] Source: UNCTAD calculations, based on data from Clarksons Research, as at 1 January 2020 (estimated current value).
[7] Note: Value is estimated for all commercial ships of 1,000 gross tons and above.

Europe – Asia via Suez preserved its main trade routes, but this flow direction has changed to the opposite side.

Figure 1. Percentage Share of Loaded & Unloaded Goods of Regions Regarding Maritime Trade in 2019

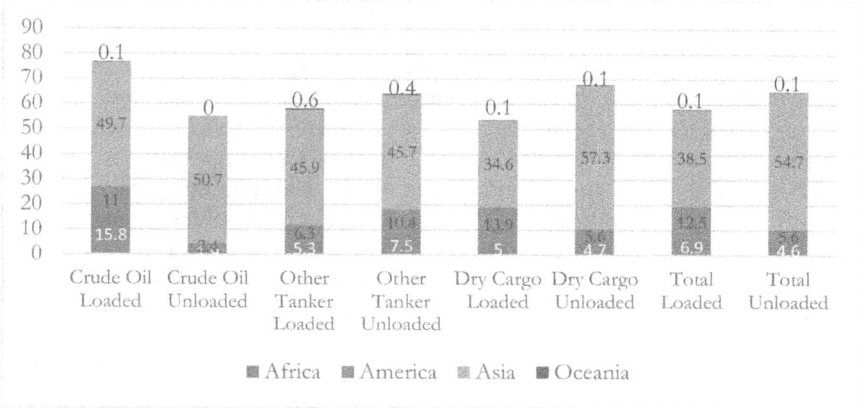

(Source: UNCTAD Data[8], compiled by author)

Figure 2. Maritime Trade Capacity (Million tons loaded) (Source: UNCTAD Data[9], compiled by author)

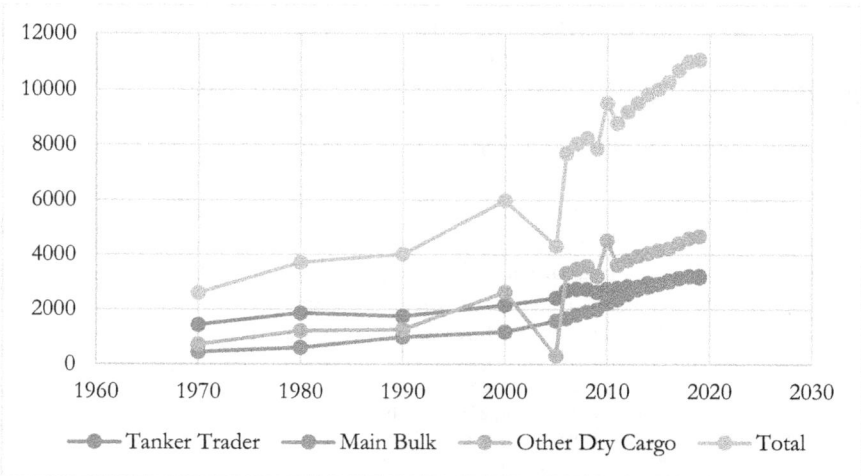

---

[8] UNCTAD (2020), Review of Maritime Transport 2020, United Nations Publications, New York, ISBN 978-92-1-112993-9, pg.4, https://unctad.org/system/files/official-document/rmt2020_en.pdf (Accessed, May 13, 2021)

[9] UNCTAD (2020), Review of Maritime Transport 2020, United Nations Publications, New York, ISBN 978-92-1-112993-9, pg.4, https://unctad.org/system/files/official-document/rmt2020_en.pdf (Accessed, May 13, 2021)

Evaluation of World Maritime Transport Lanes

There are three major routes for world maritime trade.[10] These are Southern Corridor[11], Eastern Corridor[12] and Northern Corridor.[13] Potentially, there may be an infinite number of shipping routes available for maritime trade, but the configuration of the global system is relatively simple. The main axis is an equatorial corridor connecting North America, Europe, and Pacific Asia with the Suez Canal, Malacca Strait, and the Panama Canal. Main routes are shipping routes that support the most important commercial transport flows serving major markets. Alternative secondary routes are mostly links between smaller markets. The Panama Canal, Suez Canal, Hormuz Strait and Malacca Strait are important and priority key chokepoints in the global commodity and commodity trade. Although the Strait of Magellan, Dover Strait, Sunda Strait, and Taiwan Strait are of secondary priority, they are essential chokepoints for maritime trade.[14] Freight rates have declined significantly after the 2008 crisis until today. However, the main maritime trade routes have not changed. Considering the countries that supply and demand goods and commodities, the most economical routes pass through these chokepoints. There are essential ports in Europe, East Asia, and East America. Especially in Netherlands, Japan, Shanghai, Singapore, Hong Kong and the eastern coasts of the USA, there is an intensive commercial flow for all commodities subject to sea trade. The actors playing leading roles in the maritime industry are summarized in Table 1 below.

Although it is a slow mode of transport, sea shipping constitutes a robust service network that connects all ports in the world. Raw materials are supplied from North and South America and South Africa to produce intermediate goods in Europe. Since intermediate goods exported from Europe, Australia, and Japan to become final products into Asia, these regions have perpetuate their strategic importance. Even, Asia is a rising value, it still retains its interdependence to keep peace and prosperity. The final output of shipyards is the ships. Ships consist of two main structures, hull, and outfitting. Asian countries such as China and South Korea are the leading actors in shipbuilding. Suppose a flag is affixed to each part of a ship consisting of tens of thousands of pieces of equipment. In that case, it will be seen that that ship is not of Chinese origin because high technology producers are the leading suppliers of component materials and also outfittings.

---

[10] Theo Notteboom, Athanasios Pallis and Jean-Paul Rodrigue, "Port Economics, Management and Policy: Main Maritime Shipping Routes", New York: Routledge, 2021, (accessed, 31.05.2021) https://porteconomicsmanagement.org/pemp/contents/part1/interoceanic-passages/main-maritime-shipping-routes/#:~:text=Among%20those%20are%20the%20Panama,trade%20of%20goods%20and%20commodities

[11] They are routes from the Suez Canal in the Red Sea to the Indian Ocean and the Strait of Malacca.

[12] They are the routes that extend from the Malacca Strait to the East China Sea through the South China Sea and Taiwan.

[13] The North Sea Route is the Northwest Passage, the Transpolar Sea Route and the Arctic Bridge Sea Route that will extend from Russia to Canada.

[14] Jean-Paul Rodrigue and Theo Notteboom, "Port Economics, Management and Policy: Interoceanic Passages", New York: Routledge, 2021, https://porteconomicsmanagement.org/pemp/contents/part1/interoceanic-passages/ (Accessed, 01.05.2021)

Table 1. The Actors Playing Leading Roles in The Maritime Industry[15] (compiled by author considering UNCTAD 2018 Data[16])

Newbuilding (91%)	Ownership (38%)	Registration(4 2%)	Operations (30%)	Scrapping (95%)	F&I[17]	GTO[18]	Seafahrers (30%)
China	China	Liberia	Denmark	Bangladesh	Scandinavia	Hong Kong	Indonesia
Japan	Japan	Marshall Islands	Switzerland	China	United Kingdom	Netherlands	Philippines
South Korea	Greece	Panama		India		Singapore	Ukraine
	Germany			Pakistan		UAE	
				Turkey			

The reason why Asia comes to the fore in production is due to the cheap labor cost. The basis of peacekeeping condition is interdependency. Recently, a spider web has been knitted between supply chain management and manufacturers, intermediaries, and final customers. Geography does not always facilitate the development of maritime trade. The distances are too far; the vast sea is not always dead calm. In addition, narrow passages, canals, straits, artificial and natural canals, regions close to coastal waters are not so cute for safe navigation. Besides, illegal piracy activities that suddenly appear in the vicinity of chokepoints can endanger the security of the ship, cargo, and crew. As it is known, chokepoints constitute primary *(Panama Canal-Gibraltar-Turkish Straits-Suez Canal-Bab el Mandab-Strait of Hormuz- Strait of Malacca-Cape of Good Hope)* and secondary *(Yucathan Channel, Windward Passage, Mona Passage, Magellan Passage, Northwest Passage, Doverstrait, Oresund, Sunda, Lombok, Makassar, Torres, Luzon Strait, Taiwan Strait, Tsugaru)* geographical constraints. Especially at canal and strait crossings, traffic separation schemes can be established, and the obligation to get an escort or a pilot may be applied. The special transition regime of the flag state can be used in these channels and straits, as well as international agreements can be established a legal status. Generally, strong currents, sharp course alterations, and unpredictable weather conditions make it more challenging to navigate safely throughout the channels or straits. Since the chokepoints are within the sovereignty of a single country or two or more coastal countries, the transit passage regime, which is considered to be applied between two exclusive economic zones, is not possible in some cases. As stated in Table-2 below, the traffic density of the ships coming from a vast ocean area to chokepoints increases, according to the geographical characteristics of these narrow passages, navigational hazards arise. In some of them, ships exposed to the piracy attack on approaching lanes face the risk of losing their life and cargo safety. An essential strategic waterway of maritime trade to Africa, Oceania, Asia, and Europe, connecting the Pacific and Indian Oceans, is the South China Sea. South

---

[15] Jean-Paul Rodrigue, "The Geography of Transport Systems: The Maritime Transport Life Cycle and Main National Actors", New York: Routledge, pg.177, ISBN 978-0-367-36463-2, https://transport geography.org/contents/chapter5/maritime-transportation/life-cycle-maritime-transport/ (Accessed, May, 15, 2021)

[16] UNCTAD (2018), Review of Maritime Transport 2018, United Nations Publications, New York, ISBN 978-92-1-112928-1, pg.22, https://unctad.org/system/files/official-document/rmt2018_en.pdf (Accessed, May 13, 2021)

[17] F&I: Financing and Insurance

[18] GTO: Global Terminal Operatorss

China Sea is surrounded by important primary and secondary chokepoints such as Lombok, Makassar, Luzon Strait, and Taiwan Strait indicated in Table 2.

Table 2. Major Oceans[19] Relevant to Circulation of Maritime Trade and Chokepoints

Oceans	Pasific	Atlantic	Indian	Mediterranean	Baltic Sea	Arctic
Surface Area (in Millioon Square Meters)	161,76	85,13	70,56	2.97	0,41	15,56
Primary Chokepoints						
Panama Canal	X	X				
Gibraltar		X		X		
Turkish Straits				X		
Suez Canal			X	X		
Bab el Mandab			X	X		
Strait of Hormuz			X			
Strait of Malacca	X		X			
Cape of Good Hope		X	X			
Secondary Chokepoints						
Yucathan Channel	X	X				
Windward Passage	X	X				
Mona Passage	X	X				
Magellan Passage	X	X				
Northwest Passage	X	X				X
Doverstrait		X			X	X
Oresund		X			X	X
Sunda	X		X			
Lombok	X		X			
Makassar,	X		X			
Torres	X		X			
Luzon Strait,	X		X			
Taiwan Strait	X		X			
Tsugaru	X		X			

The existence of strategic energy resources in the South China Sea has also brought about maritime jurisdiction conflicts on South China Sea Islands, and the Spratly Islands. The total area of the South China Sea is 350 square kilometres. The South China Sea contains over 230 small islands, atolls, cays, and shoals, collectively known as the Paracel Islands, the Macclesfield Bank, the Pratas Islands and the Spratly Islands. China, Taiwan (China), Vietnam, Malaysia, Singapore, Indonesia, Brunei, and the Philippines surround the South China Sea. There is a conflict about maritime jurisdictions among these sovereign states and territories due to rich natural resources including oil, gas and fish[20]. Similarly,

---

[19] Statista Research Department, Surface Area of Oceans Worldwide in Million Square Kilometers, https://www.statista.com/statistics/558499/total-area-of-global-oceans/ (accessed, May 16, 2021)
[20] Chang, Yen-Chiang, The South China Sea Disputes: An Opportunity for the Cross Taiwan Strait

there are disputes in the Mediterranean and Aegean Sea regarding the sharing of maritime jurisdictions due to natural and living resources. In addition, the stable environment of the Black Sea has the potential to turn into intercontinental war due to the frozen conflicts.

Another geopolitical hot zone is the Caribbean Sea. The Caribbean Sea is lying among Panama Canal, Yucatan, Windward, and Mona Passages. In addition, The Caribbean Sea is a sea of geostrategic value that connects the Atlantic Ocean and the Pacific Ocean. The Caribbean, which consists of many small islands, is also a geopolitically important maritime jurisdiction areas. It is a strategic geography where high-value cargoes including drugs, weapons and nuclear material are passed. Economic constraints, security weaknesses, unfavorable climate, weather, and sea conditions make up the favorable environment to illicit activities[21]. Before looking at the geopolitical and geostrategic transformations, it can be seen that in which regions of the world there are already hot conflicts and maritime jurisdiction problems, the struggle to get a share from new energy resources lies in the background of these conflicts. It will be possible to say that illegal activities have increased due to the instability of areas of struggle. Another factor is irregular migration movements. Compared to the major oceans, the area of the Mediterranean basin is one percent of the world's seas. However, twenty-five percent of the total maritime trade is carried over the Mediterranean[22].

The Mediterranean is a transcontinental waterway that connects Europe, Asia, and Africa is located at the center of the strategic fault lines of the Balkans, the Caucasus, the Middle East, and North Africa, with its rich energy resources. Hot conflicts in Crimea, Ukraine, Iraq, Syria, Palestine, Israel, Yemen, and Kashmir, as well as maritime jurisdiction area disputes among various states worldwide, have strengthened the allegations[23] of the return of geopolitics. The intention to revive geopolitics and its beneficial tool on the seas, gunboat diplomacy, is nothing but taking the easy way out of wrapping the movie back and playing the same game again. This situation means returning to the bipolar world order or the status quo of the cold war era. Another geopolitical struggle area of the world is the polar regions. But the difference of this geopolitical scenes from the others is not the rich boy, the blind and the poor girl scenario, it is a difficult geography where the superpowers will enter into a tough struggle. Moreover, even if it is assumed that the icebergs will completely melt in the 2070s, naval presence will not be needed to establish dominance in a short time.

Relationship, 2018, pg.50, DOI: 10.1163/9789004379633_004.

[21] Jacqueline Braveboy Wagner, "Spaces and Places: The Impact of Geopolitics on Caribbean International Relations and Foreign Policy", 2014, pg.3 https://www.researchgate.net/publication/329488915 (accessed, May 19, 2021)

[22] Jean-Paul Rodrigue (2020), The Geography of Transportation Systems: Domains of Maritime Circulation, New York: Routledge, pg. 171, ISBN 978-0-367-36463-2, https://transportgeography.org/contents/chapter5/maritime-transportation/domains-maritime-circulation/

[23] Simon Dalby, Anthropocene Geopolitics: Globalization, Security, Sustainability, University of Ottawa Press, Canada, 2020, pg.10, ISBN 9780776628899

As a matter of fact, risky regions such as the Mediterranean, the Black Sea, the Persian Gulf, and the South China Sea, where hot conflicts can arise, are conflict areas. Therefore, navies need to maintain a persistent forward presence, conduct sea control and sea denial, and enable power projection. In the 21st century, instead of defending the country, it is necessary to make excuses in accordance with international law to seek national interests outside her exclusive economic zones, thousands of nautical miles from the homeland, and even in the foreign countries exclusive economic zones. Otherwise, riparian countries will be irritated by the foreign navies operating nearby continental shelfs and will be alert their navy because of national security.

Evaluation of the Status of Merchant Ships and Warships in the Context of Freedom of the High Seas, and Maritime Jurisdiction Areas

Although it is known that Egypt (3200 BC) and China (10th and 15th centuries AD) played an active role in the world maritime trade history, Portugal, Spain, the Netherlands, France, and England carried out colonial activities between the 15th to 19th centuries respectively. Maritime trade intensified around the Caribbean, the Mediterranean, the Indian Ocean, Pacific Asia, and the North Atlantic due to the colonial countries' Navies served on oceans. These regions, where maritime trade is interconnected, continue to be important today, and maritime transportation networks are more frequent among these main centers.

On the other hand, the situation that changes geopolitics and geostrategy or increases / decreases its effect is forming a global supply chain with the developments in technology and the shape of a logistics network that creates added value with integrated transport modes. Although circum equatorial routes retain their traditional value, north-south connectors, trans-oceanic connectors, polar routes, landbridge routes bypass the main shipping lanes and make trans-shipment markets cost-effective. However, the principle of freedom of the high seas is vital for a reliable, safe, and time-oriented maritime trade. In fact, initiatives for the freedom of the high seas have long been a problem area for League of Nations.

The practices of the states in order to establish an order on the seas became customary after a reasonable time. These practices eventually developed within the framework of customary law. Since the 20th century, various conventions have been signed regarding the principle of freedom of high seas. Main principles determining the legal regime of high seas; the freedom of the high seas and the nationality of ships and the exclusive jurisdiction of the flag state. Freedom of the High Seas Principle entered the literature with the 1958 Geneva Convention on the law of the sea and 1982 The United Nations Convention on the Law of the Sea (UNCLOS). Since these conventions contain general provisions regarding maritime jurisdictions, the principle of equity and conscience cannot be applied, and the boundaries of special waterspaces cannot be determined.

Some states do not sign UNCLOS conventions as persistent objectors, do not enforce them even if they do, or do not sign at all. These states are not incompatible with or not to be against the rules of international law. Since the current international law rules are insufficient regarding exclusive maritime areas, sovereign states must first solve maritime jurisdiction areas problems bilaterally or multiples. If necessary, they should duly apply to international courts with their consensual. However, countries that have achieved their acquisitions to the extent prefer to preserve the status quo and increase tension when necessary.

The maritime trade is disrupted sometimes, contrary to the principle of freedom of the high seas due to regional problems. The high seas are ultimately interrupted geographically at the primary and secondary chokepoints. In addition, they are restricted by transit, innocent, or special passing regimes between the exclusive economic zones. Besides, customs, fiscal, immigration, or sanitary laws and regulations of the coastal state are also additional restraining obstacles. Consequently, the flag state is given the authority to enforce the right to cabotage in territorial waters, inland waters, and ports. In summary, merchant ships are subject to some restrictions in terms of navigation, except high seas. In addition, the status of foreign warships is restricted due to security reasons, especially in maritime jurisdictions areas, and innocent passage or transit passage is allowed in a way that does not hostile intentions and hostile acts. However, if there is a special passage regime established by bilateral or multiple agreements, special passage rights are applied in the strait, passage and canals subject to these agreements.

Within the international maritime law, international regulations, flag states jurisdictions, and practices, warships, and commercial ships can sail freely in all world seas. But here it is necessary to ask a childish question, as if no truth is known. Since merchant ships can sail freely and carry out their commercial activities, for what reason can foreign warships operate within the exclusive economic zone of a country without a United Nations resolution or any other official invitation? In ancient times, piracy was the official state policy. At that time, there was not yet a sharp distinction between merchant ships and warships. Therefore, ships were not only trading with another country, but also clashing on their routes and with the sovereign state's port cities.

The concept of territorial waters is an output of the period of piracy. Since the port cities have established coastal artillery batteries to defend themselves and the guns have a maximum range of three nautical miles, the concept of territorial waters has been naturally included in the literature as three nautical miles. Since ancient times, the law of the sea has been developing, and although various rules have been adopted in terms of customary law, the most comprehensive and multinational legal bases related to maritime jurisdictions have been established with *"1958 Geneva Conventions on the Law of the Sea"* and, also reinforced with *"1982 United Nations Convention on the Law of the Sea (UNCLOS)"*. It was observed that they made a general definition regarding the determination of maritime jurisdictions considering the letter and spirit of the two regulations.

But, the resolution of the disputes subject to international courts after 1958 and 1982 was not uniform, and the courts had political consequences according to the geopolitical situation. In summary, while another decision was made in the Tunisian-Libyan Arab Jamahiriya case[24] or Libyan Arab Jamahiriya-Malta case[25] and another decision was made in the Canada-France case[26]. Whichever case examined, it is not the outcome of the case. It will be important in which move the geopolitical chessboard is a tool that will meet the strategic goals of the global powers. In a world where needs are unlimited and resources are scarcity, one of the methods applied by global actors who want to maintain their power to access resources is to act in harmony with international law, and the other is to gain the political support of the world public opinion. Where resources are in a country's mainland or maritime jurisdiction areas, global or regional actors are required to provide a reasonable justification. Otherwise, there will be an intervention that does not comply with international law. Note that while resources are never mentioned, soft power tools such as democracy and human rights do not fall off the agenda in every political environment and on every state of affairs. Political and military activities in the Middle East and Eastern Mediterranean result from these understandings. Recently, any person or institution that takes the map and pen in their hands determines the exclusive economic zone boundaries in the eastern Mediterranean. These individuals or institutions carry out so-called academic studies and create areas of economic interest by referring to the 1982 UNCLOS in a way that benefits a country or a global actor. Sevilla University is the best example of this. The Sevilla university is famous for the Exclusive Economic Zones drawn on The eastern Mediterranean Map. At first glance, the EEZ maps seem innocent, as if they are in accordance with the 1982 UNCLOS. When looking at the European Union Economic Area, it seems that it coincides with the EEZ maps in question. However, in these maps, it is understood that Turkey was confined to its territorial waters, hydrocarbon deposits were left to Greece and Greek Cypriot Administration. Therefore, it is evaluated that energy transmission lines to be laid from the Middle East to Europe were planned to pass through the EU countries' EEZs. The Mediterranean Sea is a semi-enclosed sea, not a homogeneous region and riparian states belong to three continents.

There have been many reasons for historical conflicts among Mediterranean littoral countries, and these historical conflicts eventually extended to the problem of sharing maritime jurisdictions areas. The Mediterranean basin does not have a simple nature that can be resolved with delimitation methods determined by a general international convention. Every country or union will naturally think about its interests and future. However, since many countries have had harrowing tragedies since the colonial period, they do not want to make

---

[24] International Court of Justice , "Case concerning the continental shelf", Libyan Arab Jamahiriya/Malta, Vol.1, 1982, https://www.icj-cij.org/public/files/case-related/63/9511.pdf

[25] International Court of Justice, "Case concerning the continental shelf", Tunisia/Libyan Arab Jamahiriya, Vol.1, 1985, https://www.icj-cij.org/public/files/case-related/68/9565.pdf

[26] United Nations, "Case concerning the delimitation of maritime areas between Canada and France", Vol. XXI pp. 265-341 Decision of 10 June 1992, https://legal.un.org/riaa/cases/vol_XXI/265-341.pdf

available their resources to someone else again. It is thought that those who still want to revive a classical concept such as geopolitics in this century are desperately seeking a solution to stop or reverse the process of collapse. In the Anatolian territory, there is a saying that if antiquated were in demand, splendor would rain on the flea market. Nowadays, at least a hundred pieces of warships belonging to the navies of foreign countries that do not have a coast on the eastern Mediterranean are patrolling in the east Mediterranean each day all around the year. In addition, proxy wars continue in the Middle East, North Africa, and the Caucasus, color revolutions are triggered one after another, frozen conflicts are melted, and the region remains on the steam like an atomic bomb ready to explode at any moment. This strategic planning package is applied simultaneously in all crisis areas of the world in its classical form.

The Mediterranean is an indispensable geopolitical area for global and regional powers as it is the major routes of maritime trade, energy resources and black-money traffic. The main reason for signing international agreements should not be to provide legitimacy to the interests of global and regional powers, but to establish permanent peace both regionally and worldwide. Internal turmoils loom in all crisis regions around chokepoints globally, and these countries are forced to divide into two or more parts. Civil wars, human rights violations, and even significant tragedies that lead to genocide prepare the ground for the great powers to concentrate their capacity to peace enforcement in the region. There is a very significant correlation between world trade, technological developments, industrial production, and naval dominance as a foreign policy tool. While it is necessary to increase the interdependence to establish permanent peace, countries with a large foreign trade deficit and unilaterally dependent countries either prefer mandate and patronage. Otherwise, they enter a very rapid disintegration process if they do not participate in an alliance that protects their survival. Both solutions create unstable geography that cannot provide peace and prosperity for a long time compared to a country that can independently stand on its own feet. Countries with geopolitical and geostrategic interests benefit from this unstable environment. Because global and regional powers can open the doors to access the resources they need due to instability. One of the most important international agreements that ensure lasting peace is the 1936 Montreux Convention, which covers the Turkish Straits, the Marmara Sea and the Black Sea. Turkey unilaterally renounced some of its sovereign rights and became a party to the Montreaux Convention[27].

The convention allows the balance policy in the Black Sea to be ensured, the freezing of unresolved conflicts, the safe operation of maritime trade, the restriction of the presence of foreign warships in the Black Sea, and allowing passage to the Black Sea under certain conditions. The balance policy established by the Montreux Agreement is tried to be eroded from time to time by the

---

[27] Republic of Turkey Ministry of Foreign Affairs, Implementaton of the Montreaux Convention, https://www.mfa.gov.tr/implementation-of-the-montreux-convention.en.mfa (accessed, May, 27, 2021)

European Union, the USA, and the RF. Although the Russian Federation is satisfied with the current situation, it is observed that it has taken an aggressive attitude in some periods because its ambition to go down to warm seas has not stopped historically. The two closest examples of this are the military operations it developed against Georgia in 2008 and its current active role in Syria. The USA, which is not a party to the Montreux Agreement, has been trying to create a Black Sea Region that can penetrate by including the countries outside the Black Sea basin from the Balkans to the Caucasus with its wider black sea concept. After Bulgaria and Romania became members of NATO and the European Union, the EU could expand its sphere of influence in the Black Sea. Although the political processes necessary for Ukraine and Georgia to become members of NATO and the EU continue, the political stance of the Russian Federation increases the tension. One of the dominant countries that shaped the political-military situation in the Black Sea is the Russian Federation, and the other is Turkey. Many security mechanisms have been developed to ensure lasting peace in the Black Sea. Although these mechanisms sometimes remain dysfunctional, they have maintained the balance policy and lasting peace to date. Only riparian countries should determine the fate of the Black Sea region and should not allow foreign interventions. This region has dangerous dynamics that will start the third world war, and foreign interventions only disrupt the peaceful environment. For this reason, the Montreux Convention should not be eroded by excuses such as the right of transit passage regime, and the peace environment established in the Black Sea should not be detoriated.

The RF should not scratch Crimea or other frozen conflicts and historical disputes with former Warsaw Pact members because this region has a structure that can be the scene of greater tragedies than the Middle East. Another strategic power in the region as effective as the USA, EU, and RF is China. With its long-spectrum strategic target plans, China continues to acquire its millennial targets step by step. Sun Tzu's The Art of War manifests itself in almost every field. Already playing a leading role in global logistics and supply chain management, China is increasing its dominance in the region day by day and strengthens its influence in history with a modern version of the historical silk road. A small country that thinks itself as a strategic partner with China will be able to acquire interests as much as a tick bite a horse and suck its blood. Countries that change their geopolitical and geostrategic goals as if they have found a new ally will not be different from a frog being slowly boiled alive. When establishing inter-state agreements, the rights of not only parties to the deal but also the rights of third parties should be considered. For example, if two states with opposite coasts decide to increase their territorial seas from 6 nautical miles to 12 nautical miles, international waters become narrower.

International law regards bilateral agreements as legitimate and respects an agreement that both countries have mutually agreed upon third parties' rights. There is no international mechanism to monitor violations of third parties' rights or reject the said bilateral agreement. Because legally, the sovereign rights of states are superior to the powers of all organizations. There are gaps in international law for third parties. Therefore, the limitation of maritime jurisdiction areas should be subject to special conditions, and consortia should be given priority in the face of the excessive demands of states with a maximalist approach in special waterspaces. The Exclusive Economic Zone (EEZ) concept, which came into force with the 1982 UNCLOS, was included in the convention to strengthen the principle of freedom of the high seas and allow the transit passage regime between the EEZs. If the transit regime is viewed from a naval perspective, submerged submarines can navigate due to the right of transit passage regime, fighters can fly over chokepoints, and warships can navigate where transit passage regime is permitted.

On the surface, there seems to be no problem. However, compared to the innocent passage regime granted to foreign warships in territorial waters, warships have more freedom in waterspaces where the transit passage regime is applied. Countries with geopolitical and geostrategic goals can reach the point they want in the world's oceans relatively more freely and operate in the seas thanks to the transit passage regime. No coastal country likes the presence of a stronger navy than itself, even if it is an ally in its maritime jurisdiction areas. The presence of a foreign navy may even be perceived as a threat by the opposing country, unless it is a previously planned or informed activity through diplomatic means or within the scope of military cooperation.

In some cases, conducting multinational exercises for demonstrating force in areas close to the coastal waters of another country may cause the rules of engagement to be enforced in the direction of escalation. There are many reasons for deploying naval forces outside of their area of responsibility and engaging in activities to achieve national interests at any point in the oceans. But the main goal is to establish world peace, and these activities can sometimes turn into a war-fueling monster. Because strategic interests often conflict with other countries' ones. Global powers always have the ability to make strategic raids and power projection capabilities. This situation cannot be prevented by the national power of a country. Since no one wants to swim in a lake with alligators, how can the security of maritime trade be guaranteed in such an environment? Moreover, the activities of submarines, which no one knows but is always aware of their existence, are a mystery. As can be seen, to ensure peace and stability worldwide, international law should be reconsidered, and United Nations security mechanisms should be made functional. Otherwise, in a global environment where the strong are right, every country will seek an alliance to feel safe, and these groupings will not bring peace to the world.

Considerations on The Geopolitics of The Mediterranean as A Witch's Cauldron

Due to its central location connecting Europe, Asia, and Africa, the Mediterranean is the board for all chess games to be played in the strategic power struggle. The Mediterranean is geopolitically subject to three separate geographical divisions. The area between Gibraltar and Malta is accepted as the Western Mediterranean. The longitude 27° E is the Central Mediterranean. The sea basin to the east of the longitude 27° E is internationally recognized as the Eastern Mediterranean. Because of the geostrategic fault lines that trigger each other, the Eastern Mediterranean should be considered together with the Adriatic Sea, Red Sea, Aegean Sea, Marmara Sea, Turkish Straits, and the Black Sea. However, it is also necessary to examine each of the above-mentioned geographical areas, especially the Aegean Sea, by considering their legal sui generis characteristics.

One of the countries bordering the Red Sea with the Balkans, Middle East, Caucasus, riparian countries of Black Sea, Southern and Eastern European countries, North African countries, the Turkish Republic of Northern Cyprus (TRNC), and the Greek Cypriot Administration (GCA) are within the hinterland of the Eastern Mediterranean. A political and/or military mobilization that occurs in one or more of them affects the entire region. The recent Syrian Crisis is the best example to explain the mentioned horror film. Therefore, when the Eastern Mediterranean is referred to, it is thought that looking at the geography only as the sea basin and its riparian countries may cause irreversible mistakes in terms of strategic decision processes. Although the word geopolitics includes geography and politics, at first glance, it is perceived as a political struggle of neighboring powers. When waterspaces such as the sea and ocean are involved, overseas countries can penetrate particular geography for the sake of their political goals. Thus, the relationship between geography and politics becomes much more complex. Therefore, It is considered that geopolitical interventions leading to world wars have witnessed significant conflicts throughout history, especially in a watershed like the Eastern Mediterranean, and triggered all strategic fault lines around it. The Mediterranean appears to be the geopolitical area of around twenty countries in a narrow sense.

However, the Eastern Mediterranean, surrounded by superpowers such as the USA, the European Union, the Russian Federation, China, and India, is the most tensioned region in the world geopolitically. The Mediterranean, with its land and sea basin, is around 7000 km². The Eastern Mediterranean basin, where both trade lines and underground and surface riches are concentrated, is a nodal point where strategic interests such as energy, water, food, transportation, and logistics can turn into conflict. The factors that may cause crisis and war in the Eastern Mediterranean are as follows;

• The richness of hydrocarbon deposits,

• Availability of fossil fuels,

• Existence of qualified and young population that can make a technological leap forward,

• Drugs, human trafficking,

• Organized crimes,

• Illegal activities, including proliferation of nuclear, biological and chemical weapons,

    • Increasing severity of asymmetric threats such as terrorism day by day,

    • The existence of low peace indexed countries in the region,

    • Fostered ethnic and sectarian conflicts,

    • Dirty alliances turning into ever-changing conflicts of interest,

    • The project of the clash of civilizations, which was created artificially at the beginning and which has no basis, was put into practice in some way, causing the Arab Spring and its derivatives.

For the reasons mentioned above, the mobility of irregular migration has occurred in the vicinity of the Eastern Mediterranean. It has created political, social, economic, cultural, military, technical, and other problem areas that are very difficult to solve in the 7000 km².

Conclusions

Before examining all the issues in the world in-depth, it is necessary to consider the economic situation. The only reason behind strategic decisions that do not coincide with logic, humanity, emotion, and universal values are economic imperatives. All utopian ideas developed by philosophers are romantic, sympathetic, or ideal. It is much easier to live with utopias that are never attainable than to face reality. The economic tools invented today have lost their function.

The most critical output determined by Kondratiev in the conjuncture institute established in the 1920s is that communism will never succeed. Sometimes the right ideas can cost a person's life. Kondratiev's end was no different. Today, the same allegation applies to capitalism. As the production volume in the world shrinks and trying to prevent the recession by clinging to defense technologies is not an ethical way. A war economy is an essential tool for geopolitical approaches. Geopolitical approaches also dictate the achievement of geostrategic goals. This situation requires the use of military capacity. In summary, some people have to die for other countries' economic prosperity or access their own country's resources to survive. In the long run, the structural thaw of the states under geopolitical tensions will have been inevitable. The disintegration of the giant state organizations would be a natural consequence. The division of the USA, China, India, and again the RF into smaller parts are in the nature of things. As these giant structures divide, others can't preserve their existence. The next century will be the century of cantons. International organizations or multinational NGOs will be much stronger than state organizations, the concepts of state sovereignty or state power will be weakened. Sovereignty requires complete domination; if a gap is created, someone will definitely fill it. Terrorist activities are increasing in every brittle fracture of the world, commercial activities revival in these hot spots and maritime trade carries wood to these witch cauldrons. Soft power elements shape the operational environment across the globe. Not a third world war with tanks, rifles, and rockets, but a civil and permanent war economy in which the power elements are concentrated on the strategic centers of gravity will capsize the world order.

Hybrid wars, hybrid alliances, microlateralism will form the complex political infrastructure of the new world order, and macro geopolitical approaches will leave their place to micro ones. Not all institutions and organizations related to maritime trade are transparent. Therefore, the forecasting of maritime markets to manage strategic decision-making mechanisms is so important. Countries that are capable of processing artificial intelligence in big data will also be able to manage geostrategy. Since the International Law of the Sea, which has developed from the jurisprudence of the colonial era to the present day, thanks to the events in both maritime trade and the naval warfare history, it is designed in favor of global powers, the principle of fairly and proportionately in the rights of third parties cannot be fully met. The fact that the two sovereign states agree on the maritime jurisdiction areas may harm the interests of other parties sharing the same sea and third parties.

The Montreux Agreement is an exemplary model for twenty-six primary and secondary chokepoints worldwide. Thus, while merchant ships can pass freely and safely through straits, on the one hand, The Convention also restricts the activities of foreign warships that may disturb the military balance of the region. Restrictions should be placed on the operation of foreign warships in another country's exclusive economic zone unless there is a UN resolution. The law should work for the benefit of humanity. Littoral States Border/Coast Guard Agencies Cooperation mechanisms can ensure the safe conduct of maritime trade. It should be provided that The Common Operational Picture (COP) and Consistent Tactical Picture (CTP) is globalized and that the flag states or relevant merchant ships requests protection by contacting the appropriate border/coast guard coordination centers when necessary. As long as warships move freely all over the world, the arms race will continue.

The defense industry has always been a savior in preventing the structure of the capitalist economy from recession, which has been flawed above. For this reason, artificial crisis zones have been created in the world. Public opinion is inured to spiraling crime against humanity. Maritime jurisdiction areas cannot be shared by the principles of equity and conscience (ex aequo et bono) even between two states that have reciprocal coasts in a particular maritime area, such as the Aegean Sea. Therefore, an unnecessary arms race is being conducted, and this situation is not in favor of them. However, suppose Turkey and Greece could jointly ensure the security of the Aegean Sea by declaring a joint EEZ in which they can share living and non-living resources with collaborative consortia. In that case, investments will be made in education, health, art, or other fields. As people become civilized, their willingness to fight will decrease, and permanent peace would be brought to the region. If EEZ cannot be shared with equity and conscience, and countries are on the brink of war artificially, littoral countries must establish a common EEZ, and share all living and non-living resources fairly and proportionately with criteria such as; the size of the country, the population, and the length of the coastline, etc. The same logic would serve as an exemplary model for the South China Sea. The ambition of one or all of the parties brings harm to the region and the whole world. When global powers are also involved in these problems, it becomes more challenging to establish perpetual peace.

The world is enough for everyone as long as there isn't an irresponsible state that covets more than it needs. Religions and morals are for civilization. Despite this, there has been an increase in the number of states waging proxy wars using terrorist organizations as a tool when some people dilute areas such as religion and morality to create a clash of civilizations. For lasting world peace, international mechanisms need to evolve to benefit humanity, and instruments that can curb those countries with global ambitions should be established. The world community cannot tolerate re-polarization with the ambition for access to energy resources and an arms race that can cause deaths by restarting gunboat diplomacy with geopolitical means.

Everything should be for peace and humanity. The republic model and the concept of *Peace at Home, Peace in the World* put forward by Mustafa Kemal Atatürk, the most successful leader the world has ever witnessed, are exemplary models that will ensure lasting peace. If this model, which Turkey has still been trying to implement fully, is realized, it will be possible to prevent the state from being destroyed by individualization. If the world really wants to get rid of selfishness and make peace, brotherhood, and love prevail, every country must compromise its self-interest. If there are still hungry people in this century, if there are still mass migrations, and if those victims are killed to be faster, more profitable, and more robust, this terrible tragedy occurred is a brutal crime against humanity. This shame is even more severe than genocide. Every prosperous person needs to think about a piece of food that goes through his throat and question his level of civilization because he has more than he needs. It is time for a new world humanity revolution. If this revolution cannot be carried out, humanity will find its solution, and the world states would be divided into cantons. As a result, geopolitical and geostrategic approaches should be abandoned for the revival of the maritime economy. The seas should be shared fairly and proportionately, and policies that support the lack of solution and escalate terrorism in crisis regions should be avoided.

MARITIME SPATIAL PLANNING FOR GLOBAL COMMONS

Dinçer Bayer*

Introduction

Sea has many resources which are called as global commons. Global commons are resource domains that are legally accessible to all nations such as open seas[1]. The commons might be managed by international organizations established by different institutions instead of governmental authorities. In essence, commons should be handled in having an objective to make all nations freely use their common resources.

Global commons are also specified as the common heritage of mankind, a term used by UNESCO and International Seabed Authority. Governance of global commons is shared among many regional or global multinational agreements. Their governance process is not centrally established[2].

The sea areas beyond the limits of national jurisdiction may be called as global commons are defined by the United Nations Convention on the Law of the Seas (UNCLOS) such as.

- The water column beyond the exclusive economic zone or beyond the territorial sea in case no exclusive economic zone has been defined, called the "high seas" in accordance with the Article 86 of the UNCLOS and

- The seabed which lies beyond the limits of the continental shelf, determined in conformity with Article 76 of the UNCLOS, defined as "the Area".

The area and high seas are the common spaces for all. Everybody has rights of free navigation, overflying, making research and use of the natural resources in the high seas and in the area in conformity with part VII of the UNCLOS.

The high seas are not linked to the sovereignty of any state and its usage is free for all states. The main principle is that the use of the high seas must be carried out in such a way that this usage is not obstruct the interests of other states. The high seas are called also the open seas and open for the common

---

* Asst. Prof. Dr. Piri Reis University, Maritime Higher Vocational School, dbayer@pirireis.edu.tr
[1] Kutay Kutlu (2020) Global Commons. In: Romaniuk S., Thapa M., Marton P. (eds) The Palgrave Encyclopedia of Global Security Studies. Palgrave Macmillan, Cham. https://doi.org/10.1007/978-3-319-74336-3_407-1
[2] Tomas Zuklin (2019) International Governance of Global Commons in the Context of SDG 17. In: Leal Filho W., Azul A., Brandli L., Özuyar P., Wall T. (eds) Partnerships for the Goals. Encyclopedia of the UN Sustainable Development Goals. Springer, Cham. https://doi.org/10.1007/978-3-319-71067-9_7-1

usage[3].

The area is called as the "common heritage of mankind". The International Seabed Authority ("ISA)" is the UN's body entitled to act on behalf of the humanity (Article 137 (2) of UNCLOS) and to provide administrative principles for the common heritage of mankind by establishing the cooperation and collaboration opportunities for the common interests on the management of mineral resources (Part XI of UNCLOS)[4].

The high seas and area cover 2/3 of the ocean and provide human being many possibilities by including in a great amount of biodiversity and natural resources[5].

United Nations expert group from World Commission on Environment and Development on Environmental Law prepared a report in 1987 titled as "Our Common Future" express that the natural resources in sea spaces are under stress because of "overexploitation, pollution, and land-based development". The Report states as "The common resource characteristics of many regional seas make the local management essential"[6]. Therefore, administrative and cooperative arrangements and organizations in all common areas are needed to make the mutual benefit of mankind.

Sea areas except ABNJ are delimited and sea borders are determined by states by applying different procedures based on the geographical, historical and political situations. However, sea traffic, fish species, pollution threats and many industrial activities, cable networks or pipelines do not respect national boundaries at sea.

UNCLOS Articles 15, 74 and 83 provide guidance to states on the delimitation of the sea areas. There are many factors effecting delimitation of sea areas. The delimitation is made based on two principles notably (1) that land dominates the sea, by (2) intermediary of the coast[7]. One study made by Qiu et al on the role of land domination and natural prolongation related to maritime delimitation issue over the exclusive economic zone (the EEZ) and continental shelf, claims that the natural prolongation with respect to the delimitation of continental shelf does not only points out the continental margin but also

---

[3] Dorota Pyć (2019) The Role of the Law of the Sea in Marine Spatial Planning. In: Zaucha J., Gee K. (eds) Maritime Spatial Planning. Palgrave Macmillan, Cham. https://doi.org/10.1007/978-3-319-98696-8_16

[4] Susanne Altvater, Ruth Fletcher and Cristian Passarello (2019) The Need for Marine Spatial Planning in Areas Beyond National Jurisdiction. In: Zaucha J., Gee K. (eds) Maritime Spatial Planning. Palgrave Macmillan, Cham. https://doi.org/10.1007/978-3-319-98696-8_17

[5] UNEP-WCMC (2017). Governance of areas beyond national jurisdiction for biodiversity conservation and sustainable use: Institutional arrangements and cross-sectoral cooperation in the Western Indian Ocean and the South East Pacific. Cambridge (UK): UN Environment World Conservation Monitoring Centre. 120 pp. Retrieved from: https://www.unep-wcmc.org/ (Access 14.05.2021).

[6] WCED. (1987). Report of the World Commission on Environment and Development: Our Common Future. Retrieved from: http://www.un-documents.net/ourcommon-future.pdf (Access 14.05.2021).

[7] Bjorn Kunoy (2006). The Rise of the Sun: Legal Arguments in Outer Continental Margin Delimitations. *Neth Int Law Rev* 53, 247–272 (2006). https://doi.org/10.1017/S0165070X06002476

specifies the EEZ coverage area limits[8]. According to Ndiaye, seaward projections of the shores of the coastal state and the effect of these projections on those at sea of the other coastal state determine the maritime delimitation between those two states[9].

When sea areas are considered, several overlapping sea spaces are mentioned about each of which has its very own exclusive relationships. For example, territorial seas are normally located in exclusive economic zones. Their status differs from others and spatial divisions naturally require different approach and methods because each one of these sea areas has different regimes.

If there are more than two states having interest in delimitation of a sea area, it is much more difficult to achieve an agreement. For example, in determining of Malta-Libya boundary limitation a short section of boundary with Greece created difficulty depending on the precise terminus of the Italy-Malta and Libya-Malta boundaries[10]. The similar boundary determination problem exists in the eastern Mediterranean between neighboring states such as Turkey, Libya, Greece and Egypt. Many potential EEZs are in disputed status. The exclusive economic zones declared by states based on bi-lateral agreements are not accepted by the other neighboring states. All the nations adjacent or neighboring each other in the eastern Mediterranean are required to reach a common agreement on delimitation to solve the problem. It is so difficult because the source of the problems is not only legal but also historical and political in nature.

The southeastern part of the Mediterranean is also largely unregulated. There is also a contention for the potentials of area between Syria, Cyprus, Lebanon, Egypt, Israel, and the Palestinian state where gas fields (Leviathan, Gaza Marine) have been explored[11]. A multinational agreement is a must in the region.

Many maritime boundaries in global scale are not delimited. Jenisch stated in the year 2012 that an estimated number of 100 sea areas in the world are disputed or unresolved. The typical causes of delimitation problems are territorial claims, resources, and shipping route requirements. Whereas the total number of potential maritime boundaries was 420 in 2015, only about 200 boundary agreements existed[12]. These statements show that many disputed sea areas are not regulated or governed because of nonexistence of the responsible states in accordance with UNCLOS regulations.

---

[8] Wenxian Qiu, Xiangland Jin, Yinxia Fang and Kui Wang (2017). Effect of natural prolongation with geological features on maritime delimitation. *Acta Oceanol. Sin.* 36, 35–42. https://doi.org/10.1007/s1313 1-017-1002-6

[9] Tafsir Malick Ndiaye (2015). The judge, maritime delimitation and the grey areas. *Indian Journal of International Law* 55, 493–533. https://doi.org/10.1007/s40901-016-0027-2

[10] Gerald H. Blake (1997). Coastal state sovereignty in the Mediterranean Sea: the case of Malta. *GeoJournal* 41, 173–180 (1997). https://doi.org/10.1023/A:1006849310995

[11] Uwe K. Jenisch (2012). Old laws for new risks at sea: mineral resources, climate change, sea lanes, and cables. *WMU J Marit Affairs* 11, 169–185. https://doi.org/10.1007/s13437-012-0018-1

[12] Tafsir Malick Ndiaye (2015). The judge, maritime delimitation and the grey areas. *Indian Journal of International Law* 55, 493–533. https://doi.org/10.1007/s40901-016-0027-2

The coastal states have exclusive rights such as exploration and exploitation of natural resources in their EEZs[13]. These rights are to be understood as the responsibilities for the protection and rational management of these resources. The coastal state is to act in its EEZ as manager of all the resources[14]. For the disputed waters, there is no such an authority to manage the EEZ or continental shelf areas.

Piedra et al[15], evaluate the delimitation issues from the Hobbes point of view by stating that, disputes take its source from the different views of neighboring or adjacent states of disputed waters, expecting to obtain more resources or spaces at sea. They claim that conflicts may be resolved in the existence of an agreed power represented by an international organization or an authority, but not entirely eliminated. That is because of the human's nature.

Even if UN has some mechanisms to resolve the disputes between states on delimitation issues, the states do hesitate in applying to courts because of thinking the issues are linked to their sensitive national interests. For example, The International Tribunal for the Law of the Sea (ITLOS) is the UN's court adjudicates on disputes relating to the explication and implementation of the UNCLOS. The UNCLOS grants the Tribunal jurisdiction to resolve a variety of international law of the sea disagreements such as the delimitation of maritime zones, fisheries, navigation and the protection of the marine environment[16].

UNCLOS Article 197, prescribes that States shall cooperate on a global or regional basis, for the protection and preservation of the marine environment. Even though only the high seas outside of national jurisdiction is truly commons, other commonly used sea areas require more effective management because their common usages. According to mare liberum concept, which was developed in the17th Century by Hugo Grotius, sea areas are common property. Its freely usage is a natural right for all especially for transportation needs.

UNCLOS takes into accounts the traditional rights such as freedom of navigation and also emerging rights such as sovereignty and sovereign rights over resources within AUNJ. UNCLOS defines the concept of ocean governance evolved as well[17]. The preservation of oceans is the foremost requirement of

---

[13] Mohammed M. Rahman (2019) Exclusive Economic Zone (EEZ). In: Romaniuk S., Thapa M., Marton P. (eds) The Palgrave Encyclopedia of Global Security Studies. Palgrave Macmillan, Cham. https://doi.org/10.1007/978-3-319-74336-3_331-1

[14] Dorota Pyć (2019) The Role of the Law of the Sea in Marine Spatial Planning. In: Zaucha J., Gee K. (eds) Maritime Spatial Planning. Palgrave Macmillan, Cham. https://doi.org/10.1007/978-3-319-98696-8_16

[15] Luis Piedra, T. Guarda and R. Armijos (2018) Evolution of the International Regime for Oceans Under the Hobessian Image View. In: Rocha Á., Guarda T. (eds) Developments and Advances in Defense and Security. MICRADS 2018. Smart Innovation, Systems and Technologies, vol 94. Springer, Cham. https://doi.org/10.1007/978-3-319-78605-6_17

[16] International Tribunal for the Law of the Sea (ITLOS). (2018) In: The Statesman's Yearbook 2018. The Statesman's Yearbook. Palgrave Macmillan, London. https://doi.org/10.1007/978-1-349-70154-4_45

[17] Pradeep A. Singh and Mara Ort (2020). Law and Policy Dimensions of Ocean Governance. In: Jungblut S., Liebich V., Bode-Dalby M. (eds) YOUMARES 9 - The Oceans: Our Research, Our Future. Springer, Cham. https://doi.org/10.1007/978-3-030-20389-4_3

ocean governance itself. An effective spatial planning is the main practice to preserve and protect seas in general.

The UNCLOS regime which has been applied since 1995 was not able to solve many problematic issues especially on the traditional common resource of fish stocks and fisheries. Fish stocks are one of the examples have long been exhausted, because of the principle of mare liberum. The introduction of the EEZs by the UNCLOS regime did not bring any relaxation for fishing. Many EEZs are in disputed status within sea areas encircled by more than one state. The domestic fishers have not limited themselves with the EEZs and followed harvesting the stocks in the international waters and other EEZ's. They claim that the fish stocks are mobile across different EEZs or high seas. Therefore, a more cooperative management is needed in sea areas even they are delimitated or not.

In this chapter, the status and current governance structure of ABNJ including disputed EEZ and continental shelves are to be examined and maritime spatial planning requirements will be brought around.

Maritime Spatial Planning and Its Current Applications

Maritime spatial planning (MSP) is a public process of analyzing and allocating the spatial and temporal dispersion of human activities in marine areas to achieve ecological, economic and social objectives that are usually determined based on political decisions[18]. MSP is a convenient way to make and apply a rational organization in the use of ocean spaces[19].

Flannery et al. explain the MSP as a process for performing ecosystem-based management in the marine environment, a mechanism for decreasing user conflict, a means of improving the environmental protection and a work for facilitating the growth of maritime economies by getting the views some other authors as well[20].

MSP is accepted as a principal mechanism to get more effective planning and management of human- sea interactions. Kidd et al, define the MSP in their study as a public work of analyzing and sharing out the spatial and interim distribution of human activities in marine areas to acquire ecological, economic and social objectives that have been identified through a political process[21].

[18] Jacek Zaucha and Kira Gee (2019) Maritime Spatial Planning: Past, Present, Future. Springer, e-book. ISBN 978-3-319-98696-8 (eBook) https://doi.org/10.1007/978-3-319-98696-8
[19] Dorota Pyć (2019) The Role of the Law of the Sea in Marine Spatial Planning. In: Zaucha J., Gee K. (eds) Maritime Spatial Planning. Palgrave Macmillan, Cham. https://doi.org/10.1007/978-3-319-98696-8_16
[20] Wesley Flannery, Hilde Toonen, Stephen Jay and Joanna Vince (2020). A critical turn in marine spatial planning. *Maritime Studies* 19, 223–228. https://doi.org/10.1007/s40152-020-00198-8
[21] Sue Kidd, Hannah Jones and Stephen Jay (2019) Taking Account of Land-Sea Interactions in Marine Spatial Planning. In: Zaucha J., Gee K. (eds) Maritime Spatial Planning. Palgrave Macmillan, Cham. https://doi.org/10.1007/978-3-319-98696-8_11

Over the last 20 years, MSP has developed from a concept to a widely use currently more than practice of 20 nations to moving towards sustainable development in the oceans[22]. Moreover, Flannery et al. asserts that over the last 10–15 years maritime spatial planning has become the dominant marine planning technique.

Oceans emerge as spatial expressions and a way of structuring the sensation of the social as created by mutual initiative[23].

Oceans provide many resources for human use such as marine species, tourism, shipping, renewable energy, seabed mining, biotechnology medium, aquaculture, offshore oil and gas capabilities. When these possibilities are considered, it is realized that the sea is very valuable, indispensable and must be preserved. Therefore, collective protection of oceans is the foremost requirement even they are delimitated or not. We are not able to preserve and protect seas without having an effective spatial planning in general. The common lack of coordination for risk and uncertainties in MSP applications is still exist.[24]

Vince and Day propose several principles in making MSP effectively. They listed 21 principles in their study, by stating that the managers and planners making the planning for the sea area need to consider all the principles, and then choose and priorities those that are relevant to their area.[25]

Altvater et al, state that the UNESCO considers MSP as a "public process" capable of defining the different human activities in the marine environment and distribute them in a rational and sustainable way to reduce possible negative effects[26].

The UNCLOS expresses in its preamble that "the problems of ocean space are closely interrelated and need to be considered as a whole". This preamble emphasizes great importance for MSP, especially in the adjacent and interacting areas of EEZs or the continental shelves and ABNJs including disputed sea areas[27].

States should consistently coordinate, cooperate or collaborate to create a legal document for protecting the marine environment, especially since the

[22] Charles Ehler, Jacek Zaucha, and Kira Gee (2019) Maritime/Marine Spatial Planning at the Interface of Research and Practice. In: Zaucha J., Gee K. (eds) Maritime Spatial Planning. Palgrave Macmillan, Cham. https://doi.org/10.1007/978-3-319-98696-8_1

[23] Kira Gee (2019) The Ocean Perspective. In: Zaucha J., Gee K. (eds) Maritime Spatial Planning. Palgrave Macmillan, Cham. https://doi.org/10.1007/978-3-319-98696-8_2

[24] Xander Keijser, Hilde Toonen and Jan van Tatenhove (2020). A "learning paradox" in maritime spatial planning. Maritime Studies 19, 333–346. https://doi.org/10.1007/s40152-020-00169-z

[25] Joanna Vince and Jon C. Day (2020). Effective integration and integrative capacity in marine spatial planning. Maritime Studies 19, 317–332. https://doi.org/10.1007/s40152-020-00167-1

[26] Susanne Altvater, Ruth Fletcher and Cristian Passarello (2019) The Need for Marine Spatial Planning in Areas Beyond National Jurisdiction. In: Zaucha J., Gee K. (eds) Maritime Spatial Planning. Palgrave Macmillan, Cham. https://doi.org/10.1007/978-3-319-98696-8_17

[27] Dorota Pyć (2019) The Role of the Law of the Sea in Marine Spatial Planning. In: Zaucha J., Gee K. (eds) Maritime Spatial Planning. Palgrave Macmillan, Cham. https://doi.org/10.1007/978-3-319-98696-8_16

oceans do not have physical borders and ship movements, economic interests of nations and environment pollution risks do not necessarily stay within delimited sea areas. The MSP technique could make possible an effective maritime management and create new ways of managing the sea that not only takes into consideration the human activities but also considers the interactions between the marine ecosystems[28].

Various aspects of marine areas are evaluated with different scientific disciplines such as physics, biology, geography, economy, political, spatial, sociology, philosophy and cultural dimensions. Therefore, managing the sea areas requires a broad scientific and political approach and is very much complicated job. The necessity for using a multidisciplinary approach is caused from the nature of marine space as a multi-dimensional concept requiring understanding from many scientific disciplines and types of knowledge[29].

According to Pyc, the World seas are a universal and common space for mankind. It is difficult to determine whether the ocean will separate us in the future or bring us closer together[30].

Sea space is still a research area for humanity for different reasons. Many types of national or multinational research have transboundary nature as well. Therefore, a multidimensional spatial approach to each sea area is a necessity. In addition to the delimitation of sea areas, maritime spatial management, even in delimited areas or in ABNJ requires close coordination, cooperation and agreements between states. Today, many global economic activities have strong transboundary dimensions. Therefore, more international maritime networks such as underwater communication cable systems, transnational oil and gas pipelines and new shipping routes are emerging in particular, in enclosed seas such as the Mediterranean and the Black Sea.

Even if delimitation of sea areas is not able to be achieved due to historical, geopolitical and economic reasons and a new term of disputed waters for some continental seas is getting common; complex economic and environmental issues require the cooperation of regional states.

European Union has a project aiming smart, sustainable and inclusive economic and employment development from the oceans, seas and coasts called as blue growth policy for the maritime pillar of the Europe 2020 strategy. The role of MSP was found in this project as an important facilitator and enabler for fostering the development of maritime sectors. A pre-impact study

---

[28] Susanne Altvater, Ruth Fletcher and Cristian Passarello (2019) The Need for Marine Spatial Planning in Areas Beyond National Jurisdiction. In: Zaucha J., Gee K. (eds) Maritime Spatial Planning. Palgrave Macmillan, Cham. https://doi.org/10.1007/978-3-319-98696-8_17

[29] Charles Ehler, Jacek Zaucha, and Kira Gee (2019) Maritime/Marine Spatial Planning at the Interface of Research and Practice. In: Zaucha J., Gee K. (eds) Maritime Spatial Planning. Palgrave Macmillan, Cham. https://doi.org/10.1007/978-3-319-98696-8_1

[30] Dorota Pyć (2019) The Role of the Law of the Sea in Marine Spatial Planning. In: Zaucha J., Gee K. (eds) Maritime Spatial Planning. Palgrave Macmillan, Cham. https://doi.org/10.1007/978-3-319-98696-8_16

commissioned by the European Commission pointed the economic effects of MSP as it results in higher efficiency, cost reductions and investment incentive creator. Therefore, MSP is evaluated as a motivator role in development and economic growing in the EU.

MSP for coastal sea areas requires a coordination and collaboration of all regional states. For example, The Baltic SCOPE Maritime Spatial Planning Project organized bring together MSP representatives from six Baltic Sea countries to increase the cross-border interactions and coordination of spatial planning activities in the Baltic Sea[31]. The main aim of the project was to create the planning options to transboundary issues and develop the maritime spatial planning activities. The countries were Sweden, Denmark, Germany, Poland, Latvia and Estonia. Other project partners were the international organizations Helsinki Commission (HELCOM) and Vision and Strategies Around the Baltic Sea (VASAB) and the two research organizations NordRegio and the Finnish Environment Institute. By activation of this project, a coordinated Baltic Sea MSP was achieved providing also inputs for national spatial planning efforts. In the Baltic Sea region, the improvement of collective principles belongs to MSP, such as linked, ecologic, prudent and responsible management was accomplished with the involvement of all interested parties and organizations.

Another EU maritime spatial planning project made with the name of the SUPREME, was collectively exercised by Italy, Croatia, Slovenia and Greece in the Eastern Mediterranean. In the project, five different sea areas were scrutinized closely (one area for each country). For the Greek coastal waters, the project was made in two pilot areas first within the Inner Ionian Sea and Corinthian Gulf and second within the Myrtoon Pelagos Passage of Kythera. The studies in the Greek pilot areas were supervised by the Hellenic Ministry for the Environment and Energy and carried out by three Greek universities. According to Papageorgiou et al., SUPREME project has been evaluated as valuable to both the competent Greek authority for maritime spatial planning and the Greek academia[32]. Papageorgiou et al. recommend that the cross-border and international cooperation among countries in the Eastern Mediterranean in addition to the other key issues that need to be addressed to accelerate MSP implementation.

MSP has already been established within the UK both national and regionally, for coastal areas and open seas, at different usage purposes[33]. According to the Ritchie and McElduff, more analysis is needed on issues of the marine problems

---

[31] Baltic Scope Project (2017). The EU Project for the Baltic States Maritime Spatial Plans, Retrieved from: http://www.balticscope.eu/about-baltic-scope/ (Access: 31.1.2021).

[32] Marilena Papageorgiou *et al.* (2020). Implementation challenges of maritime spatial planning (MSP) in Greece under a place-based approach. *Euro-Mediterr J Environ Integr* 5, 39. https://doi.org/10.1007/s4120 7-020-00172-0

[33] Heather Ritchie and Linda McElduff (2020). The whence and whither of marine spatial planning: revisiting the social reconstruction of the marine environment in the UK. *Maritime Studies* 19, 229–240. https://doi.org/10.1007/s40152-020-00170-6

is constructed which are vital to understand the current, and future, maritime governance and its relationship to other agendas such as blue growth and/or regimes such as territorial planning in order to achieve the social development of the marine environment.

France has been executing a Project called as integrated ocean and coastal zone management since 2011. The project is set to become a reality in 2022. In this Project, the planning of maritime activities around French coasts requires an effective global approach and integrated initiative[34].

Belt and Road Initiative (BRI) proposed by China in 2013 and the most well-known global initiative is a strategic level spatial planning project. From the geographical perspectives, the BRI is a new revolutionary comprehensive trans-regional and multilateral project connecting the optional and optimum transportation routes. In this BRI model, spatial interaction describes and predicts spatial flows of people, commodities, capital and information are associated with locations in geographic space[35].

MSP is to be made multilaterally by taking into account potential benefits of all parties which may have interests within the space. "Turner" studied the construction of spatial regional identities especially for the Baltic and found that many actors outside of the regions such as China, Russia and some other countries may also have interests in the Baltic Sea[36].

Geographic limits should not be an obstacle in effective cooperation. For example, geographic and other boundaries have been evaporated in the European Union for the interest of all EU member states[37].

Maritime Spatial Planning is a planning activity that provides the spatial order in seas. MSP should accept and arrange the presence of multidimensionality and interdependencies of activities in the marine environment taking place because of interaction of various occurrences assumed in it, including economic activities[38].

One study was made in the Aegean Sea to assess the possible locations for offshore wind farms. The study investigated the challenges for renewable energy facilities, maritime spatial planning techniques and environmental conservation

---

[34] Annie Cudennec (2020) Integrated Ocean and Coastal Zone Management in France: Some Perspectives. In: Chircop A., Goerlandt F., Aporta C., Pelot R. (eds) Governance of Arctic Shipping. Springer Polar Sciences. Springer, Cham. https://doi.org/10.1007/978-3-030-44975-9_16

[35] HUANG Qinshi, ZHU Xigang, LIU Chunhui, WU Wei, LIU Fengbao and ZHANG Xinyi (2020). Spatial-temporal Evolution and Determinants of the Belt and Road Initiative: A Maximum Entropy Gravity Model Approach. *Chin. Geogr. Sci.* 30, 839–854.

[36] Barnard Turner (2010). The construction of spatial regional identities: the case of the Baltic in a global context. *Asia Eur J* 8, 317–326 (2010). https://doi.org/10.1007/s10308-010-0270-y

[37] Paul Meerts (2011) Boundaries in Bargaining: A Multidimensional View. *Group Decis Negot* 20, 155–164. https://doi.org/10.1007/s10726-010-9198-2

[38] Dorota Pyć (2019) The Role of the Law of the Sea in Marine Spatial Planning. In: Zaucha J., Gee K. (eds) Maritime Spatial Planning. Palgrave Macmillan, Cham. https://doi.org/10.1007/978-3-319-98696-8_16

in the areas belong to Turkey and Greece (Countries have different legal, political, and socio/economic characteristics). The study recommends making more detailed feasibility analysis at appropriate offshore wind energy regions in future in the two study areas under Greek and Turkish jurisdictions[39]. This requirement shows that collaborations not only require in areas beyond national jurisdiction but also in areas under national control.

MSP Requirements and Current Initiatives

UNCLOS Article 123 requires the cooperation efforts of states bordering confined seas, to manage, conserve, explore and make use of the living resources of the sea while protecting and preserving the marine environment.

Preservation of natural and environmental aspects of ocean is also a human interest. Marine species, flora and fauna are decreasing and even under the extinction danger threatened by maritime activities and land-based industry. Delimited maritime areas are not able to put limits to obstructs these dangers. Additionally, economic activities such as shipping, offshore oil and gas extractions, tourism, aquaculture are expected to grow in the future. National or transnational activities such as seabed mining, renewable energy and bio technologic facilities within sea areas are expected to increase.

It is a mutual knowledge that the oceans provide primary resources for human life. This dependency requires international rules to be developed to regulate the complicated human activities in the oceans[40].

Zaucha and Gee put stress on the need for improving the collaboration efforts between the countries, to provide:

- Regulating the fishing and improving the sustainable management of fish resources.

- Regulation of sea traffic routes specifically in narrow waters and ship traffic congested sea areas.

- Reduction of ship collisions and environmental accident risks to an acceptable level; and

- Management of conflicts that might arise from the extraction and transportation of oil and natural gas resources[41].

In addition to the above-mentioned threats, migratory nature of fish and

---

[39] Emre Tercan *et al.* (2020). A GIS-based multi-criteria model for offshore wind energy power plants site selection in both sides of the Aegean Sea. *Environ Monit Assess* 192, 652 (2020). https://doi.org/10.1007/s10661-020-08603-9

[40] Pradeep A. Singh and Mara Ort (2020). Law and Policy Dimensions of Ocean Governance. In: Jungblut S., Liebich V., Bode-Dalby M. (eds) YOUMARES 9 - The Oceans: Our Research, Our Future. Springer, Cham. https://doi.org/10.1007/978-3-030-20389-4_3

[41] Jacek Zaucha and Kira Gee (2019) Maritime Spatial Planning: Past, Present, Future. Springer, e-book. ISBN 978-3-319-98696-8 (eBook) https://doi.org/10.1007/978-3-319-98696-8

marine species require much more attention and a close coordination of neighboring states. International cooperation and collaboration efforts beyond national delimited sea areas is necessary for humanitarian, economic and ecologic reasons. Therefore, zonal management and maritime spatial planning should be considered altogether for the sea governance for ABNJ.

The law of the sea is categorized under two parts as the zonal and sectoral approaches. The zonal approach relates to the states controlling the sea area or having the authority to establish regulations and practice them, whereas the sectoral approach deals with the type of actions to be organized. This differentiating shows that the ocean management or ocean governance is a complicated notion that requires expressing trans-boundary and cross-sectoral concerns altogether[42].

The sectoral approach accepts the assumption that zonal obligations defined on boundary lines are insufficient and requires be amplified with specific agreements and regulations that is applied on the related activity. Because of that, the law of the sea includes in various sectoral regimes such as shipping, fishing, mining and recreational activities exposed each of them with separate suits of laws. The sectoral arrangements become mainly evident in trans-boundary sectoral activities such as shipping and fishing. Particularly in the case of fisheries, the improving regional regulations are also one of the fast-growing activities.

Governance of ABNJ and disputed sea areas include the sustainable and coverage management of the sea areas among many maritime zonal and sectoral issues. This management requires an effective spatial planning and demonstrates the applicability of various concepts and means to achieve different objectives and mainly defines the requirements to improve coordination, cooperation and collaboration issues between different partners and institutions that have interests in the activities at sea.

The Intergovernmental Oceanographic Commission of UNESCO (IOC) is the United Nations institution has 150 member states responsible for supporting global ocean science and services. The IOC coordinates the activities of various institutions of states on maritime spatial planning globally. Since it was established in 1960, the IOC has improved the procedures on management of oceans, coastal regions and marine ecosystems. The IOC also supports all its members to establish their scientific and institutional capacity to accomplish the United Nations Sustainable Development Goal 14[43]. The IOC also integrated its spatial planning ventures as part of the Integrated Coastal Area Management Strategy (ICAMS) and continued to document the international employment of maritime spatial management around the world, synthesizing lessons learnt,

---

[42] Pradeep A. Singh and Mara Ort (2020). Law and Policy Dimensions of Ocean Governance. In: Jungblut S., Liebich V., Bode-Dalby M. (eds) YOUMARES 9 - The Oceans: Our Research, Our Future. Springer, Cham. https://doi.org/10.1007/978-3-030-20389-4_3
[43] The Intergovernmental Oceanographic Commission. (2021). Retrieved from; https://ioc.unesco.org/ (Access 12.02.2021).

defining priorities and updating technical guidance in various perspectives of MSP project and enforcements.

The International Seabed Authority (ISA) is an international organization has 167 member states which was established under the UNCLOS and the 1994 Agreement relating to the Implementation of Part XI of the UNCLOS. EU is one of the partners of ISA. ISA is tasked to coordinate, manage, regulate and control the mineral-related activities in the sea area for the benefit of human being[44].

There are some regional initiatives considering the common environmental protection measures such as the Barcelona Convention of 1976 for the Protection of the Marine Environment and the Coastal Region of the Mediterranean. The Barcelona Convention is a good example of legal and regional agreement for the regulation and protection of the Mediterranean marine spaces and coastal zones[45].

UNEP -MAP (www.unepmap.org) which is an UN environment project, and the first regional marine program includes 21 partner states bordering the Mediterranean Sea. Its founding aim is to improve the regional and private efforts to achieve sustainable development in marine areas. One report prepared by UNEP-MAP on marine litter in the Mediterranean provides suggestions to the states that several proposed issues should be considered to provide a scientific and technical background for a consistent environmental monitoring, a better environment management system and science-based pollution reduction measures[46].

Discussion on Resources and Activities to be Considered in Relation to Maritime Spatial Planning for ABJN

Shipping:

Shipping is ensured to be freely executed everywhere based on the mare liberum concept. MSP should provide all the ship routes open in ABNJs including disputed EEZs and continental shelf areas all over the world by considering the current and the future shipping requirements. Therefore, planners must have enough knowledge about the current and potential routes by having information and/or estimation on future port developments, ship maintenance facilities and recreational as well as tourism-oriented shipping. There will be a need also to allocate separate and exclusive routes may be required for the future autonomous transport vehicles. One of the basic challenges for

---

[44] The International Seabed Authority (2021). Retrieved from; https://www.isa.org.jm/home (Access 12.02.2021).

[45] Barcelona Convention. (1995). Retrieved from; https://wedocs.unep.org/bitstream/handle/20.500.11 822/7096/Consolidated_BC95_Eng.pdf (Access 20.02.2021).

[46] UNEP MAP. (2015). Marine Litter Assessment in the Mediterranean, ISBN No: 978 -92 -807 -3564 2, Retrieved from; https://wedocs.unep.org/bitstream/handle/20.500.11822/7098/ (Access: 20.02.2021).

autonomous sailboats and autonomous vessels is how to plan secure routes to enable a safe navigation[47].

The security of maritime shipping of global supply chain is vulnerable from the port of loading and on the high seas to the port of unloading[48]. Supply chain sea transport routes will provide a reference for route planning.

Martínez de Osés and Uyà Juncadella assert in their study that there will be a need for a creation of global maritime traffic services to be covered all the transportation routes for the future. This system will consider the creation of an ocean-based vessel traffic services, where all personnel would exchange information, without state borders, between ships and onshore centers worldwide[49].

In a study made by Han and Yang, a mathematical framework based on Automatic Information System (AIS) track data of transiting ships is proposed to automatically generate ship planning routes for maritime emergency search and rescue planning and operations[50]. This proposed method might also be deemed appropriate to be used in the route localization in the maritime spatial planning.

Fishery:

Fishery is not an easy sector to integrate into MSP processes, as those cannot be forced to fish in a geographic area because many fish species are migrant and generally not exclusive for a defined sea area. Planners need to have knowledge which enable them to determine the most suitable areas for fishing and fish species according to their life cycle. Fishery sector planning including trans-boundary considerations should take place at an early phase to integrate in a better way in the MSP processing. MSP is also used to supplement other fishing regulations. For example, Norway uses sea space regulation as governing instrument to support its fish-quota management arrangements. The instruments used in sea space regulation are varied from technical regulation of use of gear in certain areas via specific zones for certain vessel sizes to protect the areas[51].

[47] Wei Jing *et al.* (2020). Path Planning and Navigation of Oceanic Autonomous Sailboats and Vessels: A Survey. *J. Ocean Univ. China* 19, 609–621. https://doi.org/10.1007/s11802-020-4144-7

[48] Richard R. Young and Gary A. Gordon (2020). Intermodal maritime supply chains: assessing factors for resiliency and security. *J Transp Secur* 13, 231–244. https://doi.org/10.1007/s12198-020-00224-0

[49] F. Xavier Martínez de Osés and Àfrica Uyà Juncadella (2021). Global maritime surveillance and oceanic vessel traffic services: towards the e-navigation. *WMU J Marit Affairs.* https://doi.org/10.1007/s13437-020-00220-0

[50] Peng Han and Xiaoxia Yang (2020). Big data-driven automatic generation of ship route planning in complex maritime environments. *Acta Oceanol. Sin.* 39, 113–120. https://doi.org/10.1007/s13131-020-1638-5

[51] Jahn Petter Johnsen (2017). Creating political spaces at sea – governmentalization and governability in Norwegian fisheries. Maritime Studies 16, 18. https://doi.org/10.1186/s40152-017-0071-7

Coastal and Cruise Tourism:

Coastal and cruise tourism is continuously growing globally, and its infrastructure requirement is also increasing. Planners should consider the current and potential cruise tourism routes by estimating the potential developments in the sector as well.

Offshore Wind Facilities:

The wind sector at sea has improved fast since marine environment provides suitable conditions for wind energy facilities. During the planning process of a MSP in a sea area, it is needed to consider that once the wind energy infrastructure installed in a place, this facility effects the other maritime usages long time.

Cables and Pipelines:

The location of current electricity and communication cable and pipeline networks in addition to the potential installation locations of new submarine cables and pipelines and their possible environmental effects must be taken into account in making an effective Maritime Spatial Planning.

Oil and Gas:

Integrating the current oil and gas extraction sites, their transportation ways and their effects to environment and to other related maritime activities has to be taken into account in the spatial planning. The potential oil or gas areas should also be considered.

Marine Aquaculture:

Planners and the marine aquaculture sector have to work together to define the new and suitable regions for aquaculture.

Marine Seabed Mining:

Seabed mining facilities, sand and gravel extraction sites have substantial environmental impacts. Environmental effects of the infrastructure to other resources or activities should be taken into considerations in spatial planning.

Group Study: Brainstorming on Common Resources and Activities required to be regulated for ABJN

One study group established in the Piri Reis University to discuss the MSP issues for common areas and to define the resources and activities to be regulated in the ABJN. Group was included in 8 members who each one is maritime lecturer from Piri Reis University. Therefore, the group is assumed as an expert group on maritime.

The group was given the resources and activities such as "shipping, fishery, coastal and maritime tourism, offshore wind facilities, cables, pipelines, oil and gas facilities, aquaculture, seabed mining" issues discussed in the previous section and asked for defining the other subjects required for an effective spatial planning for sea areas beyond national jurisdiction including disputed EEZs and continental shelves. Additionally, the group was also requested to prepare a prioritization list for all the subjects to be defined.

After a detailed and careful brainstorming, the group proposed the following issues as the preferential resources and activities to be taken into consideration in spatial planning to be carried out in marine areas beyond national jurisdiction including disputed EEZs and disputed continental shelf areas.

- Current and potential international shipping routes and separate routes for autonomous vessels of future.

- The installations of submarine electricity and telecom cables and pipelines.

- Scientific research and observation areas.

- Navy training areas.

- Search and rescue coordination areas.

- Vessel - Source Pollution Prevention Areas (ECA, Special Areas, Ballast Water Discharge Areas).

- Current and potential oil and gas extraction facilities and their potential transportation means such as pipelines or shipping routes.

- Marine mining resources, current or possible facilities.

- Possible migration and refugee movement and migration management areas and routes.

- Fishery areas, marine species and fish protection areas and cross-border fish migration routes.

- Current and potential marine aquaculture facilities.

- Renewable energy installations such as offshore wind potential areas, potential solar, current or tidal electricity production facilities.

- Current and possible sea sport areas and recreational facilities, yachting routes and installations.

Conclusions

The preservation of oceans is the foremost requirement. Natural resources in sea spaces are under stress because of "overexploitation, pollution, and land-based development".

Sea traffic, fish species, pollution threats and many industrial activities, cable networks or pipelines do not respect national boundaries at sea and require coordination and cooperation of regional states. The common resource characteristics of many regional seas make the local management essential. Administrative and cooperative arrangements and organizations in all common areas are needed for the mutual benefit of mankind. Even though only the high seas outside of national jurisdiction is truly commons, other commonly used sea areas including disputed waters require more effective management because their common usages. An effective spatial planning is the main practice to preserve and protect seas in general.

The following issues are recommended to be spatially defined by regional states neighboring in a sea area for an effective MSP preferably with the initiative, cooperation, collaboration and coordination of global or regional international institutions. This responsibility lays under the international organizations for the main global commons such as open seas.

a) Current and potential international shipping routes and separate routes for autonomous vessels of future.

b) The installations of submarine electricity and telecom cables and pipelines.

c) Scientific research and observation areas.

d) Navy training areas.

e) Search and rescue coordination areas.

f) Vessel - Source Pollution Prevention Areas (ECA, Special Areas, Ballast Water Discharge Areas).

g) Current and potential oil and gas extraction facilities and their potential transportation means such as pipelines or shipping routes.

h) Marine mining resources, current or possible facilities.

i) Possible migration and refugee movement and migration management areas and routes.

j) Fishery areas, marine species and fish protection areas and cross-border fish migration routes.

k) Current and potential marine aquaculture facilities.

l) Renewable energy installations such as offshore wind potential areas, potential solar, current or tidal electricity production facilities.

m) Current and possible sea sport areas and recreational facilities, yachting routes and installations.

BLUE ECONOMY AND BLUE GROWTH

İ. Melih Baş*

Introduction

Sustainable development (SB) was defined by Brundtland Commission of the United Nations in 1987.[1] Based on SB mentality the term "green economy" appeared in a report titled as 'Blueprint for a Green Economy' prepared by Pearce, Markandya and Barbier in 1989.[2] This report translated into even Turkish. Subsequently, interest in green economy has spread worldwidely.

UNEP has been a pivot organization in that sense, publishing most important partitions of green economy literature. Green Economy Report published in 2011 by UNEP was a landmark. A huge set of reports are published by UNEP in the following years.[3]

Definition of 'green economy' seems an ongoing assessment. Short of long saying, it may be defined as a triple bottom line (TBL) integration of development axis as economic performance, ecologic performance and social performance. In other words, they must be included in the aim equation, improving human wellbeing and social equity, reducing ecological risks as well as economic

---

* Prof. Dr. İ. Melih Baş, İstanbul Arel University, E-mail: melihbas@arel.edu.tr, ORCID ID: 0000-0003-1455-9529

[1] United Nations Brundtland Commission, Our Common Future. UN, 1987.

[2] Pearce, D. W., Markandya, A., & E. Barbier. **Blueprint for a Green Economy**. Earthscan, 1989.

[3] United Nations Environment Programme (UNEP). SCP Indicators for Developing Countries. A Guidance Framework. Paris: UNEP, 2008; Integrated Policymaking for Sustainable Development. A Reference Manual, 2009; Green Economy: Developing Countries Success Stories. UNEP, 2010; Towards a Green Economy: Pathways to Sustainable Development and Poverty Eradication. Nairobi, 2011; Organic Agriculture. A step towards the Green Economy in the Eastern Europe, Caucasus and Central Asia region. UNEP, 2011; Inclusive Wealth Report 2012: Measuring progress towards sustainability. Cambridge University Press, 2012; Green Economy Scoping Study – Barbados. UNEP, 2012; Measuring Progress Towards an Inclusive Green Economy. UNEP, 2012; Green Economy Scoping Study – Azerbaijan. UNEP, 2012; Green Economy Scoping Study – Mexico. UNEP, 2012; Green Economy Sectoral Study: BioTrade – A catalyst for transitioning to a green economy in Peru. UNEP, 2012; Green Economy Sectoral Study: BioTrade – A catalyst for transitioning to a green economy in Namibia. UNEP, 2012; Green Economy Sectoral Study: BioTrade – Harnessing the potential for transitioning to a green economy – The Case of Medicinal and Aromatic Plants in Nepal. UNEP, 2012; Using Indicators for Green Economy Policy Making. UNEP, 2013; Green Economy and Trade – Trends, Challenges and Opportunities, 2013; Using Models for Green Econommy Policy Making. UNEP, 2013; Green Economy Modelling Report of South Africa. Focus on Natural Resource Management, Agriculture, Transport and Energy Sectors. UNEP, 2013; Green Economy Modelling Report of South Africa: Focus on natural resource management, agriculture, transport and energy sectors. UNEP, 2013; Kenya Green Economy Assessment. UNEP, 2014; Using Indicators for Green Economy Policymaking. UNEP, 2014; Using Models for Green Economy Policymaking. UNEP, 2014; United Nations Environment Programme (UNEP) & United Nations Development Programme (UNDP), Assessing the impact of green economy investments in Bosnia and Herzegovina (BiH): A sectoral study focused on energy and mountains (agriculture and livestock), 2013.

performance (like income equality etc.). The optimal balance (equity, fairness, just) between those three variables in terms of internationally, nationally, regionally, intergenerationally is the vision.

It seems difficult to fix it with 5W1H questions set! As it is known widely, they are 'what, when, where, why, who/for whom and how as well. Perhaps the most critical one is H, because of huge debates on the answer. As a hint for that, it may be illustrative to remind a popular answer conflict: Under capitalism or transition to socialism. Even in that sense there are embedded concepts: ecosocialism and ecocapitalism (green capitalism). After a while 'blue economy' is introduced as a sister (baby?) of 'green economy'.

Blue Economy: Definition

The terms 'blue economy' and 'blue growth' are used together. The terms 'blue economy' and 'maritime sector' are used instead of each other in literature somehow.

The Blue Growth agenda, published in 2012 by the European Commission (EC), sets the opportunities for marine, maritime and coastal sustainable growth, transferring the concept of a 'Green Economy' into the 'Blue World' i.e., the 'Blue Economy'.

Blue economy is defined as 'all those activities that are marine-based or marine related' in EU Blue Economy Report 2020:[4]

Marine-based activities: include the activities undertaken in the ocean, sea and coastal areas, such as *Marine living resources* (capture fisheries and aquaculture), *Marine minerals, Marine renewable energy, Desalination, Maritime transport* and *Coastal tourism.*

Marine-related activities: activities which use products and/ or produce products and services from the ocean or marine-based activities like seafood processing, biotechnology, *Shipbuilding and repair, Port activities*, technology and equipment, digital services, etc.

To date, although it is a generally accepted thought that the oceans have an economic value, it is very complex to quantify, in terms of provision of resources, habitat for marine life, carbon sequestration, coastal protection, waste recycling and storing, and processes that influence climate change and biodiversity.

Blue Economy Sectors

Blue economy covers a wide range of interlinked established and emerging sectors. Established sectors are sectors with long-term proven contribution to the economy. These established sectors and sub-sectors are classified as follows:

- Marine living resources (primary production, processing of fish

---

[4] European Commission. **The EU Blue Economy Report 2020**, European Union.

products, distrubition of fish products)

- Marine non-living resources (oil and gas)

- Marine renewable energy (wind energy)

- Port activities (Cargo and warehousing, port and water projects)

- Shipbuilding and repair (shipbuilding, equipment and machinery)

- Maritime transport (passenger transport, freight transport, services for transport)

- Coastal tourism (accommodation, transport, other expenditure)

- Emerging sectors are new sectors showing high potential for future development. These emerging sectors are listed as follows:

- Blue bioeconomy

- Ocean energy

- Desalination

- Maritime defence

- Cables

- Research and education

- Marine observation

Blue Growth

According to "Report on the Blue Growth Strategy Towards more sustainable growth and jobs in the blue economy" by European Commission, the blue economy can be a driver for welfare and prosperity.[5] This idea was introduced in Blue Growth Strategy adopted by EC adopted in 2012.

Based on this idea, many initiatives are launched in many policy areas related to oceans, seas and coasts, facilitating the cooperation between maritime business and public authorities across borders and sectors, and stakeholders to ensure the sustainability of the marine environment.

In this context, five innovative, high-potential maritime sectors (blue energy, aquaculture, coastal an maritime tourism, blue biotechnology and sea-bed mining) was underlined.

This Blue Growth approach aimed at supporting on their way new technologies and sectors that had not yet made their mark on the maritime economy. From the very outset, action on Blue Growth did not rely on regulation

---

[5] European Commission. Report on the Blue Growth Strategy Towards more sustainable growth and jobs in the blue economy. Brussels: European Commission 31.03.2017.

but on enabling market forces, by removing the barriers and market failures that prevent innovation and investment.

European Commission initiated private-public fora, such as the "Ocean Energy Forum" or the "Blue Economy Business and Science Forum" bringing together industry, finance, academia and public authorities to identify practical solutions and make investment more attractive.

In the same vein, the sea-basin strategies (in the Atlantic Ocean, the Baltic and the Adriatic and Ionian Seas) and other regional initiatives (for instance in the Mediterranean, the Black and North Seas) have been bottom-up vehicles to trigger regional cooperation towards the blue economy.

It is crucial that, in our quest for natural resources and economic growth, we do not repeat the same mistakes on sea as we did on land. In that sense for a sustainable blue growth, healthy seas is sine qua non. Fortunately, blue growth is still in its early stages. Human responsibility is to make sure that maritime economic development leads to a sustainable and competitive blue economy.

The ocean economy and blue growth ideas has moved up the international policy and also political economy agenda. At the Rio+20 Summit, for the first time, the conservation and sustainable use of the oceans were addressed along with the world's other most pressing sustainability challenges.

The output of the global ocean economy was estimated at EUR 1.3 trillion in 2017 by EC and this could more than double by 2030.

Sustainable Development Goals and Blue Economy

Perhaps the most important concept in the global agenda is Sustainable Development and Sustainable Development Goals (SDGs).

The SDGs may be acronymed also as 5Ps as a pentagon (Don't confuse it with Pentagon – the headquarters building of US Department of Defence, please). These letters are explained by UN as follows:

"People: We are determined to end poverty and hunger, in all their forms and dimensions, and to ensure that all human beings can fulfil their potential in dignity and equality and in a healthy environment.

Planet: We are determined to protect the planet from degradation, including through sustainable consumption and production, sustainably managing its natural resources and taking urgent action on climate change, so that it can support the needs of the present and future generations.

Prosperity: We are determined to ensure that all human beings can enjoy prosperous and fulfilling lives and that economic, social and technological progress occurs in harmony with nature.

Peace: We are determined to foster peaceful, just and inclusive societies which are free from fear and violence. There can be no sustainable development without peace and no peace without sustainable development.

Partnership: We are determined to mobilize the means required to implement this Agenda through a revitalised Global Partnership for Sustainable Development, based on a spirit of strengthened global solidarity, focussed in particular on the needs of the poorest and most vulnerable and with the participation of all countries, all stakeholders and all people.

The interlinkages and integrated nature of the Sustainable Development Goals are of crucial importance in ensuring that the purpose of the new Agenda is realised. If we realize our ambitions across the full extent of the Agenda, the lives of all will be profoundly improved and our world will be transformed for the better"[6]

Because of the main topic of this book is "migration", I could go beyond the limit, if i allocate pages for explanation of the SDGs. However, for the readers it will be fruitful to submit a short definitions box for SDGs as follows.[7]

Table 1. SDGs (Resource: UN, un.org, Access 30.5.2021)

Box 1: Sustainable Development Goals
Resource: United Nations, https://sdgs.un.org/2030agenda, (Access 30.5.2021).
Goal 1. End poverty in all its forms everywhere
Goal 2. End hunger, achieve food security and improved nutrition and promote sustainable agriculture
Goal 3. Ensure healthy lives and promote well-being for all at all ages
Goal 4. Ensure inclusive and equitable quality education and promote lifelong learning opportunities for all
Goal 5. Achieve gender equality and empower all women and girls
Goal 6. Ensure availability and sustainable management of water and sanitation for all
Goal 7. Ensure access to affordable, reliable, sustainable and modern energy for all
Goal 8. Promote sustained, inclusive and sustainable economic growth, full and productive employment and decent work for all
Goal 9. Build resilient infrastructure, promote inclusive and sustainable industrialization and foster innovation
Goal 10. Reduce inequality within and among countries
Goal 11. Make cities and human settlements inclusive, safe, resilient and sustainable
Goal 12. Ensure sustainable consumption and production patterns
Goal 13. Take urgent action to combat climate change and its impacts*

---

[6] UN Department of Economic and Social Affairs, "Transforming Our World: the 2030 Agenda for Sustainable Development", https://sdgs.un.org/2030agenda (Access 30.05.2021).
[7] İbid.

Goal 14. Conserve and sustainably use the oceans, seas and marine resources for sustainable development
Goal 15. Protect, restore and promote sustainable use of terrestrial ecosystems, sustainably manage forests, combat desertification, and halt and reverse land degradation and halt biodiversity loss
Goal 16. Promote peaceful and inclusive societies for sustainable development, provide access to justice for all and build effective, accountable and inclusive institutions at all levels
Goal 17. Strengthen the means of implementation and revitalize the global partnership for sustainable development

These SDGs are illustrated with some symbols and short slogans as follows also.

One of the Sustainable Development Goals which followed up the Summit is to conserve use the oceans, seas and marine resources sustainably titled as "Life Below Water (SDG 14)". It is determined to turn these commitments into action and to be at the frontline in improving the way oceans are managed, reducing human pressures on our oceans and investing in science. This will ensure that marine resources are used sustainably, for healthy marine eco-systems and a strong blue economy.

Principles for a Sustainable Blue Economy

Does "blue economy" mean the use of the sea and its resources sustainable economic development or does it simply refer to any activity in the maritime sector, whether sustainable or not?

Blue economy must respect ecosystem integrity, and that the only secure pathway to long-term prosperity is through the development of a circular economy. So there is a need for principles describe how a sustainable blue economy must be steered and managed.

WWF has developed a set of "Principles for a Sustainable Blue Economy." WWF urges all Blue Economy actors to use these Principles to:

"**Communicate** about the blue economy with stakeholders in decision-making processes, as well as in educational or awareness-raising settings.

Guide decision-making about the Blue Economy in both the public and private sector.

Inform assessment processes that track progress in developing a sustainable Blue Economy.

Support stakeholder dialogues with a common definition and frame of reference on the blue economy.

Mobilize commitment by government and all relevant stakeholders to the vision of a sustainable turn that vision into reality".[8]

These Principles provide a definition of a Sustainable Blue Economy (SBE) and a roadmap to help us get there. They are universal and can be applied to any part of the oceans, seas or coasts, as well as used by any actor involved in the economic development of the sea, including all the stakeholders like governments, private and financial sector actors, international agencies, and civil society groups.

These WWF principles include definition, government rules and actions as well.[9]

Definition: A sustainable blue economy is a marine-based economy that provides social and economic benefits for current and future generations, by contributing to food security, poverty eradication, livelihoods, income, employment, health, safety, equity, and political stability; restores, protects and maintains the diversity, productivity, resilience, core functions, and intrinsic value of marine ecosystems – the natural capital upon which its prosperity depends; is based on clean technologies, renewable energy, and circular material flows to secure economic and social stability over time, while keeping within the limits of one planet.

Government Rules

A sustainable blue economy is governed by public and private processes that are:

Inclusive: A sustainable blue economy is based on active and effective stakeholder engagement and participation;

Well-informed, precautionary and adaptive: Decisions are based on scientifically sound information to avoid harmful effects that undermine long-term sustainability. When adequate information and knowledge are missing, actors take a precautionary approach, actively seek to develop such knowledge,

---

[8] WWF. Principles for a Sustainable Blue Economy. panda.org. 2015.
[9] İbid.

and refrain from undertaking activities that could potentially lead to harmful effects. As new knowledge of risks and sustainable opportunities is gained, actors adapt their decisions and activities;

Accountable and transparent: Actors take responsibility for the impacts of their activities, by taking appropriate action, as well as by being transparent about their impacts so that stakeholders are well-informed and can exert their influence;

Holistic, cross-sectoral and longterm: Decisions are based on an assessment and accounting of their economic, social and environmental values, benefits and costs to society, as well as their impacts on other activities and across borders, now and in the future;

Innovative and proactive: All actors in a sustainable blue economy are constantly looking for the most effective and efficient ways to meet the needs of present and future generations without undermining the capacity of nature to support human economic activities and wellbeing.

Actions: To create a sustainable blue economy, public and private actors must set clear, measurable, and internally consistent goals and targets for a sustainable blue Economy. Governments, economic sectors, individual businesses and other actors must all set relevant and measurable goals and targets for a sustainable blue economy to provide their planning, management and activities with a clear direction. Goals and targets for different economic, social and ecological areas – as well as related policies and activities – must be made as integrated and coherent as possible, to avoid conflicts and contradictions;

Assess and communicate their performance on these goals and targets: The goals and targets for a sustainable blue economy must be regularly monitored and progress communicated to all stakeholders, including the general public, in a transparent and accessible way;

Create a level economic and legislative playing field that provides the blue economy with adequate incentives and rules: Economic instruments such as taxes, subsidies and fees should be aimed at internalizing environmental and social benefits, costs and risks to society. International and national laws and agreements, including private agreements, should be framed, implemented, enforced, and continuously improved in ways that support a sustainable blue economy;

Plan, manage and effectively govern the use of marine space and resources, applying inclusive methods and the ecosystem approach: All relevant uses of marine space and resources must be accounted, planned, managed and governed through forward-looking, precautionary, adaptive and integrated processes that ensure the long term health and sustainable use of the sea, while also taking into account human activities on land. Such processes must be participatory, accountable, transparent, equitable and inclusive, in order to be responsive to present and future human uses and needs, including the needs of minorities and the most vulnerable groups in society. To make informed trade-offs, such processes should also use appropriate tools and methods to capture the range of benefits that ecosystem goods and services can bring to different stakeholders;

Develop and apply standards, guidelines and best practices that support a sustainable blue economy: All actors — including governments, businesses, non-profit enterprises, investors and consumers — must develop or apply the global sustainability standards, guidelines, best practices, or other behaviors that are relevant to them. For organizations, application of such standards should not only ensure that their activities are conducted in a responsible way, but also improve their own performance and competitiveness, today and in the future;

Recognize that the maritime and land-based economies are interlinked and that many of the threats facing marine environments originate on land: To achieve a sustainable blue economy in the seas and coastal regions, land-based impacts to marine ecosystems must be addressed and actors must also work to promote the development of a sustainable green economy on land;

Actively cooperate, sharing information, knowledge, best practices, lessons learned, perspectives, and ideas, to realize a sustainable and prosperous future for all: All actors in a sustainable blue economy have a responsibility to participate in the process of implementation, and to reach out across national, regional, sectorial, organizational, and other borders, to ensure collective stewardship of our common marine heritage.

Blue Economy / Blue Growth and Es & Ges

The blue growth agenda targets maritime economic activities that have the sea and the coasts as drivers. These activities are supported by marine Ecosystem Services (ES) in combination, or not, with abiotic outputs from the marine natural capital. Lillebo et al. analysed blue growth activities with regards to the demand and supply of marine ES and Good Environmental Status (GES) in a paper.[10] The results of their paper show that marine provisioning ES support aquaculture and blue biotechnology, while blue energy is supported by marine provisioning ES and by abiotic provisioning, and abiotic provisioning supports extraction of marine mineral resources. Maritime, coastal and cruise tourism is supported by cultural marine ES and cultural settings dependent on marine abiotic structures. All these multi-sectoral economic activities depend on healthy marine and coastal ecosystems that are provided by regulating and maintenance ES combined with the abiotic regulation and maintenance by natural marine physical structures and processes. In order to balance concurrent sectoral interests and achieve sustainable use of marine resources there is the need to consider indicators for demand for ES, which are social and economically driven, and for the supply, which are dependent on ecosystems capacity to provide the

---

[10] A.I. Lillebø et al. "How can marine ecosystem services support the Blue Growth agenda?" http://dx.doi.org/10.1016/j.marpol.2017.03.008, (Access 30.5.2021).

required marine ES. Some of the actions foreseeing GES are already anticipated in legislation that underpin Blue Growth, whilst others could benefit from additional regulation, particularly in what concern the exploration and exploitation of marine mineral and biological resources. Blue Growth options require navigating trade-offs between economic, social and environmental aspects.

FIGURE 1 given below shows that the demand for ES is social and economically driven, and in the case of the blue growth agenda, there is the demand for: fish protein for human consumption; active compounds for nutraceutics, cosmetics and pharmaceutics; reduction of the dependency on non-renewable abiotic energy sources; cultural experiences, and demand for rare earth elements, commonly used in industrial metals and non-renewable energy.

Figure 1. Schematic representation of how natural capital supports the Blue Growth activities following the Common International Classification of Ecosystem Services (CICES), (Source : Lillebo et al.)

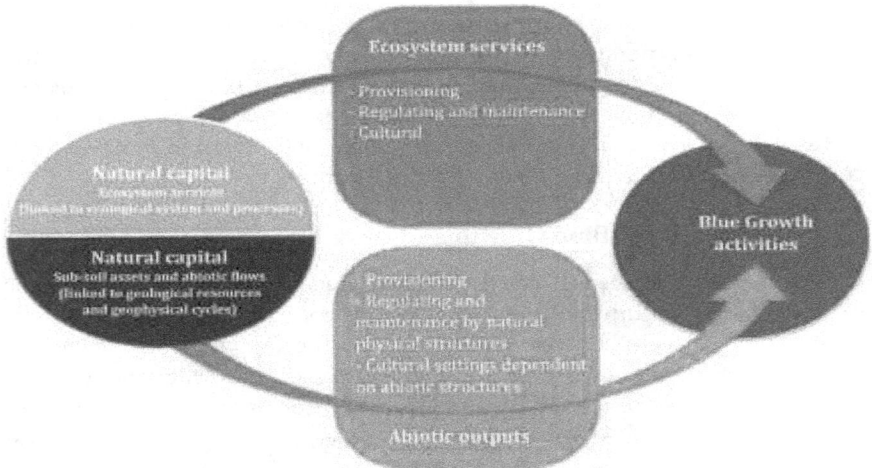

As schematized in Figure 2 given above marine ES supply biomass from plants and animals for marine aquaculture, and biomass from all biota for direct use or processing for biotechnology. Both ES and the abiotic outputs from seas and ocean supply energy from algae biomass or from renewable abiotic sources (blue energy). They also provide interactions with environmental or with physical settings for maritime, coastal and cruise tourism. Abiotic outputs supply abiotic substances, materials and energy as marine mineral resources. However, the capacity for marine ecosystems to supply the required services in a sustainable way requires actions that are regulated by legislation. In this way human well-being can be linked to GES. Shortly saying, blue growth requires navigating trade-offs between economic, social and environmental aspects underpinned by marine ES.

Figure 2. Schematic representation of how marine ecosystem services (ES) can support the Blue Growth agenda, taking into account the demand for marine ES and the actions regulated by legislation that are needed for the supply of the required services in a sustainable way. (Source: Lillebo et al.)

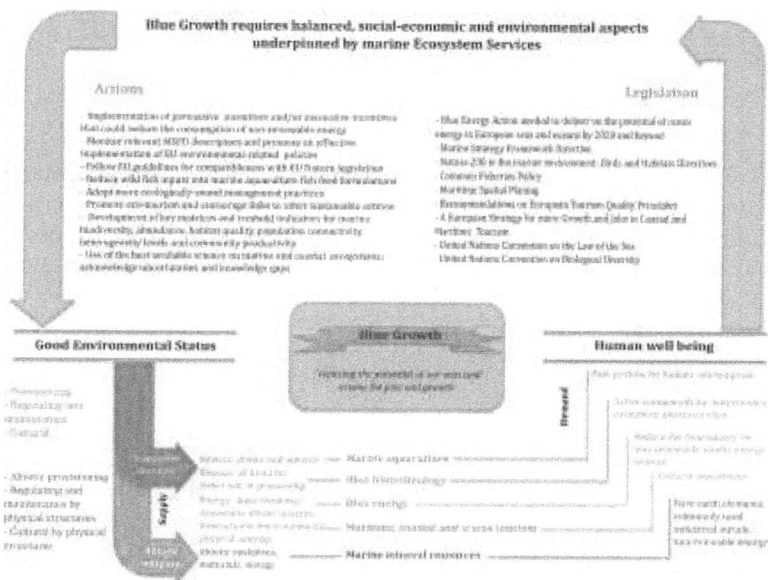

Deep Sea Mining: A Discussion

Deep sea mining is conidered as advanced level of blue economy. But there are some discussions about pros and cons of it.

Some scientists warn that deep sea mining could lead to inevitable and irreparable harm in our oceans, including damage to the natural processes that store carbon. Yet a handful of private companies are leading the charge, heavily influencing the UN regulator and lobbying governments to carve up the international seabed for profit and destruction – and sometimes, remarkably, even speaking on behalf of governments in political negotiations. Despite serious misgivings about the fundamental viability of the industry, deep sea mining companies claim that giving them access to mine the global oceans would benefit poorer nations and future generations. But by tracking the ownership and beneficiaries of the companies with nearly a third of the exploration contracts, this report raises important questions about who stands to benefit – and who is left at risk – if deep sea mining is allowed to begin.

A Greenpeace International Report about deep sea mining, demonstrates how mineral exploration of the deep sea, a global commons, has become monopolised by a small number of corporations headquartered in the Global North, working through subsidiaries, partners and subcontractors in an effort to

427

maintain the illusion that deep sea mining can be a public good.[11]

Meanwhile, the few developing nations that are sponsoring these companies' exploration contracts are exposed to significant liabilities and risk as a result of the opaque and complex corporate structures of their foreign private contractors.

Key findings of this report is summarized below:

"Commercial exploration of fragile global commons is iincreasing despite serious environmental and economic misgivings.

→ As the deep sea mining industry develops and governments negotiate rules to potentially open up the international seabed to commercial mining, it is increasingly clear that far from fulfilling lofty ambitions to boost global development and benefit humanity, deep sea mining would magnify the inequities and environmental harm of previous extractive industries if it is allowed to begin.

→ An area roughly the size of France and Germany combined has already been opened up to exploration for deep sea mining. To date, 30 contracts to explore for deep sea mining viability, covering over a million square kilometres of the international seabed, have been given out by the International Seabed Authority (ISA). Nearly a third of these contracts involve private companies, largely headquartered in North America and Europe, including some with links to the fossil fuel, terrestrial mining and other polluting sectors.

→ Deep sea mining will cause serious and irreversible damage to the ocean biome, risks driving biodiversity loss and could potentially damage an important carbon sink: the deep ocean.1 Impacts experienced from increasing risks to food security will fall disproportionately on developing countries. The emerging deep sea mining industry faces mounting opposition, including from civil society groups in small island nations who have called out foreign private companies for leaving their nations environmentally threatened and financially liable.

Murky corporate practices which obscure lines of profit and liability.

→ Investigating the corporate structures of the leading proponents of deep sea mining reveals that the concentration of ISA exploration contracts are in the hands of a few private companies whose management, directors and those in line to profit are based overwhelmingly in the Global North. The States sponsoring these companies, largely Small Island Developing States (SIDS), are exposed to liability and financial risk. Developing States also risk the disproportionate burden of environmental harm.

Numerous contractor compliance issues have already been reported in the exploration phase but details remain confidential.

---

[11] Greenpeace International. **Deep Trouble The Murky World of the Deep Sea Mining**, Greenpeace Int. 2020.

→ Half of the 16 contracts to explore for minerals in the Pacific's Clarion-Clipperton Zone are now dominated by just four entities – including three private companies. By working through networks of sub-contractors, partnerships or subsidiaries, the dominance of Canadian-registered DeepGreen, Belgian corporate Dredging, Environmental and Marine Engineering

NV (DEME), and US arms manufacturer Lockheed Martin, is not immediately obvious or accountable.

→ The obscure workings and acquisitions of Canadian corporation DeepGreen to gain exploration contracts via ostensibly local entities sponsored by Nauru, Kiribati and Tonga, casts doubt over the extent to which sponsoring States would financially benefit from any deep sea mining.

→ DeepGreen, DEME and Lockheed Martin subsidiaries have sought arrangements with SIDS to allow these North American and European parent companies to Access areas of international seabed 'reserved' for developing nations. Despite calls for disclosure, details of the arrangements between the companies and the governments remain secret, making it difficult to ascertain what benefit, if any, the States will derive from the partnership in return for the risks taken.

→ The murky acquisitions of ISA contracts by a small number of parent companies raises pertinent questions over transparency, accountability and equity in the international regime for deep sea mining. The development of the deep sea mining industry in practice stands at odds with governments' legal obligations to ensure that any mining in the international seabed would benefit humankind overall, especially developing nations.

Undue influence of deep sea mining companies on government policy.

→ Greenpeace investigations suggest that some governments are basing their estimates of the economic value of deep sea mining solely on industry calculations. The British government, for example, has presented as a fact that the UK stands to benefit to the tune of £40 billion, apparently based only on an estimate provided by weapons giant and mining prospector Lockheed Martin, without any independent analysis to substantiate the figure.

→ A revolving door exists between senior staff in sponsoring States and deep sea mining companies, with a former minister who supported exploration applications later joining a company as an advisor, ministers serving on deep sea mining company boards as 'citizens' while in office, and a company lawyer advising government delegations in international tribunal hearings.

Corporate capture of the international regulator.

→ The industry's regulator (the ISA) has consistently prioritised the development of deep sea mining over the preservation of the deep ocean. This has enabled a deep sea mining industry to develop with limited controls on corporate changes of ownership and the ensuing risks to both the environment and equity.

→ Private sector mining companies appear to exert a heavy influence over the international negotiations determining the future of the seabed, lobbying governments to urgently finalise rules that would allow for full-scale mining of the deep ocean to begin, with a financial regime that would maximise corporate profits. To date there has been inadequate discussion between governments as to where and to whom the corporate share of any profits from deep sea mining will ultimately flow.

→ While senior staff at the ISA make increasingly pro-mining comments and amplify private companies, the ISA's powerful advisory commission includes experts employed by deep sea mining contractors.

Controversially, spokesmen from DeepGreen2 and DEME3 have quite literally spoken on behalf of governments, addressing ISA meetings from Nauru and Belgium government seats respectively. Governments face key political decisions in the next 12 months – including whether to open up the largest ecosystem on Earth, the international seabed, to commercial mining. In making these decisions, governments must consider whether the deep sea mining industry may simply direct any profits to a handful of companies in the Global North while the brunt of environmental harm, legal liability and financial risk is faced by nations in the Global South".[12]

Greenpeace International's advice is "to protect against this, governments must ensure that the deep ocean remains off-limits to deep sea mining and instead agree a Global Ocean Treaty that can put protection at the heart of ocean governance".[13]

A Research Agenda for the Future

Fundamental research into extreme environments including the deep-sea, as well as Polar and remote regions, is critical as long as these vast ocean areas remain unknown. The deep-sea in particular is already yielding resources of potential commercial and medical benefit to industry and human health. Fully comprehending these extreme environments, and the impacts of exploration, extraction and economic activities, is important to preserve them and their associated ecosystem services for future generations. Better understanding of oceanographic processes is essential in developing greater renewable energy opportunities from the ocean as well as offshore aquaculture. If managed well, such developments can provide economic and livelihood opportunities without compromising the environment. Fundamental new knowledge is also needed about our changing ocean environment, including climate-induced changes.[14]

---

[12] İbid.
[13] İbid.
[14] Erika Techera and Gundula Winter, "Addressing the challenges and harnessing the benefits of marine extremes", **Marine Extremes**, Erika Techera and Gundula Winter, (Eds). Routledge, 2019, pp. 219-225.

Growing literature on blue economy in different disciplines is shining brightly.[15] 72 percent of surface of the earth is consits of seas and oceans, so the Earth is a blue planet. The economy of the blue planet is blue economy? Doesn't it sound? But instead of a cowboy economy, it would be better a spaceship economy, namely a sustainable blue economy! Does it seem impossible? Be realistic and demand impossible! It is good for 5Ps (People, Planet, Prosperity, Peace, Partnership).

---

[15] Liesl Hotaling & Richard W. Spinrad. Preparing a Workforce for the New Blue Economy: People, Products and Policies, Elsevier, 2021; Iftikhar Ahmed Rao. Elements of Blue Economy, IPS Press, 2020; Nick Lambert et al. Technology and the Blue Economy: From Autonomous Shipping to Big Data, Kogan Page, 2019; Gunter Pauli. The Blue Economy 3.0. The Marriage of Science, Innnovation and Entrepreneurship Creates a New Business Model that Transforms Society, Xlibris, 2017.